Working with Students with Emotional and Behavioral Disorders

A Guide for K-12 Teachers and Service Providers

Daniel S. Sciarra, PhD
Hofstra University
Vance L. Austin, PhD
Manhattanville College

with

Elizabeth J. Bienia, EdD

Series in Education

VERNON PRESS

www.vernonpress.com

In the Americas:
Vernon Press
1000 N West Street, Suite 1200
Wilmington, Delaware, 19801
United States

In the rest of the world:
Vernon Press
C/Sancti Espiritu 17,
Malaga, 29006
Spain

Series in Education

Library of Congress Control Number: 2022939777

ISBN: 978-1-64889-563-0

Also available: 978-1-64889-220-2 [Hardback]; 978-1-64889-521-0 [PDF, E-Book]

Cover design by Vernon Press. Cover image created by freepik / www.freepik.com.

Table of Contents

	Preface	*v*
Chapter 1	**Introduction**	1
Chapter 2	**Conduct Disorder**	47
Chapter 3	**Oppositional Defiant Disorder**	89
Chapter 4	**Attention-Deficit Hyperactivity Disorder**	121
Chapter 5	**Specific Phobia, Separation Anxiety Disorder, and Social Anxiety Disorder**	165
Chapter 6	**Post-Traumatic Stress Disorder, Generalized Anxiety Disorder, and Obsessive-Compulsive Disorder**	213
Chapter 7	**Eating Disorders**	257
Chapter 8	**Depressive Disorders, Bipolar Disorder, and Suicide Prevention in School-Age Children and Youth**	305
Chapter 9	**Autistic Spectrum Disorders**	345
Chapter 10	**At-Risk Behaviors and Emotional Disturbance**	395
Chapter 11	**Conclusion**	467
	Author Bios	*501*
	References	*503*
	Index	*569*

Preface

The authors first discussed this book project in depth in 2003 and began working on the earlier version in 2006. Vance Austin was both a part-time high school special education teacher and full-time college professor and Daniel Sciarra was a full-time college professor as well as a practicing clinical psychologist at the time. We shared a passion for the work of both investigating the causes and characteristics of students with emotional and behavioral disorders and helping to improve their social-emotional well-being and, ultimately, their lives.

In 2006, we agreed to produce a book on this important subject and completed the manuscript in 2009. The book was subsequently published in 2010. We were very gratified by the supportive feedback we received from teachers, college professors, school administrators, and even parents. Dan and I had several requests from college professors for a newer edition. In response, we developed a second book that included a focus on attachment theory and relational approaches in addition to our emphasis on the value of cognitive-behavioral theory (CBT). Nevertheless, we really wanted to revisit and update our first book to include some new "best practices" and address current issues impacting school-age children and adolescents. We felt that that book conveyed, most effectively, the knowledge and skills critical to teachers and related service providers working with students with emotional and behavioral disorders. To ensure that the book accurately reflected the most recent research and read smoothly, we invited Elizabeth J. Bienia to join our writing team. Liz has written extensively on topics from preschool to PhD, she has been an adjunct college professor, and currently works as an elementary school principal in Massachusetts. Her assistance has been invaluable.

The product of our collaboration is this thoroughly updated and revised book designed to help teachers and service providers work successfully with children who exhibit emotional and behavioral disorders affording them a repertoire of valuable, evidence-based interventions. Furthermore, because the book represents a synthesis of expertise, written from the dual perspectives of an experienced clinician and an educator, the school professional who reads it will better understand the role of both teacher and service provider, thus optimizing the coordination and effectiveness of the services that are critical to the success of these students. The book also blends the cognitive-behavioral approach to intervention with the important relational perspective provided in attachment theory.

The book explores the most prevalent behavioral disorders encountered by school professionals as they work with today's students. These high-incidence behavioral disorders will be addressed by type, and each will include a discussion of the relevant characteristics, causes, assessments, and treatment strategies. Features that are unique to this book include its acknowledgement of the need for a collaborative approach to these problems by all school professionals as well as the coordination of services provided by the classroom teacher and other service providers working with students with emotional and behavioral challenges. To date, few books, if any, have provided this holistic perspective.

Finally, the book is primarily intended as a guide for K-12 teachers and related service providers (i.e., school psychologists, school social workers, speech language pathologists, guidance counselors, and occupational therapists) working with children and youth that are experiencing emotional and behavioral problems. Since it is designed to inform, familiarize, and help prepare school professionals to work effectively with these students, it could be considered a prerequisite for more advanced clinical preparation. Much of the material has been class-tested in various counseling courses as well as a preliminary graduate course designed to familiarize general education teachers with approaches to working more effectively with students with emotional/behavioral disorders.

Chapter 1

Introduction

Focus Questions

- *Why is it so difficult to provide a comprehensive definition for "emotional disturbance," and what are some of the contributing factors?*
- *Is there a behavioral profile of a child that warrants the classification "emotionally disturbed"? If so, what are the characteristic traits?*
- *What is a functional behavior assessment, and how is it applied to classroom intervention?*
- *What are some typical nontherapeutic teacher responses to misbehavior in the classroom, and how can these be positively transformed?*
- *How can teachers avoid conflict and help build a sense of community or shared responsibility in the classroom?*

Defining Emotional and Behavioral Disorders

Providing a comprehensive definition for emotional and behavioral disorders (EBD) is very difficult, primarily due to the following factors:

- Subjectivity in determining abnormal behavior, that is, what constitutes an atypical level of severity (intensity), duration, and frequency, and how we differentiate between abnormal behavior caused by abnormal or mitigating circumstances and abnormal behavior exhibited under normal or near-normal circumstances
- Effects of developmental change on the behavioral and emotional stability of an individual
- The tendency of federal and state education agencies to exclude children and youth who are considered "socially maladjusted" or who are "court adjudicated"
- The controversy surrounding certain diagnoses whose presenting characteristics are not deemed to be primarily emotional or behavioral (e.g., ADHD, autism spectrum disorder)

- The amorphous nature of the field and special education, in general
- The inclusion or exclusion of schizophrenia and other psychiatric diagnoses, depending on the predisposition of a particular state

Subjectivity in Determining Abnormal Behavior

The recommendation of experts in the field of EBD is to develop a profile of what normal behavior is under a certain set of circumstances and then to compare it to the behavior of a child in question. If there is a significant disparity, then it can be justifiably concluded that the child's behavior is abnormal and in need of remediation. Similarly, some researchers (Kauffman & Landrum, 2018) have recommended analyzing the child's behavior according to three evaluative criteria: (1) duration, (2) intensity, and (3) frequency. Problems exist, however, in the interpretation of what constitutes an excess in these three areas of analysis. In other words, "how long is too long?" in the case of a child who is depressed, for example, or what level of a behavior is "too" intense and indicates abnormality. Finally, how many times must a behavior be evident over a period of time to be considered "too" frequent? What are the lines or levels that demarcate unacceptable from acceptable behaviors? Can or should there be constant measurements for all behaviors and emotions, or must they be adjusted according to the different types of emotions and behaviors?

The Effects of Developmental Change on the Behavioral and Emotional Stability of an Individual

Equally confounding to the identification of EBD are the effects of physiological development that are particularly evident in preadolescence and adolescence. Most children, in fact, experience significant emotional and behavioral instability during this developmental metamorphosis. Kauffman and Landrum (2018) pointed out that most adolescents engage in some form of delinquent behavior and commit what might be referred to as "status" offenses. This mercurial state associated with adolescent development further complicates and obscures the notion of what constitutes "normal" behavior at this stage. Most adolescents, for example, engage in some form of risk-taking behavior that may include smoking cigarettes, underage drinking, early sexual activity, truancy, driving a car without a license or outside the restrictions imposed by the license, and the recreational use of controlled substances, to name but a few. Because a majority of youth participate in one or more of these "delinquent" behaviors, they compose the profile of normal behavior for adolescents; thus, a young person who engages in or exhibits these behaviors should not be considered aberrant or "emotionally disturbed."

The Tendency of Federal and State Education Agencies to Exclude Children and Youth Who Are Considered 'Socially Maladjusted' or Who Are 'Court Adjudicated'

Youth who are considered to be socially maladjusted characteristically evidence behavior that conforms with conduct disorder. Many experts in the field have argued that if children and youth commit chronic acts of vandalism, property destruction, and violence in the community and display no concern for laws or the rights of others, such behavior is pathological and therefore evidence of an emotional disturbance (Borduin et al., 2017). Indeed, it seems rather paradoxical to imagine that such egregious behavior could be confined to expression in only one setting or social context.

The Controversy Surrounding Certain Diagnoses Whose Presenting Characteristics are not Deemed to be Primarily Emotional or Behavioral (e.g., ADHD, Autism Spectrum Disorder)

When experts in the field of special education consider appropriate classification, they usually evaluate the pathological characteristic that profoundly affects learning. Accordingly, some have argued for the inclusion of students who have attention-deficit hyperactivity disorder (ADHD), predominantly hyperactive-impulsive type, as well as more severe levels of autism spectrum disorder, as the behavior of children with these disorders tends to impede learning as well as socialization.

The Amorphous Nature of the Field and Special Education

The field study of EBD continues to be anomalous because of the varied and often discrepant views of its researchers and expert stakeholders regarding the requisite characteristics of its constituents. This lack of anonymity is evident when one reviews the major textbooks available on the subject. There appears to be significant variation in what types of disorders are included or excluded. Perhaps what is needed is a more concise universal federal definition of what constitutes the essential criteria of an EBD. The absence of such a definition has resulted in confusion in diagnosis and treatment as well as in the determination of incidence and prevalence rates.

The Inclusion or Exclusion of Schizophrenia and Other Psychiatric Diagnoses, Depending on the Predisposition of a Particular State

Several states do not recognize psychiatric disorders, such as childhood-onset schizophrenia, as appropriate for inclusion in the category of "emotionally disturbed." Those states that do so hold that, in particular, due to its emotional lability and behavioral volatility, schizophrenia is appropriately included in this category.

The Implication of Including Socially Maladaptive Students

As mentioned earlier, many experts (Cloth et al., 2014; Kauffman & Landrum, 2018) have regarded the exclusion of socially maladaptive students from the category of "emotionally disturbed" as counterintuitive or paradoxical as these students display pathological behavior in the community and are often referred to as "juvenile delinquents." The fact that these students, either through truancy or expulsion, are not well represented in schools does not obviate the fact that they are emotionally disturbed. In fact, the behaviors they display in the community are the same as those that characterize oppositional defiant disorder and conduct disorder, two subtypes of EBD that are found in students who receive special education services in the school.

Some authors (Cloth et al., 2014; Kauffman & Landrum, 2018) have contended that the reason for the exclusion of students deemed "socially maladapted" is rather insidious and relates to the fiscal restraints endemic to rising school budgets and sharp constituent criticism. Many investigators have suggested that including students who are currently considered "socially maladjusted" would increase the number of students receiving special education services by 3 percent, resulting in a substantial increase in school budgets (Gresham, 2005). Yet others have noted that simply not acknowledging the real social problem these delinquent youth represent is to deny the reality of our present situation, tantamount to hiding one's head in the sand (Barnett, 2010).

The fact remains that, in states where children and youth deemed "socially maladjusted" are currently excluded from classification as "emotionally disturbed," they become constituents of another and far more costly system—the penal and corrections complex (Musu et al., 2019). A comparison of the two systems reveals that the educational one has a far better rehabilitation rate than the juvenile justice system (Musu et al., 2019). In addition, the estimated per-student cost of educating a child with special education services averages, depending on the district, $10,000 per year. The estimated cost to incarcerate an individual in a state correctional facility or juvenile detention center is "$588 per day, or $214,620 per year, a 44 percent increase from 2014" (Justice Policy Institute, 2021, n.p.), while the rate of recidivism can be as high as 75% in three years (Seigle et al., 2014). This high rate of return to custody is due, in part, to the poor job of rehabilitation done by these correctional facilities. In fact, experts suggest that incarcerating a youth in one of these facilities for a minor offense accomplishes one thing with certainty - the individual will learn criminal type behaviors and emerge more likely to offend again (Jeong et al., 2014; Seigle et al., 2014).

In contrast, there is evidence that if effective school-based and family-based interventions are applied early for children and youth deemed "socially maladjusted" or "delinquent," these individuals gain the academic and social skills necessary to avoid criminal prosecution and lead socially productive lives (New York State Division of Criminal Justice Services, 2003). For this reason, if "socially maladjusted" youth are included in the category of emotional disturbance, there is an increased probability that these individuals will be contributors to society rather than wards of it. In the long run, this proposition will almost certainly prove more cost-effective as well; alleviating any guilt of being short-sighted or 'penny wise and pound foolish' when it comes to the lives of children and youth and the betterment of society as a whole.

A Growing Field

Even with the exclusion of socially maladjusted children and youth from the category, the number of students classified as 'emotionally disturbed' continues to increase significantly (Williams et al., 2018). Part of this remarkable surge is a result of the increase in the identifications of children and youth with anxiety disorder; specifically, eating disorders, obsessive-compulsive disorder, and posttraumatic stress disorder (Williams et al., 2018). The rise in the number of students affected by these disorders is a result, in part, of the increase in environmental stressors such as the perceived proliferation of terrorism, the elevated toxicity levels in air, water, and foods, and the increase in society's use of food as a means of control, escape, a measure of self-esteem, and as a reinforcement (Norton & Abbott, 2017).

Likewise, the number of students diagnosed with various types of pervasive developmental disorder, especially autism spectrum disorder, has risen sharply in the last decade (Xu et al., 2018). Though part of this is explained by more precise diagnostic identification criteria, some researchers have pointed to rising levels of environmental toxins and related genetic factors (Xu et al., 2018).

Furthermore, the increase in the number of students who have attention-deficit hyperactivity disorder has arguably contributed to the increase as well, particularly the 'combined type' and 'hyperactive-impulsive type' subcategories. The reasons attributed to the increase in the number of children and youth diagnosed with ADHD are controversial; however, most experts agree that there are many more bonafide cases of the disorder identified per capita today than there were ten years ago (Danielson et al., 2018).

Finally, perhaps the fastest-growing contributors to the growing incidence of EBD are those described as 'defiance disorders' or 'antisocial' behaviors. Principal among these is 'conduct disorder' and its precursor, 'oppositional defiant disorder.' Most clinicians and experts agree that these disorders are closely correlated with ineffective parenting behaviors and family factors such as abuse and neglect on the part of parents or guardians (Szentiványi, & Balázs, 2018). Some research findings have pointed to the increase in single-parent households, which often imply diminished supervision, loss of same-sex role models, and decreased income and financial resources, as a principal contributor to the rise in conduct disorder among children and youth (Szentiványi, & Balázs, 2018). In addition, investigators have noted that the higher cost of living experienced nationwide, necessitating dual incomes and reduced child supervision, may also factor into the increase in the incidence of antisocial behaviors in children and youth in the United States (Szentiványi, & Balázs, 2018).

The Importance of Understanding Attachment Theory in Working with Students With Emotional and Behavioral Disorders

Attachment Theory as a Basis for Understanding

Many authors believe that attachment theory (Bowlby, 1969; 1980) can assist in understanding and intervening more effectively with students with emotional and behavioral disorders. Attachment theory posits that from early experiences with the primary caretaker/attachment figure, the child develops an attachment style, and this book suggests that the display of student's difficult behaviors may have the child's attachment style (especially one that is insecure) as an underlying factor (Bowlby, 1980). Not all emotional disturbance is the result of insecure attachment because behavior is and always will be multifactorial. Attachment theory, however, places the emphasis on environment and nurturance in contrast to the neurobiological theories of behavioral disorders.

Introduction to Attachment Theory

Darwin was very influential in Bowlby (1969) who understood attachment to mothers (primary caretakers) as a means of survival; securely attached children were more likely to survive and be less in danger. Over time, the child learns the best way to establish closeness with the mother even in the face of an unavailable or abusive parent (Rees, 2007). This results in different attachment styles all designed to help the child survive. The child is either securely or insecurely attached based on the perception of the mother's availability; for example, a child whose repeated attempts at closeness with the mother have resulted in failure may withdraw and engage in deactivating strategies, a shutting down of the attachment system. While this would be considered an insecure attachment style, it is, nevertheless, the result of the child's need for survival and an attempt to feel securely attached. In this scenario, difficult behaviors manifested later in life are interpreted as attempts to keep others away, of cutting off relationships thus helping the individual feel safe based on their early experiences with the primary caretaker.

Attachment styles follow us through life and thus have a determining effect (Bowlby, 1980). The good news is that attachment styles can be changed, and teachers can play a crucial role in effectuating a child's transition from insecure to secure by providing a safe holding environment. This book considers teachers as attachment figures, and the relationship with student's as attachment bonds, ties that one individual has to another perceived as stronger and able to provide protection and help in times of need.

A secure attachment style is key to a healthy survival because Bowlby (1969, 1980) believed that the attachment system is related to other systems of survival, most notably the exploratory system. Secure children operate from a secure base and learn to explore the world early on through play and later through relationships with other children and the larger environment. This does not mean that such children are without fear. Their fears, however, are not excessive, and they are better able to manage the fears they do have.

While attachment theory can serve as an antidote to the genetic-biological determinism of disordered behavior so much in vogue today, there is the question as to whether the quality of the attachment bond is determined more by the infant's behavior or the mothers. In other words, an infant's difficult behavior could create an insecure parent because they would not know how to deal with such behaviors; therefore, a very difficult child temperament could compromise attachment. This is the nature side of the argument. The nurture side posits that a secure parent will provide sensitive and protective care even with a difficult child. Here, temperament is not primary, but rather the parent's ability to establish a secure attachment bond. In short, attachment theory places the emphasis on the primary caretaker because of the relative position she has in shaping the quality of the attachment bond (Bowlby, 1980).

The Strange Situation: The Emergence of Attachment Theory

Mary Ainsworth, a disciple of Bowlby, moved to Uganda in 1953 and began observations of Ugandan families where she recognized three distinct patterns of attachment: infants who cried little and in presence of their mothers explored easily; infants who cried a lot even when held by their mothers and did little exploration; and infants who were seemingly indifferent to the presence of their mothers. From this experience, Ainsworth (1969) developed the "Strange Situation" experiment (Ainsworth, 1969), a 20-minute drama divided into segments: (1) mother and infant are in the playroom and joined by a strange female; (2) the stranger plays with the infant while the mother leaves; (3) mother returns and leaves with the stranger and the infant is alone; and (4) the stranger returns followed by the mother.

It comes as no surprise that the infants did more exploration of the playroom in the presence of their mothers rather that in the presence of strangers. More interesting, however, was the infants' reaction upon reunification with mother. Some were angry after separation from mother and wanted contact but only to kick and scream. Ainsworth (1969) labeled this group ambivalent (later known as anxious or resistant). A second group avoided contact with mother upon reunification and was labeled avoidant. Later on, a third group of insecure attachment was added, disorganized/disoriented, to describe infants who exhibited fearful, odd, and conflicted behaviors such as such as falling to the floor, huddling and disoriented behaviors like freezing as if they were in a trance (Main & Solomon, 1990). This resulted in four distinct categories of attachment.

Secure Attachment

These children tend to be confident, attentive, eager, and resourceful explorers of the world around them. In the "Strange Situation," they initiate contact upon reunification (activation of the attachment system) but then return to exploratory play (activation of the exploratory system). Their mental representation of the attachment figure is one who available when needed.

Resistant Attachment

These children often appear distressed and preoccupied with the parent that prevents exploration. They suffer from hyperactivation of the attachment system constant seeking contact but not comforted by it. They tend to be clingy, demanding, helpless, and dependent (Bergin & Bergin, 2009). As they mature, children with an anxious/resistant attachment style tend to have boundary issues, for example, always wanting to sit next to an adult or the teacher. As adults, they are hypervigilant, dependent, and tend to score lower on self-reports around job and view of self (Richards & Schat, 2011).

Avoidant Attachment

These infants were not distressed over the separation from their parent in the Strange Situation and tended to treat the stranger in the same way as the primary caretaker. While resistant children suffer from hyperactivation of the attachment system, the opposite is true for avoidant children. The deactivation of the attachment system is their defense mechanism against an attachment figure whom they perceive as uninvolved and unresponsive. Deactivation is lost hope for responsiveness from the mother. As they grow older, these children employ distancing strategies in dealing with others. They see others in a negative light, have difficulty with trust, and rely heavily on rational thinking. They tend to be very independent and avoid intimacy. In school, they tend to sit by themselves and rarely initiate contact with others. Based on their early attachment experience, they expect rejection from others leading to withdrawal and sometimes aggression since they tend to suppress their anger.

Disorganized Attachment

Labeled as such because they lack an organized attachment strategy, these children tend to come from high-risk environments. In the "Strange Situation," they evidence fear without solution becoming frozen, trancelike, clinging effusively or the opposite, leaning away avoiding any eye contact with the parent (Hesse & Main, 2000). This is the result of experiencing the attachment figure as frightening with physical and verbal abusive behaviors.

Children with a disorganized attachment style are highly represented in clinical samples and evidence more severe forms of psychopathology (e.g., dissociation, and borderline personality disorder). Further observations of disorganized children led to the classification of two types: punitive-controlling and caregiving-controlling (Main & Solomon, 1990). The first group tends to engage in hostile and aggressive behaviors designed to humiliate the parent into submission.

The second group are more internalized and want to protect the parent by being overly happy, helpful, or polite (Moss et al., 2005). The majority are the controlling type. They employ fight or flight defenses alternating between severe aggression and withdrawal to deal with their feelings of helplessness when confronted with frightening events. Since they feel they cannot rely on the attachment figure for protection, their extreme behaviors are a form of coping.

Internal Working Models

Early attachment experiences create expectations as to how one will be treated by others. Bowlby (1980) believed that these expectations result in internal working models (IWMs). Children with secure attachment histories tend to see the world as safe, good, responsive and themselves as worthy of respectful treatment by others. Those with insecure attachment histories tend to see the world as not safe, unpredictable, and insensitive, and they deserve to be treated in kind. IWMs shape expectations from other attachment figures, (e.g., teachers) and therefore shape behaviors towards such figures.

For the purposes here, the question arises as to whether IWMs can be changed. The answer is probably yes, but it is not easy. Those with secure attachment histories can revise IWMs to meet the needs of a changing world, but those with insecure attachment histories find it much more difficult to do so. Bowlby (1969, 1980) had an interesting concept of trauma where he coined the term *defensive exclusion* that many children with insecure attachment histories engage in due to some form of trauma history. It is common belief that traumatic memories are stored differently in the brain in what is referred to as episodic memory as opposed to semantic memory. What the child wants to believe or what the parent wants him or her to believe about the traumatic event is stored in semantic memory, but the actual event is stored in episodic memory. When episodic memory erupts into semantic memory, children with a history of attachment trauma will begin to evidence difficult and hard to understand behaviors.

The good news is that teachers can play a role in the revision of IWM's as close relationships that serve as an antidote to insecure attachment can go a long way in contributing to the development of a more secure relational self (Simpson et al., 2007; Sroufe et al., 2005). Such individuals are labeled *earned secure.*

Attachment Theory and Development

The accepted belief among attachment theorists is that the early relationship with the primary caretaker has a significant effect upon the developing brain. These relationships form the basis for self-regulation (the ability to control emotional responses) and through observation of the attachment figure how to behave in relationships (Weinfield et al., 2008). Anger and anxiety are the two most common reactions to an unavailable caretaker and will follow the child through his or her development.

Academic Development

Emotional regulation is key to academic success; therefore, insecurely attached children will have greater difficulty succeeding the school. Their anxiety or anger makes them focus less on what the teacher is saying and more on threats to their safety. These children tend to have much higher absentee rates than securely attached children, another ingredient to academic failure.

Social Development

Securely attached children and adolescents have more stable, longer-lasting relationships than those with histories of insecure attachment. In the case of bullying, so common in schools, avoidant children tend to be perpetrators; Resistant children, victims; and secure children not involved in bullying one way or the other (Kurth, 2013).

Development of Psychopathology

Bowlby (1980) posited that the child's reaction to the unavailable caretaker had two phases: protest and despair. The first is marked by constant crying with the hope that the attachment figure will return and provide the safety that the child yearns for. The second, despair, is the realization that the situation is hopeless. The definition of attachment trauma is the child's experience of the primary caretaker as a potential source of danger rather than safety. The traumatic reaction is one of "detachment"; however, if this is unsuccessful in avoiding painful memories and emotions, the child can do the opposite: show intense hatred and aggression toward the parent and parent-like figures (i.e., teachers) (Kobak & Madsen, 2008). Teachers are encouraged to keep in mind that when students exhibit such rage towards them, it may be the result of attachment despair and/or a paradoxical attempt to contact an attachment figure (Johnson, 2008).

In the world of attachment theory, an emotional and behavioral disorder, much like the concept of its opposite (resilience), is not considered an inherited, immutable trait but the result of interactions and transactions between individuals and their environment. The interplay between environment and brain chemistry is the key to accepting attachment theory's explanation of disordered behavior.

Attachment Theory in the Classroom

Bowlby (1969) held that another person and/or institution could replace the primary attachment figure. Schools and teachers can be subordinate attachment figures and help insecure students find a safe haven for exploration. Howes and Ritchie (1999) explored the attachment behaviors of more than 3000 early schoolers and concluded the following:

1. Avoidant children were more interested in classroom materials than in the teacher or other children. They did not approach the teacher, so the teacher easily lost track of them. When the teacher approached, they acted as if they did not hear or notice the teacher. If requested to come to the teacher, they did so, but

quickly left. They did not call out to the teacher to show something. When hurt or upset they did not seek the teacher and even moved away if the teacher tried to comfort them.

2. Resistant children were irritable and fussy with the teacher for no apparent reason. These students often cried and were difficult to console, resisted classroom routines like cleaning up, and they clung to the teacher and cried if the teacher attempted to leave the room. Every bump or scratch brought tears. Students were easily frustrated by difficult tasks, they were demanding and impatient with the teacher, and often not satisfied with the teacher's attempt to respond to them.

3. Secure children accepted comfort if hurt or upset, molding their bodies to the teacher if held. They were apt to spontaneously hug the teacher, touch the teacher gently during play, and readily shared their activities with the teacher, showing things and welcoming entrance into play. Students asked for help if they needed it, read the teacher's face for information, and easily followed directives and acted sorry if the teacher spoke firmly to them. Finally, students made transitions smoothly and they were glad to see the teacher at the beginning of the day.

4. Near secure children displayed moderate avoidant behaviors and some secure behaviors. They distrusted their teachers, but conformed readily to classroom procedures, such that teachers did not perceive a problem in their relationships. This category could be thought of as 'attachment in the making.'

(Adapted from Bergin and Bergin, 2009)

The concept of parallel process can help us appreciate the challenges for teachers in developing supportive relationships with insecure students (American Psychiatric Association [APA], 2020). Parallel process means that children tend to recreate the same kind of relationship with attachment-like figures (i.e., teachers) that they had with their primary attachment figure. They behave in such a way to elicit the same response from the attachment-like figure that they experienced with the primary attachment figure. Schools are the primary place where children reenact and recreate their childhood memories; yet more important than what the child says or does, is the teacher's response that can ameliorate or worsen the behavior.

Response of Teachers

Secure teachers can create secure students! Their classroom environment allows for exploration where students feel comfortable challenging themselves, asking questions, and making mistakes from which they learn. All this leads to an increase in self-confidence and self-efficacy. The acceptance of a peer-rejected child and the provision of safety and support for a disorganized child has a positive impact on the student's school performance and aggressive behaviors. To meet these challenges effectively, the teacher will need to reflect on their own attachment histories.

Teachers with an avoidant attachment style, for example, will tend to have relationships with students that lack warmth, empathy, or trust. Remember that those with an avoidant attachment history have learned to be very independent and self-reliant that can result in having unrealistic expectations for students in regard to maturity and independence (Kennedy & Kennedy, 2007). On the other hand, teachers with an anxious, or resistant, attachment history run the risk of overinvolvement with students in contrast to the under involvement of teachers with an avoidant history. They replace the rigid boundaries of the avoidant teacher with diffuse boundaries because they want to be 'close' to their students, and they need their students to like them. In the most extreme cases, they will rely on their students for help with their own personal needs (Kennedy & Kennedy, 2007). To reiterate what has been said before about the contrast between these two groups, avoidant teachers will suffer from a deactivation of the attachment system, while anxious teachers suffer from a hyperactivation of the attachment system.

Mentalization for Teachers

To effectuate positive relationships with difficult students from an attachment perspective, teachers need to engage in mentalization. Mentalization is the ability to intuit mental states in oneself and another and, as a result, understand better each other's behaviors (Slade, 2008). "Mentalization is the opposite of being reactive; for example, when confronted with a student's difficult behavior, teachers who mentalize might ask themselves: what made this student talk like that to me? Is it something internal to them? Maybe they have a good deal of self-hate and their comment to me is simply a splitting off and projection of their own self-hate. Or maybe the vicious comment is the result of something going on between the two of us? Maybe it is linked to something in our past that has never been dealt with" (Austin & Sciarra, 2016, p. 27). Secure teachers are more likely to mentalize; while insecure teachers are more likely to react. Teachers who mentalize do not allow difficult student behavior to dictate their own behavior. They do not react; they reflect; they mentalize! "From an attachment perspective, teacher mentalization might ask the following about a student's behavior: what is this behavior about? Does it appear to be the result of anger, anxiety, deactivation of the attachment system, hyperactivation of the attachment system? What, if anything, have I done to make the interaction better or worse? What is my first internal response? Do I want to rescue this student (usually the result of dealing with a highly anxious student)? Do I want to run away from this encounter (usually the result of an angry, hostile student)?" (Austin & Sciarra, 2016, p. 28).

Mentalization requires being in touch with one's feelings that are provoked by another's behavior. The anxious, or resistant, student may provoke in teachers a feeling of wanting to rescue immediately the student, a response that replicates the early attachment dynamics. "A mentalized response might be "I can't help you right now, keep trying on your own and in a little while I will take a look and review it with you" (Austin & Sciarra, 2016, p. 28). This response is designed to delay the immediate gratification so often sought for by students with an anxious attachment style.

Avoidant students can be very challenging since they are often dismissive of a teacher's efforts to help and support. "If the teacher personalizes this rejection (very likely for an insecure preoccupied teacher), the relationship can become quite toxic. How often have we heard a teacher saying something like the following: "I did so much for that student; I went out of my way to help; and look at the thanks I got" (Austin & Sciarra, 2016, p. 28). A secure teacher who mentalizes might intuit that this is an avoidant student and allow the student a certain amount of independence and simply state that if they want help, they can ask. If this response is reiterated, an avoidant student might be surprised that their rejection of the teacher is not met with the teacher's rejection, but the opposite. In this way, the teacher helps to create a more secure base.

Finally, there are the most challenging of all students - those with a disorganized attachment history. The hallmarks are extreme emotional dysregulation and behaviors that provoke fright in others, including teachers who tend to worry about the student's emotional stability. The fearful situation provokes the fight/flight response. Neither option is effective. If teachers want to flee, it is a pretty sure sign they are dealing with a disorganized student; however, a teacher who mentalizes will not react; rather, they will understand that such behaviors come from a history of pain and trauma.

Secure teachers have empathy for even the most difficult behaviors knowing they most likely reveal an abusive history. In the heat of the moment, it is impossible to reason with these students. "The best the teacher can hope for is to calmly deflect the behavior by saying something like the following: Now is not the time for us to discuss your behavior, but we both know something is very wrong, and perhaps with time we can figure it out. If it's ok with you, I'd like to get back to teaching" (Austin & Sciarra, 2016, p. 29). Remember an antithetical mentalized response is infinitely better than the provoked response.

Summary

This section on attachment theory has tried to make the case that it can be beneficial to teachers dealing with difficult behaviors to know the different kinds of student attachment styles, the teacher's own attachment style, and increasing their capacity for mentalization. Good teaching involves establishing good relationships even with challenging students. The authors believe that attachment theory can help to meet those challenges. The chapters that follow will integrate attachment theory into the various case examples to give the reader a more useful understanding of attachment theory and the dynamics involved in dealing with specific difficult behaviors.

Trauma Informed Teaching

Trauma-informed practice or teaching requires educators to recognize the prevalence, impact, and indicators of childhood trauma and to respond to student behavior in ways that support traumatized youth (Thomas et al., 2019). Furthermore, trauma-informed school practices require that educators receive training about childhood trauma and ways that it may manifest in students' behavior (Crosby et al., 2018). It also requires that teachers reflect this knowledge in their classroom management and instruction practices. Administrators must also work to develop a culture of support for students and teachers alike (National Child Traumatic Stress Network, 2017). Essentially, trauma-informed teaching acknowledges the ways in which a student's life is fundamentally impacted by trauma and use trauma-sensitive strategies in opposition to the traditional, more punitive, and insensitive ones (Crosby et al., 2018).

Some Effective Trauma-Informed Teaching Strategies

According to Minihan (2019), there are eight strategies that are most effective in teaching practices to include:

- Expect Unexpected Responses: Seemingly innocent or benign events can trigger an unanticipated behavioral response in students that have been traumatized, being aware of this possibility and being prepared to address the behavior with patience and understanding are key to helping the student process the event and regulate her emotions.

- Employ Thoughtful Interactions: It is important that teachers become aware of the student's perception of their interactions with them and seek to mitigate the potential for misperception by never embarrassing the student, for example, slipping them a note rather than criticizing them in public or providing choices as opposed to an ultimatum.

- Be Specific About Relationship Building: As teachers develop successful relationships with students affected by trauma, they might convey the strategies that proved most effective in the form of a brief report or tip sheet to other teachers and caregivers that have contact with the student and might benefit from that information.

- Promote Predictability and Consistency: Teachers need to provide "predictable positive attention" to all their students, especially those who have experienced trauma and may need the reassurance and emotional comfort afforded by predictable, scheduled support and "check-ins."

- Teach Strategies to "Change the Channel": Provide students who have trouble staying focused or on-task with cognitive distractions or thought breaks. Minihan (2019) suggests having trivia games or "madlibs" available for these students. The goal is to provide an alternate learning activity to help the student refocus and return to the lesson refreshed and ready.

- Give Supportive Feedback to Reduce Negative Thinking: To help ensure that students do not misinterpret positive feedback as negative, offer explicit encouragement at the beginning and end of a learning task (the "positive sandwich approach") replete with a positive affect (smile).

- Create Islands of Competence: Helping to develop a sense of self-efficacy is critical in working successfully with students that have experienced trauma. Asking the student to tutor younger students is one effective strategy in helping to improve self-esteem, another is to employ the "orbital" technique whereby the student is asked to share their passion or favorite pastime with the class. They can use a power point or slide deck, pictures, videos, or show artifacts to enhance their brief five to ten-minute presentation. They are the "resident expert" for perhaps the first time in their lives.

- Limit Exclusionary Practices: Kohn (2006) extolled the importance of including every student in the class as a valued member of the "classroom community." Because many of our students have experienced abandonment or neglect or have been excluded from activities and events for various reasons, it is important for teachers to include these students in all class activities. Their inclusion or special attention from the teacher should never be contingent on compliance with a request or attainment of a specific goal, such as getting all their homework completed in exchange for having lunch with the teacher.

Let us think about three students each of whom is described in great detail in *Chapter Five: Anxiety Disorder.* Nicola, a student with a chronic phobia, Visalia, a student manifesting separation anxiety, and Julia, a student with social anxiety, and consider ways in which trauma-informed teaching might benefit each of them.

Nicola's co-dependency relative to her mother and her perseverating about the college and flying present a challenge for her teachers. Understanding the mother-daughter dynamic and the trauma that the notion of being separated will cause presents an opportunity for attentive 'trauma-informed' teachers to employ a strategy to address Nicola's fears. The strategy that might be helpful from the eight described above would be "Create Islands of Competence" (Minihan, 2019). Employing this strategy, teachers might ask Nicola to share her interest in engineering, thereby emphasizing the value of attending a good school that will enable her to achieve her goal of becoming an engineer, while minimizing the fact that she needs to fly to Pittsburgh to attend the college.

In Visalia's case, the trauma of being separated from his mother and home may be ameliorated to some extent by employing three of the recommended strategies; namely, "Be Specific About Relationship Building," "Give Supportive Feedback to Reduce Negative Thinking," and "Limit Exclusionary Practices" (Minihan, 2019). Visalia needs to be encouraged to think differently about school and understand its significant benefits that are not a threat to his relationship with his mother.

Finally, we turn to Julia, our student with social anxiety disorder. Julia's fear of performing might benefit from the following strategies described by Minihan (2019); specifically, "Expect Unexpected Responses," "Be Specific About Relationship Building," "Give Supportive Feedback to Reduce Negative Thinking," and "Create Islands of Competence." Julia might vigorously refute her singing talent and might become reactive to those that insist otherwise. An astute teacher will anticipate this reaction and not become entangled in the debate understanding that, for Julia, this is a non sequitur. Likewise, Julia might feel especially close to her music teacher, given their similar interests and experiences. The music teacher then might provide others with suggestions about the best way to work with and encourage Julia. When Julia is self-deprecating and insists she does not have the talent to preform publicly, teachers can gently assert that they have heard her sing on various occasions and have truly enjoyed her talent without overemphasizing that fact. Lastly, Julia could be asked to help coach younger vocal protégées, which might help her recognize and acknowledge her own vocal talents and inspire her to perform again.

Social Emotional Learning (SEL) as an Effective Intervention for Trauma and Anxiety

Sugai and Horner (2006) have called for students to be taught, supported, and surrounded with social-emotional learning (SEL) practices at the individual and environmental level. In fact, according to the U.S. Department of Education: Regional Educational Laboratory Program [USDOE] (n.d.),

> *Research suggests a positive association between students' social and emotional skills—such as self-awareness and responsible decision making—and their academic and career outcomes. Reflecting these findings, the Every Student Succeeds Act (ESSA) allows states and districts to use federal funds on evidenced-based programs that promote students' social and emotional learning (SEL)* (n.p.).

SEL concentrates on developing within students the ability to recognize emotions, their own as well as the emotions of others, while providing them the skills necessary to communicate this emotional understanding. School systems acknowledge the need to integrate SEL curriculums into the educational programming for students as one way to foster the development of resiliency (Zenner et al., 2014).

Resiliency, thought to be a characteristic of normal development (Masten & Barnes, 2018), enables everyone to hold an attitude of optimism and basic trust during times of uncertainty and "reflects the degree to which an individual's personal resources match or exceed their reactivity to internal or external stress" (Prince-Embury, 2013, p. 1). Research in this area has identified many protective factors such as an easy temperament, emotional support, positive relationships, and good school experiences (Masten & Barnes, 2018). If resiliency is part of normal development, then it is possible that these qualities can be cultivated in all children and environments. Researchers have identified factors of resiliency that show resourcefulness and flexibility as effective responses to environmental stressors, noting that individuals who exhibit higher levels of resiliency, experience less emotional dysregulation (Masten & Barnes, 2018; Prince-Embury, 2013).

Research suggests that better instruction in Social Emotional Learning (SEL) may improve school connectedness, and help students become better learners (Jones & Bouffard, 2012; New York State Education Department, 2018; Osher & Kendziora, 2010). To facilitate access to quality SEL instruction, the New York State Education Department (2018) identified the following SEL learning benchmarks for their public schools.

- "Develop self-awareness and self-management skills essential to success in school and in life" (New York State Education Department, 2018). Being aware of one's emotions and knowing ways to manage and express them constructively are essential life skills. These skills can help students to manage stress, control impulses, and self-motivate to succeed when faced with personal, academic, or work-related challenges.
- "Use social awareness and interpersonal skills to establish and maintain positive relationships" (New York State Education Department, 2018). The capacity to recognize the thoughts, feelings, and perspectives of others, and to seek to understand others from diverse backgrounds, is essential in establishing positive relationships. Equally important is the ability to collaborate with classmates, engage in civil discourse, and resolve conflicts with others.
- "Demonstrate ethical decision-making skills and responsible behaviors in personal, school, and community contexts" (New York State Education Department, 2018). The ability to make ethical decisions and behave responsibly, considering the rights and well-being of others as well as one's own, are vital to the survival of a civil society and is the bedrock of responsible citizenship in a democratic society.

Nine SEL programs employed in U.S. school systems have been identified as having an evidence base of effectiveness, to include, "Roots of Empathy," "Positive Action," "Responsive Classroom Approach," "Second Step," "4Rs (Reading, Writing, Respect, & Resolution)," "Resolving Conflict Creatively Program," "Meditation ('Mindfulness')," "Service Learning," and "School Wide Positive Behavior Support (SWPBS)" (Vega, 2015). Explicitly embedding SEL goals in educational curriculum can help students develop emotional self-awareness and self-management, providing students with tools to manage their thinking (CASEL, 2022). The practice of mindfulness is designed to direct the individual's thoughts with the goals of (1) self-regulation of awareness, (2) directing internal and external attention, (3) metacognition, and (4) the adoption of a non-judgmental attitude (Bishop et al. 2004). Loosely defined, mindfulness is the deliberate act of paying attention in the moment while withholding judgment; more specifically, it is "...moment-to-moment, non-judgmental awareness, cultivated by paying attention in a specific way, that is, in the present moment, and as non-reactively, as non-judgmentally, and openheartedly as possible" (Kabat-Zinn, 2005, p. 108).

A literature review concluded that mindfulness activities could elevate positive psychological feelings, improve functioning, and help to alleviate psychological distress through the direction of self-regulatory processes (Hart et al., 2013). Furthermore, studies have found that mindfulness activities can convey significant benefits to children evidencing difficulties with social competence (Flook et al., 2015), as well as those suffering from social anxiety disorder (Carlton et al., 2020), and difficulties modulating attention (Semple et al., 2010).

In addition to the benefits of mindfulness practice in clinical settings, research supports the use of mindfulness activities in school settings (Zenner et al., 2014), reporting beneficial results in academic improvement, increased attendance rates, and decreased suspensions, in addition to a sense of increased well-being in many students. Some schools around the country have gone as far as implementing full mindfulness curriculums into the school day with the goal of improving educational outcomes and school climate for all students. Two specific curriculums with documented success in schools are Quiet Time, utilized successfully in the San Francisco school district (Dierke, 2012), and Mind UP, a curriculum in place at schools in Vancouver, British Columbia (Wickelgren, 2012).

It is important to note that mindfulness techniques need not be done on a school-wide basis. Individual teachers can employ mindfulness techniques in their classrooms in order to avail students of its documented benefits. Any teacher with a little knowledge, training, and motivation can and should be able to embed this or a similar social-emotional learning technique into her own classroom curriculum.

Let us think about the three students mentioned earlier and how they might benefit from a social-emotional learning technique such as mindfulness. First, Nicola, who has a chronic specific phobia relative to flying might employ one of the techniques described in a mindfulness curriculum like, "Learning to Breathe" (Broderick, 2019). One mindfulness exercise that might be helpful to Nicola is to simply close her eyes and focus exclusively on her breathing while shutting out competing thoughts. Arguably, it will take practice for Nicola to master the technique, but research is clear that it can help reduce the kind of stress her fear of flying creates.

The same is true for Visalia, the student that experiences separation anxiety. He might benefit from a technique informally referred to as emotional sandwiching (Land, 2011). Whenever Visalia comes to school, he is greeted by a preferred classmate or teacher and provided with encouragement and a sense of belonging. Likewise, as he prepares to return home, hopefully at the conclusion of the school day, he receives an encouraging word from that classmate or teacher such as, "Visalia, it was great having you in class, you really did well today, I look forward to learning with you tomorrow!"

Lastly, Julia, our talented student with social anxiety. According to Jones et al. (2018) mindset is one of the quintessential social and emotional learning skills and relates to Julia's fear of performing, perhaps truly, her acute fear of failing. Developing a mindset that acknowledges her talent in singing while also being tolerant of imperfection and occasional failures is key to Julia's emotional well-being. Her teachers and classmates might institute a regular meeting in which each student is asked to lead or facilitate a discussion about issues that affect them both in and out of school. A specific technique is the "racoon circle" in which everyone sits or stands in a circle, joins hands, or holds on to a circular rope. The facilitator asks a question, and everyone is encouraged to respond. A question might be, "Tell us something about you that is unique and makes you feel fulfilled." Julia might come to realize that her talent is acknowledged and valued by others and, more importantly, by herself.

A Final Word on the Importance of Trauma Informed Teaching

According to the Centers for Disease Control and Prevention [CDC] (2019), trauma is arguably the greatest public health threat facing today's children. Typically, traumatic events include abuse, neglect, experiencing a natural disaster, living in a war-torn region of the world, and being exposed to violence, but trauma can result from "factors such as racism explicit, implicit, and systematic; and microaggressions as well as poverty, peer victimization, community violence, and bullying" (Portell, 2019, n.p.). The effects on our students are challenges in self-regulation, negative thinking, being on high alert, difficulty trusting adults, and inappropriate social interactions (Terrasi & de Galarce, 2017). These actions can feel inimical to teachers who do not understand the real cause of the student's maladaptive behavior, which can lead to misunderstanding, ineffective interventions, and obstacles to learning (Minahan, 2019).

Students are unable to learn if they do not feel safe, known, and cared for within their schools (Aupperle et al., 2012). Teachers can make a difference in reducing the emotional and psychological effects of trauma by being aware and proactive in addressing the needs of affected students by creating a classroom climate in which every student feels safe and valued, in short, in which every student is made to feel that they belong. Small, manageable changes to the classroom structure and teaching pedagogy that help to foster successful learning (Minahan, 2019).

Students carry their traumatic experiences with them and, of course, bring them into school. Teachers may not always know about these traumatic experiences; however, by creating a connection between SEL interventions and trauma-informed approaches, educators can increase the effectiveness of both types of interventions (Elias & Leverett, 2011). Just as the field of SEL adopts much of the pedagogy of special education instruction (Elias, 2016), it also must begin to adopt the principles of trauma-informed instruction.

Accordingly, nothing is more important than developing better supports for the teachers who work in schools. Teachers and staff need to work in a healthy school culture, in which they can learn to regulate their emotions, build stronger relationships with colleagues, and model for the students that school is generally a safe place, where exposure to traumatic events is minimized (Pawlo et al., 2019).

Profile of a Child with an Emotional or Behavioral Disorder

Most of the disorders associated with the category of emotional/behavioral disorder can be organized into two types either externalized behaviors, which describes those that are overtly displayed; or internalized behaviors, defining behaviors that are more difficult to observe (Liu et al., 2011; Liu, 2004). Subtypes of EBD that are predominantly externalized are those whose characteristics involve observable actions or behaviors that are antisocial, that is, impulsive, aggressive, disruptive, destructive, and in violation of the laws and rules or norms of society (Liu, 2004). Subtypes of EBD in which behaviors are primarily internalized and thus not as readily apparent include mood disorders such as depression, anxiety disorders such as posttraumatic stress disorder, and thought disorders/psychiatric diagnoses such as schizophrenia (Liu et al., 2011).

A typical profile of an individual with an externalized EBD is Jack, an adolescent with a conduct disorder. Jack, a tenth grader at a local high school, comes from a very abusive household. His father is currently serving time in a state prison for assault with a deadly weapon. He has a history of abuse towards Jack's mother, and there is some suspicion that he has physically abused Jack, as well. Since his father's incarceration, Jack's mother has had to work two jobs to make ends meet, leaving Jack to fend for himself.

At school, Jack is the classic bully, threatening and intimidating other students and staff with his size and propensity for violence. He has been suspended twice so far this year, both times for fighting with other students on school grounds. His behavior in the community has been equally violent. In one instance, Jack fought with an older man who claimed Jack had intentionally damaged his car. Jack did not deny the charge, but he severely beat up his accuser in retaliation for what he perceived as the man's bad attitude. The assault-and-battery case is awaiting trial, and if he is found guilty, Jack may do hard time in an adult prison.

Jack's behavioral profile fits that of an individual with conduct disorder, an externalized type of emotional/behavioral disorder. He represents a real challenge for his teacher and administrators, some of whom would like to see him locked up.

The Functional Behavioral Assessment and its Applications

The term functional behavioral assessment (FBA) refers to a systematic process used in identifying the function or purpose of a specific misbehavior or inappropriate action. According to behaviorists including Skinner (1969), all behaviors serve a purpose for the actor; therefore, if practitioners and caregivers can successfully identify that purpose, a relevant and effective intervention can be developed. The danger in not understanding the purpose or root cause of an undesirable behavior is to inadvertently compound the problem by either reinforcing the pathological behavior or wasting time and resources treating a misidentified one.

Throughout the chapters in this book, the authors provide a model of how an FBA is conducted relative to a representative case example. In each case, the FBA exemplar is used to develop an effective behavioral intervention plan (BIP). Because identification of the root cause of a misbehavior or, more accurately, the function that a misbehavior serves for an individual, it is important to establish a valid and reliable process for conducting an FBA (Gresham et al., 2001).

Several studies have demonstrated the efficacy of a well-executed FBA in the development of effective behavioral interventions (Cook et al., 2012). The need for a research-based behavioral assessment process that can be effectively employed by the classroom teacher has prompted the authors to employ a model that conforms to the recommendations of this research and includes critical elements identified in these studies. This model is derived from the recommendations offered by Barnhill (2005) as well as Cook et al. (2012) and includes the following key components (1) identify and describe the problem behavior, (2) collect baseline data and academic performance information, (3) describe the environmental and setting demands, (4) complete a direct observation, (5) develop a hypothesis, and (6) test the hypothesis by assessing the effectiveness of the behavior intervention plan in reducing the undesirable behavior and increasing the more appropriate behavioral response (see the Functional Behavioral Assessment Worksheet below).

Functional Behavioral Assessment Worksheet

Student Name: ____
Date: ____________________

Target Behavior: Operationally define the behavior that most interferes with the student's functioning in the classroom. Include intensity (high, medium, or low), frequency, and duration.

____

____

When, where, with whom, and in what condition is the target behavior least likely to occur?

____

____

Setting Events or Context Variables (i.e., hunger, lack of sleep, medications, problems on bus):

____

____

Immediate Antecedents & Consequences
Antecedents Problematic Settings Consequences
__ Demand/Request Unstructured setting Behavior ignored
__ Difficult task Unstructured activity Reprimanded
__ Time of day Individual seat work Verbal redirection
__ Interruption in routine __ Group work __ Time-out (duration: __)
__ Peer teased/provoked Specials Loss of incentives
__ No materials/activities Specific subject/task Physical redirection
__ Could not get desired item Crowded setting Physical restraint
__ People ________ Noisy setting Sent to office
__ Alone __________ Other __________ Suspension
__ Other __________ Other __________ Other __________
What function(s) does the target behavior seem to serve for the student?
__ Escape from: demand/request person activity/task school
__ other ________________
__ Attention from: __ adult __ peer __ other __________

__ Gain desired: __ item __ activity __ area __ other ____________
__ Automatic sensory stimulation:
Hypothesis:
When ________________ occurs in the context of ____________________________
(antecedent) (problematic setting)
the students exhibits________________ in order to ____________________________
(target behavior) (perceived function)
This behavior is more likely to occur when____________________________
(setting event/context variables)
Replacement or competing behavior that could still serve the same function for the student:
____
____

Is the replacement behavior in the student's repertoire, or will it need to be taught directly? ____
If so, how will it be taught? ______________________________
List some potential motivators for student:
____
____

Source: Barnhill, G. P. (2005). Functional behavioral assessment in schools. *Intervention in School and Clinic,* 40(3), 131–143.

A successful behavioral assessment depends on collaboration among the student's teachers, parents, and related service providers and their willingness to collect accurate baseline data. In addition, the multidisciplinary team (or Individualized Education Plan [IEP] team) must prioritize problem behaviors and target the most serious for change. Furthermore, the student, when appropriate, should be an active participant, both in the FBA process as well as the development of a viable BIP. Finally, the target behaviors identified by the FBA must be ones that can be readily addressed by a BIP in both the school and home environments; they must be measurable and regarded as high priority. In short, the more painstakingly and thoroughly the FBA is conducted by teachers or caregivers, the more effective the BIP will be, because the most debilitating behavioral obstacle will have been identified and targeted (Crone et al., 2015).

Developing an Effective Behavioral Intervention Plan

According to Gresham (2004) and Lewis et al. (2016), most school-based behavioral interventions can be conceptualized using four broad theoretical categories (1) applied behavioral analysis, (2) social learning theory, (3) cognitive behavior therapy, and (4) neobehavioristic stimulus–response (S-R) theory. A brief discussion of each approach follows.

1. *Applied Behavioral Analysis.* The applied behavioral analysis (ABA) approach fits quite nicely within the framework of a functional behavioral analysis. The goal of ABA is to determine the function that a problem behavior serves for an individual and then to replace that dysfunctional behavior with a more socially appropriate one.

2. *Social Learning Theory.* Social learning theory is based on the notion of reciprocity between the behavior of an individual and the environment (Bandura, 1986). The concept of modeling really emanates from this approach, and modeling is effective in teaching/generalizing desired behaviors to students who have not learned appropriate responses to ambivalent situations.

3. *Cognitive Behavior Therapy.* The essence of the cognitive behavior therapy (CBT) approach is the assumption that behavioral responses to the environment are mediated by the thoughts or thinking of an individual. Thus, teaching more effective or self-affirming ways of thinking about one's environment can positively affect the way an individual behaves within/toward it. Techniques such as self-talk, self-evaluation, problem solving, and self-instruction all emanate from this approach and are used primarily as therapeutic interventions with students who experience anxiety and mood disorders.

4. *Neobehavioristic Stimulus–Response Theory.* Neobehavioristic S-R theory is based on classical conditioning as presented by Skinner (Powers & Franks, 1988). In essence, the individual, through behavioral conditioning based on an environmental stimulus, learns a new and more appropriate behavioral response that will continue indefinitely in the presence of the stimulus. Systematic desensitization and exposure-based treatments are derived from this learning model.

Some of the maladaptive behaviors displayed by students who have EBD might be more effectively addressed by one of the aforementioned models, whereas others might be better served by a multisystem approach. For teachers and school personnel, the important consideration is ease of application, or practicality, and the effectiveness of a particular intervention in the classroom setting. The potential for misuse of interventions by teachers is high because research has suggested that, frequently, teachers continue to use techniques that are easy to employ but may not be effective (Walker et al., 2004). Gresham (2005) examined the efficacy of matching the intensity of the intervention to the severity of the problem, which involves organizing the intervention into three levels: primary, secondary, and tertiary. The purpose of intervention at the primary level is preemptive; at the secondary level, it is to reverse the deleterious effects of maladaptive behavior; and finally, at the tertiary level, intervention serves to contain the damage inflicted by the misbehavior and reduce harm.

Furthermore, Gresham (2004) identified three levels of intervention intensity (1) universal intervention, (2) selected intervention, and (3) targeted/ intensive intervention. Universal interventions are described as being directed toward all students in the same manner and under similar conditions. Examples of such plans include school-wide discipline plans, district-wide zero-tolerance plans, and social skills training provided consistently within a school system. Selected interventions are those that apply to noncompliant students, at-risk individuals, and, generally, those for whom the universal interventions were ineffective. Finally, targeted, or intensive interventions refer to those extraordinary measures that target a very small percentage of students who cause the majority of behavioral disruptions and that require intensive treatments.

The goal of universal intervention is to facilitate the student's academic and social development. Selected interventions are intended to significantly change ineffective or undesirable behaviors or behavioral responses through reinforcement, that is, behavior modification. Similarly, the purpose of targeted interventions is to decrease the frequency and intensity of very serious behaviors and, hopefully, teach the individual more appropriate alternative ones (Gresham, 2004).

According to Lewis et al. (2016), an effective way to determine which of the three intervention levels is most appropriate for a student is through a decision-making model referred to as response to intervention (RTI). In essence, the RTI model uses a student's lack of response to a seemingly appropriate research-based intervention as the starting point for revising or modifying it. If an initial behavioral intervention does not produce a measurable improvement in a student's behavior within a reasonable time period, it should be carefully reviewed using a functional assessment model such as applied behavioral analysis (ABA), appropriately revised, and then reassessed to determine its overall effectiveness.

Buck et al. (2000) noted that the systematic response to behavioral problems as described in the federal Individuals with Disabilities Education Act (IDEA, 2004) is predicated on two key assumptions:

1. Behavior problems are best addressed when their cause is known, and that cause is most effectively determined/identified through a functional behavioral assessment.

2. Behavior interventions that involve positive reinforcements are more effective than punitive ones, and those behavior interventions, to be effective, need to be thoughtfully designed, systematically implemented, and periodically evaluated to ensure that they are successful.

Once the FBA has been completed, the resulting deductions inform the design of an effective behavioral intervention plan. Fad et al. (1998) recommended five procedures in the development of a viable BIP to include (1) review of the behavior targeted in the FBA, (2) identification of the behavioral goal that will cause an increase or decrease in the frequency of a targeted behavior, (3) determination of individualized and appropriate intervention strategies, and the designation of the individual or individuals responsible for their implementation, (4) determination of the dates for its review and evaluation, and (5) selection of appropriate evaluation methods and criteria.

The Behavior Intervention Plan Template below provides the authors' example of a behavioral intervention plan template that can be easily used by the classroom teacher to record and evaluate behavioral data relative to a target behavior and its executor.

Behavior Intervention Plan Template

Name of Student ______________________ Start Date ______________________
Age __________ Grade __________ Homeroom Mr./Ms. ______________________
Specific Behavioral Goals:
1.
Oversight ________
2.
Oversight ________
3.
Oversight ________ For each goal above:

1. What antecedents, events, and consequences can I change to increase/decrease the behavior?
2. What strategies, curricular adaptations, and physical design modifications can I use to increase/decrease the behavior?
3. Which of these changes are most likely to be effective?

Evaluate the Plan:
How is it working? If it is not working, what changes or modifications are needed to make it work?

Elements of Behavior Support Plans

Horner et al. (1999) and Sugai and Horner (2016) have identified six key elements that are integral to an effective BIP (1) learn how the student perceives or experiences events in his or her environment, (2) invest in preventing occurrences of problem behavior, (3) teaching is the most powerful behavior support strategy available in schools, (4) avoid rewarding problem behavior, (5) reward positive behaviors, and (6) know what to do in the most difficult situations (see Behavior Support Plan Checklist).

Behavior Support Plan Checklist

Student: ______________________________
When developing and implementing behavior support plans, judge the degree to which each of the following has been considered:
G = Good, O = Okay, P = poor, N = not applicable
Date: ____________
Functional assessment:
Develop understanding of problem behavior.

1. Describe problem behavior in operational terms.
2. Identify problem routines.
3. State complete functional assessment hypothesis.
4. Collect data to confirm hypothesis statement.

Foundations:
Consider factors that go across routines.

1. Health and physiology.
2. Communication.
3. Mobility.
4. Predictability.
5. Choice.
6. Social relationships.
7. Activity patterns.

Prevention:
Make problem behavior irrelevant.

1. Modify activity schedule.
2. Adapt curriculum.

3. Modify design of instruction.
4. Adapt instructional procedures.
5. Add prompts for appropriate behavior.
6. Precorrect for typical problem.

Teaching:
Make problem behavior less efficient.
1. Teach specific replacement skills.
2. Teach adaptive social skills.

Extinction:
Make problem behavior less effective.
1. Minimize positive reinforcement for problem behavior.
2. Minimize negative reinforcement for problem behavior.

Reinforcement:
Make appropriate behavior more effective.
1. Select range of effective positive reinforcers.
2. Maximize schedule of positive reinforcement for appropriate behavior.

Crisis Intervention Plan:
Prevent injury.
1. Arrange environment and practice procedures to prevent crisis and emergency situations.
2. Arrange environment and practice procedures to respond to crisis and emergency situations.

Ensure Contextual Fit:
Match intervention to social and treatment context.
1. Consider values and expectations of adults.
2. Assess skill level and fluency of adults.
3. Determine budget.
4. Assess time requirements.
5. Secure administrative support system.
6. Give priority to best interests of student and family.

Evaluation and Assessment:
Make plan more effective, efficient, and relevant.
1. Specify what questions need to be answered.
2. Specify information to be collected.
3. Develop measurement system.
4. Establish schedule for collecting data.
5. Collect and evaluate data.
6. Use data to improve plan.

Source: Horner, R. H., Sugai, G., Todd, A. W., & Lewis-Palmer, T. (1999). Elements of behavior support plans: A technical brief. *Exceptionality*, 8, 205–215.

Each element is explained here in more detail to provide the reader with a better understanding.

Learn How the Student Perceives or Experiences Events in His or Her Environment

Teachers should take the time to ascertain medical, physiological, and social factors that might affect the way in which a student is experiencing the classroom.

Invest in Preventing Occurrences of Problem Behavior

Be aware of antecedents that trigger misbehavior. Some of the more typical of these include (a) poor or deficient communication skills, (b) mobility challenges and poor ambulation, (c) lack of and familiarity with a clear routine, (d) lack of choice in daily activities, (e) social isolation, (f) access to a limited number of activities, and (g) does not receive positive reinforcement, attention, or acknowledgment. In addition, teachers should be aware of and be willing to alter or remove environmental or aversive events and facilitate the attainment of perceived rewards, as appropriate.

Teaching Is the Most Powerful Behavior Support Strategy Available in Schools

Teaching new, adaptive skills is considered by many to be the single most effective behavioral intervention. Often, students engage in misbehavior simply because they do not know a more appropriate way to achieve their goals; therefore, an integral part of every effective behavior intervention plan should be explicit strategies for teaching pro-social behaviors such as social skills instruction, with informative corrections, and high-frequency positive reinforcement for displays of desired alternative behavior.

Avoid Rewarding Problem Behavior (Malcontingency)

It is important that teachers clearly understand the process of identifying the problem or target behavior and only reward behaviors that approach the more appropriate replacement behavior. Preferably, teachers should design BIPs that alter the environment so that undesirable behaviors are unattainable.

Reward Positive Behaviors

Skilled and effective teachers need to identify motivators or incentives that encourage extra effort on the part of students to try to achieve an academic or behavioral goal. Students should receive positive acknowledgments for engaging in appropriate learning and social skills. However, positive reinforcement and praise to reward student effort needs to be meaningful and therefore should reference a concrete, viable achievement.

Know What to Do in the Most Difficult Situations

A good behavior intervention plan should describe, in detail, the appropriate response by teacher and family members to instances of severe misbehavior or misconduct. In addition, teachers and parents must be prepared for the possible reoccurrence of this behavior, because the most reliable predictor of severe misbehavior in a child is the evidence of such behavior in the past.

Monitoring and Evaluation

Teachers and caregivers who design and implement a behavior intervention plan have an obligation to monitor its effectiveness through systematic evaluation. Those with oversight of the BIP should always be observing the plan and the individual for whom the plan was designed, to ensure a good contextual fit among the elements of the plan, the skill level and motivation of the plan implementers, and the quality of environmental support. For a BIP to be implemented effectively, stakeholders must be involved in the development of the BIP, have the skills and knowledge to implement it, have sufficient time and resources to accomplish the plan's objectives, and, most important, believe that the plan can and will be effective.

Typical Nontherapeutic Teacher-Caregiver Responses

Without proper training and preparation, teachers, parents, and community members will respond inconsistently to inappropriate or maladaptive behaviors of school-age children and youth. How they respond will depend on several personological factors, such as (1) perceived competence in behavior management, (2) tolerance of predisposition/sensitivity to the offending behavior, (3) personal and professional management of stress, (4) perceived goodness of fit between the student of concern and the classroom or school culture, (5) the caregiver's affinity for or intuitive connection with the child, (6) school, community, or family policy regarding the type and severity of the misbehavior, and (7) the notion that behavior management is not the purview of teachers (Coleman & Weber, 2002; Cullinan, 2002; Jensen, 2005; Kohn, 2006; Lane et al., 2002; Rosenberg et al., 2004). Each of these factors will be discussed, in brief.

Perceived Competence in Behavior Management

Many teachers and parents complain that they feel unprepared to deal effectively with problem behaviors and therefore abdicate responsibility for dealing with them or direct the student to someone they perceive to be better trained or more capable, such as a special educator, building administrator, or school counselor (Baker, 2005).

Tolerance of Predisposition/Sensitivity to the Offending Behavior

Despite efforts to the contrary, teachers and parents are often subjective in their consideration of misbehavior or aberrant behavior as well as in their tolerance of certain personality types in children. For each of us, there is that one child who seems to be proficient at 'getting under our skin.' Even with the objectivity that should be provided by a systematic screening process, teachers, and parents who respond subjectively or reactively often exacerbate the misbehavior by inadvertently reinforcing it. Occasionally, teachers and parents allow themselves to be drawn into a game of escalating threats and counterthreats, which can negatively affect their authority and influence (Coleman & Webber, 2002; Cullinan, 2002; Jensen, 2005).

Personal and Professional Management of Stress

The effects of personal and/or job-related stress on a teacher's or parent's tolerance level is often overlooked. Today's teachers and parents are under a significant amount of stress caused, in part, by high expectations imposed by each of these roles; for example, teachers are typically involved with more than academic instruction; they are frequently role models, unofficial social workers, and occasionally surrogate parents for their students. These additional unofficial responsibilities, combined with the pressures imposed by standardized tests and increased state and local certification requirements, place a daunting burden on the classroom teacher. Likewise, parents are often struggling with the increased demands of work, the high cost of living, and the pressures imposed by their guilt feelings at not spending enough quality time with their children. All of these personal and professional pressures, as well as many others, combine to create a potentially volatile psycho-emotional state for teachers and parents, one that provides little room for patience and tolerance toward misbehaving students (Herman et al., 2018).

Perceived Goodness of Fit Between the Student of Concern & the Classroom/School Culture

Some studies have demonstrated the importance of 'goodness of fit' in relation to the successful inclusion of a student into a preexisting classroom or school culture. Typically, students who exhibit atypical behaviors, such as those observed in students who have emotional or behavioral disorders, are ostracized by both their classmates and their teacher (Jones et al., 2004). In fact, one study indicated a tendency of students to eschew classmates who were disliked by their teacher (Sachs, 1999). Many students who have behavioral disorders exhibit oppositional and sometimes defiant behaviors, and it is very difficult for parents and teachers to treat them with equanimity; nevertheless, teachers who exhibit consistent intolerance and negativity toward these students invariably escalate the problem.

The Caregiver's Affinity for or Intuitive Connection with the Child

Occasionally, some teachers and parents display preferential treatment toward particular students, even ones who present behavioral challenges. The reason they sometimes give for this exclusive treatment is an intuitive connection or empathy for a particular child. This discriminatory treatment is inconsistent with professionally sound, research-based practice and can result in inconsistent treatment of misbehavior, depending on the teacher's or parent's predisposition toward a particular student. Best practice, of course, requires the teacher to conduct a functional assessment and then to develop an appropriate intervention based on the findings of that nondiscriminatory assessment.

School, Community, or Family Policy Regarding the Type and Severity of the Misbehavior

Many schools and school districts have adopted zero tolerance policies in the aftermath of the Columbine tragedy (Austin, 2003). In addition, some community and family cultures are less tolerant of students who display emotional or behavioral disorders. This low tolerance often results in indiscriminate rejection, alienation, or prescriptive punishment of individuals who engage in aberrant or antisocial behavior. Schools, communities, and families that hold conservative views regarding rule-breaking behavior, and that support the punishment of misbehavior as an effective deterrent, typically have a low tolerance for children and youth who engage in misbehavior. Teachers and other caregivers within these social organizations tend to recommend punishments that are swift and severe, albeit usually ineffective.

The Notion That Behavior Management is Not the Purview of Teachers

There is a pervasive notion among some teachers that behavior management is somehow outside their job description. In other words, these individuals insist that their mandated responsibilities begin and end with teaching and that behavior management is the responsibility of parents, administrators, school counselors, and sometimes the special educator. This flawed perception has led some to abdicate responsibility for managing misbehavior, like the ostrich burying its head in the sand, through planned ignoring. Unfortunately, this attitude sends the wrong message to children and youth with emotional or behavioral disorders. The message it conveys is, essentially, "I don't care about you enough to challenge you to correct your misbehavior." In addition, it allows students to escape the consequences of misbehavior and, in so doing, inadvertently reinforces it (Farmer et al., 2018).

Developing the Right Approach: Some Tips for Avoiding Conflict and Building Community in the Classroom

This book is not intended to be a 'how to' panacea that provides prescriptive responses to specific behavioral problems. On the contrary, presented are research-based practices and interventions that provide teachers with valuable tools and approaches to help students who have EBD be more successful in the classroom and, consequently, in life. To a degree, however, is the book has been written from a constructivist perspective in that the authors firmly believe that all students, including those with EBD, affect and are affected by their social milieu. It is critical to our philosophy of behavioral intervention that, to the greatest extent possible, any intervention developed enhances the individual's ability to be a viable member of his or her community, whether that community be a classroom or society at large.

Furthermore, it is our contention that if behavioral interventions ostracize or alienate a student from his or her teachers or classmates, they will prove ultimately ineffective and counterproductive. Behavioral interventions must therefore be carefully developed to preserve the student's sense of belongingness to the community in the classroom. Such membership is critical in the development of a sense of shared ownership or investment in the classroom and the social responsibility that is created. Likewise, ownership and responsibility within the classroom community fosters a sense of self-empowerment, which obviates the learned helplessness that springs from the external locus of control that is characteristic of most students who have EBD.

It can be argued that many students who engage in antisocial behavior do so because they feel alienated from society. They are often expressing anger, internally or externally, at being excluded and disenfranchised, just as many adults express anger toward the government when they feel disempowered and ignored. Although including these students as viable members of the classroom community will not act as a panacea for their deep-seeded emotional or behavioral problems, it will go a long way toward building trust and relationship, both of which are fundamental criteria for meaningful behavior change. Like the old joke that asks, "How many psychiatrists does it take to change a light bulb?" and replies with the punch line, "Only *one*, but the light bulb has to *want* to change," the student who has EBD must acknowledge the detrimental effects of his or her ineffective behavior and want to change it.

Such an epiphany and resulting transformation can be best achieved in the presence of two antecedents (1) a community that welcomes the student and whose memberships he or she values and (2) the use of a behavioral intervention that is research-based, relevant, and effective. The latter of these predispositions will be carefully explored in the subsequent chapters in relation to specific emotional or behavioral disorder; the former was nicely encapsulated in the work of Kohn (1996; 2006), and some of its key elements are described next.

In his book, *Beyond Discipline: From Compliance to Community*, Kohn (1996; 2006) identified five criteria that are crucial to building community among students and teachers in the classroom; the first of these is a relationship with the adults. Kohn (1996; 2006) suggested that, far too often, teachers isolate themselves from their students, believing the old teacher adage that teachers should not smile at their students until winter vacation. Instead, Kohn (1996; 2006) suggested, teachers should ask students what they think about a topic and then care about the answers the students give. Teachers who form truly caring relationships with students are both helping to meet those students' emotional needs and setting a powerful example. A teacher who listens patiently to student responses or news, apologizes for a misperception or misinformation, or shows genuine concern for the problems expressed by a stranger is modeling the civil behavior that demarcates a caring community. Many children with EBD have no such models and have rarely experienced such civil behavior.

A second criterion suggested by Kohn (1996; 2006) relates to building connections between students. Teachers should provide opportunities for students to interact with every other student in the classroom across a variety of experiences and situations. Teachers, Kohn (1996; 2006) asserted, should provide activities that promote an understanding of another's perspective. Darwall (2004) suggested that an appreciation for another person's point of view is the foundation of community building.

Third in Kohn's (1996; 2006) list of criteria was the promotion of class-wide and school-wide activities. He elaborated on this statement by explaining that students in classrooms and schools should be encouraged to meet en masse and discuss issues of relevance and importance to them and their well-being.

Kohn's (1996; 2006) fourth criteria involves the use of community-building activities to facilitate academic instruction. The author suggested that skillful teachers can integrate academic lessons with group activities. A prime example of this is assertion is the cooperative learning approach, whereby a small group of students (no more than four or five) work together on a project such as a report on the practice of medicine in ancient Egypt. A way to promote an equitable division of labor in these endeavors is to employ Kagan's (1990) numbered heads together approach. In this model of cooperative learning, each student in the various small groups is able to choose a specific task that is integral to the cooperative assignment, and that individual must share her results with the group as a whole and, ultimately, participate in a presentation to the entire class. The student is supported in this endeavor by the rest of the group and receives the same evaluative score as the other members of the team. This type of activity promotes cooperation and teamwork, both essential elements in community-building.

Finally, Kohn (1996; 2006) extolled the value of decision-making. He asserted that this aspect promotes autonomy and self-efficacy, both of which are important factors in character development and the promotion of good citizenship. In short, students in the classroom should be given the autonomy to make responsible, informed choices about the design and development of their classroom community. Research has long advocated the importance of choice for students who have EBD, for whom choice is typically not an option (Patall et al., 2010). The opportunity to participate in the decision-making process is both empowering and community-building because it implies ownership and requires collaboration. In truth, autonomy and community membership are both essential elements of democracy, and the inclusion of students who have EBD in these processes will encourage their responsible participation and positive contribution to society (Kohn, 1996; 2006).

In conclusion, although this book references the disability model as elaborated in IDEA (2004) and the American Psychiatric Association's *Diagnostic and Statistical Manual of Mental Disorders*, 5th edition [DSM-V] (2013), it is used only as far as it provides us with a way of understanding emotional and behavioral disorders and providing help for the children who display it. We do not view children and youth as labels or broken toys that need to be fixed, nor do we recommend a one size fits all approach to behavioral intervention.

The purpose of this book is simply to help teachers work effectively with students who behave in ways that are detrimental to their learning and general well-being. The strategies described are research-based and have been shown to be effective in the classroom, and they are presented in a way that is clear and understandable, with real-world examples that suggest their most effective application. Further, it is acknowledged that, although our approaches represent those currently recommended in the literature, it is very likely that they will not be effective every time for every student who has a particular disorder: There are, of course, no magic bullets in this business. The most powerful and effective intervention protocol is *you*, the teacher, and your thorough *understanding* of each of your students' needs allied with the positive *rapport* you have established with each of them.

Fundamental to this approach is a firm belief in the importance of valuing all individuals, appreciating their unique characteristics, and establishing a caring, respectful relationship with them. Furthermore, we recognize the importance of using a systematic and thoroughgoing approach in identifying both the problem behavior and, most importantly, the function it serves for these individuals. In addition, we strongly advocate the use of research-based interventions that are appropriate for an individual, given his or her specific behavioral characteristics and needs, and that these interventions must be periodically reevaluated and, if necessary, modified to ensure their positive effect.

Finally, in concert with the tenets of inclusion, we believe that each student is a valuable constituent in the classroom and will benefit from the autonomy derived from choice and the responsibility of belonging inherent in that membership. In short, all students must be so empowered, and all students must feel valued.

The subsequent chapters in this book examine nine categories of EBD. Each begins with a description of a relevant case example and is followed by a discussion of the characteristics, prevalence, etiology, and research-based interventions that are relative to the disorder. Then, in accordance with IDEA (2004) and our research-based approach, we use the introductory real-life case study to develop a relevant functional behavioral assessment from which we develop an effective behavioral intervention plan. We conclude each chapter with a concise summary, a section called *Tips for Teachers* that offers easy-to-implement practice-based strategies, and study questions with recommended responses.

This format follows a logical progression and provides a practical application predicated on the real-life case example. It is our hope that this text will help you develop your own individualized behavioral intervention plans that are effective and easily implemented in your classroom. We believe your students will benefit from this research-based, programmatic approach that can and should be tailored to the needs of *your* students.

From the Field

George Giuliano, J.D., Psy.D

George Giuliani is a child psychologist, a legal expert on special education, executive director of the National Association of Special Education Teachers

(NASET), and a professor in the Graduate School Program in Special Education at Hofstra University.

What is 'state-of-the-art' in special education today? Can you tell us about innovations or modifications that, in your opinion, have had the biggest effect on the field?

The state of the art in special education today centers around the concept of inclusion. The focus of our work in the field is primarily about how we can include children with special needs in the general education setting as opposed to segregation. The field is not that old, with the first federal law of P.L. 94-142 only enacted in 1975.

But the major principles of this law still stand true. And two, the concept of "zero reject" and "least restrictive environment" has led to the idea that children with disabilities should be educated with their non-disabled peers to the maximum extent appropriate. As the field of advances, these concepts become ever more important.

What do you think are the most important things a special education teacher should know about IDEIA (2004) and NCLB (2001, 2006)?

I think the answer lies in the question. So many teachers would be better served if they really understood what both laws represented and what they actually do to protect children with disabilities. Too often, we as professionals forget that almost everything we do in special education is primarily guided by federal law. Teachers need to be aware of what the laws allow for, as well as what not. Ultimately, teachers need to understand the general principles of each law, and then be able to apply it to their classrooms.

The question needs to be "How do these laws impact me as a teacher in my classroom?" "How do they affect the children in my class?" "How do they affect the school in which I teach?" "How do they affect the overall state of education?" Only when teachers really understand the impact of the laws can they better be served by them.

What would you say about the importance of making and understanding the distinctions between students with emotional disorders, students who have behavioral disorders, and socially maladjusted students?

I think that the most important thing for teachers to understand is that each child is unique. Some children will exhibit only "symptoms" of behavioral problems, while others will be classified as students with an emotional disturbance. Regardless, the key lies in understanding why the children do what they do, and then what you, as a teacher can do about it. Teachers need to understand behavior, as well as the antecedents and consequences behind it. Furthermore, they have an obligation to learn about the disorders that exceptional children have in their classroom. The reality of "emotional disturbance" is that it tells us very little. It is probably the "vaguest" of all the disabilities. Does the child have depression, anxiety, conduct disorder, schizophrenia, etc.? The list is endless. So, telling me a child is classified with ED, only tells me that the child has emotional/behavioral issues. But what does it really mean? In the end, teachers need to understand each child as a unique entity and learn what motivates the child.

What sort of advice would you offer a new teacher about creating functional behavioral assessments? What sort of advice would you offer a new teacher about creating effective intervention plans?

I have combined these two questions because I believe that the answer is the same. No one expects teachers to be able to write an FBA or BIP on their own. It's not their sole responsibility. Their primary role is to implement whatever is prescribed by the FBA and/or BIP. Teachers need to be very aware of what comprises these very important tools. They need to be giving the other special education professionals, especially the school psychologists, information that can make the plans as effective as possible. New teachers have so much on their plates, but the truth is that when you work with students in special education, you are going to have to work harder. That is the reality. The rewards are wonderful, but you will definitely have to work harder; therefore, it is your responsibility to learn about FBAs and BIPs, look at models of effective ones, and really understand their rationale and purpose.

What sort of advice would you offer a new teacher about communicating with students with emotional disorders, students who have behavioral disorders, and socially maladaptive students?

The bottom line is that you need to be competent and confident. Working with children with ED or similar related disorders and disabilities requires a knowledge base in the field. You need to know how to implement behavior modification plans, provide positive reinforcement, and know how to use punishment and discipline so as to be effective. Students with ED have often had very poor experiences in school. So, when they get a teacher or teachers who genuinely care about their well-being and know that they are there for them 100%, they will often have great respect for them. It will not be easy, but the satisfaction in getting a child with ED to respond is often greater than any other teaching experience, but the only way it works is by understanding the student. You do this by becoming competent in the field, learning about what research has suggested works with children like the ones in your classes, and ultimately knowing how to teach them.

If you could impress something upon the readers of this book—something they often miss but that, if they understood it, would prepare them more effectively for their work—what would it be?

Never lose sight of the fact that you are a teacher and the leader of the classroom. All students will look to you for leadership. Often times, teachers will say "I'm scared of working with those kids with behavioral problems." Well, if you are, then those students are almost assuredly going to recognize that fear. You need to feel good about working with students with ED. You want to be able to work with them and let them know that you understand and want them in your classroom. Students want to succeed and want to feel like they are important. Too often, repeated failure inhibits children with ED to try at school. Your job is to find out what motivates these children and get them to reach their fullest potential.

What changes to you see on the horizon for special education. What do you think are the aspects of the field that most need changing?

The change in the field is definitely one of the school districts moving towards inclusive classrooms. That's a given. We are taking students who used to be in special education classrooms for most/all of the day and now integrating them into the general education classroom for most/all of the day. So, the change is obvious. We as educators at the university and State levels, need to give our general education teachers more courses and more professional development in working with exceptional children. Teachers will be much more effective if they are learning the latest state of the art research in the field. We need to level the playing field and educate all teachers in the field of special education so that they can feel competent when they are working with these children in the general education setting.

Focus Questions Revisited

Why is it so difficult to provide a comprehensive definition for "emotional disturbance," and what are some of the contributing factors?

A Sample Response: Providing a comprehensive definition for emotional disturbance is complicated by several key factors, including:

- Subjectivity in determining abnormal behavior, that is, what constitutes an atypical level of severity (intensity), duration, and frequency, and how we differentiate between abnormal behavior caused by abnormal or mitigating circumstances and abnormal behavior exhibited under normal or near-normal circumstances.

- Effects of developmental change on the behavioral and emotional stability of an individual
- The tendency of the federal and state education agencies to exclude children and youth who are considered "socially maladjusted" or who are "court-adjudicated"
- The controversy surrounding certain diagnoses whose presenting characteristics are not deemed to be primarily emotional or behavioral (e.g., ADHD, autism spectrum disorder)
- The amorphous nature of the field and of special education in general
- The inclusion or exclusion of schizophrenia and other psychiatric diagnoses, depending on the predisposition of a particular state.

Is there a behavioral profile of a child that warrants the classification as emotionally disturbed? If so, what are the characteristic traits?

A Sample Response: Providing a general profile or set of characteristic traits to facilitate a classification of emotionally disturbed is virtually impossible; nonetheless, most of the disorders associated with this category of disability can be organized under two subcategories: externalized, which describes behaviors that are overtly displayed; or internalized, defining behaviors that are more difficult to observe. Subtypes of EBD that are predominantly externalized are those whose characteristics involve observable actions or behaviors that are antisocial, that is, impulsive, aggressive, disruptive, destructive, and in violation of the laws and rules or norms of society. Subtypes of EBD whose behaviors are primarily internalized and thus not as readily apparent include mood disorders such as depression, anxiety disorders such as posttraumatic stress disorder, and thought disorders/psychiatric diagnoses such as schizophrenia.

What is a functional behavior assessment, and how is it applied to classroom intervention?

A Sample Response: The term functional behavioral assessment (FBA) refers to a systematic process used in identifying the "function" or purpose of a specific misbehavior or inappropriate action. According to Skinner (1969) and other behaviorists, all behaviors serve a purpose for the actor; therefore, if practitioners and caregivers can successfully identify that purpose, a relevant and effective intervention can be developed. The danger in not understanding the purpose or root cause of an undesirable behavior is to inadvertently compound the problem by either reinforcing the pathological behavior or wasting time and resources treating a misidentified one.

What are some typical nontherapeutic teacher responses to misbehavior in the classroom, and how can these be positively transformed?

A Sample Response: Without proper training and preparation, teacher, parents, and community members may respond inconsistently to the inappropriate or maladaptive behaviors of school-age children and youth. All too often, untrained, or unenlightened teachers react to maladaptive and disruptive behavior with a knee-jerk response, interpreting the misbehavior as intentional and vindictive and therefore assessing a punishment that is frequently subjective and countertherapeutic. How they respond will depend on several personological factors, including (a) perceived competence in behavior management, (b) tolerance for or predisposition/sensitivity towards the offending behavior, (c) personal and professional management of stress, (d) perceived goodness of fit between the student of concern and the classroom culture, (e) the caregiver's affinity for or intuitive connection with the child, (f) school, community, or family policy regarding the type and severity of the misbehavior, and (g) the notion that the task of behavior management is not the teacher's purview. Proper training in effective behavior management techniques can obviate many of these counterproductive teacher responses.

How can teachers avoid conflict and help build a sense of community or shared responsibility in the classroom?

A Sample Response: Kohn (1996; 2006) identified five criteria that are crucial in building community among students and teachers in the classroom, in and reducing conflict. The first of these is a relationship with the adults. Second, teachers should provide activities that promote an understanding of another's perspective. Feshbach et al. (1983) suggested that an appreciation for another person's point of view is the foundation of community building. Third, skillful teachers can integrate academic lessons with group activities. An example of this type of participative activity is represented in the cooperative learning approach. Fourth, students in the classroom should be given the autonomy to make responsible, informed choices about the design and development of their classroom community. Finally, research has long advocated the importance of choice for students who have EBD, for whom choice is typically not an option (Cullinan, 2002; Jensen, 2005; Kauffman, 2005). The opportunity to participate in the decision-making process is both empowering and community building because it implies ownership and requires collaboration.

Key Terms Used in the Chapter

Socially Maladjusted:
An ambiguous term used frequently to describe children or youth who engage in delinquent acts in the school or community. Occasionally, the term is used interchangeably with the term emotionally disturbed, which is problematic because some states exclude students adjudged "socially maladjusted" from eligibility to receive special education services.

Schizophrenia:
Psychotic disorder characterized by distorted thinking, abnormal perception, and bizarre behavior and emotions observed for at least six months.

Lability:
Unstable, mercurial, or volatile emotional state.

Juvenile Delinquents:
Minors who engage in antisocial or illegal behavior or who commit more serious crimes and misdemeanors.

Externalized behaviors:
Acting-out behavior, such as fighting, typical of students diagnosed with conduct disorder or another disruptive disorder.

Internalized Behavior:
Behavior typically associated with social reticence, as in the case of a child identified with an anxiety or mood disorder.

Functional Behavioral Assessment (FBA):
Refers to a systematic process used in identifying the function or purpose of a specific misbehavior or inappropriate action.

Response to Intervention (RTI):
Refers to a process that emphasizes how well students respond to the changes in instruction. The essential elements of an RTI approach are the provision of scientific, research-based instruction and interventions in general education; monitoring and measurement of student process in response to the

instruction and interventions; and use of these measures of student progress to shape instruction and make educational decisions.

Nondiscriminatory Assessment:
Refers to a comprehensive individual assessment that is free from bias and used to determine eligibility for special education services.

Zero Tolerance:
Refers to the policy of schools, developed during the last decade in response to a series of violent acts of school grounds, to impose mandatory and, in some cases, severe punishments for school infractions of school regulations relative to the health and safety of students and school personnel.

Behavioral Intervention Plan (BIP):
Refers to a relevant, individualized treatment or approach designed to address and mitigate the adverse effects of a specific maladaptive behavior or series of related behaviors, based on the determination of the functional behavior assessment.

Community in the Classroom:
A term coined by Kohn (1996; 2006) to describe a classroom climate that fosters and sustains belongingness, one wherein each student, including individuals with emotional and behavioral disorders, is a valued constituent.

Maladaptive Behaviors:
Behaviors that represent a pathological or antisocial set of actions designed to achieve a desired goal. Such behaviors are often habituated and learned from a high-stakes peer or role model who engages in them.

Chapter 2

Conduct Disorder

Focus Questions

- *What are the defining characteristics of a conduct disorder?*
- *How can I effectively diffuse a behavioral crisis in my classroom that involves a student who has a conduct disorder?*
- *Students who have conduct disorder can be defiant and verbally confrontational. What is the best way to deal with these behaviors when they occur in the classroom?*
- *Because many students who have conduct disorder are co-diagnosed with ADHD, how can I deal effectively with their impulsiveness and off-task behavior?*

Introduction

Students who have been classified as *emotionally disturbed* typically receive counseling as a related service along with special education in either an inclusion or self-contained setting. In fact, teacher surveys have revealed that counseling is the preferred intervention for serious classroom problems (Walker, 1995). With the proliferation of the inclusive model in schools within the United States, increasing numbers of students who emotional behavioral disorders (EBD) such as conduct disorder, oppositional-defiant disorder, and attention-deficit hyperactivity disorder (ADHD) are being educated in general education classrooms (Austin, 2001). This means that now both the special and general education teachers may work with students who have EBD. Affected teachers will be required to participate in the development of these students' Individualized Education Plans (IEPs) and, where possible, coordinate with other service providers.

Unfortunately, because service providers are outside the classroom, there is little opportunity for the teacher to confer with them about issues relevant to a particular student. In addition, many teachers feel absolved of responsibility in providing meaningful interventions for these students because they believe that students who have emotional or behavioral disorders will change simply by gaining insight into the causes of their maladaptive/anti-social behavior (Walker et al., 2004).

Typically, service providers focus on helping students who have conduct disorder and other emotional or behavioral problems identify and understand the reasons for their maladaptive behavior and change it. Often, these students demonstrate an awareness of the inappropriateness of their behavior, but there is little empirical evidence to correlate awareness with behavior change (Dryfoos, 1990). Whereas awareness of a behavior problem and an understanding of its cause is a critical step in the process of behavior change, conscientiously applied, effective behavior change strategies as well as cognitive behavior therapies must be practiced in the classroom, home and community to ensure the permanence and generalizability of the results (Elliot et al., 2002).

This chapter addresses the need for greater reciprocity and collaboration between key stakeholders in the provision of services for students who have conduct disorder -specifically, the classroom teacher, related service providers, and the affected child. Each has an important role in providing therapeutic interventions and therefore should strive to work together to optimize the treatment benefit to the student. To do this effectively, each stakeholder should clearly understand her role as well as that of her colleague.

This chapter provides the information necessary to begin this emerging collaborative process and begins with an overview of conduct disorder: its characteristics, causes, assessment issues, and treatment strategies. A case example follows that will serve as a paradigm for addressing a student who has conduct disorder in the classroom. Two further sections then divide interventions into instructional and behavioral approaches. The chapter ends with a question-and-answer format designed to address the most common problems experienced by teachers in working with children and youth who have conduct disorder.

Case Example: Lucas: A Student with Conduct Disorder

Lucas, a fourteen-year-old student currently enrolled in a residential treatment program in the Hudson Valley Region of New York State displays behaviors that are characteristic of a child with conduct disorder.

Lucas comes from a rural area in south-central New York State, often referred to as the 'southern tier.' Lucas's father, an itinerant laborer, left when Lucas was only two-years of age, and his mother has had a succession of boyfriends and has worked legitimately as a beautician but supplemented her income by selling marijuana and cocaine on the side. She has been arrested and jailed several times for solicitation and drug possession with the intention to distribute.

At five years of age, while enrolled in a local preschool Lucas's teachers reported to Child Protective Services (CPS) that he seemed neglected, his clothes always filthy, his hair matted and unwashed, and he appeared undernourished. He was also observed squirreling away some of the bread and fruit provided at no cost to the students. He seemed food insecure, afraid that he would not be given any more food at home.

After an extensive investigation by CPS, Lucas was removed from his home and was placed in foster care. Unfortunately, Lucas continually fought with his foster parents' children, was very disrespectful toward adults and one evening, started a small fire in his bedroom. The fire starting was the final straw and subsequently, Lucas was transferred to a new foster home in a small town further upstate. During this time, which encompassed a year, he had not been permitted to see or visit with his birth mother because she had been in and out of jail and was currently in an in-patient rehabilitation program.

The second foster care placement fared little better. Lucas continued to fight with the other foster children, and break toys, furniture, and appliances whenever he was disciplined by his new foster parents, which was frequent. The breaking point was an incident in which he fought with one of the other children in the home and was severely punished. After a disingenuous apology, Lucas was sent to his bedroom. Later that night, he crept downstairs to the kitchen, removed a paring knife from the utensil drawer and quietly entered the bedroom of the child with whom he had fought with earlier. The child awoke to find Lucas astride him with the paring knife pressed against his throat. Lucas whispered to him, "If you ever tell on me again, you'll be very sorry!" The child promised not to but relayed the incident to the foster parents the next morning. Lucas was taken to a child psychologist the next day and after extensive evaluation, was placed in a residential treatment program for children with learning and adjustment difficulties within a few weeks.

For the first month or so at the school, Lucas was relatively compliant, seeming to adjust to the new routine and surrounded by scores of children who exhibited behaviors much like his own. By the end of the first quarter in November, however, Lucas began to distinguish himself as a 'leader' who, because of his size and athleticism, was able to intimidate most of his classmates. Whenever he was challenged by another boy, Lucas would wait for an opportunity to ambush and 'sucker punch' the rival. As a result of his aggressive behavior, Lucas was given one of the few single rooms in the residence hall. He was also prescribed several medications to help him control his aggression and violent tendencies - none had any effect at all on Lucas.

Most of his peers were clearly afraid of him and many of teachers and residence staff gave him a wide berth. While Lucas did attend class and usually participated in required after-school activities (since most involved playing a team sport such as basketball and he loved most sports), he continued to hold the dubious distinction as the record-holder for the most fights, most restraints employed to subdue him, and the greatest loss of points and privileges of any child in the program. He was the unrivaled 'baddest' kid on the block. Sadly, during his time in the school, which quickly amounted to years, his birth mother never attempted a visit or tried to contact her son - she had essentially abandoned him.

The following incident epitomizes Lucas's propensity for violence. One afternoon last fall, Lucas was especially disruptive and disrespectful to his homeroom teacher. The teacher felt he could no longer effectively teach with Lucas's disruptive influence and so summoned the crisis-intervention team to forcibly remove him to the quiet room, a room with nothing but padded walls and floor and a locked door with a Lexan window. As Lucas was being escorted into the room he passed another student who was just being released to return to class. In an instant, before the staff could react, Lucas grabbed the hapless student, who was much smaller and weaker and placed him in a chokehold, threatening to break his nose if he (Lucas) was not released immediately. When the crisis staff did not comply with his ultimatum, Lucas viciously punched the poor victim in the nose. The audible snapping sound was nauseating. Having broken the nose of the unoffending student, Lucas turned to the two members of the crisis team and casually reprimanded them for their inaction, explaining nonchalantly that it was their fault the student was injured; after all, he had told them what he would do if his demand was not met.

This incident provides a glimpse of Lucas's window on the world. He sees everyone as a potential threat and consequently is justified in anticipating the worst and acting on that premonition. This is the classic misperception of students with a conduct disorder.

Mr. Leone: A Therapeutic Response to Lucas's Maladaptive Behavior

Mr. Leone is Lucas' homeroom teacher and is well-liked by all his homeroom students. He is genuinely interested in each one and what is going on in their lives and at home. He makes an effort to get to know each of his student's interests, challenges, and day-to-day status both in school and in the residence hall. His colleagues have warned him about Lucas and how mercurial and volatile his temperament can be. They have recommended that he not trust Lucas and have recounted several incidents to support this contention. Some of the teaching staff have even tried to enlist Mr. Leone to sign a petition that will be delivered to school administrators to have Lucas removed from the school and placed in an upstate juvenile detention facility, citing Lucas' propensity for violence, repeated rule violations, and destruction of property.

Mr. Leone has taken these requests and recommendations under advisement, but after studying Lucas' family and academic history and conferring with the social worker and psychologist assigned to Lucas, he felt that more than anything else, Lucas needed to feel cared for and valued as a student and a human being - something that life had never conferred on him.

Mr. Leone has taken the time to learn about Lucas's talents and interests and has developed an academic curriculum that incorporates both. The result has been remarkable. Lucas has responded to Mr. Leone's strategy and has begun to take a real interest in his studies. He also displays more compliance with classroom and school rules and seems to really value and seek the approval of Mr. Leone and other staff, clearly wanting to succeed socially and academically.

This positive trend is not without the occasional setback and Lucas is far from achieving the academic and behavioral goals Mr. Leone has set for him; nevertheless, he is making significant progress in several of his classes, and that has never happened before.

Ms. Sawyer: A Non-Therapeutic Response to Lucas's Maladaptive Behavior

Ms. Sawyer, Lucas' grade eight science teacher, recently retired from public school after thirty years of successful teaching as a middle school science teacher. Toward the end of her career as a public school teacher, Ms. Sawyer enrolled in and successfully completed the requisite courses to obtain her special education certification. Subsequently, Ms. Sawyer served for five years as an inclusion science teacher, providing instruction for both students with and without disabilities. During that time, her belief was that given quality instruction, every child can succeed whether or not they have a learning or behavioral challenge. Most of her students responded positively to that philosophy. She brought this optimistic belief to her new second career, teaching students with emotional and behavioral disorders in a residential treatment setting.

From day one, Lucas chaffed Ms. Sawyer. He refused to respond to her best efforts to entice him to enjoy the sciences. He was consistently defiant and insubordinate engaging in aggressive behavior that would have triggered a 45-day manifestation determination hearing and possible expulsion in her old school - emotionally disturbed or not! She acknowledged that things were categorically different in this 'special' residential school, but she simply could not ignore the disrespectful behaviors of this very troubled and troubling student.

Routinely, Ms. Sawyer would summon the crisis team to remove Lucas to the quiet room for even the slightest provocation; for example, the other day, during a lesson about cell division, she asked the students to sketch a dividing cell. Lucas provocatively drew a very inappropriate cartoon depicting a couple engaged in coitus. When confronted by a furious Ms. Sawyer and asked how he could imagine his drawing was on task and appropriate, Lucas replied without pause, "Oh, I think having sex makes a lot of cells divide!" whereupon the rest of the class erupted with laughter.

Ms. Sawyer immediately called for his removal from class and warned him, as he was being escorted to the quiet room, that if he continued to behave like an animal, he would never pass science eight or graduate from middle school. She intimated, not too subtly, that he might soon end up somewhere else even more restrictive and unpleasant.

Commentary

Lucas clearly meets the criteria for conduct disorder (see DSM-V Diagnostic Criteria for Conduct Disorder), and his early developmental history would suggest that he has a disorganized attachment style. As mentioned in the introduction, disorganized was added to classify infants who lacked any organized attachment style with the premise that their basic experience of the attachment figure was frightening. As a result, they experience the world as threatening and therefore must deal with others accordingly. Lucas hurts others both physically and emotionally as his way of survival. Abandonment by father, succession of mother's boyfriends, a series of mother's imprisonment along with multiple foster care placements all indicate a complete lack of attachment security evidenced by early signs of neglect. Even basic needs like food seem to have gone unmet. It is no wonder that he often engages in proactive aggression to establish a sense of security in a world that early on proved to be anything but secure. The larger issue, however, is what is the most effective way to deal with a student like Lucas. This is not an easy question.

Both Ms. Sawyer and Mr. Leone want to help Lucas, but there is a difference between them. Ms. Sawyer, to her credit, believes all students, with an enthusiastic and dedicated teacher, can not only learn but actually enjoy the material. This did not work with Lucas, and it was only a matter of time before he exhibited the same insubordinate, aggressive, and frightening behaviors. Ms. Sawyer resorted to a common intervention - often calling the crisis team with the eventual demand that he be removed from her class. This is thought to be the only solution to a sociopathic child - if you commit the crime you pay the fine. A more empathic approach will not work since a student like Lucas is thought to be devoid of empathy and will only use such an approach to manipulate and achieve his own selfish interests. In the world in which

Lucas lives, no one can be trusted, not even, and perhaps most especially, those who show love and support.

Mr. Leone, on the other hand, is able to see beyond Lucas' behavior a child, who despite all his frightening behavior, is frightened himself and therefore needed to be cared for and valued. From an attachment perspective, we would say that Mr. Leone, if he is able to resist getting caught up and derailed by Lucas' provocations, is trying to provide him with security that was completely absent in his childhood. For Mr. Leone, setbacks in his work with Lucas are not an invitation to personalize rejection of his efforts and give up but an opportunity to remain steadfast in his approach. One thing Mr. Leone should be clear about is that he is not going to replicate the rejection of so many others; rather, he will give Lucas an alternate response with the hope that his worldview can be shifted to one that is more secure and consequently diminish his need to annihilate others. There are no guarantees in this approach, but it is a strategy worth employing as it does not replicate the abandonment that Lucas' behavior pulls for.

Characteristics of Conduct Disorder

Conduct disorder (CD), along with oppositional defiant disorder (ODD), is recognized as a major diagnostic category among disruptive behavior disorders (DBDs) in childhood and adolescence. CD is one of the most common reasons for referral to children and adolescents to mental health treatment centers (Cunningham et al. 2016). According to Mohan et al. (2021), "conduct disorder is more common in boys than girls, and the ratio could range from 4:1 as much as 12:1. The lifetime prevalence rate in the general population could range from anywhere between 2 to 10% and is consistent among different race and ethnic groups" (n.p.).

According to the *Diagnostic and Statistical Manual of Mental Disorders*, (DSM-V) (American Psychiatric Association, 2013), CD is "a repetitive and persistent pattern of behavior in which the basic rights of others or major age-appropriate societal norms or rules are violated" (p. 469). The fifteen criteria listed below in the DSM-V Diagnostic Criteria for Conduct Disorder (American Psychiatric Association, 2013) reveal the basic symptomatology of CD. In order to distinguish simple aggressive behaviors from CD, the frequency, intensity, and degree of functional impairment must be considered as it is estimated that 70% of adolescents participate in some delinquent behavior (Mangold & King, 2020). The DSM-V (American Psychiatric Association, 2013) understands CD as violating both the rights of others and societal norms on a consistent basis, stipulates that at least three of the fifteen criteria must be present during the last twelve months, and at least one criterion must have been present in the last six months, for a diagnosis of CD.

DSM-V Diagnostic Criteria for Conduct Disorder

1. Bullies, threatens, or intimidates others
2. Initiates physical fights
3. Uses a weapon(s) that can cause serious physical harm to others
4. Has been physically cruel to people
5. Is cruel to animals
6. Confronts a victim and steals
7. Forces others into sexual activity
8. Sets fires with the intention of causing serious damage
9. Destroys other's property
10. Breaks into someone else's house, building, or car
11. Lies to obtain goods or favors or to avoid obligations
12. Steals items of nontrivial value
13. Stays out at night despite parental prohibitions, beginning before age 13
14. Runs away from home overnight at least twice while living in parental or parental surrogate home
15. Often truant from school, beginning before age 13 years.

Adapted from DSM-V by the American Psychiatric Association, 2013.

In order to distinguish conduct problems in general from CD in particular, researchers and theorists have developed various subtypes of aggression. The DSM-V (American Psychiatric Association, 2013) distinguishes three subtypes based on age (childhood-onset type and adolescent-onset type), limited prosocial emotions (lack of remorse or guilt, lack of empathy, unconcerned about performance) and three levels of severity (mild, moderate, and severe) based on the number of conduct problems presented. The case example of Lucas at the beginning of the chapter provides a realistic profile of a student with a more intense level of CD to better illustrate the characteristics as manifested in the home and at school.

Age of onset is a significant factor in determining the future course of CD. The adolescent type develops after age 10 and usually with the onset of puberty. Well over 50 percent of those with early onset (before age 8 years) continue with serious problems into adulthood, marked by disrupted and violent relationships, vocational problems, and substance abuse (Fairchild et al., 2019), and anywhere from 25 to 40 percent develop adult anti-social personality disorder (Docherty et al., 2019). They are more likely to drop out of school.

On the contrary, about 85 percent of those with adolescent-onset type show an absence of antisocial behaviors by their early twenties (Bakker et al., 2017). Additional subtypes of conduct problems, though not included in the DSM-V (American Psychiatric Association, 2013), include aggressive versus nonaggressive behaviors, reactive versus proactive aggression, and overt versus relational aggression (Kimonis & Frick, 2006). Non-aggressive behaviors such as being stubborn, angry, defiant, and touchy are more characteristic of ODD (see Chapter 3), whereas bullying, fighting, property violations such as vandalism, cruelty to animals and fire setting are more indicative of CD. Overt aggression involves hitting, pushing, kicking, and threatening, in contrast to relational aggression designed to damage relationships and peer group affiliations through gossiping and spreading rumors (Fairchild et al., 2019).

Research shows that children evidence either reactive or proactive aggression (Rieffe et al., 2016). Proactive aggression is carefully planned and designed with a clear purpose in mind; for example, to obtain some material benefit (robbery), power over others (bullying), or to increase one's social status (risk-taking behaviors) (Rieffe et al., 2016). Reactive aggression, on the other hand, is retaliatory and based on real or perceived threats (Rieffe et al., 2016). These children evidence deficits in social information processing, with a tendency to employ a hostile attribution bias to ambiguous situations (van Bockstaele et al., 2020). A reactively aggressive child can turn a neutral encounter into a fight, often with deleterious consequences. Proactively aggressive children tend to have a more positive prognosis when it comes to decreasing the frequency of aggressive behaviors.

A final subtype of children with conduct disorder behaviors are termed *callous* and *unemotional* (Caputo et al., 1999; Frick et al., 2000). They tend to be more proactive in their aggression, suffer from an absence of guilt, like to participate in novel and exciting risk-taking behaviors, and are by and large insensitive to punitive consequences for their behaviors (Frick et al., 2003; Pardini et al., 2003).

Prevalence of Conduct Disorder

Among community samples, the prevalence rate for males with CD is between 2 and 4-5 percent, while for females, the range is between 0.5 percent and 4.5 percent (Moore et al., 2017). Difficulties in estimating prevalence rates for CD include the use of different criteria, the methods used to assess these criteria (child reports versus parent reports) and variations that occur at different ages and among different subgroups such as males versus females. Childhood-onset CD is more common among boys; however, before the age of 5, rates are more or less equivalent for both sexes (Fairchild et al., 2019). CD increases significantly during adolescence with significant differences in rates of CD among ethnic groups. African-American youth have higher rates of CD compared to White youth (Cunningham et al., 2016). Such differences might be contextual, as a greater percentage of children of color live in neighborhoods with higher rates of crime, poverty, and violence. Evaluator bias can also play a role in assessing clients of color more or less severely (Gushue, 2004; Gushue et al., 2008).

Comorbidities

Children and adolescents with CD often suffer from other disorders, the most frequent of which are Attention Deficit Hyperactive Disorder (ADHD), learning disabilities, anxiety, and depression. Of these, ADHD is the most common co-morbid disorder. ADHD is more frequent among those diagnosed with childhood-onset CD, and this subgroup tends to display more chronic delinquency, more severely aggressive acts during adolescence and more violent offenses in adulthood. It is not known whether the high rate of learning disability among those with CD is due more to the comorbidity of ADHD and less to the conduct problems. There is most likely an interaction effect as some children with learning disabilities who do not have ADHD develop conduct problems later during adolescence.

Children with CD have high rates of anxiety and/or depression. Estimations are that anywhere from 15 to 31 percent of children with CD have depression (Erskine et al., 2016). Among community samples, between 22 percent and 33 percent have an anxiety disorder, and this rate increases to between 60 and 75 percent among clinic samples (Erskine et al., 2016). Those who are depressed are at an increased risk for suicidal ideation. Children with CD have pervasive relationship problems; therefore, the high rates of anxiety and depression could be the result of interpersonal conflicts (Munene & James 2017).

Etiology of Conduct Disorder

In general, the literature has divided the risk factors for developing CD into three categories to include biological, psychological, and social. Multiple risk factors play a role in the development of CD. Kimonis and Rick (2014) suggested three methods for understanding the influence of multiple risk factors to be cumulative, interactionist, and multiple pathways. In the *cumulative* method, one is concerned simply with number of risk factors; the more risk factors one has, the more likely one is to develop CD. The *interactionist* perspective emphasizes the significance of certain risk factors interacting with others, and it is the combination rather than the accumulation of factors that result in CD. The *multiple* pathway method suggests that different causal processes are involved in the development of CD, and each involves a different set of risk factors. Childhood-onset of CD, for example, has more to do with personality/dispositional factors than adolescent onset and may result in adolescent rebellion taken to an extreme (Taubner et al., 2019).

Biological Factors

Biological factors can be subdivided into genetics, hormonal, neurotransmitter dysfunction, neurological, and prenatal toxin exposure (Heatly & Lee, 2018).

Genetic Factors

Studies examining a genetic link have found a high correlation for CD among twins and between family negativity and adolescent antisocial behavior (Holz et al., 2018). Among those with adolescent-onset CD, family environment had more of an impact, in contrast to younger children with CD in whom the genetic influence was a more significant factor (McCart et al., 2014). Studies have supported a strong association between parental antisocial behavior and preadolescent onset of CD and parental psychopathology such as mother's substance abuse, anxiety, or depression (Heatly & Lee, 2018).

Hormonal Factors

In general, studies have found hormone levels, particularly high levels of testosterone and its derivatives, to be associated with CD with specific attention paid to high levels of dehydroepiandrosterone (DHEAS), the precursor to testosterone, similar to boys with oppositional defiant disorder (Bakker-Huvenaars et al., 2020).

Neurotransmitter Dysfunction

The role of neurotransmitter dysfunction has also been studied in the development of aggression in children, adolescents, and adults. Abnormal function of serotonin, the neurotransmitter implicated in the expression and regulation of affect and impulse control, has been found to play a role in aggression and lack of impulse control as have low levels of 5-hydroxyindoleacetic acid (metabolized serotonin) in the cerebrospinal fluid. In addition, low levels of the neurotransmitter, serotonin, have been linked to aggression in children (Clanton et al., 2017).

Neurological Factors

The relatively new research in neuroanatomy and CD has consistently shown frontal lobe damage in subjects prone to violence and aggression (Darby, 2018). Underarousal of the autonomic nervous system (i.e., slower heart rate) is associated with adolescent antisocial behavior and later criminality (Sijtsema & Garofalo, 2019).

Prenatal Toxin Exposure

Prenatal and perinatal complications and maternal smoking and/or substance abuse during pregnancy have also been associated with behavioral problems (Scott-Goodwin et al., 2016). Finally, exposure to environmental toxins, such as lead, is also associated with delinquency and aggression (Jackson et al., 2017).

In summary, there exists a host of biological factors for which empirical research has established a link, not necessarily with CD specifically; rather with violence and aggression in general, which are the prominent characteristics of CD. A combination of these biological factors are more likely than any one factor to contribute to a diagnosis of CD.

Neuropsychological Factors

Burke et al. (2002), in their review of the literature on CD, categorized psychological factors as temperament, attachment, neuropsychological functioning, intelligence and academic performance, reading problems, impulsivity and behavioral inhibition, social cognition, sociomoral reasoning, and pubertal/adolescent development. For many of these factors, contradictory findings exist. The more consistent and stronger associations with CD are neuropsychological deficits, especially in the area of executive functioning (Schoorl et al., 2018), low achievement and school failure (Powers et al., 2016). Intelligence level is mediated by other factors.

Many of the functional factors may serve as pathways rather than predictors of behavioral disorders. Even the stronger associated factors appear to be mediated by confounding factors such as ADHD and early psychosocial factors discussed below. In general, children with CD have lower-than-average IQs and, more specifically, have deficient verbal IQs. Studies have also shown impairment in executive functions (concentration, attention, planning sequencing, and inhibition) (Schoorl et al., 2018) along with deficits in reading (Cederlöf et al., 2017).

Psychosocial Factors

Among the most notable psychosocial factors in the development of CD are parenting (including abusive practices), peer effects, and neighborhood/socioeconomic determinants (Burke et al., 2002).

Parenting

Poor family management (i.e., inconsistent and severe discipline, poor supervision, and failure to set clear expectations) is among the most powerful predictors of later delinquency (van Gelder et al., 2018). Another pathway to conduct disturbance seems evident - children whose parents are hostile, negative, and neglectful are at risk for developing all sorts of mental health problems, which in turn lead to patterns of antisocial and violent behavior (Rajyaguru et al., 2019). Undoubtedly, when children are exposed to violence in the home, they come to understand violence as an acceptable way of dealing with conflict and solving problems. Exposure to high levels of family and marital conflict increase the risk for later violence.

Peer Effects

Peer-related factors in predicting conduct problems have been examined in terms of having delinquent siblings, delinquent peers, and gang membership. All three have been found to have a positive link to disturbances in conduct (Utržan et al., 2018).

Neighborhood and Socioeconomic Factors

The factors hypothesized as contributing to conduct disorder in youth are poverty, community disorganization, availability of drugs and firearms, neighborhood adults involved in crime, exposure to violence and racial prejudice, and violence in the media (Jennings et al., 2018).

Conclusions about Risk Factors

One of the difficulties in predicting CD is that most of the research has examined factors contributing to CD in conjunction with symptoms of other diagnoses such as Oppositional Defiance Disorder (ODD) and ADHD. Another problem is that most studies have looked at aggression and delinquency as outcomes and, for the most part, have left unexamined nonaggressive antisocial behaviors (Burke et al., 2002). Research is far from complete on youth violence and delinquency. More research is needed to study the interaction effects of different factors as predictors of other problems. The greater the number of risk factors, the more likely it is that a youth will receive a diagnosis of CD. The percentage of youth convicted for conduct violations increased from 3 percent for those with no risk factors to 31 percent for youth with four risk factors (Farrington et al., 2017). Helpers must be especially vigilant of those students who evidence more than one factor.

Assessment

Many consider a diagnosis such as CD to be overused; therefore, assessment needs to be both multimethod and multi-informant. Most experts recommend at minimum the use of an interview, rating scales, and observational data.

Interviews

Interviews can be either unstructured or structured. The unstructured interview most often used by clinicians helps to build rapport but is questionable in term of reliability and validity (Kelley et al., 2016). The skilled provider, however, will know what questions to ask, intuit the client's capacity for victim empathy and realize the degree of manipulation. Some adolescents who have CD actually don't mind talking about their egregious acts. Others will refrain from talking because they see the sharing of information as giving up control.

Several semi-structured interviews exist for diagnosing conduct problems. Sections on the *Child Assessment Schedule* (CAS; Hodges et al., 1982) and the *Schedule for Affective Disorders and Schizophrenia for School-Aged Children* (K-SADS; Spitzer et al., 1998) that deal with conduct problems can be helpful in recognizing and diagnosing CD.

Structured instruments (instruments that do not allow for any additional follow-up or probes) for assessing CD that use the DSM-V criteria exist. The most well-known are the *Diagnostic Interview Schedule for Children* (DISC-IV; Shaffer et al., 2000) and the *Diagnostic Interview for Children and Adolescents* (DICA-I; Welner et al., 1987). The disadvantage of the structured interview is that they are time-consuming and often do not include normative data (Loney & Lima, 2003).

Rating Scales

Numerous rating scales exist for the assessment of CD that are either self-reports or reports by significant others. Rating scales have the advantage of being relatively fast to administer and use normative data. One widely used measure is the Behavior Assessment System for Children (BASC; Reynolds & Kamphaus, 1992). It is a multi-informant measure for parent, child and teacher that measures adaptive functioning and other clinical categories (e.g., depression, anxiety) as well as tapping into CD.

Self-reports are frequently used among adult populations. Their use among children and adolescents is questionable because these populations often see themselves as not having a problem and can be poor historians. As a result, greater reliability is attached to reports from significant others. For parents of those suspected of CD, a frequently used measure is the *Eyberg Child Behavior Inventory* (ECBI; Eyberg & Pincus, 2022) that primarily assesses problems at home such as fighting and other oppositional behaviors. It also has a teacher-report form, *Sutter-Eyberg Student Behavior Inventory* (SESBI; Eyberg & Pincus, 2022). General, broadband measures of psychopathology can also be used to confirm a diagnosis of CD. One of the most widely used for parents is the *Achenbach System of Empirically Based Assessment* (ASEBA; Achenbach &

Rescorla, 2004). The ASEBA also has a *Teacher Report Form,* as does the *School Behavior Checklist,* another widely used general measure of psychopathology.

Direct Observation

Behavioral observations are advantageous because they are less biased than child, parent and even teacher reports; however, they can be time-consuming and complicated due to observation schedules for coding classroom and group interactions, in addition to the parent reports. After a designated time period, the observer completes a checklist of behavioral indicators. Many of the behaviors associated with CD are infrequent and covert in nature; therefore, some have called into question the reliability of direct observation to assess CD (Thornton & Frick, 2018). Manipulation and deceit, often characteristic of CD, can reduce reliability in observation.

Direct observation of the parent and child together is also recommended for differentiating a diagnosis of CD. Typically, parent and child are observed in both a structured and unstructured activity for communication patterns, positive parenting behaviors, and child's response to parental demands. The three common approaches are free-play, parent-directed play, and parent-directed chore situations (Roberts & Hope, 2001). For older children and adolescents, an argument-producing discussion topic or a problem-solving task can be substituted for play activity (Freeman & Hogansen, 2006). One of the more well-known parent-child observation scales is the *Dyadic Parent-Child Interaction Coding System* (DPICS; Nelson & Olsen, 2018).

Summary

The formal diagnosis of CD is not an easy task. Some symptoms can overlap with other diagnoses, and there is a high degree of co-morbidity that complicates the diagnostic picture. Because deceit forms a part of symptomatology, even the more astute helper can be fooled; therefore, assessment of CD should occur over time and be multimodal. Helpers are encouraged to make every effort to gather as much information as possible through observation, both formal and informal, along with reports from parents as well as academic and clinical records.

Treatment Strategies

Effective treatment strategies for CD can be divided into four categories to include individual cognitive-behavioral, family-based, multisystemic, and psychopharmacological. The following paragraphs describe and evaluate these four approaches to the treatment of CD.

Cognitive Behavioral Treatment

Cognitive-behavioral treatment (CBT) focuses primarily on thought processes and employs behavioral techniques to change those processes that are seen as being responsible for problematic behavior. The therapist attempts to engage the client in new ways of thinking that will result in new ways of feeling and behaving. Aggressive youth tend to perceive neutral acts by others as hostile; therefore, the helper can work with them on their perceptions and change some of their faulty thinking (Harris, 2019). The teaching of problem-solving skills and relaxation training can also form part of the treatment. Problem-solving strategies are a multi-step process that involves:

1. A description of the problem and major goals for the solution;
2. Generation of alternate solutions;
3. Evaluation of these alternatives in terms of how well they will assist in the achievement of the goal;
4. Selection and enactment of the best strategy identified; and
5. Evaluation of the degree of success of the outcome (Southam-Gerow, 2003).

The *Coping Power Program* (Powell et al., 2017) treats both child-level factors (poor decision-making skills, poor self-regulation, poor ability to resist peer pressure, and reading social skills appropriately) and contextual factors (poor parental caregiver skills and discipline). The skills imparted through the *Coping Power Program* are usually through a group modality.

Empirical studies over the years have found CBT to be moderately effective in treating CD and less effective than family-based and multisystemic treatments; for example, problem-solving skills have been found to be an effective treatment, but not as effective in combination with parent management training (Pooravari et al., 2016). The American Psychological Association concluded that child-focused CBT did not meet the criteria for well-established treatment status, in contrast to parent-focused interventions, which did (Matthys & Schutter, 2021). By focusing on the child, CBT may not sufficiently consider family influences in the development and maintenance of CD (Gatti et al., 2019).

Family-Based Interventions

Family-based interventions can be divided into two categories to include those that focus on parenting and work exclusively with the primary caregiver(s) in terms of parent management training and those that work with the entire family system.

Parent Management Training

Parent management training (PMT) is used primarily for preschool and elementary school children who are evidencing conduct problems. The theoretical basis for PMT is the assumption that conduct problems are developed and sustained in the home by maladaptive parent-child interactions (Kazdin, 2018). The trainer works with the parents to alter their interaction with the child by teaching the parents to give clear rules and commands, positive reinforcement for compliance, time-outs, and loss of privileges for non-compliance, negotiation, and contingency contracting with consistent consequences for unwanted behavior (Kazdin, 2017).

PMT is perhaps the most empirically investigated technique for reducing symptoms of CD. Numerous studies have shown PMT to be effective in both the short and long term (Colalillo & Johnston, 2016; Ollendick et al., 2016; Thijssen et al., 2017). Greater effects are associated with longer-term programs. Programs with less than ten hours of PMT indicate negligible benefits. In spite of the overwhelming evidence in favor of PMT, parental resistance and psychopathology are impediments to treatment. The availability of numerous manuals makes PMT a simple and effective approach to treating CD, especially with younger children. If the helper can engage the parents into this form of treatment, it is likely they will successfully reduce much of the problematic behaviors associated with CD.

Family Systems Therapy

Treating the entire family (defined as those living together) for one member with CD results from the conceptualization that the identified symptom serves a systemic function; for example, a family counselor might view CD as the system's need for avoiding interpersonal contact or distract mother and father from their own relationship problems. Functional family therapy (FFT) consists of three phases to include engagement and enactment, behavioral change, and generalization (Sexton, 2017).

During the first phase, the provider meets with the family, knowing that within a short period of time, the family will demonstrate its familiar ways of behaving. The provider is alert to patterns of communication, coalitions, and boundaries being either too diffuse or too rigid. In the second phase, the provider begins to interrupt these familiar patterns and restore power and authority to the executive subsystem. In the third phase, the family members are taught to apply their new learning by anticipating problems, practicing, and preventing themselves from relapsing into old and familiar ways of relating.

The advantage of FFT is its short-term focus - anywhere from six to twelve sessions. Two disadvantages are the difficulty of engaging the entire family system and the lack of helpers sufficiently trained to work with the entire family. Over the years, family counselors have become known for their direct and sometimes confrontational style, which is often at odds with the traditional training one receives in working with individuals. A number of studies, however, have shown that FFT can be effective in reducing recidivism rates among adolescents with delinquent histories and improving the functioning of those with conduct problems (Gottfredson et al., 2018; Humayun et al., 2017; Sexton, 2019).

Multisystemic Treatment

More recently, multisystemic treatment (MST) for conduct disorder has shown the greatest success. MST goes beyond family treatment because it considers the family system as an important but only one of a number of systems in which a child is embedded (Henggeler, 2017). These other systems include peers, school, and neighborhood. Because not only family relations but involvement with deviant peers, school difficulties, and neighborhood/community factors are strong contributors to delinquency, successful treatment of CD should include these other systems.

At the family level, MST will employ some form of FFT outlined above. At the peer level, interventions attempt to diminish the association with deviant peers and replace those relationships with more positive ones by facilitating membership in organized athletics, after-school activities, and church youth groups (Henggeler, 2017). At the school level, the provider develops strategies to help parents monitor school performance by opening lines of communication between parents and teachers and structuring time at home to go over homework and other school-related activities.

When biological factors are involved, MST employs the use of psychopharmacology, an intervention discussed in a separate section below. MST is broad-based and flexible to consider and deal with any and all factors contributing to CD; for example, a parent's stress because of unemployment complicating the task of effective parenting, would also be addressed by the provider.

Research examining the effectiveness of MST has shown it to be superior to other forms of treatment for general delinquency (Boxer et al., 2017), violent and chronic offenses (Borduin et al., 2017, 2018; Corrado et al., 2019), substance use and abuse (Calix et al., 2018) and sexual offenses (Grant et al.,

2016). In spite of its documented success, however, MST is not always the preferred mode of treatment for CD. One disadvantage is that MST is time-consuming and practical concerns such as insurance reimbursement for a provider's time spent outside the traditional therapeutic encounter make it difficult for some clinics and programs to implement MST.

Psychopharmacological Intervention

As mentioned previously, recent literature has established a genetic and neurobiological link in the development of CD. This has led to an increased consideration of psychopharmacological intervention with this population. Although a number of different drugs have been shown to be effective, the difficulty of doing randomized controlled studies (RCT's) with children and adolescents caution circumspection in the use of drug therapy.

The most prescribed medications for conduct problems are stimulants, most especially methylphenidate (Ritalin being the most popular). CD is highly comorbid with ADHD; therefore, stimulants known to be effective for reducing the impulsivity associated with ADHD have effectively reduced conduct problems in children with both CD and ADHD (Bakker et al., 2017; Joseph et al., 2019). Even when ADHD was controlled, stimulants helped in reducing symptoms of CD.

Although there is some evidence for the effectiveness of several medications in reducing the symptoms of CD, the support is far from conclusive. At most, medications are partially helpful, and more effective results require the need for complementary treatment modalities. When psychosocial treatment is combined with medication therapy for conduct problems, the rate of improvement is far higher (Cornacchio et al., 2018). In addition, the benefits of medication must always be considered in conjunction with the cost of side effects.

Summary

In spite of studies showing the effectiveness of different interventions for CD, a number of challenges and limitations exist in achieving success with this population. A significant number of children do not improve. Improvement is difficult to sustain over time and across settings, and rarely does a child with CD reduce behaviors to a normative level. Children under the age of 8-years-old show the greatest improvement, which emphasizes the need for early intervention and suggests that interventions with older children and adolescent are less effective (Kyranides et al., 2018; Murrihy et al., 2017). Schools work with children on a daily basis, and those institutions that have developed school-based intervention programs for children with CD have the greatest chances of success in reducing aggressive behaviors.

School-Based Interventions

Thorough coverage of the characteristics, prevalence, causes, assessments, and treatment strategies that are currently recommended concerning children and adolescents who have conduct disorder is provided throughout this book. This information will provide the reader with a sound knowledge base from which to embark on the next phase of our investigation: the application of theory and research to classroom practice. This process involves two distinct stages (1) assessing the problem and (2) developing an effective intervention plan, as required by the federal Individuals with Disabilities Education Act (IDEA, 2004). Both stages will be described in detail in the passages that follow, and a suggested intervention plan for Lucas, the case example for this chapter, will be elaborated.

Assessing the Problem

The behavioral assessment, in this case a functional behavioral assessment (FBA), is based on the hypothesis that specific environmental factors are related directly to problem behavior, these variables or factors can be identified through assessment, and addressing these factors systematically can reduce the problem behavior and/or support the development of more functional, pro-social behavior.

In the case of a child or youth with a conduct disorder, this assessment approach is particularly useful to teachers, because it helps them identify the purpose the maladaptive behavior serves. The FBA can be direct, through actual teacher observation and recording of the target behavior, or indirect, through what other sources such as peers, family members, and others may say. A simple way of establishing a direct FBA assessment is through the use of an A-B-C record sheet. (A=Antecedents; B=Behavior; C=Consequence; see A-B-C Recording Form below).

A-B-C Recording Form

Student's Name: ______________________ Date: ____________ Class: ____________

Teacher: __________________ Consultant: ____________________ Time: ____________

In the Behavior column, note codes for target behaviors as they occur. You can also record additional information about the behavior, such as the name of the student who was hit when the behavior "hitting" occurred.
In the Antecedent column, record the code for the classroom activity and any specific list codes and their definitions here:

Antecedent	Behavior	Consequence

Source: Witt, J.C., Daly, E., & Noell, G.H. (2000). Functional assessments: A step-by step guide to solving academic and behavioral problems. Longmont, CO: Sopris West.

An example of the use of the A-B-C record sheet is for a child who consistently hits other children in class. The teacher would record the incidents of hitting (the target behavior) over the course of the day and also pays close attention to the activities or specific events that occurred just prior to the target behavior. Next, the teacher records the events that occurred just after the target behavior, using codes or brief narration.

The result of this behavior recording is the development of a hypothesis that should include (1) setting events, (2) immediate antecedent events, (3) problem behavior, and (4) maintaining consequences (outcomes that help maintain the behavior - which may be positive or negative). If it is hypothesized, for example, that the child hits to stop verbal antagonism from a classmate, the consequence might be that the antagonism stops, thus negatively reinforcing the hitting (i.e., an aversive, the antagonism, is removed by hitting). If the child derives gratification through the intimidation of peers by hitting, however, then the fear and intimidation produced in the victims serves as a positive reinforcement for the behavior (hitting).

In the case of Lucas, three types of assessment were used (1) a formalized interview; namely, the *Diagnostic Interview for Children and Adolescents* (DICA-IV; Welner et al., 1987), (2) rating scales, in this case, the *Achenbach System of Empirically Based Assessment* (ASEBA; Achenbach & Rescorla, 2004), and direct observations. As noted earlier, assessment of CD should occur over time and be multi-modal. The results of these assessments helped to confirm the diagnosis of conduct disorder and provided Lucas with special education services under the classification: *emotional disturbance*.

Based on the extensive evaluation, Lucas's behaviors targeted for treatment included (1) physical and verbal intimidation and aggression, (2) unprovoked anger and hostility toward others, and (3) blatant disregard for the rights and property of others. The purpose or function served by these behaviors was hypothesized to be Lucas's need to expiate his anger towards his mother as well as his own sense of alienation from the community.

A behavioral intervention plan was subsequently developed to effectively address these behaviors and their root causes. Lucas's positive response to this plan confirmed the correctness of the functional hypothesis and therefore this behavioral intervention plan was incorporated into his IEP.

Developing an Effective Intervention Plan

Most teachers have few resources or the time to conduct elaborate behavioral assessments, despite the recommendations of some researchers. Often, these researchers fail to understand the complexities of the modern classroom, which are often overcrowded (especially in urban schools), have insufficient resources, and include several children with special needs. To compound these concerns, typical preadolescent and adolescent students often engage episodically in antisocial acts as a function of psychosocial and physiological development aggravated by environmental factors.

In the real world of the classroom, teachers, in the moment of crisis, need strategies they can employ with reasonable effectiveness and immediacy given the time constraints of the typical class period. Unfortunately, much of the current literature has not been classroom-tested and does not take into consideration these limitations.

Students with conduct disorders often manifest aggressive, intimidating, and coercive behaviors and are therefore perceived as threats to safety and good order. For these reasons, they are often expelled during the middle or high school grades. This tendency underscores the importance of effective assessment at the earliest opportunity to determine the presence of challenging, antisocial behaviors as well as academic deficiencies. Students who exhibit these behaviors consistently are more likely to be removed from the school experience or drop out voluntarily (Walker et al., 2014).

Before a student can be provided an effective intervention, the teacher must gain an understanding of the interpersonal dynamics of the student, include academic and social strengths and weaknesses as well as personal preferences. Next, teachers must take a personal inventory of their own prejudices toward this type of child and find the motivation to work with these students for the duration of the school year. Finally, the teacher must seek out and develop a support group consisting of other teachers who work successfully with students who exhibit maladaptive behavior.

Recommended interventions for the teachers who provide instruction for students who have conduct disorder can be divided into two categories, those of instructional and cognitive-behavioral. The first step in selecting an appropriate intervention, however, is to establish a rapport with each of the students in the class. Taking the time to learn a little about the students and including them in decision-making helps establish the trust necessary to ensure that an affected student will participate in an intervention. This alliance may, in some cases, obviate the need for a more formal intervention.

An effective way for teachers to achieve the trust and respect of their students is to develop a sense of community in the classroom. A teacher can facilitate this goal by providing opportunities for meaningful student input and participation, teaching, and practicing active listening skills, presenting the students with purposeful learning experiences, and promoting student choices (Elias, 2016).

Instructional Approaches

All instructional approaches are designed to provide the student who has CD challenging and meaningful learning experiences. This presupposes that the student's academic strengths and weaknesses have been clearly identified.

Motivation To Learn

For students who have emotional and behavioral disorders, motivation is essential to learning. An effective model to use in increasing a student's motivation to learn is represented by the *expectation X value theory* (Ping et al., 2006). This theory postulates that the extent to which people become actively involved in an activity is dependent on (1) whether they believe they can be successful at a task, and (2) the degree to which they value the rewards associated with successful task completion. A third component, *climate*, addresses the importance of relationships within the task setting experienced during task engagement.

Students who have EBD are not likely to be motivated to learn unless all three components are present; normally, (1) they must feel they can accomplish the task, (2) they find value in the task, and (3) they can complete the task in a climate that is supportive of their basic needs. Sometimes it is more expedient for the teacher to find other tasks than to try to motivate students to do tasks that do not meet these three criteria.

Some of the ways successful learning and the ensuing academic achievement can be accomplished include (1) matching instructional methods and cultural styles to optimize student engagement; and (2) helping students understand what it means to be an effective learner. This can be seen in the graphic below entitled *Defining a Successful Learner.*

Defining a Successful Learner

Looks Like	Sounds Like
Eyes focused on speaker	Gives encouragement
Concentrates on their work	Uses appropriate voice level
Is well organized	Asks questions
Cooperates with others	Asks for help when needed
Follows classroom rules and procedures	Shares their ideas with others
Sets goals	Comments are on-task
Stays calm when having a problem	Is courteous to others
Uses time wisely	Uses problem solving
Learns from mistakes	
Shares materials	
Does not give up	

A successful learner is someone who works hard, cooperates with others, takes risks, sets goals, makes a good effort, asks for help if needed, doesn't give up, and learns from his or her mistakes.

Source: Vernon F. Jones and Louise S. Jones. (2017). *Comprehensive Classroom Management: Creating Communities of Support and Solving Problems,* Sixth Edition. Published by Allyn and Bacon, Boston, MA. Copyright Pearson Education.

It is very important that students who have a conduct disorder understand and practice the behaviors associated with good attending and successful learning (e.g., eyes focused on the speaker, asking questions, asking for help when needed, cooperating with others) (Jones et al., 2017).

Identify Strengths and Abilities

Teachers need to help students with EBD understand their individual learning strengths or special abilities; for example, a student who has a conduct disorder may not have strengths in interpersonal or intrapersonal functioning, but he or she may have artistic/spatial aptitudes that provide unique opportunities to explore learning and develop knowledge. Understanding and accommodating the different learning styles of students who have EBD facilitates learning for them. Some students may learn most effectively when a passage of text is read to them, whereas they are unable to process information from a printed source; thus, providing an opportunity for oral reading or reviewing a tape-recorded lecture or lesson would really help her to learn. Further, allowing students to organize their learning environment to some degree may prove helpful; for example, some students with conduct disorder evidence a high degree of distractibility and prefer working in a "low-stimulus" environment. For these students, a study carrel might be a preferred situation (Jones et al., 2016).

Provide Appropriate Strategies

Many students who have conduct disorder do not seem to know how to learn so, providing them with suitable strategies to do so can be of great help. One such approach involves teaching these students some study skills. Cognitive interventions needed in accomplishing a specific task can be taught; examples of such skills include underlining, highlighting, using a mnemonic, outlining, and summarizing. Metacognitive interventions include selecting and monitoring one's use of strategies and determining when and under which circumstances one strategy is preferable to another.

Finally, students who have conduct disorder should be taught behaviors that reflect the right attitude to learning and that show a willingness to participate cooperatively in the learning process (Kavale & Mostert, 2004). When teaching these learning skills, it is important to tie them to the lesson requirements of the day or week within a specific context, rather than to generalize skills.

Provide Real-World Learning

Research with students who have conduct disorder and other emotional or behavioral impairments has suggested the importance of incorporating real-world learning in the academic curriculum. An example of this approach is 'real-world problem solving,' in which students work together to solve problems that are relevant to their lives and their communities. Students might work in small groups to identify a need within their school or community and develop a solution, in which they must participate or contribute.

A derivation of this notion is the concept of service-learning used in various colleges and universities as an extension of their course curricula. The intention here, as with the concept applied to schools, is to provide enriching experiences and constructive interactions between students and their community. A suggested checklist for developing such a program within a school curriculum might include (1) choosing a problem to work on, (2) creating a vision, (3) studying the problem, (4) accepting the risks, (5) making a commitment, (6) planning the project, and (7) executing the plan (Jones & Jones, 2017).

Adaptations, Accommodations, and Modifications

Another important aspect of effective instruction especially relevant to students who have conduct disorder is the provision of adaptations, accommodations, and modifications.

- *Adaptations* are essentially changes made to the environment, curriculum, instruction, and/or assessment that help to ensure success for the learner.
- *Accommodations* are alterations in presentation and response format, timing, environment, and/or scheduling that do not affect level, content, or performance criteria but do provide the student with equal access to learning as well as demonstrating what is known.
- *Modifications* represent changes in instructional level, content, and performance criteria that provide students with an opportunity to participate meaningfully and effectively in learning experiences (Jones & Jones, 2017).

Effective curriculum and environmental adaptations for students who have EBD are predicated on the following assumptions (1) that such adaptations are for all students; (2) that the adaptation is not new; (3) that adaptations are best developed through collaborative problem solving; (4) that they start with individual pupil goals; (5) that they maximize the participation of the student in the standard curriculum; and (6) that they can be supported by instructional strategies (Shore & Rastelli, 2006).

Some specific areas that lend themselves to adaptation include (1) the size of the task (e.g., the number of problems assigned may be reduced to relieve the perceived pressure and tedium associated with excessive work volume); (2) time allotted for learning, completion, or testing (e.g., allotted time can be increased); (3) level of support (e.g., students may be provided more individualized attention through peer tutoring or by an instructional aide); (4) input of information (e.g., students may be provided with more examples, instructions can be repeated and reinforced); (5) difficulty of the skill, problem, or rule (e.g., students may have the skill or task broken down into more manageable segments or steps); (6) output, or how students can demonstrate mastery (e.g., students can provide evidence of mastery through a portfolio, project, graphic model, demonstration, report, etc.); (7) participation (e.g., students who cannot by reason of their disability participate in traditional ways, can do so by alternative methods; for example, they may help construct a model rather than write a report (Shore & Rastelli, 2006).

Improve Communication Skills

Research suggests that many students who have EBD lack the basic skills to communicate effectively (Olson, 2016). For students at the middle and high school level, a strategy-based approach has demonstrated effectiveness in improving language and literacy skills. The reason for this success is thought to be its focus on increasing metacognitive and metalinguistic skills; for example, students are taught how to learn, not just what to learn. One strategy that helps students comprehend unfamiliar words is called by the acronym DISSECT. The steps of the strategy represented are (1) Discover the content (skip difficult words), (2) Isolate the prefix, (3) Separate the suffix, (4) Say the stem, (5) Examine the stem, (6) Check with someone, (7) Try the dictionary (Lenz & Hughes, 1990).

A similar strategy, the LINCS technique, helps students focus on the key aspects of vocabulary and then use visual imagery, mnemonic devices, and self-evaluation to facilitate encoding and recall. Each letter of the LINCS, accordingly, represents part of the strategy L=List the parts, I=Imagine the picture, N=Note a reminding word, C=Construct a LINCing story, and S=Self-test, respectively. In teaching the strategy, students are asked to write the new vocabulary on the top half of an index card with the definition on the other side. Next, they are told to choose a reminding word and to write that word on the bottom of the front of the card (e.g., if the vocabulary word is "sari," the student might choose "sorry" as the reminder word) and create a sentence about the meaning of the vocabulary word. In the last step, Self-test, the student says both the vocabulary word and the reminder word while thinking of the LINCing sentence and the image created, states the meaning of the new word, and checks for correct spelling (Harris et al., 2011).

Cognitive-Behavioral Approaches

Walker et al. (2020) recommended several principles to communicate to students who have conduct disorder that they have value and teachers care about them. Many of the following approaches may be helpful in working with students like Lucas, the student profiled in the case example for this chapter.

Establish a Positive Climate

Kohn (2006) elaborated on the idea of establishing a positive climate in his assertion that the classroom is a community, which he describes as "a place in which students feel cared about and are encouraged to care about each other. They experience a sense of being valued and respected; the children matter to one another and to the teacher" (p. 101). Given the antisocial nature of the student who has conduct disorder, whose experiences at home and typically at school are primarily of rejection and exclusion, a supportive, inclusive classroom is critical to their rehabilitation.

Create High Expectations

A second principle that is relevant to teachers working with students who have conduct disorder is to establish and communicate high expectations in achievement and behavior for all students. Students who have conduct disorders are often very adept at manipulating teachers to lower standards, whether through intimidation, coercion, or negotiation. It is important that these students learn these are ineffective approaches and they will be expected to produce consistently high-caliber work as is required of every student in the class.

Structured Learning Environment

Teachers should provide a structured learning environment in which students know what is expected of them and to whom to go to for assistance with social and academic issues. Research supports the importance of providing structure in the lives of students who have conduct disorder because, generally, their lives and families are in disarray, which increases their frustration and behavioral volatility (Hallahan et al., 2020).

Cooperative Learning

Teachers are encouraged to employ cooperative learning strategies that permit small diverse groups of students to interact, problem-solve, and develop collaborative skills. Most students who have conduct disorder adopt a 'me against them' attitude in social situations. Assigning them to work with a small group of students who are congenial and empathetic can help the student with CD feel valued and connected and begin to develop necessary social skills.

Positive Reinforcement

Research and experience support the value of showing appreciation for the small behavioral gains made by students with CD. Encouragement and praise, when related to a specific gain or accomplishment, are very powerful reinforcers because these students are more often criticized and admonished for failures and ineptitude. Teachers can demonstrate care for these students by communicating a genuine interest in their academic progress and personal development.

Social Skills Training

Behavior-change programs have not shown great success with students who have conduct disorder, but some social skills training programs have shown better results (Walker et al., 2020). When implementing any form of social skills training, it is important that the training be conducted in the natural environment. If the targeted skill involves appropriate communication between students and authority figures, for example, students should have an opportunity to practice the skill in authentic conversation with parents, teachers, and administrators.

Social skills training should encompass the following areas (1) cooperation (e.g., helping others, following rules), (2) assertion (e.g., asking others for information), (3) responsibility (e.g., caring for property or work of self or others), (4) empathy (e.g., showing respect for others' feelings and ideas), and (5) self-control (e.g., responding appropriately to teasing and name-calling, compromising) (Walker et al., 2020). Likewise, selected social skills interventions should promote skill acquisition, enhance skill performance, remove or reduce competing problem behaviors, and facilitate the generalization and maintenance of the acquired social skills (Gresham, 2007).

Three key approaches used to teach appropriate social skills are coaching, modeling, and behavioral rehearsal. Coaching involves teaching social skills in three consecutive steps: (1) presenting social concepts, (2) providing opportunities for practicing the targeted social skills, and (3) providing specific informational feedback regarding the student's performance. Essentially, coaching involves telling a student how to perform a specific social skill and providing oral feedback about the student's performance (Giordano et al., 2020).

Modeling is based on the principles of observational learning and vicarious reinforcement (Bandura, 1977). In essence, observers (in this case, students who have CD) learn a behavior by being vicariously reinforced as they watch the model (teacher or caregiver) receiving reinforcement for effective social skills performance. The modeling should be conducted in a naturalistic setting - when and where this behavior typically occurs. For example, the teacher can model appropriate respectful dialogue with an authority figure by asking the school principal to visit the classroom during a lesson and then soliciting a discussion about the nature of the exchange with the class afterwards.

Lastly, behavioral rehearsal involves the practice of a newly acquired social skill in structured role play. The advantage of this approach is that it provides the students with an opportunity to practice the social skill without being concerned about negative consequences that might result from mistakes. This safeguard is particularly helpful in encouraging students who have conduct disorder to try out a new social skill without fear of negative social repercussions or rejection. Behavioral rehearsal can be conducted in three ways: covert, verbal, and overt. In *covert rehearsal*, the student imagines or thinks through the use of the social skill in a specific situation. *Verbal rehearsal* requires that the student talk through the social skills application, and *overt rehearsal* requires that the student actually perform the social skill within a hypothetical situation (Gresham, 2007).

The behavioral intervention plan developed for Lucas, based on the results of his functional behavioral assessment, focused primarily on learning strategies and cognitive-behavioral approaches. Concerning learning strategies, Lucas's teachers were encouraged to provide him with reasonable academic goals, meaningful learning tasks, assignments that optimized success and thus increased self-confidence, alternative assessments, as well as choices in the selection of curriculum. The underlying assumption was that if Lucas could be provided the opportunity to succeed academically, his self-esteem would also flourish. It was believed that much of Lucas's aggression and hostility was fueled by his own lack of confidence and self-worth.

The cognitive-behavioral approaches employed by Lucas's teachers included the use of positive reinforcement to encourage his participation in classroom social and learning activities. In addition, his teachers deliberately involved him in all aspects of classroom routine, from cooperative group activities to everyday duties and responsibilities. Lastly, Lucas's teachers used teachable moments to reinforce the social skills training that he was receiving in the Coping Power Program (Stromeyer et al., 2020), an after-school program that is part of Lucas's multisystemic therapy. Lucas's teachers are provided support from the school psychologist as they encounter behavioral challenges from Lucas that exceed their capability. He has been a valuable resource in the implementation of the behavioral intervention plan.

From the Field

Lisa Goldberg, MSED.

Lisa Goldberg is a Special Education Teacher at a High School for Students who have emotional and behavioral Disorders.

Lisa, can you provide our readers with your "sense" of the typical student you work with who has been identified as having a conduct disorder?

Students who have conduct disorder tend to be smart, capable individuals who refuse to comply with classroom rules, school guidelines, or behave in a socially acceptable way despite intellectual ability. Frequently these individuals are identified as "bad kids" that are regularly in trouble. These students are commonly found to come from backgrounds that include abuse, traumatic experiences, haphazard parenting, and school failure. Typically, these individuals have a history that includes initiating physically aggressive behavior towards others, bullying, threatening and intimidating behavior, property destruction, and show little empathy or concern for others, feelings, wishes or the well-being, and they blame others for their own behavior. They are the students who require a great deal of your attention and management. These students can be aggressive or act in a passive-aggressive manner, rebelling against your every effort to effectually change, shape and create new behavior patterns.

In your estimation, what are the greatest challenges these students pose to teachers and teaching?

These students frequently disrupt the regular pattern of the classroom, to spite of all of the behavior modification techniques you employ. These students generally attract a lot of attention from both classroom staff and peers alike. Frequently, students who have conduct disorder will employ any means they can to draw the attention of their peers in order to increase their own status and diminish the control of the teacher. Maintaining ongoing continuums of learning can be very challenging with these individuals in the population of a classroom. In addition, these students have generally developed a history that includes ongoing fear and distrust of adults. All of this adds to a student's well-developed poor self-image. Their habit is to fail and be in trouble, and changing their normal, which is the heart of effectively teaching them new behaviors, is the greatest challenge a teacher faces when working with these individuals.

What are some potential mistakes that new teachers can make when working with a student who has conduct disorder?

New teachers may initially see the child's behavior as being personally about them and act in a reactionary manner. It is important for all teachers to be proactive and have interventions in place for handling the student's behavior. Educators need to maintain awareness that a student's oppositional behavior is frequently a way for that individual to manage his or her anxiety to perceived demands by the teacher and the school setting in general. These students are in desperate need of positive learning and success experiences. Recognition of this is key to changing the pattern of failure these students are accustomed to.

Can you provide a few of your most effective strategies for working successfully with these students; for example, tips that you wish someone had given you when you started working with this population?

Being able to identify a child's "island of competence", that which they truly enjoy and do well, can be a huge factor in providing initial success experiences for these individuals. A proactive environment that is adaptable to the student's needs and provides short-term, somewhat easily achievable goals will give the student quick sense of success, which can be transferred, over time, to those behaviors that are targeted for change.

It is extremely important to remember that in order to make long-term changes in these individual's behavior, specific target behaviors must be identified and worked on consistently. Consistent positive reinforcement will, over time, effect change in a more permanent manner than those behavior modification techniques that are merely disciplinary. Positive incentives may initially have to be tangible, as intrinsic values are not generally developed in these students, as they are uncommonly instilled in their at-risk environment.

Teachers and students should be working on goals that can be achieved over a relatively short time, providing near-immediate success initially, and over time, extend those goals to things that require a greater period to achieve, always keeping in mind that positive reinforcement, catching them doing something good and rewarding it, is going to be more effective than punishing these individuals. Punishment has been their whole world; it is our job to change that pattern and provide new experiences for them to relish.

Finally, Lisa, could you share an anecdote from your teaching repertoire that highlights one of your most memorable successes in working with a student who has a conduct disorder?

Teaching students with conduct disorder has been one of the greatest challenges I have experienced, but it's yielded some of the most rewarding experiences I've had. While working in a residential treatment center for inner-city, court-mandated students who had piled up failure experiences and seen more of life's difficulties by 15 than others might see in a lifetime, *challenge* was the name of the game. I spent years developing a program for students with significant gaps in their education, reading levels that were a minimum of five years below grade level, patterns of failure in the classroom, and experiences with court interventions and incarceration.

Teaching these students, who were mainly, but not totally male, ranging in ages from 15 to 21, required me to build a program that redeveloped success patterns, provided proactive interventions, taught them, through modeling, good examples and their own experiences, how to develop positive relationships with both peers and adults, and be ready to learn in a structured environment. Teaching my students to trust, for many of them, the first time in their lives they had anyone they could trust, was a key factor in providing them with the initial success experiences necessary to breaking the pattern of failure that they had become so accustomed to. Accommodating all students, and individualizing curriculum, learning pace, and measurable expectations lay the groundwork for successful learning experiences such as these young people had not yet encountered.

Consistent positive reinforcement, rules, and - most importantly - consistent expectations eventually began to pay off. Students who, when they came to me, were nearing societal exile and a future that would almost definitely include incarceration, were able to learn acceptable behavior patterns that enabled them to participate in work-study programs, off-campus jobs and eventually graduate from high school, many with model of behavior that would allow them to be good citizens and members of the world community, not the burden they were bound to become prior to arrival in my program.

One of the most memorable of these students was Joey. Joey came to me at age 15, reading a K.9 level [Kindergarten, ninth month of the school year]. He did not recognize his own name in writing, did not know his address, and had already been incarcerated in high-level juvenile facilities prior to his arrival. Joey had spent much time out of school, because of his continued deteriorating pattern of behavior as well as mere school avoidance. From his perspective, he was already so far behind that even a day or two was so overwhelming to face the huge task in front of him, in order to catch up with his peers, that he avoided school altogether and ran the streets instead. Joey was very accustomed to adults belittling him, reminding him of his failures, his inabilities, and intimidation had become his way of life.

Teaching Joey involved finding something that he would be able to focus on; that he did well and even minimally could admit he enjoyed in order to provide him the immediate success experiences he so desperately needed. We quickly learned, although through discussion of his criminal escapades, that Joey was very automotively intuitive. He could tell you anything you needed to know about a car, inside out, diagnose, and solve any problem he encountered related to the automobile. Identifying this 'island of competence' was key in providing Joey with an initial increase in self-esteem and identifying intact skills that we focused on transferring to other areas of the curriculum. In addition, modeling positive relationships was another key factor in Joey's reentering society in an effective manner.

Although students did not normally remain in our program for very long, Joey was with us for a little over two years. In that time, I was able to build a positive relationship with him, and help him improve his self-esteem, which in turn allowed him to risk venturing into areas that he had previously found overwhelming. Joey was able to target key behaviors and begin the process of shaping them and extinguishing problem behaviors that he had developed in his many years of running the streets. Using behavior modification techniques like positive reinforcement, cost response systems, and tangible rewards, I was able to assist Joey in developing a series of successes, positive behaviors, and coping strategies for him to use when encountering situations that would otherwise have thrown him into old, well-formed habits.

At the end of Joey's stay in my program, Joey had grown to an individual who was able to read and write at a fourth-grade reading level and hold down a job. He successfully stayed off of probation and no longer faced legal ramifications from his pattern of behavior. Three years after leaving my program, Joey came to visit with his mechanic's certification in hand, successfully holding down a job in a reputable station, and maintaining his own residence. He had become an effective member of the community.

Summary

This chapter began by providing an overview of conduct disorder, an emotional or behavioral disorder that creates challenging management situations for classroom teachers in particular and school personnel in general. The etiology of CD is more often than not multifactorial, and, in clinical settings, a number of treatment modalities have been shown to be relatively effective. In the school setting, however, it is important to carefully determine the purpose served by the problem behavior as it pertains to the classroom and school environments in order to provide more relevant, effective interventions. This investigative process is referred to as a functional behavioral assessment or FBA (IDEA, 2004).

In working with students who have CD, teachers can employ several effective interventions. The most helpful of these involve both instructional and cognitive-behavioral approaches such as those described in this chapter. It is also important that teachers find ways to establish rapport with these students. One way is to include them in all aspects of the classroom, accept and welcome them as constituents in the classroom community, and engage them in meaningful learning activities.

Frustration, anger, and resentment are often the feelings that teachers use to describe the intuitive effects produced by students who have conduct disorders. If teachers can better understand the nature of this disorder and have available a repertoire of effective, research-based interventions, they are much less likely to feel overwhelmed by the disruptive behaviors exhibited by affected students.

Tips For Teachers

To conclude, teachers are urged to keep in mind the following strategies to improve the quality of their interactions with students who have CD:

- Build a sense of community and belonging that includes every student in your classroom.
- Establish rules of conduct as a class and include yourself and their expectations of you in the discussion.
- Provide meaningful and appropriate choices.
- Triage the crises - some, such as fistfights, require immediate attention; others, such as an epithet uttered under the breath, do not.
- Provide *meaningful* praise and positive reinforcement. Connect the praise to a discrete accomplishment or behavior *not* to some vague or future possibility.
- Find a reason to appreciate every student in your class. There must be some quality the student possesses that can be viewed as a positive or strength.
- Get to know the likes and dislikes, the hobbies and pastimes, the passions and dreams of these students - this will help build relationships and no one can truly provide help without relationships. Similarly, a teacher cannot be simultaneously uncaring and effective - not with a student who has CD.
- Provide meaningful learning experiences for your students; connect the lesson to real-life applications.
- Ignore small annoyances and disruptions. Students who have CD will try to provoke their teacher—they expect to be disliked. Try not to fall prey into a contest of wills.

Be consistent and fair with each student. Treating each student fairly, especially those with CD, does not mean treating each student the same. Would it be fair to expect a student with cerebral palsy to run competitively in a race with physically able students? Essentially, being consistent with rewards and consequences means just that (adapted from Cavin, 1998).

Although teachers clearly have the most sustained contact with students in their classrooms, teachers cannot provide the therapeutic interventions that have shown the greatest promise in treating CD. In fact, a multisystemic treatment strategy that has demonstrated the greatest benefit for these students. This approach incorporates family systems therapy and takes into account other systems affecting the students. School personnel are in a unique position to facilitate these interventions and provide coordination of services with families and other social units.

Lamentably, research has suggested that there is often little coordination between the teacher and other helpers (Walker et al., 2020). Our hope is that the information provided in this chapter will facilitate the collaboration of the teacher and other professionals who both play significant roles in the therapeutic process. Perhaps then, students who have a conduct disorder, like Lucas, will be provided a coherent, effective intervention plan that will help them experience success in school and in life.

Focus Questions Revisited

The final section of this chapter comprises a brief question-and-answer discussion of typical concerns raised by teachers who work with students who have CD. It might be particularly helpful for preservice and less experienced teachers to consider the behavioral profile of Lucas presented in the case example, when considering these questions.

What are the defining characteristics of a conduct disorder?

A Sample Response: The following represent the key characteristics that help to identify a conduct disorder: a repetitive and persistent pattern of behavior in which the basic rights of others or major age-appropriate societal norms or rules are violated, as manifested by the presence of three (or more) of the following criteria in the past twelve months, with at least one criterion present in the past six months:

- Often bullies, threatens, or intimidates others
- Often initiates physical fights
- Has used a weapon that can cause serious physical harm to others (e.g., a bat, brick, broken bottle, knife, gun)
- Has been physically cruel to people
- Has been physically cruel to animals
- Has stolen while confronting a victim (e.g., mugging, purse snatching, extortion, armed robbery)

- Has forced someone into sexual activity
- Has deliberately engaged in fire setting with the intention to cause serious damage
- Has deliberately destroyed others' property (other than by fire setting
- Has broken into someone else's house, building, or car
- Often lies to obtain goods or favors or to avoid obligations (i.e., "cons" others)
- Has stolen items of nontrivial value without confronting a victim (e.g., shoplifting, but without breaking and entering; forgery)
- Often stays out at night despite parental prohibitions, beginning before age 13
- Has run away from home overnight at least twice while living in parental or parental surrogate home (or once without returning for a lengthy period (DSM-V; APA, 2013).

How can I effectively diffuse a behavioral crisis in my classroom that involves a student who has a conduct disorder?

Sample Response A: One method that has been successful in many schools is the Life Space Crisis Intervention (LSCI) (Long et al., 2001). This approach to a perceived or real crisis involving a student allows the teacher to use a classroom conflict to provide the student with insight into the problem, thus enabling him to regain emotional control and make rationale choices. LSCI is used to help students who are dealing with a crisis that is of such intensity they cannot be supported by the traditional tactics used by their teachers. LSCI can empower the teacher to turn a conflict into a meaningful learning experience for the student by determining what fuels his behavior and by defining the purpose served by the behavior (Long et al., 2001).

According to Long et al. (2001), LSCI can help the student discover that: (1) a crisis does not mean adult rejection or alienation; (2) an adult can still see potential for growth and positive attributes despite the student's loss of control during the crisis; (3) there is relationship between perception and behavior; (4) he exhibits a chronic pattern of nonproductive behaviors; (5) he can accept responsibility for his behavior; and (6) he can trust professional caregivers and teachers.

There are six stages in implementing a LSCI:

1. The student's crisis stage and the staff's de-escalation stage (i.e., help define the child's irrational volatility)
2. The student's timeline stage and the staff's relationship skills (i.e., have the student develop a detailed, step-by-step narrative of the entire incident, beginning with events that preceded it)
3. The student's central issues stage and the staff's differential diagnosis skills (i.e., identify the central issue and determine whether the issue represents a pattern or is merely an isolated episode)
4. The student's insight stage and the staff's clinical skills (i.e., carry out the appropriate intervention, which should provide the students and staff with insights regarding the undesired behavior, prompting a discussion of more effective and appropriate behavior alternatives)
5. The student's new skill stage and the staff's empowering skills (i.e., an opportunity for the teacher to present alternative pro-social skills)
6. The student's transfer-of-training stage and the staff's follow-up skills (i.e., establish expectations for the student to return to class and participate meaningfully) (Jones et al., 2016).

This technique may have a viable application in a case such as Lucas's when a student has physically or verbally assaulted another student, threatened a student or teacher, or damaged or destroyed school property.

Sample Response B: Another strategy that may be effective in addressing a serious crisis in the classroom, such as a fight between two students, is to isolate the combatants by insisting that other students leave the classroom. The teacher then asks one of the more responsible students to get help from the school's crisis intervention team. It is important to note that no teacher should attempt to break up a serious altercation between two adolescents without the assistance of other adults. Even physically smaller youth can cause serious injury to an adult (often the student who escapes restraint). One teacher, alone, can effectively restrain only one student (if the student is physically less powerful than the teacher), leaving the other student free to assault the restrained student without impedance. Teachers are cautioned that, ideally, two physically fit adults are required to safely restrain one typical adolescent. When the safety of staff and students cannot be assured, teachers should call for the assistance of law enforcement officers.

For crises that have not escalated to involve physical aggression or assault but that have become seriously disruptive and antagonistic (e.g., verbal assaults, temper tantrums, verbal tirades, oppositional defiance, and threats), once again, the authors recommend isolating the antagonist by asking them to leave the room; however, state, and federal laws have established that teachers are responsible for the safety and supervision of all students assigned to them for the duration of the class period (New York State Education Department, 2021; New York State Education Department, 2017). The teacher or teacher's aide should always accompany a student sent into the hall or to the office for corrective purposes. Nonetheless, if the angry, agitated, or hostile student can be calmed sufficiently, it is preferable to continue with the classroom activity, allowing the student the opportunity to sit calmly and regain composure. The nature and cause of the crisis should be addressed as soon as possible after class (perhaps employing an LSCI).

Students who have conduct disorder can be defiant and verbally confrontational. What is the best way to deal with these behaviors when they occur in the classroom?

A Sample Response: If a student who has CD or oppositional defiant disorder makes an offensive comment or uses patently offensive language, the best strategy is to ignore the behavior if possible; however, if the behavior persists and becomes disruptive to the learning environment, the student should be confronted firmly and calmly. One of the authors simply describes the offensive behavior and why it is so disruptive to the class, asks the offending student to refrain from the behavior, and reminds the student of the prescribed consequence if the behavior persists. The important aspects of this process are consistency and certainty: If the behavior is not curtailed, the student will incur the appropriate consequence. That the appropriate consequence will be administered by the teacher is certain—there can be no exceptions or deviations; however, it is important to note two things here (1) The classroom rules of conduct should be meaningfully determined by the students and teacher in keeping with the desire to build community in the classroom; and (2) the teacher must, at all times, maintain composure and explain the rules and consequences in a matter-of-fact way. Giving way to outrage, frustration, or fear will provide a student who has a conduct disorder an insight into the teacher's vulnerabilities, which he might exploit later.

Because many students who have conduct disorder are co-diagnosed with ADHD, how can I deal effectively with their impulsiveness and off-task behaviors?

A Sample Response: It may be unreasonable to expect these students to remain seated, calmly working on a task for forty-five minutes. One of the authors has established a signal whereby a student who exhibits hyperactivity and impulsive behaviors can obtain a pass to the bathroom or be assigned an 'important' errand that will allow him to legitimately leave his seat and move around. Furthermore, providing meaningful and interesting learning tasks that can be completed in a ten-to-fifteen-minute interval helps maintain student interest and provides the novelty and change the student needs to maintain focus.

Research has suggested that students who have CD and ADHA are seldom given options or choices; they are thus deprived of opportunities to participate in planning (Hallahan et al., 2020). Providing preselected choices or options for assignments or thematic units is a way to instill in these students a sense of ownership and empowerment. When provided such an option by one of the authors, one student seemed quite moved and stated, "I've never in my life been given a choice before, except do I want to be expelled or sent to "Juvy" (Juvenile Hall)."

Key Terms Used in the Chapter

Executive Functioning:
Refers to a set of high-level cognitive abilities that have to do with planning, organizing, strategizing, paying attention to, and remembering details. Those with good executive functioning are able to anticipate outcomes and adapt to changing situations. Concept formation and abstraction are also considered under the meta construct of executive functioning.

Cognitive-Behavioral Treatment or Therapy (CBT):
Refers to a therapeutic approach that teaches the individual to "think" about events in a different way, often from another's perspective, and provides strategies that facilitate this (e.g., using an acrostic or acronym such as "STOP" to remind the individual to use a set strategy).

Contingency Contracting:
Refers to a prearranged system of consequences (reinforcers and punishers) designed to increase appropriate behavior and decrease inappropriate behavior.

Multisystemic Treatment:
A multiple-system treatment approach to many emotional and behavioral disorders that typically combines family therapy with individual and peer-oriented therapies, acknowledging the importance of affecting behavior change in all these important milieus.

Randomized Controlled Studies (RCTS):
Refers to the random allocation of interventions to different subjects. The most reliable RCTs are double-blind, where the researcher does not know to what intervention group a subject has been assigned. Double-blind studies are the best way to control for researcher bias.

Antecedent-Behavior-Consequence (A-B-C) Record Sheet:
Recognized as important information in assessing the purpose served by maladaptive behaviors, the A-B-C record sheet provides the teacher with a convenient and efficient means of identifying and recording the events that trigger the target (maladaptive) behavior as well as the consequences of that behavior that serve to maintain it.

Setting Events:
Refers to antecedent events that "trigger" or provoke the target or undesired behavior.

Maintaining Consequences:
Refers to consequences that facilitate the perpetuation of the target or undesired behavior.

Coaching:
Coaching involves telling a student how to perform a specific social skill and providing oral feedback about the student's performance (Giordano, Eastin, Calcagno, Wilhelm, & Gil, 2020).

Modeling:
Describes an intervention in which observers, ostensibly, students who have an emotional or behavioral disorder, learn a behavior by being vicariously reinforced as they watch the model (teacher or caregiver) receiving reinforcement for effective social skills performance. The modeling should be conducted in a natural setting—in other words, when and where this behavior typically occurs.

Behavioral Rehearsal:
Involves the practice of a newly acquired social skill within structured role play. The advantage of this approach is that it provides students with an opportunity to practice a social skill without concern for the negative consequences that can result from mistakes.

Chapter 3

Oppositional Defiant Disorder

Focus Questions

- *Why is it so important that we address oppositional defiant disorder (ODD) behaviors observed in our students quickly and effectively?*
- *What characteristic behaviors are symptomatic of ODD?*
- *What does research say about the probable causes of ODD?*
- *How is ODD appropriately assessed?*
- *According to the best practice evidence provided in this chapter, which treatment option appears to be most effective? What are its principal strengths?*
- *Suppose you have a student in your classroom who has ODD. What are some interventions you might employ to help him control and, ultimately, reduce his defiant behaviors while simultaneously increasing his pro-social ones?*
- *What other professional support might you solicit in your efforts to help a student who has ODD?*

Introduction

Many researchers have regarded *oppositional defiant disorder* (ODD) as a term that identifies a separate category of emotional or behavioral disorder related to conduct disorder, whereas others view it as an antecedent (McNeilis et al., 2018). Students with ODD display characteristic behaviors that often include (1) frequent loss of temper, (2) frequent arguing with adults, (3) refusal to comply with rules or requests of authority figures (adults), (4) exhibiting intentionally annoying behavior, (5) blaming others for his or her mistakes, (6) being easily annoyed by others, (7) being frequently angry or resentful, and (8) engaging in spiteful or vengeful behaviors (American Psychiatric Association, 2013, p.102). This chapter examines the characteristics, causes, and prevalence that delineate ODD, and, most importantly, describes some of the most effective interventions to assist teachers in working successfully with these individuals. A research-based intervention plan is also provided that is predicated on a systematic assessment of the disruptive behavior in order to determine its ultimate purpose.

Students who engage in disruptive disorders are unquestionably among the most challenging children to teach. Current studies on the cause of teacher attrition have indicated the primary cause to be the necessity of working with students who are defiant and disruptive (Nygaard, 2019; Stohmann et al., 2020). In addition, research on the academic performance of these students has shown that they typically perform poorly in school and have higher dropout rates than students without these problems (National Center for Learning Disabilities [NCLD], 2017; University of California - Davis - Health System, 2010).

A search for causes, in most cases, points to ineffective parenting practices such as lax supervision, inconsistent discipline, excessive punishment, volatile discipline, and inflexibility in discipline practices (Tams, 2017). Logically, therefore, the most recommended interventions involve, to some degree, the parents of these children. There are several popular treatment programs for individuals with ODD to include Parent-Child Interaction Therapy (PCIT), joint Problem-Solving Skills Training (PSST) and Parent Management Training (PMT) (Kazdin, 2017), and the Incredible Years Training Series (IYTS) (Webster-Stratton & Bywater, 2019).

Students who have ODD unquestionably represent a challenge to all teachers. They are often narcissistic, unpleasant to deal with, and disruptive to the lesson; however, contrary to the predictions of some of our colleagues, these students are not lost causes, nor should we simply try to bravely teach over, around, or in spite of them as some teachers have suggested (NCLD, 2017). These children often present oppositional defiant behaviors in the classroom because they feel safe to act out the accumulated frustrations acquired at home; for example, they know that most teachers typically will not react violently as their parent might or, conversely, provide inconsistent discipline. If the true underlying cause of ODD is understood, educators may stop feeling singled out, or exploited, stop feeling abused and indignant, and instead start to see that they are uniquely positioned to make a difference in the life of a very misunderstood and misrepresented child - for teachers the saying 'the buck must stop here!' has never been truer.

Case Example: Elan, A Student With ODD

Elan, a 10-year-old child born in Romania in 2010 was adopted by Herbert and Anita Hamilton shortly after his birth and brought to live with them in the U.S. According to his adoptive parents, Elan's early years were typical, and he met all the usual developmental milestones within the normal time ranges.

His early school years were, for the most part, uneventful. Elan's teachers described him as 'inquisitive, and precocious' but was never quick to comply with teachers' requests or expectations. In the 5th grade, Elan's teacher, Mrs. Burr, expressed concern over his increased distractibility and non-compliant behavior.

Eventually, given the significant changes in Elan's behavior, Mrs. Burr requested that the school social worker contact Elan's adoptive parents. Ms. Lacey, the social worker, learned from Elan's mother that Elan recently had begun exhibiting more oppositional behavior at home and his father, always very strict with Elan, was battling more and more Elan's defiance and had resorted, on several occasions, to the use of corporal punishment. She suspected that this increasingly punitive and 'stronger than you' response might account for Elan's increased oppositional behavior at school.

Mrs. Burr shared with the school psychologist and Elan's parents that, in the classroom, he can easily explode when reprimanded or told to do something and when things do not go his way; for example, she cited a recent incident in which the physical education teacher reported that after Elan's team had lost a basketball scrimmage due to a student's missed free throw, Elan flew into a rage and assailed the unfortunate student with epithets and ridicule and was ordered to leave the gym and return to his homeroom.

Similarly, he exhibits little patience when a classmate with whom he is partnered makes a mistake or is slow to comprehend a new concept or acquire a new skill. Last week, for example, during a unit test in math, Elan's 'study buddy' could not solve one of their assigned word problems and Elan became so frustrated that he broke his pencil and tried to tear up his partner's paper.

On another occasion, while in the library, Elan's cell phone rang and instead of silencing it, he proceeded to engage in an animated conversation with the caller. When one of the librarians asked him to end the call and silence his phone, Elan loudly declared that "it was an important call from my mother and I am allowed to take calls from her anywhere at any time!" The librarian asked him to leave the library and as he left, Elan continued to protest and assert his perceived right to use his cell phone. He proclaimed loudly, along with a few expletives, "I'm right about this, you're wrong - go check with Mr. Phillips (the principal), he said it was ok - I'll get you fired!"

Mr. Mattot's Response to Elan's Oppositional Behavior

Mr. Mattot, Elan's 5th-grade social studies teacher, has explicit classroom rules, foremost of which is the importance of mutual respect. As an army veteran, he is a stickler for adherence to these rules and applies them frequently and consistently. In his view, there is no excuse or exception for violating any of them, especially the one about respect. In some ways, he is similar to Elan's father, Mr. Hamilton.

After months of assigning detentions to Elan for insubordinate behavior and frequent calls home to complain to Elan's parents, Mr. Mattot has requested that Elan be removed from his class for the balance of the school year, citing the disruption to learning caused by his frequent outbursts and his inability to follow directions. Mr. Phillips has acceded to Mr. Mattot's request both to keep the peace and because Mr. Mattot is a veteran teacher, highly respected by the faculty, and he is also the school's teacher union representative. Before being reassigned to another class, however, Elan is determined to make Mr. Mattot's life miserable and is doubling his efforts to be disruptive and non-compliant.

Mrs. Burr's Therapeutic Response to Elan's Oppositional Behavior

In contrast with Mr. Mattot's unsuccessful relationship with Elan, Mrs. Burr has taken the time to learn a bit about Elan's family history and the social dynamic of his home life. While she makes allowances for these mitigating factors, she continues to hold Elan accountable for his insubordinate behavior; yet she does so in ways that are non-adversarial, always acknowledging and rewarding Elan for instances of compliance and acceptance of responsibility when he fails to comply. Most especially, she has found ways to make Elan feel 'in charge' by inviting him to perform certain tasks that would be helpful to her and the other students. Rather than getting into a power struggle with Elan, she has reduced the power differential by having him perform prosocial jobs.

Mrs. Burr has invested effort in getting to know Elan on a personal level and has thus learned about his passion for computer games. She even knows about his favorite game called *League of Legends* and has learned a bit about its processes and rules. With permission from Elan's parents and the school administration, and in consultation with the school psychologist, she has received approval to initiate a reward system involving providing him with additional game 'enhancements.' Mrs. Burr, in collaboration with Elan, developed a point system for him that provides 'rewards' for compliance with classroom rules as well as engagement in prosocial behaviors versus angry and argumentative responses. Once Elan achieves sufficient points, he can earn a specified number of enhancements for use in his game. At present, Mrs. Burr has collected sufficient data to confirm the efficacy of her positive behavioral intervention. Unlike Mr. Mattot, Mrs. Burr does not view Elan's defiance and non-compliance as inviolable traits but as mutable behaviors that, with patience and the right approach, can be transformed for the better.

An Attachment Perspective

From an attachment perspective, little is known about Elan's pre-adoptive history and whether he began life from a secure base to explore the world around him. Oppositionality results in the hyperactivation of the attachment system. Both Mr. Hamilton and Mr. Mattot's response to Elan exemplify this. Both appear to have a more military style to effectuate compliance form Elan. This is completely contraindicated for responding effectively to those with ODD. In this case, the hyperactivation of the attachment system results in engaging in a power struggle with the child. More often than not, the child will win this battle as seen in Mr. Mattot's 'defeat' that demanded Elan be transferred to another class. If anything, such a move would only embolden Elan's oppositional behavior. Excessive rule-based authority devoid of emotion is often an indication of an avoidant attachment style. This is a bad mix with someone like Elan.

Mrs. Burr represents a different approach. More secure than that of Mr. Mattot, she is not afraid to allow Elan some freedoms and privileges earned through a contingency management plan. Her nurturing approach is made possible because she is not threatened by Elan's behavior. Rather than engage in a power struggle, she ceded power to Elan by giving him prosocial responsibilities to feel in charge and important. Her bonding intervention, learning the game *League of Legends*, further serves to offer Elan a different version of authority. Whether it is sufficient to counteract his other experiences of authority, harsh and punitive, no one can really know. All teachers can do is try to remind themselves that they are attachment figures upon whom students will project their own attachment style and vice versa. Only teachers who operate from a secure base stand a chance to deal effectively with a student like Elan. Through mentalization they can intuit the provocation to engage in a power struggle and rather than cede to that provocation respond in an antidotal fashion. In the case of Elan, it meant allowing him to feel that he was in charge.

Oppositional Defiant Disorder: An Overview

ODD is one of several disorders in the more general category of disruptive behavior disorder (DBD), and along with conduct disorder (CD) is the most prevalent. There has been considerable controversy over the years as to whether ODD and CD are separable disorders. The DSM-V (American Psychiatric Association, 2013) has maintained them as two distinct disorders, yet it does not allow for ODD to be diagnosed in the presence of CD—an indication that ODD might be considered a precursor to CD.

Research has been inconclusive as to whether ODD and CD should be considered separately or together. What is clear, however, is that not all children and adolescents who are diagnosed with ODD progress to CD (Husby & Wichstrøm, 2017). Approximately two-thirds of children diagnosed with ODD do *not* develop CD, and there are adolescents who develop CD without having had an earlier diagnosis of ODD (O'Leary & Solano, 2018). The progression from ODD to CD appears to depend on three classes of risk factors to include (1) child characteristics, (2) parenting practices, and (3) family organization problems (Burke & Loeber, 2017). Early onset, greater severity, frequent physical fighting, parental substance abuse, and low socioeconomic status are factors that increase the risk of ODD progressing to CD (Shader & Beauchaine, 2020).

Prevalence and Comorbidity

Prevalence rates for ODD range anywhere from 1 to 11 percent with an average estimate of 3.3 percent (American Psychiatric Association, 2013). This wide range is due to the historical lack of precision in diagnosing ODD and the difficulty in distinguishing mild ODD (e.g., tantrums, crying, screaming) from normal, developmentally appropriate behavior (Burke & Romano-Verthelyi, 2018). ODD is more prevalent in boys than in girls, and it is most frequently diagnosed in children under age 8.

ODD rarely exists alone and is highly comorbid with ADHD. Approximately 80 percent of those diagnosed with ODD have ADHD and about 60 percent of those diagnosed with ADHD have ODD (Hudec & Mikami, 2018). In addition to ADHD, significant comorbidity exists between ODD and mood disorders as well as anxiety disorders (Mohammadi, Salmanian et al., 2020). Studies have also indicated a strong association between language impairment and ODD (Thompson et al., 2017). Finally, because a defining characteristic of ODD is social impairment, studies have looked at the overlap between ODD and autism spectrum disorder (ASD) (Pijper et al., 2016).

Characteristics of Oppositional Defiance Disorder

As the diagnostic label suggests, the defining characteristics of ODD are opposition and defiance that follow a behavioral pattern and are developmentally inappropriate with high levels of negativistic, disobedient, and hostile behavior, especially toward authority figures.

Specific behaviors associated with ODD include temper outbursts; persistent stubbornness; resistance to directions; unwillingness to compromise, give in, or negotiate with adults or peers; deliberate or persistent testing of limits; and verbal (and minor physical) aggression (Greene, R., 2006). It is interesting to note that "these behaviors are almost always present in the home and with individuals the child knows well, and they often occur simultaneously with low self-esteem, mood lability, low frustration tolerance, and swearing" (Cunningham et al., 2016, p. 233).

To gain more clarity about the diagnosis, differentiating ODD from ADHD and CD can be helpful. Although some symptoms of ADHD (interrupting others, blurting out, etc.) may overlap with ODD, the distinction lies in the purposefulness of the behavior. Such behavior in children with ADHD results from restlessness and is generally unintentional, whereas in children with ODD, behavior is most often purposeful (El Ouardani, 2017). Children with ODD tend to have a hostile attribution bias that causes them to react aggressively to otherwise neutral environmental stimuli. The aggression associated with ODD is often the result of a perceived threat or provocation. In contrast, the aggression associated with CD is more proactive (Schoorl et al., 2016), that is, one that anticipates a reward. Furthermore, social problems in children with ODD are, for the most part, with authority figures, whereas children with ADHD and CD have social problems that are more generalized.

Etiology of Oppositional Defiance Disorder

Etiological factors in the development of ODD can be divided into biological factors, parenting and familial factors, and the child's social-cognitive processes.

Biological Factors

Most etiological studies have focused on aggression in general and/or CD; while fewer studies have examined the causes of ODD as distinct from CD. Most studies suggest that genetic factors interact with psychosocial and environmental factors to produce a diagnosis in the realm of disruptive behavior disorders (Barker et al., 2017). To our knowledge, the study of Comings et al. (2000) is the only one to mention ODD specifically, along with CD and ADHD, as having a strong association with adrenergic genes.

The same can be said for hormonal factors and their effect on adolescent behavior. In general, studies have found hormone levels, particularly high levels of testosterone and its derivatives (e.g., dehydroepiandrosterone (DHEAS), to be associated with conduct problems (Bakker-Huvenaars et al., 2020).

The role of neurotransmitter dysfunction has also been studied in the development of aggression in children, adolescent, and adults. Abnormal function of serotonin, the neurotransmitter implicated in the expression and regulation of affect and impulse control, has been found to play a role in aggression and lack of impulse control (Çetin et al., 2017) as has low levels of 5-hydroxyindoleacetic acid in the cerebrospinal fluid (da Cunha-Bang et al., 2016).

Minor neurological deficits have been found to correlate with conduct problems; for example, studies have shown a consistent association between low IQ and disruptive behavior (Rydell & Brocki, 2019). Most studies have focused on CD and have shown a relationship with reduced temporal-lobe volume resulting in deficits of executive function and inhibition (Efferson & Glenn, 2018).

Finally, studies have shown that prenatal toxins, such as nicotine and alcohol, have an association with disruptive behavior (Lebel et al., 2019). In conclusion, few studies have examined the biological bases of ODD specifically. If, however, one accepts the position that ODD is a precursor to CD, then many of the biological bases for CD would logically apply to ODD. As mentioned previously, though, only about one-third of those diagnosed with ODD progress to CD.

Parenting and Family Factors

Studies have consistently established a link between parenting and family characteristics and the development of ODD. Family dysfunction, lower levels of family income, higher levels of authoritarian parenting, lower levels of parental warmth and supervision, and inconsistent discipline have all been implicated in the development of ODD (Hayden & Patterson, 2018). In addition, insecure attachment to the primary caregiver has also been associated with ODD (Hornstra et al., 2019). The most attention has been paid to patterns of parental discipline and the role of coercion in the development of ODD. The social interaction model developed a typology of parenting (see list below) thought to be responsible for the development of ODD.

A Typology of Parenting Based on the Social Interaction Model

1. *Inconsistent discipline.* Parenting that lacks follow-through with commands and consequences and inconsistent responses to positive and negative behaviors. The parent gives in when the child argues and changes the expectations and consequences for noncompliance.
2. *Irritable explosive discipline.* Parenting that is marked by a high rate of commands, use of intense strategies such as yelling, hitting, and threatening. Makes derogatory and humiliating comments about the child. These practices increase the possibility of defiant behaviors by the child.
3. *Low supervision and involvement.* Parenting is disengaged. Parents know very little about their children—their whereabouts, friends, performance at school,

etc. Their children lack supervision even when they are participating in high-risk or delinquent activities.

4. *Inflexible, rigid discipline.* These parents have limited capacity for utilizing various strategies. They rely on a sole means of discipline without considering the severity of the transgression and contextual factors responsible for the transgression. They do not listen to their children and do not explain the reasons for their disciplinary actions.

Adapted from Chamberlain, P., & Patterson, G. R. (2002).

Child Characteristics

Originally, the social interaction model placed almost exclusive emphasis on parenting practices as the cause for a child's conduct problems, without considering how child characteristics might contribute to parent-child interactions. More recently, experts have emphasized the need to pay greater attention to child characteristics such as the capacity for emotional regulation, frustration tolerance, adaptation, and problem-solving skills (O'Kearney et al., 2017). The failure to possess such skills results in a lack of compliance, defined as the inability to delay one's own needs and wants in deference to those of an authority figure. If compliance is the result of having learned a complex set of social-cognitive skills, oppositional behavior (understood as a lack of compliance) can be understood as the child having a learning disability, that is, an inability to learn the skills needed for compliance (Griffith et al., 2019).

To further this argument, this lack of executive skill is also present in the psychiatric disorder most often comorbid with ODD (ADHD), leading to the conjecture that ADHD may set the stage for ODD (Greene, R., 2006). A deficit in the area of executive skills such as *working memory* (the ability to hold events in order to learn from them and act appropriately), *self-regulation* (the ability to regulate arousal to achieve a goal-directed action), *shifting cognitive set* (the ability to shift from rules and expectations in one situation to those of another situation), and *problem-solving* (the ability to generate possible solutions, choose the most appropriate, and enact a plan) can easily result in noncompliance. With regard to ODD, the child is not able to learn from past events nor anticipate the consequences of his or her actions (working memory), responds with a high level of emotion such as screaming or swearing (emotional regulation), has trouble responding immediately to adult requests (shifting cognitive set), and is limited in the repertoire of alternative responses (problem-solving skills) (Greene, R., 2006).

A similar argument is made for the high comorbidity between ODD and language disorders as "Those children compromised in the capacity to label emotions (such as frustration and anger) may have difficulty identifying and internalizing an adaptive repertoire of behavior strategies for responding to such emotions" (Greene, R., 2006, p. 287). In addition to these cognitive deficiencies, studies have also identified cognitive distortions that tend to exist in children with ODD (Daly et al., 2018). Children with antisocial tendencies, when presented with ambiguous social situations, tend to attribute hostile intentions to others and are more likely to support activities that are damaging to interpersonal relationships (Hartmann et al., 2020). In contrast to proactive aggression, the reactive aggression often associated with ODD is the result of misinterpreting other's behavior as being hostile.

The most significant deficit among those with ODD is in problem-solving skills. Children with ODD have trouble encoding social cues, generating alternative solutions, and choosing the most appropriate response (Motavalli Pour et al., 2018). Their preferred means of solving conflicts is through aggression, as cognitively it is the only means available to them.

In summary, the etiological component of ODD has been investigated through two dimensions to include parent/family characteristics and child characteristics. The controversy is around which is primary; that is, do child characteristics associated with ODD result from certain parenting practices, or the reverse? The most likely explanation is that there is an interaction effect between child and parent where the parents' response to a lack of compliance can increase frustration and arousal in the child (Frick & Brocki, 2019).

Assessment of Oppositional Defiance Disorder

The assessment of ODD should come from multiple sources and take place across settings, people, and events. If the emergence of ODD is the result of a poor match between a child's behavior and the parent's response to that behavior, assessment must then take into consideration information about the child, the parent, and environmental circumstances that contribute to the oppositional interactions (Greene, R., 2006). This is true for interactions that take place at home with the parent as well as those that take place in the school with the teacher and other school personnel. Questions such as "Who is the child interacting with when the behavior occurs?" "What is the child doing when the behavior occurs?" "Where do such behaviors tend to occur?" "What are the precipitating events that result in oppositional episodes?" all need to be part of the assessment of ODD.

To complete the ODD assessment, a thorough developmental, school, and treatment history should be gathered. The developmental history should focus on early temperament, attachment history, family history, and trauma history. The school history needs to ascertain the degree of oppositional behaviors across situations and teachers. The purpose of the treatment history is to find out what behavioral interventions have been tried and assess their effectiveness.

Treatment Strategies

The effectiveness of different treatment interventions for conduct problems has garnered a great deal of attention in recent years. One difficulty has been that the majority of studies are designed to assess the effectiveness of interventions for conduct problems in general and do not report findings disaggregated for a particular diagnostic group. Few studies have been limited to or report separately for ODD.

Outcome studies are generally divided into five categories:

- Individually based behavioral parent training
- Group-based behavioral parent training
- Behavioral parent training with a social support component
- Video modeling–based behavioral parent training
- Behavioral parent training combined with child-focused problem-solving skills.

Metanalytic reviews (Mouton et al., 2018) indicate that different treatments are more effective than no treatment at all. Behavioral parent training combined with child-focused problem-solving skills training appear to be the most effective intervention for ODD and more effective than either of these components alone.

Treatment Programs

The three most popular treatment programs for ODD are *Parent-Child Interaction Therapy* (PCIT) (Zisser-Nathenson et al., 2017), joint *Problem-Solving Skills Training* (PSST) together with *Parent Management Training* (PMT) (Kazdin, 2018), and the *Incredible Years Training Series* (IYTS) (Webster-Stratton & Bywater, 2019).

Incredible Years Training Program

This program has a teacher training component. Although all three programs enjoy empirical support, the IYTS is perhaps the most well-known and has the most empirical support. Its use of videotaped modeling has proven especially effective, and the fact that it has a teacher training component makes it especially attractive to those who work or plan to work in schools with young children, especially children ages 6 through 10, for whom the program was designed. It can, however, be adapted to older children. The IYTS has three different types of programs: one for parents, one for children, and one for teachers.

Parent Intervention Training Program

The goal of parent training is to increase competency and strengthen families through (1) increasing parents' positive parenting, nurturing relationships with their children, and general self-confidence about parenting; (2) replacing critical and physically violent discipline with positive strategies such as ignoring, natural and logical consequences, redirecting, monitoring, and problem-solving; (3) improving parents' problem-solving skills, anger management, and communication skills; (4) increasing family support networks and school involvement/bonding; (5) helping parents and teachers work collaboratively to ensure consistency across settings; and (6) increasing parents' involvement in children's academic-related activities at home (Webster-Stratton & Reid, 2018).

The basic parent training is videotaped-based, whereby participants watch vignettes of modeled parenting skills, a total of 250 vignettes that last from one to two minutes and shown in parent groups of eight to twelve members. They are designed to demonstrate social learning and child development principles and to teach parents the use of child-directed interactive play, praise, and incentive programs. Parents learn through discussion of the vignettes under the facilitation of a trained therapist. The program takes approximately twenty-six hours to complete over the course of thirteen to fourteen weekly two-hour sessions.

There is also an advanced parent training program that consists of fourteen sessions based on watching sixty videotaped vignettes that emphasize the following three components:

- *Personal self-control.* Parents are trained to replace their angry, depressive, and blaming self-talk with coping and positive self-talk as well as practicing anger-management techniques.
- *Communication skills.* Parents are taught to identify the deficits in their communication style and instead replace it with effective interaction skills for dealing with conflict.

- *Problem-solving skills.* Parents are taught effective strategies for coping with conflict from others to include children, family members, significant others, and employers (Webster-Stratton & Reid, 2018).

The school-parent training component is designed to help parents promote children's self-confidence at school, foster good learning habits, deal with discouragement, participate in homework, use teacher-parent conferences to advocate for their children, as well as how to discuss a school problem with their child.

Teacher Training Intervention Program

As mentioned previously, children with ODD have problems with peer socialization and authority figures in the school. Often, teacher reactions exacerbate the difficulties of disruptive children. For this reason, the IYTS includes a teacher component that is appropriate for teachers, school counselors, and psychologists. The goals of the training are to increase teachers' use of effective classroom management strategies for dealing with disruptive behaviors, promote positive relationships with difficult students, strengthen social skills in the classroom and beyond, and strengthen collaboration between teachers and parents (Webster-Stratton & Bywater, 2019; Webster-Stratton & Reid, 2018). School personnel are also taught effective problem-solving strategies to help children with ODD improve their peer relationships and, at the same time, help their peers respond more effectively to those with ODD.

Child Training Intervention

The Child Training Intervention Program (see goals listed below) runs for twenty-two weeks, during which the children meet weekly for two hours in groups of six and watch over one hundred hours of videotaped vignettes that teach problem-solving and social skills in response to real-life conflict situations at home and in school. Ideally, the parent training program runs concomitantly. All three training programs are video-based, which is a unique aspect of the IYTS, and research supports the effectiveness of the program.

Although the IYTS makes use of role play, practice activities, and live feedback, videotape "provides a more flexible method of training than didactic instruction or sole reliance on role play; that is, we could portray a wide variety of models and situations" (Webster-Stratton & Reid, 2003, p. 230). Models used in the videotapes reflect a diversity of age, culture, socioeconomic status, and temperament.

Models are often unrehearsed and show both the right and wrong approaches to interacting effectively with children with ODD. All presentations of videotaped vignettes are followed by focused discussions designed to promote learning and mutual support among members of the group. The inclusion of training for different constituencies (parents, children, and teachers) results from the premise that the origin of ODD and its maintenance is the result of a complex interaction where the outcome depends on the interrelationships between children, parents, teachers, and peers (Webster-Stratton & Reid, 2018).

The Child Training Program in the Incredible Years Training Program: Goals

- Strengthening children's social skills and appropriate play skills (turn-taking, waiting, asking, sharing, helping, and complimenting)
- Promoting children's use of self-control strategies such as effective problem-solving and anger management strategies
- Increasing emotional awareness by labeling feelings, recognizing the differing views of oneself and others, and enhancing perspective-taking
- Boosting academic success, reading, and school readiness
- Reducing defiance, aggressive behavior, and related conduct problems such as noncompliance, peer aggression and rejection, bullying, stealing, and lying
- Decreasing children's negative cognitive attributions and conflict-management approaches
- Increasing self-esteem and self-confidence

Source: Webster-Stratton, C., & Reid, M. J. (2018). The Incredible Years Parents, Teachers and Children Training Series: A multifaceted treatment approach for young children with conduct problems. In A. E. Kazdin & J. R. Weisz (Eds.) (3rd Ed.), *Evidence-based psychotherapies for children and adolescents* (pp. 122-141). New York: Guilford Press. Copyright Guilford Press. Reprinted with permission.

School-Based Interventions: Elan

The first step in developing an effective school-based intervention that will be appropriate for Elan is to determine the purpose or function of his oppositional defiant behaviors. This determination needs to be made for each specific behavior described in the case example at the beginning of the chapter. One way to conduct such an informal assessment is to (1) determine specific antecedents, events that preceded the disruptive or defiant behavior, (2) operationally describe the behavior itself (in measurable terms), and then (3) identify the results or consequences of the misbehavior that serve to reinforce it. This process is referred to as the A-B-C approach to identifying the purpose served by the target behavior, in this case, Elan's defiant behavior. Ideally, this approach will facilitate the development of hypotheses regarding the functions served by Elan's engaging in these problem behaviors and thereby help his teachers construct an effective behavioral intervention plan.

Assessing the Problem

From the scenario presented in the case example, it appears that the behaviors that most seriously affect Elan's classroom performance include (1) disrespectful, insubordinate behavior displayed in talking back to the teacher and making threats, (2) ridiculing and denigrating others when frustrated or angry with authority figures or classmates in the school (we need to identify these behaviors), and (3) impatient with classmates and intolerant of others' mistakes (again, we need to know more about the specific behaviors that demonstrate his impatience with others).

When working with a student like Elan, who presents an array of problem behaviors, it is necessary to prioritize them according to their impact on learning and classroom performance. Consequently, based on what we know about Elan's classroom conduct, the primary target behaviors to address are (1) insubordination (talking back or speaking disrespectfully to the teacher), (2) ridiculing others, and (3) impatience with others. These target behaviors have to be operationally defined to facilitate their identification and recording.

To provide the necessary baseline data for each of these target behaviors, Elan's teachers, in conjunction with the multidisciplinary evaluation team, are asked to provide anecdotal data consisting of written observations of the targeted behaviors identified within a specific time frame as well as event recording, noting the frequency with which the target behaviors occur (reference the Behavior Intervention Checklist below and the Functional Behavioral Assessment Worksheet found on page 24). In addition, these teachers are asked to conduct systematic observation of the target behaviors relative to a specific situation (e.g., Mrs. Burr's class), across various settings (e.g., content-area classes, specials, extra-curricular activities and postschool events), and at different times of the day (e.g., homeroom, before lunch, lunch, after lunch, dismissal, and departure).

Once the baseline for each of these behaviors has been established, Elan's teachers need to deduce the following:

1. The circumstances in which the behavior appears most likely to occur.
2. Various contributing factors

3. The consequences of the specific behavior for the student or the benefits derived by the student from engaging in the problem behavior
4. Circumstances in which the student is least likely to engage in the problem behavior
5. Any other contributing factors (Ingram et al. 2005).

Subsequently, Elan's teachers, in coordination with the multidisciplinary evaluation team, will determine the primary function or purpose served by each of the target behaviors and design an intervention plan that will address each one effectively. A behavioral intervention plan (BIP) should be judiciously derived from the child's functional behavioral assessment and address short-term prevention, teaching of alternative skills, responses to problem behaviors, and long-term prevention (Barnhill, 2005).

Behavior Intervention Checklist

Student's Name: ____________________

Target Behaviour: ____________________

Put an "X" in the space that corresponds to the time and date of each observed behaviour. If plotting more than 1 behaviour, use another letter.

Dates: ____________________

Monday	Tuesday	Wednesday	Thursday	Friday	Comments
8:30					
8:45					
9:00					
9:15					
9:30					
9:45					
10:00					
10:15					
10:30					

10:45					
11:00					
11:15					
11:30					
11:45					
12:00					
12:15					
12:30					
12:45					
1:00					
1:15					
1:30					
1:45					
2:00					
2:15					
2:30					
2:45					

Source: Barnhill, G. P. (2005). Functional behavioral assessment in schools. *Intervention in School and Clinic,* 40(3), 131–143.

Developing an Effective Intervention Plan

Using the case example of Elan, the team will develop an appropriate intervention plan as a model. First, clearly address each of the target behaviors in priority order. In this instance, the team will begin with insubordination (talking back or speaking disrespectfully to the teacher).

Short-term Prevention (Insubordination). Oppositional defiance disorder, like conduct disorder and ADHD, does not appear to be affected in the short term. The only immediate intervention that might provide some behavioral improvement would be the change in teacher attitudes and approaches relative to affected individuals, which are components of the teacher training in the Incredible Years Training Series (IYTS) (Webster-Stratton & Bywater, 2019). This intervention is currently both the most popular and empirically supported of the treatment programs designed to help individuals with ODD.

Insubordination, distinguished by disrespectful speech, is characteristic of the child with ODD. The tone and quality of the teacher's response can do much to exacerbate or mitigate a potentially volatile situation. The Old Testament aphorism: "A gentle answer turns away wrath, but a harsh word stirs up anger" (Proverbs 15:1, New American Standard Version) still holds relevance; particularly for this situation. Remember, the student who has ODD is often reacting to the position of power and control that the teacher holds and is rarely a personal attack. This can sometimes help the teacher maintain composure and provide the student with a model of civility and respect—important attributes we want the student who has ODD to acquire.

Teaching of Alternative Skills (Insubordination). The goals of the child training program component of the IYTS are clearly the teaching of alternative skills to replace the undesirable and antisocial ones associated with ODD. As outlined in the treatment section of this chapter, some of these substitute skills include (1) strengthening children's social skills and appropriate play skills (turn-taking, waiting, asking, sharing, helping, and complimenting), (2) promoting children's use of self-control strategies such as effective problem-solving and anger management strategies, (3) labeling feelings, recognizing the differing views of oneself and others, and enhancing perspective-taking, and (4) increasing self-esteem and self-confidence (Webster-Stratton & Bywater, 2019).

Responses to Problem Behaviors (Insubordination). Research has supported the importance of providing immediate response to problem behaviors, especially those that involve verbal and/or physical aggression (Kauffman, 2015; Kauffman & Badar, 2013). The roots of oppositional defiant behavior are generally found in ineffective and sometimes abusive caregiver relationships; therefore, it is important that the teacher establish a firm but caring and respectful rapport with the student who exhibits such behaviors. This does not mean that the student displaying ODD behaviors should be treated deferentially; on the contrary, evidence suggests that meaningful consequences should be swiftly applied. Students who have ODD need to know that insubordinate behavior will not be permitted in the classroom and will be met with consequences that are predictable and sure (Gresham, 2011; Walker & Hoyt, 2015).

Long-Term Prevention (Insubordination). Restitution should also be an integral part of any behavioral intervention plan for students who engage in ODD behaviors (Mullet, 2014). Unlike the child with a conduct disorder, the child with ODD will most typically engage in verbal aggression and insult, or blatant disrespect expressed verbally. As a consequence, the insult or injury inflicted by these children tends to be felt on an emotional level. Restitution, in this case, typically means an apology, written or verbally expressed or both. The apology does not preclude additional consequences as in a case involving a physical threat, racist or sexually explicit epithets, or property damage that occurs inadvertently as a result of the oppositional or defiant behavior.

The most effective responses to children who are disrespectful, however, are ones that model respect and civility—the ones that display grace under fire. Engaging in heated verbal exchanges with these children invariably escalates the frequency and intensity of the very behaviors we want to extinguish. Once again, there appear to be no quick fixes for behavior problems that have developed over time, incubated in an unhealthy or pathological home environment. The best deterrent for ODD behaviors is a teacher–student relationship that has been nurtured on trust, has been time-tested, and is predicated on compassion.

The next set of behaviors to address is Elan's ridiculing and denigrating of others when frustrated or angry with authority figures or classmates. These exhibitions include (a) using epithets to harangue and humiliate, and (b) damaging or destroying property to express frustration with another.

Short-Term Prevention (Ridicule/Denigrate). Similar to disrespectful behavior, ridicule and denigration are expressions of frustration and anger that may be misplaced but nonetheless must be swiftly and effectively addressed. Typically, the use of such antisocial communication is not tolerated in the classroom, and the guilty party is subject to some sort of established consequence. This level of deterrence is usually effective for most students, for whom such behavior is an anomaly; however, for students who have ODD, punishment is often ineffective because the acting-out behavior is frequently a demonstration of deep-seated anger that cannot be expressed to the child's parents.

The Incredible Years Training Program (IYTP) (Webster-Stratton & Bywater, 2019) provides effective intervention for this behavior set through promoting children's use of self-control strategies such as effective problem-solving and anger management techniques, increasing emotional awareness by labeling feelings, recognizing the differing views of oneself and others, and enhancing perspective-taking, reducing defiance, aggressive behavior, and related conduct problems such as noncompliance, decreasing negative cognitive attributions and conflict management approaches, and increasing self-esteem and self-confidence. Likewise, the teacher-training component of IYTP equips the teacher with the skill set to allow the teacher to see beyond the antisocial, distasteful behaviors to the need for acceptance and affirmation on the part of the child with ODD.

Teaching Alternative Skills (Ridicule/Denigrate). This is an important component of the IYTP program. Depending on the age of the child exhibiting the problem behavior, the teacher can use the infringement to conduct a social skills autopsy (LaVoie, 2005). This may be a more effective approach for younger children because they are less constrained by image and peer pressure. In essence, the social skills autopsy involves on-the-spot analysis of the misbehavior to determine (1) the specific misbehavior and why it occurred, (2) its effect on the student and others, and (3) the socially appropriate behavior to be implemented next time.

In the case of the child's display of rude gestures, the student might be taught to use appropriate replacement behaviors such as speaking with the teacher about situations that are perceived as stressful, frustrating, or provocative, using a prearranged signal to notify the teacher of the need to take a time-out from an activity that is becoming tedious or a situation that is exceptionally stressful. An older student might be asked to confer with the teacher immediately after the misbehavior to allow the student to decompress and also to permit the teacher to explain the negative consequences of the problem behavior, investigate possible antecedents, and collaborate to identify and implement an appropriate alternative behavior response for the future.

Responses to Problems (Ridicule/Denigrate). In the case of a very challenging student like Elan, the teacher is often pushed to the limits of tolerance and, in that aggravated state, can behave unprofessionally toward the offending student. There have been cases in which typically effective professionals have succumbed to the relentless provocations of a student like Elan. For a few, a careless and unprofessional response was a career-ender, whereas others, a bit more established and resilient, were able to weather the unpleasant repercussions. There is never a circumstance that is so dire that a teacher cannot ask a colleague for some assistance. All of us, at one time or another, reach the end of our tether. The real professional wisdom is to acknowledge those moments and, however uncomfortable, ask for a few minutes of relief from an understanding colleague. At no time should the teacher engage the student in a power game of threats and counterthreats.

In any event, the correct response to the provocations of someone like Elan is always one tempered by restraint and reason - the reaction of the teacher should be swift, firm, and brief. In response to rude gestures, for example, the teacher might move to a position beside the offending student rather than in front, to avoid an escalation of the problem behavior. The teacher then should assume a lower body stance (i.e., a squat or support on one knee) and quietly but firmly remind the individual that such behavior is unacceptable and will not be tolerated in the classroom. At this point, the student should be provided the opportunity to speak with the teacher about perceived antecedents outside the classroom or, if the improper behavior was unprovoked, the student should be reminded about relevant consequences. If the student persists in engaging in defiant, disruptive behavior, he needs to be escorted to a designated time-out room, and the incident should be anecdotally recorded.

Long-Term Prevention (Ridicule/Denigrate). Many times, students who have ODD, like Elan, continue to engage in the same inappropriate or offensive behaviors because they simply do not know a better way to achieve the objective they want. There is evidence suggesting that if students who have ODD are simply taught more appropriate ways to attain those ends, many will stop behaving badly; they simply lack the skills repertoire that would offer them more socially acceptable choices (Gresham, 2011; Walker & Hoyt, 2015). Also, through treatment programs, such as the Incredible Years Training Program, students who have ODD learn self-control strategies such as effective problem-solving and anger management strategies, enhancing perspective-taking, and conflict management approaches, all of which can ultimately lead to an increase self-esteem and self-confidence.

The last of Elan's target behaviors that needs to be addressed in the classroom is impatience with classmates and intolerant of others' mistakes. Clearly, this behavior contributes to Elan's isolation from his peers as well as his own sense of alienation. What child wants to associate with a classmate that constantly criticizes them for the slightest mistake? The irony here is that, as much as children like Elan insist they do not care about being socially excluded by his classmates, the fact remains that they are deeply affected.

Short-Term Prevention (Impatience). Students who have ODD, like Elan, simply do not have the self-awareness or the intrapersonal skills to understand and control their innate feelings of frustration and anger (Patterson et al., 2006). Whatever a teacher can do to help reduce the alienation brought about by the self-destructive behavior of students like Elan may help break a vicious cycle and restore the child's sense of belongingness (Perry & Lavins-Merillat, 2018). One technique that is used effectively in schools is peer mediation. This approach requires that both students involved in a fight or disagreement work through their problems with the aid of a trained peer mediator. A teacher, who has also been trained in the intervention, provides adult oversight; however, as long as the disputants comply with the rules of mediation, formal school sanctions are not applied.

Teaching Alternative Skills (Impatience). The functional behavioral assessment conducted by the multidisciplinary team should identify a plausible purpose for Elan's provocative behaviors. This information is critical to his instructors and caregivers, who will be teaching and modeling alternative behaviors. Let us assume that, in Elan's case, these behaviors serve two primary purposes, first to gain attention and recognition, albeit negative, from peers; and secondly, as retribution for being ostracized by his peers. In response, then, teachers must first model proactive rather than reactive responses to stressful events; for example, rather than shouting at Elan in reaction to his verbal outbursts, teachers should speak calmly and firmly, directing Elan away from the contentious situation and into a less stimulating environment, such as the hallway or designated time-out or quiet room.

Once removed from the stressful situation and after Elan has regained his composure, the teacher can deconstruct the event and suggest ways that Elan might constructively handle similar situations in future. He might be taught a self-management technique to help him deescalate a potentially volatile situation, something as simple as POST: Pause, consider Options, Seek help, Try a new way. If the situation is too volatile, the student might be provided a signal that will enable him to surreptitiously remove himself from the demands of the setting and relocate to a predetermined neutral location (Webster-Stratton & Bywater, 2019).

Responses to Problems (Impatience). As in the case of Elan's other target behaviors, teachers need to remember to respond therapeutically, not overreacting or personalizing his defiant remarks. Teachers must understand that they are simply safe targets of opportunity, ones that will not reciprocate in kind. That does not mean that they cannot or should not confront the behavior, dispensing swift and sure consequences for the child's misbehavior. The important thing to remember is that, ultimately, the child must not feel that he or she has been ostracized or rejected; on the contrary, the child with ODD must understand that her membership in the class is inviolable.

Long-Term Prevention (Impatience). Like the other two target behaviors, the most effective means of preventing a recurrence of peer aggression is through the child and her caregivers' participation in an effective intervention program such as the Incredible Years Training Program (IYTP). Specifically, the IYTP teaches the student effective strategies that help the affected individual reduce defiant behaviors as well as related conduct problems such as noncompliance and peer aggression and rejection, among others. To reiterate, the eventual goal of any school-based intervention relative to the child who exhibits oppositional and defiant behavior is the effective replacement of those undesirable behaviors with ones that are pro-social and self-affirming.

From the Field

James Slavet, Ph.D.

James Slavet is a clinical psychologist at the Manville School, which is part of Judge Baker Children's Center in Boston, Massachusetts. He earned a Ph.D.

from UMass–Amherst in 2004, where he focused on research and training opportunities with court-involved youth. He was an intern in the Department of Public Behavioral Health and Justice Policy at the University of Washington and a postdoctoral fellow at Brown University and the Rhode Island Training School. His current interests include the application of evidence-based practices to therapy with children and families.

You have worked with a large number of students who were both oppositional and defiant. How would you describe the behaviors of these children?

Typically, students diagnosed with ODD disobey rules and regulations, argue with authority figures, and disrupt teaching classroom activities. Students presenting with oppositional and defiant behaviors are often struggling with other emotional and/or learning problems. It is important to generate hypotheses regarding the function of oppositional and defiant behaviors for an individual student (Why are they acting this way?); for example, some students may exhibit these behaviors while they are angry, others might act this way when they feel as though they have little control over their environment, and still others may be modeling behaviors of peers or siblings. Understanding the function of behavior can help you plan an appropriate intervention for an individual student.

In your experience, what are is it about the oppositional-defiant child that presents the greatest challenge to the teacher and to teaching?

I think that the greatest challenge for teachers is forming a solid relationship with oppositional-defiant children. It can be extremely frustrating when a child defies classroom rules, disrupts the class, and is openly hostile towards the teacher, and it is very challenging not to take this behavior personally. If a teacher is able to disapprove of the behavior, while still showing that he or she cares about the student, it can go a long way to building respect and a positive relationship. This kind of positive teacher–student relationship is especially important with students who have oppositional and defiant behaviors. Typically, these students have been often punished both at school and at home and have internalized these experiences into their identity. A positive relationship with an adult focused on their strengths and pro-social behaviors can be the key to shifting behaviors.

As a novice, I am sure that you, like all of us, made a few mistakes with these students. For the benefit of the new and inexperienced teachers who are reading this, could you share one or two of these missteps with us so that we can be aware of and, hopefully, avoid them?

My biggest mistake has been trying to reason with a child who is exhibiting oppositional or defiant behavior. Rarely is a child available for a rational conversation when he or she is behaving this way. When I've tried to reason with students during an instance of problematic behavior, it has only led to an increase in the intensity of the problem. I remember one occasion, during my first year working at Manville School, a teacher and I debated the utility of school rules over and over again with a particular student. It turned out that this student ended up liking debating the rules with us much more than going to class. It took us a while to figure out that he was purposely acting out to get out of class so that he could get our attention!

Can you provide a few of your most effective strategies for working successfully with these students? For example, tips that you wish someone had given you when you started working with this population?

I believe that the most important strategy in working successfully with students who are displaying oppositional defiant behavior is to shower them with positive reinforcement when they are not displaying problematic behavior. This is difficult and at times counterintuitive. People often say, "Why should I reward a kid for doing what he or she is supposed to do anyway?" It is important to realize that doing the right thing and the effective thing is sometimes different.

Ignoring problematic behavior is critical, but sometimes the behavior is so bad that a student needs to be removed from the class or consequenced in another way. But for these students, the way in which the consequence is handed out is just as important as the consequence itself. Whenever possible, giving a verbal consequence in front of the class in a pejorative tone should be avoided. Writing students a note clearly describing the consequence usually works pretty well; in my experience, they find it harder to argue with a clearly written statement!

Finally, could you share an anecdote from your teaching repertoire that highlights one of your most memorable successes in working with a student who has a conduct disorder?

Several years ago, I was working with an adolescent girl who was incarcerated. Her behavior problems were among the most intense that I have worked with. When I first met her, she refused to follow most of the staff rules, often fought verbally and physically with peers, and had conflictive relationships with most of her family members. In therapy, I was able to engage her in a discussion of her strengths, her goals, and, and her interpersonal relationships. We spent almost no time discussing her 'bad' behavior. I was also able to include her mother in therapy sessions. While we had intense discussions and talked about some important issues, she remained oppositional at times in therapy and had very little immediate behavior change outside of therapy.

Therapy ended after she was transferred to a different facility, due mostly to her bad behavior. Months later, I received a letter from her thanking me for the work we had done together. She told me of the great changes that she had made in her behavior and her upcoming return to living in the community with her family. In the letter, she repeated back several phrases that I had used with her in therapy and she had seemed to internalize these concepts. She taught me the important lesson that people change their behavior on their own schedule, and while our work might not have led to an immediate change in her behavior, it ultimately did help her. Classroom teachers don't have the luxury of the time afforded by therapy, but they may still benefit from this lesson. As I mentioned earlier, a positive relationship with an adult who ignores negative behaviors as much as possible while focusing on and reinforcing strengths and pro-social behaviors can be the key to shifting behaviors.

Summary

Perhaps the most challenging students that teachers must instruct are those with defiance disorders. Some researchers have suggested that oppositional defiant disorder is a precursor to its more serious manifestation, conduct disorder. If this is so, it then follows that teachers are in a unique position to intervene in the development of the disorder and prevent its pernicious evolution.

Prevalence rates for ODD range anywhere from 2 to 16 percent (American Psychiatric Association, 2013) because of the historical lack of precision in diagnosing ODD and the difficulty of distinguishing mild ODD from normal, developmentally appropriate behavior (Burke & Romano-Verthelyi, 2018). ODD is more prevalent in boys than in girls, and it is most frequently diagnosed in children under age 8. Moreover, ODD is highly comorbid with ADHD and with anxiety and mood disorders. Finally, because a defining characteristic of ODD is social impairment, some studies have looked at the overlap between ODD and autism spectrum disorder (ASD) (Pijper et al., 2016).

The principle characteristics of the ODD are opposition and defiance that have become a developmentally inappropriate pattern of behavior, with high levels of negativistic, disobedient, and hostile behavior, especially toward authority figures. These behaviors include "temper outbursts, persistent stubbornness, resistance to following directions, unwillingness to compromise, give in, or negotiate with adults or peers; deliberate or persistent testing of limits; and verbal (and minor physical) aggression" (Greene, R., 2006, p. 285). In addition, children with ODD tend to have a hostile attribution bias that causes them to react aggressively to otherwise neutral environmental stimuli. The aggression associated with ODD is often the result of a perceived threat or provocation and are for the most part directed at authority figures, whereas children with ADHD and CD have social problems that are more generalized (Schoorl et al., 2016).

Etiological factors in the development of ODD can be divided into biological factors, parenting and family factors, and the child's social-cognitive processes. Studies have consistently established a link between parenting and family characteristics and the development of ODD (Hayden & Patterson, 2018). Family dysfunction, lower levels of family income, higher levels of authoritarian parenting, lower levels of parental warmth and supervision, and inconsistent discipline have all been implicated in the development of ODD (Hayden & Patterson, 2018).

Researchers have agreed that the assessment of ODD should come from multiple sources (Hendren & Mullen, 2006). Clinicians and other professionals have relied on diagnostic interviews, rating scales, and reviews of school records to gather information enroute to making a diagnosis of ODD. The assessment of ODD must also take place across settings, people, and events. If the emergence of ODD is the result of a poor match between a child's behavior and the parent's response to that behavior, assessment must take into consideration information about the child, the adult, and environmental circumstances that contribute to the oppositional interactions (Greene, R., 2006). This is true for interactions that take place at home with the parent as well as those that take place in the school with the teacher and other school personnel. A thorough developmental, school, and treatment history should be gathered as well.

Lastly, in this chapter, we identified several research-based interventions that have demonstrated success in mitigating the behaviors of ODD in school-aged children. One of the more popular of these is the *Incredible Years Training Program* (Webster-Stratton & Bywater, 2019), which provides explicit training programs for all key stakeholders—teachers, parents, and affected children. Using a case example, we developed an assessment plan that helped identify target behaviors and their specific functions and, as a result, an effective intervention plan to address each of the problem behaviors.

Tips for Teachers

- Do not allow the child to draw you into an argument that can escalate. Likewise, be careful not to use ultimatums (e.g., "If you say one more word, I will assign you a thirty-minute detention," or "Get up out of your seat and leave the room at once—I want you out of here!"). These kinds of responses often force the child to choose between compliance (sometimes viewed as a sign of weakness) and insubordination that will invariably result in punishment.

- Plan a regular conference time for the student during which his or her comments and expressed feelings will not be subject to censure or sanctions. This will show the student that there are socially appropriate times and places for expressing anger and frustration.
- Investigate the causes of the student's agitation. Take immediate steps to provide relief from the source, and help the student select a more appropriate behavioral approach.
- Praise the student frequently for making appropriate behavioral choices; remind the individual that, ultimately, he or she is responsible for both the good and bad ones.
- Become an "expert" in identifying the verbal and nonverbal signals characteristic to the individual that precede a behavioral incident.
- Say what you mean and mean what you say! If you must give the student a warning or an ultimatum, make sure that you follow through. Sometimes teachers feel compelled to give the student an "if, then" condition: "If you do this, or if you do not do that, then . . . (name a consequence)." Occasionally, such an admonition is a reaction to what is perceived as "outrageous" behavior; frequently, it is simply a human response to what ostensibly is disrespect. Nevertheless, if you do assign a consequence, then you are duty-bound to deliver. The same is true for the promise of a reward. Students who have ODD are used to inconsistency in dealings with authority figures and the meting out of consequences, good or bad. This inconsistent treatment is often a factor in the development of their defiant behavior (Hayden & Patterson, 2018).
- Set boundaries around the inappropriate behavior. Speak privately with the child and, keeping in mind that defiance of authority is a sign not of strength but of a fragile ego, establish yourself as the benevolent authority. Explain that although you understand that the child may have underlying issues and that you will help him or her try to understand them, you will not tolerate the inappropriate behavior. Stress the seriousness

of the situation and the consequences if it persists (Pierangelo & Giuliani, 2016).

- Try to help the student understand why she is defiant. Encourage her to verbalize what she is feeling or why she does what he does. If she cannot give voice to her feelings, you may want to provide her with some descriptors; for example, you may want to say that you have seen other students defy authority because they felt they were not doing well in school, had problems at home, or felt rejected by peers (Pierangelo & Giuliani, 2016).

- If the defiant behavior follows a consistent pattern, confer with the student's parents to obtain information about any issues at home. Consult with the school counseling or social work staff or the school psychologist about developing a behavioral contract for the student. Parent involvement will be important. Finally, if the problem is severe and persists, consult the school's pupil personnel or child study team (Pierangelo & Giuliani, 2016).

- Arrange for a safe and supervised "time-out" or "chill space." The purpose of such a place is to provide a neutral site where the student can "cool off" when he becomes aware that he is about to "lose it." Give him a laminated "chill pass" to show you before he leaves the room. Praise him for his self-awareness and good choice in removing himself from the classroom and taking a positive time-out rather than succumbing to his volatile and unpredictable emotions. If the student seems to abuse this privilege, discuss your concerns in a private conference and negotiate the number of times he may use the pass, encouraging him to reduce the frequency of its use as he learns to employ more appropriate coping strategies. Suggestion: Because students who exhibit defiance disorders often prefer to receive praise or criticism in private, avoid publicly 'spotlighting' them with public display of praise and criticism (Pierangelo & Giuliani, 2016).

Focus Questions Revisited

Why is it so important that we address oppositional defiant disorder (ODD) behaviors observed in our students quickly and effectively?

Sample Response. It is important that we address these defiant behaviors for two reasons: (a) because the defining characteristics, which can include temper outbursts, persistent stubbornness, resistance to following directions, unwillingness to compromise, deliberate limit testing, and verbal aggression, make teaching these students very challenging, if not almost impossible; and (b) because a significant number of children with ODD sometimes progress to the more serious diagnosis of conduct disorder(Shader & Beauchaine, 2020).

What characteristic behaviors are symptomatic of ODD?

Sample Response. Characteristic behaviors include negativistic, hostile, and defiant behavior lasting as least six months, during which four (or more) in any of the following categories are present:

- **Angry/Irritable Mood**: often loses temper; is often touchy or easily annoyed by others; is often angry and resentful;
- **Argumentative/Defiant Behavior**: often argues with authority figures or for children and adolescents, with adults; often actively defies or refuses to comply with adults' requests or rules; often deliberately annoys people; often blames others for his or her mistakes or misbehavior;
- **Vindictiveness**: is often spiteful or vindictive at least twice within the past 6 months (American Psychiatric Association, 2013).

What does research say about the probable causes of the disorder?

Sample Response. Research has established a link between parenting styles—specifically, patterns of discipline and the role of coercion—and the integrity of the family unit in the development of ODD (Hayden & Patterson, 2018). Similarly, some investigators (Chamberlain & Patterson, 2002) have identified specific parenting traits that may be instrumental in the genesis of ODD. These traits include: (a) inconsistent discipline, (b) explosive discipline, (c) low supervision and involvement, and (d) inflexible, rigid discipline. In contrast, other research has pointed to child characteristics—in particular, the capacity of the child for emotional regulation, frustration tolerance, adaptation, and problem-solving. These studies regarded the affected child as simply unable to learn the skills needed for compliance (Griffith et al., 2019). A more popular explanation contends that ODD may be more accurately described as a recursive effect created by these two dynamic variables, that is, the interaction effect between child and parent (Frick & Brocki, 2019).

How is ODD appropriately assessed?

Sample Response. As is the case with all emotional behavioral disorders, assessment of ODD should come from multiple sources. Professionals should administer rating scales, conduct diagnostic interviews, review school records, and examine the structured and unstructured observations of teachers, parents, and other stakeholders to confirm a diagnosis of ODD (Hendren & Mullen, 2006). Furthermore, because the disorder is often linked to the quality of the child–parent interaction, the assessment process should investigate the nature of the parental relationships of the child in question (Greene, R., 2006).

According to the best practice evidence provided in this chapter, which of the treatment options appears most effective? What are its principal strengths?

Sample Response. The most popular and well-supported intervention described in the chapter is the Incredible Years Training Series (IYTS; (Webster-Stratton & Bywater, 2019). The principal strength of this program is its recognition of the importance of long-term commitment on the part of all three stakeholders: the parents, the child, and the teachers. For example, the goal of the parent intervention training component is to increase competency in parenting skills relative to the affected child, improve parent–child communication, and strengthen the family unit through the development of support networks that include collaboration with teachers and other professionals. Similarly, the teacher training intervention component stresses the importance of increasing collaboration with parents. It also provides the teacher with training in effective classroom management techniques, especially those that address working with disruptive behaviors, promote positive relationships with difficult students, and strengthen social skills (Webster-Stratton & Bywater, 2019).

Finally, the child training intervention component helps to strengthen the child's social skills, promotes greater self-control through the acquisition of problem-solving strategies, increases emotional awareness by enhancing perspective-taking and teaching the child to label feelings, teaches conflict-management strategies, and helps to improve academic success by focusing on key skill areas, thereby reducing the child's innate sense of failure, and increasing self-esteem and self-confidence (Webster-Stratton & Bywater, 2019).

Suppose you have a student in your classroom who has ODD. What are some interventions you might employ to help him control and, ultimately, reduce his defiant behaviors while simultaneously increasing his pro-social ones?

Sample Response. Acknowledging, of course, that every child is unique and will most assuredly present distinctive problem behaviors, the child with ODD will likely present one or two of the behaviors identified in the example case of Elan. Of course, one must conduct a functional behavioral assessment, both to identify and confirm the target behaviors and to identify the purpose served by each one. Accordingly, the interventions employed must be research-based and address effectively the identified target behaviors and their functions. Suppose, for example, that the student is similar in his expression of oppositional-defiant behaviors to the case example of Elan. In such a case, the following approaches might be tried: (a) plan a regular conference time for the student during which his comments and expressed feelings are not subject to censure or sanctions, which will show him that there are socially appropriate times and places for expressing anger and frustration; (b) investigate the causes of the student's agitation and take immediate steps to provide relief from the source and help the student select a more appropriate behavioral approach; (c) praise the student frequently for making appropriate behavioral choices and remind him that, ultimately, he is responsible for both the good and bad ones; (d) become an "expert" in identifying the verbal and nonverbal signals characteristic to the individual that precede a behavioral incident; (e) set boundaries around the inappropriate behavior; (f) speak privately with the child and, keeping in mind that defiance of authority is a sign not of strength but of a fragile ego, establish yourself as the benevolent authority; and finally, (g) try to help the student understand why he is defiant and encourage him to verbalize what he is feeling or why he does what he does—if he cannot give voice to his feelings, you may want to provide him with some descriptors.

What other professional support might you solicit in your efforts to help a student who as ODD?

Sample Response. If the defiant behavior follows a consistent pattern, confer with the student's parents to obtain information about any issues at home. Consult with the school counseling or social work staff or the school psychologist about developing a behavioral intervention plan for the student. Finally, if the problem is severe and persists, consult the school's committee for special education (CSE) or child study team (CST), and solicit their help in addressing the difficulty.

Key Terms Used in the Chapter

Adrenergic Genes:
Hormonal genes that carry adrenalin.

Dehydroepiandrosterone Erone (DHEAS):
A natural steroid produced from cholesterol that undergoes conversion to produce testosterone in males and estrogens in females.

5-Hydroxyindoleacetic Acid:
The principal metabolized form of serotonin.

Cognitive Distortions:
Refers to dysfunctional thinking.

Operationally Defined:
Refers to target behaviors that must be carefully delineated to ensure consistent identification for recording purposes.

Anecdotal Data:
Behavior recording consisting of written observations of the targeted behaviors identified within a specific time frame.

Restitution:
A behavioral consequence that involves a meaningful and substantive reparation on the part of the transgressor or perpetrator to help make amends to the victim as well as to ensure that the transgressor takes responsibility for his or her behavior and acknowledges its destructive consequences.

Peer Mediation:
An approach that requires both students involved in a fight or disagreement to work through their problems with the aid of a trained peer mediator. A teacher, who has also been trained in the intervention, provides adult oversight; however, as long as the disputants comply with the rules of mediation, formal school sanctions are not applied.

Chapter 4

Attention-Deficit Hyperactivity Disorder

Focus Questions

- *Differentiate the three types of attention-deficit hyperactivity disorder (ADHD) as presented in the DSM-V. Which of the three poses the greatest challenge in the classroom and why?*
- *As the teacher of a student who has ADHD, would you advocate for the use of a pharmacological intervention?*
- *What can the teachers of a student suspected of having ADHD do to provide meaningful data to help inform the multidisciplinary team and thus facilitate the referral process?*
- *Discuss the controversy surrounding the classification of ADHD. Based on your knowledge of the disorder, should ADHD be classified as an emotional/behavioral disorder, a health impairment, a learning disability, or is it distinctive and therefore deserving of a separate category?*
- *Why do many "experts" contend that arriving at a correct diagnosis of ADHD is one of the most challenging tasks for clinicians?*
- *After reviewing the section in the chapter on pharmacological interventions used in the treatment of ADHD, what are your impressions of its efficacy?*

Introduction

Research presently contends that there are two *somewhat* distinctive "types" of the disorder; namely, *predominantly inattentive type* and *predominantly hyperactive-impulsive type*, yet a third type comprised of a combination of the characteristics of these two is becoming increasingly prevalent. All three subtypes of ADHD share the same purported etiologies, are assessed using the same instruments, and are similarly treated. Accordingly, this chapter begins with two cases examples, that of Alice, diagnosed with ADHD, combined type; and Matt, diagnosed with ADHD, predominantly inattentive type.

Included in this chapter is an extensive review of the use of pharmacological interventions in the treatment of ADHD. The coverage of this aspect of treatment may appear to be excessive; however, the reason should be apparent given the ubiquity of methylphenidate (marketed as Ritalin) as the preferred treatment for the disorder. Methylphenidate, the most widely prescribed drug for children, is also acknowledged to be among the most abused drugs by school-age children in the United States (Weyandt et al., 2016). Furthermore, due to the prodigious lack of research concerning the effects of the prolonged use of methylphenidate, it is vital that the reader is fully informed both as to the potential for harm as well as the recommended procedures for its prescription and use.

Attention Deficit Hyperactivity Disorder Introduced

Attention Deficit Hyperactivity Disorder (ADHD) has been described as the most common neurobiological disorder of childhood (CDC, 2020). Its cause is believed to be primarily a malfunctioning of neurotransmitters that facilitate the transfer of signals from one neuron to another. Specifically, there appears to be a deficiency in a specific neurotransmitter known as dopamine (Duggal, 2020). As a result, this inefficient neurotransmission in response to the reduced levels of dopamine impairs the executive functioning of the brain, which is reportedly focused in the prefrontal cortex. Although this perspective is debated, a majority of researchers support it (Gold et al., 2014).

Just as controversial is the classification of ADHD under the Individuals with Disabilities Education Act (IDEA; U.S. Department of Education, 2004). Currently, many students who have been diagnosed with ADHD receive special education and related services under the category, "Other Health Impaired," whereas others, whose symptoms may not be as severe or affect their educational performance to a degree considered appropriate for classification under IDEA (U.S. Department of Education, 2004) may receive accommodations under Section 504 of the Rehabilitation Act of 1973 (United States Department of Health, Education, and Welfare, Office for Civil Rights, 1978). Many practitioners, however, still consider ADHD to be primarily an emotional/behavioral disorder given that its presenting symptoms appear to be principally behavioral. In contrast, other investigators have contended that ADHD affects the cognitive processing areas of the brain and should therefore be considered a learning disorder (Semrud-Clikeman et al., 2010). The following two cases provide the reader with helpful examples of actual students that have been diagnosed with ADHD.

Case Example: Alice, ADHD Combined Type

Alice is a fourteen-year-old girl attending Grace Academy in Grover's Mills, NE. She is currently in the eighth grade and has been retained due to substantial academic deficits in mastering the eighth-grade curriculum. Her parents are frequently embarrassed by her "childish" antics and numerous suspensions from school for everything from insubordination to roughhousing and damaging school property. Alice's parents despair over the very real possibility that she will fail to graduate from high school and are considering a placement in a "special" school for students with learning and behavioral challenges. They seem ill-equipped to address Alice's challenges and she is constantly compared to her two older siblings who excelled in school and in their postsecondary pursuits.

Alice is emotionally immature and, in addition to her academic deficits in reading and math, she exhibits poor impulse control and poor judgement. Her teachers have expressed concern that she 'has no filter, she just says whatever pops into her mind.' In social studies, for example, the class was viewing a film on the subject of slavery in the U.S., and one of the actors portraying a slave master used the n-word in reference to his slaves. After the film, Alice approached Mr. Jenkins, the social studies teacher who is also African American and asked him if he would have been called a n------- back then. Mr. Jenkins thoughtfully replied that, sadly, he had been called that word many times even today. Alice really did not mean her question to be offensive, she just did not seem to appreciate the effect caused by her insensitive questioning.

Due to behaviors like this, Alice is the least popular student in her class, and this often makes her feel alienated and sad. She wants so badly to be accepted and included in social activities, but she is ostracized due to her impulsivity and immature behavior. As an example of her poor social skills, last week the school announced the annual "Sadie Hawkins" dance to which the grade seven and eight girls are encouraged to invite a boy to attend with them. Alice, who has long had a crush on Ned, a very amiable but extremely shy classmate, was determined to ask him to accompany her to the dance. Ned was a bit disconcerted by her very direct, public invitation and immediately declined, offering an excuse to spare Alice further embarrassment. Alice, however, followed Ned around all day pestering him and repeatedly asking him to be her date. When at last Ned declined more emphatically, using an expletive to emphasize his displeasure at her incessant nagging, Alice slapped him across the face. Both Ned and Alice were sent to the principal's office and required to serve a detention for the altercation.

As another example of Alice's impulsivity, the prior week the maintenance crew finished painting one of the stairwells at the end of the hallway leading to Alice's homeroom and roped off the staircase posting large signs warning students and staff not to touch the walls or banisters or use the staircase until further notice. Alice, in typical fashion, ignored the warning signs and boldly approached the freshly painted banisters, which were glistening with still wet paint and gripped them with both hands. Without hesitating, Alice, her hands covered with black paint, slapped two of her classmates squarely in the back, leaving her handprints on each. Her parents were summoned for a meeting with the principal and school superintendent to discuss a more suitable placement for Alice. Clearly, neither her parents, teachers, nor school administrators know how best to work with a student with this level ADHD (combined type).

Case Example: Matt, ADHD Predominantly Inattentive Type

Matt, a senior at West King's High School in Great Falls, MT is a gregarious and popular student with peers and teachers alike. He is the star center for the varsity basketball team, standing 6'10" in height. Fans come from the surrounding counties to see him play in Friday night games at the high school. Already scouted by several ranked colleges and universities, Matt has received provisional scholarship offers from many schools, but his clear preference is Villanova, which won the NCAA Championship two years prior.

Ever since kindergarten, Matt has experienced significant challenges with his ability to focus and attend to academic tasks, which have negatively impacted his ability to learn. As a result of these challenges, Matt has been held back twice in elementary school to enable him to acquire the necessary academic skills to advance. In contrast, athletically he has excelled, enhanced by his size and native abilities. From first grade onwards, Matt's best subject has consistently been physical education. Once introduced to basketball in third grade, Matt found his niche and true love and he has never looked back. In subsequent years, he has competed as a member of travel and school teams in leagues that incorporated students much older than himself...and he has consistently been a star performer.

His parents are unable to understand his tendency to procrastinate in completing school assignments and his forgetfulness in completing assigned tasks both at home and at school, which is in stark contrast to his laser focus on the basketball court. They marvel at his ability to follow the coach's set plays to the letter and his ability to retain the intricacies of the game as opposed to his ineptitude in the classroom. Matt is so easily distracted by irrelevant enticements except when he is engaged on the court in a practice session or a game.

Until recently, Matt never had time to participate in extracurricular activities outside of basketball. He had never attended social events such as school dances or class parties; however, recently, he has become interested in a cheerleader, Sara, who is also on track to become this year's valedictorian. She is scrupulously organized and has made Matt her 'pet' project, helping him to organize his notes, focus on the most salient points of lectures and assigned readings, maintain a schedule of classes and assignment due dates, and ensure that he complies with the various deadlines.

Since they have become an 'item,' Matt's grades have improved significantly. Sara has begun working with him to improve his overall GPA to ensure that he will qualify for admission to his dream school, Villanova, on a four-year athletic scholarship to play basketball. Fortunately, for Matt, Sara has also applied and received early acceptance to Villanova. Matt has, inadvertently, discovered an 'accommodation' to address his academic deficiencies caused by his ADHD and, concurrently, a life partner to help him in the process.

Characteristics Of Attention Deficit Hyperactivity Disorder

ADHD is identified symptomatically in the *Diagnostic and Statistical Manual for Mental Disorders* (DSM-V; American Psychiatric Association, 2013) according to criteria for inattentiveness, hyperactivity, and impulsivity (see list below).

DSM-V Criteria for ADHD

People with ADHD show a persistent pattern of inattention and/or hyperactivity–impulsivity that interferes with functioning or development:

Inattention: Six or more symptoms of inattention for children up to age 16 years, or five or more for adolescents age 17 years and older and adults; symptoms of inattention have been present for at least 6 months, and they are inappropriate for developmental level:
Often fails to give close attention to details or makes careless mistakes in schoolwork, at work, or with other activities.
Often has trouble holding attention on tasks or play activities.
Often does not seem to listen when spoken to directly.
Often does not follow through on instructions and fails to finish schoolwork, chores, or duties in the workplace (e.g., loses focus, side-tracked).
Often has trouble organizing tasks and activities.
Often avoids, dislikes, or is reluctant to do tasks that require mental effort over a long period of time (such as schoolwork or homework).
Often loses things necessary for tasks and activities (e.g. school materials, pencils, books, tools, wallets, keys, paperwork, eyeglasses, mobile telephones).
Is often easily distracted
Is often forgetful in daily activities.

Hyperactivity and Impulsivity: Six or more symptoms of hyperactivity-impulsivity for children up to age 16 years, or five or more for adolescents age 17 years and older and adults; symptoms of hyperactivity-impulsivity have been present for at least 6 months to an extent that is disruptive and inappropriate for the person's developmental level:

Often fidgets with or taps hands or feet, or squirms in seat.
Often leaves seat in situations when remaining seated is expected.
Often runs about or climbs in situations where it is not appropriate (adolescents or adults may be limited to feeling restless).
Often unable to play or take part in leisure activities quietly.
Is often "on the go" acting as if "driven by a motor".
Often talks excessively.
Often blurts out an answer before a question has been completed.
Often has trouble waiting their turn.
Often interrupts or intrudes on others (e.g., butts into conversations or games)
In addition, the following conditions must be met:
Several inattentive or hyperactive-impulsive symptoms were present before age 12 years.
Several symptoms are present in two or more settings, (such as at home, school or work; with friends or relatives; in other activities).
There is clear evidence that the symptoms interfere with, or reduce the quality of, social, school, or work functioning.
The symptoms are not better explained by another mental disorder (such as a mood disorder, anxiety disorder, dissociative disorder, or a personality disorder). The symptoms do not happen only during the course of schizophrenia or another psychotic disorder.
Based on the types of symptoms, three kinds (presentations) of ADHD can occur:

Combined Presentation: if enough symptoms of both criteria inattention and hyperactivity-impulsivity were present for the past 6 months
Predominantly Inattentive Presentation: if enough symptoms of inattention, but not hyperactivity-impulsivity, were present for the past six months
Predominantly Hyperactive-Impulsive Presentation: if enough symptoms of hyperactivity-impulsivity, but not inattention, were present for the past six months.
Because symptoms can change over time, the presentation may change over time as well.

Diagnosing ADHD in Adults

ADHD often lasts into adulthood. To diagnose ADHD in adults and adolescents age 17 years or older, only 5 symptoms are needed instead of the 6 needed for younger children. Symptoms might look different at older ages. For example, in adults, hyperactivity may appear as extreme restlessness or wearing others out with their activity.

Source: American Psychiatric Association. (2013). *Diagnostic and statistical manual of mental disorders, 5th edition.* American Psychiatric Association. Content Source: National Center on Birth Defects and Developmental Disabilities.

In addition, some of those symptoms need to have been evident before age 7. Furthermore, some of the symptoms need to be observable in two or more settings (e.g., school, home, work, or in community activities). Similarly, the symptoms must significantly impair social, occupational, or academic performance and they cannot be better accounted for as a mood disorder, anxiety disorder, dissociative disorder, or a personality disorder. ADHD comprises, essentially, three sub-types to include (1) predominantly inattentive, (2) predominantly hyperactive-impulsive, and (3) combined (types 1 and 2) (American Psychiatric Association, 2013).

ADHD, Predominantly Inattentive Type

Students who have ADHD, predominantly inattentive type, typically perform poorly in school, and 35-50 percent could be appropriately co-diagnosed with a specific learning disability (Brown, 1996). These students typically make careless mistakes in school, and they have real difficulty staying on task and screening out irrelevant stimuli. An example of this type of ADHD is provided in the case example of Matt.

ADHD, Predominantly Hyperactive-Impulsive Type

Students diagnosed with ADHD, predominantly hyperactive-impulsive type, seem to have boundless energy and have great difficulty staying in one place for extended period of time: They cannot seem to sit still. In school, this often results in disciplining referrals, which only exacerbate the problem. Paradoxically, as a result of the time spent out of class caused by frequent disciplinary referrals, students with this type of ADHD tend to miss important aspects of the curriculum. Such absences seriously impact the affected students' academic performance and identify them as "troublemakers" as well.

In conjunction with the symptom of hyperactivity, students with this type of ADHD also experience disinhibition. This suppression of the inhibitory response mechanism in the cerebral cortex often results in impulsivity (Ninivaggi, 2017). This impulsiveness can manifest in poor choices in the classroom; for example, affected students may blurt out answers in the classroom, they may intrude on or interrupt the activities of other children, and they experience real difficulty with turn-taking (American Psychiatric Association, 2013).

ADHD, Combined Type

Students displaying the characteristics of both hyperactivity-impulsivity and inattention represent the fastest-growing and most prevalent diagnostic category of ADHD (Furman, 2005). They display, in varying degrees, several of the behaviors of hyperactivity-impulsivity as well as inattention described in the DSM-V and, as a result, present teachers with a significant challenge to manage the unproductive behaviors associated with hyperactivity and impulsivity while helping the student stay focused (Aebi et al., 2010; Austin, 2003; Kauffman, 2005).

Universal Characteristics

It is not surprising, based on these behavioral characteristics, that children and youth with ADHD experience significant academic challenges. Typically, these educational problems occur in strategic areas that include written expression, listening skills, reading, general knowledge, and social functioning (Loe & Feldman, 2007). In addition, children with ADHD perform slightly lower on general intelligence tests than same-age peers, which may account, in part, for the increase in hyperactivity (Anderson et al., 2012). Furthermore, it is estimated that 30 percent of children with ADHD repeat a grade at school, 30 to 40 percent are classified under IDEA to receive special education services, and approximately 56 percent need academic tutoring. Finally, between 10 and 35 percent of these students may fail to graduate from high school (Anderson et al., 2012).

Cognitively, students who have ADHD evidence deficits in executive functioning that involves planning, organizing, inhibitory responses, mentally representing a task, switching strategies, and self-regulation.

Social skills deficits are consistently present in a majority of students who have ADHD. These are exacerbated by estimates that suggest that 50 to 70 percent of students who have ADHD have concomitant emotional or behavioral disorders; principally, conduct disorder (30 to 50 percent) and oppositional defiance disorder (35 to 70 percent), which are characterized by poor or deficient social skills (Daly et al., 2016; Kauffman, 2005). In addition, studies suggest that about 25 percent of these children also have anxiety disorder, which is also highly correlated with poor social skills development (Daly et al., 2016). As a result of poorly developed social skills and undesirable behaviors exhibited by students who have ADHD such as poor turn-taking, lack of focus, hyperactivity, and forgetfulness - students who have ADHD are often the least popular and most disliked by peers and teachers (Daly et al., 2016).

Lastly, and perhaps most important, students who have ADHD pose significant problems for the family and its relationship to them. The principal problem seems to be one of perception: Mothers and fathers as well as siblings tend to view the inattentive, hyperactive-impulsive behaviors of the family member with ADHD as volitional - intentionally oppositional and defiant or adversarial. This leads to disaffection and alienation of the child with ADHD and a tendency to view her or him as the "black sheep" of the family. However, there is growing evidence that supports the heritability of ADHD, and thus many of the behaviors viewed as undesirable by the parents may, in fact, be shadowy reflections of their own behaviors (Barkley, 2003; Larsson et al., 2014). In any event, family systems theory, popularized in the 1990s suggests that dysfunction affecting one member of the family, in this case, the child with ADHD, invariably affects to some extent every member of the family (Wicks-Nelson & Israel, 2005).

In addition, a point of interest is the fact that, compared with control groups, children who have ADHD experience significantly more accidental injuries. For example, 7 percent of students who have ADHD suffered accidental poisoning, compared with 3 percent of students who do not have ADHD; similarly, 23 percent had bone fractures in contrast to only 15 percent of students who do not have ADHD (Khanjani et al., 2020).

Prevalence and Comorbidity

Kauffman (2005) notes that the difficulty experienced by stakeholders in reaching a consensus about what are viewed as universal characteristics for ADHD makes it very difficult to estimate how many school-age children actually have ADHD. Estimates of prevalence of between 3 to 5 percent of school-age children qualify it as one of the most common reasons for referral for special education (Hallahan et al., 2005). Boys are identified three times as often as girls and this disparity may be explained, in part, by gender bias, but may also be a function of fundamental behavioral differences between boys and girls (Kauffman, 2005; Smith, 2015).

ADHD is frequently comorbid with other types of emotional and behavioral disorders. For example, research has suggested that between 10 and 92 percent of children with ADHD could also be identified as having a learning disability. This may be a result of differences in diagnosis and in discriminating between both the conditions in individual studies. A recent study displayed the relationship between learning disabilities and ADHD, predominantly in the inattentive type. An earlier study revealed that an LD was present in 70 percent of the children with ADHD. Interestingly, an LD in writing was more than two times as common (65 percent) than an LD in reading, math, or spelling (Gnanavel et al., 2019).

Another concomitant disorder is oppositional defiant disorder (ODD). According to Harvey et al. (2016), more than half of children with ADHD have ODD as well, making it the most frequently identified comorbid condition. Finally, according to Pliszka (2003) a strong majority children under the age of 12 years who meet the criteria for ODD or CD will meet the criteria for ADHD. Among adolescents, CD is more commonly comorbid with about one-third meeting the criteria for ADHD; however, it has been our experience that most children with ADHD behave in a manner that is impulsive, yet the consequences of these behaviors are seldom malicious or premeditated. As noted in Chapter 2, children with conduct disorder typically engage in behaviors that are disruptive or destructive with intentionality. Consequently, the high rate of comorbidity suggested by Harvey et al. (2016), and others seems to be counterintuitive.

Etiology of Attention Deficit Hyperactivity Disorder

Although no single cause of ADHD has been identified and substantiated, there are several hypotheses concerning its etiology. The most popular cause of ADHD is believed to be neurological dysfunction or genetic predisposition; however, some researchers have posited other causative hypotheses (Hallahan et al., 2020). These include brain structure and activity, pregnancy and birth complications, poor nutrition and dietary concerns, environmental factors (e.g., lead exposure), and psychosocial factors (family factors) (Hallahan et al., 2020).

Brain Structure andActivity

Some researchers have suggested that individuals with ADHD have brain abnormalities; that is, that the brain of these persons are anatomically different from that of persons without ADHD; for example, one study found that the total brain volume of boys with ADHD is 5 percent less than boys without the condition (Krain & Castellanos, 2006). Similarly, the corpus callosum and the cerebellum are sometimes smaller in individuals with ADHD (Krain & Castellanos, 2006).

These anomalies would help account for the problems with motor coordination and certain kinds of memory recall experienced by individuals with the disorder. The most prevalent anomaly, however, is the measurably smaller right fontal area of the brain referred to ask the caudate nucleus as well as the globus pallidus (Jacobson et al., 2018). Finally, investigators are now focusing on the role of neurotransmitters on brain functioning – specifically norepinephrine, dopamine, and serotonin (Banerjee & Nandagopal, 2015).

Pregnancy and Birth Complications

There is evidence to support a correlation between low birth weight and attention problems as well as increased activity and impulsivity (Thapar et al., 2013). Similarly, maternal alcohol and substance abuse also correlate to increased activity level, attention deficits, and organizational problems in the developing infant. Medical investigators continue to hypothesize a connection between pregnancy and birth complications; to date, however, little evidence supports this contention (Thapar et al., 2013).

Poor Nutrition and Dietary Concerns

In the 1970s, Benjamin Feingold and others posited a theory that linked hyperkinesis or hyperkinectivity to excess sugar and preservative intake on the part of children. Feingold (1975) claimed that 25 to 50 percent of children affected with chronic hyperactivity and learning disabilities could be effectively treated with nutritious diets that conscientiously excluded sugars, artificial dyes, preservatives, and salicylates. Subsequent research has failed to support Feingold's claims (Rojas & Chan, 2005).

Environmental Factors

Researchers have also speculated as to the deleterious effects of environmental toxins such as lead (in lead paint and pipes), air pollutants (e.g., fluorocarbons and CO_2). To date, however, no significant studies have supported the effects of teratogens as a viable cause of ADHD (Thapar et al., 2013).

Genetic Factors

Research has supported a strong correlation between genetic transmission and ADHD. Recent studies, for example, have found that between 10 to 35 percent of immediate (first degree) family members are likely to have ADHD, and the children of parents or a parent with ADHD are at a higher risk of experiencing the disorder (Sciberras et al. 2017). Twin studies indicate on average heritability of .80, thus, establishing a clear link between genetic heritability and ADHD transmission (Sciberras et al. 2017).

Psychosocial Factors (Family Factors)

Studies have found evidence that suggest a link between family factors such as parental malaise, marital discord, adversarial child-parent relationship, as well as family adversity, and the development of ADHD (Froehlich et al., 2011). Similarly, incompatibility between mother and child also correlates with ADHD. One study found that inconsistent, intolerant, and authoritarian parenting styles also were more predictive of ADHD in children (Woodward et al., 1998). Another study pointed to characteristic depression and/or anxiety in mothers and ADHD diagnoses in fathers as strong predispositions for ADHD in their children (Kashdan et al., 2004). These studies must be interpreted with caution; for example, some of the negative parent behaviors may be attributed to their reaction to having a child with ADHD, not a cause of it. Likewise, teacher behaviors may affect a child's attentiveness or exacerbate preexisting conditions of hyperactive-impulsive behavior (Legato, 2011).

Despite all the research to understand and identify the etiology of ADHD, it appears that the most likely and defensible cause is in the area of the neurobiology of the child. Future research is needed to better understand the connection between neurology and the development of ADHD in order to advance new treatments that are more effective.

Assessment of Attention Deficit Hyperactivity Disorder

Experts consider the process of arriving at a correct diagnosis of ADHD to be singularly difficult - in fact, perhaps one of the most challenging diagnoses to make. In order to ensure that the identification process is accurate, a sequence of steps is essential. These steps involve assessment instruments that have been normed and standardized as well as parent, child, and teacher interviews, careful observations, and a thorough medical and psychological evaluation. Such a comprehensive process typically includes the following steps:

1. Administering and collecting rating scales from relevant persons
2. Orienting the family and the student to the evaluation
3. Interviewing the student
4. Administering normed tests such as IQ, achievement, and continuous performance tests
5. Conducting direct observations in several settings, including school, community, and home if possible
6. Interviewing the parent(s)
7. Conducting a medical evaluation
8. Integrating all the data
9. Giving feedback and recommendation to the team (Werts et al., 2007).

Typically, the school psychologist presides over the data collection process. A similar sequence of assessment is suggested by the Council for Exceptional Children's Task Force on Children with ADHD (1992). The CEC guidelines are as follows:

Step 1. Document behavior observed by both parents and teachers that is indicative of ADHD.

Step 2. Reevaluate tests to determine whether they are accurate measures of potential or whether poor performance may be the result of attention problems. A physician may be consulted to see whether an identifiable physical condition is causing inattention or hyperactivity.

Step 3. Attempt classroom management to correct or control behavior leading to poor academic performance. If such attempts are unsuccessful, request a referral for ADHD placement.

Step 4. Conduct psychological evaluation to see whether the student meets criteria for ADHD placement. Administer individual tests and behavioral rating scales. Review medication recommendations.

Step 5. Have the team, including the child's parents, plan for the special educational needs of the child.

Step 6. Implement the Individual Education Plan.

Checklists and rating scales are helpful in providing certain insights relative to a child's inattention or hyperactive behavior; however, the results are very subjective and provide only a snapshot of a limited behavioral domain. The most commonly used checklist is the *Child Behavior Checklist* (Achenbach & Edelbrock, 1991). The *Conners' Rating Scale 3rd ed.* (Conners, 2008) is another very popular instrument used in evaluating the problem behaviors associated with ADHD. It offers versions that are specifically tailored for administration to students, parents, and teachers. Another relevant instrument is the *Attention Deficit Disorders Evaluation Scale - 5th ed.* (ADDES-5; McCarney & House, 2019), which has a parent and teacher version and identifies and differentiates the three types of ADHD as described in the DSM-V (American Psychiatric Association, 2013).

Systematic observation conducted in natural settings also provides valuable information in determining a diagnosis of ADHD. Direct observation should be conducted in various school settings, including the classroom, the playground, the lunchroom, and the hallways. In addition, careful daily records of academic performance should be maintained (Hallahan et al., 2020).

Similarly, interviews should be conducted with parents and teachers to facilitate the diagnostic process. These stakeholders typically have valuable information to pass on regarding the student's aberrant behaviors and academic deficiencies.

Lastly, the student assessment should include a complete medical examination to rule out medical or health causes for the behaviors that appear to be symptomatic of ADHD. The hyperactive component of ADHD, for example, may be simply an adverse effect produced by the medication taken to relieve the symptoms of a health impairment such as asthma.

Treatment Strategies

A number of interventions have been recommended in the treatment of ADHD. These include psychosocial training for parents and teachers, cognitive strategy training, pharmacological interventions, and multisystemic therapies.

These interventions are usually more effective with young children and involve some form of positive reinforcement for the performance of desired behavior or, conversely, a negative consequence (punishment) such as response cost. A timeout should never be used as a punishment; ideally, it represents the removal of all stimuli to facilitate the child's return to emotional stasis, or balance. It is important that, to the extent possible, all behavioral interventions be conducted in the natural setting where the target behaviors are most likely to occur (Wicks-Nelson & Israel, 2005).

Psychosocial Training for Parents and Teachers

The goal of parent and teacher training is to help these key stakeholders learn to deal with the challenging behaviors of children with ADHD and to cope more effectively with their own nontherapeutic behaviors. Therapists or psychologists typically involve parents and teachers in an intervention plan that generalized to the settings of the home and school. In addition, parents and teachers are taught to develop greater tolerance for the perseverating behaviors of the child with ADHD and are helped to understand that she or he is not displaying these disruptive behaviors willfully, but can, nonetheless, learn to reduce their frequency and severity. This understanding can reduce the indifference that parents and teachers sometimes express towards students with ADHD as well as the tendency to blame these children for their disorder, thereby increasing tolerance and understanding. The change in appreciation and attitude on the part of teachers and parents can help affected children improve their self-esteem (Anderson et al., 2012; Moldavsky & Sayal, 2013).

Cognitive Strategy Training

Cognitive strategy training encompasses self-instruction, self-monitoring, self-reinforcement, and cognitive-interpersonal problem solving (Pullen et al., 2008). Although research has not demonstrated significant benefit from these approaches in reducing the undesirable symptoms associated with ADHD; self-monitoring and self-instruction will be described because, in conjunction with behavioral approaches and pharmacological treatments, they can be beneficial.

Self-monitoring functions as a reminder by prompting the student to ask themselves if they were paying attention to the lesson. Typically, the student is provided with a checklist of desirable target behaviors and prompted by an audible signal at timed intervals, chooses "yes" or "no" in response. Ostensibly, over time, the student internalizes this external control and, hopefully, the desirable behaviors become part of the student's repertoire.

Self-instruction teaches students to talk to themselves about their behaviors in relation to a classroom task. At first, the teacher, who talks aloud, describing, for example, the steps in solving a math problem, models the procedure. Next, the student follows suit, verbalizing aloud each step of the process. Later, the goal is for the student to employ the self-instruction techniques where needed, sub-vocally (Hallahan et al., 2020).

The use of mnemonics, another cognitive strategy, is helpful in providing the student with a way of organizing information so that it can be effectively stored and easily retrieved later, when needed. Examples of mnemonic strategies include the use of the silly story, the Roman room, and acrostics designed to be spoken or sung that represent or include the target information. An example of one such acrostic, PEMDAS (Please Excuse My Dear Aunt Sally), which represents the order of operations in solving algebraic equations.

Pharmacological Interventions [1]

A clinical expert who is a consultant in the school district on matters regarding ADHD diagnoses provided the families of Alice and Matt with a brief explanation of the plausible relationship between various therapeutic drugs and ADHD symptoms. The expert explained that research on the effects of popular psychostimulants such as Ritalin and Adderall suggested that these drugs may accelerate the production of norepinephrine, an important neurotransmitter responsible for the transfer of messages from one part of the brain to another (Valente, 2001). Investigators have also established that the increased availability of these neurotransmitters improves brain function, which includes attention and focus as well as the ability to control impulsivity (Brown, 2000; Kollins et al., 2001). Some studies have pointed to a lack of dopamine and norepinephrine production as a possible cause of ADHD; therefore, the benefit of such stimulant drugs is evident (Kollins et al., 2001).

The procedure for determining which drug is right for an individual involves a process of elimination (Szymanski & Zolotor, 2001). Methylphenidate (Ritalin), for example, has demonstrated effectiveness in controlling undesirable symptoms such as inattentiveness and impulsivity for approximately 70 percent of the persons diagnosed with ADHD to whom it was prescribed. In addition, it is generally well tolerated; therefore, it is usually the first course of medication prescribed (Szymanski & Zolotor, 2001).

Typically, the initial dose is administered once daily and the effects of this dose on predetermined behavioral and educational objectives such as focus, time on task, and impulse control are carefully monitored. If a higher dose is needed to achieve these treatment objectives, then the amount is increased incrementally until the desired outcomes are obtained. The effects of methylphenidate are of short duration (three to four hours) and the length of the school day may exceed six hours; therefore, a second dose is often recommended to be taken at lunchtime. Occasionally, if undesirable behaviors develop after the noontime dose begins to wear off (a rebound effect); a third dose may be prescribed. Newer, slow-release preparations such as Concerta have been formulated to address the need for a longer-lasting, sustained dose (Greenhill et al., 1999).

If an individual is unresponsive to the effects of a particular psychostimulant such as Ritalin, another type, such as Adderall may be tried; however, if it appears that stimulants in general are ineffective in improving the effects of ADD, then tricyclic antidepressants such as bupropion hydrochloride (Wellbutrin) and venlafaxine (Effexor) may be used, both of which increase the availability of norepinephrine and dopamine. In addition, desipramine and imipramine have demonstrated effectiveness in treating the symptoms associated with ADD; however, the potential for life-threatening side effects in children generally preclude their consideration as a treatment option (Greenhill et al., 1999).

Other medications, such as the alpha-blockers, clonidine (Catapres) and guanfacine (Tenex) help to reduce aggressive behaviors and feelings of hostility, anxiety, and frustration. Similarly, beta-blockers and low doses of antiseizure medications can be helpful, but when a comorbid condition such as conduct disorder is evident, or when tics become troublesome, major tranquilizers such as risperidone (Risperdal) may prove helpful (Szymanski & Zolotor, 2001).

It is important to acknowledge that any substance introduced artificially into the human biosystem presents the potential for adverse effects. Each of these popularly prescribed medications can produce some undesirable conditions ranging in severity from mild discomfort to death. These drugs, the possible beneficial and adverse effects, and the typical dosage and duration of action are provided below (see Table 4.1).

Table 4.1. Drug Specifications Relative to the Treatment of ADHD

Name of Drug	**Dosage**	**Potential Benefits**	**Potential Adverse Effects**
Methylphenidate (Ritalin)	2.5-20 mg	Reduction of hyperactivity, impulsivity, and inattentiveness	Loss of appetite, sleeplessness, rapid heartbeat, tics, risk of liver cancer
Methylphenidate SR 20 (sustained release)	20 mg	Same as for methylphenidate	Same as for methylphenidate

Methylphenidate (Concerta) Sustained release	18 mg, 36 mg, 54 mg Duration: 10-12 hours	Same as for methylphenidate	Same as for methylphenidate
Mixed salts of a single-entity amphetamine product (Adderall)	5 mg, 7.5 mg, 10 mg, 12.5 mg, 15 mg, 20 mg, 30 mg Duration: 3.5-8 hours	Same as for methylphenidate	Same as for methylphenidate
Dextroampheta mine (Dexedrine, Dextrostat)	2.5 mg – 10 mg Onset: 20-30 min. Duration: 4-5 hours	Same as for methylphenidate	Same as for methylphenidate
Pemoline (Cylert)	18.75 mg, 37.5 mg, 75 mg Duration: 8-10 hours	Same as for methylphenidate	Potential for serious liver damage-frequent monitoring of liver function required
Imipramine and desipramine (Tofranil and Norpramin)	10 mg, 25 mg, 50 mg, 100 mg Onset: 1-3 weeks Duration: 24 hours (not abruptly stopped)	Low doses improve focus and control, higher doses may stabilize mood	Similar to methylphenidate; may produce arrhythmia and change blood count
Bupropion (Wellbutrin)	75 mg, 100 mg Duration: 6-8 hours	Same as for methylphenidate and helps relieve depression	Headaches and difficulty sleeping
Clonidine (Catapres)	Patches or tablets of 0.1 mg, 0.2 mg, 0.3 mg Duration: patch-5-6 days Tablets: 4-6 hours (not abruptly stopped)	Improves hyperactivity and insomnia; may decrease facial or vocal tics; reduces hostility	Fatigue, dizziness, dry mouth, hyperactivity, and irritability
Guanfacine (Tenex)	1 mg tablet Duration: 6-8 hours	Reduces facial and vocal tics as well as hostility and oppositional behavior	Dizziness, dry mouth, hyperactivity, irritability, and other behavior problems

Source: CHADD (2022). Fact Sheet No. 3. Medical management of children and adults with AD/HD. Retrieved from https://chadd.org/understanding-adhd/adhd-fact-sheets/.

After presenting this information to Alice and Matt's families and teachers, the consultant discussed the findings of several recent studies conducted to assess the efficacy of pharmacological interventions in the treatment of

ADHD (Anand et al., 2017; De Crescenzo et al., 2017; Hodgkins et al., 2012; Moreno-García et al., 2019). She did this in a very informal and practical manner to ensure that all the individuals present understood the benefits of medication in the treatment of ADHD as compared with other interventions. The principal study described involved the largest and longest trial ever conducted with children diagnosed with ADHD: the Multimodal Treatment of ADHD (MTA) Study, sponsored by the National Institute for Mental Health (MTA Cooperative Group, 2004). Based on the results of this study, which involved over 500 school-age children diagnosed with ADHD conducted over fourteen months, medication alone - specifically, methylphenidate - was found to be superior to behavioral and educational interventions, combined pharmacological and behavioral treatments, and treatment in the community (MTA Cooperative Group, 2004). Further studies recommend the value of a combined, multimodal approach involving behavioral as well as pharmacological interventions (Döpfner et al., 2004).

Unfortunately, as the consultant pointed out, in some cases, psychostimulants and other pharmacological interventions are being prescribed with little adherence to the American Academy of Pediatrics (AAP) guidelines (Bright, 2008; Lakhan & Kirchgessner, 2012; Wilens et al., 2008), which include the following important recommendations:

- Primary care physicians should establish a management plan that recognizes ADHD as a chronic condition and should serve as a resource and clearinghouse for information, collaborating with children, families, teachers, nurses, psychologists, and counselors to develop child-specific treatment plans. Furthermore, physicians should maintain currency about new research on treatment efficacy and innovation.
- The treating physician, family members, child, teachers, and psychologist should establish three to six treatment goals that encompass realistic and measurable outcomes that may include improvements in relationships, self-esteem, and school performance as well as a decrease in disruptive behaviors.
- The physician should recommend psychostimulant medication and/or behavior therapy as a first-line treatment, based on the overwhelming body of research that supports their effectiveness in the treatment of ADHD.
- Individuals, families, and teachers should be informed that the long-term effect of stimulant use has not been determined.

- The use of pemoline is not recommended due to rare, but potentially fatal, liver damage (hepatoxicity). In addition, second-line treatments include the tricyclic antidepressants (imipramine and desipramine) and bupropion (Wellbutrin).
- Physicians are advised to adjust the dosage upward from an initial low dose until treatment objectives are met. Conversely, if side effects and no further benefits are experienced by the patient; the physician is encouraged to adjust the dosage downward in order to identify a dose that achieves the optimal treatment objectives with minimal adverse effects.
- In the case of children taking stimulant medications such as Ritalin, a lack of success at the highest safe dose suggests considering another approved stimulant medication such as Adderall.
- Concomitant behavior therapy should be employed whose goal is to adjust the physical and social environments to change behavior through positive reinforcement, with effective reinforcers acquired through response-cost inventories, and/or token economies.
- Family members, teachers, and other caregivers should be appropriately trained to implement these behavioral interventions.
- If the multimodal intervention plan is ineffective, it may be the result of misdiagnosis, a misidentification of pertinent symptoms, the presence of a comorbid condition, a lack of adherence to the recommended treatment regimen, or treatment failure.
- A systematic follow-up should be conducted periodically by the physician for the child with ADHD relative to the achievement of treatment objectives and presence of adverse effects, based on input from teachers, family members, and the child (Chatfield, 2002; Leslie et al., 2004).

Furthermore, the medical consultant cautioned the families and teachers of Alice and Matt about the credibility of findings from studies funded by pharmaceutical companies such as Ciba-Geigy (manufacturer of Ritalin) and Shire Richwood, (manufacturer of Adderall) (Findling et al., 2009; Wigal, 2009). The consultant explained that many of the studies used by pharmaceutical companies and others to support the efficacy and safety of a particular medication used to treat ADHD often involve small sample sizes of from twenty to thirty participants or fewer (Catala-Lopez et al., 2017). This limitation significantly affects the usefulness of the findings; yet to the inexperienced consumer, results so obtained can sound conclusive and authoritative.

Finally, and most importantly, the consultant informed the families of Alice and Matt as well as their teachers that no research has been conducted on the long-term effects of psychostimulants such as methylphenidate and dextroamphetamine (Kollins et al., 2001). She also noted that because these drugs affect and alter an individual's neurobiology, it is reasonable to predict that, if used consistently for twenty or thirty years, some adverse effects might develop.

The consultant assured the families and teachers that she was not an advocate of pharmacological intervention exclusively; rather, her professional experience as well as much of the research on interventions for ADHD supported the carefully monitored use of psychostimulants in conjunction with effective educational and behavioral approaches (Döpfner et al., 2004). Based on the information presented, it was noted, the family members of one or both children might choose to forego pharmacological interventions in favor of psychosocial or behavioral ones. The important thing in determining an intervention for Alice and Matt, it was stressed, was its endorsement by the families, the teachers, and the students themselves as well as its effectiveness in helping each of these students achieve the desired treatment outcomes.

In concluding her recommendations concerning pharmacological interventions, the medical consultant asserted the importance of accurate information about the beneficial and adverse effects of the various medications used in the treatment of ADHD. She further elaborated best practices that teachers and families can use collaboratively to monitor and assess drug effects. The first of these is to ensure that the child has had a thorough physical and psychological examination that includes height and weight determination, the presence of any cardiological anomalies, the potential for side behavioral effects, any evidence of seizure disorders, tics, and tests of liver function (Kollins et al., 2001). Families, teachers, and clinicians should assess the symptoms of ADHD using several of the following instruments: the *Child Behavior Checklist/Teacher Report Form* (Achenbach & Edelbrock, 1991), the *Attention Deficit Disorders Evaluation Scale - 5th ed.* (ADDES-5; McCarney & House, 2019), the *ADHD-IV Rating Scale* (DuPaul et al., 1999), the *Disruptive Behavior Rating Scale* (Barkley & Murphy, 1998), and the *Conners Rating Scales – 3rd ed.* (Conners, 2008).

Researchers have suggested that, before making the decision to use medication, family members and teachers should review the information provided by the following questions:

- How old is the child? It should be noted that although psychostimulants are increasingly prescribed for pre-school-age children, methylphenidate, otherwise known as Ritalin or Concerta, has never been approved for children under the age of six (Braaten, 2016).
- Have other interventions been tried and, if so, why were they ineffective?
- How severe are the child's current symptoms?
- Can the family afford the costs associated with pharmacological intervention?
- Can family members adequately supervise the use of medication and prevent abuse?
- What are the attitudes and cultural perspectives of family members toward medication?
- Is there a substance-abusing family member in the home?
- Does the child have concomitant disorders such as tics or mental illness?
- Is the child overly concerned about the effects of the medication?
- Does the physician seem committed to appropriate follow-up and monitoring?
- Is the child or adolescent involved in competitive sports or planning on entering the military? The reason for this question is that the medication will be detected and considered a controlled substance in the course of urinalysis (Kollins et al., 2001).

Families and teachers are also valuable monitors of the effectiveness of a particular medication as well as the dosage level. Researchers recommend a double-blind procedure wherein family members, teachers, and the student do not know the dose level of the prescribed medication or if it is in fact a placebo. Their weekly reports using a teacher/family ratings scale as well as the side-effects questionnaire (Barkley & Murphy, 1998) would then be more likely to reflect true drug effects than the phenomenon referred to as practice effects; which refers to the tendency of family members and teachers to rate the behaviors of students receiving medication as significantly improved once the regimen has begun.

Similarly, teachers can assess the effects of medication in the treatment of ADHD with the use of continuous performance tests such as the presentation of a symbol (e.g., a letter or number) at varied intervals within a series (Parsons et al., 2019). The use of restricted academic tasks has demonstrated validity in confirming optimal medication doses for children and may help to identify the effects of incremental medication changes and adjustments on carefully structured academic problem sets (Fischer & Newby, 1998). Moreover, research suggests that a functional analysis of behavior may allow teachers to identify and control for antecedent and consequent events, which can help them assess the impacts of these conditions on the effects of medication as it relates to the child with ADHD (Karama et al., 2009).

Finally, teachers can use curriculum-based measurement (CBM) to measure the effects of medication on behaviors that impact academic function (Haraway, 2012). When using CBM, students become their own controls, and comparisons are made between their performance on an academic task before and after treatment with medication. Significant changes in either a positive or negative direction are noted and reported to the physician as one indicator of the effectiveness of the medication and dosage level.

Multisystemic Therapies

Pharmacological treatment appears to be the single most effective therapy for students with ADHD, but it often comes at a cost in the form of adverse side effects. Behavioral approaches also have drawbacks and require intensive, time-consuming monitoring. Similarly, cognitive-behavior therapies have demonstrated limited success in reducing undesirable ADHD behaviors, perhaps because they require some level of executive function and self-control, qualifications many children with ADHD simply do not seem to possess.

Researchers looked to a multisystemic treatment that combines pharmacological therapy with a behavioral intervention. Some studies supported the efficacy of multimodal therapy in maintaining treatment benefits over time (Borys et al., 2015; MTA Cooperative Group, 2004). More recently, the National Institute of Mental Health (NIMH) conducted an investigation of a multisystemic treatment regimen that included medication plus psychosocial intervention consisting of tutoring, social skills training, organization training, parent training, counseling, and limited contingency management. Results of the study showed improvement in all outcome measures; however, when the participants were taken off medication, their behavior regressed (Kapalka et al., 2018). These findings engendered optimism about the use of multisystemic treatments. It is important to note, however, that this optimism is based on the awareness that any such treatment regimen must be tailored to the specific needs of the individual with ADHD and these needs vary greatly from individual to individual depending on the degree and type of ADHD.

School-Based Interventions

After considering the preceding clinical review of ADHD, teachers can, in consultation with the school or child psychologist, develop a practical intervention plan for a student with the disorder. Such an intervention plan, as we noted, cannot be successfully designed without a thorough understanding of the root causes of the problem behavior; that is, what function or purpose the behavior serves for the child, if any, and what contingencies help maintain it. This section offers suggested approaches for the case examples of Alice and Matt.

As with other emotional and behavioral disorders, the logical first step in developing an effective treatment or intervention plan is to identify and describe the presenting undesirable behavior accurately.

The step-by-step process developed by Barnhill (2005) is one way to reach an effective intervention plan. We will use this process to develop behavioral intervention plans for Alice and Matt, based primarily on the findings of their functional behavioral assessments.

Assessing the Problem: Alice (ADHD, Combined Type)

Identify and Describe the Problem Behavior

Alice's teachers and parents have observed and documented frequent episodes of hyperactivity and impulsivity that seem to be increasing in frequency and intensity. Examples of some of the more severe of these include unsolicited and unwanted physical contact, mercurial and volatile temper, verbal abuse, concomitant academic failure, and inability to complete tasks and remain focused. These undesirable behaviors appear to be escalating despite the application of psychosocial interventions.

Collect Baseline Data and Academic Information

The school psychologist has administered the Brown *ADD Scale for Adolescents* (Brown, 1996) as well as the *Conners-Wells Adolescent Self-Report Scale* (Conners et al., 1997), which helped to confirm the diagnosis of ADHD, combined type. The psychologist obtained observation data from all of Alice's middle school teachers as well as her parents; teachers also provided completed child behavior checklists.

Describe the Context in which the Behavior Is Observed

Behavioral observations involving teachers were made in the school and classroom. In a similar vein, Alice's parents conducted observations in and around the home. Both contexts revealed similar behavioral characteristics; namely, episodes of heightened activity, inattention, and lack of focus, as well as impulsive behavior that included unsolicited touching and aggression.

Complete a Functional Assessment Form (FBA) and/or Behavior Rating Scale

Both of these protocols were completed and are presented below.

A Functional Behavioral Assessment Template

1. Identify the Problem Behavior:
2. Define the Behavior
3. Collect Data About the Frequency, Duration, and Intensity of the Behavior:
4. Perform an Antecedents-Behavior-Consequences (ABA) Analysis: (What are the triggers that precipitate the behavior? What are the consequences of the behavior that may be reinforcing it?)
5. Analysis of Data and Development of Hypothesis Statement(s):
6. Develop the Behavioral Intervention Plan (BIP).

Behavioral Intervention Plan

Name of Student ______________________________ Start Date ______________________
Age ____________
Grade ___________
Homeroom Mr./Ms. ____________________________

Specific Behavioral Goals:
1.
Oversight ____________________________________
2.
Oversight ____________________________________

3.
Oversight ______________________________

For each goal above:
1. What antecedents events and consequences can I change to increase/decrease the behavior?

2. What strategies, curricular adaptations, and physical design modifications can I use to increase/decrease the behavior?

3. Which of these changes are most likely to be effective?

Evaluate the Plan:

How is it working? If it is not working, what changes or modifications are needed to make it work?

Conduct a Direct Observation

As mentioned earlier, direct observations were conducted by both Alice's parents and teachers and the recorded data was analyzed. The findings were used to help confirm the diagnosis and develop a viable treatment plan.

Develop a Hypothesis

Based on the data from multiple assessments, Alice's diagnosis of ADHD, combined type was confirmed. Alice clearly requires structure and guidance to be successful in the classroom. She tends to become unruly and uncooperative unless she is provided with stimulating, meaningful tasks. She also suffers from a lack of self-esteem, which is exacerbated when she acts out and is alienated from teachers and students. The multidisciplinary committee has recommended a multimodal approach that includes social skills training, cognitive behavioral therapy, parent, and teacher training, as well as titrated medication therapy (recommended but as yet untried).

Test the Hypothesis and Modify as Necessary

A behavioral intervention plan has been implemented for Alice; however, but it has not yet been reviewed.

Developing an Effective Intervention Plan

Alice's behavioral intervention plan, as recommended, will be multimodal and include cognitive-behavioral therapy, parent, and teacher training, and a carefully monitored medication regimen.

Alice's teachers employ a cognitive approach that includes self-monitoring and self-instruction. To facilitate the first of these two strategies, her teachers have developed a list of desirable target behaviors that they provide to Alice at the start of each class. They then start a small alarm mechanism, which is designed to give off an audible signal at timed intervals. When Alice hears the alarm, she is prompted to check 'yes' or 'no' to indicate whether or not she performed or engaged in the desired behavior.

Alice's teachers model self-instruction or self-talk by describing aloud the steps or procedures required to conduct an experiment in science class, for example. Alice is encouraged to employ the same procedure for all the tasks that require steps or involve formulas. Eventually, the goal is for Alice to internalize these steps.

A third cognitive approach that her teachers employ to help Alice encode information to facilitate retrieval is the use of mnemonic devices and semantic webs or other graphic organizers; for example, to assist her recollection of the five Great Lakes as discussed in her social studies class, the teacher has taught her to use the acronym HOMES, in which each letter represents the first letter of the names of each of the Great Lakes (e.g. Huron, Ontario, Michigan, Erie, & Superior).

Alice's teachers, directed by the school psychologist, also provide social skills training whenever possible, using the teachable moment as the pretext for such instruction; for example, Alice wanted to ask a male classmate to accompany her to a middle school dance, but after offering the invitation, proceeded to comment on his acne and suggest some topical medication she uses. She was genuinely surprised when he took exception to her 'well-intentioned' advice and declined her invitation; however, after an astute teacher explained how her forthright and unsolicited comments might be misperceived, she seemed truly remorseful and apologized to the young man, who later accepted her invitation.

Some well-supported behavioral approaches that Alice's teachers employ include increasing the use of positive reinforcement (McCluskey & McCluskey, 1999) and using a daily report card (Pisecco et al., 2001). With regard to positive reinforcement, it has been observed that many teachers are negatively predisposed toward students who have ADHD. This is not an indictment of their professionalism, because students who have ADHD, like Alice, who exhibit extreme hyperactivity and often act impulsively, present a real challenge for teachers. Research has shown, however, that teacher comments towards and interactions with students who have been diagnosed with ADHD are significantly more negative than their comments and interactions with students who do not have ADHD (Lawrence, K. et al., 2017). Clearly, such negative treatment is counterproductive and merely aggravates these undesired behaviors. Instead, Alice's teachers employ positive verbal reinforcement such as "Wow, you've completed half the page, I know you'll get the rest done by the end of the period." Alice responds well to these positive comments, as evidenced by her increased productivity as well as the quality of her work.

Pisecco et al. (2001) demonstrated the effectiveness and teacher preference for the daily report card (DRC). The daily report card involves the collaboration of parents and teachers in first identifying from three to five problem behaviors. A report card is then developed that consists of daily goals that address each of the target behaviors in a positive manner. The student takes this report card home and earns rewards for meeting these daily goals both at school and at home. Ideally, there should be a seamless transition from the school to the home in the supervision and reinforcement of this valuable behavioral intervention.

Alice's teachers work hard to provide viable connections between what Alice already knows (has mastered) and new concepts being taught. Research has supported that providing such as bridge between the known and the new facilitates the student's ability to incorporate or integrate what she is currently studying and ensures that she will generalize the new information to related applications (Reis, 2002). Similarly, the teachers require that Alice use focus journals to facilitate the application of concepts and principles learned in class to the reality of her daily life. One example of the use of a focus journal is to have Alice write a brief reaction or reflection to a teacher's daily journal focus question that includes support for her response.

These various behavioral and cognitive interventions have been effective in helping Alice maintain focus and reduce her off-task behavior and impulsivity; however, her therapist, the school psychologist, and her teachers feel that her hyperactivity, attentiveness, impulsivity, and most importantly, the physical acting out would be greatly improved with the use of a carefully titrated pharmacological intervention such as methylphenidate. Her parents' resistance to this treatment option represents a real roadblock to Alice's ultimate success in overcoming the significant behavioral and academic challenges posed by her ADHD.

Assessing The Problem: Matt (ADHD Predominantly Inattentive Type)

Identify and Describe the Problem Behavior

Matt displays distractibility and occasional inattentiveness both in school and at home. These episodes of inattention and disorganization began to increase in frequency during the middle school grades, prompting the recommendation that he be evaluated for special education services to address these areas of concern. An outside child psychologist with experience in diagnosing and treating children with ADHD determined that Matt had ADHD, predominantly inattentive type.

Collect Baseline Data and Academic Information

At school, the multidisciplinary referral team reviewed records and conducted tests such as the *Conners Parent and Teacher Rating Scales - 3rd ed.* (Conners, 2008) and were satisfied that Matt had been appropriately diagnosed with ADHD and would benefit from special education services under the category of "Other Health Impaired."

Describe the Context in Which the Behavior Is Observed

Behavioral observations involving teachers were made in the school and classroom. In a similar vein, Matt's parents conducted observations in and around the home. Both contexts revealed similar behavioral characteristics; periods of inattention, lack of focus, distractibility when not meaningfully engaged, and disorganization in terms of schoolwork and tasks he was asked to do at home.

Complete a Functional Assessment Form and/or Behavior Rating Scale

The *Conners Parent and Teacher Rating Scales – 3rd ed.* (Conners, 2008) was administered during the referral process. In addition, the child psychologist Matt has been seeing has administered several tests that have helped confirm the diagnosis.

Conduct a Direct Observation

As noted earlier, direct observations were conducted by both Matt's parents and teachers and the recorded data were analyzed. The findings were used to help confirm the diagnosis and develop a viable treatment plan.

Develop a Hypothesis

Based on the data from multiple assessments, Matt's diagnosis of ADHD, predominantly inattentive type was confirmed. Matt clearly requires structure and guidance to be successful in the classroom. He needs to use graphic organizers, daily and weekly planners, memory aids; in addition, a laptop will enable him to record notes and important dates. His inability to focus and attend is being addressed through the use of Adderall, a stimulant that is effective in improving focus and concentration.

Test the Hypothesis and Modify as Necessary

A behavioral intervention plan has been implemented for Matt; but it has not yet been reviewed.

Developing an Effective Intervention Plan

Matt's behavioral intervention plan will be multimodal and consist primarily of academic interventions that would be complimented by the use of Adderall. Since Matt's social and interpersonal skills are unaffected and represent areas of strength, behavioral interventions are considered unnecessary; however, cognitive-behavior strategies such as self-management using checklists and memory aids as well as mnemonics to improve information storage and retrieval would be used and reinforced by his classroom teachers.

To assist Matt in developing organization and management skills, he goes to the resource room for one period each day. During this period, he is taught various research-based organizational skills; for example, he uses the silly story memory technique to prepare for an upcoming term test in U.S. history. This technique features the pairing of a viable history term from the unit he is studying with an exaggerated or silly visual cue or image; Matt then creates a story that includes each of these embellished terms in a desired sequence. He is encouraged to use bizarre imagistic connections to help encode the data for easy retrieval later. This technique seems to be working well for him.

Another organizational approach that Matt has learned to use effectively involves a graphic organizer referred to as a semantic word web or mind map. This technique involves the use of pictures or geometric shapes to create a chart or graph of the main ideas of a lecture, book chapter, or term paper outline. The shapes or graphic images help Matt, whose preferred learning modality is visual and tactual/kinesthetic, to 'see' the structure of the learning task. He is then able to convert this graphic structure to the more abstract organization of print. Matt uses speech-recognition software to convert his speech to print. He has mastered this technology and can actually word-process more efficiently using this software. He finds that he actually enjoys subjects such as English and social studies that were previously an anathema because, thanks to this assistive technology, he can be successful in them. He is thus able to explore topics he finds interesting and meaningful via the internet and integrate the data he uncovers into his research projects.

Lastly, Matt has been taught to use a reading comprehension strategy called reciprocal reading to improve his comprehension of print and increase his ability to sustain focus and concentration (Palincsar & Brown, 1986; Palincsar & Klenk, 1992). The technique is predicated on the effective use of a self-questioning strategy. The student is taught to ask four types of questions concerning a written passage or story: literal types, clarifying types, predicting types, and summarizing types. An important component of the strategy is that the user must actually teach a familiar passage to a classmate using the questions types as prompts to enhance the partner's understanding of the passage. Matt has shown significant improvement in reading comprehension as a result of this strategy, and he is able to use it in all his subjects, for math word problems.

From the Field

Vincent D'Amico, PsyD.

Vincent D'Amico, a clinical psychologist, doctor of integrative medicine, certified nutritional consultant, and interfaith minister, is an expert in the field of attention-deficit disorder (ADD)/ADHD. He is director of the ADD/ADHD Diagnostic & Treatment Center, the Family Stress Reduction Institute, and the Discovery Summer Program. He is in private clinical practice utilizing various treatment protocols that have been found to be safe and effective in working therapeutically with students who have these disorders. He is the author of The Sacred Journey of *Parenthood* and *Renato's Quest*, both self-published books. He has conducted research on brahmi (Bacopa monniera), an herb, and its effect on attention, impulsivity, concentration, short-term auditory memory, working memory, and sympathetic nervous system arousal in ADHD children. Initial results are promising.

Discuss approaches that you have found successful in your practice relative to students diagnosed with ADD or ADHD.

Approaches that I have found useful in working with students diagnosed with ADD/ADHD are those that offer encouragement, empowerment, and self-control. Before I discuss the approaches/interventions, it is important to note that each individual is unique. I do not know of any single approach that works for everyone. It is critical to understand the students' individual and unique personalities—their unique strengths, weaknesses, and temperaments.

First and foremost, form a working, therapeutic relationship with the student. Without a working relationship based on mutual respect, most interventions are likely to fail. In an effective mentoring relationship, a student feels understood, not judged. He or she is more likely to benefit from feedback, a crucial factor in working therapeutically with ADD/ADHD students. Many students with ADD/ADHD suffer from low self-esteem and can be terribly sensitive to criticism. An atmosphere of support, encouragement, and teamwork will likely help them to lower their defenses and be more receptive to feedback to help correct weaknesses. When we demonstrate our confidence in them, they begin to believe in themselves.

There are many interventions that I have found effective with students who have ADD/ADHD after a working relationship has been formed. These interventions empower the student. The goal is to expose the student to various interventions and help them to choose those that they like most. These can be included in a "virtual toolbox" and utilized as needed. Just as a mechanic, surgeon, carpenter, mason, computer software programmer, and plumber need tools to perform their respective tasks, ADD/ADHD students also require tools for success.

One such approach is to teach the student to develop an internal dialogue or "self-talk." This takes the form of "talking out loud" at first. Then, the dialogue becomes internalized, so the student learns to work problems through in their mind. This helps to reduce impulsivity and anxiety and improve concentration. In modeling this type of problem-solving approach, coupled with words of inspiration and encouragement, the student learns to become their own coach.

Another approach is to find the optimal time interval that the student is able to attend and perform assignments. I recommend using a timer, such as the "Time Timer," which has a large red dial that provides a visual reminder of the passage of time. The timer can be set at the optimal length of time (e.g., 10, 20, or 30 minutes). Then, when the time is up, the timer is set again for a rest break. Each student is unique, so the amount of time will have to be determined based upon their current ability to work effectively. Then, in time, the length of time can be increased.

Another tool that I have found effective in helping ADD/ADHD students to develop mental stamina is EEG biofeedback, also known as neurofeedback. The brain produces electrical patterns in the cerebral cortex called brainwaves. Brainwaves are measured in cycles per second (cps). The slower brainwaves (theta) are "daydreaming" brainwaves. The very fast brainwaves (high beta) are "hyperactive/frustration/anxiety" brainwaves. Sensory motor rhythm is a brainwave that is associated with attention, concentration, and peak performance. Therefore, different brainwaves are associated with different conscious states. Neurofeedback teaches students how to control their brainwaves. Brainwaves are electronically monitored, recorded, and analyzed by a computer. Visual and auditory feedback is provided by a simple video game. Success in the game is based on the student's ability to regulate the brainwave pattern. Through feedback, the brain learns how to produce more or less of the desired/undesired brainwave.

Another useful technique is progressive muscle relaxation (PMR) and diaphragmatic breathing. PMR is a way to self-monitor by training the body and mind to engage the body's relaxation response. It involves a series of exercises where different muscle groups are first made tense for several seconds, then the tension is released. At the same time, the student engages in deep, diaphragmatic breathing where inhalation takes place in the abdominal area. They are instructed to breathe in as if they are filling their belly like a balloon. Then, they exhale pulling their abdomen in, squeezing the air out. This is repeated throughout the exercise. Daily practice helps to reduce impulsivity and anxiety, while increasing attention, concentration, and overall mental stamina. Practicing this technique, combined with stretch and rest breaks during school hours, will likely increase academic achievement.

Effective communication is vital in working therapeutically with ADD/ADHD students. By the therapist/teacher's modeling ways to communicate clearly and concisely, the student is more likely to both understand directions and learn ways to communicate clearly. Here are some guidelines.

- Be brief and to the point.
- Keep it simple and address one issue/lesson at a time.
- Establish an interactive dialogue and avoid monologues.
- Ask questions and enlist their involvement in solving the "problem."
- Demonstrate that you are in this together, that you are on the same team.
- Match language with maturity. Talk with, never down, to students. Never speak above or below the student's level of maturity. Ask them to paraphrase what you said to ensure that the message was understood the way you intended it to be. This is a way to identify and correct miscommunication/misunderstanding.
- Be patient and avoid strong reactions such as anger or disappointment, suspending judgment and being mindful of your own need to control and be effective. As Leonardo Davinci once said, "Patience serves as a protection against wrong as clothes do against cold. For if you put on more clothes as the cold increases, it will have no power to hurt you. Grow in patience when you meet with great wrongs, and they will then be powerless to vex your mind."

I would also like to add a note about the importance of nutrition. The old adage 'You are what you eat' is profound wisdom. In order to function optimally, the absorption of proper nutrients is essential. Proper nutrition includes a balance of proteins, amino acids, healthy fats, vitamins, minerals, and complex carbohydrates. Today's fast and highly processed foods have greatly depleted our bodies of essential nutrients; for example, sugar consumption in the United States has risen dramatically. Refined sugars stress the blood sugar control mechanism. It sets the student up for metabolic roller coaster rides that can include mood swings, excessive energy, fatigue, and concentration and memory difficulties. Sugar, in the short term, can have a stimulant effect. This then rebounds into an exaggerated fatigue response. Also, some ADD/ADHD students respond negatively to wheat (gluten) and dairy (casein). They may have food allergies/sensitivities. There are tests that a clinician can perform to determine this. A general rule of thumb is to eat fresh, organic fruits and vegetable, meats that are organic, and free-range and organic grains, dairy, and nuts.

What about approaches or interventions that you would not recommend for those working with students with ADD or ADHD?

I would not recommend approaches that create power struggles, such as authoritarian 'do it or else' types of systems. Punishment is not effective in the long term; in time, it causes more harm than good. Resentment builds and learning suffers. This does not mean that natural consequences are not built into the learning system. If homework is not handed in, certainly a consequence is appropriate; however, it is important it understand whether the homework was not completed due to boredom or lack of understanding. If the student grasps the concept, then giving less is better. If they do not understand the assignment, a review is needed until comprehension is mastered. A general rule of thumb with ADD/ADHD students is to give less homework but ensure comprehension.

What about success stories? Can you tell us a personal anecdote that illustrates a successful treatment experience?

One success story that stands out in my mind is a student I will call Bill (his name has been changed). I first saw Bill when he was 15 years old and diagnosed with ADHD. He was failing nearly all his subjects, and he suffered from low self-esteem and social anxiety. He also suffered from inattention, impulsivity, limited concentration, poor organizational skills, and deficits in memory. He had been in cognitive-behavioral therapy for years with no observable improvement. He had also taken many different medications that included Ritalin, Adderall, Celexa, Prozac, Paxil, and Lexapro. I inherited Bill on my caseload when I took over as director of an ADD/ADHD center.

As I looked over his chart before meeting him, I had doubts about his treatment. Reminding myself that a new person and different perspective can have a positive impact, I threw away the textbooks, so to speak, and began to get to know Bill. I created a supportive, empathic, safe environment where Bill could say everything. Bill began to talk about his troubles at home and at school. He began to trust me with secrets he never told anyone before. He told me how he was bullied; how afraid he was to tell anyone; and how he suffered in silence. He described how difficult it was for him to keep track of assignments, and how frustrated he was with his poor academic performance.

After several months, Bill decided to make some changes. He showed interest in learning strategies to help him to focus and relax. He learned and practiced progressive muscle relaxation, diaphragmatic breathing, and visual imagery. These techniques helped him to quiet his mind enough to have the mental stamina necessary to focus and attend in school. He also participated in EEG biofeedback (neurofeedback), which further helped him to pay attention and focus. After two years, he stopped taking all medication. He graduated high school and went to a community college, where he became interested in journalism.

He took an interest in diet and nutrition. He began taking vitamin/mineral supplements. He also took an herb called brahmi (Bacopa monniera), which he reported helped him to concentrate better. He graduated from the community college and was accepted to and earned a scholarship at a four-year accredited university, where he graduated with nearly all A's. He successfully participated in several internship programs, wrote articles for the school newspaper, and had articles published in several magazines. He is currently pursuing a master's degree in fine arts.

When Bill was asked what helped him most, he said, "All the things I learned from you were helpful; the visual imagery, neurofeedback, nutrition, the brahmi, and all that stuff. But from the beginning, I think what was most helpful was that you listened to me. You became a friend, a father figure. You gave me advice my own father could not give me. You have been a great friend, and coach. You helped motivate me to help myself."

Never underestimate the power of listening. Listening is in itself therapeutic. If we listen deeply to our students, they will be more likely to learn from us. In my years of working with students, I have learned this: Students choose their teachers. You can place them in front of hundreds of "teachers," but they will choose who they will learn from. They are more likely to choose us if we listen to them. Our Creator gave us one mouth, but two ears. We need to talk less and listen more.

What strategies or approaches would you recommend as an expert in the field that the teacher of a student who has ADHD might try to improve that student's academic success?

First, let the student know that you are on the same team. Make yourself available before and after school to meet with the student. During the day, place your hand on his or her shoulder when asking him to perform a task.

Second, utilize strategies that allow for movement in the classroom. This can take the form of stretching, simple yoga postures, deep breathing, and jumping in place. Also, give special tasks to the ADHD student. For example, ask him or her to assist in handing out materials, or cleaning up after an activity. Also, several passes can be given to the ADHD student for use when he or she needs a break. This increases the locus of control within the students. Often, students require less frequent breaks because they know they have a pass that they can use when they need to.

Third, ensure that all homework is written down. If the student is forgetful, recommend a checklist to review with you at the end of the day to ensure that all assignments are written down. Make sure to break large assignments into smaller, clear steps. Some children prefer auditory interventions. In this regard, a microcassette tape recorder can be suggested and assignments recorded verbally. If books are continuously forgotten, a second set of textbooks to keep at home can be made available.

Fourth, alternate creative tasks with structured ones. For example, after a lesson in social studies which the ADHD student might find boring, include a guessing game or a series of funny riddles or jokes during a 5-minute break. Also, make as many lessons as possible hands on. If you are teaching the 50 states and their capitals, rather than simply reading, and memorizing them from a book or sheet, use a large puzzle and have the AHDH student arrange the pieces together. This increases their attention, participation, and retention. Associate the name of the state and the capital with something humorous; for example, the capital of New York has many rabbits: "All Bunny" (i.e., Albany); the capital of New Jersey has ten people named "Trent" (e.g., Trenton); etc.

Fifth, utilize a vertical accordion file system to organize assignments by subject. Give each subject a different color sticker on the tab to help differentiate each one and to assist in organizing work.

Sixth, an academic incentive plan can be created between the teacher and student, and between the parents and student. For example, rewards can be given for completed assignments, grades, class participation, staying on task in the classroom, etc. The student can earn time in, where he or she earns free time which can be taken at scheduled times during the day. Points, stickers, tokens (e.g., marbles, poker chips) can be earned and exchanged for time in where the student can choose something he or she likes to do for a period of time (e.g., listen to music, read a comic book, play cards, etc.). Parents can reward the student with other incentives (e.g., going out to a movie, a toy, money, etc.).

Seventh, let the ADHD student know that you will call on him or her the next day to answer a question. Tell him the question and let him be prepared to answer it the next day. This strategy helps improve attention, retention, and self-esteem, as the student is prepared when called upon to answer the question.

Eighth, avoid power struggles. Implement a collaborative teaching paradigm, treating the ADHD student as an equal partner in learning.

Summary

ADHD continues to be among the most challenging disabilities to diagnose and remediate. Current estimates suggest that from three to five percent of school-age children in the United States are impacted by this disorder. Although there is no single definitive cause for ADHD, it appears to be primarily neurobiological and thus not attributable to poor parenting or as a convenient excuse for laziness, egocentricity, or incorrigibility.

The DSM-V (American Psychiatric Association, 2013) differentiates three sub-types of ADHD: (1) predominantly inattentive, (2) predominantly hyperactive-impulsive, and (c) combined type (1 and 2). This diagnostic manual provides behavioral criteria unique to each of these sub-types as well as several universal criteria that include: (1) behavioral characteristics evident by age 7, (2) some of the symptoms need to be evident in 2 or more settings (e.g., school and home), and (3) the symptoms must significantly impair social, occupational, or academic performance and cannot be better explained by a mood disorder, anxiety disorder, dissociative disorder, or a personality disorder.

Students who have ADHD, predominantly inattentive type, experience significant academic problems, and 30 to 50 percent could be co-diagnosed with a learning disability. These students also have difficulty maintaining focus and screening out extraneous stimuli. In contrast, students who have ADHD, predominantly hyperactive-impulsive type, seem to have an inexhaustible supply of energy and have real difficulty saying in one place for an extended period of time. In addition, the disinhibition associated within the impulsivity of these children impels them to make rash choices that after cause accidents and result in disciplinary referrals.

Not surprisingly, the behaviors associated with ADHD create a host of social problems, resulting in stigmatization and, ultimately, in alienation. This social isolation often leads to low self-esteem, poor self-efficacy, a heightened sense of loneliness, and "learned helplessness".

The difficulty in accurately diagnosing ADHD; therefore, assessment needs to be thorough and employ valid and reliable instruments. The process involves several steps and is both time-consuming and costly. Typical instruments used in the diagnostic process include: checklists and rating scales, parent, teacher, and student interviews, direct observation of target behaviors by parents and teachers, and a complete medical examination to rule out medical or health-related causes for the symptoms.

Effective interventions include behavioral ones, such as contingency reinforcement schedules, and daily report cards, cognitive ones, such as self-monitoring and self-instruction; academic ones that provide organizational aids such as graphic organizers and semantic webs; as well as information-encoding/retrieval strategies such as mnemonics and memory enhancements.

Finally, the single most effective intervention is the prescription of medication such as methylphenidate (Ritalin). Effective pharmacological intervention must follow stringent procedures and be closely monitored to ensure minimal adverse effects and optimal treatment benefits.

As we learn more about the causes of ADHD, we will be better prepared to develop more effective academic and behavioral interventions. Despite the controversy surrounding our current diagnostic protocols and interventions, new research is helping to illuminate the many misperceptions and mysteries surrounding this enigmatic and often controversial disorder. Although teachers are not typically involved in this research, they can influence and improve the academic and behavioral approaches used to help students with ADHD achieve success in school and in life.

Tips for Teachers

- Whenever possible, avoid steps with more than one instruction, and also avoid giving multipart assignments. Allow the child to finish one assignment or follow one direction at a time before offering him the next.
- Designate a specific location where the child should deposit completed assignments. If the child is capable at this stage, teach her to keep a daily homework journal or prepare a copy of the homework assignments to give to the child at the end of the day.

- Give shorter but more frequent assignments to increase success rates. Break long-term projects into short-term assignments. Reward the child for completing each step. Remember, confidence builds through repeated successful experiences.
- Ask parents to help the child get organized each night before school. Encourage them to develop a checklist so the child's clothes, books, assignments, and so on are ready for the next morning.
- If necessary, have the child finish all assignments at school.
- Require the child to clean out her desk each day.
- Use boxes, bins, or other organizers to help the child separate and store various items.
- Encourage the use of binders or individual folders to help keep schoolwork organized.
- Set up a special place for tools, materials, and books. Organization and routine are critical to success.
- If possible, do not place the student near distracting stimuli, such as an air conditioner, heater, high traffic areas, doors, or windows. Create a stimuli-reduced study area. Let all students be allowed to go to this area so that the student with ADHD will not feel self-conscious or singled out.
- Avoid planning numerous transitions and changes throughout the day. Clearly list and explain the daily schedule to help the child deal with change.
- Stand near the student while lecturing. This is called *proximity control.*
- Try to preempt the child's behavior, especially during changes in the schedule. Inform the child of the change about 5 minutes beforehand and define your expectations for appropriate behavior.
- As appropriate to the age and situation, identify strengths in the child you can publicly announce or praise. This will help the other students develop a more positive perception of the child.

- If the child takes any mediation, protect her privacy (e.g., by avoiding publicly reminding her to go down to the nurse's office to take it).
- Encourage the use of word processing, typing, spell checking, and other computer skills.
- Create chances for peer interaction and cooperative learning for academic tasks that do not require sitting for long periods of time.
- An effective management system concentrates on a few behaviors at a time, with new behavior patterns added when the student masters the first ones.
- Reinforce appropriate behavior with something the student is willing to work for (or to avoid); for example, give or remove points immediately, according to the behavior, so the child understands why he is or is not being rewarded. While older children may be willing to work toward a deferred reward, younger children generally need more immediate reinforcement (Pierangelo & Giuliani, 2008).

Focus Questions Revisited

Differentiate between the three types of ADHD as presented in the DSM-V. Which of the three, poses the greatest challenge in the classroom and why?

A Sample Response. Essentially, the three are differentiated as follows:

- ADHD, predominantly inattentive: These students typically make careless mistakes in school, and they have real difficulty staying on task and screening out irrelevant stimuli.
- ADHD, predominantly hyperactive-impulsive: These students seem to have boundless energy and have great difficulty staying in one place for an extended period of time. They cannot seem to sit still. In conjunction with hyperactivity, students who have this type of ADHD also experience disinhibition. This suppression of the inhibitory response mechanism in the cerebral cortex often results in impulsivity.

- ADHD, combined type: Affected students display the characteristics of both inattention and hyperactivity and impulsivity. Students diagnosed with the combined type may represent the greatest challenge in the classroom, because they display both of these detrimental characteristics.

As Alice's teacher, would you advocate for the use of a pharmacological intervention? Provide a rationale for your response based on her presenting behaviors.

A Sample Response. I would do so reluctantly, but only because Alice appears to be unresponsive to all other interventions and research supports the stand-alone efficacy of stimulant medication, such as methylphenidate, in improving focus and reducing impulsivity.

What can teachers of a student suspected of having ADHD do to provide meaningful data to help inform the multidisciplinary team and facilitate the referral process?

A Sample Response. In accordance with the steps suggested by Culatta et al. (2003), teachers can do the following in order to produce meaningful and informative data concerning a student in the referral process:

- Administer and collect rating scales from relevant persons.
- Orient the family and the student to the evaluation.
- Interview the student.
- Administer normed tests such as achievement and continuous performance tests.
- Conduct direct observations in several settings, including school, community, and home if possible.
- Interview the parent(s).
- Recommend a medical evaluation.
- Integrate all the data.
- Give feedback and recommendation to the team.

Discuss the controversy surrounding the classification of ADHD. Based on your knowledge of the disorder, should ADHD be classified as an emotional/behavioral disorder, a neurodevelopmental disorder, a learning disability, or is it distinctive and therefore deserving of a separate category? Provide a justification for your position.

A Sample Response. Some investigators have expressed concern at the recent proliferation in the incidence of ADHD among school-age children in the United States, citing inadequate and faulty assessment practices or the lack of creditable science to make a case for a discrete category of ADHD. Others claim that it is a convenient construct that provides billions of dollars in profit to the pharmaceutical industry, which commissions flawed studies that justify its existence. I agree that ADHD is frequently misdiagnosed and overidentified, partly, because of a lack of thorough assessment; however, I believe that a sufficient number of credible studies exit that demonstrate its viability. I think, based on the neurological nature of its most prominent characteristics, it can appropriately be considered a neurodevelopmental disorder.

Why do many "experts" contend that arriving at a correct diagnosis of ADHD is one of the most challenging tasks for clinicians? What are some of the most perplexing factors? What are the potential ramifications of a misdiagnosis?

A Sample Response. The reason that experts consider ADHD to be among the most challenging diagnosis to make is due in no small way to the universality of its purported characteristics: many disorders and illnesses can "mask" as ADHD based on its identifying criteria. Also, ADHD is comorbid with several other and potentially more serious disorders. Clinicians are then faced with a task of triage: determining the most serious disorder and treating it first. The detrimental effects of misdiagnosis are the stigmatizing effects of the classification and the likelihood of receiving ineffective treatment.

Review the case example for Matt. If you were the clinician, would you arrive at a similar diagnosis? Explain your answer.

A Sample Response. Yes, I would. The confirmatory data are the report card comments from elementary school that reveal the concerns of teachers early on regarding Matt's ability to focus and screen out extraneous stimuli. The results of extensive neurological tests ruled out the possibility of brain injury, which provides further support for the diagnosis of ADHD predominantly inattentive.

What academic and/or behavioral accommodations would Matt need to be successful in your class/in your school?

A Sample Response. Matt would need to be provided the opportunity to use a laptop in class to facilitate note taking. He might benefit from a "study buddy" or peer tutor to ensure that his notes are organized and relevant and that he is clear on the requirements and time frame for assignments (use a pocket organizer of some type). Matt would likely require extended time and an alternate location, free of excessive stimuli, to enable him to be successful on major tests, exams, and assignments. He might benefit, as well, from the provision of a period in the resource room each day in him stay current on all assignments and get help with his organization and management skills.

What academic and behavioral interventions wouldAlice need to be successful in your class/in your school?

A Sample Response. Alice appears to be relatively unresponsive to the behavioral interventions that have been provided her to date. I do believe that she needs firm and consistent setting of limits as well as a well-defined routine to enable her to succeed in the classroom. Of course, I believe she would respond most dramatically to the application of medication; specifically, methylphenidate. Whether that is a viable option for her remains to be seen.

After reviewing the section in the chapter on pharmacological interventions used in the treatment ofADHD, what are your impressions of its efficacy? Are there students for whom it might be appropriately prescribed? Provide an example of one. What are some counter indications that make the decision to prescribe a pharmacological agent a very deliberate and painstaking one?

A Sample Response. Alice seems to represent an exemplary case for the prescription of medication. Her hyperactive-impulsive behaviors would clearly benefit from a drug that helps her focus, stay on task, and reduce impulsive behaviors. A medication like Ritalin, which offers significant improvements in these areas, might represent Alice's best treatment option. Clearly, the adverse effects of any of the medications used in the treatment of ADHD are potentially very serious, as delineated in Table 4.1. Consequently, even for Alice, who might benefit from an optimal dose of Ritalin, the health risks, both in the short-term and long-term, are real and the decision to prescribe the drug as well as the determination of the optimal dosage level must be made only after carefully weighing these risks.

[1] Much of the material in this section is adapted from Austin, V. L. (2003). Pharmacological interventions for students with ADD. Intervention in School and Clinic, 38 (5), 289–296. Copyright 2003 by Sage Publications. Adapted with permission.

Key Terms Used in the Chapter

Methylphenidate (Ritalin):

A prescription stimulant commonly used to treat attention-deficit hyperactivity disorder (ADHD). It is also one of the primary drugs used to treat the daytime drowsiness symptoms of narcolepsy and chronic fatigue syndrome. The drug is seeing early use to treat cancer-related fatigue.

Neurotransmitters:

The chemicals that account for the transmission of signals from one neuron to the next across synapses. They are also found at the axon endings of motor neurons, where they stimulate muscle fibers to contract.

Dopamine:

An important neurotransmitter (messenger) in the brain that is classified as a catecholamine (a class of molecules that serve as neurotransmitters and hormones). It is a monoamine (a compound containing nitrogen formed from ammonia by replacing one or more of the hydrogen atoms with hydrocarbon radicals). Dopamine is a precursor (forerunner) of adrenaline and a closely related molecule, noradrenaline.

Prefrontal Cortex:

The very front of the brain located right beneath the forehead. It is in the anterior (front) region of the frontal lobes. Besides being the front of the brain physically, it is responsible for the executive functions, which include mediating conflicting thoughts, making choices between right and wrong or good and bad, predicting future events, and governing social control—such as suppressing emotional or sexual urges. The prefrontal cortex is the brain center most strongly implicated in qualities such as sentience, human general intelligence, and personality.

Dextroamphetamine (Adderall):

A pharmaceutical psychostimulant, Adderall is composed of mixed amphetamine salts. The drug is used primarily to treat attention-deficit hyperactivity disorder (ADHD) and narcolepsy. Adderall has also been used successfully to manage severe cases of treatment-resistant depression. It is a Schedule II controlled substance, meaning that it has been deemed to have a high potential for abuse and addiction, but it has accepted medical uses.

Disinhibition:

Loss of inhibition, as through the influence of external stimuli such as drugs or alcohol, or as a result of brain damage.

Intentionality:
A behavior or act that is thoughtfully planned and executed; it is not carried out impulsively

Norepinephrine:
A stress hormone, norepinephrine affects parts of the brain where attention and responding actions are controlled. Along with epinephrine, norepinephrine also underlies the fight-or-flight response, directly increasing heart rate, triggering the release of glucose from energy stores, and increasing blood flow to skeletal muscle.

Serotonin:
A hormone, also called 5-hydroxytryptamine, in the pineal gland, blood platelets, the digestive tract, and the brain. Serotonin acts as a chemical messenger that transmits nerve signals between nerve cells and also causes blood vessels to narrow. Changes in the serotonin levels in the brain can alter mood. For example, medications that affect the action of serotonin

Hyperkinesis:
A state of overactive restlessness in children. It is also a medical condition resulting in uncontrolled muscle movement, akin to spasms.

Perseverating Behaviors:
Many children with severe disabilities, particularly those on the autism spectrum, perseverate. Perseverating means they do certain actions over and over again, such as repeating a phrase, shutting a door, twiddling fingers, lining up toys, rubbing their hands together, or spinning objects.

Concerta:
An extended-release central nervous system stimulant (methylphenidate) that is used to treat children and teens with attention-deficit hyperactivity disorder (ADHD). It can be prescribed to children who are more than 6 years old, although because it is a pill that must be swallowed, younger school-aged children may have problems taking it.

Chapter 5

Specific Phobia, Separation Anxiety Disorder, and Social Anxiety Disorder

Focus Questions

- *Suppose a child who has a specific phobia, such as a morbid preoccupation with death, was assigned to your class. What might you do to facilitate his acceptance and integration?*
- *List some specific fears experienced by children. What differentiates the pathological ones that characterize a phobia from those that are common to many children who are able to function successfully without special treatment?*
- *How common is separation anxiety disorder in children? How can a teacher determine whether a child's symptoms represent a bona-fide disorder or will simply disappear in time?*
- *What can a classroom teacher do to help a child who is experiencing separation anxiety disorder?*
- *How do you define social phobia or social anxiety disorder as it pertains to school-age children?*
- *What are the five most feared situations for children who have social anxiety disorder, and how can a teacher facilitate the student's participation in them?*
- *Describe the Social Effectiveness Therapy for Children (SET-C) cognitive behavioral intervention and identify its strengths in helping students who have social anxiety disorder.*

Introduction

The comprehensive media attention given to the threat of terrorism intensified the sense of foreboding and dread that permeated American society after the catastrophic events of 9/11 (Silver, 2021). This was further complicated by the COVID-19 pandemic with its changes in social interactions (Okabe-Miyamoto & Lyubmoirsky, 2021). This climate of fear may help account for the significant increase in the identification of social phobia and generalized anxiety disorders in children and adolescents. Similarly, dropout rates continue to pose a challenge for educators, especially among students with disabilities (National Center for Education Statistics, 2021; National Center for Education Statistics, 2020; Pacer Center, 2022).

These sociocultural triggers and the corresponding increase in phobias among school-age children demand that teachers and related service providers be especially aware of and familiar with the characteristics of these disorders as well as the most effective school-based interventions. This chapter offers a practical approach to identifying childhood phobias and the most effective school-based interventions. Where possible, case-examples drawn from actual practice will be used to provide teachers and related service providers with authentic applications of school-based interventions.

To facilitate clarity and understanding, the chapter examines the most prevalent phobias that affect school-age children: specific phobia, separation anxiety disorder, social anxiety disorder, and generalized anxiety disorder. Each of these diagnoses will be introduced with a relevant case example, followed by an elaboration of the characteristics, causes, and recommended interventions for the specific disorder, and concluding with a behavior intervention plan as required by Individuals with Disabilities Education Act, otherwise known as IDEA (U.S. Department of Education, 2004).

Specific Phobia (SP)

Case Example: Nicola, a High School Senior with a Specific Phobia

Nicola, a high school senior, lives in Seattle, Washington with her mother, a preschool teacher, her father, an aircraft mechanic with Boeing, and two younger brothers. Nicola has always enjoyed an especially close relationship with her mother, Lois, who is obsessively protective of her and jealous of her affections and attention. Lois suffers from "pernicious anemia," which made childbirth especially difficult and Nicola was born three months premature and spent those months in an incubator in the prenatal ICU of the local hospital. Nicola's survival was very much in question and when it became clear that she would and was ready to be taken home, Lois lavished her with all her attention, after all, she was her *very special* and *only* daughter. Thereafter, her mother never let Nicola out of her sight and agonized when she came down with a cold or the flu or any other of the typical childhood illnesses. Her overprotectiveness has only intensified during Nicola's high school years and her mother made it very clear that a steady boyfriend was simply out of the question. Nicola is an excellent student with a very bright future and, in her first semester as a senior year in high school has been applying to colleges and universities that offer degrees in engineering. Her dream has always been to gain acceptance at Carnegie Mellon, one of the top engineering schools in the country, located in Pittsburgh, PA.

Last week, Nicola learned that she had been accepted - an incredible accomplishment in a school with an acceptance rate of less than 17 percent. Needless to say, her parents, teachers, friends, and siblings were ecstatic as was Nicola, that is, until she realized that she would need to fly out for new student orientation over winter break. Nicola experiences a specific phobia referred to as aerophobia or fear of flying. Many people share a healthy fear of flying, but with a little fortification, such as that provided by sedatives or alcohol, they are able to endure the discomfort. Unlike these folks, however, Nicola is paralyzed with fear at even the thought of flying, a fear that is symptomatic of a larger, more insidious issue; namely, her pathological interdependence with her mother.

There is a two-pronged dilemma, therefore, the first caused by the fact that there are only three means of travel from Seattle to Pittsburgh; train, automobile, or aircraft, and Nicola has a limited amount of time. Travel by train or car would be an estimated two-week round trip whereas air travel would cover the same distance in about four hours, each way. The second, and more terrifying, is the realization that for the first time in her eighteen years, Nicola will not be worried over or attended to by her closest friend, her mother. To make matters worse, Lois continually reminds her of that fact and has tearfully asked that Nicola consider living at home and attending a local college for at least her freshman and sophomore years.

Nicola is heartbroken at the thought of being unable to attend her dream school, but the thought of flying there and being so far from her mother terrifies her. Her father, teachers, and friends think she is being oversensitive and unreasonable and though they are aware of her diagnosis, find it difficult to understand how she could pass up this once-in-a-lifetime opportunity for an irrational fear.

Her therapist and school psychologist are both aware of her dilemma, which is causing her even further anxiety, and are exploring some extraordinary and extraordinarily costly therapies. One of them involves exposure therapy that actually consists, of all things, flying in an airplane. The other requires courage and sensitivity and will take much longer than a few sessions with a therapist as Nicola and her mother need to address their unhealthy interdependence.

Lois's (Nicola's mother) Response

Lois loves her daughter dearly and has been very supportive and understanding of her struggles with specific phobia - aerophobia. She has made numerous allowances for her fear of flying, agreeing to drive her long distances to special events, visits with relatives, and vacations but she balks at this latest challenge. How can her only daughter and closest friend consider attending a college so far from her mother? Who would be there to help her, if she became ill or needed some emotional support or buoying up? She must convince Nicola that she knows what is best for her daughter and the better alternative would be to stay at home and attend a local college. Mother knows best!

Nicola's father has explored various ways that she could safely travel by plane by taking prescribed sedatives, engaging in exposure or cognitive behavioral therapies, or using a therapeutic travel companion, but Nicola refuses to consider any of them insisting that she will have a breakdown and does not want that indelible experience, obscuring her greater fear, that of leaving her mother.

Nicola's mother has always enjoyed a close relationship with her daughter and feels she truly understands her; however, this travel issue is creating friction and is becoming a constant source of conflict, which threatens to poison the amicable mother-daughter relationship. Lois is an emotional wreck at the thought of her daughter leaving home and uses her anguish to elicit guilt in Nicola and thus, influences her decision.

The Therapist's Approach

Nicola's therapist, Marissa, has worked with her since grade school and understands the cause of her phobia - never downplaying its seriousness. She has employed cognitive behavioral therapy to help Nicola think more positively about flying and tactfully begin to address the underlying relational issue involving her codependence with her mother and their unhealthy relationship. Nicola insists they not discuss the latter issue, effectively ending the potential benefit provided by the CBT approach.

An Attachment Perspective

A close relationship with the primary caregiver is not necessarily problematic; however, when the closeness prevents the activation of the exploratory system, the attachment is insecure and therefore impedes normal development. Nicola's mother was very protective of her, but this seemed not to be a problem throughout her early development, which was somewhat understandable given Nicola's premature birth. When the time came for a period of significant physical separation (i.e., going off to college), Nicola developed a fear of flying making it impossible for her to attend a far away, yet prestigious university. Her mother's immediate solution was to keep her close to home and prevent her from exploring the world. A resistant (also known as anxious) attachment style is the result of an interaction effect between the primary caretaker and child. Nicola's imagined separation causes extraordinary anxiety in her mother which in turn increases Nicola's own anxiety. The result is the development of specific phobia in Nicola that finally translated into a significant impairment in functioning.

As mentioned in the case, exposure (discussed later in the chapter) is a well-supported intervention for phobias. Lois is resistant to such an intervention and sees the best solution as Nicola staying close to home. Nicola is also resistant to interventions that might help reduce her anxiety about flying and pursue her plans of attending Carnegie Mellon. It is not surprising given the attachment history that both mother and daughter would resist these interventions. The resistant attachment style derives its name from the kind of relationship between caregiver and child that resists the intrusion of the outside world, hyperactivates the attachment system and deactivates the exploratory system.

Given the dynamic between mother and daughter, any intervention with Nicola should probably include her mother. The end goal is for Lois to do what all parents must do - lunch their children into the world. After all, does Nicola really belong to her mother or does she belong to the world? Healthy development and a secure attachment history would have us believe that the correct answer is the latter.

Characteristics of Specific Phobia

Specific phobia is "a marked and persistent fear that is excessive or unreasonable, cued by the presence or anticipation of a specific object or situation (e.g., flying, heights, animals, receiving an injection, seeing blood" (American Psychiatric Association, 2013, p. 197). It rarely exists in isolation but is highly co-morbid with other anxiety disorders, depressive disorders, and disruptive disorders. Studies suggest comorbidity rates as high as 60 percent in general and as high as 75 percent specifically with other anxiety disorders (Coelho et al., 2020). Separation anxiety disorder is the most common comorbid disorder with SP. In addition, it is important to distinguish SP from normal fear, because all children have fears, which are considered a normal part of the developmental process.

Marks (1969) articulated four distinguishing characteristics of a phobia to include (1) it is out of proportion to the demands of the situation, (2) it cannot be explained or reasoned away, (3) it is beyond voluntary control, and (4) it leads to avoidance of the feared situation. Marks' (1969) definition did not distinguish between phobias in adults and children; however, Miller et al.

(1974) suggested that there were three characteristics specific to phobias in children, which included (1) it persists over an extended period of time, (2) it is unadaptive, and (3) it is not age- or stage-specific.

These seven characteristics formed the basis of the DSM-V (American Psychiatric Association, 2013) definition of a SP, which does allow for distinguishing characteristics in children, most notably through the expressions of crying, tantrums, freezing, or clinging.

The manifestation of SP is through a triple response system: behavioral, cognitive, and physiological (Muris, 2017). The most common behavioral manifestation of SP in children is avoidance of the feared stimulus. Some examples include:

- Avoiding or escaping certain situations such as feared places in the home (e.g., the basement);
- Keeping the light on when sleeping or insisting on sleeping with parent(s) to escape darkness;
- Avoiding eating for fear of choking; and
- Refusing to attend a doctor's appointment for fear of a needle.

Cognitive responses usually include scary thoughts ("I'm afraid"), negative self-statements ("I can't do it"), and the expectation of some catastrophic result ("I'm going to die from the lightening"). Physiological responses include sweating, stomach upset, dry mouth, increased heart rate, shakiness, muscles tension, and even fainting associated with blood-injection type of SP (American Psychiatric Association, 2013).

Prevalence

SP is present in approximately 5 percent of children and increases to 16 percent in 13 to 17-year-olds (American Psychiatric Association, 2013). Evidence has suggested that girls have higher rates of SP than boys (Liberman & Öst, 2016), but differences across racial/ethnic groups are not significant. A diagnosis of SP is given only when other anxiety disorders have been ruled out, especially fear-related to separation (separation anxiety disorder), social situations (social phobia), dirt/contamination (obsessive-compulsive disorder), a traumatic event (post-traumatic stress disorder) or fear of having an attack (panic disorder) (Samra & Abdijadid, 2020). Developmentally, specific phobias are known to occur before the age of 7, especially those related to animals, darkness, insects, and blood/injury whereas those of the natural-environment type more commonly begin around age 11 or 12.

Etiology of Specific Phobia

The etiology of childhood fears in not completely understood (Pittig et al., 2018). Previously, it had been thought that all fears in children came about through Rachman's (1976, 1977) pathways to fear acquisition: direct classical conditioning, vicarious conditioning, and information/instruction. More recent studies suggest, however, that not all fears can be accounted for through an individual's learning history and that other factors (e.g., biological/genetic and parenting influences) must also be considered in the causality of SP.

Learning Factors

The earliest thinking about phobia acquisition concentrated on aversive classical conditioning. A child would experience a trauma around a certain stimulus and then associate the same trauma with any future experience of the same stimulus. The well-known case of 'Little Albert' (Watson & Raynor, 1920) concerned a boy who developed a fear of rats after paring an aversive sound with the sight of the rat. Although trauma can certainly cause a phobia, it is not the only learning pathway to developing a phobia. Social learning factors can also play a part. A child may observe a phobic reaction in someone else (e.g., another child) or learn about the phobic reaction of others through reading and various media outlets (Lindström et al., 2018).

Most of the research on the etiology of phobias has been retrospective; for example, investigating adult or adolescent reports many years after the development of their phobias. Relying on Rachman's tripartite theory of fear acquisition, Ollendick & King (1991) studied 1092 Australian and American children (ages 9 to 14) and found the most common pathways to be vicarious and instructional rather than direct conditioning. Rarely was only one factor responsible for the development of the fear, and in most cases, there was an interaction between two of the factors proposed by Rachman (1977).

In a study with parents of water-phobic children, Menzies and Clarke (1993) found that only 2 percent attributed the fears of their children to direct conditioning events; 26 percent attributed them to vicarious conditioning. Furthermore, the majority of parents (56 percent) believed that their child's fear of water was present from the very beginning and could not attribute it to any conditioning event. Findings such as these have led theorists to conclude that although various forms of conditioning are important factors in the development of specific fears in children, they do not tell the whole story, and that other causal factors must be considered. These other factors include heritability of phobias, biological-constitutional factors, and parenting influences (Oar et al., 2019).

Heritability of Fears

Inherited phobia proneness is a controversial hypothesis that has escalated the debate around the causality of specific fears. Du to their early development, specific phobias are considered to have the lowest heritability, as opposed to, for example, agoraphobia (fear of open spaces), considered to have the highest heritability estimate because of its relatively late onset. Genetic factors play a part in the development of fears, but not an overwhelming one. The role of genetics appears to be more related to an individual's propensity to fear, and environmental factors play the part of manifesting this propensity in the form of a specific fear.

Constitutional Factors

Certain temperamental characteristics (shyness, introversion, withdrawal, etc.) are thought to play a role in the development of childhood fears. Kagan et al. (1989) used the term *behavioral inhibition,* to describe a child who is constitutionally disposed to acquire phobias. Differences in the sympathetic nervous system activation responses of behaviorally inhibited children lend support to the neuropsychological basis of anxiety disorders in general and phobic disorders in particular (Luis-Joaquin et al., 2020).

Familial Influences

Increased rates of behaviorally inhibited children born to parents with anxiety and phobic disorders raise the question not only of a genetic connection but also an environmental one. Children, constantly exposed to the influence of anxiety-disordered parents, may develop behaviorally inhibition characteristics such as cautiousness, uncertainty, and fearfulness in new and different situations (Johnco et al., 2016). Phobic parents may model avoidance behaviors, thwart risk-taking behaviors, and discourage exploration by their children. Direct behavioral observations of the interaction between parent and child in stressful or difficult situations confirmed that phobically-inclined parents tend to use insulating and protective behaviors (Capriola-Hall et al., 2020).

In summary, the literature surrounding the etiology of specific phobia suggests that it is multifactorial and that a number of factors such as genetics, temperament, parental psychopathology, parenting practices, and individual conditioning histories interact in the development and maintenance of childhood phobias (Oar et al., 2019).

Assessment of Specific Phobia

Most experts on childhood phobia have agreed that its assessment needs to be multi-informant and multi-method. There are three assessment approaches for the diagnosis of phobias in children to include diagnostic evaluation/interview, fear rating scales, and behavioral tasks with observation.

Diagnostic Evaluation/Interview

Interviews for the diagnosis of SP can be structured, semi-structured, or unstructured. Structured interviews have the most reliability. Of all the structured interviews designed to assess psychiatric diagnosis in children, only one has been designed specifically to assess SP and other anxiety disorders in children - the *Anxiety Disorders Interview Schedule for DSM-V, Child, and Parent Versions* (ADIS-C/P; Albano & Silverman, 2016). ADIS-C/P diagnoses other anxiety disorders in addition to SP; therefore, it is useful in cases of comorbidity. The interview process usually begins with the child and uses a time frame of the preceding year. The questions are organized around type (i.e., animal, natural environment, blood-injection/injury, situational, and other type). Both the parent and child versions use a 0-8 Likert-scaled format to assess the degree of fear in relation to a specific object or event. To control for variability in language across subjects, the ADIS-C/P utilizes a feelings thermometer to help children rate the tasks.

Fear Rating Scales

Fear rating scales are self-report, standardized measures that allow a child or someone else to rate the degree of fear in relation to a particular object of event. The most well-known and widely used is the *Fear Survey Schedule for Children-Revised* (FSSC-R; Muris et al., 2014). The FSSC-R includes eighty items with a five-factor underlying structure:

- Fear of the unknown
- Fear of failure and criticism
- Fear of minor injury and small animals
- Fear of danger and death
- Medical fears

Gullone and King (1992) developed the *Fear Survey Schedule for Children and Adolescents* (FSSC-II), which consists of seventy-eight items with the same underlying factor structure as the FSSC-R but includes more contemporary events such as nuclear war and AIDS (acquired immunodeficiency syndrome).

In addition to these instruments that measure a broad spectrum of fears, a number of instruments have been developed that assess a specific fear, such as fear of darkness, snakes, tests, medical procedures/hospitals, and dental procedures.

Fear rating scales can be used for several purposes. They are helpful in determining a child's level of fear and therefore can be used to establish a baseline level of fear. Subsequent administration will determine the level of improvement. General fear rating scales can also determine the range of fears from which a child may suffer. Most of the scales are easy to administer, have good reliability, and can help to distinguish anxious from normal youth (Heiser et al., 2009). Fear rating scales, however, should not be used to make differential diagnoses, especially among children who have psychiatric disorders as the discriminate validity of these scales is still a work in progress.

Behavioral Tasks

Another form of child phobia assessment is the *Behavioral Avoidance Task* (BAT) (Castagna et al., 2017; King et al., 2005). The BAT requires a child, under observation, to enter a room and approach the feared stimulus in gradual fashion. Assessment results from the determination of how close the child can get to the feared stimulus, at what point (if any) the child freezes and refuses to approach any closer, time spent in the presence of the feared stimulus, and the number of approach responses. The external validity of the BAT is questionable because the controlled setting allows the child the nearby support of the researcher and a caregiver. In addition, the BAT usually employs fairly safe exercises. As a result, a child's fear may be assessed as lower than what corresponds to a real-life, everyday situation.

Treatment Strategies

Four methods have been used to treat children with specific phobia: behavioral, cognitive-behavioral, psychodynamic psychotherapy, and medication. By far, the most popular and researched methods are behavioral and cognitive-behavioral, so we begin with those.

Systematic Desensitization

Systematic desensitization is a counterconditioning, behavioral intervention which has three forms to include in-vivo, imaginal, and emotive. First developed by Wolpe (1958), it is based on the theory that phobias are classically conditioned responses and therefore can be unlearned through counterconditioning procedures. Systematic desensitization basically has three parts (1) the induction of an incompatible response; for example, muscle relaxation, imagery, or meditation); (2) the presentation of a fear-producing hierarchy from the least to the most fearful; and (3) the systematic, graduated pairing of items in the hierarchy with the incompatible response (Wolpe, 1958). In-vivo systematic desensitization uses a real-life stimulus and an incompatible response. With imaginal systematic desensitization subjects are asked to imagine the feared stimulus. A third form of systematic desensitization is emotive, where the participant, instead of an actual anxiety inhibitor such as muscular relaxation or edibles, is asked to imagine something exciting or pleasant (e.g., the child's favorite hero). All three forms have shown to be effective, but greater effectiveness appears to be with the first two, where an actual anxiety inhibitor is employed (Higa-McMillan et al., 2016; Muris, 2017).

Modeling

Based on Bandura's (1973) Theory of Social Learning, modeling makes use of observational learning to reduce and/or eliminate childhood fears. Modeling can be symbolic (e.g., the child watches a film or studies a picture), live, or participating, where the child is invited to engage in the same behavior as the model in relation to the feared stimulus. All types of modeling have been shown to be more effective than a nonintervention control group, and participant modeling was shown to be more effective than symbolic or live modeling without participation (Ollendick, 2017).

Contingency Management

Based on the principles of operant learning, contingency management is a behavioral intervention designed to reduce childhood fears by managing consequences. The assumption is that the fear is being maintained and reinforced through consequences. Its elimination, therefore, must be based on the removal of reinforcers. A simple example is the child who is afraid of the dark and cannot fall asleep. As a result, parents allow the child to sleep in their bed. This child's fear is being reinforced by getting him or her what he or she wants: closeness and connection with parents. Under contingency management, the parents would be instructed not to allow the child to sleep with them, encourage the child to deal with the fear, and reward the child with their presence every time the child is able to face the fear on their own. Unlike systematic desensitization, anxiety reduction is not a pre-requisite for confronting the stimulus. Contingency management is considered a well-established psychological procedure for dealing with childhood phobias (Muris, 2017).

Cognitive-Behavioral Interventions

Cognitive-behavioral interventions include any intervention designed to alter the child's distorted, fear-producing cognitions through verbal self-instruction that generate positive self-statements. The main goal is for the child to develop a plan to deal with the feared stimulus through problem-solving strategies and relaxation. Children, for example, who are afraid of dogs might be taught to tell themselves, "I am a brave person -- I know I can take care of myself;" "Dogs can be fun to watch and play with--they do many interesting things." Cognitive-behavioral intervention, while effective, does not seem to rise to the effectiveness level of contingency management (Sigurvinsdóttir et al., 2020).

Psychodynamic Psychotherapy

Psychodynamic psychotherapy and psychoanalysis continue to be used in the treatment of childhood anxiety and phobias (Preter et al., 2018). There is a paucity of studies on the effectiveness psychodynamic/psychoanalytic treatment for childhood phobias, yet some evidence exists that suggests this method is better than no treatment at all (Weitkamp et al., 2018).

Medication

Relatively little evidence exists for the effectiveness of pharmacological intervention with childhood phobia. Antidepressants and anti-anxiety medications have been used for the treatment of a number of anxiety disorders in children; however, there are few reliable outcome studies for specific phobia (Patel et al., 2018). Among adults, selective serotonin reuptake inhibitors (SSRIs) have become the preferred class of drugs for dealing with phobias and other anxiety-related disorders. There is some evidence of the effectiveness of SSRIs among children who have a specific phobia (Patel et al., 2018).

Summary

Silverman and Moreno (2005) recommended a three-phase treatment for children who have a specific phobia:

- The education phase
- The application phase
- A relapse prevention phase

In the education phase, both the child and the parents are given information about fears, the key ingredient to overcoming them (i.e., exposure), and, especially for parents, an understanding of contingency management. In the application phase, the child learns relaxation training as part of systematic desensitization, cognitive restructuring, self-evaluation, and reward (King et al., 2005). Finally, fears are not expected to be conquered once and for all, because most children will relapse after having made some progress. To minimize relapse, helpers should try to anticipate future events that might cause the child to become afraid. By creating 'what if' scenarios, helpers work with the child in applying already learned skills to future events.

School-Based Interventions

This section provides practical, effective strategies for working with students who have a specific phobia. To make the recommended school-based interventions described in this section as real and pertinent as possible, we present both the assessment of the behavior and the appropriate behavioral intervention in relation to Nicola, the student described in the preceding case example.

Assessing the Problem

In this book, an array of emotional and behavioral disorders are addressed. Some of these involve primarily internalizing behaviors, which require extensive treatment protocols that engage the participation of all the child's caregivers, particularly the school psychologist. Remember that any purposeful assessment of problem behavior is essentially a problem-solving process conducted to identify the purpose of a behavior so as to develop a plan that will mitigate it effectively. The steps involved in any such plan should include

1. identifying and describing the problem behavior,
2. collecting baseline data and academic information,
3. describing the context in which the behavior is observed,
4. completing a functional assessment form and/or behavior rating scales as appropriate,
5. conducting a direct observation, (6) developing a hypothesis, and
6. testing the hypothesis and modifying it as necessary (Barnhill, 2005).

Once a viable hypothesis has been established, the teacher can develop a behavioral intervention plan (BIP). Teachers are required to provide such assessment as a precursor to the development of an effective BIP (IDEA,

2004). Using the case example of Nicola, the high school senior with a specific phobia related to flying, an appropriate functional behavioral assessment will be described.

First, relative to identifying and describing the problem behavior, Nicola's teachers have agreed that the principal undesirable behavior she manifests involves her fear of flying. This perseverating behavior significantly impairs her ability to travel as well as the unique opportunity to attend a prestigious college.

Next, in terms of collecting baseline data and academic information, Nicola's teachers have begun to use a behavior checklist to record the number of times during the school day that Nicola talks about her fear of flying or asks questions to assuage her worries. She is currently speaking about her fear of flying and her quandary with attending Carnegie Melon, which her classmates find both annoying and "elitist" on average five times per school day, as observed by her teachers. In addition, Nicola's grades have been declining noticeably since she began to obsess about her flying dilemma.

It is also beneficial to describe the environments and setting demands in determining the function served by a problem behavior. It appears that Nicola is indiscriminate with whom she shares her fears. There does not seem to be a specific environmental trigger for her disclosures. Nicola seems to initiate a conversation involving her fears associated with a flight to Pittsburgh in an opportunistic way. She waits for a sympathetic listener and then 'unloads' her phobic preoccupation.

A functional behavioral assessment and a behavior rating scale were completed in addition to annotated teacher-conducted behavioral observations that are ongoing. After conducting a rigorous assessment to determine the function of the targeted maladaptive behavior, Nicola's teachers, in coordination with the school psychologist, developed a hypothesis about its function as a prerequisite to developing an effective behavioral intervention plan.

Based on the antecedent and current behavioral data, it seems logical to assume that Nicola will continue to obsess about her fear of flying until an effective school-based intervention is identified and employed. Nicola is currently receiving therapy from an outside psychologist who specializes in the treatment of phobias and will share her treatment regimen with Nicola's family as well as school personnel.

As a preliminary step, the proposed behavioral intervention plan will be implemented, monitored, and evaluated to ensure its efficacy. The multidisciplinary team, in conjunction with the outside psychologist, have recommended the implementation of what is hoped will be an effective school-based intervention. School personnel have just started to employ it, however, and they feel that more time is needed to assess its effectiveness in helping to mediate Nicola's perseverating fear. If it is successful, the treatment plan will be written into Nicola's Individualized Education Plan (IEP) as a behavioral intervention plan. A multidisciplinary team meeting with Nicola and her parents is scheduled for next month, to allow sufficient time before then for the newly instituted BIP to produce measurable results.

Developing an Effective Intervention Plan

The Individuals with Disabilities Education Act (IDEA, 2004) requires that school personal develop a behavioral intervention plan (BIP) for students who experience significant emotional or behavioral problems in school (Killu, 2008). This BIP should (1) be research-based and relevant; (2) only be implemented after informed consent has been provided by the child's parents; (3) document the steps of the intervention plan, including who will be responsible, when and where it will occur, and for how long; (4) establish realistic and measurable goals; and (5) establish a method to measure progress. After the BIP has been implemented for a reasonable period of time, it should be evaluated to determine the extent of behavior change and, thus, the plan's overall effectiveness (Crone et al., 2015).

For Nicola, our case example, a research-based intervention developed in response to the results of the behavioral assessment will most likely be a behavioral and/or cognitive-behavioral one. Considering all the recommended interventions described earlier in the chapter, the most effective intervention plan for use in school will include contingency management and verbal self-instruction. These two are preferred as they can be effectively and easily implemented and monitored in the classroom. The former technique was used initially in the classroom as it did not require training; the latter one was used after Nicola had been trained in verbal self-instruction.

Specifically, in Nicola's case, contingency management involved ignoring her when she began to perseverate about flying. Teachers and students were instructed to walk away or immediately change the subject. Teachers also were asked to maintain a behavior checklist to record the frequency of the target behavior (i.e., talking about or asking questions about flying and her preoccupation with Carnegie Mellon) in order to monitor the effectiveness of systematic ignoring.

The cognitive-behavioral management technique selected for use with Nicola involved a problem-solving strategy employing verbal self-instruction or self-talk as reinforcement. Explicitly, Nicola was taught to remind herself that flying is one of the safest modes of transportation and according to the U.S. National Safety Council "the odds of dying as a plane passenger at 1 in

205,552. That compares with the odds of 1 in 4,050 for dying as a cyclist; 1 in 1,086 for drowning, and 1 in 102 for a car crash" (Munro, 2018, n.p.).

Initially, Nicola was told to reinforce herself perceptibly (aurally) so that teachers could monitor her use of this intervention. Nicola was taught that when intrusive, morbid thoughts about flying permeated her mind, she was to remind herself about the inherent safety in flying with a commercial airline. Teachers were asked to provide prompts if Nicola perseverated about her fears or started to mention topics related to her impending flight to Pittsburgh. The prompt was "Nicola, remember that flying is safer than any other mode of transportation."

Finally, teachers were provided with contingencies should Nicola's specific phobia relapse. In this eventuality, teachers were prepared to help Nicola reassert control over the fear induced by various stimuli. Nicola, for example, will likely hear about a plane crash via the media, either through television programs, movies, or radio programs dealing with the subject. These exposures might result in a reemergence of fear-related behaviors, but Nicola can, once again, be reminded to use the strategies she has learned to regain control.

Tips for Teachers

- Do not allow the student to perseverate about her fear.
- Do not allow the student to monopolize your attention with her fearful obsession; instead, reinforce the prescribed intervention plan or use planned ignoring.
- Avoid deviating from the treatment plan by acceding to the student's requests to call home.
- Provide established prompts if the student appears fearful or mentions feeling afraid.
- Immediately change the subject if the affected student becomes preoccupied with her phobia.
- Be prepared to provide a rational explanation to help allay the child's fear.

Separation Anxiety Disorder

Case Example: Visalia, A Student with Separation Anxiety Disorder

Visalia and his family recently immigrated to the U.S. from Kazakhstan. They were fortunate to obtain legal immigration status and resident alien cards before immigration restrictions were imposed by the new administration. Visalia was regarded as a very bright, precocious student in his native Kazakhstan and had been promoted to the equivalent of grade seven in the U.S. educational system-a full two years ahead of his peers. Visalia also learned English in conjunction with his advanced-level schooling. He is more fluent in English than either of his parents or older sibling, a sister, Magheet.

The family, as are most families in Kazakhstan, is very close knit and interdependent. The need for family closeness and support is intensified by their arrival in a new country with strange and unfamiliar customs and language. Visalia has always enjoyed a very close relationship with his mother, Svetlana. As the only son, in a culture that is still staunchly patriarchal, Svetlana is especially protective of Visalia. Visalia is fluent in speaking, reading and writing in English and performed very well on placement tests in English and math; therefore, he was placed in a general 7th-grade classroom.

His American teachers and classmates noted a difference in his clothes and meal preferences but were warm and receptive. Visalia responded positively to the warm reception and politely thanked his classmates and teachers for welcoming him and including him as a bona fide member of the class. The students and teachers even dedicated a period of study to a question-and-answer session, during which they asked Visalia to tell them about life in Kazakhstan, including the culture, customs, language, and food. Visalia was delighted at the opportunity to share information about his native land. That is the Kazakh way. One never complains to others or shares how they are truly feeling, especially in a foreign country; respect is so important. To cause a 'loss of face' for your host is unthinkable!

In contrast, at home Visalia was sharing a different perception with his parents and Magheet. He especially disliked being separated from his mother, Svetlana. She was always a friend and counselor, who provided encouragement when he encountered a challenge in his studies and provided a safe harbor from the storms of his father, who could be very demanding and especially abusive when he drank. He felt overwhelmed with homesickness and longed to return to his homeland and the familiar way of life and right now his mother was, as always, his sole refuge and he simply couldn't be without her.

To compound Visalia's difficulties, because his father, a medical researcher, had just started a new job with a large research firm and his mother was currently unemployed, the family had no health care coverage to pay for counseling services even if such support had been considered.

Visalia's anxiety in attending school became so acute that he began experiencing nightmares in which the specter of the new school and teachers left him breathless, and he awoke in the night wet with perspiration and hyperventilating. On school-day mornings, Visalia would experience feelings of dread accompanied by nausea so severe he would actually throw up. Svetlana would dutifully inform the school that her son was ill and would not attend that day, which brought immediate relief to Visalia.

On very rare occasions when he attempted to go to school, Visalia could not bring himself to enter the building and feigned illness. His mother seemed to welcome this outcome and, as she had on every other occasion, brought him home immediately and called the school attendance office to confirm her son's persistent illness. This was becoming an untenable dependency brought on by his very real anxiety.

Response by Dr. Tucker, the School Principal

After a week of Visalia's absences, Dr. Tucker called Visalia's home to check on his disposition. Unfortunately, since Visalia's parents could not speak English, he was unable to communicate his concern and determined to obtain the services of an interpreter provided through the school district office. In the meantime, he alerted the school social worker and asked that she scheduled a visit with Visalia's parents accompanied by an approved interpreter.

Dr. Tucker had never encountered a problem like this before and, without any knowledge of Kazakh culture mistakenly assumed his parents were likely neglectful and ignorant of the U.S. law regarding mandatory school attendance until 16 years of age and were therefore unsupportive of their son's educational progress. A devout Catholic, Dr. Tucker had heard that Kazakhs were primarily Muslim and generally opposed to democratic principles, as citizens of a former Soviet Republic. He was determined to ensure that, going forward, Visalia would attend school every day and acquire the values inherent in the American way of life; after all, wasn't that why the family had immigrated to the US in the first place?

Mrs. Buell and Dr. Scofield's Approach

Mrs. Buell, the school social worker, in collaboration with Dr. Scofield, the school psychologist, have investigated the situation with Visalia and his family and understood the social dynamic caused by the extreme changes in location culture and lifestyle. They had visited Visalia and his family at their home and, with an interpreter, conveyed their genuine concerns to his parents. Showing sensitivity for the cultural differences they explained that they can help Visalia gradually adjust to the new school environment through a plan that would involve incremental exposure by first providing him with a Chromebook and an online connection service.

What both Mrs. Buell and Dr. Scofield noticed and remarked on later was the unusual interdependence between Svetlana and Visalia. They observed that Visalia sat beside his mother with his head on her shoulder for the entirety of their meeting with the family. Svetlana placed her arm around her son's shoulders and unconsciously stroked his hair. This behavior made them feel a little uncomfortable, but they reasoned that it might be endemic to the Kazakh culture.

An Attachment Perspective

The case of Visalia is more complicated due to the inclusion of a strong cultural component that could normalize his behaviors. One may not be able to apply the same standards of individual autonomy to a family from Kazakhstan. Prior to coming and in the early days in his new country, all seemed to be fine. There is, however, some important details about the family dynamic, such as Visalia's father's drinking and his abusive and demanding nature. Visalia now longs to return to his native country and cannot tolerate being separated from his mother.

These details would suggest a resistant (anxious) attachment style where a mother and son bond closely, in this case, as a form of protection from an abusive father. Was such a dynamic present before coming to the United States? Whether it be the difficulty adapting to a new culture or the family dynamic or a combination, the end result is Visalia has become a school refuser, a behavior little tolerated in his new country because of strict laws regarding school attendance. His panic-like and somatic symptoms related to attending school suggest extreme anxiety relieved only by his mother calling the school to tell then that Visalia would not be going.

From a behavioral perspective, one would say that mother is reinforcing the bad behavior. From an attachment perspective, one would infer that mother's needs are also being met by keeping her son at home. This is quite common in separation anxiety disorder. While at school, Visalia cannot know how mother is doing. This might be a frightening experience for a son who believes that his mother may be in danger from an abusive, possibly drunk, father and dealing with her own struggles of adapting to new culture. The interesting question is whether this family dynamic would have yielded the same result in Kazakhstan. One could argue that the familiarity of his native culture would have provided a sense of safety for Visalia and allowed him to attend school even though there was a history of insecure attachment, resistant type. Nevertheless, in this country, school refusal can lead to severe consequences for the family as evidenced in the response of the school's principal.

Dr. Tucker considers Visalia's excessive absences a form of neglect and therefore sends the school social worker to the home to apprise the family of the consequences, a report to the appropriate child welfare agency. After exhausting other possible remedies, Dr. Tucker would be well within his rights to do so; however, the details about his view of Kazakh/Muslim culture combined with his own devout Catholicism seem to support assimilation as his preferred mode of cultural adaptation rather than integration and/or the promotion of biculturalism. This, of course, would require some flexibility and deeper understanding of the difficulties inherent in cultural adaptation. Dr. Tucker is a 'by the book' kind of guy, and most principals need to be that way to avoid escalating problems in their school. On the other hand, he may be the product of an avoidant attachment history that wants to remove emotion from the equation and not make distinctions for those whose culture creates a different set of challenges.

Mrs. Buell and Dr. Scofield espouse a different approach, and one that is grounded in supported effective interventions for school refusers - start with getting Visalia connected to school in the least threatening way possible. Rather than demand he attend physically all classes every day, start small and build gradually till he overcomes his fear. Adults who are open-minded, flexible, try different approaches and appreciate cultural difference, usually the products of a secure attachment history. Additionally, if mother is also colluding in the school refusal, interventions must also be provided that would allow her son room to separate without causing her overwhelming anxiety. A referral to a skilled multicultural counselor would help but is complicated by the family's culture and lack of insurance; thus, the school is in the best position to help this family negotiate the sometimes-perilous waters of cultural adaptation.

Characteristics of Separation Anxiety Disorder

The focal point of SAD's symptomatology is a child's excessive fear and anxiety related to being away from home and/or attachment figures, and tremendous worry that harm will come to themselves or their parents while they are separated (Spence et al., 2018). Many children have fears of separation; therefore, it is important to distinguish between normal separation anxiety and that which constitutes a disorder. The differential diagnosis is made according to the type, severity, duration, and impact of symptoms on the child's functioning.

Most children who suffer from SAD develop symptoms between the ages of 8 and 12 years. Social phobia is more prevalent in adolescents than in children, yet the reverse is true for SAD (Spence et al., 2018). Symptom expression differs across age groups in that adolescents with SAD tend to report physical complaints on schools days; older children (ages 9 to 12) tend to report excessive distress upon separation, and younger children (ages 5 to 8) tend to report nightmares about separations (Silove et al., 2016).

Among clinical samples, SAD is highly comorbid with other anxiety disorders especially generalized anxiety disorder and specific phobia. About half of children who have SAD are also diagnosed with one of these two disorders, and about a third are diagnosed with depression (Mohammadi, Badrfan et al., 2020). Refusal to attend school is often a symptom of SAD; however, there can be many other causes and should not be considered an automatic indicator of the disorder (Elliott & Place, 2019). SAD is the most common diagnosis among school-refusing children (Elliot & Place, 2019).

When compared to other anxiety disorders in children, SAD has been found to have one of the highest recovery and lowest stability rates (Kodal et al., 2018). With the proper interventions, the prognosis of children who have SAD is very good. There has been some suspicion that SAD may be linked to the development of panic disorder and/or agoraphobia in adulthood (Silove et al., 2016). Although some adults with panic and agoraphobia report retrospectively the existence of SAD in childhood, this is not true in all cases. It is also possible that SAD in children can persist into adulthood, albeit at very low rates. Such persistence is most likely the result of biological factors and/or the experience of continued insecurities in primary attachments (Deveci Şirin, 2019).

Prevalence of Separation Anxiety Disorder

SAD is one of the most common anxiety disorders among children, estimated to constitute about a third of all anxiety disorders. Twelve-month prevalence rates are estimated to be 4 percent in children and 1.6 percent in adolescents (American Psychiatric Association, 2013). In general, studies have found higher rates of SAD in girls; yet boys who show symptoms of SAD are more likely to be referred to treatment (Santarossa et al., 2019; Zagoloff & Bernstein, 2017). In contrast to other anxiety disorders, for which children tend to come from middle to upper-middle-class families, 50 to 75 percent of children who have SAD come from low-socioeconomic-status families (Ramphal et al., 2020).

Etiology of Separation Anxiety Disorder

Silverman and Dick-Niederhauser (2004) identified six developmental pathways for SAD to include biological factors, cognitive factors, family processes, parental anxiety/depression, and caregiver stress. Following is a brief explanation along with empirical support for each of these factors.

Biological Factors

Overall, genes appear to play less of a role in the development of SAD than environment; however, a marked gender difference appears to exist in the heritability of SAD, with girls having a much higher estimate than boys (Bandelow et al., 2016; Silove et al., 2016). Higher rates of SAD exist among behaviorally inhibited children than among uninhibited children (Morales et al., 2017).

Cognitive Factors

In general, children who have anxiety disorders manifest more negative thinking than non-anxious comparison groups, and children who have SAD are no exception. Research has not discovered any cognitions that would distinguish children who have SAD from children who have other anxiety disorders (Silove et al., 2016).

Family Processes

Family dynamics and parenting styles have long been studied as factors in the development of SAD (Lavallee & Schneider, 2019). One long-standing consideration has been an enmeshed relationship between mother and child, the result of a dysfunctional marital relationship that forms a coalition between the two against father. Other psychodynamic explanations include the sexually inhibited mother who prefers the affective fulfillment she receives from the relationship with her child to that provided by her husband. The lack of research to support such hypotheses has turned attention away from psychodynamic explanations to the investigation of parenting styles.

According to Lavallee and Schneider (2019), two possible parenting pathways can lead to the development of SAD. The first is the pairing of a difficult child with an ambivalent caregiver who is only sporadically available to the child. This heightens the child's insecurity, who then seeks to attach him/herself to the caregiver in order to attain comfort.

This exaggerated effort to seek comfort from a parent reduces the possibility of the child's exploration, and the child becomes unaccustomed to dealing with new and different situations. In addition, the parent becomes anxious in dealing with the difficult child; the child picks up on this anxiety and seeks to comfort the parent by attaching himself to her. This increases the parent's anxiety, setting up a cycle of reinforcement for attachment behaviors.

The second pathway proposed is the parent's inability to provide a consistent model for dealing with stress. Often, this parent is ill, and the child becomes preoccupied with the health and well-being of the parent and eventually develops SAD.

Parental Anxiety and Depression. Children who have SAD are known to come from families with a high incidence of anxiety disorders and depression (Liberman & Öst, 2016).

Caregiver Stress. Caregiver stress, whether caused by the marital relationship or something outside the family, is known to result in insecure attachment between parents and their children (Dark-Freudeman et al., 2016). Some studies have sought to examine maternal employment and placement in daycare with insecure attachment. To date, no study has been able to show a direct link between the mother's employment status and attachment style (Choi et al., 2020). Parent background variables (age, degree of support, education) are more predictive of anxiety in mothers than employment status. Mothers who were younger, less educated, and received less support were found to be more anxious and have more insecure attachment styles (Choi et al., 2020).

Assessment of Separation Anxiety Disorder

Assessment of SAD is done through diagnostic interviews, clinician rating scales, and self-report measures.

Diagnostic Interviews

Diagnostic interviews may be either structured or unstructured. A structured interview, specific to the diagnosis of SAD, does not exist, but can be accomplished using more general interview formats to include

- Schedule for Affective Disorders and Schizophrenia for School-Age Children (K-SADS; Ambrosini, 2000)
- Diagnostic Interview Schedule for Children (DISC-IV; Schaffer et al., 2000)
- Child and Adolescent Psychiatric Assessment (CAPA; Angold & Costello, 2000)
- Interview Schedule for Children and Adolescents (ISCA; Sherrill & Kovacs, 2000)
- Children's Interview for Psychiatric Symptoms (ChIPS; Weller et al., 2000)
- Anxiety Disorders Interview Schedule for DSM-5, Child Version, Child, and Parent Interview Schedules (ADIS; Albano & Silverman, 2016).

A separate category of diagnostic interviews is pictorial in nature. Valla et al., (2000) developed the Dominic-R for White children and the Terry for African American children. There is also the Pictorial Instrument for Children and Adolescents (PICA-III-R; Ernst et al., 2000). A computer version also exists for the Dominic-R, and it has been translated into Spanish, German, and French. The PICA-III-R serves a broader range of children (ages 6 to 16) than the Terry or the Dominic-R. Most of the instruments mentioned above generally have good psychometric properties in relationship to the diagnosis of SAD and can be used with a degree of confidence.

Clinician Rating Scales

There are two clinician rating scales appropriate for assessing levels of anxiety to include the Anxiety Rating Scale for Children—Revised (ARC-R; Bernstein et al., 1996), and the Pediatric Anxiety Rating Scale (PARS; Research Units, 2002). Both measures yield overall anxiety scores, yet neither is designed to diagnose SAD specifically. The ARC-R, however, does have a separation anxiety item: "When you're not with your folks, are you afraid or worried about something bad happening to them?" It is recommended that clinician rating scales be used in conjunction with other assessment techniques.

Self-report Measures

There are a number of self-report measures that specifically assess for separation anxiety symptoms. The Multidimensional Anxiety Scale for Children (MASC; March et al., 1997) has a nine-item separation anxiety subscale with high internal consistency and test-retest reliability. Validity, both convergent and discriminate, has been supported by comparison with other anxiety and depression measures. The Screen for Child Anxiety Related Emotional Disorders (SCARED; Birmaher et al., 1997) has both child and parent versions with an eight-item separation anxiety subscale. It also has good psychometric properties. Lastly, the Spence Children's Anxiety Scale (SCAS; Spence et al., 2003) has a six-item SAD subscale, which has been shown to have adequate reliability and validity.

The use of self-reports as a screening tool and a first step toward the diagnosis of SAD is appropriate. These measures, however, suffer from the problems of all self-report measures: participants may want to present themselves in a favorable light (Perwien & Bernstein, 2004). These measures should always be used in conjunction with other forms of assessment.

The differential diagnosis of SAD can be problematic. Social phobia and school refusal due to other causes can complicate the diagnostic picture, as can the high comorbidity rates between SAD and other anxiety disorders.

Assessment should rule out any medical conditions that might simulate SAD, be multi-informant (child, parent, and teacher), and be multimethod (interview and at least one rating scale).

Treatment Strategies

Therapeutic Interventions

As mentioned previously, cognitive-behavioral therapy (CBT) is the treatment of choice for anxiety disorders in children and enjoys the most empirical support and investigation. Often, CBT is used in conjunction with other interventions, such as educational support, family management, and group therapy. Exposure therapy is a key component of the CBT approach (West et al., 2020).

Mendlowitz et al. (1999) studied the effects of a twelve-session group intervention on children who have anxiety disorders. Participants were assigned to one of three groups: child-only intervention, parent-only intervention, and parent-and-child interventions. Parent groups were basically psychoeducational, and the child groups incorporated a number of CBT interventions such as relaxation training, teaching of coping self-statements, and self-reinforcement. All three groups showed a decrease in anxiety-related symptoms, but the parent and child intervention groups improved the most. These results are consistent with other studies that support the added benefits of a parent component.

Six- and twelve-month follow-ups revealed that 70 percent of those who received a CBT workbook intervention did not meet the criteria for an anxiety disorder, compared to 96 percent of those who received the CBT intervention plus family management (Barrett et al., 2019). Flannery-Schroeder and Kendall (2000) investigated a group CBT intervention by comparing it to an individual CBT intervention for children aged 8 to14. After an eighteen-week workbook intervention, a significant number of children in both groups (73 percent of the individual modality versus 50 percent for the group modality) no longer met the criteria for an anxiety disorder when compared to a control group, in which only 8 percent did not meet the criteria.

Research has not supported a consistent significant difference between group and individual treatment for anxiety disorders in children. Both are effective, and some studies have shown one to be more effective than the other. Schools that have a number of children who have anxiety disorders can use a group intervention, knowing that research supports its effectiveness. Keep in mind, however, that the addition of a parent component has been shown to be the most effective together with either group or individual treatment.

Pharmacological Intervention

In recent years, selective serotonin reuptake inhibitors (SSRIs, e.g., Lexapro, Zoloft, Prozac) have been the pharmacological treatment of choice for SAD and several studies have supported their effectiveness (Dobson et al., 2019; Hussain et al., 2016; Strawn et al., 2018, 2019).

In summary, successful treatment of SAD is usually multimodal, consisting of some combination of individual and or group CBT, family therapy and psychoeducation, consultation with teachers, and possibly medication for the more dysfunctional cases. Presently, the first choice of medication appears to be the SSRIs. For SAD, as for many of the other anxiety disorders in children, training in contingency management for parents and school personnel is also necessary. Reinforcement for SAD symptoms must be eliminated and reserved for the successful management of anxious feelings.

School-Based Interventions

Teachers who have students in their classes who have SAD in their classes can, in collaboration with the school psychologist, develop effective behavioral interventions for the disorder. As we have consistently recommended, such intervention plans cannot be successfully developed without a thorough understanding of the root causes of the problem behavior; that is, what purpose is served by the behavior, and what contingencies help maintain it. This section offers a suggested functional behavioral assessment for Visalia, the student described in the case example.

Assessing the Problem

Following are the outcomes of the behavioral assessment for Visalia, a student who has SAD, organized according to the steps recommended by Barnes et al. (2020). In terms of identifying and describing Visalia's problem behavior, based on observation, that would be his constant desire to be with his mother, as manifested dramatically by his inability to leave her to attend school. He also exhibits the following symptoms associated with SAD when he is, or thinks he will be, separated from his mother; physiological symptoms such as nausea, hyperventilating, excessive perspiration; and psychological symptoms that include a pervasive sense of impending calamity or dread.

Relative to data collection, Visalia's teachers and the school psychologist have begun to work on a plan to facilitate his gradual reintroduction to school. Baseline data and academic information are currently unavailable because of Visalia's high rate of absenteeism. As Visalia is able to stay in school for progressively longer periods without panicking, his teachers will be able to provide duration recordings of his on-task behavior and length of time in school. Teachers will also maintain accurate records of Visalia's academic performance, starting from his first day back in school, noting improvement or regression.

In describing the demands exerted by environment and setting, Visalia's SAD symptoms are exacerbated by any attempt to separate him from his mother. Proximity to the school building and perceived "abandonment" there create the acute symptoms of anxiety.

A functional assessment form was completed after Visalia's first week back at school. In addition, behavioral assessment measures that included the Multidimensional Anxiety Scale for Children (MASC; March et al., 1997) as well as the Screen for Child Anxiety Related Emotional Disorder (SCARED; Birmaher et al., 1997) were administered to Visalia during his first trial week back in school (half-day schedule). The results from these self-report measures correlated highly with separation anxiety and provided a first step toward formal diagnosis.

Research has indicated the importance of a multimethod assessment that includes teacher and parent observations as well interviews conducted with the child, parent, and teacher. Observations of Visalia during the modified trial return to school revealed three phases of behavior: (1) initial separation anxiety characterized by physiological symptoms such as nausea, and persistent requests to be allowed to call his mother or to go home; (2) a gradual cessation of these symptoms followed by a willingness to be distracted and attempts to reengage in school work; and (3) a gradual escalation of the earlier symptoms of anxiety that seemed to dissipate when his mother returned to the school to take him home.

From a review of the precipitating event as well as antecedent and consequent stimuli, it appears that Visalia has developed SAD, the actual cause of which is hypothesized but not confirmed at this point. A systematic research-based approach must be developed and implemented to get Visalia back in the classroom and ensure that he stays there.

In cooperation with parents and related services providers, Visalia's teachers will implement the behavioral intervention plan that has been developed by the multidisciplinary team. After sufficient time has elapsed, the effectiveness of the plan will be assessed and, if necessary, it will be modified. If the intervention plan is revised or modified, the improved plan will be trialed; this process will continue until the desired results have been achieved.

Developing an Effective Intervention Plan

Recommended treatments for children who have SAD are multivariate. Cognitive-behavioral therapy, which involves various self-management techniques, which may include relaxation training, teaching of coping self-statements, and self-reinforcement, appears to be the single most effective intervention as well as the one most easily employed by the classroom teacher.

Visalia's therapist has developed an effective CBT approach to help reduce and regulate his separation anxiety and assist him in resuming a normal school routine. This intervention has been developed to be effectively implemented and monitored during the school day. Visalia's teachers have received training in supporting his treatment plan, which will be implemented both in school and at home.

As part of this plan, his teachers encourage Visalia to use coping self-statements such as "I am here with teachers who care about me and I'll see Mom at 3:30 p.m.," and "All the other kids love and often miss their mothers, but they can wait until school is over to see them," and finally, affirming statements such as "School is cool. I can learn new things and spend time with my friends." When these self-talk strategies are ineffective, such as during times of high stress and anxiety, Visalia can call his mother at a prearranged time and speak with her for a maximum of five minutes. This option is only available in an emergency when Visalia is feeling out of control. His teachers must confirm this exceptional circumstance.

In addition, his teachers are advised to remind Visalia of his mother's admonishment to him, that "Your [Visalia's] job is to attend school Monday to Friday all day, from 8:30 a.m. until dismissal at 3:30 p.m. If you feel sick or anxious during the day, you need to follow the plan." The plan specifies that if Visalia is truly ill, he will be referred to the school nurse, who will determine the severity of his illness and call his mother, who will then come and pick him up at her earliest opportunity. Visalia is to remind himself or be reminded that his mother must find work to help provide the money they need to live; he cannot stay home alone but must attend school. There are no other options.

The teaching staff and related services providers in the school are supportive of this plan. Visalia's mother has agreed to comply with the plan and will insist that he attend school for the full day. Thus, a coordinated plan that provides consistent reinforcement is in place both at school and at home. Parents and teachers have recourse to meet if some part of the behavioral intervention plan is not working or the plan needs to be revised.

Tips for Teachers

- Show support and encouragement and provide positive reinforcement for even small achievements such as going through the school day without a panic attack, emotional outburst, or request to call home.

- Maintain a firm position relative to the child's requests to call a parent or be sent home. The child will only begin to accept school attendance as compulsory if there are no alternatives.
- Give the child encouragement, let her know you truly care about her and are committed to her success in school. Help her feel valued and to have a sense of belonging.
- Encourage the child who has SAD to make friends in class. Provide cooperative learning opportunities, consider pairing the student with a peer tutor or "study buddy."
- If the student is absent for any reason, let her know when she returns that she was truly missed.
- If the student is absent for any reason, call home to let the child know you missed her and want her to return as soon as possible.
- Never shame or punish the child for an emotional outburst. Instead, try to comfort and isolate the student until she can regain her composure.
- Hold the student accountable for all work missed because of absence; the student must take responsibility for her school performance.
- Ensure that you understand the behavioral intervention plan instituted for this child and participate in it as directed. For example, if the key intervention is CBT, know the self-statements or prompts and encourage the student to use them; provide reinforcement where possible.
- Develop an effective rapport with the child's parents or guardians to enhance collaboration and facilitate the exchange of relevant information concerning the student's target behavior.
- Speak to your other students before the child who has SAD returns to your classroom, to help them understand their classmate's challenges and solicit their support.
- Perhaps most important to the success of a school-based intervention is the individualization of treatment. For the teacher, this means making a special effort to develop a positive relationship with the child. Research has supported the importance of this individualized approach in the reduction of SAD behaviors (Ollendick et al., 2006).

Social Anxiety Disorder (Social Phobia)

Case Example: Julia, a High School Student with Social Anxiety Disorder (SAD)

Julia has been told by many, from a very young age, that she has a natural talent for singing and a beautiful voice. Her mother, Joyce, in contrast, has always been very critical of her daughter, finding fault in everything she does, especially, her singing. Because of her vocal talent, Julie has been asked to sing solos at her church and does so regularly. People who do not normally attend church come when Julia is advertised to sing. Similarly, at school Julia has been considered a rising star. She has been a featured performer in all the school musical productions, vocal recitals, and choral presentations.

Julia seems to thrive on the success of her singing and the public adulation that she received as a result. Throughout her school career, until a recent event changed everything, Julia has participated in numerous talent shows and has even performed, to great acclaim, in a regional 'search for the rising star' show produced by a local television network. Not surprisingly, she placed first in every one of these contests.

Indeed, throughout her very young career, the only times she has ever struggled in reaching a note or performing a solo well were those in which her mother was present. Julia knew that she would need to endure a stinging critique of her performance that would invariably end with tears and a loss of self-confidence, making performing again a real challenge.

Despite Joyce's disparaging influence, Julia appeared to be on her way to a very successful singing career, until a recent calamity, that occurred in her high school musical production of *Jesus Christ Superstar,* in which she had been cast as Mary Magdalene. As Julia was preparing to sing the iconic number, "I Don't Know How to Love Him," she glanced furtively at the audience and caught her mother's critical grimace. All at once, she experienced a sensation of dread and was stricken with a fear that she would fail and humiliate herself, her mother, the cast, and the school in front of an audience of several hundred. When her musical introduction finished, she froze, paralyzed with fear. The musical director noticed her panic-stricken face and thinking that Julia simply missed her cue or temporarily blanked on the lyric, signaled the conductor to replay the song's introduction. When Julia failed to pick up her cue the second time, she was quickly ushered off stage and the actors continued with the next scene. Julia was asked what happened by the director and she replied that she did not know, she just blanked, and then began to sob uncontrollably. It was clear that Julia was unable to continue the performance and was immediately replaced by her understudy.

Julia's cast members were very supportive and tried to console her after the performance and while Julia appreciated their genuine attempts to buoy her up, she sensed somehow that she could never again perform in front of an audience. Her dream of becoming a professional soloist was over. Julia's memory of her mother's displeasure, her public breakdown, and the subsequent humiliation and embarrassment it caused, would haunt her for years.

Response from Joyce, Julia's Mother

Julia's breakdown confirmed for her mother that Julia's vocal talent was never going to get her on the professional stage. Joyce had once been extolled for having a lovely voice, but her dream of becoming a professional performer had been dashed by a local critic. She was determined not to let that happen to her daughter. Joyce would ensure that Julia's illusions were dispelled early on so that she would be spared her mother's suffering. After all, who knew Julia better than her mother!

The Music Director's Response

Mrs. Smithland, director of the recent musical, *Jesus Christ Superstar,* has a different point of view. A few days after Julia's 'fiasco' onstage, Mrs. Smithland asked to meet with her. Asked how she felt about performing again, Julia tearfully insisted that the very thought of performing in front of an audience made her feel ill and she actually began to experience the same sense of dread as when she froze on stage during the live performance! Mrs. Smithland shared a similar personal experience and a few other anecdotes, recalling other performers she had directed or coached who experienced stage fright. She also assured Julia that everyone's experience was unique and, in time, her fear might be overcome with therapy and support. Mrs. Smithland provided the name and number of a therapist she had used and found very helpful in the past, just in case Julia was interested in exploring that type of support.

What Mrs. Smithland did not mention, to spare Julia embarrassment, was that she, too, had noticed her mother's disparaging look. In fact, several times, she had observed the detrimental effect Joyce's presence had on her daughter's performances. She attributed it to mother-daughter envy or perhaps something even more insidious, but since she was not a qualified psychologist, she thought it best to hold her tongue.

After much reflection, Julia decided to see the therapist referred by Mrs. Smithland. The therapist, who specialized in treating persons with social anxiety disorder (SAD), spent several sessions exploring Julia's acute fear of performing, which caused her to experience a deep sense of loss and to question her self-worth. Now she felt that part of her life had been taken away for reasons she did not understand. What the therapist was beginning to learn, as they talked, was Julia's deep-seeded need for her mother's approval and an infallible belief in her judgement.

An Attachment Perspective

You need not be a mastermind in psychology to know that a parent's constant and consistent criticism will result in an insecure child. No amount of talent (and Julia had plenty of it) can overcome such criticism even though Julia enjoyed years of early success and admiration from her audiences. What makes this case interesting is that the mother's purpose was to prevent her daughter from having the same experience, that of her hopes dashed by a harsh critic. Of course, Joyce is guilty of overidentification with her daughter - what happened to me will happen to you! Joyce operates out of fear and instills fear into her daughter to sabotage her career as a singer.

What the reader may see as spiteful behavior, Joyce sees as loving her daughter and protecting her. Parental protection overdone is always an indicator of an insecure/resistant/anxious attachment style. This hyperactivates the attachment system and limits the exploratory system. Julia will no longer be able to explore the world of singing with its infinite challenges and possibilities. Joyce's belief that Julia could never handle a career so publicly evaluated is probably correct because the seeds of insecurity were sown early on and continued through her development.

The reader may be thinking about another possibility in that Joyce sabotaged her daughter's career not out of fear, but resentment. Because she failed, so will her daughter. This dynamic, however, is less evident of a resistant attachment style and more evident of a disorganized one. Fear, not anger, seems to be the hallmark emotion of what is taking place between Julia and her mother.

There is no doubt that therapy can help Julia and probably needs to be more psychodynamic in orientation for Julia to work through the complicated relationship with her mother. The danger is that Julia's mother might work also towards sabotaging the therapy her daughter is receiving. Mrs. Smithland, the music director, while supportive and nurturing toward Julia, can only do so much. The therapist can take on the role of a surrogate mother figure offering Julia many of the qualities that were absent in her mother that could ensure a successful career and allow Julia to handle the public criticism that goes along with such a career. Insecure attachment styles can be reorganized when the world provides alternate experiences. More often than not, those experiences are provided by teachers!

Characteristics of Social Anxiety Disorder

The child who suffers from a social phobia is often referred to as shy. Much of the research on social phobia has been done with adults. Approximately 1 percent of the adult population is diagnosed with social phobia, but most experts agree that social phobia has its precursors in childhood, and the prevalence rate is likely the same or higher in children (Beidel et al., 2014). Unlike some of the other anxiety disorders, the most common age of onset for social phobia is adolescence, particularly early to middle adolescence. Beidel et al. (2014) studied fifty children (age range 7 to 13 years; average age 10 years) with social anxiety disorder and reported their five most feared situations to include reading in front of the class, a musical or athletic performance, joining in on a conversation, speaking to adults, and starting a conversation.

Approximately 60 percent of socially distressing events occur at school. When distressed, children who have social phobia manifest physical symptoms such as heart palpitations, shakiness, flushes, chills, sweating, and nausea (Beidel et al., 2014). Social anxiety can be distinguished from other forms of social withdrawal when it is ego-dystonic, that is, the child recognizes a problem and wishes that he or she were not that way. The socially anxious child wants to engage socially and feels distressed at not being able to do so.

In a sample of preadolescent children who have social anxiety, Beidel et al. (1999) found that 60 percent also had one of several other disorders to include generalized anxiety disorder (10 percent), attention-deficit hyperactivity disorder (10 percent), specific phobia (10 percent), selective mutism (8 percent), separation anxiety disorder (6 percent), obsessive-compulsive disorder (6 percent), depression (6 percent), panic disorder (2 percent), or adjustment disorder with anxious and depressed mood (2 percent).

In adolescence, the disorder may take the additional forms of poor social networks, underachievement in school and work, and poor social skills (Davidson, 2016). Age of onset appears to be the strongest predictor of recovery from social anxiety. In retrospective studies with adults, those who reported developing social anxiety after the age of 13 were nine times more likely to recover than those who reported an onset before the age of 7 (Davidson, 2016).

Etiology of Social Anxiety Disorder

Most experts agree that the development of social anxiety disorder is multi-factorial and the risk of developing social anxiety during high school increases with the number of factors. Chartier et al. (2003) studied those with social phobia between the ages of 15 and 64 and found risk factors to include:

- Lack of a close relationship with an adult
- Not being the first born (males only)
- Marital conflict in the family of origin
- Parental history of mental disorder
- Moving more than three times as a child
- Childhood physical and sexual abuse
- Juvenile justice and child welfare involvement
- Running away from home
- Failing a grade
- Special education before age 9
- Dropping out of school

Traditionally, risk factors have been categorized as either psychological or biological.

Psychological Factors. Among the psychological factors, direct conditioning, social learning, and information transfer are considered pathways for the development of social phobia (Beidel & Turner, 2007). A significant number of adults attribute their social phobia to a direct traumatic event (Bjornsson et al., 2020). Although it may be a risk factor, direct conditioning is not sufficient to explain the development of social phobia for two simple reasons – a significant number who reported a conditioning event did not develop a social phobia and among those who developed a social phobia, a significant number reported no such conditioning event (Beidel & Turner, 2007). Having a parent who is shy, reticent, or avoidant of social situations is also considered a risk factor because of the modeling and social learning it provides to the child (Bjornsson et al., 2020).

Information transfer, the third psychological factor in the etiology of social anxiety disorder, refers to family communication patterns through which the child may have received messages emphasizing shame and/or an exaggerated concern for the opinions of others (Norton & Abbott, 2017). The current focus is on parent-child interactions to determine the significance of information transfer in the development of social anxiety and avoidance behavior.

Biological Factors. As in the case of other anxiety disorders, genetic disposition and temperament are thought to play a role in the development of social anxiety. Many experts believe there is an interaction effect between biological and environmental factors. If a child is behaviorally inhibited by temperament, a parent may feel compelled to protect the child from challenging social situations and therefore reinforce what is a genetic disposition.

Assessment of Social Anxiety Disorder

Many children shy away from strange situations until they gain a sense of comfort, which makes the assessment of clinical levels of social anxiety somewhat challenging; therefore, when assessing for social anxiety, the developmental age of the child must be taken into consideration. Younger children, for example, have stranger anxiety, which normally decreases as the child gets older.

Another difficulty is differentiating social anxiety disorder from other disorders, particularly generalized anxiety disorder. The key to differentiation is the theme of the child's anxiety. With social anxiety, fears are limited to a negative evaluation, rejection by others, or humiliating oneself in front of others. Some children may suffer from clinical levels of social anxiety, which can be explained by environmental factors such as living in a high-crime neighborhood, coming from an abusive home, and so on.

An investigation into the child's school history may help to distinguish anxiety that is more reactive to environmental stimuli as opposed to being a long-standing part of the child's presentation. With these considerations in mind, many of the self-report and behavioral assessment scales recommended previously to diagnose clinical levels of anxiety can also be used to diagnose social anxiety disorder.

Treatment Strategies

Many of the empirically supported treatments for children who have social anxiety disorder have very small sample sizes, because they are usually part of a much larger sample of those with anxiety disorders in general.

Individual/Group Treatment. Albano et al. (1995) were the first to develop Group Cognitive-Behavioral Treatment for Adolescents, otherwise known as CBT or GCBT-A, designed specifically for socially phobic children. In a design of five case studies, Albano et al. (1995) found that after treatment, four children had subclinical levels of social anxiety. As with fears in general, exposure therapy is a treatment of choice and, for the most part, has been successful (Radtke et al., 2020). Peer-based interventions that include peer paring and social skills training have been used successfully for social anxiety disorder (Coplan et al., 2018).

Family Treatment. As with other anxiety disorders, parent education and contingency management for children who have social phobia can be an important part of the treatment process (Asbrand et al., 2016).

Pharmacological Treatment. Like many of the CBT studies, pharmacological studies use samples of children who have a variety of anxiety disorders. It is difficult in some of these studies to decipher drug effectiveness specifically for children who have social anxiety. Several studies, however, have supported the effectiveness of SSRI's for children and adolescents with social anxiety disorder (Frick et al., 2018, Frick et al., 2020; Jakubovski et al., 2019; Nordahl et al., 2016).

School-Based Interventions

Once again, after carefully reviewing the information provided in the previous section about the characteristics of and recommended treatment strategies for this disorder, teachers and caregivers should conduct a systematic evaluation as a precursor to developing an effective behavioral intervention. The intervention process is therefore two-staged, consisting of a data-based assessment and a relevant research-based intervention based on the target behavior identified in the assessment.

Assessing the Problem. As with any case involving a child who exhibits inappropriate or unproductive behavior, teachers should conduct an analysis of behavior. A hypothetical assessment based on Julia's case is provided below.

The first step in the evaluative process is to identify and describe the problem behavior. Julia had recently begun to avoid public situations, ostensibly fearing criticism and rejection. This has had a negative effect on her school performance because she is unwilling to participate in musical or theatrical productions, which are a key part of her junior year electives. As noted, Julia has lost interest in the performing arts, which her teachers believe was instrumental in helping her develop and maintain self-esteem. As a result of these behavioral changes, Julia has become excessively self-conscious and introverted.

A second step in the process is for teachers to collect behavioral and academic information. Accordingly, Julia's teachers report that she is unable to participate in public events, becoming panicky and complaining of nausea. She expresses a palpable fear of being criticized or judged for her ineptitude. This pervasive fear of social situations generalizes to classroom as well as extracurricular activities and includes interactions with peers as well as with teachers and other adults.

Julia's recent refusal to participate in small-group or cooperative activities has negatively affected her academic performance in several of her classes. Prior to the onset of the disorder, for example, Julia consistently earned an A in social studies and English; afterwards, her grades in both these favorite subjects dropped to B-. Moreover, her withdrawal from and avoidance of social situations has adversely affected her self-esteem and eroded her confidence.

The third stage in the process entails describing the environmental and setting demands. Julia seems very uncomfortable presenting or reading in front of the class. Similarly, she has dropped out of the school chorus and drama club, explaining to the music and theater directors that she has to make up schoolwork. In addition, her teachers and mother report that she appears to be very uncomfortable speaking with adults. She 'clams up,' responding with one- or two-word utterances when asked a question. Classmates, too, have noticed a significant change in Julia—from gregarious and outgoing to shy and retiring, except in the presence of her mother or very close friends.

As the next step in the assessment process, a functional behavioral assessment was completed in October of last year. In addition, the school psychologist administered a self-report measure, the Spence Children's Anxiety Scale (SCAS) (Spence, 1998), as well as the Fear Inventory—Children (Cautela et al., 1983). The results of these tests helped to confirm the diagnosis of social anxiety disorder or social phobia. The data from these assessments provided the information necessary to develop an effective behavioral intervention plan.

Julia's mother and teachers maintained anecdotal records based on observations of anxiety displayed in social situations. These observations revealed an adolescent who has experienced a dramatic behavioral change, moving from gregarious and outgoing to guarded and fearful in social situations. They further confirm the results of behavior rating scales as well as Julia's own expressions of fear and social anxiety.

After reviewing the data as well as identifying the environmental triggers, it appears that Julia has developed social anxieties in relation to classroom and extracurricular performance that involve, in particular, her singing. This condition is further aggravated by the need to speak to adults, or a group of individuals and the conversation always seems to center on what a vocal talent she possesses. Based on this hypothesis, it seems prudent to identify and implement an effective school-based intervention as soon as possible.

In response to the development of the hypothesis described above, it is critical that Julia's caregivers select an appropriate, research-based intervention that will help reduce her fear of participating in social situations and especially in performing as a singer. In response to this need, a behavioral intervention plan will be developed and implemented for a prescribed duration, long enough to be able to assess its effectiveness. Necessary modifications will be made, if warranted, after evaluating the success of the plan.

Developing An Effective Intervention Plan. Crone et al. (2015) have identified the following key components needed for an effective behavioral intervention plan:

1. Learn how the student perceives or experiences events in his or her environment.
2. Invest in preventing reoccurrences or problem behavior.
3. Include instructional objectives, realizing that teachers can and should provide relevant social skills instruction in class.
4. Always reward positive behavioral responses.
5. Develop contingency plans that cover most emergencies relating to the problem behavior and the individual responsible.

After reviewing recommended interventions for adolescents and children who have social phobia, the two that were identified and implemented as most appropriate for Julia included a group cognitive-behavioral intervention and family treatment. The first intervention selected was social effectiveness therapy for children (SET-C), which consists of group social skills training, peer-generalization experiences, and individual in-vivo exposure.

In conjunction with SET-C, Julia joined a group of adolescents who shared similar social phobias and participated in musical events, presentation activities with the support of peers, and practiced speaking to adults as well as initiating conversation. Julia's teachers played a significant role in this treatment strategy by providing supported and safe opportunities for her to engage in rehearsed class discussions and solo performances.

The SET-C intervention was conducted in conjunction with family treatment that involved Julia's mother. This extracurricular intervention involved teaching Julia's mother about the causes and characteristics of social phobia as well as relevant contingency management and the identification and avoidance of malcontingencies. Here, too, Julia's teachers played an important role by inviting her mother to classroom presentations or small recitals that featured her daughter. In addition, they encouraged Julia's mother to share her insights and offer suggestions regarding Julia's behavior at home.

This bimodal treatment plan has achieved measurable success in helping Julia overcome her social anxiety. To date, she has made significant progress in initiating conversations with adults and groups of peers. Julia is also able to sing again in front of a small group of classmates. Her progress has been steady and consistent. Julia's therapist and teachers, as well as her friends, have expressed delight at her newfound confidence.

Tips for Teachers

Classroom interventions that may be helpful to a student who has social phobia, like Julia, include the following.

- Assign the individual a study buddy to help him with coursework and projects.
- Encourage the student to participate in small-group discussions of four to six students.
- Encourage the individual to find outlets for nonacademic skills and interests, typically ones that involve membership in after-school programs and extracurricular activities.
- Make a point of speaking to the student every day in both academic and social contexts to desensitize the student and demystify the experience of speaking with an adult or authority figure.
- Help the student identify school- or community-based clubs that help individuals who are socially withdrawn or shy gain self-confidence and poise (e.g., the toast masters club; the school debating society; the speakers' bureau; drama club).
- Teachers might consider presenting a unit or a series of lessons on verbal and nonverbal communication skills that would benefit all students in the class, especially a student who has social phobia.
- Teachers should avoid embarrassing the student or inadvertently creating anxiety by arbitrarily calling on the student without advance notice. Teachers should consider rehearsing a planned question with the student before class, to allow the individual to prepare and then be able to respond with confidence. Similarly, the teacher and student might establish a nonverbal cue that would signal the teacher's intention to ask the student to respond. The student could then signal her willingness to do so or decline surreptitiously and thereby avoid embarrassment.

From the Field

Justin R., Student

Justin is an 18-year-old white male from a major metropolitan area in the Northeast. He has been attending the Apex School, a private residential treatment facility for adolescents experiencing learning and adjustment difficulties, for the past two years. Justin has clearly benefited from the services offered as well as the relationships formed during his stay at Apex, and, with graduation imminent and having been accepted to a prestigious university, he shares some of his insights regarding this experience.

Justin, can you provide a brief overview of the challenges you faced in public school and your referral for special education services?

In public high school, I suffered from clinical depression and anxiety. The depression was not diagnosed until fifth grade and the anxiety not until late middle school. I would refuse to attend school because I was terrified to attend, but for no legitimate reason.

What circumstances led you to choose or be referred to a special school for your high school education?

After being sent to Restwell, a psychiatric facility, for having thoughts of suicide, I was sent to multiple alternative high school settings. After that, I was sent to the psychiatric ward of Saint Peter's Hospital twice for the same suicidal desires. I was held back in eighth grade because my mom didn't think I was ready for high school, and after half a year in public high school, along with other attempts at alternative settings, I was sent to Apex School, a residential treatment facility.

Can you provide a brief description of life at this special high school? What is a typical day like?

We are woken up at 7:30 a.m. by the staff member that stays in our cottage (or dorm) overnight. At around 8:00 breakfast opens downstairs, and we are required to be out of our rooms by 8:30. Homeroom begins at 8:45, first period at 9:00. We have 50-minute periods, seven a day, with school ending at 2:55. We have a point system, boys starting with three points at the beginning of the day. If you misbehave or break a rule, a staff member will remove points from your point sheet and the staff members in your cottage will impose appropriate penalties.

At 3:00 we return to our cottages and get settled. By 3:15 we should be out of our rooms and attending one of the various activities around the campus.

Activities generally close at 5:00, and the different cottages have dinner at different times, the earliest being 5:00, the latest being 6:30. After dinner, we have a 45-minute quiet time where we are required to stay in our rooms. If we aren't up to date in our classes, we have double quiet time, requiring the student to be in his room for an hour and a half. We are allowed to stay out of our cottages until 9:00 and must be in our rooms by 10:45. Lights out is at 11:00 p.m.

In your opinion, what are the major drawbacks to receiving a high school education in this setting?

There are many restrictions set in place that greatly limit the enjoyment of daily life; for instance, we are only allowed to be off-campus until 5:00 p.m., but it takes about 15–30 minutes to get into town or to the mall, allowing for only about an hour or so to ourselves. My cottage is given specific shower times which becomes problematic when I have very limited time to spend with some friends. I must shower at my shower time or suffer consequences, even though I know I will be responsible and can be accountable for showering on my own. Also, we must attend dinner. I usually do not eat the food served at dinner (I am a very picky eater), but I must go down and sit with my cottage for 15 minutes, regardless of whether I am eating there or not. In my experience, most drawbacks are in the residential aspect, though there are academic drawbacks, as well. As an example, there are very few teachers to teach any specific subject, meaning that if you don't get along with any given teacher, or maybe you aren't suited to that teacher's teaching style, you are limited in your ability to switch classes.

By way of contrast, can you share the major benefits of such an educational experience?

The limitations described prior are not entirely negative. I, as a senior, have overcome most of the challenges I faced earlier in my attendance. When I first arrived at Apex, I still suffered from depression and did not care much about myself or my appearance. I would not shower regularly because I did not think that people realized or cared that I did not clean myself. After the shower times were implemented, I began to shower regularly, and started to pay more attention to other people that did not clean themselves. It allowed me to understand the importance of taking care of myself and the effect it has on how people view me and treat me.

It would be very helpful for our readers if you could provide representative examples of each of the following:

- **A teaching approach or approaches that you found counterproductive or unhelpful:** With such small class sizes, teachers are able to cater to individual students that may not understand the material. While this is in a sense a positive thing, the students that are able to learn faster or grasp the concepts of a certain content area better than others are the ones now left behind, so to speak. They are unable to proceed through the class as quickly as they would be able to or would like to.
- **A teaching approach or approaches that you found very helpful in improving your social and academic experience at this high school:** One of the first things students need to get used to at Apex is the fact that we are on a first-name basis with nearly every teacher. The teachers here are not only our teachers; they are our friends. At a public high school, things are very formal. Sometimes students are reluctant to ask for assistance from a teacher. Maybe they are embarrassed to do so. Asking a friend for help is much easier. It also eases tension in the classrooms. Students also feel more obliged to do work for their friends than for their teachers.

Finally, nothing is more instructive than an anecdote or personal story that highlights an individual's most significant life experiences. Could you take a moment to reflect on and share such an experience from your life as a student at this high school?

I would say that the school as a whole has been a significant life experience. I can't put my finger on one specific event that had some profound effect on me, but I know that this school definitely provided me with an experience that I would not have received in a public high school. Living exclusively with students, for example, who are generally more difficult to live with than many, if not most, of the students that I will encounter in college has prepared me for the worst, so to speak. My transition to college will be easier because I am used to living away from home, as well. But most importantly, it has provided me with the ability to graduate. This in and of itself is reason enough for me to appreciate the time I have spent there.

Summary

In this chapter, we have examined three of the more prevalent childhood phobias, specific phobia, separation anxiety disorder, and social anxiety disorder. Our three real-life case examples provided vicarious experiences to use in applying appropriate identifying criteria, becoming familiar with effective assessments used in diagnosis, learning about recommended research-based interventions, and, most important, gaining practice in the development of relevant behavioral intervention plans predicated on the results of purposeful behavioral assessments. In each case, the most effective treatments turned out to be behavioral and cognitive-behavioral interventions, but the critical factor in effective intervention must always be the teacher's familiarity with the specific behavioral needs of the child. This knowledge is best determined through the application of a thorough behavioral assessment that will ensure the development of an effective behavioral intervention plan.

Nicola's specific phobia expressed in a morbid fear of flying, Visalia's sudden and seemingly inexplicable panic at the possibility of being separated from his mother, and Julia's dread of social situations and performing after her panic attack on stage are examples of childhood phobias that teachers will encounter in their classrooms today. Indeed, children are bombarded every day with the fears and stressors exerted by a world that is increasingly perceived as less safe, one in which their country is at war with terror, and media that constantly reinforce these fears with news and images of existential threats and impending disasters. Under these conditions, it is inevitable that many children will develop phobias as they are vicariously affected by the proliferation of our adult fears.

In response to the anticipated increase in students who are diagnosed with phobias, it is incumbent on today's teachers to be equipped to help identify and treat these debilitating disorders as they arise in the classroom.

Focus Questions Revisited

Suppose a child who has a specific phobia, such as Nicola, who has a paralyzing fear of flying, was assigned to your class. What might you do to facilitate her acceptance and integration?

A Sample Response: It would be important to invite the school psychologist to explain and discuss phobias and anxiety disorders with the class and then advise them that a student who has a specific phobia will be joining them shortly. Depending on the maturity of the students in the class, describing the characteristics of Nicola's phobia could be helpful. It would also be vital to provide strategies that have been effective in helping Nicola control her fears and solicit their support. It might be beneficial to ask for a volunteer to act as a class partner or peer mentor to assist Nicola in acclimating to the classroom. Last, pointing out that we all experience fears and anxieties that others might regard as silly or unnecessary; nevertheless, to those affected, these seemingly harmless triggers can be very troubling. For these reasons and more, all individuals involved should be understanding and supportive of others' struggles to overcome fears.

List some specific fears experienced by children. What differentiates the pathological ones that characterize a phobia from those that are common to many children who can function successfully without special treatment?

A Sample Response: Some fears might compel a child to avoid or escape certain situations; for example, avoiding places in the home (e.g., the basement) that are perceived as scary, keeping the light on when sleeping or insisting on sleeping with parent(s) to escape darkness, avoiding eating for fear of choking, refusing to attend a doctor's appointment for fear of a needle, and so on. Cognitive responses usually include scary thoughts ("I'm afraid"), negative self-statements ("I can't do it"), and the expectation of some catastrophic result ("I'm going to die from the lightning"). Although most children experience these feared events to some extent and at some time, the degree to which they prevent the child from engaging in daily activities such as school and home routines, as well as experiencing a sense of well-being, demarcates a phobia.

How common is separation anxiety disorder in children? How can a teacher determine whether a child's symptoms represent a bonafide disorder or will simply disappear in time?

A Sample Response: Separation anxiety disorder is one of the most common anxiety disorders among children, estimated to constitute about a third of all anxiety disorders. Prevalence rates have been estimated to be between 3 and 5 percent in children and adolescents. A recent study found the prevalence rate to be 3.6 percent (American Psychiatric Association, 2013).

As with any emotional or behavioral disorder, the identification of a bonafide disorder is accomplished by examining the anxiety associated with leaving a caregiver or the security and comfort of home that is typical of children who are the same age as the individual of concern. If that child's anxiety is significantly greater (intensity), experienced much more frequently (frequency), and has been manifest for a significantly long time (duration)—e.g., six months or longer— then a teacher will have reasonable cause to suspect an anxiety disorder and refer the child for evaluation by a qualified diagnostician (psychologist or psychiatrist).

What can a classroom teacher do to help a child who is experiencing separation anxiety disorder?

A Sample Response: As with any behavioral intervention, the classroom teacher must comply with the plan developed by the IEP team incorporating the recommendations of the school psychologist. To the extent feasible, the classroom teacher should implement this plan to help the affected child in the classroom. In general, teachers working with students who are experiencing SAD should provide good instruction and engage them in meaningful work. In addition, students who have SAD should not be allowed to call home other than at previously arranged times that do not interfere with instruction or the students' class schedule. The teacher should provide clear expectations that the individual will remain and participate in classroom activities for the duration of the school day. In the event of tantrums or more severe behavioral manifestations, a prearranged emergency plan should be initiated. Such a plan might include sending the student to the school psychologist's office or to the school nurse to help the individual to regain self-control and decompress.

How do you define social phobia or social anxiety disorder as it pertains to school-age children?

A Sample Response: Children who have social phobia manifest physical symptoms when under distress, such as heart palpitations, shakiness, flushes, chills, sweating, and nausea. Social anxiety can be distinguished from other forms of social withdrawal when it is ego-dystonic. The socially anxious child wants to engage socially and feels distressed at not being able to do so. The child who suffers from social phobia typically may be referred to as shy. In adolescence, the disorder may take the additional forms of poor social networks, underachievement in school and work, and poor social skills. Age of onset appears to be the strongest predictor in recovery from social anxiety. Unlike some of the other anxiety disorders, the most common age of onset for social phobia is adolescence (Beidel et al., 2014), particularly early to middle adolescence.

What are the five most feared situations for children who have social anxiety disorder, and how can a teacher facilitate the student's participation in them?

A Sample Response: Beidel et al. (1999) studied fifty children (age range 7 to 13 years; average age 10 years) with social anxiety disorder and reported their five most feared situations as reading in front of the class, musical or athletic performance, joining in on a conversation, speaking to adults, and starting a conversation. Using reading in front of the class and starting a conversation as examples, a teacher might facilitate the student's participation in them in the following ways.

- **Reading in front of the class**. One way to facilitate this desired participative goal is to have the student read to a friend to develop the self-confidence to take the next step, which would involve reading to a small group of select peers who are supportive of the individual's goal. Finally, after the individual expresses sufficient confidence, he or she would be scheduled by the teacher to read a rehearsed passage in front of the entire class. The teacher would also prepare the class by apprising them of the student's fear and enlisting their support in being an attentive, sympathetic audience.
- **Starting a conversation**. The student could be provided with a set of generic conversation starters, or questions that require more than a yes/no response. These could include questions about the weather, such as "How are you enjoying the lovely weather?," or about some common themes relative to school such as "What do you think about the new principal?," "How are you coming with the history paper?," or sport- or activity-related questions such as "What do you think of the Yankees' chances of winning the World Series this year?" Once the individual is adept at starting a conversation, they should then be taught ways to sustain one by asking probing questions that elicit voluntary elaborations. These kinds of questions should encourage the social partner to share some personal information. This provides opportunities to extend the dialogue and facilitates reciprocity, the hallmark of true conversation.

Describe the Social Effectiveness Therapy for Children (SET-C) cognitive behavioral intervention and identify its strengths in helping students, like Julia, who have social anxiety disorder.

A Sample Response: SET-C consists of group social skills training, peer-generalization experiences, and individual in-vivo exposure. The focus of this intervention is to expose the individual with SAD to controlled, safe group experiences. Students like Julia, who lack confidence and become anxious when faced with social situations that carry risk, such as when public speaking or performing, can practice with a sympathetic audience that consists of students who are similarly affected. Once the individual feels comfortable speaking or performing in front of the peer group, they are ready to engage in a similar real-life experience, with the support of the therapist and group members. To ensure success, the initial experience or trial should be well-rehearsed and brief; for example, Julia might choose to read a favorite short poem to the class, demonstrate a simple dance step, or play an abbreviated selection on the piano as a first step. Emboldened by this success, Julia's next public experiences would involve incrementally greater risk and longer public exposure; ideally, in time, her self-confidence would be fully restored.

Key Terms Used in the Chapter

Classical Conditioning:
A paradigm in which an unconditioned stimulus is paired with a conditioned stimulus to evoke a conditioned response; for example, a child who approached a dog and was bitten would learn to avoid all dogs and/or places where there might be dogs.

Vicarious Conditioning:
An operant response that is strengthened or weakened as a result of consequences that are either reinforcing or punishing. For example, children's fears may get them what they want—care and comfort from their parents.

Sympathetic Nervous System:
A part of the autonomic nervous system that becomes more active during stress. It is responsible for the fight-or-flight response to fear-provoking situations.

Discriminate Validity:
The ability of a test or scale to discriminate a concept (e.g., fears) from another concept that is theoretically different and should not be similar.

Reliability:
The ability of a measure to produce consistent results. Test-retest is one way to determine reliability.

External Validity:
The ability of a test or experiment to generalize to the broader population and not be limited to the controlled, idiosyncratic settings in which the measure was administered.

Selective Serotonin Reuptake Inhibitors (SSRIS):
A class of drugs used in the treatment of depression and anxiety. They block the reuptake of serotonin, the neurotransmitter responsible for mood regulation, making it more available to the brain.

Chapter 6

Post-Traumatic Stress Disorder, Generalized Anxiety Disorder, and Obsessive-Compulsive Disorder

Focus Questions

- *Which related services providers and other knowledgeable persons can provide critical advice and support to the teacher of a child who has posttraumatic stress disorder (PTSD)?*
- *How would you, as the teacher of a child diagnosed with PTSD help that child succeed in the classroom?*
- *What are some plausible causes of PTSD in school-age children in U.S. schools today? Which of these, do you think, would be most typical and why?*
- *How can you, as a classroom teacher, differentiate between a student who is simply "overanxious" or a "worry wart" by nature and a student who has generalized anxiety disorder? What diagnostic "tools" do you have at your disposal?*
- *What could you, as a classroom teacher, do to reduce the maladaptive behaviors represented by (a) perfectionism and (b) excessive fear of perceived threats in one of your students diagnosed as having generalized anxiety disorder?*
- *If you were assigned a child who has obsessive-compulsive disorder (OCD), what might you do to help him feel valued and included in your classroom?*
- *What might be some good questions to ask the school counselor or school psychologist about a child in your class who has been diagnosed with OCD? Similarly, what questions might you ask family members to help you work more effectively with this child in your classroom?*

Introduction

Posttraumatic stress disorder, generalized anxiety disorder, and obsessive-compulsive disorder are becoming more prevalent among school-age children and youth (Anxiety & Depression Association of America [ADAA], 2019). These anxiety disorders can have a significant impact on a student's academic performance, to say nothing of their effect on an individual's well-being. The reasons for the increase in identification are, to a significant degree, attributable to environmental factors that include increased stress in our society due to the proliferation of drugs, violence in the media, instability in the home and parental anxiety, pervasive climate in response to a perceived increase in the incidence of fear of crime and terror (ADAA, 2019).

These disorders can be ameliorated, to a great extent, by effective behavioral intervention applied by the teachers in the classroom. This chapter provides an understanding of these disorders as well as recommended research-based interventions that are effective in reducing the undesirable behaviors associated with these anxiety disorders, which can be easily implemented in the classroom.

Similar to the other chapters in this book, there is first a discussion of each of these disorders with a real-life case example that typifies a student who has the disorders followed by an elaboration of characteristics, causes, and research-based interventions. A fully developed functional behavioral assessment and relevant behavioral intervention plan (BIP) appropriate to the student profiled in the introductory case example is shared next. This feature should prove particularly helpful for teachers of students diagnosed with any of these disorders, as behavioral intervention plans may be integral to the Individualized Education Plans (IEPs) of these students and, likewise, a thorough understanding of the construction and implementation of a BIP is expected of these teachers.

Post-Traumatic Stress Disorder

Case Example: Anisa, A Student with Post Traumatic Stress Disorder (PTSD)

Anisa, a 15-year-old girl recently arrived from Aleppo, Syria has been struggling of late, both at home and in school. A very proficient student, Anisa is fluent in Arabic, French, and English. Her education in Aleppo, prior to the shelling by Syrian forces, was advanced and upon arrival in the U.S. with refugee status, she easily tested on grade level academically. Anissa, however, has been suppressing a year of horrific memories involving the destruction of her neighborhood by Syrian troops as well as maltreatment at the hands of the security forces. As her father, Ahmed, worked desperately to connect with a brother in the U.S. to obtain refugee status for his family as well as visas to facilitate legal immigration to America, Anisa and her family were forced to relocate to a refugee camp near the Turkish border. Every day she could hear the sounds of gunfire and see the smoke from bombs exploding in and around Aleppo to the south. Before their relocation, Anisa had both witnessed and experienced other horrors, terrible, unspeakable things that soldiers did to innocent civilians.

When the news came that her uncle had obtained and sent the requisite visas and provided the funds for their relocation to America, Anisa and her family were overjoyed! Unfortunately, for Anisa, that joy was short-lived. After a few days at her uncle's home in Philadelphia, Anisa began to experience nightmares that deprived her of sleep. One evening, as the city prepared to celebrate July 4th, she was terror-stricken by the sounds of fireworks in the streets around her uncle's home. She kept her fear to herself; however, not wishing to alarm her family or embarrass her uncle.

Anisa also experienced flashbacks that immediately transported her to Aleppo and those terrible days prior to relocation to the refugee settlement. She could hear her heart pounding as she recalled the events in vivid detail, as though they were happening again. Ironically, although she had always felt close to and protected by her father, Ahmed, she now avoided him and cringed when he would kiss or embrace her. He, her mother, and her siblings became reminders of the horrors of the civil war in which she had been a hapless victim.

In better times, before the civil war, Anisa was known for her gregariousness. She loved people and people loved her. Now, however, she mistrusted everyone, especially strangers who she assumed wanted to harm or exploit her. She now viewed the world as an evil place full of danger and she felt detached even from those she used to love. She preferred the safety of her room to the uncertainty of the school or the community.

Normally a very attentive and engaged student, Anisa experiences real difficulty concentrating and in place of her exemplary patience and joy in helping people, she has become irritable and short-tempered with everyone. Sadly, the school she attends in Philadelphia is under-resourced and is unable to provide mental health support. Even though several of her teachers notice her tendency to withdraw from social activities, they assume that it must be the result of culture shock and have agreed to give her room and time to acclimate to the new surroundings. They can only imagine things must have been difficult for her in Syria; yet they really have no idea how difficult.

Anisa's parents are not well educated, Ahmed was a rug merchant and her mother a seamstress in Aleppo-between them, they made just enough to support the family. Because of their poverty, life in Aleppo, even before the outbreak of civil war, was a drudgery requiring long hours of hard labor with very little family time. The children had to grow up early to take responsibility for the household chores and frequently to help out with their parents' work. Now, in the U.S., with very poor English, and no marketable skills, Ahmed must depend on his older brother for support until he can find work as a laborer. There is no money for luxuries, like a therapist, and they do not understand what could be wrong with their gifted daughter, Anisa!

Anisa from an Attachment Perspective

Given the historical events Anisa experienced, she is most likely suffering from Post-Traumatic Stress Disorder (PTSD). It is easy to think that anyone who experienced what Anisa did would have PTSD; however, it is well-known that two people may experience the same traumatic event(s) with one developing PTSD while the other does not. One theory put forth for this is strength of spirit and character that some individuals are just more resilient than others. Part of resilience is due to a secure attachment style. In other words, those with a secure attachment history may be less likely to develop PTSD. Someone with a secure attachment history, however, can still develop PTSD when their experience of the world, previously secure, becomes unsafe, and they must deal with the consequences of an unsafe world.

Either is possible in the case of Anisa. The case mentions that even before the outbreak of civil war, the family's poverty required the children to grow up very fast and take on great responsibilities at an early age. Her parents were always extremely busy trying to make ends meet. Could this result in an inconsistent attachment experience that allowed Anisa to explore (or not explore) the world from an insecure-anxious base? If so, the horrific experiences of the Syrian civil war and resulting relocation would be fertile ground for the development of PTSD.

Another attachment explanation, however, is possible. Anisa could have had a secure attachment style that was seriously disrupted by the traumatic events that she experienced. PTSD is multifactorial and even someone who has even the most secure attachment experience could develop PTSD especially if the traumatic event is very serious. If this explanation is correct, the prognosis for Anisa's recovery would be better than if she had an insecure attachment history. If the traumatic event serves to confirm the world as an already experienced insecure/unsafe place, the recovery from PTSD is more complicated.

Characteristics of Post-Traumatic Stress Disorder

Most experts agree that PTSD has been widely overlooked in children (Cohen & Mannarino, 2004). Incidents of sexual abuse, physical assault, domestic violence, serious illness, accidents and natural or man-made disasters can easily result in PTSD in children. These children may become avoidant, amnestic, drug-abusing, and engage in other self-destructing behaviors to numb their emotional pain (Cohen & Mannarino, 2004).

Hyperarousal is also a common reaction and may include "angry outbursts, irritability, sleep disturbance, difficulty concentrating, shortened attention span, feeling jittery or displaying motor hyperactivity, somatic complaints such as stomachaches or headaches, increased startle response and hypervigilance" (Cohen & Mannarino, 2004, p. 406).

There are two types of trauma, type I, and type II (Streeck-Fischer, 2020). Type I includes sudden, unexpected, and unpredictable single-incident stressors, while type II includes expected, repeated, and chronic stressors such as child abuse, bullying, and more. Distinguishing between these two types of traumatic events can help to develop more appropriate interventions (Streeck-Fischer, 2020).

Prevalence and Comorbidity

Among the adult population, it is estimated that 60 percent of men and 50 percent of women experience at least one traumatic event in their lifetime (National Center for PTSD, n.d.). More than two-thirds of children report a traumatic event by the age of 16 (Substance Abuse and Mental Health Services Administration, 2020). Common traumatic events among school-aged children may include seeing someone killed, shot, stabbed and/or being a direct victim of a violent crime.

Although it is clear that children quite commonly experience events that can cause PTSD, it is less clear just how many children actually are diagnosed with PTSD (National Center for PTSD, n.d.). Those who experience a life-threatening event are more likely to develop PTSD. Other variables in developing PTSD include physical proximity to the event, disordered cognitive processing during the event and, with regard to type II traumas, the duration of the experience.

PTSD in children has significant comorbidity with other disorders (van der Merwe et al., 2019). Depressive spectrum disorders have especially high comorbidity, for example; children who develop PTSD in response to child abuse are more at risk for developing major depressive disorder. Researchers have also found a high rate of anxiety disorders in children who have PTSD (van der Merwe et al., 2019). Pre-event anxiety levels have a significant effect on the development of PTSD, and those with higher anxiety levels were more predisposed to developing PTSD (van der Velden et al., 2020).

Attention-deficit hyperactivity disorder (ADHD) is frequently diagnosed in children who have been exposed to a traumatic event. A number of researchers found that trauma-exposed children more frequently present with ADHD before PTSD (Gibbons, 2020; Schilpzand et al., 2018). Because hyperarousal is also a symptom of ADHD, it may be that PTSD children are misdiagnosed with ADHD or that children who have ADHD are more disposed to traumatic experiences. More research is needed to understand the relationship between ADHD and PTSD.

Disruptive disorders (such as ODD and CD) have been found in children who have PTSD (Kessler et al., 2018). One hypothesis concerning this relationship is that children who develop PTSD from violent PSTD-qualifying events are more likely to develop anger and behavioral problems than children who experience nonviolent events (Kessler et al., 2018). Substance abuse also has been found to have a significant relationship with PTSD. Adolescents with PTSD will often turn to drugs as a form of self-medication. Data also exists that documents comorbidity between PTSD and dissociative disorders (Swart et al., 2020) and borderline personality syndrome (Frost et al., 2020). This is especially true for adolescents who have been physically or sexually abused.

The differential diagnosis of PTSD can be complicated. A child may present with the symptoms of PTSD but a traumatic-qualifying event cannot be identified. Even when a traumatic event is identified, one must distinguish the symptoms of PTSD from other disorders, either premorbid or developing after the traumatic event. Stress from a traumatic event can cause any preexisting disorder to reappear. A careful history might also reveal that the child had PTSD symptoms before the event. Many children are exposed to a PTSD-qualifying event without developing PTSD. There could be any number of reasons for this. Children may be more resilient, underdiagnosed, or develop symptoms related to another preexisting disorder.

As children mature, they are more likely to manifest a wider range of PTSD symptoms. Very young children may report only a very few PTSD symptoms and may resemble children who have generalized anxiety disorder (Barbano et al., 2019). Again, some experts believe that the lack of qualifications in the DSM-V for PTSD in children make it an inappropriate diagnostic tool for this population. A differential diagnosis must be based on a thorough premorbid history as well as the development of symptoms after experiencing the traumatic event.

Etiology of Post-Traumatic Stress Disorder

For a diagnosis of PTSD in adults and children, the DSM-V (American Psychiatric Association, 2013) has established five criteria:

1) Exposure to a PTSD qualifying event
2) A re-experiencing of the traumatic event
3) Persistent avoidance of stimuli associated with the trauma along with a numbing of general responsiveness
4) Negative alterations in cognitions and mood
5) Persistent increased arousal.

If symptoms last for more than three months, the PTSD is labeled 'chronic;' if less than three months, 'acute;' and if the onset of symptoms is at least 6 months after the event, 'with delayed onset' (American Psychiatric Association, 2013).

Re-experiencing can include intrusive memories, thoughts, and perceptions of the event, recurring dreams, flashbacks, and distress over exposure to cues that recall the traumatic event (American Psychiatric Association, 2013). It is not uncommon for children with PTSD to engage in traumatic play and reenactment behaviors and have frightening dreams whose content may or may not be related to the traumatic event (American Psychiatric Association, 2013). Avoidance can be:

- Cognitive—thoughts, feelings, or conversation associated with the trauma
- Behavioral—people, places, or activities that recall the trauma
- Amnestic—inability to recall aspects of the trauma
- Emotional—feelings of detachment and restricted range of emotion along with a sense of foreshortened future.

More than feelings of numbness, children who have PTSD often report feelings of aloneness or even wanting to be alone to keep their emotions in check (American Psychiatric Association, 2013). Hyperarousal includes sleep disturbance, irritability, difficulty concentrating, hypervigilance, and exaggerated startle response. The child with PTSD may constantly seem on alert (American Psychiatric Association, 2013).

Assessment of Post-Traumatic Stress Disorder

A difficulty in assessing PTSD is the unreliability of children's self-reports and, in cases of domestic violence and child abuse, that of the parents or alleged perpetrator. Evaluator suggestibility and the inadequacy of childhood memory create the need for evaluations that are independent of both child and parent (Cohen et al., 2017). In many areas, for example, sexual abuse response teams exist that allow the children to recount their story one time before a team of experts who observe from behind a one-way mirror. This is in contrast to previous methods of evaluation, when children were forced to tell their story multiple times to different constituencies that often resulted in different and contradictory versions of the event, not to mention additional trauma (Cohen et al., 2017).

Once the reliability of the reported traumatic event has been determined, the next step in the assessment of PTSD is the evaluation of symptoms. The clusters used by the DSM-V (American Psychiatric Association, 2013) can help structure the assessment interview. There are two widely used structured assessment instruments for PTSD (both require that the parent and child be interviewed separately) to include the Clinician-Administered PTSD Schedule for Children and Adolescent (CAPS-CA)(Pynoos et al., 2015; Weathers et al., 2004) and the PTSD section of the K-SADS (Ambrosini, 2000; Birmaher et al., 2009). In addition, numerous child and parent self-reports exist to evaluate the symptoms of PTSD in children. Some of these include the PTSD Reaction Index (Kaplow et al., 2020), the Child PTSD Symptom Scale (Foa et al., 2001), and the Children's PTSD Inventory (Saigh et al., 2000). All three have good psychometric properties and, because of their brevity, are especially appropriate for the school setting.

As mentioned previously, both the overdiagnosis and underdiagnosis of PTSD is a real problem. Overdiagnosis is the result of the evaluator simply discovering a traumatic event in the life of the child and then looking for symptoms of PTSD. On the other hand, some evaluators are reluctant to pursue questioning about trauma because of the discomfort it can generate in both the child and the parent. Further complicating the assessment of PTSD with children is the DSM-V (American Psychiatric Association, 2013) requirement that symptoms exist across clusters that some experts feel may be mutually exclusive. For children who are manifesting avoidant and numbing responses to the trauma, the assessment might conclude, for example, that they are not being affected by the trauma, when in reality these symptoms are simply hiding more positive PTSD symptoms (Tedeschi & Billick, 2017).

Treatment Strategies

Compared to other anxiety disorders in children, less research has been done on treatment effectiveness for children with PTSD. Treatments that have been studied include cognitive-behavioral therapy, eye movement desensitization and reprocessing (EMDR), nondirective supportive therapy, psychological debriefing, and pharmacotherapy (Cohen & Mannarino, 2004). CBT is the treatment that is most supported by the empirical studies.

Trauma-focused Cognitive-Behavioral Therapy

Trauma-focused CBT includes many of the basic interventions, including gradual exposure, cognitive processing of the event, psychoeducation, and stress reduction through positive self-talk and relaxation (Watkins et al., 2018). March et al. (1998) developed an eighteen-week treatment protocol called*Bounce Back* for children diagnosed with PTSD. 'Bounce back' means helping children feel they have some control as opposed to feeling controlled by PTSD. The session outline for the Bounce Back program is listed below.

Bounce Back Program for Children Diagnosed with Posttraumatic Stress Disorder (PTSD): Session Outline

Session 1	Overview of treatment, information gathering, and "bouncing back PTSD" by giving it a silly nickname
Session 2	Anxiety management: muscle relaxation
Session 3	Anxiety management: diaphragmatic breathing
Session 4	Anxiety management: use of the fear thermometer to manage distress
Session 5	Anger control: monitor self-statements and perspective taking
Session 6	Anger control: conflict resolution through role play
Session 7	Bounce back PTSD: positive self-talk and realistic risk appraisal
Session 8	Bounce back PTSD: positive self-talk and PTSD
Session 10a	Overview of exposure and response prevention
Session 10b	Individual pull-out exposure sessions
Session 11	Narrative exposure: each member tells their story to the group
Session 12	Imaginal exposure
Session 13	Introduce in-vivo exposure
Session 14	Exposure targets through verbalizing "worst moment" possible
Session 15	Confront dysfunctional beliefs and substitute helpful beliefs
Session 16	Relapse prevention and generalization: how to keep bouncing back PTSD
Session 17	Graduation party

Source: March J. S., Amaya-Jackson, L., Murray, M. C., & Schulte A. (1998). Cognitive-behavioral psychotherapy for children and adolescents with posttraumatic stress disorder after a single-incident stressor. *Journal of the American Academy of Child and Adolescent Psychiatry, 37,* 587.

Psychological Debriefing

In recent years, psychological debriefing has come under scrutiny both for the adult and child populations (Twigg, 2020). Its effectiveness with the child and adolescent population still needs to be determined. How, when, where, and with whom are variables that can determine the effectiveness of psychological debriefing. Helpers should not consider this intervention as an automatic first-line approach to treatment for children who have PTSD (Twigg, 2020).

Eye Movement Desensitization and Reprocessing

EMDR is a newer treatment and a form of exposure therapy that has been used to treat a variety of populations, including children, who have experienced a traumatic event. After a history taking, assessment, and educational phase, the intervention consists of imaginal exposure, verbalization of the negative cognition, and attention to physical sensations. Exposure is limited, as little as less than one minute to the most disturbing part. During this time, the client is instructed to visually track the helper's index finger as it moves back and forth rapidly and rhythmically across the client's line of vision for anywhere from 12 to 24 times. The client is instructed to block out any negative experience, breathe deeply, and express what he or she is imagining, thinking, and feeling (Valiente-Gómez et al., 2017).

The second part of the treatment, known as the installation phase, focuses on replacing the negative cognition with the positive one identified by the client. Once installed, the client is instructed again to imagine the traumatic event, but this time with a positive cognition and scan the body for any tension. The goal is to experience as little bodily tension as possible.

Pharmacological Treatment

Dopamine blocking agents such as Risperdal and SSRI's such as Citalopram (Celexa) have been used to treat PTSD in children and both have been shown to reduce symptoms of PTSD in children (Huemer et al., 2017). The paucity of research in pharmacotherapy for children who have PTSD requires that such an intervention be used sparingly, as a last resort, and monitored very carefully.

Summary

The importance of assessing and monitoring children for PTSD cannot be overemphasized. Child abuse, domestic violence, natural disasters, and accidents continue to occur and maintain their frequency in the lives of today's children. The COVID-19 pandemic and the ever-present possibility of other disasters increase the need to be vigilant for partial and full-blown indications of PTSD in children. Assessment and diagnosis is difficult and can often be overlooked in view of the unreliability of self-reports. If the presentation is not clear or not sufficient to meet the criteria for a formal DSM-V diagnosis, a rule-out diagnosis of PTSD can be recorded, and the child can be monitored and assessed again at a future point in time. CBT treatment for children who have PTSD has proved efficacious, making help for these children readily available.

School-Based Interventions

Armed with the information we have provided about the characteristics, causes, and recommended treatment strategies for students with PTSD, you, the classroom teacher, are ready to learn an effective model for (1) identifying key or target behaviors that you wish to change in a student who has this disorder, and (2) developing an effective behavioral intervention plan to address target behaviors so identified.

Assessing the Problem

Again, the most effective approach in determining a school-based intervention is a systematic assessment of the behaviors of concern and the function they serve for the student. As noted earlier, the function of some maladaptive behaviors may be symptomatic of a specific disorder and therefore be difficult to assess using a functional behavioral assessment protocol. An individual with a psychiatric disorder such as schizophrenia, for example, may exhibit bizarre behaviors that preclude learning and can be occasionally harmful to that individual or others. Conducting a functional behavioral assessment for behaviors produced by disordered thinking processes would be fruitless, because the undesired behavior is driven by a biochemical imbalance.

For Anisa, an older child with PTSD, a functional behavioral assessment would be appropriate in identifying target behaviors that could be changed or modified with the application of a behavioral intervention plan. Such a functional behavioral assessment might conform to a model like the one developed by Barnhill (2005), which consists of seven steps that are considered important for the development of an effective behavioral intervention.

As a reminder, these steps are (1) identifying and describing the problem behavior or behaviors, (2) collecting baseline data as well as academic information, (3) describing the context in which the behavior is observed, (4) completing a functional assessment form and/or behavior rating scales, (5) conducting a direct observation, (6) developing a hypothesis, and (7) testing the hypothesis to confirm effectiveness or modify accordingly.

Let's apply this investigative model to Anisa's case. Accordingly, the first step is to identify and describe the problem behavior. Anisa's teachers have indicated concerns about her distrust of her classmates and teachers as well as increased irritability, her frequent inability to focus in class and her emotional volatility.

Next, we systematically collect baseline data and academic information. Anisa's academic performance has dropped significantly in all subject areas because of her lack of ability to focus. Using a behavior checklist, her teacher reports that she is off-task approximately 50 percent of the allotted class time. She must also excuse herself at least two times per week, because of an emotional outburst. She usually misses the entire period of instruction. When this occurs, her school performance and consequently her grades are affected. In Aleppo, prior to the civil war, Anisa was averaging a B+ in all her subjects; after immigrating to the United States, her grades dropped significantly. Currently, her overall average hovers around the C- level.

Third, we need to describe the environment and setting demands that affect Anisa's behavior. Anisa is affected by several stimuli in the classroom environment, including (1) the sound of a fire alarm or fire engine, (2) anything or anyone who frustrates her, (3) sudden noise or movement around her, which triggers a panic response, and (4) televised news reports about terrorism or the ongoing wars in Syria and Afghanistan.

Fourth, we should complete a functional assessment form and/or behavior rating scale. Both of these have been completed with regard to Anisa's presenting behavioral concerns.

The next step recommended by Barnhill (2005) is to conduct a direct observation. To this end, Anisa's teachers and caregivers have conducted several direct observations over time, and they have consistently revealed a girl who is constantly fearful and anxious. Anisa appears tentative and unsure of herself in class and always 'looks like she expects imminent disaster,' according to her homeroom teacher, Mrs. Mansfield.

Ultimately, we must develop a hypothesis and then test its validity through an assessment of the efficacy of the interventions we employ. Based on the data and observations, Anisa's PTSD seems to have been exacerbated by events related to the Syrian civil war. Furthermore, it seems that using trauma-focused CBT, as described earlier in this chapter, will be the most effective school-based intervention.

Teachers who have used the trauma-focused CBT intervention with Anisa report that it seems to have helped, citing her positive response to the cognitive processing of the event as well as to the use to self-talk. These techniques will be discussed in greater detail in the next section of this chapter. This treatment approach has been added to Anisa's behavioral intervention plan, which is integral to her IEP. Recent examination of the behavioral data revealed a significant reduction in her trauma-related fears and anxieties. This reduction in symptoms is credited to the effectiveness of the interventions.

Developing an Effective Intervention Plan

As mandated by the federal Individuals with Disabilities Education Act (IDEA; 2004), the multidisciplinary team has developed a behavioral intervention plan based on trauma-focused CBT. This approach involves gradually exposing the child to the traumatizing situation and cognitive processing of the event, in which the individual revisits the event and is coached through the more unsettling, traumatizing aspects.

Her teachers have been taught to assist Anisa with positive self-talk, whereby she is able to verbally rationalize the fear-inducing event and acknowledge the inability of this imagined fear to affect her safety and well-being in the present. In addition, Anisa has been encouraged to use relaxation techniques, including controlled breathing, visualizing a favorite place and activity, and, in extreme circumstances, going to a "safe place" within the school (i.e., the school psychologist's office) to sit and discuss her feelings, look at a favorite movie, or listen to relaxing music.

Once Anisa feels ready to rejoin class activities, she is encouraged to do so in order to minimize time away from studies. She is expected to make up missed work and is responsible for getting notes from her study partner, another student who has been assigned to help Anisa remain up to date in her schoolwork. The classroom teacher keeps a record of the frequency, duration, and intensity of Anisa's panic attacks or episodes of extreme anxiety as well as the time she spends out of class. This information is shared with the school psychologist, Anisa's mother, and the multidisciplinary team. Presently, these interventions are proving effective in helping Anisa cope with her bouts of anxiety and fear and to remain in class. Her teachers hope that, eventually, Anisa will internalize the CBT techniques and no longer require time away from the classroom.

Tips for Teachers

Teachers may employ the following strategies in the classroom to help students like Anisa who have PTSD symptoms.

- Ensure that the child feels safe and supported in the classroom.
- Consider assigning a classmate to act as a study partner or study buddy to take notes and collect assignments and handouts for the child with PTSD when the individual is absent from class.
- Follow the strategies prescribed in the behavioral intervention plan (BIP) in the students' IEP.
- Speak with the child's counselor to provide updates on the individual's classroom behaviors. Also, ensure that you know how to apply the recommended techniques, such as trauma-focused CBT.
- Stay in close contact with the child's parents to monitor changes in behavior at home and, likewise, to apprise them of the student's classroom performance.
- Maintain a record of the student's behaviors relative to PTSD, noting the intensity, frequency, and duration of each episode.
- Try to avoid including or emphasizing stimuli that trigger an anxiety attack or phobic reaction in the child (e.g., showing graphic film clips of battles, using professors will assist students in learning basic skills, detailed accounts of tragic events, realistic descriptions of scenes that depict a traumatic event).
- Provide positive reinforcement, such as praise, when the child displays resilience in the presence of an anxiety-provoking stimulus. Always model a confident and rational demeanor when helping the student process a fearful event.

Generalized Anxiety Disorder (Overanxious Disorder)

Case Example: Liam, A Ten-Year-Old Boy with Generalized Anxiety Disorder

Liam is an otherwise 'normal' ten-year-old boy growing up and attending elementary school in Madison, WI. His family is fairly well off and he enjoys a good life, with plenty of games, toys, books, a laptop, and the latest electronic gadgetry, to include an Apple 11 cell phone. An average student in school, Liam does just enough to get by and avoid being 'grounded.' At first glance, it might appear to the casual observer that Liam has an enviable life...except for his pernicious anxiety.

Two years ago, just after his eighth birthday, Liam's mother was diagnosed with an aggressive form of breast cancer and it had already progressed to stage four. Always a 'mama's boy,' the news and her subsequent passing was devastating to young Liam and he was inconsolable. His father took him to a therapist that specialized in counseling grief-stricken children and Liam was also encouraged to join a group of child 'survivors' known as the Rainbow Club that met weekly to share feelings and engage in volunteer activities, like helping deliver meals to the elderly shut-ins. Despite all the support and sympathy, however, Liam was unable to shake off his grief at the loss of his best friend, his mother.

Mr. Gavin, Liam's father, began to date a year after the loss of his wife and hoped that Liam would warm to his new fiancé and that she might, over time, fill the void left by the mother Liam had lost. It was clear, however, from their first date, that this was not going to be an easy transition for Liam. Liam's relationship with his father had always been rather dispassionate and impersonal and was overshadowed by his devotion to his mother. Friends of the family described Mr. Gavin as a decent man, but one that did not display an emotional attachment to any of his children, especially his oldest son, Liam.

Liam's therapist prescribed medication to help improve his mood, but the medication only made him drowsy and caused him to become irritable and gain weight. To add insult to injury, at the same time, Liam began to worry excessively that his father might develop cancer and he would be orphaned.

Despite therapy and countless reassurances from his father and the family physician, Liam continued to worry that his father would succumb to some form of cancer. He felt his father and the doctor were concealing the truth from him to shield him from the inevitable fact that his father was dying. While he did not feel close to his father, the thought of becoming an orphan terrified him. His fears multiplied to the point that he no longer slept more than an hour or two at night and constantly checked his father's bedroom to ensure he was still breathing.

His anxiety over his father's imagined fragile health soon began to generalize to fears about the health of his two younger siblings, his favorite teacher, and even himself. The anxious feelings persisted without abatement at school, making it almost impossible for him to concentrate on schoolwork. He had difficulty staying focused when people were speaking to him because his attention and thoughts invariably drifted back to his anxiety over his health and the health of those he cared about.

Instead of doing his homework or playing his favorite games with friends, Liam would search the internet to find out about various cancers and their symptoms and convince himself that he or a loved one must have it.

Eventually, as he searched WebMD and other related online sites, he became aware of other insidious illnesses that one could contract unwittingly and succumb to before obtaining a cure. All of this irrational fear caused insurmountable anxiety in Liam - he even learned that excessive worry could cause stress that creates inflammation in the body and can lead to a surfeit of illnesses, some of them fatal. Liam's anxieties are legion and he truly needs help to effectively address them.

Liam From An Attachment Perspective

It is not uncommon for a child to experience severe anxiety as the result of a parent's illness. More unusual is the fact that his anxiety has not abated in spite of multiple interventions and numerous support people in his life. This could be explained by an anxious (resistant) attachment style so extreme that no one else is able to provide the comfort and support that he was accustomed to getting from his mother. The lack of emotional support from his father could have contributed to the excessive closeness with his mother. Remember that children with a resistant attachment style seek constant contact with the attachment figure but are never truly comforted by such contact. This explains why the many interventions provided Liam have not worked and substitute attachment figures (e.g., teachers) have not resulted in lessening his anxiety. Because the anxious attachment was not resolved before mother's death, Liam suffers from complicated grief. It is not unusual that he now fears that others in his life will get sick and die. Near the end of the case, we find out that he has also included himself among those who might die. There are two approaches for dealing with Liam, and they should be combined. First, from a behavioral perspective the adults in his life must be careful not to reinforce the anxiety by constantly protecting and allowing him to avoid facing his fears. Also needed is constant provision of reassurance with facts that his fears are unfounded. Sooner or later Liam will show some minimal signs of dealing with his anxiety and for this he should be immediately reinforced.

Characteristics of Generalized Anxiety Disorder

The anxiety disorders discussed so far have all been relatively focused. Generalized Anxiety Disorder (GAD) is more pervasive and is marked by excessive worry in any number of areas—for example, health, safety, performance, the safety of others, the future, keeping to schedules, family finances, and relationships (Sutherland-Stolting et al., 2020). Perfectionism is another sign of GAD, which can result in an overwhelming reaction to a small mistake or refusing to do anything that might be evaluated publicly (go to the board, read aloud, etc.). To defend against their anxiety, children who have

GAD may adhere rigidly to social norms, be eager to please, and behave like adults, often creating an illusion of maturity that allows the adults around them to appreciate some of their behaviors (Kendall et al., 2004). When they are stressed, children who have GAD can become oppositional. A common symptom is somatic complaints such as headaches, stomach upset, muscles aches, and sleep disturbances for which there are no known medical causes (Kujanpää et al., 2017). Older children tend to have more symptoms than younger children.

The greatest challenge in making a diagnosis of GAD is differentiating it from other anxiety disorders; for example, some of the social problems associated with GAD are similar to social phobia. As indicated previously, the anxiety in social phobia is confined to social interactions, which is not true in GAD. Similarly, in specific phobia, the fear is limited to a specific object or situation. The anxiety produced by GAD is not related to obsessions and compulsions, as it is in obsessive-compulsive disorder. Finally, to make a diagnosis of GAD, the excessive fear or worry must be present for at least six months.

Prevalence of Generalized Anxiety Disorder

Using strict diagnostic criteria, the prevalence rates for GAD are about 1 percent for adolescents and 3 percent for adults in the United States (American Psychiatric Association, 2013). In children ages 9 to 13, there are no gender differences in the diagnosis of GAD. There is, however, a marked gender difference among older adolescents and adults. In clinical settings, those with GAD are 60 percent female with epidemiology rates of about 66 percent female (American Psychiatric Association, 2013).

GAD is highly comorbid, especially with other anxiety disorders (Moscati et al., 2016). The type of comorbidity is often related to age as younger children tend to be also diagnosed with separation anxiety disorder or ADHD, whereas older children tend to be diagnosed concurrently with simple phobia or major depression (Moscati et al., 2016). Even if they do not meet the clinical criteria for major depression, children who have GAD often have low self-esteem and suicidal ideation (Boston Children's Hospital, 2022).

Etiology of Generalized Anxiety Disorder

Etiological factors in the development of GAD are no different than those of other anxiety disorders in children and include attachment issues, temperamental characteristics (e.g., behavioral inhibition), parental anxiety, and parenting characteristics that reinforce avoidant behaviors (Newman et al., 2016). Recent research has often focused on cognitive-processing variables such as negative self-talk, expectations of danger, and self-questioning (Newman et al., 2016).

Assessment of Generalized Anxiety Disorder

Circumspection must be used to avoid the overdiagnosis of GAD as a certain amount of fear and worry is normal in children and adolescents. As with other anxiety disorders, assessment should focus on cognitive, behavioral, and physiological symptoms. Clinical interviews, clinician rating scales, and self-reports are all recommended for the assessment of GAD. Many of the instruments designed to diagnose anxiety disorders in general and mentioned previously in Chapter 5 are appropriate for use in diagnosing GAD. The recent emphasis on cognitive processing factors in the etiology of GAD has generated measures of anxious cognitions. Two measures specifically designed to assess cognitive processing in children are the *Negative Affectivity Self-Statement Questionnaire* (NASSQ; Ronan et al., 1994; Sood & Kendall, 2007) and the *Coping Questionnaire for Children—Child (or Parent) Version* (CQ-C, CQ-P Crane & Kendall, 2020). The NASSQ is designed to measure negative affect as well as cognitions of anxiety and depression. It has an underlying four-factor structure: depressive self-statements, anxiety/somatic self-statements, negative-affect self-statements, and positive-affect self-statements. The NASSQ can be a valuable diagnostic tool in that it distinguishes between anxious and depressive self-talk.

The CQ-C and CQ-P are designed to assess a child's perceived ability to cope with anxiety in certain situations. The CQ-P offers the advantage of gathering data from other sources. Teacher reports are also important, and the teacher version of the *Child Behavior Checklist* (Achenbach, 2000) can be used. Structured observations using behavioral avoidance tasks are also important in the diagnosis and assessment of GAD. As with other anxiety disorders, the assessment of GAD needs to be multi-informant and multimethod. If there is suspicion that the cause of the child's anxiety lies in family functioning, the evaluator can use family assessment tools such as the *Family Adaptability and Cohesion Evaluation Scale IV* (FACES-II; Nogales, 2007).

Treatment Strategies

Studies have shown CBT to be effective with children diagnosed with GAD (Borza, 2017; Gosch et al., 2018). Education and skill-building are two fundamentals in the treatment of GAD, which can begin with the development of the four-step FEAR plan as outlined below. The FEAR plan is designed for children ages 8 to 13 and is adapted from the Copycat Workbook (Kendall, 1992). The child's primary caregivers need to be included in the treatment so they can extend the child's practice at home of newly taught or acquired skills.

The Four-Step FEAR Plan for the Treatment of Generalized Anxiety Disorder

- ***Feeling frightened?*** The helper works with the child to develop awareness of her anxious responses and to use such awareness to begin relaxing.
- ***Expecting bad things to happen?*** The child is taught how to identify cognitions that result in anxiety and modify those cognitions through rehearsal, social reinforcement, and role-playing.
- ***Attitudes and actions.*** The child learns problem-solving skills and develops a plan for coping with anxiety. The counselor helps the child to brainstorm and evaluate the consequences of alternative behaviors.
- ***Results and rewards.*** Together, the child and helper evaluate the plan and make any necessary adjustments. The child also learns how to self-reward for successfully managing anxiety.

Source: Adapted from Kendall, P. C. (1992). *Copycat workbook.* Ardmore, PA: Woodstock, p. 50.

School-Based Interventions

This section discusses school-based interventions for students who have GAD using the case example of Liam described earlier.

Assessing the Problem

An assessment of Liam's problem behaviors, conducted by the multidisciplinary team, revealed the following information organized according to the steps we have been using consistently throughout this book.

First, with regard to *identifying and describing the problem behavior,* Liam's most challenging behaviors seem to be organized in one area, that is his generalized fear of losing those close to him to cancer or some other chronic, life-threatening illness.

Next, teachers need to *collect baseline data and academic information.* In performing this task, Liam's teachers have provided assessment data that substantiate the frequency of Liam's refusal to participate in any activities he perceives to be potentially dangerous as well as the number of incomplete assignments in all core subjects.

Relative to the *generalizability of environment and setting demands*, Liam's anxieties occur across settings—that is, at home and in the community, as well as in school. School appears to be a Petrie dish for various diseases and accidents, which generates extreme anxiety in Liam.

As required by the IDEA (U.S. Department of Education, 2004), a *functional behavioral assessment* was conducted relative to Liam's anxiety in school, and the results confirmed the diagnosis of GAD and pointed to parental factors in the development of the disorder (e.g., his mother was diagnosed with GAD as a child). In the same way, both the *Negative Affectivity Self-Statement Questionnaire* (NASSQ) and the *Family Environment Questionnaire* were administered to Liam and his family to provide further data to inform the diagnosis and possible treatments.

In addition, Liam's teachers conducted systematic observations to identify the frequency, duration, and intensity of the behaviors related to his anxiety. An examination of these observations revealed a student who is overanxious and perfectionist; as one teacher observed about Liam's in-class behavior, "He is afraid of his own shadow." Similarly, another teacher reported that, while observing Liam write an essay in English, she noticed that its theme was related to the impact of plagues and pandemics on human mortality and that he became easily frustrated and destroyed several pages of work because he considered it substandard. As a result, he was unable to complete written assignments on time. In some instances, the teacher would actually retrieve his discarded draft from the waste can and provide a grade based on the preliminary draft; otherwise, Liam would not have completed the revision in time to receive *any* grade.

The next stage in the assessment process is to *develop a hypothesis* or *supposition* about the purpose that the problem behavior serves for Liam. Based on the data from direct observation as well as his academic performance, it appears that environmental triggers or catalysts induce Liam's chronic anxieties. Based on this understanding, it seems that his generalized anxiety may be best addressed through cognitive-behavioral training, such as the FEAR plan (Kendall, 1992), as outlined in the Four-Step FEAR Plan above.

The final confirmatory step involves testing the validity of the hypothesis. If our initial guess is, Liam's anxious behaviors should diminish significantly with the application of CBT. Similarly, observing Liam's response to the use of praise, encouragement, and positive reinforcement to help generalize appropriate replacement behaviors will further confirm the accuracy of our hypothesis.

Developing An Effective Intervention Plan

The behavioral intervention plan for Liam involves the following school-based treatment approach and includes his primary caregiver. Research supports the effectiveness of instituting a four-step FEAR plan (Kendall, 1992). The plan will be fully explained to Liam's teachers by the school psychologist and then will be incorporated into their classroom routines.

The first step in the FEAR plan involves asking the student whether they are feeling frightened. If the answer is "yes," the teacher asks whether the student expects bad things to happen. If the student affirms this, the teacher can briefly explore the specific negative expectations and provide a rationale that will help expel them while simultaneously replacing them with positive ones.

Next, the teacher, following the recommendation of the school psychologist, will help Liam employ problem-solving skills to help reduce anxiety; for example, if Liam procrastinates on handing in an assignment for fear that it is substandard and might receive a failing grade, the teacher can (1) edit the rough draft without grading it, (2) provide Liam with an example of acceptable work as a guide as well as an assessment rubric, or (3) break up the larger assignment into more manageable components and grade each of these components separately, ultimately providing a cumulative grade for the entire project (Salend, 2005; Smith, 2007; Smith et al., 2006).

Lastly, the teacher should evaluate the plan with Liam, make necessary adjustments, and provide positive reinforcement for overcoming or managing the fear; for example, Liam might be rewarded for completing and submitting an assignment, regardless of its quality. This reward might be in the form of bonus points that can be exchanged for a desired secondary reinforcement at a later time or, preferably, an additional assessment component that will provide points for assignment completion (Pierangelo & Giuliani, 2008).

Tips for Teachers

- Consult with the school psychologist in developing the behavioral assessment and intervention plan and apply the intervention plan conscientiously.
- Always provide the affected student in your class with a safe, structured environment in which to learn.
- Provide consistent praise and positive reinforcement for every effort the student makes to control the targeted behaviors.
- Never demean or disparage a student who has GAD for expressing 'unreasonable' fears.

- Get to know *all* of your students. Building positive relationships with your students is the single most important step in the development of an effective school-based intervention plan.
- Read the student's case file and become knowledgeable about the behavioral and academic goals described in the student's IEP.

Obsessive-Compulsive Disorder (OCD)

Case Example: Karim, A Student with Obsessive Compulsive Disorder (OCD)

Karim is an eleven-year-old boy living in Columbus, GA and currently attending Shelbourne Elementary School as a sixth grader. His parents, Dayyaan and Haniya emigrated from Pakistan in 2003 and Karim and his sister were born later in the U.S. As a devout Muslim, Dayyaan is determined to raise Karim with strict adherence to Sharia law. Dayyaan believes in disciplining his children and not coddling them. Haniya acquiesces and has acknowledged her husband's dominance as head of the house.

Karim has always sought to please his father but is frequently rebuked for failing in one area or another-not doing his chores to his father's liking, underperforming in school, and sometimes forgetting to pray five times a day as required by the Koran. From the age of four or five, Karim's parents and teachers began to notice anomalies in his behavior, the tendency to order his crayons by color, touch pencils and utensils five times in a very ritualized way, and, as he learned to recite prayers in Arabic at the mosque, he would utter a prayer often in conjunction with the counting.

This ritualized, repetitive behavior increased and intensified over time and now, at age eleven, they seem to be compulsions that are manifest in every aspect of his life. When they first appeared, Dayyaan punished Karim, hoping that it would deter these compulsive behaviors, but they only intensified. Karim's teachers also began working with the school psychologist to address the behaviors that were now interfering with his ability to engage in many activities and to complete assignments on time. His classmates, warned not to tease him, were quick to do so surreptitiously and outside the classroom, which caused Karim to lash out aggressively, further alienating him from them.

His father is unsympathetic believing that his son is looking for attention or may even be oppressed by an evil spirit and has taken him to see the Imam at their mosque who conducted a purification ceremony, which was unsuccessful in stopping Karim's compulsive behaviors. Getting ready for school or for bed may take hours because Karim must count out each item of clothing five times as he puts them on in the morning or disrobes before bed.

It also takes much encouragement and cajoling to get Karim out of the shower. His usual shower routine takes at least an hour as he first organizes all the personal toiletries and then washes himself in a very ritualized manner, counting each time he scrubs a body part with the washcloth. Any disruption of his routine invariably results in a major meltdown, and he is compelled to repeat the process from the beginning. All of this ritualized preparation creates havoc in the home and causes Karim to be chronically late for school. He typically arrives after first period, more than an hour late, which adversely affects his academic performance.

Karim desires to please people, especially his father and other authority figures like his teachers and the Imam, but he seems oblivious to his compulsions. His teachers suspect that his compulsive behaviors might have been caused by his desire for approval from his father who they consider to be far too authoritarian and demanding. They reported to the school psychologist that his compulsive behaviors seem ritualized and almost like a religious ceremony as his counting and sorting are always accompanied by a prayer whispered in Arabic. "It's almost as if his rituals are a mantra for approval and acceptance," observed one of his teachers, "the poor kid really needs help and not just in school!"

Karim from an Attachment Perspective

It may be tempting to think of OCD as the result of an anxious/resistant attachment style, but research has indicated that it is more a function of an avoidant/ambivalent attachment style (Zakiei et al., 2017). The primary caretakers often do not give the necessary attention to children, and the result is a belief that they are unreliable. This belief later extends to themselves and the outside world that is not to be trusted and devoid of optimism. In this view, the obsessions and compulsions are an attempt to restore orderliness within a disordered, pessimistic worldview. The thoughts and behavior, however, never achieve their desired end, and so the individual may develop OCD.

In the case of Karim, the relationship with his authoritarian father who demands perfection and a mother who seemingly acquiesces is key in understanding his OCD from an attachment perspective. The parental demandingness coupled with the strict adherence to Sharia law most likely allowed Karim to understand the world as a not-so-safe place, especially if the rule of law is not followed precisely. The social impediments are obvious, and the interaction effect between Karim's quirky behaviors and peer rejection only serve to exacerbate his distrust in those who inhabit the world around him.

Karim evidences all of the typical symptoms of OCD. His father's reflexive response to punish Karim for these "bad" behaviors is another contributor to

Karim's pessimistic worldview. Dayyaan's decision to take Karim to see the Imam for a purification ceremony should be respected given the family's strict religiosity. Unfortunately, this intervention did not work even though we might say it was worth a try. It probably only contributed to Karim's poor sense of self by not pleasing authority figures and being a good boy.

There are many individuals who have experienced avoidant attachment styles from the primary caretaker and do not develop OCD. The strictness of the home environment coupled with low resiliency most likely has led Karim to obsessions and compulsions to try and make things right and feel safer in an unsafe world, yet this is a losing battle. Given the family's cultural/religious background, getting Karim professional help may be a challenge. One piece of leverage is that Dayyan tried a religious intervention, and it did not work. Perhaps it is time to try something else.

Characteristics of Obsessive-Compulsive Disorder

To receive a diagnosis of OCD, a child must have either obsessions, compulsions or both. The DSM-V (American Psychiatric Association, 2013) defines obsessions as "recurrent and persistent thoughts, impulses, or images that are experienced, at some time during the disturbance, as intrusive and inappropriate and that cause a marked anxiety or distress," while compulsions are "repetitive behaviors (e.g., hand washing, ordering, checking) or mental acts (e.g., praying, counting, repeating words silently) that the person feels driven to perform in response to an obsession, or according to rules that must be applied rigidly" (p. 237).

A compulsion is designed to neutralize an obsession. What distinguishes OCD from a thought disorder is that the person recognizes that the obsessions and compulsions are unreasonable and senseless. This recognition requirement, however, is waived for children because of the understanding that children, more than adults, may see OCD symptoms as somewhat reasonable.

The most frequent obsessions in children are:

- Concern with dirt, germs, or environmental toxins
- Something terrible happening (fire, death, or illness of self or loved one)
- Symmetry, order, or exactness
- Scrupulosity (religious obsessions)
- Concern or disgust with bodily wastes or secretions (urine, stool, saliva)

- Lucky or unlucky numbers
- Forbidden, aggressive, or perverse sexual thoughts, images, or impulses
- Fear of harming oneself or others
- Concern with household items
- Intrusive nonsense sounds, words, or music (Herren & Berryhill, 2018)

The most frequent compulsions children are:

- Excessive or ritualized hand washing, showering, bathing, tooth brushing, or grooming
- Repeating rituals (going in and out of a door, up or down from a chair)
- Checking (doors, locks, appliances, emergency brake on car, paper route, homework
- Ritual to remove contact with contaminant
- Measures to prevent harm to self or others
- Ordering or arranging
- Counting
- Hoarding or collecting rituals
- Rituals of cleaning household or inanimate objects
- Miscellaneous rituals (such as writing, moving, speaking)

Many children who have OCD have more than one obsession and compulsion, and symptoms most likely will change over time (Nota et al., 2020). Most young children have some obsession or compulsion (e.g., a bedtime ritual); therefore, it is important to distinguish between OCD and normal developmental behaviors. Most experts have agreed that timing, content, and severity are the most important considerations (Nota et al., 2020). Normal obsessive-compulsive behaviors occur early in childhood, do not interfere with everyday functioning, and are appropriate to the developmental need for mastery and control over the child's environment.

Prevalence of Obsessive-Compulsive Disorder

Obsessive-compulsive disorder affects about 1 percent of the child and adolescent population at any given time and has about a 2 percent lifetime prevalence rate (James et al., 2017). Among younger children, boys outnumber girls; however, by adolescence there appears to be no gender difference. The mean age of onset is around age 10 though some children develop the disorder as early as age 7 (James et al., 2017). Among adults with OCD, one-third to one-half developed the disorder during childhood (Rapoport et al., 2000). OCD is highly comorbid, with only 26 percent of children and adolescents having OCD as the sole disorder (Rapoport et al., 2000). The most common comorbid disorders are other anxiety disorders, ADHD, developmental disabilities, conduct and oppositional disorders, substance abuse, and depression (American Psychiatric Association, 2013). Tourette syndrome or other tic disorders also commonly occur with OCD.

Etiology of Obsessive-Compulsive Disorder

Early psychoanalytic and learning theories about the etiology of OCD have given way to the understanding of OCD as a neurobiological condition. Imaging studies have shown the areas of the brain most affected in those who manifest symptoms of OCD to be the orbital frontal cortex, the anterior cingulated areas, and the head of the caudate nucleus (Grant & Chamberlain, 2020). Pharmacological and genetic studies have furthered the understanding of OCD as a neurobiological disorder.

The strongest evidence implicates the neurotransmitter serotonin because drugs that block the reuptake of serotonin have been very effective in reducing symptoms of OCD (Zhang, K. et al., 2019). The other neurochemical hypothesis involves the neurotransmitter dopamine since there is evidence suggesting that some forms of OCD are related to Tourette syndrome. Drugs that control the level of dopamine in the body have been effective in reducing Tourette and associated OCD symptoms (Burton et al., 2020).

The relatively strong relationship between OCD and tic disorders (TDs) led to the discovery that OCD and TD symptoms can arise or worsen with GROUP A beta-hemolytic streptococcal infection (GABHS), a strep infection. This combined symptomatology is labeled "pediatric autoimmune neuropsychiatric disorder associated with strep (PANDAS)" (Sigra et al., 2018). An exacerbation of OCD symptoms is also found in pediatric patients with Sydenham chorea, a neurological variant of rheumatic fever (Cunningham & Cox, 2016). Five criteria must be met for a diagnosis of PANDAS to be made:

1. The presence of OCD, a tic disorder, or both
2. Prepubertal onset
3. Episodic course of symptom severity
4. Association with GABHS
5. Association with neurological abnormalities (Xu et al., 2020)

When dealing with children who show symptoms of OCD, helpers need to rule out the existence of PANDAS, which can be done through a review of the medical history.

Finally, twins and family studies have suggested that OCD has a strong genetic component. In general, twin studies have shown higher rates of OCD among monozygotic (identical) twins compared to dizygotic (fraternal) twins (Purty et al., 2019).

Assessment of Obsessive-Compulsive Disorder

Several general scales used to assess anxiety disorders can also be used for OCD (e.g., the ADIS-C, the MASC). There are, however, a number of assessment instruments designed specifically for OCD, for instance, the *Children's Yale-Brown Obsessive-Compulsive Scale* (CY-BOCS; Scahill et al., 1997), which can be administered with or without a parent present. The authors caution that, especially in the case of sexual obsession, a child or adolescent might feel uncomfortable giving accurate information in the presence of a parent. *The Children's PCD Impact Scale* (COIS; Piacentini et al., 2007) can be used to assess the degree of functional impairment in an individual with OCD.

Treatment Strategies

As with most other anxiety disorders, CBT is the nonpharmacological treatment of choice for children who have OCD.

Cognitive-behavioral Treatment

The two fundamentals of treatment are exposure and response prevention (Öst et al., 2016). Exposure is based on the principle that repeated and sustained contact with the feared stimulus will reduce the associated anxiety. A child, who obsesses about dirt or germs might be instructed to touch something dirty. Response prevention consists of blocking the habitual response (i.e., the compulsion); for example, the child is prevented from washing his or her hands, and the provider helps the child to work through the anxiety that otherwise would be mitigated through hand washing. This working through is done through constructive self-talk, cognitive restructuring, and minimizing the effects of thought suppression. Exposure to the feared stimulus is either gradual or flooded (an extreme form of exposure) since both have been shown to be effective (Jacoby & Abramowitz, 2016). The final part of treatment focuses on generalization and relapse prevention.

Franklin et al. (2003) developed a twelve-week, fourteen-visit protocol for working with children who have OCD. Visits 1 through 4 include psychoeducation about OCD, cognitive training, and understanding the stimulus hierarchy (most feared to less feared). Sessions 5 through 12 provide the intervention exposure and response prevention, and the last two sessions deal with generalization and relapse prevention. Parents are involved in sessions 1, 7, and 11. They are given homework assignments to help with response prevention at home and to provide positive reinforcement. Successful treatment depends on the presence of rituals, the motivation to eliminate them, compliance with treatment, the child and/or parents' ability to report symptoms accurately, and the absence of severe comorbid disorders.

Comprehensive studies on the effectiveness of CBT in cases of OCD are currently underway. In many of these studies, CBT was combined with pharmacological intervention in the form of SSRIs (Öst et al., 2016).

Pharmacotherapy

Today, SSRIs have overtaken the drug treatment of choice for OCD. In general, SSRIs has been shown to be efficacious in the treatment of pediatric OCD (Varigonda et al., 2016). According to meta-analyses, SSRIs result in about a 30 percent reduction of OCD symptoms; effects appear in as early as two to three weeks and level off at between ten and twelve weeks; and there is no placebo effect in OCD as there is in depression (Varigonda et al., 2016).

In summary, there is less research available on treatment effectiveness with OCD than with other anxiety disorders. More controlled studies are needed that compare the stand-alone effectiveness of SSRIs and CBT and that compare combined treatments to a stand-alone treatment. In the meantime, there is sufficient evidence to encourage helpers to use CBT with OCD children and adolescents.

School-Based Interventions

After studying the preceding clinical review of OCD, teachers can, in collaboration with the school psychologist, develop a practical behavioral intervention plan for a student who has the disorder. As we consistently recommend, such an intervention plan cannot be successfully designed without a thorough understanding of the root causes of the problem behavior—that is, what purpose the behavior serves for the child and what contingencies help maintain it. This section provides a suggested approach relative to Karim, the child described in the case example

Assessing the Problem

As a preliminary step in developing a behavioral intervention plan to be implemented in the classroom, teachers must conduct a data-based behavioral assessment. A viable behavioral assessment for Karim should be conducted systematically in accordance with standard protocols similar to that described in the following.

The first step in any such process is to *identify the target or problem behaviors.* The principal concerns that affect Karim's academic performance are the compulsive behaviors he uses to 'neutralize' his obsessions, which result in chronic tardiness, difficulty completing assignments on time, and an inability to participate in school activities that involve any sort of physical contact with other students. These target behaviors include excessive hand washing and showering, checking behaviors, and counting.

For Karim, these target behaviors include constantly asking to use the bathroom to wash his hands, and taking forty-minute showers after gym class, which often causes him to miss the next class period entirely. In addition, he painstakingly checks over assignments, which often results in a lower grade for late submission. Sometimes, his checking behaviors become a source of embarrassment and humiliation; for example, several weeks ago, he was asked by the classroom teacher to turn off the lights in preparation for a video presentation; in complying with the teacher's request, he performed his usual counting behavior, turning the lights on and off five times, to the amusement of his classmates. In another instance, a teacher who was not familiar with his problem behaviors asked him to make copies of an assignment. After two hours, the teacher found Karim meticulously counting each page of each copy three times before stapling the pages together.

The next step in the process involves *establishing a baseline and collecting relevant data.* Karim's teachers have been asked to keep records of the frequency of his checking, counting, and ordering behaviors as they occur in their classrooms. In addition, they record each time Karim asks to use the bathroom, presumably to wash his hands. The teachers try to pair the bathroom request with Karim's contact with a perceived contaminant such as a doorknob, another student's hand, a borrowed pen or pencil, a classroom textbook, or the keys on a computer keyboard. As a matter of procedure, the school maintains records of Karim's tardiness as well as the number of classes missed in courses that follow a gym period.

Karim's compulsive behaviors do not appear to be affected or influenced by a specific *environment* or *setting*. His home, school, and community all present stimuli that engage his obsessions and fuel his compulsions. The conditions that trigger Karim's compulsive behaviors include (1) opportunities to contact contaminants; (2) any routine situation that he associates with a potential for danger or that might jeopardize him or a loved one (e.g., unplugging an electrical appliance or turning off the gas for a burner in the science lab, or turning off the stove in life skills class); (3) his own ritualized beliefs associated with the protection provided by counting to five that are integral to his daily routine; or (4) objects, especially his own, that are out of order, which can occur in any setting.

A *functional behavioral assessment form* was completed at the start of the school year by the coordinator of the multidisciplinary team. Moreover, the school psychologist conducted two behavioral assessments for OCD, one using the *Children's Yale-Brown Obsessive Compulsive Scale* (CY-BOCS; Scahill et al., 1997), and the other using the *Children's PCD Impact Scale* (COIS; Piacentini et al., 2007), which is used to determine the level of impairment of persons with OCD. The results of these tests confirmed the diagnosis of OCD for Karim and helped to provide the information necessary to develop an effective behavioral intervention plan.

In conjunction with the more formal, objective assessments, Karim's teachers, counselor, and parents provided anecdotal evidence concerning his obsessive-compulsive behaviors. These observations followed the usual practice of identifying the frequency, intensity, and duration of targeted behaviors. It was evident from the anecdotal evidence that Karim's academic and social success is significantly affected by his obsessive-compulsive behaviors.

The next stage in the assessment process involves the development of a hypothesis regarding the function of the identified problem behaviors. After reviewing the data produced by interviews with caregivers, teachers, and Karim himself as well as observations of his behaviors at home and at school, it appears that Karim is significantly affected by the following obsessions and compulsions (1) a concern with dirt and germs, resulting in excessive hand washing, (2) a subconscious or habitual connection between checking behaviors and the prevention of dreaded or undesirable consequences, (3) a sense of well-being derived from symmetry and order in his environment, (4) a subconscious or innate correlation between counting and a sense of security. These obsessions must be mitigated by the corresponding compulsive behaviors for Karim to be able to function in the classroom and elsewhere.

The development of an effective behavioral intervention plan predicated on the carefully formed hypothesis will help to confirm or disconfirm its accuracy. An effective behavioral intervention plan must address each of the key concerns identified in the hypothesis and, most importantly, be easily administered by classroom teachers. After implementing the initial behavior plan, its success or failure will determine whether modifications are warranted and, specifically, which ones.

Developing an Effective Intervention Plan

Following the recommendations of Martin & Pear (2019), an effective behavioral intervention plan for Karim should address the following concerns:

- *How Karim perceives or experiences events in his environment.* Karim appears driven to perform his compulsive behaviors because of perceived threats to his safety and well-being as well as that of his loved ones.
- *How invested are Karim and the other stakeholders in preventing or preempting reoccurrences of the problem behaviors (compulsions).* Karim has shared on numerous occasions his desire to control his obsessive thoughts and ensuing compulsive behaviors. His teachers and other caregivers have indicated their commitment to helping him achieve this challenging goal.
- *Teachers should always include instructional objectives and provide relevant social skills instruction in class.* When it is feasible, Karim's teachers should incorporate behavioral goals in their instructional objectives relative to his disorder.
- *Teachers should always reward positive behavioral responses and approximations.* When Karim employs a therapeutic intervention or coping strategy to avoid engaging in a compulsive behavior, he should receive immediate praise or some other form of positive reinforcement. He should never be punished for exhibiting compulsive behaviors; these should be ignored, when possible.
- *Develop contingency plans that cover most emergencies relative to the problem behavior.* Although it is not so far apparent in Karim's behavioral repertoire, should he become hysterical or exhibit destructive or violent behaviors, a plan to remove him to a time-out or cool-down space should be in place.

Based on a thorough review of Karim's functional behavioral assessment, and the treatment plan instituted by the school psychologist, the following represents an appropriate school-based approach to Karim's behavioral concerns.

- Karim has been receiving therapy from a child psychiatrist outside the school, who has prescribed a minimal treatment dose of Zoloft, an SSRI that has been shown to be effective in reducing OCD symptoms.
- By adhering to the treatment plan developed by the school psychologist in collaboration with the private therapist, Karim's teachers help block the habitual responses (compulsions) associated with his OCD. Karim's teachers, for example, do not permit him to wash his hands after touching a perceived contaminant such as a classmate's hand, a desktop, or someone else's pen or pencil. Instead, his teachers provide a consistent rationale that helps him realize the irrationality of compulsive hand washing. They prompt him to consider the reality of the actual consequences of not washing by pointing out the probability that he will survive contact with a contaminant, while acknowledging the prudence of not placing his fingers in his mouth and of washing his hands thoroughly after using the toilet.
- Similarly, they do not permit him to engage in repetitive counting or checking behaviors, providing a similar rationale; for example, after preventing him from turning on and off the light switch five times, the teacher asks Karim what he thinks he might have accomplished in so doing, and what might happen if he does not. The teacher then provides concrete examples that expose the inaccuracy of his prediction and the lack of validation for his fears.
- Karim's teachers maintain a checklist that records the frequency of each of the targeted behaviors. The resulting data will be evaluated in approximately eight to ten weeks to confirm the effectiveness of the behavioral intervention plan. If the plan fails to produce a significant behavior change in Karim, another behavioral assessment will be conducted to suggest improvements to the current behavior plan or recommend a different approach altogether.

Tips for Teachers

- Never demean or punish a student for his or her obsessive-compulsive behaviors.
- Develop a climate of support and understanding in your classroom. Educate your students about OCD and ways they can help students who have OCD.
- Follow the treatment approaches outlined in the student's behavioral intervention plan conscientiously and maintain accurate records as directed.
- Find ways to reduce stress in your classroom. Be flexible with assignment completion time, model tolerance of different behaviors, and practice patience.
- Provide support for parents and other caregivers. They can and do experience burnout from overexposure to their child's perseverating behaviors.
- Be clear and firm about expectations relative to timely assignment completion and acceptable classroom behavior.
- Provide the student who has OCD with a sense of structure and routine in your classroom. This will increase the student's feeling of security and predictability; both of these factors are critical in helping students who have OCD control their compulsive behaviors.

From the Field

Mitch Abblett, Ph.D.

Mitch Abblett, a clinical psychologist, is Clinical Director at The Manville School at Judge Baker Children's Center, in Boston, Massachusetts. The Manville School is a therapeutic day school serving children aged 5 to 15 who have emotional and behavioral disorders as well as learning difficulties. In addition to direct clinical services and administrative oversight of clinical services at the school, a primary focus of his work at Manville is consultation with the teaching staff.

Dr. Abblett, can you provide our readers with your sense of the typical student you work with who has been identified as having an anxiety disorder?

At Manville School, students vary widely depending on which specific anxiety disorder fits their diagnostic profile. A common feature for any of our students struggling with anxiety is their experience of significant emotional distress in certain situations, and that they will often show behaviors aimed at avoiding these situations; for example, some of our students suffer significant anxiety in response to social situations (such as during lunch or recess). Due to their levels of distress in these settings, these kids will actively avoid social interactions with peers, and look to either isolate themselves, or spend time with adults. Other students might have significant anxiety reactions to being challenged academically and will exhibit problematic behaviors as a result. Some kids have more significant trauma histories, and fit criteria for posttraumatic stress disorder. Many of these children have a highly disrupted ability to trust that others will not cause them further harm or upset and experience a great deal of impairment in their daily lives. Again, the nature of the anxiety varies by the student, based on what has sparked the anxiety reaction in the first place.

By your estimation, Dr. Abblett, what are the greatest challenges these students pose to teachers? And to themselves?

By avoiding the situations that cause them anxiety, many of these children miss out on opportunities to develop their social and academic potential. These kids can pose difficulty in the classroom because, in order to escape the anxiety that the classroom environment might create for them, they may become disruptive to other students, making a teacher's job more difficult. Sometimes, anxiety-disordered students require a lot of one-to-one support, and often a great deal of redirection, in order to stay on task and complete their academics.

What are some potential "mistakes" that new teachers can make when working with a student who has an anxiety disorder?

First, I think it's important to say to new teachers that you *will* make mistakes, but it's very unlikely that you're going to make a mistake that is not fixable. Mistakes are best thought of as learning opportunities for you as the teacher, and for the student as well. Some of my best progress clinically with students has been after I've made a mistake, owned up to it, and authentically worked to improve myself as a therapist. Certainly, teachers with the right willingness will benefit from this same process of making mistakes, learning from them, and improving as a result.

In terms of common mistakes that new teachers might make, I would say that, particularly with anxiety-disordered students, it's tempting to consider students who repeatedly avoid their work and might even seem to be whiny in doing so, to be lazy and possibly lacking in ability. It's very common to develop a negative view of these students, to view them as intentionally trying to get out of doing their work. These negative views can get in the way of providing the best teaching and behavior management interventions that will help these kids make progress. Research studies have shown that if teachers form negative expectations of students and their capabilities, students will live down to these expectations and perform beneath their ability levels. Children who have anxiety disorders don't want to fail. Just like a diabetic needs insulin, or a short-sighted kid needs glasses, children who have emotional and anxiety difficulties need behavioral and emotional supports in order to meet their potential.

We know that these students are often very needy and can absorb a great deal of emotional energy from teachers. What can teachers do to prevent "burn-out" and get the help they may not know they need?

I would say it's very important for all teachers to pay a lot of attention to keeping themselves physically healthy and emotionally sharp. Any teacher or clinician working with anxiety-disordered children will eventually experience emotional strain. A self-care and rejuvenation routine is very helpful as a preventative tool. For me, it's writing, and running or working out. I find these activities crucial to keeping myself emotionally fit. The most effective teachers are aware of themselves emotionally, know their limits, and develop their own emotional skills in order to make themselves resilient, yet open and accessible individuals.

Working with kids who are emotionally distressed and who might act out as a result requires that teachers have a great deal of supervision and support from colleagues. It's important to talk out one's feelings and not let things fester such that they get in the way of effective work, as well as drain away one's enjoyment of teaching. It also helps reduce the stress of working with anxiety-disordered kids to develop skills for behavior management. If disruptive anxiety-related behaviors receive clear, firm, yet supportive limits, things will be much less likely to escalate, and teachers will feel more in control and confident in managing their classrooms. As a result of such effort on the part of teachers in developing their behavior management and self-care skills, burnout becomes much less likely.

Can you provide a few of your most effective strategies for working successfully with these students? For example, tips that you wish someone had given you when you started working with this population.

One thing I learned early on is to be flexible to the needs of students, but consistent in managing their behavior. Anxious kids feel out-of-control, and unable to structure their daily lives; they need an adult anchor. Teachers who can create consistent emotional support, but the behavioral limits kids need to nudge them forward, are most likely to have classrooms with an atmosphere of growth and academic/social progress. Teachers should look for ways to bring out the strengths in children; to champion these for the kids and help them feel successful and valued. A good relationship with a teacher gives an anxious child the confidence they need to risk change and face their fears.

Remember, these children are not intentionally trying to fail. They didn't wake up in the morning with a plan of disrupting your classroom. They have disorders that need support and treatment. You are allowed to "hate" the behavior, just not the kid.

Finally, Dr. Abblett, could you share an anecdote from your practice in working with these students as well as providing support for their teachers that highlights one of your most memorable successes?

Last year, I supervised a trainee—let's call her Jane—who did an impressive job of creating the support necessary for a student whom we'll call Jonathan with significant social anxiety to make progress and adjust to the school environment at Manville. Jane sought supervision and was flexible enough to take the advice she got from us about how to "shift gears" in order to strike a balance between supporting Jonathan emotionally (allowing him to set the pace of change) and nudging him toward facing his anxiety and attempting interactions with peers. Jane worked closely with Jonathan's classroom teaching staff, to help them understand the student's emotional needs, and how to best respond to his anxiety. Jonathan started his year at Manville hating school and wanting to avoid his peers, but he ended the year feeling as though he belongs at school, and that he can be successful there. A motivated caregiver such as Jane, or a dedicated teacher, can make that happen.

Summary

In this chapter, we have examined generalized anxiety disorder (GAD), posttraumatic stress disorder (PTSD), and obsessive-compulsive disorder (OCD) as they pertain to school-age children and youth. The real-life case examples of Anisa, Liam, and Karim provided practical insights about the challenges these students present to the classroom teacher. To further prepare the teacher to work more effectively with students who experience these disorders, the chapter has provided a research-based overview of each disorder, including a definition, key characteristics, causes, and recommended interventions.

Consistent with the most effective school-based interventions for phobias, students who exhibit these anxiety disorders appear to benefit from cognitive-behavioral therapies. As for any emotional or behavioral disorder that affects school-age children and youth, an individualized behavioral intervention plan that is tailored to the specific circumstances and needs of the affected child is essential. For Anisa, a child with posttraumatic stress disorder, the recommended approach was trauma-focused CBT, which involves gradual exposure to the traumatizing situation with teacher support in processing the more "unsettling" aspects, along with positive self-talk and relaxation techniques including controlled breathing, visualization, and the establishment of a "safe place" within the school. In Liam's case, involving a student who has generalized anxiety disorder, the school-based approach involved the use of a four-step FEAR plan (Kendall, 1992); and lastly, for Karim, a student who has obsessive-compulsive disorder, a response-prevention cognitive-behavioral treatment plan was instituted. By blocking the habitual response and providing a consistent rationale that helps Karim understand the irrationality of his compulsions, his teachers are helping to reduce the frequency of these deeply entrenched behaviors.

This chapter has shown once again that classroom teachers, when properly prepared, can successfully implement a behavioral intervention plan that has been instituted by the multidisciplinary team. These school-based interventions are critical in providing the student who has an emotional or behavioral disorder an integrated and effective treatment plan. Thus, teachers must ensure that they understand the behavioral dynamics of these anxiety disorders and the most effective ways to address them in the classroom.

Focus Questions Revisited

Which related services providers and other knowledgeable persons can provide critical advice and support to the teacher of a child, such as Anisa, who has posttraumatic stress disorder?

A Sample Response: The classroom teacher should be encouraged to speak with the school psychologist, as well as Anisa's parents, to gain a better understanding of how to accommodate her in the classroom.

How would you, as one of Anisa's classroom teachers, help her succeed in the classroom?

A Sample Response: I would encourage Anisa to use positive self-talk to help rationalize the fear-inducing stimulus and acknowledge the inability of this imagined fear to affect her safety and well-being in the present. In addition, I would prompt her to use relaxation techniques, including controlled breathing, visualizing a favorite place and activity, and, in extreme circumstances, going to a "safe place" within the school to sit and discuss her feelings or listen to relaxing music.

Once Anisa feels ready to rejoin class activities, I would encourage her to do so, to minimize time away from studies. I would also remind Anisa that she is responsible for making up missed work and getting notes from her study partner. In addition, I would record the frequency and duration of Anisa's anxiety episodes as well as her time out of class. This information would be shared with the school psychologist, Anisa's parents, and the multidisciplinary team.

What are some plausible causes of PTSD in school-age children in U.S. schools today? Which of these, do you think, would be most typical and why?

A Sample Response: Clearly, the effects of the recent pandemic, as well as media coverage of protests and associated violence and the graphic coverage of the wars in Iraq, Afghanistan and the civil war in Syria have accounted for much of the recent increase in PTSD identification among school-age children and youth. In addition, the heightened awareness and identification of child abuse, at the hands of both strangers and caregivers, appears to have risen sharply in the last decade, accounting for many new cases of PTSD. In the first instance, children view many hours of television each day, which will inevitably include news coverage of acts of terrorism and warfare. The latter of these two "plausible causes" appears to be proliferating because, in part, of increased attention to the problem given by the media and justice system. Statistically, the incidence of child abuse appears to be on the rise, and the likely causes are embedded in the perpetuation of poor parenting practices as well as the deleterious effects of poverty.

How can you, as a classroom teacher, differentiate between a student who is simply over-anxious or a worry wart by nature and a student who has generalized anxiety disorder? What diagnostic tools do you have at your disposal?

A Sample Response: The classroom teacher should not circumvent the school clinician (school psychologist) in diagnosing a student perceived to have GAD; however, teachers should familiarize themselves with several of the instruments that are typically used by psychologists in identifying bona-fide cases of GAD. Similar to other emotional and behavioral disorders, the three broad criteria used to differentiate GAD from the anxiety that affects many school-age children and youth are frequency of manifestation, intensity of symptoms, and the duration of the "problem" (Walker, 1995).

Many of the instruments designed to diagnose anxiety disorders in general are appropriate for use in diagnosing GAD. The recent emphasis on cognitive processing factors in the etiology of GAD has generated measures of anxious cognitions. Two measures specifically designed to assess cognitive processing in children are the *Negative Affectivity Self-Statement Questionnaire* (NASSQ; Ronan et al., 1994; (Sood & Kendall, 2007) and the *Coping Questionnaire for Children—Child (or Parent) Version*; CQ-C, CQ-P) (Crane & Kendall, 2020).

If Liam was one of your students, how might you address his inability to complete assignments? What incentives might you employ?

A Sample Response: If Liam is unable to complete or hand in an assignment, possibly because of his fear of receiving a substandard or failing grade, I could (a) edit the rough draft without grading it, (b) provide Liam with an example of acceptable work as a guide as well as an evaluation rubric, or (c) break up the larger assignment into more manageable components and grade each of these separately, ultimately providing a cumulative grade for the entire project. In accordance with recommendations in the chapter, I would discuss this plan with Liam, make necessary adjustments, and provide positive reinforcement for overcoming or managing fear. For example, Liam might be rewarded for completing and handing in an assignment, regardless of its quality. This reward might be in the form of bonus points or, preferably, a built-in assessment component.

What could you do, as a classroom teacher, to reduce the maladaptive behaviors represented by (a) perfectionism and (b) excessive fear of perceived threats in one of your students diagnosed as having generalized anxiety disorder?

A Sample Response: As the classroom teacher working with a child who has GAD and exhibits both perfectionism and excessive fear, I would address each concern as follows.

- *Perfectionism*: Assign work that must be completed in class and within a time frame that encompasses a class period or two. Display flexibility in not penalizing for lack of neatness and spelling. Offer to edit major written assignments and simply have the student incorporate those edits in revising the paper to produce a final draft.

- *Excessive fear:* Cognitive-behavioral therapy (CBT) is especially effective in providing a child with GAD new ways of think about and dealing with fear-inducing circumstances. An example of an effective CBT strategy is the four-step FEAR plan, which includes the following components:
- *Feeling frightened?* The child is helped to develop an awareness of her anxious responses and to use such awareness to begin relaxing through controlled breathing, thinking of a happy experience, and realistically appraising the perceived threat in order to minimize its emotional impact.
- *Expecting bad things to happen?* The child is taught how to identify cognitions that result in anxiety and modify those cognitions through rehearsal, social reinforcement, and role-playing.
- *Attitudes and actions.* The child learns problem-solving skills and develops a plan for coping with anxiety. The teacher or caregiver helps the child to brainstorm and evaluate the consequences of alternative behaviors.
- *Results and rewards.* Together, the child and helper evaluate the plan and make any necessary adjustments. Children also learn how to reward themselves for appropriate responses to minimize the effects of fear.

Teachers can learn to use strategies like FEAR plan in the classroom under the guidance of the school psychologist to help the student generalize the techniques of the intervention to the classroom and thus provide the student with consistency.

If you were assigned a childlike Karim, who has obsessive-compulsive disorder, what might you do to help him feel valued and included in your classroom?

A Sample Response: I might use some or all of the following strategies to help a child with OCD in my classroom:

- Never demean or punish the student for his or her obsessive-compulsive behaviors.
- Develop a climate of support and understanding in my classroom. Educate my students about OCD and ways they can help other students who have OCD.
- Find ways to reduce stress in my classroom. Be flexible with assignment completion time, model tolerance of "different" behaviors, and practice patience.
- Be clear and firm in my expectations about assignments and classroom behavior.
- Provide the student who has OCD with a sense of structure and routine in my classroom. This will increase the student's feeling of security and predictability, both of which are critical in helping students who have OCD control their compulsive behaviors.

What might be some good questions to ask the school counselor or school psychologist about a child in your class who has been diagnosed with OCD? Similarly, what questions might you ask family members to help you work more effectively with this child in your classroom?

A Sample Response: A teacher who is concerned about working with a student who has recently been diagnosed as having OCD might ask the school counselor or psychologist the following questions.

- What strategies would you recommend that would help reduce off-task behaviors associated with OCD?
- What are recommended responses to classmates who tease and mistreat this student?
- How do I address bizarre or more severe behaviors such as excessive requests to use the bathroom, inappropriate sexual obsessions, bizarre rituals, and "mantras" that are distracting to others?
- What do I do if an obsession or compulsion that is verbalized or enacted by the student might have serious or even criminal outcomes? For example, an adolescent touches another student inappropriately; a student threatens to harm someone or himself, etc.

Suppose you had a child with a behavioral profile similar to Karim's in your classroom. Would it ever be appropriate to punish this student? Explain your response.

A Sample Response: Yes, insofar as the misbehavior violates established classroom or school rules and was not a characteristic of his disorder. IDEA (U. S. Department of Education, 2004) has elaborated the process to ensure that a student who has a disability is not being "punished" for a behavioral manifestation of his disorder; such a process is referred to as a manifestation determination. For example, if a characteristic behavior of autism disorder is behavioral volatility due, in part, to sensory over-stimulation, and a child with autism suddenly tantrums in your classroom, it would be inappropriate to punish her as you might if she was able to control such a reaction. On the other hand, if a student with OCD brought a weapon or drugs to school, or caused physical harm to a teacher or classmate, that student would be liable for punishment in accordance with school policy regardless of whether these behaviors were manifestations of OCD.

Key Terms Used in The Chapter

Dissociative Disorders:
Disorders that result in disassociation (disconnection or interruption) of waking consciousness. A person may lose consciousness of his or her own identity or past.

Borderline Personality Syndrome:
A personality disorder marked by long-standing and pervasive instability in mood, relationships, behavior, and self-image. It is commonly thought to result from the lack of early bonding with the primary caretaker.

Psychological Debriefing:
Usually done with a group of victims, psychological debriefing attempts to recreate a traumatic event by having participants talk about what happened as well as their thoughts and feelings about the event. There is also discussion of strategies to deal with the stress resulting from the experienced trauma.

Behavioral Avoidance Tasks:
Children are exposed to various anxiety-producing stimuli and assessed for their degree of avoidance.

Dopamine:
A hormone and neurotransmitter that is responsible for critical brain functions such as controlled movement and pleasure. It is a precursor to adrenaline.

Tourette Syndrome:
A neurological disorder characterized by repetitive, stereotyped, involuntary movements and vocalizations called tics.

Placebo Effect:
A measurable, observable, or felt improvement in health or behavior that is not attributable to a medication or treatment that has been administered.

Chapter 7

Eating Disorders

Focus Questions

- *How are anorexia nervosa and bulimia nervosa currently differentiated, and what do researchers think about the relationship between these two eating disorders?*
- *Describe the diagnostic criteria for identifying a binge eating disorder.*
- *Imagine that you are a classroom teacher in a local middle school. You notice that one of your female students refuses to eat lunch with her classmates and routinely uses the bathroom immediately after lunch. Concerned students ask to speak with you privately and confide that they have witnessed this student throwing up on numerous occasions after lunch, which confirms your suspicions. What should you do, as a concerned teacher, to help this individual?*
- *What are some things you could do, as the teacher of a student who has anorexia nervosa, who insists that she is fat when it is obvious that she is seriously underweight?*
- *Suppose that you had a student who was grossly overweight and was a binge eater, constantly hoarding and consuming high-calorie, non-nutritious foods. What could you do to help this student?*

Introduction to Eating Disorders

In the course of the last decade, eating disorders have gone from being a 'dirty little secret' to a growing phenomenon of Western industrialized societies, preeminent among them, the United States. Thirty years ago, the death of a celebrity, such as the highly successful singer and drummer Karen Carpenter, who suffered from anorexia nervosa, was an anomaly (Latson, 2016). The fact that perhaps thousands of girls and young women attending schools and colleges in the United States, Canada, and other economically prosperous nations were struggling with the same disorder was suppressed and underreported (Striegel-Moore & Bulik, 2007). Many viewed the problem as an ephemeral one, the product of diet- and body- image-obsessed females that could be corrected with improved self-image and the infusion of some common-sense (National Institute of Mental Health, 2021; Striegel-Moore & Bulik, 2007).

Nevertheless, high-profile cases, like that of Karen Carpenter, helped to focus medical attention on a growing national problem among girls and young women. Although teachers cannot be expected to provide therapeutic interventions for their students suspected of having an eating disorder, they can learn the danger signs that warn of the presence of one.

As we will learn in this chapter, there are some misperceptions about the typical cause of eating disorders. Contrary to popular belief, they are not simply the product of a young woman's desire to be fashionably thin and therefore attractive to men. In fact, research has suggested that often these disorders are attempts to take control of one's life in an area over which the individual has absolute control—that is, the consumption of food (National Institute of Mental Health, 2021; The JED Foundation, n.d.).

During the last thirty years, eating disorders have come to the forefront of emotional and psychological concerns facing the school-aged adolescent population (National Institute of Mental Health, 2021). Although starvation has been a subject of inquiry since the fourth century, it was not until the 1970s that clinical studies led to a reexamination of eating disorders, away from unconscious conflict based on psychoanalytic thought and toward a more developmental, family, and socioenvironmental perspective (The JED Foundation, n.d.). More recently, biological factors have been studied in the causality of eating disorders. The 1970s also began the distinction of different kinds of eating disorders, namely, *anorexia nervosa* and *bulimia nervosa.* In addition to anorexia nervosa and bulimia nervosa, the DSM-V (American Psychiatric Association, 2013) added a third important category: *binge eating disorder*, previously considered a tentative diagnostic category.

Bulimia Nervosa (BN)

Case Example: Anna, A Student Diagnosed with Bulimia Nervosa

Anna is currently a senior at Portage Collegiate High School in Beauchamp, WI. Her father is the pastor of the local Assemblies of God church. All her life, Anna has been the poster child for the church, singing in the choir and soloing, collecting the offering, helping to clean the church, working in the nursery on Sunday mornings. She is also expected to be an exemplary student, never getting into trouble, not dating, never smoking, or drinking, a living testament to her Christian faith.

To her parents, teachers, and friends, Anna has lived up to those very high ideals, but when she is alone, which is rare, and in secret in the early hours of the morning unbeknown to everyone, Anna has been living a double life. Almost every night, after her parents have gone to bed, Anna prepares herself for the ritual. Ironically, it almost feels like a religious ceremony, like communion, except the food that she consumes will not be bread and wine, but an assortment of the junk foods she craves but would never consume in public.

Swiftly and quietly, Anna locks the door to her room, climbs onto a chair and carefully slides an acoustic ceiling tile back to provide access to her stash of food. She then arranges the snacks on her bed, the ones with the most calories on the right, those with the fewest on the left. She takes out the two-liter bottle of cola from under her bed and chugs a mouthful. Then, for the next hour, she gorges on twinkies, moon pies, Drake's Cakes, Cheetos, potato chips, and tortilla chips.

After the binge-eating has gone on for the better part of an hour, the guilty feelings begin to overwhelm her and she rushes to the bathroom adjacent to her room, locks the door and purges as quietly as possible so as not to wake her parents. She has become very proficient at this - purging the food she has just consumed feels good and she knows that she cannot gain an ounce from this junk food feast. There is no longer the feeling of guilt. She knows what she is doing is unhealthy, but she is able to maintain her weight and keep her figure. Though she promises herself that this will be the last time, she knows that tomorrow night, she will do it all over again. It has become a vicious cycle that she is powerless to stop.

Recently, though, others are beginning to notice. Anna's dentist commented on the loss of enamel on some of her teeth and asked her if she was smoking or drinking coffee or soda. Anna lied, of course, and said it was the soda. Her pediatrician was also a bit alarmed at her elevated blood pressure, unusual in someone so young. The final straw, though, was when her 'so-called' friends spoke to her homeroom teacher about noticing that the stall just vacated by Anna occasionally smelled like someone just threw up. The teacher contacted the school psychologist who subsequently called Anna's parents. He suggested they look for possible stashes of food in the home and Anna's mother noticed that one of the ceiling tiles was slightly askew. When she tried to reset the tile, her efforts dislodged a stash of junk foods. Further probing disclosed the half-full liter of cola and several other bottles that were unopened. The most damning and disconcerting discovery, however, was the small bottle of ipecac secreted in her accessory drawer. Perfect Anna is not so perfect, and her parents feel betrayed and humiliated. How could their Christian daughter bring such shame to the family and the church!

Anna From an Attachment Perspective

Research has supported a relationship between attachment insecurity and eating disorders (Tasca, 2019). One result of such insecurity is perfectionism that can easily result in body dissatisfaction. This appears obvious in the case of Anna who was expected to be an exemplary student, never getting into trouble. Her strong religious background certainly could have contributed.

As the reader will discover later in this chapter, CBT is often the treatment of choice for eating disorders with the main goal changing cognition about one's body, weight, and other factors. The attachment literature, however, helps to understand the quality of relationships as a contributor to disordered eating.

An anxious or avoidant attachment style can be a contributor to disordered eating. In the case of Anna, one could hypothesize that the attachment style is more avoidant since the case suggests a down-regulation of emotions. Anna does everything she is asked to with perfection and there is no evidence of complaining or any other expressed emotion. This is consistent with an avoidant attachment style that often is considered with a lack of affection from the primary caretaker(s). And lack of affection is thought to play a significant role in body dissatisfaction (Grenon et al., 2016).

Treatment, from an attachment perspective, for Anna, would focus on affect regulation (help her to express appropriately her feelings), her need for perfectionism, and the relationship with her parents to deal with issues of insecurity.

Characteristics of Bulimia Nervosa

The core characteristic of BN is a recurrent, out-of-control pattern of binge eating episodes characterized by the consumption of large quantities (1000 to 2000 calories) of high-calorie food over a short period of time (Levine, 2019). The eating episodes occur in conjunction with compensatory behaviors of either the purging or non-purging type. Those with BN often present with a history of AN, and vice versa. The current preference is to understand eating disorders as existing along a continuum and not as mutually exclusive categories (Abraham, 2018). The onset of BN is usually in late adolescence or early adulthood (American Psychiatric Association, 2013). Those with BN can be either underweight or overweight. Males with BN often have a history of overweight or obesity (Enache, 2017).

Anorexia Nervosa (AN)

Case Example: Kate, A Student Diagnosed with Anorexia Nervosa

Kate, a middle schooler, is an excellent student and is well-liked by her classmates and teachers; however, over the course of the last few months, everyone has noticed that Kate, always a diminutive and slim girl, has begun to look gaunt and rather unhealthy. A few of her closest friends have commented on this change in her appearance, which has been met with anger and alienation on Kate's part. Her teachers, aware of her heightened sensitivity to these comments, have avoided discussing the subject with Kate for fear of being similarly misunderstood. One of Kate's favorite teachers, Mrs. Beaton, mentioned her concerns to the school nurse and school psychologist, who agreed to keep an eye on her.

Both of Kate's parents are extremely successful professionals. Her father is a real estate executive and builder who specializes in commercial properties and has multi-million dollar projects underway all over the world. Kate's mother is a renowned neurosurgeon who is the chief of neurosurgery at Columbia-Presbyterian in New York City. The family owns a penthouse in Manhattan and Kate has always attended the very best private schools in the city. Kate's parents are both competitive people and have always expected the best from themselves and others. Accordingly, they expect Kate to excel in anything she does, especially academics. On the surface, Kate seems to welcome the challenge to be exceptional, but on the inside, she has been in turmoil. She wishes her parents could understand that she cannot be perfect all the time, that she is wilting under pressure, but she fears their rejection of her and does not want to disappoint them.

So, Kate is determined to develop the body type of a model (which does not exist as it is projected in the media). She is resigned to consuming fewer calories and working out twice daily, before and after school. She also eats a very light breakfast consisting of half a grapefruit and a cup of black coffee. She skips lunch and eats a salad for dinner, without any dressing, of course. On two occasions, Kate has fainted at school, once during calisthenics in gym class and another time during an exam. The school nurse called home, but both Kate's parents were at work and Kate pleaded with the nurse to not bother them while at work. The school nurse reluctantly agreed, but left a voicemail message on the home phone, requesting a call back to discuss Kate's fainting episodes.

Dr. Ephron, Kate's mother, spoke with the nurse and assured her, as a medical doctor herself, she would monitor her daughter and have some tests done to determine the cause of the fainting; however, when she spoke with

Kate about the incident, Kate insisted that she had been dehydrated and after drinking some water felt fully restored. Dr. Ephron did not pursue the matter and Mr. Ephron was out of the country on business.

Recently, the gym teacher, Mrs. Clements, conducted a height, weight, and BMI clinic and required that all her students participate. Reluctantly, Kate allowed herself to be weighed and measured. To no one's surprise, Kate's BMI was calculated at 14, considered a criterion indicating an extreme health issue. How could Mrs. Clements convey to Kate and her parents the seriousness of this indicator, without alienating them or being ignored. Without proper medical intervention, Kate's prognosis for continued good health looked very bleak.

Characteristics of Anorexia Nervosa

Although the DSM-V (American Psychological Association, 2013) allows for a wide range of symptomology, three critical components must be present for the diagnosis of an eating disorder to include (1) the problem must be related to eating, (2) include behavioral and psychological symptoms, and (3) result in significant dysfunction (Fatt et al., 2020). The core symptom of AN is a morbid desire to be thin and a fear of becoming fat.

It is common for those with AN to insist that they are too fat even if they are dangerously underweight. This distorted body image interferes with their body sensations. The individual may never feel hungry or may feel satiated after eating even a morsel of food. Excessive exercise and purging may also be part of the symptomatic picture. In fact, the DSM-V (American Psychiatric Association, 2013) classifies AN into two types - the binge eating/purging type and the restricting type, the classic form of the disorder. The bulimic features of the former type are associated with longer-term negative outcomes and demand a different treatment approach than the latter type (Reas & Rø, 2018).

Binge Eating Disorder (BED)

Case Example: Benny, A Student Diagnosed With Binge Eating Disorder

Benny is a twelve-year-old boy living in Coeur D'Alene, Idaho who attends a special residential school for students with learning and adjustment difficulties. Benny is morbidly obese and has been recently diagnosed with Binge Eating Disorder, a condition that causes compulsive eating, even after the individual feels full. Benny is embarrassed by his overeating and consequently consumes most of his food in secret out of public scrutiny. He has been teased unmercifully by both classmates and adults for most of his life and wants to be able to control his consumption and lose weight;

however, none of the diets and weight loss programs he has tried have been effective to date.

His parents, Ted, and Maureen are a very attractive couple, and image and physical appearance are very important to them. Benny's two siblings are both nice-looking children and within normal weight parameters for their ages. It is quite apparent to even the casual observer that Benny is an embarrassment to them. When he was diagnosed with an eating disorder as well as several other anxiety disorders, Ted and Maureen were very quick to insist that he receive therapeutic help and after only a few days of investigation found the perfect residential school. Although tuition and room and board at the Apex Residential School were very costly, Benny's parents seemed almost eager to pay the fees. They assured Benny, who was inconsolable at the news of his forced and imminent departure, that although he would be sorely missed by the family, this was the very best option.

His classmates at the Apex School have been cautioned about teasing Benny, but since he is a very private young man with few friends, they do not really know him and so they treat him like an oddity or a sideshow freak. They often use derogatory terms like "heavy drop," "Shamu," "Biggie Smalls," and "Porky" in lieu of his real name. His alienation and subsequent loneliness further provokes his compulsive eating. Since he is truly alone, he seeks comfort in the one 'friend' who will not reject him and who accepts him as he is - his favorite snack food.

Because Benny is currently on a very restrictive diet, his teachers and residence staff monitor his caloric intake scrupulously. This has forced Benny to be very creative and crafty in how he 'squirrels' away food. Occasionally, he is caught and the food is confiscated, but more often he is successful; for example, when he earns sufficient points to go into town, though he is prohibited from going into fast-food restaurants like McDonald's or convenience stores, he pays other residential students to purchase snack food and place it in predetermined caches where Benny can retrieve and eat the food surreptitiously and away from prying eyes.

At school, Benny is only allowed a healthy snack such as carrot or celery sticks at recess. He has attempted, on several occasions, to hide preferred, high-calorie snacks such as candy bars in his bookbag or inside his desk, but he is never successful because his classmates are happy to report him. Once alerted, his teachers confiscate the candy bars, which often causes a scene. Benny becomes angry and aggressive and typically ends up in the quiet room without access to any snack food.

In the latest incident involving Benny and his obsession with food, he was discovered missing during bed checks by residence staff and following a thorough search of the campus, Benny was discovered in the dumpster outside the school's dining hall. Apparently, he had been so hungry he tried to reach some discarded supper foods, slipped, and tumbled forward into the dumpster. Needless to say, he was unable to extricate himself and it took several male staff members to lift him out. Benny was terribly embarrassed by the debacle and wants desperately to overcome his compulsive eating, but he is powerless to do so.

Characteristics of Binge Eating Disorder

Binge eating disorder (BED) is a common phenomenon in people who are obese and who have little or no concern about their weight. BED is eating an excessive amount of high-calorie food within a short period of time. What distinguishes BED from BN is the lack of compensatory behaviors. The frequency of binge eating episodes required by the DSM-V (American Psychiatric Association, 2013) is described as being on average at least once a week for three months and may be more applicable to adults than to adolescents, whose behaviors may be more intermittent and have various periods of intensity (Lock & Le Grange, 2019).

General Characteristics of Eating Disorders

Given the strict diagnostic criteria for eating disorders in the DSM-V (American Psychiatric Association, 2013), many adolescents do not meet the criteria for either AN or BN, yet still have behaviors that can be considered an eating disorder and fall into the category of ED-NOS. In spite of the diagnostic difficulties, all individuals with eating disorders share several common characteristics that are useful to understanding eating disorders in adolescents:

- An abnormal attitude or set of beliefs about food, weight, and/or shape
- A degree of emotional, social, or behavioral dysfunction that results from these behaviors and attitudes (significant problems with school, work, social, or familial functioning)
- Evidence that these behaviors and attitudes are unlikely to change without intervention (Lock & Le Grange, 2019)

Epidemiology, Prevalence, and Developmental Course of Eating Disorders

Most studies have estimated the point prevalence rate for AN in adolescent girls to be 0.4 percent, or 1 in 200 girls (American Psychiatric Association, 2013). Incidence rates for AN have risen continuously. In the 1980s, the incidence rate of AN for women between the ages of 15 and 24 was 8 per 100,000 (Hoek, 2006). The rise in cases of AN has eliminated social class as a major predictor. It is not clear whether this rise is a true one or simply the result of improved detection, screening, and heightened awareness in both the professional and general populations.

Prevalence rates for BN are higher and have been estimated to be anywhere from 1 to 1.5 percent (American Psychiatric Association, 2013). Subclinical cases of BN are considerably more common. It is estimated that anywhere from 4 to 19 percent of young women may engage in less severe bulimic-type behaviors (Hoek, 2006). BN is also on the rise, especially among younger age groups. Adult women, however, have the highest prevalence rate, estimated to be about 2 percent. Epidemiological data for BED is rather scant, given the recent addition of this disorder. The prevalence rate for BED among adult females is 1.6 and 0.8 percent among males (American Psychiatric Association, 2013).

With regard to gender, all three eating disorders have higher prevalence rates among girls than among boys. For AN, the prevalence rate is 19:2, female to male, and for BN it is 29 to 1 per 100,000 (Mangweth-Matzek & Hoek, 2017). In general, adolescent and adult males comprise approximately 10 percent of clinically diagnosed cases of eating disorders (American Psychiatric Association, 2013). Some believe that eating disorders are significantly underdiagnosed in males because of a prevailing bias toward seeing such disorders as exclusively female. In addition, some symptoms, such as binge eating, may be more socially accepted in men than in women, and men may be less likely than women to seek clinical intervention for their disordered eating. Women are more likely than men to seek treatment for their disordered eating (Thapliyal et al., 2018). Further research is needed to determine more accurately the prevalence of eating disorders in males. Many young men suffer from acute levels of anxiety about being either too fat or insufficiently muscular. To what degree these symptoms approach subclinical and clinical problems warrants further investigation.

Developmental Course of Eating Disorders

Anorexia nervosa and bulimia nervosa appear to have different developmental courses, with the former being the more serious in terms of morbidity and mortality (Gorrell et al., 2020).

Anorexia Nervosa

Anorexia nervosa typically develops in early adolescence, around the age of 13 or 14, with the individual beginning a diet to either lose weight, eat healthier, or improve performance in some activity such as sports or dancing. The dieting usually begins with cutting out a small number of foods, such as desserts, but as time goes on, the food choices become more narrowed, with an emphasis on consuming smaller quantities. Food preparation can become quite elaborate, accompanied by an obsession over not consuming a morsel of food that is contraindicated. Often, the individual will prefer to eat by themselves.

As food consumption decreases, rigid adherence to an exercise regimen increases. Through self-induced vomiting, the individual progresses to purging even a small quantity of consumed food and may also resort to diet pills and laxatives. At some point during the process, as body fat declines, menstruation ceases in postmenarcheal females, though this varies according to the individual. Some develop amenorrhea early in the process, whereas others continue to menstruate in spite of being very underweight (Mehler, 2017b). This variability resulted in the removal of amenorrhea as a required diagnostic criterion for AN in the DSM-V. As malnutrition sets in, a number of medical problems begin to develop, which may include:

- Lowered body temperature
- Decreased blood pressure and heart rate
- Changes in skin and hair texture, including lanugo (the development of fine body hair)
- Hypogonadism, causing ovary malfunction
- Cardiac dysfunction
- Brain abnormalities
- Gastrointestinal difficulties (Couturier & Lock, 2006)

Some of these problems can become life-threatening. The most common chronic medical problems among those with AN include growth retardation and bone mass reduction (Himmerich et al., 2020).

Outcomes for persons with AN vary, as some make a complete recovery while others suffer from long-term weight gains and losses, which may lead to the development of BN. Some never recover and follow a deteriorating course that may result in death. The crude mortality rate is about 5 percent per decade (American Psychiatric Association, 2013) Most of the deaths are from medical complications. Death from AN is higher than from any other psychiatric disorder (van Hoeken & Hoek, 2020). The longer the illness exists, the greater is the chance of death.

Bulimia Nervosa

In comparison to AN, bulimia nervosa (BN) develops later in adolescence, with most cases beginning around the age of 18 (Lock & le Grange, 2006). Prior to its development, individuals typically have a history of preoccupation with their weight, and many of them suffered from mild to moderate obesity in childhood (Lock & le Grange, 2006). Their histories often include failed attempts at weight reduction, and many report that their binge eating is the result of denying themselves food through fasting and dieting. The cycle includes guilt over binging and the consequential purging to avoid gaining weight. The most common form of purging is vomiting, but the use of laxatives, diuretics, and exercise is also common.

As the illness progresses, these individuals organize their lives around opportunities to binge. Because binging is done in private, they may withdraw from family and friends, show declines in their schoolwork, and suffer from depressed mood (Cleveland Clinic, 2019). In addition to binging, those with BN may participate in other impulsive behaviors such as drug use and stealing (Lock & le Grange, 2006). Although the weight of those with BN may fluctuate rather significantly, it rarely approaches the dangerously low levels of those with AN. According to the Cleveland Clinic (2019), common medical problems, mostly the result of purging, include:

- Low potassium levels
- Tears in the esophagus
- Gastric abnormalities
- Dehydration
- Severe changes in heart rate and blood pressure

In a 2018 - 2019 study (Elflein, 2020), the mortality rate for those with BN was one 980 as compared to almost 2,700 for anorexia nervosa. It should be noted that any of the medical problems associated with BN can become severe enough to cause death. Without treatment, bulimics can sustain a regimen of binging and purging for many years. Many patients are treated successfully, with about 50 percent becoming asymptomatic and another 20 percent significantly improved (Linardon et al., 2018).

Comorbidity And Differential Diagnosis of Eating Disorders

Conditions that are comorbid with eating disorders can be both psychological and medical. The most common DSM-V disorders that are comorbid with eating disorders are mood, anxiety, substance use, and personality disorders (American Psychiatric Association, 2013). Depression is the most frequent comorbid condition for both AN and BN.

As a result of starvation, an individual with AN may exhibit many symptoms of depression, such as insomnia, irritability, fatigue, dysphoria, psychomotor retardation, and social withdrawal (Alhussien et al., 2019). When proper weight is restored, many of these symptoms tend to disappear. It is therefore recommended that assessment for depression take place when the individual is within 10 percent of normal weight.

According to de Oliveira Gonzalez et al. (2020), the most frequent personality disorders associated with AN, restricting type, are obsessive-compulsive (22 percent), avoidant (19 percent), borderline or dependent (10 percent). In contrast, the most frequent personality disorders in those with AN, binge eating/ purging type, are borderline (25 percent), avoidant or dependent (15 percent), histrionic (10 percent) (de Oliveira Gonzalez et al., 2020). Borderline is also the most frequent comorbid personality disorder for those with BN (28 percent), followed by dependent (20 percent) and histrionic (20 percent) (de Oliveira Gonzalez et al., 2020).

One of the more difficult differential diagnoses is between AN and obsessive-compulsive disorder, or OCD (Lloyd et al., 2019). Those with AN limit their obsessive-compulsiveness to food and weight. For full-blown OCD to exist, the obsessive-compulsiveness must include aspects beyond food and weight. Anxiety disorders may coexist with eating disorders and AN in particular, but a drive for thinness and extreme fear of becoming fat should not be confused with phobias and other anxiety disorders (Lloyd et al., 2019).

The high comorbidity between eating disorders and depression should be a major concern; however, depression is given as a separate diagnosis only if the depressive symptoms appear to be unrelated to the consequences of the eating disorder, such as starvation, sleep disturbance, low energy, and poor concentration (Marucci et al., 2018). Overeating can be a symptom of depressive disorders but is distinguished from overeating in BN by the absence of compensatory behaviors (Levinson et al., 2017). Similarly, weight loss associated with depression is not accompanied by intense fear of becoming fat, a critical sign of AN (American Psychiatric Association, 2013). The same may be said for body dysmorphic disorder, which is characterized by an excessive preoccupation with defects in general appearance that is not limited to body shape and size or the fear of becoming fat.

Medical conditions that are comorbid with eating disorders are numerous and are listed below. Most of these medical conditions will subside with an increase in nutrition, though some such as growth stunting and long-term risk of fractures) may persist even after a return to normal weight (Bulik et al., 2016; O'Brien et al., 2017).

Medical Conditions Comorbid with Eating Disorders

Structural brain abnormalities

- Brain atrophy
- Deficits in gray matter
- Altered serotonin levels
- Altered blood flow to the brain

Dental and dermatological abnormalities

- Dental erosion
- Skin lesions
- Alopecia

Endocrinological abnormalities

- Osteopenia
- Osteoporosis
- Metabolic irregularities

Gynecological abnormalities

- Amenorrhea

Gastrointestinal abnormalities

- Bleeding
- Peptide release
- Gastric emptying
- Gastric capacity

Source: Adapted from Terre, L., Poston, W. S. C., II, & Foreyt, J. P. (2006). Eating disorders. In E. J. Mash & R. A. Barkley (Eds.), *Treatment of childhood disorders* (3rd. ed., pp. 783–784). New York: Guilford Press.

Etiology of Eating Disorders

Etiological factors in the development of eating disorders can be divided into biological, psychological, familial, and sociocultural factors.

Biological Factors

The role of genetics has been investigated as a cause of eating disorders. Studies have found higher rates for both AN and BN in first-degree relatives of those with these disorders (Bulik et al., 2016). Twins studies have revealed higher concordance rates among monozygotic (identical) twins than among dizygotic (fraternal) twins - 50 percent versus 14 percent (Hübel et al., 2018; Wade & Bulik, 2018). The unraveling of shared and nonshared environments in the causality of eating disorders remains a work in progress, and the contribution of genetic versus environmental influences remains somewhat unclear. Although some genetic influence (O'Brien et al., 2017) may be apparent, it is not clear exactly what is being genetically transmitted (Waszczuk et al., 2019). Is a genetically inherited temperament or personality trait(s) responsible for the development of an eating disorder? The answer to this question is not really known. The safest thing that can be said about the role of genetics in the causation of eating disorders is that girls, especially girls who grow up in families in which either the mother, father, or a sister has an eating disorder, are very much at risk for developing an eating disorder of their own (Bulik et al., 2016).

Investigators have also considered the role of neurobiological factors, most especially differences in serotonin activity, among those with eating disorders. Low levels of serotonin have been found in those with BN, and antidepressants that increase levels of serotonin have been efficacious in the treatment of those with BN (Krzystanek & Palasz, 2020). If binge eating of high-calorie foods plays a role in mood regulation (i.e., increases levels of serotonin), an antidepressant regimen may very well decrease the desire for such foods. In contrast, it has been hypothesized that those with AN may suffer from an overactivity of serotonin, which would decrease the desire for food intake (Haleem, 2017). Though studies have shown an association between serotonin activity and eating disorders, a definite causal link has not been established. It is possible that the differing levels of serotonin could also be the result of an eating disorder rather than the cause (Bailer et al., 2017). Serotonin activity seems to play a role in numerous other disorders; therefore, it may be a common pathway rather than a specific link to eating disorders (Ericsson et al., 1996).

Recently, some research has investigated prenatal, perinatal, and early childhood complications as possibly having a role in the development of eating disorders (Marzola et al., 2020). Perinatal factors in the development of AN include preterm birth (less than 32 weeks of gestation), low birth weight, and birth trauma as well as pediatric infectious disease.

Psychological Factors

Personality. For many years, the role of personality patterns has been considered an important factor in the development of eating disorders. Those with AN often exhibit premorbid personality patterns of compliance, perfectionism, dependence, social inhibition, emotional restraint, obsession, self-hate, guilt, low in novelty-seeking, high in harm avoidance, and high in reward dependence (Farstad et al., 2016). Depression, poor impulse control, acting-out behaviors, low frustration tolerance, affective lability, difficult temperament, and inhibition have all been posited as personality traits that are common in those with BN (Barajas-Iglesias et al., 2017). More recent research has examined the role of attentional biases in the development of eating disorders (Jiang & Vartanian, 2018).

Early Trauma. Another line of research in the development of eating disorders is the experiencing of early trauma in the form of separation and loss, family discord and divorce, parental death, dysfunctional parental behavior, parental illness, sibling or parental pregnancy, and other types of family difficulties (Groth et al., 2019). Childhood sexual abuse has received special attention as an etiological factor (Opydo-Szymaczek et al., 2018). The greatest continuity has been between sexual abuse and BN, and there appears to be a small yet positive relationship between eating disorders and sexual abuse (Levine & Smolak, 2020). Sexual abuse has more of an indirect effect because of its association with other risk factors and is part of a complex interaction in the development of eating disorders (Van Tu et al., 2020). The relationship between traumatic events and eating disorders has extended to sexual harassment (Van Tu et al., 2020).

Adolescent Developmental Patterns. Adolescent developmental patterns have also been seen as playing a major role in the development of eating disorders. Adolescence can be a time of great insecurity, especially about one's physical appearance. Pubertal changes, especially those that result in weight gain, can leave some adolescents feeling negatively about their bodies. Some are victims of teasing. This can create a desire to be thin, especially in light of the emphasis on fashion in our society. An exaggerated focus on weight and shape may lead some adolescents to engage in extreme and various weight-loss measures (Mairs & Nicholls, 2016).

Studies have found that as many as 45 percent of children express a desire to be thinner and approximately 37 percent engage in some form of dieting or other weight-loss strategy. These rates increase in middle and high school, with some estimates being as high as 70 percent of high school girls engaging in some form of weight loss strategy. Engaging in measures that are extreme and harmful is a significant risk factor in the development of an eating disorder (Izydorczyk & Sitnik-Warchulska, 2018).

Sociocultural Factors

For many years, Western society's pressure for thinness has been held responsible for the development of eating disorders. As our society becomes more obese, thinness also becomes a rare and valued commodity (Sansone et al. 2005). Being thin has a strong connection with fashion, success, and beauty and is constantly reflected in the media. This is seen, most especially, in magazines and television shows that are popular among adolescents. Femininity and self-worth are defined in terms of body size (Weissman, 2019). This bombardment can easily result in some adolescents resorting to extreme weight-loss measures. For males, the media's portrayal of muscularity and low body fat as an indication of real manhood can contribute to body dissatisfaction and increased concerns about weight (Laporta-Herrero et al., 2018). Concern is also high for those who come from other cultures. In an effort to increase their acculturation and social acceptance in their new environment, they may internalize the cultural messages about weight, which could result in disordered eating (Warren & Akoury, 2020).

Since AN also exists in non-Western cultures where the emphasis on thinness is absent, it would appear, then, that eating disorders are not culture-bound syndromes rather that etiological factors vary across cultures (Weissman, 2019).

Family Factors

Serious attention has been given to family dysfunction as a possible cause of eating disorders. Those with eating disorders have been found to come from families that are enmeshed, conflict-avoidant, inflexible and controlling (in cases of AN;) chaotic, critical, and conflicted (in cases of BN). High incidences of weight problems, eating disorders, physical illness, affective disorders, obsessive-compulsive disorders, and alcoholism in families have all been considered risk factors in the development of eating disorders (Cerniglia et al., 2017; Husarić et al., 2018). Two things, however, must be said about these kinds of family dysfunction and eating disorders. First, not all those with eating disorders come from families with these kinds of dysfunction. Second, these types of family dysfunction have also been linked to numerous other emotional disorders. It is difficult, therefore, to isolate a family factor(s) as having a direct etiological link to eating disorders. At best, they may play an indirect role and be part of the pathway to the development of an eating disorder.

According to most studies, general family environment and family dynamics do not predict disordered eating (Pearlman et al., 2020). On the other hand, parents and family members who tend to tease, criticize, and offer weight-loss advice to a family member have been shown to contribute to negative body image and unhealthy weight-control measures (Pearlman et al., 2020).

Summary

From the above description, it seems certain the causality of eating disorders is multidetermined, and that antecedents to the disorder vary from one individual to another (Tóthová, 2019). In recent years there has been a bias in favor of biological and genetic factors. Eating disorders are most likely the result of a genetic/biological predisposition to the disorder that interacts with a number of cognitive, psychological, and environmental variables to result in symptoms as outlined in the DSM-V (American Psychiatric Association, 2013). Future research needs to examine more carefully these interacting factors to determine perhaps the pathway(s) of an eating disorder. This will help shed some light on what is currently understood as a complex and, to some extent, undetermined etiology of eating disorders.

Assessment of Eating Disorders

As for many other disorders, the assessment of eating disorders needs to be comprehensive and multimodal (Smith et al., 2018), and should include a medical evaluation, an interview with the adolescent, an interview with the parents, consultation with a dietician, and, if necessary, the administration of a standardized assessment instrument(s).

Medical Evaluation

Any individual with an eating disorder (or suspected of having one) should undergo a thorough medical evaluation by a pediatric specialist or internist. Careful attention needs to be paid to signs of malnutrition such as tooth erosion, dehydration, and lanugo (Sacco & Kelley, 2018). Blood tests are performed with special attention to liver, kidney, and thyroid functioning to rule out other illnesses that might be responsible for weight loss. In addition, an examination of the cardiovascular, endocrinological/metabolic, gastrointestinal, dermatological, and pulmonary systems is necessary (Mehler, 2017a). Electrolyte imbalance, the result of purging, can manifest through complaints of weakness, tiredness, constipation, and depression and should not be overlooked (Mehler, 2017a). The medical evaluation is a key element in determining whether hospitalization is necessary for those whose lives might be in danger due to the consequences of having an eating disorder.

Interview with the Adolescent

Engagement of adolescents with eating disorders can be difficult, as they are often in denial about their condition. The interviewer must be both empathic and challenging to break through the denial. The existence of a precipitating event, such as the onset of menses, family conflicts, starting middle or high school, dating, a romantic breakup, or knowing others in and outside the family who might be dieting (Lock & le Grange, 2006).

Second, the interviewer should obtain a detailed history of efforts to lose weight, such as counting calories, restricting consumption of fats, fasting, skipping meals, not drinking, restricting consumption of meat and protein, increased exercise, binge eating, purging behaviors (exercise, laxatives, diuretics), and use of stimulants and diet pills (both over-the-counter supplements and illegal products) (Lock & le Grange, 2006).

Individuals who have AN and those who have BN both engage in binge eating; therefore, this must also be assessed. The difference between the two disorders is that those who have AN may refer to eating a normal amount of food as binging, whereas for those who have BN, the binging usually involves eating excessive amounts of high-calorie food. The interviewer should pay attention to possible physical symptoms such as dizziness, headaches, fainting spells, weakness, poor concentration, stomach and abdominal pain, and loss of menses (Tomba et al., 2019 Lock et al., 2017). These symptoms are often the result of binging and purging behaviors.

Interview with the Parents

There are several purposes to the parent/guardian interview; therefore, the primary adults who are involved in the life of the adolescent should attend. The first purpose is to assess the adolescent's development history:

- Pre-, peri-, and postnatal complications
- Early feeding history
- Transition into preschool and elementary school
- Quality and differences of attachment to mother and father
- Early temperament
- Family problems
- Relationships with siblings and peers (Lock & le Grange, 2006)

The interviewer should also pay careful attention to signs of overprotectiveness, communication problems, and conflict-resolution strategies, which have all been implicated in the development of eating disorders (Cerniglia et al., 2017). The family's history of eating and weight-related behaviors such as dieting and whether the adolescent was a victim of insults or teasing concerning issues of weight also needs to be assessed (Pearson et al., 2017). The parent interview may also be used to assess interpersonal difficulties outside the family, as eating disorders are known to impede psychosocial development.

Consultation with a Dietician

The main purpose of this assessment is to determine the adolescent's body mass index (BMI) and to establish a weight range for recovery (Lock & le Grange, 2006) based on proper nutrition. The consultation is necessary for both the adolescent and the parents who are in charge of monitoring their child's nutrition. The dietician or nutritionist's scientific knowledge may help to challenge faulty beliefs about food that usually develop in those with an eating disorder; for example, if an adolescent accepts the idea of eating a bagel but objects to eating a poppy-seed bagel because of its additional calories, the dietician might be able to deal with such obsessiveness by providing accurate information about the additional calories in a poppy-seed bagel.

Standardized Assessment

Numerous formal instruments can be used for the assessment of eating disorders. It is beyond the scope of this chapter to discuss all of them. The majority of these measures are designed to assess cognitions and behaviors either through self-report or a diagnostic interview. Others assess outcomes expectancies associated with dieting and other eating behaviors, dietary restraint (those who have dieted many times and failed), body image, and appearance. All of the instruments listed in Table 7.1 have been published since 1988 and have sound psychometric properties.

Table 7.1. Assessment Measures for Eating Disorders

Purpose	**Domain/construct**	**Instrument**	**Authors**
Diagnostic Interview	Assess severity of eating preoccupation and rituals	*Yale-Brown-Cornell Eating Disorder Scale* (YBC-EDS)	Mazure et al., 1994
	Frequency and severity of eating behaviors and attitudes	*Eating Disorder Examination* (EDE, 12th edition)	Fairburn & Cooper, 1993
Self-report of behavioral symptoms	Frequency and severity of eating behaviors and attitudes	*Eating Disorder Questionnaire* (EDE-Q)	Fairburn & Belgin, 1994
	Severity of symptoms associated with AN and BN	*Eating Disorder Inventory-2* (EDI-2)	Garner, 1991
	Bulimia symptoms, DSM-IV criteria	*Bulimia Test-Revised* (BULIT-R)	Thelen et al., 1996

	Symptoms of eating disorders, DSM-IV criteria	*Eating Attitudes Test* (EAT)	Lavik et al., 1991
	Children's symptoms of eating disorders	*Children's Eating Attitudes Test* (ChEAT)	Maloney et al., 1989
	Symptom checklist for bulimia and binge-eating	*Eating Questionnaire-Revised* (EQR)	Williamson et al., 1989
	DSN-IV criteria for diagnosing AN, BN, and binge-eating disorder	*Survey for Eating Disorders* (SEDs)	Gotestam & Agras, 1995
	DSM-IV criteria for diagnosing eating disorders	*Questionnaire for Eating Disorder Diagnoses* (QEDD)	Mintz et al, 1997
	DSM-IV criteria for diagnosing AN, BN, and binge-eating disorder	*Eating Disorder Diagnostic Scale* (EDDS)	Stice at al., 2000
	Eating disorder cognitions and behaviors	*Sterling Eating Disorder Scales* (SEDS)	Williams et al., 1994
	Cognitions associated with eating disorders	*Mizes Anorectic Cognitions Questionnaire* (MAC-R)	Mizes et al., 2000
Assess expectancies	Expectancies related to dieting practices and losing weight	*Weight Loss Expectancy Scale* (WLES)	Allen et al., 1993
	Cognitive expectancies for eating	*Eating Expectancy Inventory* (EEI)	Holstein et al., 1998
	Cognitive expectancies for dieting and thinness	*Thinness and Restricting Expectancy Inventory* (TREI)	Hohlstein et al., 1998
Assess dietary restraint	Caloric restriction and disinhibited eating	*Restrain Scale*	Lowe, 1993
	Cognitive aspects of restrained eating	*Dutch Eating Behavior Questionnaire-Revised* (DEBQ-R)	van Strien et al., 1986
	Cognitive aspects of restrained eating	*Factor Eating Questionnaire-Revised* (FEQ-R)	Stunkard & Merrick, 1985

Assess body image	Dysfunctional beliefs about implications of one's appearance	*Beliefs about Appearance Scale* (BAAS)	Spangler & Stice, 2001
	Body image attitudes	*Multidimensional Body-Self Relations Questionnaire* (MBRSQ)	Cash, 1994

Source: Adapted from Collins, R. L., & Ricciardelli, L. A. (2005). Assessment of eating orders and obesity by In D. M. Donovan and G. A. Marlatt (Eds.), *Assessment of addictive behaviors* (pp.326–327). New York: Guilford Press.

Treatment of Eating Disorders

Depending on the possible need for hospitalization, treatment for eating disorders differs according to where the treatment takes place. Inpatient treatment is typically multidisciplinary, with the goal of restoring the patient to a noncritical weight.

Inpatient Treatment

Many good, specialized inpatient treatment centers exist for eating disorders. Weight that is 15 to 25 percent below average, significant medical problems, psychiatric emergencies (e.g., a suicide attempt), and the failure of outpatient treatment may all be cause for hospitalization (Cooney et al., 2018). A typical inpatient team includes a psychiatrist, a psychologist, a medical consultant, and a dietician or nutritionist. The primary goal of inpatient treatment is refeeding, with an initial goal of 1000 to 1600 calories per day, gradually increased to 3000 to 3600 calories per day (Hale & Logomarsino, 2019). Forced feeding through gastric tubing is rare, and the patient is encouraged to participate as much as possible in planning meals (Pennell et al., 2019) Along with the goals for caloric intake, there are also goals for weight gain of anywhere from one to three pounds per week (Ziser et al., 2018). Patient denial, comorbid conditions (e.g., depression and other medical problems), and the feeling of loss of control inherent in any hospitalization may all delay or hinder successful inpatient treatment (Ali et al., 2017).

The length of hospital stay for eating disorders is varied but, for the most part, in recent years has been trending downward, with typical hospitalization ranges anywhere from seven to twenty-six days (Isserlin et al., 2020). In some programs, patients transition to less intensive care before being fully discharged. Discharge is recommended when the patient has achieved a stable and suitable weight, is medically stable, and has identified psychological and family factors that need to be addressed in outpatient treatment (Li et al., 2020).

Individual Counseling

Individual approaches for those with eating disorders have included behavioral therapy, cognitive-behavioral therapy (CBT), and interpersonal therapy. Research has failed to identify an overwhelmingly more effective approach for treating all eating disorders. The one exception appears to be the use of CBT as an initial treatment for BN (Linardon et al., 2018).

Behavior Therapy

Techniques used in the behavioral approach to treating eating disorders include response prevention, operant conditioning, response delay, self-monitoring techniques, and stimulus control (Bartholdy et al., 2016, 2017; Lindgreen et al., 2018; Magson et al., 2020; Waller & Raykos, 2019).

Response Prevention. In response prevention, the individual is prevented from vomiting. For these individuals, vomiting reduces anxiety; therefore, the hypothesis is that those with eating disorders will not binge if they are prevented from vomiting. Empirical support for the efficacy of response prevention in treating eating disorders, however, is somewhat limited (Magson et al., 2020).

Operant Conditioning. Operant conditioning (the use of positive and negative environmental contingencies) has been used primarily in inpatient settings. Research has shown that when it is used within a comprehensive treatment plan, operant conditioning can be helpful (Waller & Raykos, 2019).

Response Delay. Response delay is designed to have the client delay the impulse to binge by participating, for example, in an alternative activity. The technique is based on the hypothesis that if the response can be delayed, the sequence of events can be altered (Bartholdy et al., 2016, 2017). Response delay is a commonly used and well-accepted technique in the treatment of eating disorders in spite of the absence of studies that support its effectiveness.

Self-monitoring Techniques. As part of a comprehensive treatment plan and not as a stand-alone treatment, self-monitoring techniques have proven useful in helping with eating disorders (Lindgreen et al., 2018). This intervention requires careful monitoring by the individual of his or her thoughts, feelings, and behaviors, both before and after the problematic behavior. This information is then used in counseling, with the goal of manipulating the antecedents that lead to the behavior.

Stimulus Control. Stimulus control involves environmental engineering to remove or reduce opportunities to participate in problematic eating; for example, favorite high-calorie foods, the preference of many binge-eaters, are not kept in the home (Bartholdy et al., 2017). Replacement strategies might include removing all candy and substituting fresh fruit. Little research has been done on the effectiveness of stimulus control, specifically. It is, however, very much a part of CBT programs, because logic suggests that reducing the opportunities to binge-eat makes sense.

Cognitive Behavioral Approaches

The primary goal of CBT is the use of techniques to restructure an individual's distorted cognitions about body image and his or her faulty beliefs that equate thinness with worthiness, strength, and success in conjunction with some of the behavioral techniques described earlier (Agras et al., 2017). Empirical support for the use of CBT, especially with BN, is very strong (Linardon et al., 2017). Studies have also found CBT and pharmacological intervention to be superior to drugs alone in the treatment of BN (Svaldi et al., 2019). With AN, CBT has been shown to be helpful in relapse prevention (Berends et al., 2018) and the use of CBT with adolescents who have AN has been studied empirically, although to a lesser extent than in adults; however, there is general support for its effectiveness (Essayli & Vitousek, 2020). Studies have shown that CBT can also be effective in treating binge eating disorder (Hilbert et al., 2007; Hilbert, Herpertz et al., 2020).

Interpersonal Counseling

Interpersonal counseling focuses on the client's relationships, based on the hypothesis that maladaptive relationships have either a direct or an indirect effect on the development of eating disorders. Research has found that this approach is as effective as CBT in treating BN, but results are obtained more slowly (Karam et al., 2019).

Family Counseling

Based on the hypothesis that maladaptive patterns of family interaction play an important role in the etiology of eating disorders, family counseling has long been a preferred mode of treatment. Family counseling is often used as a component of a comprehensive treatment package. Interventions range from simply providing education to the family about the disorder to changing a family's structural patterns. The latter approach is based on structural family therapy (SFT) and results from the hypothesis that those with eating disorders come from families that are overly enmeshed, overprotected, and conflict-avoidant (Lindblad-Goldberg & Northey, 2013). The goal of counseling is to effectuate a gradual disengagement from the family that allows the adolescent appropriate separation and autonomy. Families are helped to establish boundaries that are neither too rigid nor too diffuse.

A different approach utilizes the family as a resource in the treatment by eliciting their help in refeeding, consistent application of eating patterns, and meeting the developmental challenges of adolescence (Murray, 2019; Rienecke, 2017). In some ways, the family's role is similar to that of a nurse in that it provides parental control over eating until the adolescent is able to maintain consistent and appropriate eating alone.

Using the family as a resource may be more effective in weight restoration, yet less effective than individual treatment in dealing with some of the psychological variables responsible for the disorder. The effectiveness of family versus individual approaches may also depend on age, with older adolescents and adults doing better with individual treatment (Jewell et al., 2016). One thing, however, remains clear - whether they are seen together with or separately from their adolescent son or daughter, parents need to be involved in the treatment of eating disorders, and this is especially true for those who develop eating problems at a younger age.

Group Counseling

Over the years, group work has been used more with BN and BED and less so with AN. Until the adolescent is medically stabilized, group work is not advisable for those who have AN. Recent studies, however, have shown promising results after stabilization (Hilbert et al., 2017). Group interventions commonly employ either a feminist and/or psychoeducational perspective. In the former, participants are given the opportunity to discuss the conflicting demands placed on women. They are helped not to turn over their self-definition as women to the sexist elements of society. The psychoeducational approach provides information about the disorder, and the group members act as coaches and sources of support for each other. Although it is not suitable for everyone, the psychoeducational group approach offers efficient and cost-effective treatment (Tak et al., 2016).

Pharmacological Treatment

In general, the use of psychotropic medications for those with eating disorders is not effective. In cases of AN as some have argued that certain medications can help to stimulate appetite, whereas others have argued that lack of appetite is rarely the cause of AN (Lock, 2019). Medication is more indicated to prevent relapse after the individual has reached a healthy weight. The use of SSRIs and other antidepressants has been more common in treating BN, based on the theory that the disorder is the result of decreased levels of serotonin in the brain. Based on the current literature, the use of antidepressants can be useful for the short-term treatment of BN, yet medication alone is associated with more relapse and less overall effectiveness than CBT (Hilbert, Petroff et al., 2020)

Treatment Outcomes

Outcome literature on eating disorders reveals that about one-third of patients experience poor outcomes (Eddy & Thomas, 2019). Factors related to poor outcomes for those with AN are hospitalizations, longer duration of illness, very low weight during illness, and the presence of bulimic symptoms such as vomiting and laxative abuse. Favorable factors include early age of onset, high socioeconomic status, good parent-child relationships, short interval between onset and treatment, histrionic personality, and short duration of inpatient treatment without readmission (McCabe et al., 2019). Dobresuc et al. (2020) report that outcome literature suggests the following with regard to those diagnosed with AN:

- The mortality rate in AN averages from 5 to 6 percent.
- Full recovery occurs in only about 45 percent; 33 percent improve, and 20 percent develop a chronic course.
- A large proportion of patients evidences other psychiatric disorders throughout life (e.g., mood, anxiety, substance abuse, obsessive-compulsive, and personality disorders).
- About one-third do not achieve normal employment and education, and only a minority enter marriage or a stable relationship.

In general, those diagnosed with BN tend to have better outcomes than those diagnosed with AN or those who have AN and BN. A significant number can continue with subclinical features of BN. Based on the 22-year follow up of those with BN, the following can be tentatively said about those diagnosed with BN:

- Full recovery occurs in about 47 percent; 26 percent improve; and 26 percent are chronic cases.
- Mortality rates are less than 1 percent.
- Many have other psychiatric disorders: mood disorders (25 percent), substance abuse (15 percent), and anxiety (13 percent) (Eddy et al., 2017).

Conclusions

Eating disorders are complex, have a multifactorial etiology, and require a comprehensive treatment plan to heighten the probability of a favorable outcome. There is a need for greater understanding of eating disorders in diverse populations to assess more clearly the cultural dimension in the etiology of these disorders. Less research exists for younger populations who suffer from eating disorders. The lack of clinical trials prevents us from discovering consistently effective methods of treatment for adolescents. The research that exists suggests that family intervention should be part of a comprehensive treatment plan based primarily on a CBT approach. Those who work in schools should be adept at recognizing an adolescent who shows signs of an incipient eating disorder. The more quickly treatment can begin, the better the prognosis. Those who are already working with students diagnosed with an eating disorder need to know and maintain the pathways for these adolescents to access and participate in a comprehensive treatment plan.

School-Based Interventions

As with any emotional or behavioral disorder, before an effective school-based intervention can be identified and implemented, a functional assessment needs to be conducted. The purpose of the assessment is to determine the frequency, intensity, and duration of the problem behavior—in this case, the eating disorder—as well as the function or purpose it serves for the affected individual.

To ensure the thoroughness and reliability of the assessment, it is recommended that multidisciplinary team members employ a strategic approach that includes (1) identifying and describing the problem behavior, (2) collecting baseline data as well as information about academic performance, (3) describing the context in which the behavior is observed, (4) completing a functional assessment form and/or behavior rating scale as appropriate, (5) conducting a direct observation, (6) developing a hypothesis, and (7) testing the hypothesis and then modifying it as necessary (Barnhill, 2005). Once a valid hypothesis has been established, the multidisciplinary team can develop an appropriate behavioral intervention plan (BIP) and have reasonable confidence in its likelihood of success.

Anorexia nervosa, bulimia nervosa, and eating disorder, not otherwise specified, can have different etiologies and behavioral manifestations; therefore, we will provide an individual assessment and intervention plan for each of our three representative case examples.

Assessing the Problem: Kate

In the case involving Kate, a student diagnosed with anorexia nervosa, our assessment is as follows.

Identifying and Describing the Problem Behavior. The most serious effect of Kate's AN in the classroom is its negative impact on her health as evidenced in her fainting spells, which are clearly the result of not eating. Ultimately, these episodes will negatively impact her academic performance and given her "perfectionism," will affect her self-esteem and emotional well-being.

Collecting Baseline Data and Academic Information. Kate's teachers will closely monitor her fainting spells and ensure that she has access to a bagel and some fruit if she appears to be on the verge of passing out or states that she feels dizzy or light-headed. They will also provide remedial support in the event that she needs to miss class for health reasons or requires the re-teaching of missed curriculum.

Describing the Context in Which the Behavior Is Observed. Kate's fainting spells seem to occur most often in the morning and, when asked about what she ate before coming to school, Kate typically reports that she "doesn't eat breakfast." She seems to "perk up," according to her classroom teacher once she has eaten a piece of a bagel or fruit under the supervision of the school nurse.

Completing a Functional Assessment and/or Behavior Rating Scales as Appropriate. A daily log is maintained by Kate's lunch monitor that documents both the start and end times for her lunch, determined by the time needed to achieve her target calorie intake. The monitor also provides an anecdotal entry describing Kate's demeanor and disposition throughout the meal. Periodic reviews of the log reveal changes in eating behavior and are used to plan or adjust treatment approaches as well as target calorie intake levels. Kate is weighed daily at school by the nurse to monitor weight loss and gain, and to be sure that her body weight does not drop below the minimum level prescribed as "acceptable."

Conducting a Direct Observation. Lunch period is the only context in which the target behavior is observed and that observation is carefully recorded by Kate's lunch-time monitor; therefore, further direct observation is unnecessary.

Developing a Hypothesis. Kate's lack of proper daily nourishment that provides sufficient calories to enable her to function effectively in school is the primary behavioral issue. It is hoped that, as her treatment plan proves effective in helping her overcome her fear of gaining weight and her desire to maintain a subnormal body weight, Kate will take less time to attain her target calorie level, thus enabling her to function successfully in school.

Testing the Hypothesis and Modifying it as Necessary. This aspect of the assessment can only be addressed once an appropriate behavioral intervention plan has been developed and implemented. Such a plan, once employed, will confirm, or disconfirm the validity of the hypothesis.

Developing an Effective Behavioral Intervention Plan for Kate

According to the sound protocols established by Ryan, Halsey, and Mathews (2003), an effective BIP should address the following criteria (1) research-based and relevant, (2) only be implemented after informed consent has been given by the individual's parents, (3) document the steps of the intervention plan, including who will be responsible, when and where it will occur, and for how long, (4) establish real and measurable goals, and (5) establish a method to measure progress.

In Kate's case, the treatment plan established by her doctor and therapist involves a bi-modal approach consisting of a prescribed antidepressant, fluoxetine, and cognitive-behavioral therapy. Although teachers have no direct part in the administration of medication, they can provide important anecdotal observations about Kate's response to the prescribed medication in terms of weight gain, a reduction in obsessive thoughts about food, improved mood, and reduced abnormal eating behavior. Furthermore, teachers can record instances during the school day, and particularly during her supervised lunch period, when Kate monitors her thoughts, feelings, and behaviors, to track her assumptions about expressing emotions, forming close relationships, and the significance of a low body weight.

The behavioral goals for the school staff in conjunction with Kate's BIP are (1) a significant reduction in expressed and observed obsession with specific low-calorie foods as well as calorie totals, (2) an increase in positive statements about her body and a greater acceptance of clinically normal body weight, and (3) a less perfectionist and critical view of herself and others, leading to greater acceptance of others and improved interpersonal connections.

A secondary target goal is a significant reduction in the time required for Kate to consume the number of prescribed calories lunch; ultimately, Kate should be able to do so within the standard time allotted for lunch. An indirect benefit of this goal would be Kate's ability to attend the full class periods every day, thus obviating the need for extracurricular tutoring.

Teachers and other school staff are encouraged to support the treatment plan at every opportunity by providing positive reinforcement when Kate displays an appropriate perception of body image as well as a healthy attitude toward food. Furthermore, staff members are encouraged to reinforce any expression that suggests acceptance of less than perfect performance on Kate's part as well as for her tolerance of the imperfections of others. Lastly, teachers should also support Kate's efforts to socialize and communicate with peers and school staff.

Assessing the Problem: Anna

In the case involving Anna, a student diagnosed with bulimia nervosa, our assessment is as follows.

Identifying and Describing the Problem Behavior. Anna is very careful to avoid eating in front of others at school. In fact, she restricts her snacking as well as lunch to her car, which she is allowed to bring to school and intentionally parks in an isolated space far away from other students. She has been observed on several occasions dumping plastic bags, presumably containing food wrappers and containers into the school's dumpster. An additional concern for teachers and administrators are reports that, immediately after lunch, Anna uses the bathroom. Female classmates consistently notice the unmistakable odor of vomit after she leaves the bathroom.

For these reasons, the concerns are twofold (a) that Anna seems to be binging in secret, in violation of her treatment plan, and (b) that frequently, immediately after eating, she may be purging in the girls' bathroom.

Collecting Baseline Data and Academic Information. Anna's teachers have been asked to closely monitor the frequency with which she goes to her car as well as the number of times she is observed discarding trash bags. According to these observers, she unobtrusively goes to her car an average of three times during the school day, always providing a plausible explanation to her teachers. A female teacher's assistant has been assigned to confirm the likelihood that Anna has purged after consuming food, and she reports the frequency of this as concurrent with the number of trips Anna makes to her car—on average, three times during the school day.

Describing the Context in Which the Behavior Is Observed. Anna's binging and purging behaviors occur in secret, while in her car in the school parking lot, or in a bathroom cubicle. She is very discrete and painstakingly disguises these behaviors; for example, after purging, she brushes her teeth and gargles with mouthwash she brings in her handbag, and she covertly disposes of the plastic garbage bag she uses to discard food wrappers and containers.

Completing a Functional Assessment and/or Behavior Rating Scales as Appropriate. A functional assessment has been conducted that identifies the purposes served by Anna's binging and purging as being beyond the scope of school-based interventions; however, teachers can support Anna's treatment plan by monitoring her bathroom visits after lunch or snacks and ensuring that she eats with her classmates and is not permitted an opportunity to isolate herself or be unaccounted for during lunchtime and breaks.

Conducting a Direct Observation. Several teachers and teacher assistants have observed Anna binge-eating in her car, and both a female teacher and the teacher's assistant have entered the girls' bathroom on several occasions while she was purging.

Developing a Hypothesis. Although the reasons for Anna's binging and purging are complex and multivariate, the important thing about this behavior that teachers should know is that it involves both an obsession with weight loss and food as well as a feeling of disgust with her overeating and relief produced by purging—a chronic cycle of self-abuse.

Testing the Hypothesis and Modifying it as Necessary. The hypothesis has been confirmed by clinical practitioners after careful and reliable assessments.

Developing an Effective Behavioral Intervention Plan for Anna

As discussed previously, Anna's maladaptive behaviors are symptomatic of her diagnosed condition, bulimia nervosa. The behavioral intervention plan that was developed for implementation in the school involves several components. In order to ensure that Anna does not engage in binge eating during the school day, a one-to-one aide is assigned to ensure that she does not leave the school building, does not access her locker, or use the snack machines. Furthermore, she is restricted to two snacks and a specific lunch menu that has been prepared by the school dietitian to meet Anna's unique nutritional requirements. The aide sits with her during lunch to ensure she consumes sufficient calories and adheres to the prescribed diet. In addition, the aide ensures that Anna does not use the washroom for at least one hour after eating lunch, to ensure the absorption of nutrients; after the compulsory one-hour wait, the aide accompanies Anna to the bathroom to prevent her purging.

Assessing the Problem: Benny

Our third case example involves Benny, a student who has a binge eating disorder.

Identifying and Describing the Problem Behavior. Benny is a compulsive eater, who is obsessed with thoughts of food and an irresistible desire to consume. His obsession with food has negatively impacted his ability to make friends as well as his academic progress, which is compounded by his frequent removal from class.

Collecting Baseline Data and Academic Information. Teachers have recorded each time Benny was found eating in class or stashing food in his desk or backpack. Similarly, teachers have noted the scores of tests taken in all content areas, and these provide continuous evaluations of his academic performance throughout the escalation of his binge eating behavior.

Describing the Context in Which the Behavior Is Observed. Benny is compulsive in his eating behavior, taking advantage of any opportunity to consume food, even attempting to consume snack foods in class. Driven by his compulsion, Benny will consume available food until it is gone. He does not have the behavioral controls to stop, and this excessive behavior is negatively impacting his academic performance as well as his social life.

Completing a Functional Assessment Form and/or Behavior Rating Scales as Appropriate. The underlying function of Benny's binge eating behavior is multifaceted and thus very complex, yet it is clear that the consumption of food provides a powerful oral gratification that produces a feeling of mild euphoria and satisfaction. The results of assessments such as the *Survey for Eating Disorders* (SCOS; Gotestam & Agras, 1995) and the *Eating Disorder Diagnostic Scale* (EDDS; Stice et al., 2000), when compared with the behavior checklist completed on a daily basis by Benny's teachers, underscore the severity and detrimental effects of his binge eating.

Conducting a Direct Observation. Benny's teachers have been careful to record any observed binge eating, defined as attempts, successful or not, to consume food during class or outside of the lunchroom.

Developing a Hypothesis. Benny's eating is clearly the result of his disorder, which causes him to obsess about food and compels him to consume it without restraint. The goal for school-based intervention is to employ teachers as external controls to help reduce, if not stop, Benny's binge eating while in school. The task facing the multidisciplinary team is precisely how best to help Benny control his compulsive eating during school. With the help of the school psychologist, Benny's therapist, the school dietitian, and the input of Benny's pediatrician, the team has developed an intervention plan that they believe will prove effective in reducing the frequency of his binge eating as well as provide a replacement behavior to mitigate the frustration caused by the restrictions placed on his food intake.

Developing an Effective Behavioral Intervention Plan for Benny

While Benny is engaged in the treatment plan developed by his therapist, which involves cognitive-behavioral approaches and self-monitoring techniques, the recommended intervention to be employed by teachers and school staff involves both self-monitoring (Lindgren at al., 2018) and cognitive behavioral therapy (Hilbert et al., 2020).

Self-monitoring requires the individual to carefully monitor their thoughts, feelings, and behaviors, both before and after the problematic behavior, in this case, binging. This information is used by the counselor to manipulate the antecedents that trigger the problem behavior.

The goal of cognitive-behavioral therapy (CBT) is the use of techniques to restructure an individual's distorted thoughts about the use of food to mitigate their faulty beliefs about their self-worth, inner strength, and the ability to achieve success in life (Agras et al., 2017). Thus far, these two interventions seem to be helping to reduce the target behaviors, identified as impulsive binging on unhealthy snack foods and the emotional outbursts and consequential physical restraint and removal from class that frequently results when Benny is denied these snacks.

From the Field

Leah DeSole, Ph.D.

Leah DeSole is a licensed clinical psychologist and an expert in the field of eating disorders. She is affiliated with the New York City Eating Disorder Resource Center, and she is a member of the editorial board of Eating Disorders: The Journal of Treatment and Prevention. She also has served as adjunct faculty at Columbia University and Hunter College. In her private practice, Dr. DeSole advocates a multidisciplinary team approach incorporating, as needed, the support of specialists in the fields of nutrition, medicine, acupuncture, and psychiatry. Together with clients, she advocates creating a personalized plan to move toward recovery utilizing cognitive-behavioral therapy and psychodynamic psychotherapy. Dr. DeSole is a co-author of *Making Contact: The Therapist's Guide to Conducting a Successful First Interview* (DeSole et al., 2006).

Dr. DeSole's responses here benefited from the help of David Steinmetz, a family systems therapist with a private practice in New York City. Dr. Steinmetz earned degrees in Family Constellations at The Bert Hellinger Institute, USA, Redding, Connecticut, and in Integrated Kabbalistic Healing at A Society of Souls, Lebanon, New Jersey. He has extensive training in 'voice dialogue' with Dr. Jodi Prinzivalli at The School of Energetic Psychology, Ramsey, New Jersey; 'visualization/imagery techniques and dream work' with Dr. Catherine Schainberg at The School of Images, New York, New York; and 'object relations and psycho-spiritual development' with Drs. Alexis Johnson and Judith S. Schmidt at the Center for Intentional Living, South Salem, New York.

The problem of eating disorders appears to be growing exponentially among adolescent and preadolescent girls in schools, a trend you must be seeing in your practice. To what do you ascribe this alarming increase?

Epidemiological research cannot confirm the problem of eating disorders is growing exponentially in society; however, it can be stated with certainty that more cases of eating disorders are being reported nationwide among adolescent and preadolescent girls. Let me add that I believe the fact that more cases are being reported nationwide reflects success in the field. It suggests that there is greater community awareness regarding the signs and symptoms of eating disorders among students, teachers, and administrators in schools. It also suggests that the stigma associated with eating disorders, such as binge eating disorder, bulimia nervosa, and anorexia nervosa, is beginning to lessen. Word is spreading that eating disorders are legitimate illnesses, effective treatment is available, and recovery is possible. Whether or not it can be proven that the problem of eating disorders is growing exponentially in a sense is a moot point: *What matters most is that people who need help increasingly are getting help.*

One of the most widely discussed theories regarding why we are seeing more adolescent and preadolescent girls presenting with symptoms of eating disorders argues that it results in no small part from societal pressure. We are living in a society that progressively has placed greater emphasis on beauty, or appearance, as an essential aspect of one's well-being. In common parlance, "To look good is to feel good." Moreover, increasingly, people who are viewed as beautiful are also seen as better people than those who deviate from society's standard beauty ideals. They are seen as smarter, more competent, and more successful than their physically less attractive counterparts. Making matters worse is society's shifting definition of what constitutes beauty. Over the years, it has steadily shifted to a more and more slender figure for preadolescent and adolescent girls alike. Paralleling the development of this new, narrower beauty ideal has been development of a $50 billion diet industry and an exponential rise in the popularity of plastic surgery. As a matter of fact, weight-loss competitions, plastic surgery challenges, and modeling contests are currently listed among the nation's top-rated television shows. Shows like these simply did not exist in prior generations.

Why the alarming increase of eating disorders specifically among preadolescent and adolescent girls in the schools today?

Preadolescents and adolescents are keenly aware of society's current beauty ideal. They watch these top-rated, nationally televised shows; furthermore, they are the primary consumers of women's fashion magazines. The majority of articles and advertisements in these magazines concern dieting, exercising, and how to become more attractive (hence 'happy') girls. As a consequence, preadolescent and adolescent girls are exposed to messages regarding their bodies and beauty at an intensity (and of a kind) unknown to prior generations.

And preadolescent and adolescent girls are, unfortunately, particularly susceptible to these messages. They come at a time in their development when their bodies are changing, and they are just beginning to establish a sense of personal identity. Their bodies may represent a ready canvas on which they can express themselves. For some, their bodies are the sole area in which they feel autonomous and in control - what they eat and how much they exercise is within their power. Societal messages regarding not only the importance of beauty for women but also a beauty ideal that is unhealthy set the stage for the development of eating disorders. Indeed, I fear that they may have become a socially acceptable way for adolescent girls to alleviate anxiety, enact their desire for control, and elevate their sense of self-esteem.

Could you provide an abbreviated profile of the 'typical' girl that you treat for an eating disorder?

I am tempted to say there is no 'typical' girl that I treat for an eating disorder. I think it is all too easy to lose sight of the distinctiveness of each person who suffers from an eating disorder by describing anyone as typical. Nonetheless, I see commonalities among my patients with distinct eating disorders such as anorexia nervosa or bulimia. These may be most easily described according to a biopsychosocial model, one that conceptualizes a person across three specific domains: biological, psychological, and sociological.

My sense is that many of the girls I see in my practice possess a particular cognitive set. One such cognitive set is a kind of chronic dissatisfaction and self-critique of their bodies. Typically, this is coupled with a constant fear of becoming fat, regardless of their size. Another common cognitive set I observe involves an intricately woven notion of expectancies, such as "If I reach a 103 pounds, fit into the jeans I wore three years ago, and consume only 700 calories a day, I will be happy, admired, and successful—both in relationships and at school." Given that these expectancies tend to be unrealistic, failure is likely. And this highlights another tendency I observe in my practice among adolescent girls with eating disorders. There is a tendency for patients to think in dichotomous terms - the world is black and white; there is no gray. This thinking is epitomized by the firmly held belief, regularly voiced by persons with eating disorders, that "there are good foods and there are bad foods." In addition to these cognitive sets, I observe that girls with eating disorders tend to manifest distinct temperaments. In my own practice, I can say that it is not uncommon to observe anorexic girls whom parents and teachers alike describe as having 'controlling personalities.' These girls are disciplined in their social activity, oriented toward achievement in school, and seek comfort in routine. They want to be 'good girls,' and they describe feeling strong and competent when they restrict what they eat. Often, they do not seek out self-gratification or pleasure, and they are not sexually active. In contrast, the bulimic girls whom I see in my practice more commonly describe themselves as feeling "out of control." All the while, their parents and teachers still describe them as "being controlling." Outwardly they may appear as disciplined as their anorectic peers; inwardly, they are aware of being overwhelmed by feelings, craving intense relationships, and behaving impulsively. What I observe among both groups are difficulties identifying feelings, tolerating intense states of arousal, and adequately soothing themselves without the use of food.

The typical girl whom I see in my practice is white and middle-to-upper class. That said, I am increasingly seeing Latino and Asian patients as well as young men. Religion and ethnicity often vary as well; however, within this variation, I have found that most of my patients seem to identify as "American" rather than with any particular religious or ethnic group. Moreover, few of them have a spiritual practice in their lives. With regard to family, my observation is that often an extreme exists in that either the girl is very attached to her family (i.e., "My mother is my best friend") or notably detached (i.e., "We never talk"). Patients often report that one or both of their parents have body image issues and engage in behaviors such as chronic dieting or compulsive overeating. Lastly, it is not uncommon for parents to openly discuss their children's bodies and/or eating habits. The discussion may be praise or criticism. Neither seems to matter. What matters most is that the patient experiences a kind of conditional love, such as "I like you more when you are a size 4," which is felt although it may be unsaid.

How is an understanding of the characteristic behaviors of an individual with an eating disorder helpful to the treatment process?

To understand the characteristic behaviors of an individual with an eating disorder is to understand the patient herself. It is crucial: It is the basis for empathy and comprehension of the patient's struggle and forms the foundation of the relationship between the patient and therapist—all good treatment begins from this relationship. Adolescents often come to treatment reluctantly. Many are not ready to change their behaviors, let alone allow another person (the therapist) into their world and actually tell someone what they are thinking, feeling, and doing on a daily basis. Often, they will not offer information about their disordered eating patterns unless they are specifically asked.

Knowing what to ask is very important. What may be less obvious is the importance of *knowing how to ask*. I do not ask an anorexic adolescent, for example, "Do you take diuretics?" I may say, "I know girls sometimes take water pills or diuretics when they feel bloated; how often will you take something like that? Several times a day or week?" Eating disorder specialists will know to ask the appropriate questions in a way that is most likely to yield accurate information. People with eating disorders, especially adolescents, may be reluctant to be truthful. They may fear criticism. They may worry that they will anger their parents, and they will be punished. They may not be ready to change, or they may worry that if they speak truthfully, they will be pushed to change at a rate that is unacceptable to them. They also may be unaware of their behavior, and unless they are asked questions about their behavior directly *and* in a nonthreatening manner, this information may not be available to their consciousness. This knowledge is the key to guiding treatment and establishing achievable goals for recovery.

Are you ever asked to provide information to schools, since many of the individuals you treat are school-age?

While I don't, several of my colleagues at The New York City Eating Disorder Resource Center with which I am affiliated are strong advocates for education regarding eating disorders and speak regularly at schools. The Center itself, also maintains a website listing nationwide resources for individuals, families, and organizations (www.edrcnyc.org). In addition, there are several national organizations that provide these services in a variety of educational settings across the country. These organizations include NEDA (The National Association for Eating Disorders), EDreferral.com (Eating Disorder Referral and Information Center), and AED (The Academy for Eating Disorders), to name a few.

What would you like to share with teachers, administrators, and school clinicians that might assist them in identifying and working with affected students? Could you share any caveats that might help teachers and administrators avoid making costly mistakes in working with students who have eating disorders?

These questions are important. I, myself, err on the side of caution in response. I do not believe that teachers and administrators should work with students who have been diagnosed with an eating disorder *around their eating disordered behavior*. I think the efforts of teachers and administrators should remain in the domain of academic guidance and not in the provision of psychological services to their students. In my experience, the psychological health of students is best left to trained professionals in the field. Teachers and administrators can avoid making costly mistakes by routinely making referrals to them for evaluation and treatment.

School clinicians can be an excellent resource in this regard. They are the ideal members of the school administration to refer students who may have an eating disorder for evaluation. Given their clinical training, they will know the community resources that are available, and they will know how to communicate the school's concerns to a student in a compassionate manner. In addition, my sense is that they are more likely to reach out to an affected student and be heard, since they do not grade or discipline students. I believe schools would serve their students well by targeting their efforts at the prevention of disordered eating attitudes. Intervening after an eating disorder has developed is far too challenging and costly.

Recent studies point to an increase in the identification of what is currently termed "binge eating disorder." Based on your clinical experience, do you think this is a legitimate disorder? Why is it proliferating, and what can teachers and administrators do to help prevent its growth and provide assistance to affected students?

I do consider binge eating disorder (BED) a legitimate disorder. BED is characterized by recurrent binge episodes of binge eating without the compensatory behaviors of bulimia nervosa such as purging, laxative use, or excessive exercise. A binge may be defined by several factors, such as a loss of control of one's eating (or eating more than one intended at one sitting), eating in secret, and eating while distracted or agitated. Feelings associated with BED include significant anxiety, distress, shame, and sadness.

There is a great deal of speculation about why binge eating is proliferating in society. It has been suggested that two trends are responsible for this development - increased availability of high-calorie food and the development of the fast-food industry. Perhaps unwittingly, the government supports these trends by subsidizing the production of high-calorie, non-nutritious foods rather than healthier alternatives. Indeed, a paradox exists, more government money goes to support the production of food which we are supposed to eat less of, such as meat, dairy, and high-fructose corn syrup, rather than food we are supposed to eat more of, such as fruits, grains, and vegetables. The net result is that less nutritious food is not only more available but also cheaper than more nutritious alternatives. Furthermore, research reveals that these less nutritious foods may trigger binge eating as well as overeating in general, thus contributing to the current proliferation of BED.

As with other eating disorders, I believe teachers and administrators can serve an important role in the prevention of BED by providing education. In addition, schools can make a significant impact by *monitoring the foods they make available to students* in the hallways as well as in the school cafeteria. In school cafeterias, some administrations have elected to eliminate the use of deep fryers in food preparation. More and more schools are consulting with nutritionists in the preparation of healthy lunches. Some even have opted to provide students with breakfast, out of a growing recognition that having breakfast improves students' concentration and mood. Likewise, some administrators have decided to eliminate candy and soda machines in school hallways. Studies suggest that having these machines in school invites snacking, binging, and ultimately overeating. The susceptibility of preadolescents and adolescents, in particular, to these foods and beverages has come under increasing public scrutiny. It has been proposed that once children's taste buds become accustomed to sweet, salty, high-fat foods, it is difficult for them to enjoy other foods. Only now is research being done to assess how eating these foods may contribute to the development of BED as well as be harmful to the physical development of growing adolescent bodies.

Although current research indicates that eating disorders primarily affect girls and young women, there is growing evidence that this trend might be changing to include more boys and young men. Can you speak to this recent development from your experience as a practitioner?

Increasingly I see boys and young men in my private practice who are affected by eating disorders. These include the full spectrum of eating disorders from anorexia nervosa and bulimia nervosa to binge eating disorder. I attribute this development to many factors, but essentially they all boil down to one: shifting societal norms. Just as there is for girls and young women, there is growing public scrutiny of the bodies of boys and young men. Narrowly defined standards of attractiveness based on weight that once applied only to women are now being applied to men as well. Men, conventionally, were thought to be "protected" from developing eating disorders. According to a traditional chauvinist maxim, "Men are evaluated by the size of their wallet; women by the size of their dress." This has shifted, and males are being judged by their size as well. It has become a measure of one's worth and a reflection of one's character. Thin, fit boys and young men are seen as more competent, healthy, and successful than boys and young men of a larger size; for example, male models are venerated by the current generation of boys, in stark contrast to the past, in which it was thought to be an embarrassment to be a male model. In recent decades, men's magazines have proliferated, and they are not just talking about news, sports, and sex—now they contain articles and advertisements concerning diet, exercise, and sculpting various body parts. Such topics would have been an anathema in the past for men, much like ordering a light beer in a bar in front of one's friends or date. These shifting social norms encourage young boys and men to be conscious of their weight, shape, and appearance. Sadly, the protection that they once had from developing eating disorders has eroded. Should a young boy with a biological predisposition for an eating disorder experience a stressful event, current American culture will do little to discourage him from turning to his body to provide a release from tension and sense of self-esteem. This is what I have observed in my practice. Adolescent boys who become overly reliant on controlling their weight in order to relieve tension and increase their self-confidence are at a high risk of developing a serious eating disorder.

Finally, would you share a success story from your practice that offers hope and underscores the benefits of good practice in treating school-age children and youth affected by these debilitating disorders?

I have had several success stories in my practice. The one I will share here is a composite of three patients, each of whom shares similar histories as well as paths to recovery. I will call this patient Isabelle.

Isabelle was referred to me by her medical doctor, a specialist in adolescent medicine. Her presenting problem was anorexia nervosa (AN). At the time, Isabelle was 16 years old and attending a private school in Manhattan. She was 5' 8" and 110 pounds. Like many AN sufferers, she was a white, middle/upper-class "American" girl who did not identify with a particular ethnicity or religion.

My overall approach to treatment in this case was twofold. I began with cognitive-behavioral therapy (CBT) and subsequently provided supportive psychotherapy. CBT methods focus on the thoughts and behaviors of the patient. I find that it offers much-needed relief from the initial experience of symptoms. I used supportive psychotherapy in later sessions, primarily to address relapse prevention. In my experience, supportive psychotherapy is necessary to tackle underlying stressors such as managing relationships with friends and family. It also enables patients to cope with the myriad of feelings that arise in recovery around weight gain and body image issues. In addition to using CBT and supportive psychotherapy, I take a team approach - I coordinate care with medical doctors, nutritionists, the patient's parents, and anyone else involved in treatment.

Isabelle realized that she did not really know how to convey her feelings appropriately. Indeed, she was accustomed to smiling unless she was under great duress, such as in the session with her mother. We talked about where she learned to smile all the time and how she might find ways to express her emotions without feeling overwhelmed by them. We also discussed how "fat is not a feeling," but that the associations that she makes with being fat are feelings such as sadness, anxiety, and fear.

I encouraged her to discuss the feelings she associated with gaining control over her eating disorder, such as feeling powerful and responsible. Subsequently, we widened our discussion of feelings beyond the realm of food and eating to her relationships with others. It was apparent that as she became less preoccupied with her weight, she had more time to attend to others. Later sessions increasingly focused less on food and more on the people in her life to include her friends, boyfriends, teachers, and family members.

Isabelle's weight eventually stabilized around 118 pounds. By that time, she was back on the track team. She no longer was weighed by her medical doctor, and she saw the nutritionist whenever she wished. We began to meet every other week. Eventually, we met once a month. I often joked, "Use me as needed, like aspirin." When problems arose, she would come in more often. One summer, between her freshman and sophomore year of college, she came in weekly. By then, she had the normal struggles that we all have. I consider her recovered from AN, however, it may always be her Achilles heel. During times of difficulty, it may be the way her frustration first becomes evident. Over time, I remain hopeful that one day this too may "heal."

Summary

The increase in the last few decades of identification of school-aged children and youth who have eating disorders has been alarming. Despite the temptation to ascribe this increase to the preoccupation with thinness on the part of many girls and young women in Western industrial societies, the real reasons that these young people engage in this self-destructive behavior are complex and multivariate.

Regardless of the cause or causes, the fact many girls and young women, and, to a lesser but ever-increasing degree, young men, are affected by one or more of these disorders compels school staff to become involved. Although there are clearly characteristics that are common to all eating disorders—namely, a preoccupation with eating, concomitant behavioral and psychological effects, and significant dysfunction in patterns of daily living as well as quality of life (Lock & Le Grange, 2019)—there presently appear to be three distinct subtypes: anorexia nervosa, bulimia nervosa, and binge eating disorder (American Psychiatric Association, 2013).

The most lethal of these disorders, anorexia nervosa, is typically characterized by a pathological drive to be thin and a fear of becoming fat. This obsession with being thin results in a severely restricted diet that may be exacerbated by extreme exercise and purging. If left untreated, AN can result in death as a result of organ failure (Fatt et al., 2020).

Bulimia nervosa is a prevalent eating disorder that affects both adolescents and young adults. It can be comorbid with AN, which is consistent with the current views of eating disorders as a continuum of symptom progression from less serious to more serious. The core symptoms of BN is described as recurrent, compulsive binge-eating episodes involving large quantities of high-calorie food followed, most typically, by purging (Levine, 2019).

The third, recently proposed subtype, is binge eating disorder syndrome (BEDS). The defining characteristic of binge eating disorder is eating excessive amounts of high-calorie food within a short period of time. Individuals diagnosed with this disorder are typically obese but seemingly unconcerned about their excessive weight (Lock & Le Grange, 2019).

Various causes have been hypothesized for eating disorders. Some of the more investigated ones include biological factors, psychological factors, familial factors, and sociocultural factors. Of these four, biological and genetic factors have been best supported by research; it has been shown that girls who grow up in a family in which one or both parents or a sibling have an eating disorder are much more predisposed to develop an eating disorder. It is further suspected that individuals who have eating disorders may suffer from overactivity of serotonin, which would decrease their appetite for food. In any event, a review of the research suggests that the cause of an eating disorder is multidetermined and varies greatly across individuals, suggesting that several causative variables may be in play.

The assessment of eating disorders typically involves a medical evaluation to determine the cause of weight loss, malnutrition, and electrolyte imbalance, as well as an interview with a clinical psychologist. Further evaluation can be conducted by a dietitian to determine the kinds of foods and quantities an individual suspected of having an eating disorder consumes. In addition, many standardized assessments can be used by clinicians to confirm a diagnosis.

Treatments for eating disorders range from hospitalization, in extreme cases in which the individual is health-compromised and at risk for serious health complications or death, to cognitive-behavioral therapy, which may help the affected individual reframe faulty perceptions of body image—for example, equating extreme thinness with beauty. The two treatments we have discussed in the chapter that are most easily adapted to classroom use response delay and stimulus control.

To conclude, as the number of students diagnosed with an eating disorder continues to increase, classroom teachers will inevitably work with an affected individual. Understanding the characteristics of eating disorders, their causes, developmental course, and treatment interventions, will prove invaluable to the classroom teacher in preparing to work effectively with these students.

Tips for Teachers

For Students Who Have Anorexia Nervosa

- Avoid commenting on the individual's thinness.
- Find things that you can genuinely compliment in the student (e.g., attractive dress, academic performance relative to a real accomplishment, pleasant demeanor).

- Give the student as much of your attention and positive reinforcement as possible; give generously!
- Model healthy eating practices, eat good food, and consume healthy portions.
- Display pictures of "real" people in the classroom; these should include individuals who are full-figured, of various shapes and sizes, doing everyday things. Avoid reinforcing the student's obsession with "perfectionism."
- Accept less-than-perfect work. Remind everyone in your class that learning new skills takes time and most of life consists of working through processes; ideally, we improve as we practice.
- Avoid bringing food for the individual or suggesting that she "needs to eat more" to look healthy (the student who has AN will be unlikely to eat the food and will feel embarrassed at being the focus of attention). Remember that for the student who has AN, eating is a very private ritual.
- Keep students engaged in interesting, meaningful work; hopefully, they will "discover" avocations or activities that help them enjoy life more and be more accepting of themselves as they learn that they can engage in rewarding activities and share these experiences with others.
- Stay in close contact with parents and the school counselor, dietitian, and psychologist and be ready to support the treatment plan as appropriate and where feasible.
- Keep parents and clinicians informed of any significant behavior or changes in behavior observed in the classroom (e.g., melancholia or depression, lack of interest in others or schoolwork, a morbid preoccupation with death, expressed disgust with body weight or image).

For Students Who Have Bulimia Nervosa

- Praise the student for some legitimately laudable quality.
- Celebrate the normal body type. Avoid displaying pictures of ultra-slim celebrities or models.
- Model healthy eating and stress the importance of good nutrition.

- Compliment the individual's wardrobe or "look." You can honestly say, "Those colors really make your eyes stand out," or "I really like the way you've styled your hair," etc.

- Be alert but don't overreact to the student's requests to use the bathroom.

- Support the treatment plan developed by clinicians as appropriate and feasible within the framework of the classroom and school (e.g., don't let the student cajole you into letting her use the bathroom immediately after lunch if the treatment plan prohibits it, even though the student insists that she really "has to go," unless she can be provided with one-on-one supervision).

- If the student's behavioral intervention plan calls for you or your assistant to supervise her during lunch, make it an enjoyable experience for both of you and really "enjoy" your food.

- Make sure that the student is included in class discussions and activities and provide frequent opportunities for her to choose assignments and projects. Providing choices is empowering.

- Create cooperative groups when possible and ensure that the student has opportunities to make relevant contributions to the group process.

- Ask the student for her input in class debates and discussions. Make her feel valued by reinforcing the importance you place on her contributions to the learning process and the classroom community.

For Students Who Have Binge Eating Disorder

- Avoid shaming the student for his impulsive eating.

- Substitute tactual/kinesthetic activities such as engagement in a preferred craft, such as model building, or a board game such as chess, during breaks in the academic routine, as a distraction from the compulsion to eat.

- Keep a container of dried fruit or sugar-free candy as a healthier, low-calorie substitute for traditional high-calorie snacks when the student craves a treat.

- Avoid making comments about the student's weight and ensure that the student's classmates do likewise. Instead, invite the individual to go for a walk around the school grounds with you or a peer during lunch.
- Prohibit or restrict access to snack and soda machines and lobby the administration to allow only ones that dispense healthy beverages and snacks, such as fruit juices, water, pretzels, popcorn, and trail mix.
- Avoid eating in the classroom; restrict food consumption to the cafeteria or staff room.
- Similarly, don't permit students to eat in the classroom; encourage them to eat in the cafeteria or outside the school building.
- Avoid discussing favorite foods and meals with the student, as this will only serve as a stimulus for the desire to snack.

Focus Questions Revisited

How are anorexia nervosa and bulimia nervosa currently differentiated, and what do researchers think about the relationship between these two eating disorders?

A Sample Response: The diagnostic criterion for identifying AN is the insistence of the affected individual that she is overweight, and the most typical response to this concern is a severe reduction in caloric intake. In contrast, the individual diagnosed with BN eats impulsively, consuming a great quantity of food at one time, afterwards feeling intense shame and disgust, which is mitigated by purging.

Describe the diagnostic criteria for identifying a binge eating disorder.

A Sample Response: Binge eating disorder is characterized by excessive consumption by an affected individual of high-calorie foods within a short period of time. As the disorder affects the adolescent, periods of excessive food consumption or binging may be intermittent. Furthermore, unlike individuals diagnosed with AN and BN, persons with BED appear to be unconcerned about their weight and do not engage in purging after excessive eating.

Imagine that you are a classroom teacher in a local middle school and you notice that one of your female students refuses to eat lunch with her classmates and routinely uses the bathroom immediately after lunch. Concerned students ask to speak with you privately and confide that they have witnessed this student "throwing up" on numerous occasions after lunch, which confirms your suspicions. What should you do, as a concerned teacher, to help this individual?

A Sample Response: As the teacher of this young adolescent, I would seek the help of the school psychologist. I would also contact the girl's parents to see whether they were aware of the possibility that their daughter might have an eating disorder, and whether they had observed similar behavioral characteristics, such as binging and purging, at home. If a treatment plan is already in place, I would follow it conscientiously; however, if none had been developed, I would convey my concerns to the school's multidisciplinary team and request a preliminary evaluation. Finally, once a diagnosis had been confirmed and a treatment plan developed, as in the case of Anna, I would ensure that she received supervision during the lunch period and restrict bathroom use to at least an hour after lunch, also monitoring her bathroom visits.

What are some things you could do, as the teacher of a student who has anorexia nervosa (like Kate) who insists that she is fat when it is obvious that she is seriously underweight?

A Sample Response: I would follow the treatment plan as developed by the student's psychologist or physician to the extent possible. Such a plan would likely require that the individual's teachers maintain a record of eating-related behaviors, including episodes of binging, preoccupation with calorie counting, and perceived body image. In addition, I would avoid making comments about weight and extolling thinness and I would point out examples of healthy body types as well as the importance of consuming healthy foods in quantity. If requested, I would monitor the student during lunch to ensure that sufficient calories were consumed. On the other hand, I would avoid passing judgment about the individual's acute thinness or exhorting her to eat more and gain weight. Furthermore, I would find meaningful ways to provide positive reinforcement for the student's achievements, affording her opportunities to make choices in the classroom and take "reasonable risks" while deemphasizing the need to be "perfect." Finally, I would ensure that the student feels accepted and valued in my class and that this acceptance is unconditional.

Suppose that you had a student who was grossly overweight and a binge eater, constantly hoarding and consuming high-calorie, non-nutritious foods both inside and outside of your classroom. What could you do to help this student?

A Sample Response: I would provide nutritious, low-calorie snacks such as trail mix, whole-wheat pretzels, and dried fruit for distribution to students both as a reward, and, in the case of the student who has BED, as healthy alternative to "junk food." In addition, I would avoid embarrassing or shaming the student by making comments about his impulsive eating or his excessive weight. In contrast, I would try to model healthy eating habits by selecting nutritious foods, enjoyed during scheduled breaks outside of the classroom. Finally, I would provide alternative activities to replace the student's cravings for food, such as, a doodle pad, a favorite board game, Lego blocks, or similar tactual/kinesthetic materials that could be played with during class breaks, lunch period, or other free time.

Key Terms Used in the Chapter

Anorexia Nervosa (AN):
A serious, often chronic, and life-threatening eating disorder defined by a refusal to maintain minimal body weight within 15 percent of an individual's normal weight. Other essential features of the disorder include an intense fear of gaining weight, a distorted body image, and amenorrhea (absence of at least three consecutive menstrual cycles when they are otherwise expected to occur).

Bulimia Nervosa (BN):
An eating disorder in which the subject engages in recurrent binge eating followed by feelings of guilt, depression, and self-condemnation. The sufferer then engages in compensatory behaviors to make up for the excessive eating, which are referred to as "purging." Purging can take the form of vomiting, fasting, the use of laxatives, enemas, diuretics, or other medications, or overexercising.

Binge Eating Disorder (BED):
A newly recognized condition that probably affects millions of Americans. People with binge eating disorder frequently eat large amounts of food while feeling a loss of control over their eating. This disorder is different from binge-purge syndrome (bulimia nervosa) in that people with binge eating disorder usually do not purge afterward by vomiting or using laxatives.

Eating Disorder, Not Otherwise Specified (ED-NOS):
A diagnostic category that is frequently used for people who meet some, but not all, of the diagnostic criteria for anorexia nervosa or bulimia nervosa. For

example, a person who shows almost all of the symptoms of anorexia nervosa, but who still has a normal menstrual cycle and/or body mass index, may be diagnosed with ED-NOS.

Chapter 8

Depressive Disorders, Bipolar Disorder, and Suicide Prevention in School-Age Children and Youth

Focus Questions

- *How would you differentiate between a student who has major depression and one who has dysthymia?*
- *What are the characteristics of bipolar disorder II, and how might they affect a student's academic and social performance?*
- *What steps would you take if you suspected that a child in your class might be clinically depressed?*
- *What related services personnel might be important resources to you as the classroom teacher of a child with a mood disorder? How might these personnel provide support and/or assistance?*
- *Which of the models of depression would be most helpful to you as a classroom teacher? Provide a rationale for each of your selections.*
- *How is knowing about comorbidities (e.g., between bipolar disorder and attention-deficit hyperactivity disorder) potentially helpful to you as the classroom teacher of a child or adolescent who has a mood disorder?*
- *What observation protocol might be helpful to classroom teachers in providing relevant data for a child assigned to them who is suspected of having a mood disorder?*
- *What are some of the warning signs you would look for in assessing a student's risk of suicide?*

Introduction

Mood disorders, which include major depressive disorder and bipolar disorder, are clearly more prevalent among school-age children and youth today (Geller et al., 2001; Reichart et al., 2004). The reasons for this increase in identification may include, in part, the improved screening instruments developed within the last decade as well as a better understanding and delineation of the characteristics that define these disorders (Reichart et al., 2004). Correspondingly, suicide and parasuicide, the two most pernicious outcomes connected with mood disorders, are also on the rise among children and adolescents (Becker & Correll, 2020; Minino et al., 2002).

This chapter provides current, research-based information about depressive disorders, bipolar disorder, and suicide prevention, and a model of assessment and recommended interventions using real-life case examples and anecdotes for each. After this thorough introduction, enhanced by illustrative cases, further suggestions for effective intervention and review are offered. It is vital to the effectual integration of students who have these debilitating disorders that their teachers are knowledgeable about the characteristics and research-based interventions that can enhance their chance for success in school and in society.

Characteristics of Mood Disorders

Mood disorders, also known as affective disorders, are abnormalities and disturbances in the regulation of mood. There are basically two types of mood disorders to include depressive disorders, characterized by sadness and/or irritability and bipolar disorders, characterized by alternating moods of sadness and mania (American Psychiatric Association, 2013). The consideration and diagnosis of mood disorders in children has had a noteworthy historical development. Before the 1960s, when the field of psychology was dominated by psychoanalysis, children were considered incapable of being in a state of depression because of insufficient formation of personality structure (Schutte, 2019). In the 1960s, Glasser (1965) advanced the idea of *masked depression* in children, whose manifestation of depression, in contrast to adults, can be irritable, agitated, and disruptive.

By the 1980s, the prevailing opinion was that childhood depression was not all that separate from adult depression, yet it did have some singular characteristics such as conduct problems and school refusal. Some even put forth the idea that childhood and adult depression are mirror images of each other (Sabatino et al., 2001). Depression exists across the life span, but its diagnosis requires age-level consideration as symptom manifestation is different for different age groups. The DSM-V (American Psychiatric Association, 2013) has resolved this conflict with the inclusion of new depressive disorder called Disruptive Mood Dysregulation Disorder.

Case Example: Lashaun, A Student Diagnosed with Major Depressive Disorder

Lashaun is a junior at Westmore Regional High School in Tulsa, OK. His father left the family when Lashaun was two years of age. His mother Misha Barkley suffers from depression and sometimes augments her prescribed medication with alcohol. Lashaun was not a planned pregnancy and Mrs. Barkley has found bonding with her son to be a very challenging process. She invariably associates Lashaun with her former, abusive husband who, she claims, regularly beat her in front of Lashaun and his siblings. Mrs. Barkley also confided to a school social worker assigned to the family that she had been repeatedly raped by her former husband for whom she now has an order of protection.

When she is able, Mrs. Barkley works three days a week in a local bakery and waits tables at a family restaurant on weekends. Until recently, Lashaun, the oldest of five children, worked at Footlocker in the mall; however, of late he has not been responding well to a new medication, Bupropion, which seems to have exacerbated his condition, making it very challenging for Lashaun to even get out of bed in the morning. Consequently, he has been absent from school for over two weeks, prompting a call from both the school counselor and social worker. At 17 years of age, Lashaun is an emancipated minor; therefore, the school is legally handcuffed.

As a footnote, Lashaun was diagnosed while a student in middle school with major depressive disorder (MDD) by a school-referred child psychiatrist. The psychiatrist prescribed vortioxetine, an SSRI, in addition to weekly therapy sessions wherein the therapist employed cognitive behavioral therapy, CBT). Lashaun has been inconsistent in taking the medication and attending the therapy sessions.

In his sessions with Dr. Lampone, the child psychiatrist, Lashaun has gradually revealed his suppressed feelings about his absent father and resentful mother. Dr. Lampone has expressed increasing concern that, given his precarious relationship with his mother and his inconsistent participation in the treatment plan, Lashaun might be at-risk for engaging in self-harm, perhaps even experiencing suicidal ideation.

In the most recent session, Lashaun conveyed that he felt despondent about his chronic depression and his deteriorating relationship with his mother. Dr. Lampone asked him if he thought about harming himself, noticing some scratch marks on his wrists and while Lashaun insisted he was not contemplating suicide, he did not sound convincing. In response, Dr. Lampone requested that he be able to call Lashaun every day at a mutually agreed upon time just to ensure Lashaun's continued safety and to provide him with an opportunity to share his feelings about his mother and his plans for the future.

Lashaun From an Attachment Perspective

It appears fairly obvious given the early history of the relationship with his mother that Lashaun suffers from insecure attachment. Insecure attachment can result in any number of different behaviors and in Lashaun's case, it is depression. From an attachment perspective, depression can result in either an anxious-ambivalent or avoidant attachment style. Lashaun seems to have adopted the latter. He has stopped working at the Foot Locker, is inconsistent in his treatment with Dr. Lampone, not attending school, and the case makes no mention of any interactions with peers. In traditional psychoanalytic thinking, depression is the result of internalized anger. This internalization translates into avoidance in attachment theory. Bowlby (1969) discovered that infants left in institutions for long periods realized after initial protest, that it did not have the desired effect of returning their mother, and they began to show signs of detachment. Consequently, the child employs deactivating strategies and shuts down the exploratory system.

This easily applies to Lashaun who felt "despondent about…his deteriorating relationship with his mother." If he had adopted a more anxious-ambivalent style, he might continuously protest and be more externalized still trying to connect with his mother. The avoidant style, however, results in deactivation that results in hopelessness and despair; therefore, Dr. Lampone is correctly concerned about Lashaun's suicidality as a possible way of dealing with the loss of relationship with his mother (and father for that matter).

For the securely attached, adolescence is a time to explore new and different relationships. Securely attached adolescents have the resilience to handle the challenges and inconsistencies typical in adolescent relationships. Those not securely attached with an anxious attachment style might engage in relationships that are self-destructive (e.g. substance abuse) or, in the case of Lashaun shut down the exploratory system because of an avoidant attachment style. Unfortunately, in the case of Lashaun, it has led to despair and even wanting to kill himself.

Prevalence of Mood Disorders

The DSM-V (American Psychiatric Association, 2013) divides depressive disorders into three major types to include the previously mentioned Disruptive Mood Dysregulation Disorder, Major Depression, and Persistent Depressive Disorder (formerly known as Dysthymia). The prevalence rate for Disruptive Mood Dysregulation Disorder Major is anywhere from 2-5 percent among children and adolescents (American Psychiatric Association, 2013). Major depression occurs in approximately 3 percent of children and 6 percent of adolescents (Spruit et al., 2020), and Dysthymia in 2 percent of children and

4 percent of adolescents (Patel & Rose, 2020). In childhood, girls and boys are equally likely to be diagnosed with depression; yet by adolescence, girls are twice as likely to become depressed. Among clinical adolescent samples, however, the gender effects of having a diagnosis of a MDD are insignificant, although there are gender differences in symptom presentation.

Most experts believe that depression in childhood and adolescence is underdiagnosed, and there are several reasons for this. As mentioned previously, the manifestation of symptoms can be different than what is typically thought of as depression such as vegetative states of psychomotor retardation, loss of appetite, and excessive sleep. Another factor is that children do not have the capacity to express in verbal terms their emotions and may present with dubious somatic complaints such as just not feeling well (Madjar et al., 2020). Depression may often be overlooked due to the fact that it is highly comorbid with other disorders.

Disruptive Mood Dysregulation Disorder

This is a new diagnosis in the DSM-V to deal with depression primarily in children and adolescents where the core symptom is irritability that is chronic, frequent, and persistent. The irritability is often accompanied by temper outbursts that can be either verbally or physical abusive in nature. For a diagnosis to be made, the outbursts must occur, on average, three or more times per week for at least a year and occur in more than one setting (American Psychiatric Association, 2013).

Previously, such chronic and persistent irritability often earned a diagnosis of bipolar disorder; however, the DSM-V makes clear the differential diagnosis. In bipolar disorder, the temper-tantrums and the like that can be construed as mania are episodic. The American Psychiatric Association wanted to confront the recent upsurge in bipolar diagnosis among children and adolescents. Disruptive mood dysregulation disorder helped to understand chronic and persistent irritability more as a manifestation of depression rather than bipolar disorder; it made practical sense. Those who are constantly and persistently irritated are not happy people; therefore, the concepts of "masked depression" and "agitated depression" are no longer needed as we now have diagnosis to fit especially children and adolescents who exhibit irritable and angry behaviors most of the day and nearly every day. This is the defining characteristic of disruptive mood dysregulation disorder since other related disorders (e.g. ODD, Intermittent Explosive Disorder) are much more episodic in nature.

Major Depressive Disorder (MDD)

According to the DSM-V (American Psychiatric Association, 2013), a child or adolescent diagnosed with MDD has had one or more major depressive episodes without ever having a manic episode. Depressed or irritable mood must be present during a two-week period along with four or more of the associated features. Although the DSM-V uses the same criteria to diagnose depression in adults and children, it does allow irritable mood to be substituted for depressed mood when dealing with children and adolescents. Depressed children and adolescents can differ in their clinical presentation. Children tend to show more symptoms of anxious and somatic complaints, whereas adolescents tend to have sleep or appetite disturbances, suicidal thoughts, or behavior, and social or school impairment. In prepubertal depression, environmental factors are more a primary influence, in contrast to adolescent depression, in which genetic factors play a more primary role.

Course of MDD

MDD is an episodic condition that can recur. If it does recur after a two-month interval, the diagnosis is MDD, Recurrent (American Psychiatric Association, 2013), and what occurs during the interval is important. Studies have found that more than 90 percent of children and adolescents recover from an initial episode of MDD within one to two years of onset. After recovery, however, children and adolescents have high rates of relapse (Grover & Avasthi, 2019).

Comorbidity and Differential Diagnosis of MDD

Comorbid diagnoses among children and adolescents with mood disorders are more the rule than the exception. Studies have revealed that anywhere from 40 to 70 percent of depressed children and adolescents have a comorbid psychiatric disorder (Hussain et al., 2018). In addition, a variety of medical conditions can produce symptoms of depression, including:

- Malignancy
- Brain injury
- Infection
- Endocrine disorders
- Metabolic abnormalities
- Acquired Immune Deficiency Syndrome (AIDS)

- Multiple sclerosis
- Chronic fatigue syndrome

A thorough physical examination is a perquisite for making a diagnosis of MDD in children and adolescents. The most common comorbid diagnoses are dysthymic disorder, anxiety disorders, personality disorder, disruptive behavior disorders, and substance abuse.

The comorbidity between MDD and persistent mood disorder (dysthymia) is found to be very high. A much higher percentage of those with MDD have dysthymia than the reverse (Calles, 2016). Those with this so-called double depression (dysthymia plus MDD) have been found to have more severe and longer episodes of depression, high rates of comorbidity, greater social impairment, and more suicidality (suicidal thoughts or ideas, not a completed suicide) (Case et al., 2018). Anxiety and depression are highly comorbid even among adult samples. It may be difficult at times to decide on a primary diagnosis because individuals can become depressed about their anxiety and vice versa. A good history-taking to decide what came first is necessary to make a primary diagnosis.

CD and ODD are also highly comorbid with MDD. Those who have both MDD and an externalizing disorder have been found to have worse short-term outcomes and to suffer more rejection by their peers (McDonald & Gibson, 2017). Depressed adolescents tend to have an earlier onset of substance abuse than substance abusers who do not have a history of MDD (Woerner et al., 2020). It is quite possible that adolescents turn to drugs to self-medicate for their depression. Substance-induced depression must also be ruled out, this is when the use of substances has caused the depression. This differential diagnosis is made by taking a careful history and assuring that no depressive episodes occurred before the use of substances. A substance-induced mood disorder usually results from long-term abuse.

Etiology of Depression in Children and Adolescents

There is no one specific cause of depression, rather a number of interacting factors can result in a child or adolescent suffering from depression. These factors are biological, genetic, and environmental. McWhirter et al. (2000) divided the suspected causes of depression into five models to include biological, psychodynamic, behavioral, cognitive, and family systems.

Biological Models. Biological models of depression are of two types, either genetic or biochemical (Beijers et al., 2019). The genetic model derives from research that found genetic factors account for approximately 50 percent of the variance in mood disorders (Moore et al., 2019). A child who has a depressed parent is about three times more likely to experience depression than one who does not and having a depressed parent is one of the strongest predictors of depression in children and adolescents (Moore et al., 2019). Biochemical models of depression explain depression as a hormonal imbalance (de Souza Duarte et al., 2017). There is some evidence that depressed children and adolescents secrete unusually substantial amounts of growth hormone (Butler et al., 2019). Others have argued that biochemical imbalances may be less the cause and more a result of depression (Ruiz et al., 2018).

This same argument can be applied to the neurotransmitters (norepinephrine serotonin, and acetylcholine) that are believed to play a part in the regulation of mood and consequently in the development of clinical depression. The antidepressants that regulate neurotransmitters in the brain—monoamine oxidase inhibitors (MAOIs), tricyclic antidepressants (TCAs), and selective serotonin reuptake inhibitors (SSRIs)—have all been shown to be effective in treating depression in adults.

Psychodynamic Models. Traditional psychoanalytic theory described depression as anger turned inward—toward the self—and connected to a judging and controlling superego. The superego is still forming in children and adolescents; therefore, Freudian theorists reasoned that depression was not possible in these age groups (Bernaras et al., 2019). More recent psychodynamic models have described depression among the young in terms of a loss that stems from childhood helplessness and the disruption of emotional bonding with the primary caregiver. The result is a loss of self-esteem. The child or adolescent has no internal sense of self-worth, relying instead on external sources for validation of his or her self-worth. When those external sources are lost, the child or adolescent becomes depressed (Bernaras et al., 2019).

Behavioral Models. Behaviorists argue that depression results from a lack of positive reinforcement for behaviors that are considered more normal. As time goes on, the depressed youngster manifests behaviors that are less likely to elicit positive reinforcement, but negative behaviors draw attention to the child and give him or her a sense of control. The symptoms of depression, then, are both cause and consequence of the lack of positive reinforcement. The key for helpers is not to reinforce the depressed behaviors, to reserve praise and encouragement for those behaviors that show improvement in both task and social functioning (Bauer, 1987).

Seligman's (1974) learned helplessness model of depression is based directly on research with behavioral reinforcement. Learned helplessness is a response to a series of failures to solve a problem or to improve a situation. In time, the individual becomes convinced that nothing he or she does or tries is effective. People who have learned helplessness have an external locus of control (their life is controlled by external forces) and an internal locus of responsibility (they blame themselves). Their feelings of hopelessness generalize to most of life's situations.

For children and adolescents, learned helplessness often revolves around schoolwork. The student has made numerous attempts and tried numerous means to improve his or her schoolwork but without success, so the student gives up, and depression sets in. There are several recommended strategies to help students overcome learned helplessness:

- Provide tasks that are small and incremental to help avoid feeling like a failure and have the child gain an experience of success.
- Give the child opportunities to choose their assignments and rewards. This will give them a sense of power.
- Be sure to provide feedback that explains the connection between the child's actions and consequences. This will help them to understand cause and effect.
- Give the child opportunities to gain confidence by having them identify behaviors and consequences (Marks, 1969).

Cognitive Models. According to cognitive theorists, depression is the direct result of negative or irrational thoughts. Beck (1967) was the first to develop a cognitive theory of depression. Some years later, he and his colleagues described a cognitive triad that they believed is characteristic of people who are depressed (Beck et al., 1979). The triad consists of three negative thought patterns, those of self, of the world, and of the future. Over time, these thought patterns develop into schemas, frameworks so much a part of the individual's cognitive makeup that they are like personality traits.

Environmental stimuli are filtered through these schemas and distorted to conform to the individual's negative view of self, world, and future. Even the most positive experiences are distorted; for example, a depressed child might respond to praise for a good grade with "The teacher probably felt sorry for me." Depressed children often make negative comments about themselves: "I always fail," "I'm not good at anything," "No one likes me."

In the cognitive model, the first step in helping a student who is depressed is to teach the student to substitute positive self-talk for negative self-statements. The helper usually gives the student a homework assignment such as "Every time you say to yourself, 'I'm a bad person,' I want you to correct that statement by saying, 'I'm a good person.' Other school-based interventions include guidance lessons that teach the relationship between thoughts and feelings, and role-play activities that focus on the problems and symptoms of childhood depression (peer rejection, feelings of guilt and failure) (Werner-Seidler et al., 2017).

Another cognitive model, Rehm's (1977) *self-control model,* explains depression as the product of deficiencies in three cognitive processes:

- *Self-monitoring*: The child pays attention only to negative events.
- *Self-evaluation*: The child frequently makes negative self-judgments. He or she sets high standards for positive self-evaluation and low standards for negative self-evaluation.
- *Self-reinforcement*: The child has a negative attribution style: Events are beyond his or her control because external forces control them or because he or she has some sort of internal deficiency.

The broad goal of intervention in this model is to help the student gain a greater sense of self-control. Helpers should begin by assigning the student small, manageable tasks and provide positive reinforcement when those tasks are accomplished. There is also some evidence that group interventions in schools can increase students' sense of self-control (Jones et al., 2018).

The Family Systems Model. Family systems theorists believe that children's behavior—even behavior that is symptomatic of depression—maintains balance (homeostasis) in the family system. Family systems theorists would not approve of treating just the child; they would argue that the family must be treated. The helper should consider family dynamics in working with a student who is depressed and should consult with the parents about their child, looking for signs during the meeting that the parents are using their child's depression in some way; for example, a child's illness allows parents to focus their psychic energy on the child instead of on other difficulties they should be resolving. If there is evidence that the child's depression is serving some function in the family, the school should facilitate a referral for family counseling.

Persistent Depressive Disorder (Dysthymia)

Dysthymia occurs in approximately 2 percent of children and 4 percent of adolescents (Patel & Rose, 2020). Early onset of dysthymia is considered a gateway to the occurrence and reoccurrence of mood disorders and a high percentage of children (upwards of 70 percent) diagnosed with MDD are believed to have underlying dysthymia (Schramm et al., 2020).

Dysthymia is less intense and more prolonged than MDD. Children who have dysthymia will have good days and bad days, days that are mixed but will rarely have sustained weeks without feeling depressed (Calles, 2016). In order for a diagnosis to be made, symptoms in children must have persisted for at least one year, there must be evidence of the consistent features as well as two or more of the variable features (American Association, 2013; Kowatch et al. 2005). These include:

Consistent Features

- Symptoms not severe enough to diagnose a major depression
- Absence of a psychotic illness
- Absence of a physiological mood-altering condition
- Impaired social and academic functioning

Variable Features

- Poor appetite or overeating
- Insomnia or hypersomnia
- Low energy or fatigue
- Low self-esteem
- Poor concentration or difficulty making decisions
- Feelings of hopelessness

Assessment of Mood Disorders

Because of high comorbidity and confounding symptoms, the assessment of a mood disorder in children must include a number of strategies and constituencies. In addition to interviewing the child and parents, teachers and even peers should be included in the assessment.

Most experts agree that the best method for diagnosing depression in children and adolescents is through the clinical interview. There are, however, a number of self-report measures that are used for screening and to obtain additional information.

Self-Report Measures

The *Children's Depression Inventory, or CDI* (Sitarenios & Kovacs, 1999) is perhaps the most widely used self-report measure. It consists of twenty-seven items that deal with affective, cognitive, and behavioral aspects of depression. Participants are asked to choose which of three alternatives best describes them during a two-week period. Research on the CDI has supported good psychometric properties (de la Vega et al., 2016).

Reynolds (2004) developed the *Reynolds Adolescent Depression Scale*-Second Edition (RADS-2) for adolescents ages 13 to 18. The scale consists of thirty items derived from symptoms of depression and dysthymia. Responses include "Almost never," "Hardly ever," "Sometimes," "Most of the time" and are weighted from 1 to 4 points, which means that scores on the RADS can range from 30 to 120. Higher scores indicate higher levels of depressive symptoms. The RADS-2 takes five to ten minutes to complete. The new edition appears to have the same sound psychometric properties as the first edition (Osman et al., 2010).

The *Reynolds Child Depression Scale* (RCDS; Reynolds, 1989) was designed for use with children in grades 3 to 6. There is only a slight difference between the formats of the RCDS and the RADS. The last item in the RCDS is a series of faces showing different emotions, from happy to sad. This item is marked on a 5-point scale, so scores on the RCDS can range from 30 to 121. Like the RADS, the RCDS is easy to administer and takes about ten minutes to complete.

The *Beck Depression Inventory* (BDI) is designed to assess the severity of depression in adolescents and adults (Beck et al., 1996). The current BDI (it was revised in 1993) consists of twenty-one items, each a statement related to an affective, cognitive, motivational, or physical symptoms of depression. Test takers are asked to rate each item a 0, 1, 2, or 3 on a severity scale. Scores can range from 0 to 63, with 0 to 9 indicating minimal depression, 10 to 16 mild depression, 17 to 29 moderate depression, and 30 to 63 severe depression. The BDI can be administered individually or in a group, in oral or written form, and it can be scored by hand or by computer (Beck et al., 1996).

Peer Ratings

Lefkowitz and Tesiny (1980) developed the *Peer Nomination Inventory for Depression* based on the theory that peers are sometimes the best sources for recognizing a troubled child. The inventory asks children to nominate peers who fit certain descriptions, such as "Who often plays alone?" "Who often sleeps in class?" There are twenty items in total, fourteen load on a depressed score, four on the happiness score, and two on the popularity score.

Observation

Over the years, a number of observational and performance-based measures have been developed to aid in the diagnosis of depression in children. Many of these are time-consuming and require special training to learn different coding symptoms. Garber and Kaminski (2000) developed the following categories that are depression-related and should be observed in social-interaction tasks:

- *Emotions*: smiling, frowning, crying, happiness, sadness, anger, fear
- *Affect regulation*: control or expression of affect
- *Problem-solving*: identifying problems, proposing solutions
- *Nonverbal behaviors*: eye contact, postures
- *Conflict*: noncompliance, ignoring, demanding, negotiating
- *Cognitive content*: criticism, praise, self-derogation
- *Speech*: rate, volume, tone of voice, initiation
- *Engaged or disengaged*: enthusiasm, involvement, persistence
- *On- or off-task behavior*
- *Physical contact*: threatening, striking, affection
- *Symptoms*: depression, irritability, psychomotor agitation, retardation, fatigue, concentration

Observational data should be gathered across several domains to include the child's play, interaction with caregivers and treatment providers, and in both familiar and unfamiliar environments.

Treatment Strategies for Mood Disorders

The treatment of mood disorders can be divided basically into two categories, psychopharmacological and psychosocial. Psychosocial treatments include cognitive-behavioral therapy (CBT), interpersonal psychotherapy (IPT), and family counseling. The goal of treatment is to shorten the duration of the mood disorder, decrease the negative consequences of depression, and restore the child or adolescent to optimal functioning (Garaigordobil et al., 2019).

Cognitive Behavioral Therapy (CBT)

Meta-analytic studies have shown CBT to be effective in treating child and adolescent depression (Keles & Idsoe, 2018; Oud et al., 2019; Rasing et al., 2017). Two structured programs for treating adolescents with depression are

Primary and Secondary Control Enhanced Training (PASCET; Weisz et al., 2003) and the Adolescent Coping with Depression (CWD-A) course (Clarke et al., 2003; Rohde et al., 2005).

The PASCET was initially tested among children in grades 3 to 6 who showed signs of mild to moderate depression. It is an eight-session program that meets in small groups and emphasizes control skills. Children are helped to identify activities that enhance their mood, change maladaptive thoughts, and learn relaxation and positive imagery. End-of-treatment and nine-month follow-up evaluations showed a significant decrease in depressive symptoms than a no-treatment control group. Regarding the CWD-A, results show that 67 percent of those who attended the CWD-A course no longer met the diagnostic criteria for depression at the end of treatment, compared to 48 percent of those on the waitlist. And at twenty-four-month follow-up, 98 percent had recovered (Cuijpers et al., 2009).

Interpersonal Psychotherapy (IPT)

Interpersonal psychotherapy treats depression through improving interpersonal functioning and enhancing communication skills in relationships with significant others. IPT addresses four areas of interpersonal functioning to include interpersonal deficits, interpersonal role conflicts, abnormal grief, and difficult role transitions. Parents are involved in all phases of the treatment. Most studies have supported the effectiveness of ITP for adolescent depression (Duffy et al., 2019).

Family Counseling

Family counseling is also recommended for the treatment of depression in children and adolescents. Based on the structural model of family therapy, Minuchin (1974) hypothesized that enmeshed relationships between children and parents were responsible for depression because they prevented appropriate levels of attachment and separation. Many individual approaches to depression in adolescents include a parent-education component, but at this time, it is not clear how much the parent component contributes to the overall effectiveness of treatment as research has yielded mixed results (Dardas et al., 2018).

Psychopharmacology

Over the years, a number of medications have been used to treat depression in children and adolescents. These fall into three groups - selective serotonin reuptake inhibitors (SSRIs), tricyclic antidepressants (TCAs), and monoamine oxidase inhibitors (MAOIs). Today, without a doubt, the SSRIs are the first-line pharmacological treatment for depression (Mullen, 2018). In spite of their popularity, the SSRIs are used with precaution in children and adolescents due to some evidence of an increased rate of suicidality (Mullen, 2018). At the present time, the U.S. Food and Drug Administration (FDA) has approved only fluoxetine (Prozac) for use with children and adolescents. For the most part, studies have proven Prozac effective in the treatment of child and adolescent depression (Lawrence, H. et al., 2017; Walkup, 2017).

With the advent of SSRIs, TCAs and MAOIs are rarely used in the treatment of depression among children and adolescents. Little has been written about the effectiveness of these drugs with this population. There are special concerns regarding TCAs because of possible cardiovascular risk, after reports of sudden death in five children who were taking TCAs.

In spite of the high regard for the combination of medication and psychotherapy, only one study to date has examined the combination of treatments in adolescents who have MDD. The Treatment for Adolescent with Depression Study (TADS) Team (TADS, 2004; March et al., 2007) compared fluoxetine, CBT, combination treatment, and placebo in 439 adolescents (ages 12 to 18) who had MDD. Based on global improvement scores, results showed that 71 percent of those on combination responded positively, compared to 61 percent on fluoxetine only, 43 percent receiving CBT only, and 35 percent receiving placebo (March et al., 2007).

School-Based Interventions

Using the knowledge gained about the characteristics, causes, and recommended treatment strategies for MDD, the next step is to develop an effective behavioral intervention for Lashaun, our case example. To ensure that the treatment approach is precisely tailored to Lashaun's needs, the first step is a careful assessment to determine both what the problem behaviors are and what function or purpose they serve for Lashaun. Once this has been accomplished, we will be able to develop an individualized behavioral intervention plan to help him deal successfully with these behavioral challenges.

Assessing the Problem

To determine effective ways to improve Lashaun's participation in school as well as his self-esteem, the multidisciplinary team will conduct a behavioral assessment. This process will ensure that all stakeholders thoroughly understand the circumstances surrounding Lashaun's disability as well as the things that exacerbate it. Furthermore, the information provided through this problem-solving process will assist his teachers and other educational professionals in developing school-based interventions to help Lashaun succeed academically and socially. These school-based interventions will complement the treatment plan prescribed by Lashaun's psychiatrist. A thorough behavioral assessment for Lashaun should include the following components.

The first step is *identifying and describing the problem behavior.* Lashaun is withdrawn in class and participates in activities with great reluctance and only when required. In addition, he seems morose all the time. This behavior is exacerbated by his lack of a male role model and his feelings of alienation from his mother.

The second step of the assessment process involves *collecting baseline and academic information.* Lashaun's teachers have been instructed by the school psychologist to use three measurements to assess his emotional state in the classroom using (1) The *Reynolds Adolescent Depression Scale* (RADS, 2004), (2) peer ratings using the *Peer Nomination Inventory for Depression* (Lefkowitz & Tesiny, 1980), and (3) observations of Lashaun's behavior in the classroom according to depression-related categories developed by Garber and Kaminski (2000).

The results of the RADS produced a score of 115 (the mean score on the RADS can range from 30 to 120, with higher scores indicating higher levels of depression). The *Peer Nomination Inventory for Depression* administered to Lashaun's classmates showed that, in the estimation of the majority of these students, Lashaun was nominated for the fourteen items that are associated with depression. The cumulative outcome of these data supports the diagnosis of major depression for Lashaun.

The third stage of the assessment process involves *describing the environment and setting demands.* Lashaun is clearly avoiding any social situations that highlight his disassociation from his mother and the lack of a father figure. He seems unable to cope with this loss and is exhibiting evidence of self-harm and possible suicidal ideation.

Next, where appropriate, affected professionals should *complete a functional behavioral assessment form and/or behavior rating scale.* On Lashaun's behalf, a functional behavioral assessment form was completed in September of Lashaun's junior year in high school. In addition, the RADS and *Peer Nomination Inventory for Depression* were administered in the same month, with results as described above.

Another important element in the assessment process is *direct observation of his classroom performance.* Accordingly, Lashaun's teachers conducted numerous systematic observations, focusing principally on the categories developed by Garber and Kaminski (2000) as described earlier in the chapter. Their observations helped to confirm the diagnosis of major depression.

A final step in the process involves *developing a hypothesis about the function or purpose of the problem behavior,* including what causes and sustains it. In Lashaun's case, the cause appears to be self-evident, that is the disassociation from his mother and the lack of a male role model. It is unclear what function his depressive symptoms serve; according to researchers, the causes are multifactorial (McWhirter et al., 2000). The symptoms are likely an organic response to mitigate the pernicious effects of these aforementioned stressors.

The various assessments conducted by school and clinical staff have supported a diagnosis of major depression for Lashaun. His depression can be treated using a research-based, multimodal approach that combines cognitive-behavioral therapy with pharmacological intervention. The hypothesis developed in the functional behavioral assessment will be *confirmed* after the treatment plan has been implemented for a reasonable period of time. If the symptoms of Lashaun's depression are sufficiently suppressed, the hypothesis will be confirmed, and the behavioral intervention plan will be continued. If, however, the plan produces results that are less than desirable (i.e., does not meet minimally acceptable goals), then the plan will be modified to achieve these objectives.

Developing an Effective Intervention Plan

In accordance with the assessment data provided by Lashaun's teachers, peers, and family members, as well as the clinical diagnosis of Dr. Lampone, his therapist, a treatment plan has been developed. The plan consists of a recommended, research-based approach that involves both cognitive-behavioral therapy as well as pharmacological intervention. Specifically, Lashaun will begin an after-school course with several other students who have also been diagnosed with depression. The program, the Adolescent Coping with Depression course (CWD-A) (Lewinsohn et al., 1996) involves 14 two-hour group sessions over a seven-week period and includes training in social skills, communication, problem-solving, relaxation, identifying and modifying negative thoughts, as well as desirable-event scheduling. In addition, Lashaun's mother will attend 7 two-hour sessions that provide an overview of the skills Lashaun is acquiring.

The second component of this multimodal intervention plan involves prescribing vortioxetine, a selective serotonin reuptake inhibitor (SSRI), which is FDA-approved for use with children and adolescents. Vortioxetine has been demonstrated to produce significant improvements in the symptoms of depression in patients to whom it was prescribed, and combined treatment appears to have an even greater therapeutic effect.

Lashaun's teachers can help by continuing to monitor his emotional state, using the depression-related categories developed by Garber and Kaminski (2000) and systematically recording any changes. They should also report any physiological changes such as visible weight gain or other adverse effects that may be attributed to the use of the SSRI. In addition, his teachers should note any increase in social activity as well as self-initiated interpersonal communication.

Bipolar Disorder

Case Example: Desiree

Desiree is currently an eighteen-year-old freshman at Columbia Community College in Phoenix City, Alabama. Throughout her high school career, she had been viewed as a very average student with above-average musical and athletic ability. Now attending the local community college and registered in six classes, she barely has time to breathe. Recently, Desiree has confided to a few of her closest friends that she aspires to become a medical doctor and would like to help defray the cost of medical school with her music, playing the piano and singing in some local clubs and, perhaps if very fortunate, securing a recording contract. Her friends acknowledge her talent noting she is very good, but not that good.

Undeterred, Desiree has auditioned for two local club managers and secured a series of 'gigs' at one of them. She is reportedly 'over the moon' about this professional 'coup.' Meanwhile, Desiree is sleeping very little as she has to balance her club work with her college overload. On many nights she is up until three or four in the morning completing overdue assignments. She insists that she only needs three or four hours of sleep a night, but her friends can see the toll these late nights are taking on her physical and mental health.

Inevitably, after weeks of this relentless, frenetic activity, Desiree 'crashes.' She does not attend classes, respond to calls or emails, or come out from her room except to eat a bagel and to use the bathroom. She is also becoming increasingly irritable and uncharacteristically intolerant of the concerned inquiries of friends and family members who simply show concern for her well-being. Then, abruptly, like the character Dr. Jekyll in the famous Robert Louis Stevenson novel, she emerges from her room, full of optimism and incentive and everything is right with the world once again. Amazingly, she always seems to land on her feet and charms her way back into the good graces of her college instructors, who reluctantly grant extensions on her overdue assignments, and that of the club owner who accepts her story about needing to help a sick relative.

Desiree is dismissive of anyone that tries to reason with her about her frenetic lifestyle and their concerns for her physical and mental health. She refers to these well-intentioned souls as 'do-gooders who are simply envious of her talents and resentful of her accomplishments.' "I am going places," she insists, "and my family and friends can either support me or get out of the way!"

Desiree's cycling behavior between her manic energy and deep despondency continued unabated for several months until last April when, after missing a gig at the club, the manager had had enough and fired her while, simultaneously, she received her semester grades and learned she had failed three of her six courses. Desiree, who never drank, began to imbibe, purchasing bottles of cheap vodka that she would consume alone in her room, further exacerbating her depression. This time, there was no emerging, she was 'down and out,' thinking dark thoughts, and in desperate need of professional help.

Fortunately, her parents were able to intervene and took her to a psychiatrist who specialized in working with individuals with mood disorders. After one visit, Desiree was formally diagnosed with bipolar I disorder and was prescribed mood-stabilizer medication and provided with cognitive behavioral therapy. Reportedly, she is faring much better. She is currently taking only two college courses and is no longer working in the clubs.

Desiree From an Attachment Perspective

Mood disorders in general, and bipolar disorder in particular, are highly hereditary. There is little research on attachment and bipolar disorder. Most of the literature is dedicated to parents with bipolar disorder and the general negative effects upon attachment security. Adults with bipolar disorder tend to fall into the category of dismissive on the Adult Attachment Interview (AAI) that most likely means they assumed an avoidant attachment style in childhood.

On the one hand, one could argue that the avoidant attachment style makes sense because both the symptoms of mania and depression prevent others from getting close. Even though in the manic stage, there can be lots of romantic activity, as in the case of Desiree, it is usually on a very superficial level. The avoidant attachment style is even more evident in the depressed stage of the disorder as we saw previously with Lashaun. Here, Desiree deactivates the attachment system and the consequential exploratory system clearly evidenced by staying in her room for most of the time.

On the other hand, an alternate interpretation of bipolar disorder can be offered from an attachment perspective. Between mania and depression, there is an oscillation between hyperactivation and deactivation of the attachment system. We all do this to a degree as the process of resolving many conflicts in life demands such oscillation. This is especially true in grief and loss when one oscillates between despair and hope until reorganization is reached. An individual with bipolar disorder is unable to reach such reorganization and lives life at the extremes of hyperactivation and deactivation of the attachment system. If one were the child of a primary caretaker with bipolar disorder, this interpretation can make even more sense. Conjecture tells us that this primary caretaker would oscillate between extreme forms of closeness and affection (manic stage) and equally extreme forms of deprivation (depressed stage).

With the right medication and a good therapist, there is hope for Desiree. The biggest challenge for those with bipolar I disorder is non-compliance with medication, which is often the result of wanting to experience the manic stage with all its euphoria and grandiosity. Unfortunately, the result is often harmful to oneself and others and rarely results in stable and satisfying attachments.

Characteristics of Bipolar Disorder

Bipolar disorder is typically characterized by the alternating presence of both depressed and euphoric moods. The DSM-V (American Psychiatric Association, 2013) distinguishes three types of bipolar disorder to include Bipolar disorder I, Bipolar disorder II, and Cyclothymic disorder. Difficulties in diagnosis make it challenging to report accurate prevalence rates. The prevalence rate of BPD in adolescents is about 3 percent (Van Meter et al., 2019). Peak onset appears to be between 15 and 19 years of age (Chia et al., 2019). The diagnosis of bipolar I disorder requires the presence of a manic episode or manic and depressive episodes. The DSM-V (American Psychiatric Association, 2013) symptomatology for a manic episode include

- Persistent elevated, expansive, or irritable mood
- Inflated self-esteem
- Decreased need for sleep
- Being more talkative than usual
- Feeling of thoughts racing
- Distractibility
- Increased goal-directed activity or psychomotor agitation
- Excessive pleasurable activity that can lead to negative consequences (e.g., buying sprees, sexual indiscretions)

Bipolar I can also include a mixed episode as long as there is evidence of a previously occurring manic or depressed episode, manic or mixed episode. A *mixed episode* is defined as meeting the criteria for both a manic and a major depressive episode. In addition, bipolar I can include a hypomanic episode as long as there is evidence of a previously occurring manic or mixed episode. *Hypomania* is defined as a distinct period of persistently elevated, expansive, or irritable mood that is not as severe as mania and lasts at least four days. If hypomania occurs with evidence of only a depressive episode, the diagnosis is bipolar II disorder. Bipolar II is two to three times more common than bipolar I in children and adolescents (Findling et al., 2018). If hypomania occurs only in conjunction with periods of depressive symptoms insufficient to meet the criteria for a major depressive episode during the course of two years, the diagnosis is cyclothymic disorder.

Assessment of Bipolar Disorder

The diagnosis of BPD is complicated by two factors, those of a high rate of comorbidity and the difficulty of distinguishing manic and hypomanic symptoms from typical childhood behaviors. The estimated rates of disorders frequently comorbid with BPD can be found in Table 8.1.

Table 8.1. Comorbidity with Bipolar Disorder

Disorder	**Prepubertal**	**Adolescent**
Attention-deficit hyperactivity disorder	70–90%	30–60%
Anxiety disorders	20–39%	30–40%
Conduct disorder	30–40%	30–60%
Oppositional defiant disorder	60–90%	20–30%
Substance abuse	10%	50–70%
Learning disabilities	30–40%	30–40%

Source: Adapted from Kowatch et al. (2005).

Attention-deficit hyperactivity disorder (ADHD) is by far the most common comorbid disorder; furthermore, the symptoms of ADHD (distractibility, irritability, increased talkativeness, risk-taking behaviors) can mimic those of mania. A differential diagnosis will be based on severity, occurrence, and age of onset. The symptoms of mania are more severe, occur episodically, and more often occur after the onset of puberty. The symptoms of ADHD are less severe, chronic, and begin typically in the preschool or early elementary school years (i.e., before the age of 7). The child who has ADHD may have difficulty sleeping, but the child with mania has less need for sleep (Passarotti et al., 2016). The overactive child with mania is goal-directed, in contrast to the child who has ADHD, in whom the overactivity is often disorganized and haphazard (Passarotti et al., 2016).

The rate of substance abuse among those diagnosed with BPD is slightly higher than among normal adolescents, estimated to be about 40 to 54 percent (Quello et al., 2005). Though many adolescents are sexually active, the hypersexuality that accompanies a manic episode can lead to risky sexual behaviors. Often not in control of their thoughts and actions, hypersexualized adolescents with BPD will not take the necessary precautions to avoid sexually transmitted diseases (Geller, 2004). Bipolar adolescents are at increased risk for suicide, a topic that is treated in depth later.

Measures to assess BPD in children and adolescents are much less developed than those for depression. Structured diagnostic interviews such as the K-SADS have been used to gather information for making a diagnosis of BPD (Wick-Nelson & Israel, 2006). Rating scales for mania are all adult versions that have been adapted for children. These include the Young Mania Rating Scale (Young et al., 1978) and the General Behavior Inventory (Depue et al., 1989). Interviews and observational data are still the recommended methods for diagnosing mania and hypomania in children and adolescents.

Psychopharmacological Treatment of Bipolar Disorder

The US FDA has approved several second-generation Anti-Psychotics (SGA) agents for the treatment of bipolar disorder in children and adolescents. Risperidone (10–17 years old) was the first SGA to receive approval in 2007, followed by Olanzapine (13–17 years old), Aripiprazole (10–17 years old), and Quetiapine (10–17 years old).

Unfortunately, few published double-blind, placebo-controlled studies exist for the efficacy of any medication for BPD with this population and critical gaps remain in identifying the most effective interventions for pediatric bipolar disorder (Washburn et al., 2011).

School-Based Interventions

Equipped with the preceding information, teachers who have a student who has BPD should assess the problem behavior with a focus on the conditions that induce and maintain it. The following intervention plan for Desiree, the case example, serves as an exemplar. A systematic approach that involves sound data collection methods and research-based interventions is recommended. Such an approach provides the best chance for success in helping a student cope with BPD in the school or college environment.

Assessing the Problem

The purpose of conducting a behavioral assessment in the context of the school environment is to establish the cause or function of the target behavior and its effect on learning. To ensure consistency and thoroughness, the multidisciplinary team should follow a well-conceived protocol such as the one recommended in this textbook (Barnhill, 2005). For Desiree, an effective one would consist of the following components.

The first step is *identifying and describing the problem behavior.* Accordingly, Desiree's family members, friends, and instructors have observed a significant behavioral change in her during the past academic year. Desiree, who displayed normal adolescent behaviors and was stable and predictable, has recently evidenced extreme polarity of behaviors, cycling fairly rapidly from periods of euphoria and frenetic activity to episodes of depression and fatigue. Her emotional volatility is negatively impacting her educational performance as well as her social life. Desiree, once an average high school student, is now in danger of failing.

The second step is *collecting baseline data and academic information.* Desiree's parents, friends, and college instructors have provided anecdotal data that documents her mood swings and behavioral aberrations. Desiree's psychiatrist has asked that her instructors complete the Young Mania Rating Scale (Young et al., 1978), which helps distinguish manic episodes. Her teachers have also been encouraged to address each of the eleven categories that are depression-related (Garber & Kaminski, 2000) in their written observational reports.

Next, from *examining the environment and setting demands,* there does not appear to be a particular environment or setting that precipitates Desiree's emotional polarity. Indeed, the impetus for these changes seems to be better explained by neurobiological factors as opposed to environmental ones.

The next step in the assessment process involves *completing a functional assessment form and/or behavior rating scales.* To this end, the functional assessment form was completed at the end of the fourth quarter of Calvin's eighth-grade year, and the *Young Mania Rating Scale* (Young et al., 1978), described earlier in the chapter, was completed at the same time.

Caregivers were encouraged to conduct direct observations of Desiree's behavior in the community and at home. In response to this recommendation, Desiree's family and caregivers conducted ongoing behavior observations, noting the frequency, duration, and intensity of both her depressive and manic episodes. In addition, as recommended by her psychiatrist, Desiree's family, friend, and caregivers also described her depressive behavior in accordance with the eleven descriptive categories developed by Garber and Kaminski (2000).

As a final step in the process, her caregivers, friends, and family members formulated a hypothesis regarding the cause of the aberrant behavior as well as its purpose. Based on the behavioral data collected by these stakeholders, a formal diagnosis of bipolar I disorder was hypothesized and, ultimately, confirmed. The organic nature of this disorder precludes the determination of a purpose or function for the behaviors that are symptomatic of this condition.

Subsequent behavior consistent with the diagnosis of bipolar I disorder was observed in Desiree that was sufficiently intense, and of significant duration, to confirm the correctness of the preliminary diagnosis.

Developing an Effective Intervention Plan

In accordance with IDEA (2004) and in conformity with the model developed by Buck et al. (2000) and Ryan et al. (2003), a behavioral intervention plan was developed for Desiree that involves multimodal treatment plan consisting of appropriate cognitive-behavioral therapy, a parent-education component, and a psychopharmacological intervention.

Desiree's caregivers, while not directly involved in these treatment regimens, nevertheless should be familiar with them and continue to provide observational data to help identify and document behavioral changes that may be associated with one or more of the treatments. In addition, these stakeholders should continue to provide Desiree with a supportive and structured classroom environment and quickly notify her family and psychiatrist if they observe any sudden or significant behavior changes. They should also be informed about the type of medication prescribed for Desiree's disorder and its possible beneficial and adverse effects. Likewise, there should be a contingency plan in place in the event that Desiree requires emergency care relative to her bipolar I disorder. Lastly, as with any individual affected by depression, Desiree's caregivers, family, and friends should be educated about the warning signs of suicide as well as suicide-prevention techniques. A comprehensive examination of the warning signs of adolescent suicide and suicide assessment is provided in the following sections.

Adolescent Suicide

Case Example: A Personal Anecdote

Marcia was a student assigned to a tenth-grade special education class in a rural school district. She was one of those students who easily "slips under the radar" because she was quiet, self-composed, and cooperative in a class of mostly boys who were anything but quiet and cooperative.

Marcia had a reading disability yet was otherwise a model student. In fact, she was mainstreamed in all her courses except English 10. Nonetheless, because she worked hard and completed all her assignments, eagerly revising her written work to achieve a better grade, she was a very successful student.

She was so pleasant to have in class that she quickly became a teacher favorite. Her teachers missed the tell-tale signs of impending suicide because she was so good, she was the 'least of their worries.' It was easy to see how they were lulled into complacency by her congeniality and compliance.

Tragically, at 5:00 a.m. on the last Monday of the marking period in June, the teacher received a call from the principal informing him that Marcia had committed suicide in the early morning hours on Sunday. It was every teacher's nightmare. The teacher was asked to come in an hour early to help support students who might have already heard the news and to be prepared for the emotional fallout when the announcement of her loss was made by the principal during homeroom that morning.

The impact on the students was similar to the detonation of a bomb. Students and teachers who were affected by the news were invited to go to preset locations to receive grief counseling; clearly, the teacher wasn't the only one who was blind-sided by this unimaginable tragedy. Nevertheless, the teacher kept wondering how he had missed the cues, the warning signs. Surely, they must have been evident. The one question that plagued him for weeks and months afterwards was, "Could I have been instrumental in preventing Marcia's death if I had been more observant and identified the signs? But what were those "signs?" He was ashamed to admit that he wasn't sure.

A few months after the tragedy, the teacher attended a meeting with several colleagues as well as the principal to discuss the issue of adolescent suicide and risk assessment. Instead of an adversarial gathering of faculty, administrators, and parents that involved finger-pointing and blame, the tone of the meeting was refreshingly cathartic. They came away determined to research the subject of adolescent suicide and develop effective in-service training as well as a fluid, responsive contingency plan.

Prevalence of Adolescent Suicide

In 2018, close to 7000 individuals between the ages of 10 and 24 committed suicide (Centers for Disease Control and Prevention, 2019). Globally, suicide is the fourth leading cause of death for people between the ages 15 and 29 (WHO, 2022). In America, for individuals between the ages of 15 and 24, the suicide rate is 14.24, and while the rate for those under 15 years of age is 0.51, that is up significantly in the last ten years (American Association for Suicide Prevention, 2022).

The 2018 National Survey of Drug Use and Mental Health (Substance Abuse and Mental Health Services Administration, 2019) reported that for youth in grades 9-12, females were almost two times more likely to attempt suicide than their male counterparts. When this same age demographic was broken down by ethnic groups, The Youth Risk Behavior Survey of 2019 (Centers for Disease Control and Prevention, 2019) Black females had the highest attempt rate at 15.2 percent, followed by Hispanic females at 11.9 percent, with White and Asian females at 9.4 percent and 8.4 percent, respectively (Centers for Disease Control and Prevention, 2019). Black males reported attempting at least one suicide attempt at 8.5 percent, while Asian males had a 7.1 percentage rate, with White males and Hispanic males at 6.4 percent and 5.5 percent, respectively (Centers for Disease Control and Prevention, 2019). Native Americans came in with the lowest percentages for both male and female (Centers for Disease Control and Prevention, 2019).

Not all adolescents who commit suicide are depressed; however, a large number of them are. That makes recognizing the symptoms of adolescent depression and helping students who manifest those symptoms all the more crucial.

The Warning Signs of Adolescent Suicide

For adolescents who complete or attempt suicide, it is seen as the only way out of an untenable situation. Although teenagers may not come right out and ask for help, they almost always hint at their desperation in words or behavior. It is critical that counselors and teachers be attuned to these cues. One caution, though, no determination that a youngster is suicidal can be made based on one event, statement or behavior. When adolescents attempt suicide, several of these variables have come together, convincing them that suicide is the only way out.

Verbal Cues

Some adolescents do communicate their suicidal intent directly ("I'm going to kill myself" or "I just want to die"), but most communicate their intentions subtly, often using metaphorical language (Capuzzi & Gross, 2019):

- "I'd like to go home."
- "I won't be around much longer."
- "They'll be sorry for what they did to me."

- "I'm very tired."
- "I wonder what death is like."
- "They'll see how serious I am."
- "Things are never going to get any better."
- "I'll always feel this way."
- "Nobody cares."
- "People would be better off without me."

These are just a few examples; there are many others. The point is that when a student says something that strikes the helper as odd or that can be interpreted in a number of ways, the helper should be quick to ask the student for clarification, "Can you help me understand a bit better what you mean when you say, 'They'll be sorry'?"

School personnel also need to be sensitive to themes that might communicate what an adolescent is thinking. The nine themes that signal thoughts of suicide on the part of adolescents are listed below. Each of these nine motivations can be categorized into one of the three primary functions of suicide: to avoid a difficult situation, to take control of one's life, or to communicate pain. All suicides serve one of these three functions.

Nine Themes That Signal Thoughts of Suicide on the Part of Adolescents

- Wanting to escape from a difficult situation
- Wanting to join someone who has died
- Wanting to attract the attention of family and friends
- Wanting to manipulate someone
- Wanting to avoid punishment
- Wanting to be punished
- Wanting to control when and how death will occur (especially for adolescents who have a chronic or terminal illness)
- Wanting to end a conflict that seems irresolvable
- Wanting revenge

Source: Capuzzi, D., & Gross, D. R. (2019). I don't want to live: The adolescent at risk for suicidal behavior. In D. Capuzzi & D. R. Gross (Eds.), *Youth risk: A prevention resource for counselors, teachers, and parents* (7th ed., p. 231). Copyright by the American Counseling Association.

Behavioral Cues

School personnel must also pay attention to certain behaviors that could signal the intention to commit suicide. Capuzzi and Gross (2019) identified a number of behaviors that are cause for concern.

Lack of Concern about Personal Welfare. At times, adolescents reveal their suicidal tendencies by putting themselves at risk--for example, by driving recklessly, accepting dares from friends, or marking or cutting themselves. School personnel should understand that these students may be in pain but unable to express that pain.

Changes in Social Patterns. Helpers should notice sudden changes in students' behavior such as a socially active student who becomes withdrawn and isolated, a normally compliant student who becomes argumentative and rebellious, a student leaves one group of friends and joins another group whose members are more daring or more rebellious.

A Decline in School Achievement. Helpers should be aware of any good student who suddenly loses interest in schoolwork, itself a symptom of depression in this population. If a student is vague or refuses to talk about the problem, the helper should not be put off, "For some kids, going from A's to C's means they're giving up. Are you giving up? Have you ever thought about or considered hurting yourself?"

Difficulties Concentrating and Thinking Clearly. Again, these difficulties are symptomatic of depression. They also can indicate that the student is focusing his or her energies on planning a suicide.

Altered Patterns of Eating and Sleeping. Although there can be many causes for disturbances in eating and sleeping, depression and suicidal tendencies are clearly among them. The helper should watch for a dramatic loss or gain of weight and should ask teachers to watch for students who are nodding off in class.

Attempts to Put Personal Affairs in Order or to Make Amends. An adolescent's efforts to put his or her affairs in order could signal that the youngster is preparing to die. Before a suicide attempt, adolescents often repair a broken relationship, call old friends, impulsively finish a project that had been put off, or give away important personal items.

Alcohol or Drug Use or Abuse. Many adolescents experiment with alcohol and drugs, but sustained use, which leads to abuse, diminishes some of the psychological defenses that protect youngsters from thoughts of suicide. Substance abuse can increase impulsivity and, at the same time, decrease the adolescent's communication skills. For the substance-abusing adolescent, then, suicide may appear to be a viable option at a particular moment in time.

Unusual Interest in How Others Are Feeling. As a defense against their own pain, suicidal adolescents may show exaggerated interest and responsiveness to the problems of others. A preoccupation with others serves a dual purpose in that it helps suicidal adolescents focus on something other than their own problem; and, paradoxically, it helps them communicate their own pain.

Preoccupation with Themes of Death and Violence. This kind of preoccupation is quite common in suicidal adolescents. Certainly, many youngsters are drawn to violence in the media; but when violence becomes a major interest, the school helper needs to be concerned. Movies, books, music, video games, drawings, and writings that focus on destruction, death, and dying could signal suicidal tendencies. Helpers might become aware of such activity through teachers who discover a student's drawings or parents who notice a change and an extraordinary interest in such themes.

Sudden Improvement after a Period of Depression. Students who show a sudden improvement after a period of depression may be at risk for suicide. Having made the decision to go ahead with the suicide, they are mobilizing themselves to carry out the plan. This is not the gradual improvement that signals a depression is lifting; this is a sudden and drastic change.

Sudden or Increased Promiscuity. Experimentation with or escalation of sexual activity can be an adolescent's way of diverting attention from suicidal thoughts and feelings. The consequences of promiscuity—for example, an unwanted pregnancy or feelings of guilt—can augment the adolescent's suicidal tendencies.

The Suicide Interview

Assessment of suicide risk should cut across four dimensions to include ideation, volition, plan, and history. The following outline is a practical guide for assessing students' risk for suicide.

1. **Suicidal Ideation.** Variability in terms of frequency, duration, and intensity of suicidal thoughts is one indicator of risk level. When a student's thoughts of suicide are frequent, last a long time, and interrupt the student's routine, the student is at increased risk of hurting himself or herself. To determine the frequency, duration, and intensity of suicidal ideation, the helper should ask the following questions:

- Over a single day, how often do you think about hurting yourself?

- When the idea of hurting yourself comes to mind, how long does the idea stay with you? How long do you dwell on it?

- When these thoughts come to you, are you able to continue with what you're doing, or do these thoughts get in the way of your everyday activities?

If the suicidal ideation is not frequent (e.g., just once a day) and does not last long (several minutes), and the student is able to continue with his or her routine, then the student's risk of suicide is low. In this case, the helper should simply alert the child's parents and give them a list of symptoms to watch for—for example, increased isolation, moodiness, the child's locking himself or herself in a room. When suicidal tendencies remain at the level of ideation, the risk of suicide generally is low.

2. **Suicidal Volition**. The key question here is "Do you want to hurt yourself?" Most students answer no, they are only thinking about it. When adolescents say they want to hurt themselves, the risk of suicide automatically increases to moderate at least. The helper must immediately alert the parents, ask them to come to the school, and direct them to take their child to the nearest medical center for a psychiatric evaluation.

3. **Suicide Plan**. Having a plan increases the risk of suicide. The question the helper needs to ask is "If you did hurt yourself, how would you do it?" If the adolescent answers, "I don't know" or "I haven't really thought about it," the risk is lower than if the student is able to give concrete details about how and when he or she plans to commit suicide. Another factor here is the lethality of the method (a gun, for example, versus pills). Volition plus a plan increase the risk of suicide to high. The helper should notify the parents immediately and, after letting the principal know what's going on, should call 911 to have the student taken for an immediate psychiatric evaluation. In extreme cases, when the helper has determined that the risk of suicide is imminent, the call to the parents can be made after the student is en route to the hospital.

4. **A History of Attempted Suicide**. A history of attempted suicide automatically increases the student's present risk. The helper should always ask, "Have you ever tried to hurt yourself in the past?" Here, too, the lethality of the earlier attempt should be investigated. There is a significant difference between taking a few pills and ending up in the hospital with a serious injury. Even in the absence of volition, if a suicidal student has made a serious attempt at some earlier time to hurt himself or herself, the helper should consider the current risk to be moderate.

This outline will help school personnel to cope in an orderly and professional manner with a suicidal crisis. The goal is to stabilize the situation by choosing an appropriate intervention based on an informed assessment of the risk to the student.

From the Field

Michelle Zagrobelny, Special Education Educator and Administrator

Michelle Zagrobelny began her career as a special education teacher and transition coordinator in Culpeper County, Virginia, after which she spent several years as an academic administrator in a residential school for students who have special needs. For the past nine years, she has served as chairperson for both the Committee on Special Education and the Preschool Committee on Special Education in New York State public school districts.

Michelle, you've been a special education professional for over fifteen years, and you've worked with many children and youth with mood disorders such as depression and bipolar disorder. We know that children who have these diagnoses are becoming more prevalent in our special education population. How would you account for this increase?

I would approach answering that question in two parts. The first part is attempting to address the argument/debate of whether children are being over-diagnosed, misdiagnosed, or prematurely diagnosed versus the idea that families are reaching out more to mental health professionals to finally discover an appropriate name for why their child behaves or feels the way they do. I have known numerous children who were given a mental health diagnosis with a prescribed pharmaceutical treatment plan on their first visit to a medical physician who didn't specialize in mental health treatment. This is very frustrating to educational staff, especially when their input was not requested or considered. Unfortunately, it isn't unusual for a child to suddenly have a behavioral diagnosis yet have no issues at all in educational settings. However, I have also worked with other families and educational teams who finally understand, or begin to understand, why a child is the way they are because their emotional needs are appropriately being treated. We can't always get away with saying children who behave poorly in school are only angry, purposely delinquent, or have poor parenting outside of school.

Now, the second part of the question is why are children who have mood disorders becoming more prevalent in special education specifically? When I was growing up, special education services were for children who have mental retardation, physical disabilities, learning disabilities, etc. Children who have emotional or behavioral problems didn't always get to stay in school: They were sent away, suspended, or expelled, or quit school. Since then, federal and state education laws and regulations have widened educational doors for these students and have increased the protection of parental and children rights. In addition, as an understanding of mental health needs increases in our general population, more children as well as adults are receiving these diagnoses. Consequently, these children are in school and may experience interruptions in education. Special education has expanded classifications to include mental health mood disorders and the appropriate supports that can be recommended and provided in the educational environment.

What are schools, such as the ones you've worked in, doing to help children affected by these debilitating conditions?

I've seen in an increase in school counselors added to schools' faculties. I'm not referring to guidance counselors. Typically, schools used to have the standard guidance counselors for mostly educational planning support. With the increase of children who have mood disorders, guidance counselors' responsibilities have increased at times to a point where neither guidance nor counseling can be effective. Thus, counselors are hired to support just the children who have mental health needs.

Schools and outside resources such as youth advocacy programs, mental health workers, and even social services at times are reaching out more to one another to support these children and their families. These interventions can be very helpful; however, much improvement and efficiency is needed to make them truly beneficial to children. Lack of funding or and personnel (in rural areas) are the biggest obstacles.

I have also seen an increase in educational staff awareness through training and communication about mood disorders. The teaching staff works directly with these children more than any other school-based professional. If they are unaware and insufficiently educated about these children, then educational success can be significantly impeded.

As a former special education teacher and the current chairperson for the Committee on Special Education in your school district, what can you share with our readers that might help them work more successfully with students affected by depression?

I would encourage teachers to increase their education and training to include how to work with and understand children who have depression or other mood disorders. The days have long gone by that teachers just teach in their specialty area. For some students to progress through school successfully, they need to be surrounded by educational staff in all learning areas that are aware and may at times allow appropriate exceptions for atypical behaviors and learn how to better accommodate these children in their classrooms. I'm not implying an unfair advantage should be provided, but they deserve at least a fair chance to be successful with an increased awareness.

What are some common pitfalls new teachers might hope to avoid as they work with these students, and how would you advise them to do so?

Quickness to judge is a common pitfall. In our everyday lives, we all either do this or really try hard not to. Also, if you are aware of a student who has mental health needs, don't assume you are able to address those needs by yourself. Always communicate with other educational or administrative staff and counseling support staff regarding specifics about the child. Don't presume that those two psychology classes you took as an undergrad qualify you to diagnose or treat what it takes trained professionals weeks to see. Even the best intentions may cause more harm than good, especially if something were to happen with a child and you may not have communicated "red flag" information to other staff or attempted your own treatment or intervention without proper input and guidance.

Finally, on a positive note, could you share a "success story" from your experience as either a teacher or administrator that highlights the benefits of effective practice relative to children and youth who have a mood disorder?

After fifteen years, I struggle to think of a single success story that is worthy of a made-for-TV movie. In real life we deal with the situations as they appear, and children who have any type of disability or mental health disorder move through school like any others. If we are truly successful, the students move on to live productive lives and feel no reason to return to say thanks. It's not because they aren't grateful but rather because the system was so effective that the practice was commonplace: That's success.

Summary

Mood disorders in children and adolescents continue to be among the most challenging conditions to diagnose and treat. This larger category encompasses major depression, dysthymia, and bipolar disorder, and the diagnosis of each of these is complicated by their high rate of comorbidity with other disorders such as ADHD, learning disabilities, oppositional defiant disorder, conduct disorder, and anxiety disorders.

Major depression is characterized by a major depressive episode that typically involves appetite and sleep disturbance, impaired social or academic functioning, depressed mood or loss of interest or pleasure, and change from usual functioning that is not due to the use of chemical substance or medical condition. Dysthymia is a condition quite similar to major depression but is distinct in degree of severity. For example, its discriminating feature is the presence of a dysphonic or irritable mood in the individual for at least a year. The alternating presence of both depressed and manic or euphoric moods distinguishes bipolar disorder.

The etiology of each of these mood disorders is not relegated to a specific cause. Rather, the cause may be more accurately attributed to the interaction of several factors, including the biology of the individual, the genetic makeup of the individual and her predisposition to the disorder, and environmental factors that include family structure and learned behaviors. Furthermore, assessment of depression and mania are primarily accomplished through observation, structured interview, and self-report measures.

Typically, observations are conducted using performance-based measures such as the depression-related categories developed by Garber and Kaminski (2000). Experts have contended that the clinical interview continues to be the most effective method for diagnosing depression in children and adolescents (Kowatch et al., 2005). Self-report measures provide additional confirmation and are relatively easy to administer. Some of the more popular of these include the *Children's Depression Inventory* (CDI; Sitarenios & Kovacs, 1999), the *Reynolds Adolescent Depression Scale* (RADS-2; Reynolds, 2004), and the *Peer Nomination Inventory for Depression* (Lefkowitz & Tesiny, 1980). A recommended scale to measure mania in children is the *Young Mania Rating Scale* (Young et al., 1978).

The most serious potential effect of depression in children and adolescents is suicide. Indeed, suicide is the second leading cause of death for individuals between the ages of 15 and 19 and has increased significantly in the past twenty years. What is more, a significant number of these suicides were committed by youth who were clinically depressed, which makes the treatment of depression a very important step in reducing the alarming number of these tragic and preventable deaths.

Warning signs are often precursors to parasuicide and suicide and include (1) verbal cues (e.g., "I won't be around much longer"; "They'll be sorry for what they did to me"; "I'm very tired"; "Nobody cares"; and "People would be better off without me") and (2) behavioral cues (e.g., lack of concern about personal welfare, changes in social patterns, attempts to put personal affairs in order or to make amends, alcohol or drug use or abuse, and a sudden improvement after a period of depression).

Research on the treatment of mood disorders recommends a multimodal approach, typically involving a cognitive-behavioral therapy such as the Adolescent Coping with Depression (CWD-A) course (Clarke et al., 2003; Rohde et al., 2005), family therapy, and psychopharmacological treatment. Vortioxetine, an SSRI, is currently one of a very few medications approved for use with children and adolescents by the FDA. Similarly, lithium is the recommended medication for the treatment of bipolar disorder in children and adolescents and, once again, the only one approved by the FDA for use with this population.

Although mood disorders continue to be among the low-incidence disorders in school-age children; nonetheless, the potential for catastrophic consequences compels teachers, clinicians, and family members to be vigilant in identifying and painstaking in assessing suspected cases. Furthermore, teachers and parents need to be well informed regarding diagnostic procedures as well as thoroughly familiar with current, research-based interventions. Each of these stakeholders plays a critical role, in collaboration with clinicians, in the journey to wellness for students who have a mood disorder.

Tips for Teachers

- Become thoroughly familiar with the characteristics, assessment procedures, and recommended interventions for students suspected to have or diagnosed with a mood disorder.
- Maintain accurate and detailed anecdotal records for any student in your class who has been diagnosed with a mood disorder. This information will be invaluable in helping medical personnel determine the effects of psychopharmacological and other cognitive and/or behavioral interventions.

- Provide a structured curriculum and establish a predictable classroom routine for students who have been diagnosed with a mood disorder. Stability that comes from routine is comforting to students who may be experiencing mood cycles, dysthymia, or a depressive episode. Their world may seem "out-of-control," but your classroom may provide a "safe haven" of predictability, understanding, and support.
- Don't try to "make it all better" or "cheer up" a student who is depressed. Provide encouragement and support and alert parents, clinical professionals, and administrators if significant changes in behavior are observed.
- Familiarize yourself with the warning signs of adolescent suicide. Carefully review the recommendations provided in this chapter, and make sure that you communicate your concerns about the student's well-being to the student, her parents, clinicians, and administrators. Experts suggest that it is important to maintain communication regarding suicidal ideation, threats, or intuited "warning signs" among caregivers and stakeholders and to "stay connected" with the student of concern.
- Avoid looking for causes for the student's dysphoria or depressed state. Usually, the student does not understand the reason for her depression—it may be biochemical and therefore beyond anyone's power to "cure."
- Most important, be firm, compassionately firm. Don't accept the student's depression as an excuse for not trying or completing an assignment. Of course, teachers need to be flexible and accommodating if the student has been absent as a result of treatment for depression or hospitalization, but it is important to help the student return to a sense of "normalcy" and routine as quickly as possible.
- If the student's depression is associated with a "trigger" or precipitating event, try to structure the classroom environment and activities so as to avoid exposing him to evocative stimuli.
- Consider reducing the student's workload. For example, provide fewer problems on a test or reduce the number of questions to be answered on a homework assignment. Similarly, provide alternative projects or assessments and give the student a

choice. Finally, give the student and extension of the due date of an assignment because many students who have mood disorders have difficulty with organizational tasks and meeting stringent deadlines—be flexible!

- Provide the student who has a mood disorder with a "study buddy" or peer tutor. This can serve two purposes: provide needed social interaction; and help the student stay on task and not feel overwhelmed by the demands of the curriculum. Finally, always include the student who is depressed in all classroom activities and ensure that he knows he is a valued member of the classroom community.

Focus Questions Revisited

How would you differentiate between a student who has major depression and one who has persistent depressive disorder (dysthymia)?

A Sample Response: Persistent depressive disorder (dysthymia) is less intense and more prolonged than major depressive disorder. Children who have persistent depressive disorder tend to exhibit irritability, but while this is similar to those for MDD, it is far less severe. Children who have dysthymia do not evidence a psychotic illness, nor do they exhibit a physiological mood-altering condition. Typically, they have good days and bad days, or they may have many mixed days, but they do not have good weeks. For a diagnosis to be made, symptoms must have persisted for at least one year (American Psychiatric Association, 2013).

What are the characteristics of bipolar disorder II, and how might they affect a student's academic and social performance?

A Sample Response: A student who has bipolar II disorder displays the characteristics of hypomania, defined as a distinct period of persistently elevated expansive or irritable mood that is not as severe as mania and lasts at least four days, as well as a depressive episode. Logically, a student who has this disorder will experience a loss of motivation and energy during the depressive episode that will impair academic and social performance. In addition, the hypomanic phase might prompt the student to take on too much in terms of academic workload or a social commitment, which might cause the individual to feel overwhelmed and therefore simply "shut down."

What steps would you take if you suspected that a child in your class might be clinically depressed?

A Sample Response: I would first alert the school psychologist or a school counselor and express my apprehension to the student. It might be prudent as well to convey my concerns to the family members of the child, who might also have noticed behaviors that suggest the individual is unhappy or despondent. Upon the recommendation of the school psychologist and with the consent of the child's parents, I would initiate prereferral interventions. If, after a reasonable period of time, these measures proved ineffective in improving the student's disposition, I would recommend that the individual be evaluated by the multidisciplinary team to determine the appropriate provision of special education services.

What related services personnel might be important resources to you as the classroom teacher of a child with a mood disorder? How might they provide support and/or assistance?

A Sample Response: The appropriate related services personnel in this instance would be the school psychologist and/or school counselor. These individuals are professionally qualified to develop effective treatment plans that can generalize to the classroom, which may involve a cognitive-behavioral strategy or a multimodal treatment approach. They also serve as consultants to the teacher regarding specific interventions that might be used in the classroom.

Which of the models of depression would be most helpful to you as a classroom teacher? Provide a rationale for each of your selections.

A Sample Response: Clearly, the cognitive model offers teachers a practical approach to helping students who have MDD by encouraging students to monitor their own behavior and reinforce desired outcomes. The other models require clinical training or are simply too involved to be of benefit to the classroom teacher.

How is knowing about comorbidities (e.g., between bipolar disorder and attention-deficit hyperactivity disorder) potentially helpful to you as the classroom teacher of a child or adolescent who has a mood disorder?

A Sample Response: The interaction of the two disorders typically results in a more involved constellation of behaviors and clearly complicates all aspects of the treatment process: from assessment to the development of an effective behavioral intervention plan. Thus, the more the teacher knows about the diagnosis and treatment of both disorders, the better prepared she will be to provide effective interventions that address both the distractibility, irritability, increased talkativeness, and risk-taking behaviors associated with ADHD as well as the mania and hypermania that are characteristic of bipolar disorder.

What observation protocol might be helpful to classroom teachers in providing relevant data for a child assigned to them who is suspected of having a mood disorder? Describe its benefits.

A Sample Response: It would be very helpful if teachers used the list of characteristic behaviors developed by Kowatch et al. (2005) and organized under three headings: discriminating features, consistent features, and variable features. These characteristics include:

Discriminating features such as

1. Depressed mood or loss of interest or pleasure
2. Change from usual functioning
3. Not due to substances or medical condition

Consistent features such as

1. Appetite and sleep disturbances
2. Impaired social or academic functioning
3. Absence of use of mood-altering substances
4. Absence of a physical condition that alters mood

Variable features such as

1. Irritability
2. Weight loss or weight gain
3. Insomnia or hypersomnia
4. Psychomotor agitation or retardation
5. Fatigue of loss of energy
6. Feelings of worthlessness and inappropriate guilt
7. Impaired concentration and change in school performance
8. Suicidal ideation
9. Diurnal variation, with worsening of symptoms in the morning

10. Unexplained somatic complaints
11. Sleep–wake cycle reverse

Of course, as with all emotional and behavioral disorders, several of these characteristics should be observed in the individual of concern, and these should be clearly evident as intense, frequent, and of significant duration (exceeding six months). This list of typical or characteristic behaviors should be organized as a checklist that can be easily used by the classroom teacher to record the frequency, duration, and intensity of the behaviors observed. The completed daily or weekly checklists could then be compared with those distributed to all the student's teachers and assessed to identify behavioral trends. This aggregated data would be instrumental in determining the need for formal screening and evaluation.

Consider the case example of Lashaun. Do you think he might develop suicidal ideations? Justify your response. What are some of the warning signs you would look for in assessing Lashaun's risk of suicide?

A Sample Response: It seems very likely that Lashaun has at least contemplated suicide as a means of escaping from his pain as a result of his mother's alienation and the absence of a male role model. Unless the treatment regimen is successful, there is, I think, a very good chance that Lashaun will need help in dealing with thoughts of suicide and will need to be closely supervised.

Key Terms Used in the Chapter

Parasuicide:
An apparent attempt at suicide, commonly called a suicidal gesture, in which the aim is not death—for example, a sublethal drug overdose or wrist slash. Previous parasuicide is a predictor of suicide. The increased risk of subsequent suicide persists without decline for at least two decades.

Major Depressive Disorder (MDD):
A depressive disorder in which symptoms cause significant impairment in social and/or occupational/school functioning.

Dysthymia:
A mood disorder on the depressive spectrum. It is considered less severe than major depression but is of a more chronic nature. It is explained more fully later in the chapter.

Chapter 9

Autistic Spectrum Disorders

Focus Questions

- *Suppose you are going to be the new classroom teacher of a student who has an autistic disorder (AD). What would you want to know about the child's classroom performance and about her learning and behavioral needs as provided by her current teacher?*
- *What would be important for you to know about the classroom performance of a student who has an autistic disorder (AD) to be fully prepared to help him learn and develop?*
- *Describe the theory of mind and what insights it provides about the functional understanding of students who have autistic disorder?*
- *As the teacher of a student who has an autistic disorder, what are some important academic considerations to facilitate his acquisition of skills?*
- *Explain discrete trial training.*
- *What is paradigm/pivotal response training (PRT), and why is it often preferred over more structured techniques such as discrete trial training?*
- *Describe video modeling and what its therapeutic implications are for children who have AD.*
- *What are "social stories," and how are they used to help students who have higher-functioning autism (HFA) acquire strategies for appropriate social conversation and emotional regulation?*
- *List the key behavioral characteristics of students who have autism spectrum disorder.*

Autistic Spectrum Disorder: An Introduction

Few behavioral disorders that affect children and youth are more enigmatic or challenging to teachers than autism spectrum disorder (ASD). The reason for this is apparent in the three principal diagnostic criteria for the disorder, which describe a child who appears both disinterested in and inept at socialization and communication. Because most people are, by nature, social creatures, this apparent lack of interest in other people on the part of most children who have ASD creates confusion and frustration in most caregivers.

Equally disconcerting is the fact that the number of children diagnosed with ASD continues to grow exponentially each year. Unless this trend abates, predictions are that, within a decade, ASD may be among the most prevalent disorders affecting school-age children. In 1992 there were 15,580 cases of ASD identified in the United States among school-age children; by 2003 that number had grown to 163,773, representing a growth rate of 393 percent (National Center for Health Statistics, 2007). Recent statistics from 2018 have revealed that the number of identified cases has almost doubled in the last three years and, currently, 1 in 44 children are identified with ASD by age 8 (Centers for Disease Control and Prevention, 2021).

These disturbing statistics, together with the challenging behaviors displayed by children who have ASD, underscore the importance of educating teachers about its characteristics and effective treatment practices. Teachers must be prepared to work effectively with students who have been diagnosed with ASD as they are compelled by IDEA to do so and, like physicians, they too are bound by a higher imperative: to help all students in their classroom to learn. Working effectively with students who have ASD requires methodical preparation both in understanding autism spectrum disorder and in providing effective remediation for those whose academic and social development have been affected by it.

The DSM-V (American Psychiatric Association, 2013) made significant changes to the understanding and diagnosis of autism. First, it eliminated Asperger syndrome and created a single diagnosis of ASD. The specifier, 'with or without language impairment' substituted for the exclusion of Asperger's syndrome that previously was defined with the absence of language impairment. Secondly, it located ASD in the category of neurodevelopmental disorders along with intellectual disabilities, ADHD, specific learning disorder and motor disorders. The commonality is their manifestation in early development that result in impairment in personal, social, academic, or occupational functioning (American Psychiatric Association, 2013).

The almost phenomenal rise in the rates of ASD in the last ten years has captured the interest of many. Whether the fact that more cases are being identified represents a real increase is a subject of controversy. Changes in definition and diagnostic criteria articulated in the DSM-V, better diagnosis at both ends of the spectrum, a growing awareness of the condition, and labeling needed for appropriate educational services may have contributed to this rapid rise (Chawarska & Volkmar, 2020).

The authors anchor the clinical presentation of characteristics, etiology, and research-based interventions with practical examples, based on real-life cases. By the end of the chapter, the reader should understand the nature of ASD as well as the learning needs of individuals so diagnosed. In addition, readers will be provided examples of functional behavior assessments (FBA) as well as a behavioral intervention plan (BIPs) developed to address real-life case examples of students who have ASD. It is hoped that these examples will provide the reader with an effective process by which to address the behavioral problems that most typically affect individuals with ASD.

Finally, readers are provided with a set of strategies to facilitate working with students who have ASD as well as relevant study questions and suggested responses to ensure their grasp of the chapter content and familiarity with effective school-based interventions.

Case Example: Stefan

Stefan is a third-grader attending the Rainbow Academy in Mastic Beach, Long Island. The Rainbow Academy is a residential school for students diagnosed with autism spectrum disorder who require significant support. Stefan's parents were reluctant to place him in a residential school so far from their home; however, the quality and extent of the services it provides convinced them that this would be a better placement for Stefan.

The last two years have taken a toll on Stefan's family as his extreme support needs and persistent insomnia were very stressful. Stefan's parents and three siblings love him dearly, but his constant demands and safety concerns necessitated a drastic intervention. Stefan's applied behavioral analysis (ABA) trained behaviorist and his pediatrician recommended that his parents search for a quality residential school that focuses exclusively on students with autism requiring level two and three supports. After months of searching, the family settled on the Rainbow Academy despite its distant location two states away and the costly tuition and expensive room and board fees.

Stefan was diagnosed with ASD at the age of four by a child psychologist in coordination with a family services support team that specialized in screening children with autism. One of Stefan's presenting behaviors that comport with the diagnostic criteria provided in the DSM-V (American Psychiatric Association, 2013) include deficits in social-emotional reciprocity; for example, Stefan rarely acknowledges his parents or responds to their frequent attempts to engage him in play or to make eye contact. Similarly, Stefan displays deficits in non-verbal communication behaviors. He consistently displays a flat affect and appears disinterested in attempts to get his attention or elicit a physical response to a behavioral prompt. Finally, when children his own age were invited for a play date, Stefan behaved as if he were alone and refused to engage in play or to interact with them in any way. He also reacts angrily to any change in routine, will only eat certain foods such as bagels, white rice, or plain noodles, and frequently engages in stereotypical movements such as hand flapping, running, and jumping, and lining up objects such as toys in a specific order, often by color.

Stefan has been determined to be functioning at severity level three, requiring very substantial support. At nine years of age, Stefan is functioning socially, emotionally, behaviorally, and intellectually like a child of four. He uses visual prompts such as a picture exchange communication system provided by symbols and pictures displayed on his tablet and on a laminated card taped to his desk. He can indicate if he needs to use the bathroom, is hungry and would like to eat a specific food, would like to engage in an activity, is bothered by a sound, a light, or a change in routine, is fatigued, or to express compliance or non-compliance with a command (request).

Stefan is learning simple nouns but cannot utter speech that is intelligible to most people, except those that have worked closely with him for a few years. He works with a behaviorist to improve social behaviors such as eye gaze and verbal responses to simple questions. He is also learning to employ simple sign language for basic requests and responses. The behaviorist uses applied behavioral analysis (ABA) techniques such as discrete trial training when working with Stefan.

Stefan also works with an occupational therapist who has helped him devise an effective 'sensory diet' that facilitates his self-regulation and reduces the frequency of off-task behavior and tantrums or meltdowns.

Stefan from an Attachment Perspective

Although attachment difficulties occupy significant space in the discussion of ASD, studies have shown that many children with ASD do develop secure attachment with their primary caregivers (Rutgers et al., 2004). Attachment difficulties among those with ASD have been looked at from both the child's impairment in social communication and parental insensitivity, the ability to understand the child's attachment signals and respond appropriately. This is a challenging task since children with ASD do not express their needs explicitly due to language and social impairments. Since ASD has a strong genetic component, the primary caretaker may have his/her own limitations in social interaction.

Stefan has a more severe form of ASD and safety concerns have led to placing him in residential treatment. The fact that he rarely responds to efforts at engagement suggest an attachment style insecure and most like disorganized. A high percentage of those with ASD fall into this category of insecure attachment. His stereotypy and OCD qualities are also quite evident; these, however, have not caused a residential placement. Case details indicate that both his parents and siblings love him dearly, yet it is not clear how difficult it was for the family to place him in residential treatment. While their safety concerns were the primary motivator for such a placement, the possible absence of a strong attachment bond with Stefan may have lessened the difficulty of placing the child in residential. Of course, we do not know this for sure, but from an attachment perspective it is worthy of consideration.

Clinical Features of Autistic Spectrum Disorders

The DSM-V (American Psychiatric Association, 2013) lists three categorical symptoms for autistic disorder to include impairment in social interaction, impairments in communication, and restricted repetitive and stereotyped patterns of behavior.

Impairments in Social Interactions

Children, adolescents, and adults with ASD have deficits in more than one aspect of social functioning. These deficits are in the areas of gaze, social speech, joint attention, imitation, play, attachment, peer relations, and affective development (Carter et al., 2005).

Gaze. Normally developing infants are predisposed to establish social relationships with the primary caregiver that begins with their ability to gaze toward faces (Korkiakangas, 2018). Gazing and making eye contact are the modes of communication between the preverbal child and the primary caretaker and provide the basis for socialization. Infants who have ASD are not able to enter into mutual gazing with the primary caretaker. This feature distinguishes ASD from those with developmental delays and mental retardation who are able to establish patterns of gaze.

Social Speech. Normally developing infants show an attraction to the human voice, especially that of the mother, over other sounds. The reverse exists for children with ASD, who prefer other kinds of sounds rather than speech. Preverbal vocalizations are atypical, and there is a limited use of communication behaviors (Pokorny et al., 2020). This lack of interest in social speech denies the child the ability to establish interpersonal patterns, leading to later problems in communication.

Joint Attention. Problems in gaze and social speech leads to interference in *intersubjectivity*, "the co-construction of shared emotional meaning between parent and caregiver" (Carter et al., 2005, p. 319). This, in turn, leads to the failure of joint attention. *Joint attention* is the ability to share with another person an object or event (Mundy, 2018). Infants often point to something (e.g., a toy) that is attractive and look back at the primary caretaker; whereas children who have AD are not able to establish these kinds of exchanges. There is an inability that appears unique to autism and is not part of the clinical presentation of other developmental disorders. If children who have ASD do engage in joint attention (e.g., pointing), it is usually for functional purposes—to get something, but not to engage the interest of another person.

Imitation. Various forms of imitation are part of the developing child and allow the child to engage in symbolic activities. This imitation usually begins with the parental behaviors. The child who has ASD does not spontaneously imitate parental actions and has particular difficulty imitating body movements and those involving body movements such as playing patty-cake and pick-a-boo (Andreou & Skrimpa, 2020)

Play. The play of a child who has ASD is distinctly different, marked by a lack of social engagement, symbolic play, and a manipulation of objects, which tends to be repetitive and stereotyped (Schwichtenberg et al., 2019).

Attachment. At the end of the first year of life, normally developing infants have learned an array of social behaviors designed to maintain closeness with the primary caregiver, whose absence causes extreme distress (Bowlby, 1969). Insecure attachment is a feature of ASD. These children generally prefer objects that are hard in nature as opposed to soft and cuddly ones (Crowell et al., 2019).

Peer Relations. Children who have ASD rarely engage in mutual or cooperative play; rather they prefer to be alone and to engage in activities that are self-stimulating (Carter et al., 2005). Achieving typical peer relationships is very rare. When they do approach others, children who have ASD sometimes prefer adults rather than other children. As they reach adolescence, and with the help of interventions, some of those who have ASD make significant gains in social skills, yet their difficulty understanding and complying with social rules and conventions remains (Cresswell et al., 2019).

Affective Development. By age 3, typical children develop the capacity to understand and name their own and others' emotional states. Children who have ASD have great difficulty doing so. Their disengagement and aloofness restricts emotional expression. When they do express emotion, children who have ASD often do so in inappropriate or unusual fashion (Sasson et al., 2017). A lack of empathy is the consequence of their inability to recognize emotional expression; therefore, it might be typical for a child who has ASD to react indifferently to someone who is in pain (van der Zee & Derksen, 2020).

It is important to note that although the above-mentioned social features exist with some consistency, there is still a great deal of variability among individuals who have ASD with regard to social functioning. Much of this variability has been observed in laboratory settings, and it is not clear at this point to what degree such variability exists in natural settings. Along with the absence of relatedness in individuals who have ASD, it is also important for future research to examine the kind of relatedness that might be typical in autism.

Language and Communication

Problems in speech are usually the first signs to parents that something is not quite right in their child's development. Language problems present a differential challenge because they overlap with many other disorders. Most children who have ASD begin to speak late and develop speech at a slower rate (Naigles, 2016). IQ can account for some differences in language development. In some cases, those who have higher IQ have better language development and those who have very low verbal IQ do not achieve functional language (Trembath et al., 2020).

For those who do speak, articulation is often normal and even advanced, and those who have HFA can score quite well on standardized vocabulary tests (Baixauli et al., 2016). Social-emotional words cause notable difficulty for those who have ASD. Echolalia, the repetition with similar tone of words or phrases that someone else has said, has always been considered a classic symptom of ASD. Not all children who have ASD, however, engage in echolalia, and it can be present with other disorders. Echolalia can serve any number of communicative and protective functions for the child who has ASD to include turn-taking, assertions, affirmative answers, requests, rehearsal to aid processing, and self-regulation (Kawashima & Maynard, 2019).

Another salient characteristic in language use among for those who have ASD is confusion about the use of personal pronouns; for example, a child may manifest a desire for ice cream by saying, "Do you want some ice cream?" Such confusion is not limited to children who have ASD, but it does exist more frequently in this population. A plausible explanation for pronoun confusion is that individuals who have ASD have difficulty distinguishing self from other (Naigles et al., 2016).

Intonation can also be peculiar. Children who have ASD often speak in a monotone, devoid of any feeling or emotion. Most children who have ASD make attempts at communication, albeit limited, but they rarely initiate spontaneous communication (Yoder et al., 2020). The most common difficulties in language use among those who have ASD include listening, talking to self, following rules of politeness, and making irrelevant remarks (Kang et al., 2020).

Reading comprehension among those who have ASD is often commensurate with overall ability. Many will learn to read words without any direct instruction, and some will manifest an early and exaggerated interest in letters and numbers (McIntyre et al., 2017). A small number of children who have ASD will manifest hyperlexia, indicated by superior word recognition and compulsiveness about reading letters or writing (Shuai Zhang & Joshi, 2019). Hyperlexia can be considered a savant skill and, like other savant skills, fails to connect to overall intelligence and function.

Recent literature has investigated the narrative storytelling capacities of verbal children who have ASD. Their stories tended to be less complex, shorter, have more grammatical errors, less likely to have a resolution or introduce new characters, and less likely to reveal mental states of the characters (Baixauli et al., 2016). They often include neologisms and idiosyncratic expressions and lack identification of the causes of their characters' internal states (Baixauli et al., 2016).

Stereotyped, Repetitive, and Ritualistic Behaviors

This is the third categorical symptom in the DSM-V (American Psychiatric Association, 2013), and these behaviors occur in both children and adults. There has been less research into these symptoms compared to social development and language. One difficulty is distinguishing the stereotypies and ritualistic behaviors of ASD from obsessive-compulsive disorder (OCD). There appears to be a development around such behaviors for those with ASD as they go from repetitive sensory motor activities at an early age to more complex and elaborate activities similar to those of OCD (Carlisi et al., 2017). These more developed symptoms are often maintained through adulthood. Some have argued that the stereotypies of ASD can be distinguished from those of OCD because their forms are less organized, less complex, and more egosyntonic (i.e., acceptable and desirable), whereas those with OCD may regard their ritualistic behaviors as ego-dystonic (Pazuniak & Pekrul, 2020).

Stereotypies and ritualistic behaviors also occur in other disorders such as mental retardation, schizophrenia, and neurological conditions such as Tourette syndrome and Parkinson disease. At least among adults with ASD, the compulsions, stereotypy, and self-injury are more frequent and more severe (Furniss & Biswas, 2020). Among other age groups with ASD, this cluster of symptoms varies greatly and appears to be related to the developmental level of the individual.

School Adjustment and Academic Achievement

Because of difficulties in social development, the school environment can be particularly challenging for children who have ASD, as they find it difficult to regulate their own behaviors and understand the expectations of their teachers and peers. These deficits can result in tremendous confusion and bewilderment. Any changes in routine can be especially difficult because of their cognitive rigidity and inflexibility (Bertollo et al., 2020). Impairments in executive functioning along with attention/concentration deficits can make it very difficult for students who have ASD to organize their time, complete homework, and tests, and so on. They are also known to exhibit symptoms of hyperactivity, which can interfere with learning. Often, their nonverbal skills are more developed than their verbal skills (in contrast to those without language impairment). Among those with HFA, mechanical reading, computational tasks, and spelling pose fewer challenges. There is a great deal of variability in the academic challenges for those who have ASD, and the best educational placement will be those that are sensitive to each individual's needs.

Prevalence of Autistic Spectrum Disorders

The prevalence of ASD has increased dramatically worldwide in recent decades. Back in 2000, the CDC instituted a monitoring system for Autism and other developmental disabilities (Chiarotti & Venerosi, 2020). According to the monitoring network, the prevalence rate for ASD per 1000 children aged 8 years was 6.7 or one out of 150 children in the year 2000 (Centers for Disease Control and Prevention, 2021). In 2016, the prevalence rate was 18.5 or 1 out of every 54 children. The system establishes prevalence rates every two years (Centers for Disease Control and Prevention, 2021). Since 2002, the rate has increased significantly every two years except between 2010 and 2012.

Etiology of Autistic Spectrum Disorders

In recent years, research on the causes of autism spectrum disorders has focused on genetics, neurochemistry, neurology, and brain functioning. Other risk factors, mostly environmental in nature, such as obstetrics and vaccinations, have also been studied.

Genetic Influences

Over the years, there have been a multitude of twin studies done on autism. These studies generally revealed a huge disparity in the concordance rates between monozygotic (MZ) and dizygotic (DZ) twins. Current estimates for the heritability index for autism are anywhere from 60 to 90 percent (Thapar & Rutter, 2020). The significant discrepancy in these studies between MZ and DZ twins strongly supports genetics as a factor in the etiology of ASD.

Neurochemical Risk Factors

The behavioral, emotional, and cognitive features of ASDs indicate that the central nervous system (CNS) is different in people who have ASD. Studies have focused on three neurotransmitters (serotonin, dopamine, and norepinephrine) and on hypothalamic-pituitary (HPA) function (Andersson et al., 2020; Pavăl, 2017; Shaw, 2019).

Serotonin. Most of the interest in neurotransmitters as an etiological factor has focused on serotonin (also called 5-hydroxytryptamine, or 5-HT) due to its role in perception and a small number of treatment studies that have indicated a positive therapeutic effect for selective serotonin reuptake inhibitors (SSRIs) in persons with ASDs. Dating back to the 1960s (Schain & Freedman, 1961), it has been generally accepted that blood levels of 5-HT are elevated in individuals with autism. Some studies have found elevated blood levels in those with ASD while others have found the opposite, low levels of serotonin. Whether high or low, abnormal levels of serotonin are well documented in individuals with ASD (Andersson et al., 2020).

Dopamine. Has also generated a good deal of interest in the causality of autism because of its regulatory role in motor function, cognition, and hormone release dopamine blockers have been shown to be effective in treating some aspects of autism (Pavăl, 2017). The results of recent studies, however, have yielded mixed and often contradictory results. Because dopamine plays a role in so many disorders, it being an etiological factor in ASDs remains controversial, and more research is needed.

Norepinephrine. The same may be said for norepinephrine (NE), a neurotransmitter that is crucially related to processes of arousal, anxiety, stress responses, and memory. NE operates in both the CNS and the sympathetic nervous system (SNS). The NE causal hypothesis is based on the indication that in some individuals who have autism, the SNS is hypersensitive to stress, and some evidence that clonidine (which lessens central NE function) has been effective in treating autism. Studies have shown that NE levels are increased on measures of acute response in individuals who have autism (Shaw, 2019).

Hypothalamic Pituitary Functioning

Studies on hypothalamic-pituitary functioning (HFP) and autism have concentrated on cortisol secretion, thyroidism, and sex hormones (Cukier et al., 2020). These all play a role in the stress response and are closely related to the sympathetic nervous system (Cukier et al., 2020).

Cortisol. Cortisol is released from the adrenal cortex in response to stress. Some studies have not shown a significant difference in cortisol levels in individuals with autism on a measure of baseline functioning (Edmiston et al., 2017; Matherly et al., 2018).

Hypothyroidism. Congenital hypothyroidism (underactive thyroid function) has been found in those who have autism. Due to small sample sizes in many studies, it is not yet clear whether the finding of hypothyroidism is coincidental or poses a major risk factor for the development of autism (Getahun et al., 2018; Maximova, 2020).

Sex Hormones. A possible inhibited release of sex hormones in people who have autism has also been studied but without definitive results, although there is some evidence of the therapeutic effect of increasing sex-related hormones in individual with autism (Ferri et al., 2018).

In conclusion, the most robust and replicated support exists for the increase in serotonin among those who have autism. Although there may be abnormalities in other neurochemicals, none of these can be considered a significant risk factor until more research is able to provide more replicated results.

Neurological Risk Factors

In recent decades, magnetic resonance imaging (MRI) has made possible the study of the cognitive and brain bases of autism and related disorders. Studies of autopsied brains of individuals who had autism have revealed an increase of brain volume and brain weight (Bonnet-Brilhault et al., 2018). Although most individuals who have autism are born with normal head circumferences, head growth appears to accelerate dramatically during the preschool years. The area of the brain that increases the greatest appears to be white matter in the frontal lobe (Hazlett et al., 2017; Piven et al., 2017).

Brain studies related to autism indicate that it is a neural system disorder that affects information processing/integration and whose onset is at about 30 weeks of gestation (Rose & Basit, 2020). These problems in neuronal connectivity appear together with later abnormal brain weight and volume.

Brain Function

In contrast to traditional MRI, functional magnetic resonance imaging (fMRI) allows studies of the brain dynamically, while it is at work. Such studies of individuals who have autism have assumed a great deal of importance in the last few years, because fMRI can detect functional aberrance. fMRI studies of people who have ASD have concentrated in the areas of language/communication dysfunction, social dysfunction, and stereotyped repetitive behaviors (Ha et al., 2015; Stigler et al., 2011).

Language/Communication Dysfunction. Studies consistently showed deficiencies in left temporal lobe language regions as the likely cause for language dysfunction. Gervais et al. (2004) found, more specifically, that subjects with ASD, when compared with controls, failed to activate voice-selective regions of the brain in response to vocal sounds in contrast to nonvocal sounds. In a study of participants with HFA, Just et al. (2004) found more activation in Wernicke's area and less activation in Broca's area, which could explain why those with ASD tend toward over-analysis and hyperlexia, yet have greater difficulties integrating words into a coherent whole, which results in poorer conceptual comprehension.

Social Dysfunction. To understand the cause of social dysfunction in individuals who have ASD, studies have concentrated on social perception and social cognition (Bi & Fang, 2017; Samaey et al., 2020).

Face Perception. Face perception forms the basis of the social perception studies. To function socially, an individual must be able to recognize identity through the structural features of another person's face and to perceive the internal state of another through the shape and changes of the face (Bi & Fang, 2017). Numerous studies have shown that those who have ASD have an impaired ability to recognize facial identity.

The area of the brain that is responsible for face selectivity is in a portion of the fusiform gyrus known as the fusiform face area (FFA), a small region in the underside of the temporal lobe. This area of the brain is responsible for the second aspect of social perception, the interpretation of social signals in the form of changing aspects of the face and body (Picci et al., 2018). Hypoactivity in the FFA area is often compensated for by overactivity in another area of the brain, the inferior temporal gyrus, which is responsible for object differentiation (Pua, 2019). Hypoactivity of the FFA has been replicated in numerous other studies (Picci et al., 2018; Pua, 2019; Samaey et al., 2020; Zhao, 2017). The evidence seems to be more in the direction that impairment of face recognition of those who have ASD is the result of hypoactivity of the FFA.

Social Cognition. Studies on the prefrontal region, the part of the brain that is responsible for social cognition (i.e., thinking about others' thoughts, feelings, and intentions) have shown dysfunction among those who have ASD (Fernandes et al., 2018). More specific studies have concentrated on the amygdala, the part of the brain responsible for processing emotional information and emotional arousal. Those who have ASD, when assigned tasks that require the recognition of facial expression, had hypoactivity of the amygdala (Ibrahim et al., 2019).

Environmental Factors

Being a monozygotic twin, obstetric complications, and vaccinations have all been considered possible risk factors in the development of ASDs. There is little evidence, to date, that being a monozygotic twin is a major risk factor.

Some studies have shown an association between autism and obstetric complications (Chien et al., 2019; Wang et al., 2017). The association between obstetric complications and ASDs may also be a consequence of a genetically abnormal fetus. In this view, the association, therefore, represents an epiphenomenon—a secondary phenomenon resulting from the condition—rather than a primary causal factor (Bjørklund et al., 2018).

In recent years there has been much talk about vaccinations, particularly the measles–mumps–rubella (MMR) vaccination, as a cause of ASD. The origin of this hypothesis was the temporal association between the time of the MMR vaccination and the first manifestation of ASD. Most studies have not been able to confirm the temporal association (Farrington et al., 2001). Furthermore, Japan discontinued the use of the MMR vaccination, which did not affect the rates of autism.

A related concern has been the effects of thimerosal, a vaccine preservative containing ethyl mercury, as a cause of ASD (Dudley et al., 2018). This causal hypothesis is based on studies that have shown mercury in high doses can cause neurodevelopmental abnormalities. Some recent studies have tested this causal hypothesis and found little evidence to support it. Denmark, for example, discontinued the use of thimerosal, but there was no decrease in the reported number of ASD (Wessel, 2017). Other factors, such as maternal and congenital hypothyroidism, and maternal cocaine and alcohol abuse, have also been considered in the etiology of ASD. Although such factors may play contributory roles, there is little evidence to suggest that they are common causal factors.

In summary, current research indicates that ASD is a complex genetic disorder with interaction effects on brain development. The previous sections have reviewed the research regarding the genetic and neurological causes of ASD. Research continues, especially with fMRI studies of the brain function of those who have ASD. With larger sample sizes and more sophisticated laboratory equipment, future studies should shed more light on the etiology and development of ASD.

Assessment of Autistic Spectrum Disorder

Due to the recent rise in diagnosed rates of ASD and the more favorable outcomes for early intervention, numerous assessment instruments are available for individuals from infancy through adulthood. For the purposes of this book and the age group associated with this discussion, only instruments that are appropriate for a school-aged population will be considered. They can be divided into three groups to include screening rating scales, diagnostic interviews, and observation scales.

Screening Measures

Screening scales are the most numerous assessment instruments for ASDs and can be divided into two types: those that screen individuals from within the general population and those that screen individuals from those at risk for other developmental disorders.

Autism Behavior Checklist (ABC, Krug et al., 2008). This is a rating scale with fifty-seven items that assess behavior in five areas to include sensory, relating, body and object use, language and social interaction, and self-help. It was originally intended to be completed by teachers for the purposes of educational planning. The ABC takes about twenty minutes to complete, and the authors recommend that the informant has known the individual for at least three to six weeks. It can be used for any individual 18 months or older. The ABC has been used widely and has the advantage of easy administration and scoring. Presently, the best use of the ABC appears to be with older children and adults.

Childhood Autism Rating Scale, Second Edition (CARS 2; Schopler et al., 2010). The CARS2 is one of the most well-known, widely used, and best documented rating scales for screening behaviors associated with ASD. It consists of fifteen items designed to discriminate between children with ASD and those with other developmental disorders. Minimal training is required to administer the CARS. Items are scored on a continuum from 1 to 4, with 30 being a suggested cutoff score for mild to moderate autism; 37 and above suggests more severe autism. The CARS2 should be used with individuals 4 years of age or older. Psychometric properties are reportedly quite good (Moon et al., 2019).

The CARS can be used for clinical observation by parents and teachers and also as part of a parent interview. The ease of scoring and administration, along with its appropriateness for the educational system, make the CARS a highly desirable instrument for screening for ASDs.

Gilliam Autism Rating Scale, Third Edition (GARS3; Gilliam, 2013). The GARS3 consists of fifty-six items grouped into four domains: early development, stereotyped behaviors, communication skills, and social interaction. Items are rated on a four-point scale ranging from "never observed" to "frequently observed." It is designed for individuals ages 3 to 22, takes about ten minutes, and can be completed by anyone who is familiar with the child's behavior, although the early development part is most appropriately filled out by the primary caretaker. In addition to screening, the GARS3 can also help in planning treatment goals and measuring responses to interventions (Minaei & Nazeri, 2018).

Reliability of the GARS3, both internal and interrater, is quite high. In general, reports of the GARS3 psychometric properties were quite good (Minaei & Nazeri, 2018).

Social Responsiveness Scale, Second Edition (SRS-2; Constantino, 2012). The SRS-2 is a sixty-five-item questionnaire to be completed by an adult (e.g., teacher or parent) who observes the child in a social situation. It is designed to measure an individual's capacity for reciprocal social interaction, and the sixty-five items load on three dimensions: communication (six items), social interactions (thirty-five items), and repetitive and stereotyped behaviors and interests (twenty items). Items are rated on a scale of 0 (not true) to 3 (almost always true) according to frequency. Studies have shown the psychometric properties to be quite good (Chan et al., 2017; Sturm et al., 2017) The SRS-2 can be an especially useful and reliable instrument if the intention is to measure difficulties in social reciprocity and odd behaviors.

Children's Social Behavior Questionnaire (CSBQ; Luteijn et al., 2000). The CSBQ is a ninety-six-item questionnaire to be completed by parents for individuals between the ages of 4 and 18. Items require the respondent to focus on behaviors within the last two months and to rate them from 0 (does not describe the child) to 2 (clearly applies to the child). The CSBQ has five factors: acting out, social contact problems, social insight problems, anxious/rigid, and stereotypical. Except for the stereotypical scale, the subscales have adequate internal consistency as well as test-retest reliability.

The CSBQ can be helpful in discriminating ASD from other PDDs. Psychometric investigations of the CSBQ are relatively scarce, but it appears to be a helpful screening measure, especially for purposes of differential diagnosis (de Bildt et al., 2009).

Diagnostic Interviews

Presently, there are two diagnostic interview schedules for ASDs worthy of review: the *Autism Diagnostic Interview–Revised* (ADI-R) and the *Diagnostic Interview for Social and Communication Disorders* (DISCO).

ADI-R (Rutter et al., 2003). The ADI-R is a revision of the *Autism Diagnostic Interview* (ADI; LeCouteur et al., 1994) that grew out of the need to include a broader range of children. The ADI-R is a semi-structured interview for caregivers of children and adults suspected of having an ASD. The instrument consists of ninety-three items and takes about two hours to complete. Some training is required to administer the ADI-R, which can be acquired through video materials. The ADI-R has been translated into many languages and is considered to be one of the most valuable instruments for the diagnosis of

ASD. Interrater reliability, internal consistency, and convergent validity are all excellent (Wigham et al., 2019; Zander et al., 2017).

The AID-R is clearly designed for diagnostic purposes and is not used to measure change. Its most appropriate use is in the hands of an experienced clinical interviewer, which can limit its use; however, the AID-R is perhaps the most reliable instrument for making a diagnosis of ASD.

DISCO 9 (Wing et al., 2002). The Diagnostic Interview for Social and Communication Disorders (DISCO) has undergone nine revisions since the original *Handicaps, Behaviors, and Skills* (HBS) schedule. Up until 2002, the use of the DISCO was limited to school-aged children, and the primary purpose was to aid in educational planning. The latest version of the DISCO goes beyond the school-age years and is designed not so much for diagnosis as to assess the pattern of development over an extended period of time, in order to help with appropriate placements and interventions for those who have ASD (Leekam et al., 2002).

The interview covers the areas of social interaction, communication, imagination, and repetitive activities as well as daily living skills appropriate to the developmental level. DISCO 10 is already in the planning stages, as the authors are constantly trying to improve its reliability. For purposes of appropriate treatment planning, placement, and interventions, the DICSO is a very valuable interview schedule in the hands of a trained interviewer.

Observation Scales

Unlike the previously reviewed instruments, which rely on information provided by a third party (teacher, parent, etc.), these next instruments assess the child through direct observation. As with other observation instruments, they can be time-consuming but provide more reliable information than that obtained from a third party.

Autism Diagnostic Observation Schedule, Second Edition (ADOS2; Lord et al., 2012). The ADOS2 is the combined product of two previous instruments - the ADOD-G, designed for use with those who have fluent speech; and the PLADOS, designed for preschool children with little or no expressive language who are suspected of having an ASD. The combined instrument allows for a standardized protocol for the observation of social and communicative behaviors. The ADOS provides a series of presses to initiate the child's social interaction, play, and communication. Immediately after the administration of a press, the behavior is coded and later scored. The context in which the behavior occurs is changed, which permits an assessment across different situations. Administration takes about forty-five minutes, and it requires some training.

Internal consistency and interrater reliability for the ADOS is excellent. Studies have found three factors in the ADOS that account for upward of 70 percent of the variance: joint attention, affective reciprocity, and theory of mind (Wigham et al., 2019). One advantage of the ADOS is its potential to differentiate ASD and PDD-NOS, because observations are based on a standardized protocol and context. The information generated by the ADOS about the social and communicative functioning of the child can be particularly valuable to parents, clinicians, and teachers (Kuhfeld & Sturm, 2018).

Psychoeducational Profile—Third Edition (PEP-3; Schopler et al., 2005). The PEP-3 is a developmental and diagnostic measure for assessing children with ASDs. It has wide dissemination and has been translated into several languages. Its most appropriate use is with children ages 3 to 7. The PEP-3 rates the following characteristics of autism: response to material (eight items), language (eleven items), affect and development of relationships (twelve items), and sensory modalities (twelve items). The PEP-3 is reported to have good convergent validity and discriminate validity and reliability (Fu et al., 2012) and high internal consistency. The PEP-3 and earlier versions have been used extensively in research. They have also been used in clinical and educational settings, but to a lesser extent.

Treatment Strategies

In recent years, treatment interventions for ASD have focused on curriculum and classroom structure, behavioral interventions to promote learning and adaptive functioning, developing early language and communication, developing social communication skills (especially for HFA), models of educational intervention, working with families, and psychopharmacology. It is beyond the scope of this book to deal with all these interventions. Appropriate to the purpose of this book, we focus on behavioral interventions, developing social communication skills, and psychopharmacology but do not include interventions more relevant to academic instruction.

Behavioral Interventions for Aberrant Behaviors

Behavioral interventions for people who have ASD have emphasized the role of antecedents, consequences, and skill acquisition.

Antecedents. Although behavioral interventions have always highlighted the role of consequences, the role of antecedents in working with individuals who have ASD has been emphasized more and more (Ledford et al., 2018). Antecedents can be either remote or immediate. Remote antecedents usually deal with the setting in which the problem behavior occurs, with the understanding that certain environmental factors are responsible for the problem behavior. Modification of these factors can play a significant role in achieving the targeted behaviors. Studies have supported that when young children who have autism are in closer proximity to normally developing peers, there is a reduction in aberrant behaviors (Rojas-Torres et al., 2020). Another example is the role of physical exercise for which several studies have shown support (Losinski et al., 2017; Yarımkaya & Esentürk, 2020).

Studies have also supported the role of immediate antecedents in effecting targeted treatment; for example, Kennedy and Itkonnen (1993) found that by oversleeping in the morning, individuals who have autism set up a chain of events that resulted in more behavioral problems at school. Another example is the use of high-probability requests as antecedents to achieve a low-probability request, that is, one that has been resisted in the past. Several studies have supported the effective use of high-probability requests as immediate antecedents (Planer et al., 2018).

Consequences. The importance of the role of consequences in the learning of new behaviors and the unlearning of old ones is universally accepted. The most effective use of consequences is in the form of a reinforcer, "a stimulus event that increases the probability that the response that immediately precedes it will occur again" (Gladding, 2018, p. 135).

Reinforcement. *Differential reinforcement* (i.e., reinforcement provided in some situations and not in others) has been employed on a wide scale in working with children who have autism. The most common form of differential reinforcement used with ASD children is *differential reinforcement of other behaviors* (DRO). DRO is designed to reinforce any response other than the targeted or problematic behaviors. It has been successfully employed in reducing stereotypy (Cividini-Motta et al., 2019; Healy et al., 2019), severe aggression and self-injury (Weston et al., 2018) and hand flapping (Ringdahl et al., 2002). Token economies have also proven successful in dealing with an array of aberrant behaviors in children who have autism (Looney et al., 2018).

Punishment. Research has shown the use of punishment as a consequence to be less effective than the use of reinforcement. Nevertheless, punishment is still widely used and in many cases is the result of a spontaneous reaction to the child's provocative behaviors. Mild punishments (i.e., verbal reprimand, overcorrection, time-out, denial of privileges) are acceptable and have proven effective in reducing undesirable behaviors (Leaf et al., 2019; Li et al., 2018).

Behavioral Interventions to Promote Learning

Aside from the use of more traditional interventions to reduce negative behaviors, behavioral interventions to promote the learning of social skills and other adaptive behaviors in children who have autism are being used more and more. Since the 1960s, it has been widely accepted that children who have autism can learn (Evans, 2014). Behavioral interventions to promote learning in children who have autism have included structured interventions, naturalistic interventions, self-management strategies, and video instruction (Lovaas, 1987; Arick et al., 2005).

Structured Behavioral Interventions. Lovaas (1987) developed structured behavioral interventions that are known as discrete trial training (DT). In discrete trial training

> skills are taught in a logical sequence building on previously learned skills. Concepts to be taught are identified and then broken down into specific program elements for instruction. Each instructional session consists of a series of discrete trials. A discrete trial consists of a four-step sequence: (1) instructional cue, (2) child response, (3) consequence (generally a positive reinforcer) and, (4) pause. Data are collected to monitor the child's progress and to help determine when a pre-set criteria has been reached (Arick et al., 2005, p. 1004).

More recently, DT has been used to develop nonacademic skills such as play and peer interaction. It is important to note that in DT, the teaching materials are selected by an adult and rarely varied. Research has consistently supported the effectiveness of DT in teaching children who have autism a variety of important behaviors (Ünlü et al., 2018). Critics of DT claim that its high structure methods prevent learning from generalizing to more natural environments, and strict stimulus control prevents the spontaneous use of the learned behaviors (Schreibman & Ingersoll, 2005).

Naturalistic Behavioral Interventions. In contrast to DT, naturalistic behavioral interventions are, as the name implies, more natural and child-centered.

This class of interventions has undergone evolution since the late 1960s, when it was originally developed by Hart and Risley (1968). According to Schreibman and Ingersoll (2005), all naturalistic behavioral interventions share certain basic components to include

(1) the learning environment is loosely structured, (2) teaching occurs during ongoing interactions between the child and the adult, (3) the child initiates the teaching episode by indicating interest in an item or activity, (4) teaching materials are selected by the child and varied often, (5) the child's production of the target behavior is explicitly prompted, (6) a direct relationship exists between the child's response and the reinforcer, and (7) the child is reinforced for attempts to respond (p. 883).

One of the more well-known and popular naturalistic interventions is *paradigm/pivotal response training* (PRT). This training is also based on a four-step sequence - cue, child response, consequence, and pause. Trials in PRT, however, are incorporated into the environment in a functional context. During PRT, the child chooses the activity or object, and the reinforcer is a natural consequence to the behaviors being rewarded. The nature of this strategy makes it possible to engage the child throughout all activities and locations throughout the day (Lei & Ventola, 2017; Vernon, 2017).

PRT's significance is its use of teaching skills that go beyond language to include symbolic play (Koegel et al., 2019) and joint attention (Mundy, 2018).

Studies comparing naturalistic techniques and more structured techniques generally have found that the former result in more generalized and spontaneous use of skills (Tiede & Walton, 2019). Other studies have found that employing the techniques of PRT has led to reduced stress and more happiness among both parents and children (Koegel et al., 2019).

Video Instruction. In light of research supporting the notion that children who have autism are visual learners and respond better to interventions that rely on visual stimuli, video instruction has become a recognized learning intervention for this population. Studies have found that modeling provided through video instruction is effective in developing skills in conversational speech (Thirumanickam et al., 2018), daily living skills (Aljehany & Bennett, 2019), verbal responding (Dueñas et al., 2020), and emotional understanding (Zhang, S. et al., 2019). Video modeling has also proven effective with self-management techniques such as self-monitoring, self-delivery of reinforcement, and self-evaluation of performance (Chia et al., 2018). Self-monitoring techniques are more appropriate for individuals with HFA, about which we will have more to say in a later section.

Researchers have also been interested in what kind of models (self vs. other, video versus live) is most effective with autism (Cardon et al., 2019). Some have cautioned, however, that video instruction should not be used to the exclusion of other behavioral interventions that are more social in nature. Overuse of video modeling would remove children who have autism from the social demands that should be included in the treatment plan.

Recent Trends. Exploration of better and more sophisticated ways to teach children who have autism is ongoing; for example, experts now believe that children who have autism are capable of learning more sophisticated behaviors such as joint attention, symbolic play, theory of mind, and reciprocal imitation. In addition, teaching through the use of social stories and picture schedules developed by the Treatment and Education of Autistic and Related Communication-Handicapped Children (TEACCH) are becoming more popular (Alotaibi, 2017).

These newer pedagogies need empirical support, a dimension that has always favored the stricter behavioral approaches that emphasize data collection and validation. The inclusion of family members and peers has become more emphasized in recent years. These newer approaches demand stronger collaboration among school, home, and community. The selection of treatment intervention should carefully consider variables not only in the child but also in the family and school personnel to select what is most appropriate and has the greatest chance of success.

Dylan, A Student with Higher Functioning Autism

Dylan is a student in the tenth grade enrolled in a specialized, alternative high school and was diagnosed with autism spectrum disorder (ASD; level 1 intensity or higher functioning type) at age five. He exhibits many of the diagnostic behavioral criteria of a student with ASD to include deficits in social reciprocity, challenges in making and maintaining friendships, highly restricted, fixated interests, and hyperreactivity to sensory input such as bright lights, loud sounds, and textures, especially those associated with certain foods.

Dylan wants desperately to be accepted by his peers; however, because he is very concrete in his thinking and is virtually incapable of identifying inferential cues or appreciating sarcasm and irony, he has become the prime target for bullies. He is often the butt of jokes and is so easily taken in by sarcasm that he is alienated by many of his classmates and has become a pariah in the school. When he is given a rare opportunity to share his interests and perspectives, he simply repeats his fixation with the Macedonian Empire and the exploits of Alexander the Great. His classmates have heard this discourse many times before and have become rather intolerant of his preoccupation with this historical passion. His conversations are not reciprocal, rather they are unidirectional rants that further alienate his classmates.

Many of Dylan's classmates simply do not understand the characteristic behaviors associated with ASD and assume, unfairly, that he is a narcissist that does not care about their needs or interests.

Dylan's speech language therapist is working with him and other students in small group sessions to help him develop reciprocity and the use of pragmatic language to communicate with classmates and teachers more effectively. His school counselor is also working with Dylan to help him both identify and better understand sarcasm and inference. Admittedly, Dylan has a difficult time empathizing with others and interpreting affective cues. To help him address these deficiencies, both the school counselor and speech language pathologist are using computer programs and avatars.

Dylan's counselor and speech therapist are providing his classmates and teachers with a series of informative podcasts to help educate them about students that are neuro-atypical and behave differently at times. Students, like Dylan, who have been diagnosed with high functioning autism are not insensitive or narcissistic, they simply require explicit direction and literal explanations and are frequently unable to accurately interpret implicit or inferential cues. It is very important for Dylan's teachers and classmates to understand that he truly wants and needs to be accepted and included by them.

Higher-Functioning Autism: Enhancing Social Competence

Those with HFA will benefit from interventions that create more awareness of the intentions and emotions of social partners and increase the predictability of unfamiliar social events (Marans et al., 2005). The goals of intervention designed to increase social and emotional competence should include increasing the individual's ability to

- "...acquire conventional verbal and nonverbal communication forms for requesting assistance and/or organizing supports.
- use specific vocabulary or conversational devices to express emotional state and arousal level.
- identify and express emotional state and arousal level as well as using regulating strategies, with and without the use of visual supports.
- understand social expectations through language-based strategies" (Marans et al., 2005, p. 986).

For interventions to succeed, those who have HFA must enjoy interpersonal support from peers, teachers and other school professionals, family, and community as well as appropriate educational and learning supports. The very nature of a social disability involves other people, and these other people are critical in providing successful outcomes and improving social competence in those who have HFA.

Interpersonal Supports

Despite their lack of social competence, people who have HFA greatly desire friendships. When attempts at friendship fail, they often turn toward adults and/or age-inappropriate peers for relationship. If age-appropriate peers are not included in the treatment, their lack of understanding for those who have HFA will result in further rejection of these individuals (Sosnowy et al., 2019). A number of programs are available to help peers modify some of their own forms of communication and gain reassurance about the difficulties they experience in interacting with those who have HFA (Carter et al., 2017, 2019; Karoff et al., 2017). Older peers can benefit from a more conceptual explanation of the disability.

For school personnel, a first step in supporting those who have HFA is to use communication that is clear and explicit. Sarcastic and idiomatic subtleties, the use of nonverbal social cues (e.g., frowning to show surprise), and the use of verbal language without visual cues may hamper successful communication (Marans et al., 2005). Not all school personnel will be able to provide the necessary supports. Interventions should target teachers, bus drivers, cafeteria workers, recess monitors, and others whose natural temperament make them ideal candidates for training that provides communicative support across various environments within the school.

Families that include a member with a social disability can experience a good deal of stress when misunderstandings and arguments become the norm. Family support for those who have HFA should include members understanding the nature of the disability and modifications they can make in their own communicative style. Emotional support for family members is also an important intervention, as is helping the family modify its goals and expectations not only for the individual who has HFA but for the family as a whole. For example, it may not be advisable to abruptly change a plan that had previously been made and communicated clearly to the individual.

Community activities for those who have HFA should be carefully selected. Parents may want their children who have HFA to participate in team activities (e.g., sports) like many other children; however, team sports require social awareness and good motor skills, which are often deficient in those who have HFA. More individual activities such as swimming, martial arts, skiing, horseback riding, or golf may be more appropriate.

Learning and Educational Supports

To enhance their communication skills, dialogue scripts are a preferred intervention. Such scripts will include the content of social conversations and may be in the form of comic scripts, video modeling, or video replay. Written schedules, especially about unfamiliar events that have yet to unfold, can be particularly helpful, along with the use of social stories to provide strategies for appropriate social conversation and emotional regulation (Gray, 2022). As a learning support, social stories are designed to help those who have HFA

- Understand their own social difficulties
- Pay careful attention to the social context
- Select the most important aspects of a social situation
- Identify appropriate behaviors and responses
- Identify the social partner's perspective
- Understand the consequences of a particular positive behavior (Marans et al., 2005).

As they are more able to understand and anticipate the sequence of events in a social situation, individuals who have HFA and ASD will become more socially competent.

Psychopharmacological Treatment

Although psychopharmacological intervention appears to be quite common for children who have ASD, the empirical support for its effectiveness is sketchy. Empirical studies have generally suffered from methodological flaws such as small sample sizes, open label, and lack of replication (Howes et al., 2018). The categories of drugs used to treat children who have autism are atypical anti-psychotics, SSRIs, stimulants, anti-anxiety, and anti-convulsants.

Atypical Antipsychotics

Clozapine (Clozaril), risperidone (Risperdal), olanzapine (Zyprexa), quetiapine (Seroquel), ziprasidone (Geodon), and aripiprazole (Abilify) are known as atypical antipsychotics (AAPs) that have come to replace the more traditional antipsychotics such as Haldol. For a review of this class of drugs in the effective treatment of irritability in those with autism, Fallah et al. (2019) has provided the most up-to-date review.

SSRIs

Fluoxetine (Prozac), fluvoxamine (Luvox), sertraline (Zoloft), citalopram (Celexa), escitalopram (Lexapro) have all been used in the treatment of autism. This class of drugs is used to treat anxiety most especially in the form of repetitive behaviors, other OCD qualities, and even aggression. The effectiveness of SSRI's in children with autism is constantly under review. Yu et al. (2020) has provided a recent metanalysis studying the effectiveness of this class of drugs for repetitive behaviors.

The SSRIs are currently used carefully with children and adolescents because of early reports of an increase in suicidality. There is limited evidence of the effectiveness of SSRIs in treating children who have autism. The more rigorous studies have been done with adults, and it appears that positive outcomes for this population are not always the same for children and adolescents.

Stimulants

The effectiveness of stimulants in the treatment of attention- deficit hyperactivity disorder (ADHD) in children and adolescents is well documented. Their efficacy and safety in the treatment of autism and PDD is less studied, but their use with this population appears to be quite common, according to community and clinic-surveys (Mayes et al., 2020). The most common stimulants used in the treatment of ASD are Ritalin and Adderall. Some have concluded that the positive response rate to stimulants among those who have developmental disabilities is lower and side effects seem to be higher than in ADHD. Research has suggested that, overall, stimulant medication can be effective in treating children who have developmental disabilities and ADHD symptoms but at this time whether such medication is effective in treating symptoms of hyperactivity associated with autism appears to be a work in progress (McClafferty, 2017).

Anticonvulsants

Are commonly used in the treatment of ASD especially when the individual suffers from seizures. They are also used to treat disruptive behaviors thought to be associated with affective disorders and epilepsy. Drugs in this category include the trade names of Depakote, Dilantin, Klonopin, and Tegretol. Research on the effectiveness of these drugs with ASD is quite limited, and the effect sizes for these drugs appear small. For a complete review on the use of anticonvulsants see Hirota et al. (2014).

School-Based Interventions

The preceding review of the characteristics, causes, and treatment options for autism spectrum disorders has provided a solid foundation from which we can select the most relevant research-based intervention for both Stefan, who has autistic disorder, and Dylan, who has higher functioning autism. In both cases, accurate assessments to determine the behaviors most detrimental to academic and social functioning are critical. Likewise, for both students, a functional behavioral assessment is appropriate and useful in identifying the target or problem behaviors and the purpose they serve for the student.

Model assessment processes and appropriate behavioral intervention plans are described below for both Stefan and Dylan.

Assessing the Problem: Stefan

A functional assessment for Stefan derived from the model developed by Barnhill (2005) might look something like the following example.

The first step is *identifying and describing the problem or target behavior(s).* Clearly, Stefan's most challenging behaviors include (1) tantruming associated with sudden changes in routine, (2) interference with intersubjectivity or joint attention (the ability to share an object or event with another person), (3) the lack of eye gaze with someone trying to communicate, and (4) an inability to communicate or express feelings and emotions, or to engage in or sustain a dialogue or conversation. Each of these behaviors will be addressed later in this section.

The second step in the process is *collecting baseline data and academic performance information* to substantiate our behavioral hypotheses and to help determine Stefan's present level of performance as well as the negative impact of these problem behaviors. Accordingly, using the *Childhood Autism Rating Checklist 2nd ed.* (CARS2; Schopler et al., 2010), the *Autism Behavior Checklist* (ABC; Krug et al., 2008), and the *Autism Diagnostic Observation Schedule* (ADOS2; Lord et al., 2012), together with teacher and parent observations and interviews and curricular-based measures, significant deficits were substantiated in all four target areas identified above.

The third step is *identifying the environmental and setting demands* that might instigate and fuel each of the target behaviors. In this case, Stefan's teachers found that, consistent with his diagnosis of AD, any deviation from his schedule or change in his environment causes frustration that triggers a tantrum in which he screams, throws things, kicks and punches persons or objects in his proximity, and engages in moderately self-injurious behavior (e.g., he bites his hand and slaps his head).

A confirmatory step is *direct observation of Stefan's behavior across settings* (i.e., in the classroom, on the playground, in the lunchroom, at activities such as gym and art, and at home). Stefan was observed in several settings (e.g., school, home, and clinic) over several weeks by various caregivers and practitioners, including his parents, his teachers at the Rainbow Academy, and his clinical psychologist. An analysis of their observations identified the following behavioral trends.

- Stefan is consistently frustrated by sudden changes to his daily routine, the sequence of steps followed in accomplishing a particular task, a change in staff or caregiver, or, in short, anything outside the familiar.

- Stefan has significant difficulty maintaining eye gaze and intersubjectivity, even with persons with whom he is very familiar.
- Stefan seems unable to initiate or sustain verbal communication with another. He is currently incapable of engaging in a conversation.
- Stefan appears to receive some form of gratification in self-stimulation such as hand flapping and the noncreative manipulation of objects.

Based on analyses of systematic observations of the target behaviors, the following *hypotheses* were developed regarding the purpose or function served by the target behaviors.

- Stefan needs a schedule routine to reduce anxiety created by change and unstructured activity. He takes comfort in the familiar and predictable. Thus, a viable routine is critical for his success in school, and any changes or modifications to that routine need to be introduced gradually to minimize anxiety and aid his adjustment.
- Stefan clearly lacks the interpersonal skills that facilitate interaction and the development of meaningful peer and adult relationships. These social and communication skills must be taught in a very authentic context and, like every other competency taught to Stefan, must be introduced incrementally in observable steps. Approximations of the target behavior must be reinforced positively.
- Stefan receives some gratification through self-stimulation behaviors such as hand flapping, twirling his hair, and the ordering of objects by color or shape. His teachers and clinicians must try to help Stefan initially reduce, and ultimately stop, engaging in these aberrant behaviors. This will be accomplished most effectively through the gradual replacement of these egocentric behaviors with more socially interactive ones.

The final step in the functional behavioral assessment is to test the validity of the hypothesis by assessing the effectiveness of the behavioral intervention plan developed expressly to address each of the proposed hypotheses. Based on the degree to which this plan is successful in reducing or transforming the target behaviors, appropriate modifications and adjustments will be made.

Developing an Effective Intervention Plan: Stefan

As suggested by Horner & Sugai (2015), any effective behavioral intervention plan should include six essential components (1) an understanding of the student's perception of antecedent events and her environment, (2) an investment in preventing reoccurrences of the target behavior, (3) the use of effective teaching as a powerful deterrent to the undesired behavior, (4) an accurate understanding of the purpose served by the undesired behavior for the individual, (5) an emphasis on positive reinforcement of appropriate behavior, and (6) a contingency plan to address more severe behavioral issues as well as reoccurrences of targeted undesirable behavior.

Stefan's behavioral intervention plan should address each of the target behaviors with an effective, research-based treatment. The following plan represents a possible set of interventions appropriate for each of the target behaviors identified for Stefan.

Target 1: Tantruming Associated with Changes in Routine. An appropriate daily routine for the classroom should be developed and implemented. This routine should be modified when necessary, and any resulting changes in the established routine should be introduced gradually over a period of several days if feasible. Each time Stefan does not tantrum in response to these incremental changes, he should receive positive reinforcement, referred to as differential reinforcement of other behaviors, or DRO. The reinforcer can be primary, such as food, or secondary, such as a token that may be exchanged later for a tangible reward. The important aspect of DRO is that the teacher, clinician, or caregiver must ensure that she is reinforcing a desired behavior and not inadvertently reinforcing the target behavior.

Target 2: Interference with Intersubjectivity or Joint Attention. A naturalistic behavioral intervention; specifically, paradigm/pivotal response training (PRT), will be employed to address these interpersonal skills deficits. As noted earlier in the chapter, PRT is very effective in helping students who have AD develop joint attention. The advantage of PRT compared with discrete trial training (DT) is that it has been shown to result in greater spontaneous use and generalizability of the skills. Furthermore, PRT is less structured than DT and is generally preferred by teachers for that reason.

Target 3: Lack of Eye Gaze with Someone Trying to Communicate. Like target 2, this targeted behavior deficit will be effectively addressed using pivotal response training (PRT).

Target 4: Inability to Initiate or Sustain a Conversation. A recommended intervention for this skills deficiency is video instruction. As noted earlier, video instruction provides effective modeling of conversational speech skills as well as verbal responding and facilitates the acquisition of these skills more quickly than in-vivo (live) modeling.

Target 5: Engages in Self-Stimulating Behaviors Such as Hand Flapping and the Noncreative Manipulation of Objects and Stereotype. In addressing this problem, the most effective nonpunitive approach is to identify preferred reinforcers for Stefan, such as food or tokens, withhold these and ignore self-stimulation episodes, then provide the preferred reinforcement only after the self-stimulating behaviors has stopped or in the complete absence of the self-stimulating behavior. An alternative approach is to use either DT or PRT to teach an appropriate alternative behavior to the self-stimulation and then provide reinforcement only for the appropriate behavior. Finally, research has also supported the efficacy of differential reinforcement of other behaviors (DRO) to provide reinforcement for any appropriate response other than the target behavior (i.e., self-stimulation, stereotypy, etc.).

Lastly, once the various interventions to address the target behavior have been implemented for a reasonable period of time, at minimum five or six weeks, those with oversight of the BIP should evaluate the efficacy of each of the component treatments as well as a 'good contextual fit' between the elements of the plan, the skill-level and personological characteristics of the plan implementers, the quality of environmental supports, and the compatibility of the child and caregiver. If any aspect of the plan is not being effective, then an alternative plan must be developed and implemented as soon as possible.

Assessing the Problem: Dylan

In accordance with the model used throughout this book, it is necessary to assess and determine the probable purpose or goal associated with Dylan's target behaviors. Once again, the first step is *identifying and describing the problem or target behavior(s).* A primary area of concern regarding Dylan's well-being is his occasional depression, which can generate suicidal ideation and threats of suicide. With the help of his therapist, Dylan has been able to understand that he becomes depressed when he is unsuccessful in attracting and retaining same-age friends. It is the behavior that interferes with this desired outcome that needs to be targeted for change.

Based on the results of the *Autism Diagnostic Observation Schedule* (ADOS2, Lord et al., 2012), as well as the observations of Dylan's teachers, parents, and psychologist, the key target behaviors include the following.

Verbosity and egocentric focus in communication that impede learning and socialization. Dylan talks incessantly about the Macedonian Empire and Alexander the Great. This perseverating behavior interferes with his ability to focus on the topic at hand and alienates peers who are simply not interested in his pedantic diatribe.

An inability to appreciate the perspectives of social partners. For example, when Dylan is actually able to engage another student in a scholarly discussion, he typically 'filibusters' his social partner's attempts to interject her impressions, ignoring her protests. He also does not seem to be able to 'hear,' let alone consider, another's viewpoint. This seeming disregard for the opinions of others usually results in a 'disconnect,' whereupon the conversational partner withdraws from the dialogue and avoids Dylan altogether, adding to Dylan's sense of alienation.

Lack of empathy as a consequence of poor insight regarding the emotions of other people. On one occasion, for example, a student was sharing a very poignant story concerning the recent loss of a grandparent with the class; Dylan, unable to provide empathy through active listening, abruptly cut off the student to share his knowledge of the Holocaust and how much greater was the loss and human suffering represented by that act of genocide. In so doing, he showed his lack of appreciation for the pain experienced by the speaker and her personal loss as well as the courage she displayed in sharing such a painful experience. The teacher and, later, several classmates rebuked him for his lack of sensitivity.

The next recommended action *collecting baseline data and academic performance information.* As noted, the results of the ADOS2 as well as observation reports collected from Dylan's teachers, parents, and clinical psychologist substantiate the diagnosis of higher functioning ASD. Similarly, Dylan's academic performance in subjects that are not of interest to him, specifically, math and science is substandard, whereas he excels in the subjects that interest him; specifically, social studies and English language arts. He is also very articulate and precocious in his use of advanced vocabulary, sometimes characteristic of students who have higher functioning ASD.

Once sufficient data have been collected, the team must investigate and describe the *environmental and setting demands* that may instigate or maintain the problem behaviors. In this regard, Dylan appears to be trapped in a cycle of self-destructive behavior. He clearly wants to be liked and to receive social acceptance from his peers; however, he dominates social interactions and fails to acknowledge the contributions of social partners. This behavior alienates potential friends and further confirms his reputation as a 'narcissistic crank.'

Because Dylan, like most students who have higher functioning ASD, is sociable and craves interpersonal attention, he constantly inserts himself into social situations to which he is unwelcome. Invariably, he sets himself up for further rejection and ridicule. Occasionally, Dylan reacts angrily to this rejection and shouts obscenities at his perceived adversary. This behavior only escalates the abuse and denigration. On one occasion, Dylan felt so hurt and angry at being rejected that he ran away from school, eluding staff and the police who were summoned, and walked all the way to his home—a distance of eight miles.

The next step is *completing a direct observation of the student.* The observations of Dylan's parents and teachers have provided invaluable data for the assessment process. Dylan's parents are divorced and living separately, although in the same town. Both parents are well educated and professionally employed. His mother is attending law school at a local university at night and tends to be more involved in Dylan's education and treatment. She has been conscientious about journaling Dylan's behavior in her home. According to his mother, Dylan displays a similarly pedantic style in communicating with her and his younger brother. She notes that he usually secludes himself in his bedroom, where he reads books on the Macedonian Empire and the exploits of Alexander the Great or watches science fiction movies, another passion. He rarely interacts with his mother; she believes this is partly caused by her absence from the home to attend law school, but she also notes that Dylan has expressed that she "doesn't understand him" or appreciate his "interests." He and his brother have little in common, in part due to their disparity in age, according to his mother.

Dylan's schoolteachers have been recording any episodes involving perseverating behavior, such as unidirectional conversation and lack of reciprocity, as well as acting-out events and escalating or provocative behavior such as verbal insults and threats.

Dr. Simmons, the resident psychiatrist at the special school Dylan attends, has reviewed all this anecdotal information and determined that it is consistent with higher functioning autism and is exacerbated by other factors including adolescent development. A necessary next step in the assessment process is *developing a hypothesis* about the purposes or functions served by Dylan's problem behaviors. After reviewing the available data on Dylan's behavior in the classroom, the IEP team advanced the following hypotheses.

- Dylan clearly seeks social interaction with classmates and wants to develop lasting friendships.
- Unfortunately, his pedantic verbosity and egocentric focus prohibit reciprocity and tend to alienate potential social partners.
- Dylan is dramatically affected by this alienation, which he interprets as rejection due to prejudice, jealousy, or misunderstanding on the part of his classmates.
- Dylan frequently experiences depression as a consequence of this rejection.
- Occasionally, when provoked, Dylan exhibits inappropriate behaviors such as rude gestures, verbal aggression and insults, and self-injurious actions. These episodes typically end with Dylan overturning his desk, throwing notebooks and pens at persons he deems to be his 'tormentors,' and running out of class. He then needs to be subdued and calmed by the crisis intervention team.

The final step in the process is *testing the hypothesis* by assessing the effectiveness of the resulting behavioral intervention plan. Accordingly, a behavioral intervention plan was developed and implemented, based on the results of the functional behavioral assessment, and resulting hypotheses. The effectiveness of the BIP in addressing the target behaviors will be carefully evaluated, and any necessary modifications or adjustments will be made.

Developing an Effective Intervention Plan: Dylan

Applying the components of an effective behavioral intervention plan as recommended by Horner and Sugai (2015) to the case example of Dylan might result in the following interventions; keeping in mind that, as with previous case examples, it is important that interventions be developed to address each of the target behaviors identified in the behavioral assessment.

Target 1: Egocentric Focus of Conversation With no Interest in Reciprocity and Subject Obsession. Dylan has been scheduled to participate in weekly group meetings involving the psychiatrist, the speech-language pathologist, and other students at the school who have ASD. The focus of this group is to teach appropriate socialization skills such as turn-taking in conversations, active listening, employing related verbal and nonverbal communication skills, appreciating another's perspective, and understanding and responding to social cues such as those apparent in body language and facial expression.

The skills taught in the group have been disseminated to all of Dylan's teachers, who will act as coaches to provide positive feedback and encouragement when he employs the appropriate social skills.

Target 2: Depression. Dylan has been prescribed an antidepressant that has been helpful in stabilizing his moods; nevertheless, teachers should provide encouragement and positive reinforcement whenever Dylan displays appropriate interpersonal behavior or attempts to engage in reciprocal communication. Teachers and other school professionals should continue to monitor Dylan's affect and demeanor in school.

Target 3: Acting Out Using Verbal and Physical Aggression. In the event that Dylan's behavior escalates to a point where he abruptly leaves or must be escorted from the classroom, a crisis intervention plan should be in place. This plan should conform to the school-wide policy for handling episodes of extreme and potentially dangerous behavior. As a minimum, all teachers should be familiar with these procedures. Typically, the teacher who is present should initiate the process, which usually begins with a call to the general office or the crisis intervention team leader. A designated, well-trained crisis intervention team then deploys rapidly to the site, providing effective intervention in the crisis as well as bystander control. Following the event, the affected teacher or staff member completes an incident report, which is filed in the school office. The members of the crisis intervention team prepare a joint report that indicates the time and date of the incident and details their course of action as well as the perceived emotional state and actions of the student in crisis. These reports, along with the accounts of student and staff eyewitnesses, are critical in identifying antecedent events that precipitated the crisis as well as the consequences of the problem behavior.

Ideally, teachers and school staff should be aware of the triggers that instigate Dylan's acting-out behaviors. Often, students exhibit behavioral warning signs that signal the escalation of aggression. If the trigger can be neutralized, by removing either the instigator or the student in crisis, then a more severe and potentially serious situation can be averted. In Dylan's case, perhaps the most critical signals are the onset of verbal threats and denigration directed toward his perceived tormentor. Teacher intervention at this point is crucial to helping Dylan regain self-control and deescalating a volatile situation.

Information about the behavioral intervention plan must be included in the student's IEP. It is the responsibility of the multidisciplinary team to disseminate this information to each of Dylan's teachers. The best way to do this is to schedule a meeting at the beginning of the school year that includes all Dylan's teachers and related services providers. A copy of the behavioral intervention plan can then be distributed to all the stakeholders, intervention protocols can be discussed, and the school psychologist can address any questions about the execution of the plan. Lastly, a contingency or crisis intervention plan should be clearly articulated to ensure that all staff members know the procedures to follow in the event of a behavioral crisis. This plan should identify key persons to be notified as well as the actions and responsibilities of each of the responders. After it has been in place for five or six weeks, the plan should be reviewed to determine its effectiveness. If the plan as a whole, or any aspect of the plan, is producing less than desired results, that feature of the plan or even the entire plan should be modified or replaced.

From the Field

Mary McDonald, Ph.D.

Mary McDonald is a professor in the Special Education Program at Hofstra University and directs Eden II Programs' Outreach and Consultation Program. She completed her Ph.D. in Learning Theory at the CUNY Graduate Center and is a Board-Certified Behavior Analyst. Dr. McDonald has nearly thirty years' experience directing programs for students with autism spectrum disorder. She presents both locally and nationally and she has published articles in the areas of self-management and social reciprocity in children who have autism. Dr. McDonald's current research interests include the use of video modeling to teach social and vocational skills and the promotion of response to intervention in education.

Currently, there is a great deal of controversy and speculation about the dramatic increase in the incidence of ASD among school-age children. Can you provide a plausible explanation or explanations for this phenomenal increase?

It is true that there has been a dramatic increase in the number of students diagnosed with autism spectrum disorders over the past 15 or so years. It is most plausible that there are a variety of reasons for this increase. In particular, Asperger's was only added to the DSM [Diagnostic and Statistical Manual] in 1994 and this change would in effect itself lead to an increase in diagnosis. In addition, there has been a great emphasis on educating the public about autism spectrum disorders, and through education, we have seen a greater number of students referred for evaluation sooner. Pediatricians are also becoming more educated about autism spectrum disorders, and autism screening is now occurring along with the general developmental screenings to ensure early detection. Lastly, although there are many specific factors that have likely led to an increase in diagnosis, the level of increase (approximately

800 percent over the past 10 years in the United States) is of epidemic proportions.

We are unsure of the causes of autism spectrum disorders; therefore, it is impossible to know why the numbers might be increasing; there are many theories, such as the idea that thimerosal in vaccines is the cause of autism. Current research shows that there is a genetic component to ASD, and we know that it is more likely in siblings. Research is continuing to determine the causes of autism, as it is believed that there is a genetic predisposition and then an environmental influence that may be the cause.

Clearly, one of the greatest challenges for both students with ASD and their teachers is the impact of the disorder on the development of social skills. Can you address this issue in light of current research?

The three main areas in which characteristics of ASD are included are communication, social skills, and behavior. Each of the areas listed may affect the social ability of an individual with ASD; for example, a student who lacks the ability to communicate verbally, to understand and respond to nonverbal social behaviors of a peer, who engages in repetitive behavior to the exclusion of any other more appropriate behaviors will have difficulty interacting with others socially. The lack of ability to engage in appropriate social behaviors and have social understanding of the world around them is a hallmark of the ASD diagnosis.

The research focuses on both theories related to the social deficits in autism, including theory of mind (Baron-Cohen, 2000), the enactive mind model (Klin et al., 2003), executive functioning (Kenworthy et al., 2008), and the effective behavioral teaching approaches to social skills (Jones et al., 2007; Scattone, 2008). The research is promising, and many students with ASD are benefiting from the use of specific teaching methods (e.g., video modeling). Current research is even examining high-tech options such as the use of virtual reality models to teach social skills to individuals with ASD, but we still have a long way to go.

Specifically, as this question relates to students with high-functioning autism, what are the implications of research relative to helping them develop the social skills needed for success in life?

The research for students with HFA is focused on understanding how students with ASD understand the social world. Specifically, areas such as eye gaze and perception are being studied to determine how students with ASD look at a social situation both physically (where do they look with their eyes, what are they focused on in a picture or social situation) and what are they thinking when they see a social situation (what are their perceptions) about what is ensuing. The research is still in the somewhat early stages but thus far has shown us that individuals with ASD are not looking at the same things their neurotypical peers are and they are not perceiving situations as being social in the way their peers would. Therefore, people with ASD are missing crucial pieces of information that would allow them to understand social situations and act accordingly.

Given that social skills or 'people skills' are clearly the most important ones in the quest for greater independence for students with autism spectrum disorders, what are some strategies that teachers can use to facilitate the acquisition of these skills by students in their classrooms who have ASD?

Students with ASD need to learn what to do in the social situation and then they need to be shown how to do it and then they need many opportunities to practice the skill and receive feedback. Teachers should first conduct a social skills assessment on their students to be sure they address the areas in need. Second, teachers should develop clear objectives related to social behavior. Third, teachers must task analyze the social skills so they can be taught to the students. Fourth, teachers should determine what teaching method to use to teach the skill, based on three factors: the research, the student's learning style, and the student's history of learning. Teachers can use some basic strategies such as reinforcing appropriate social behavior when it occurs - "catch 'em being social" - provide prompts to encourage appropriate social interactions, model appropriate social behavior for students, or use peer models in the classroom. There are a number of research-based strategies for teaching social skills, such as written or audio scripts, video modeling, or social stories. Teachers can look to the Association for Science in Autism Treatment to assist them in deciding which interventions may be based on science at this time. They have an online presence and can be found at www.asatonline.org.

Could you share with our readers the results of any current research you have conducted in this area, or, for that matter, that your contemporaries may have conducted that you consider to be important to teachers and other stakeholders in working more effectively with students who have ASD?

One of my recent research projects focused on increasing creativity in play with young students with ASD through the provision of instructions and reinforcement. Students who had difficulty engaging in creative play prior to intervention were able to play more creatively, and the social validity data showed that they were able to reach levels similar to those of their peers when their play was judged by a general education teacher.

A second research project involved promoting appropriate work-related social behaviors in adolescents with ASD through the use of video modeling. The students learned how to engage in appropriate work-related behaviors by observing them perform for them on a video. This allowed adolescents with ASD to be more independent in a work setting. I do believe it is most important for teachers to get to know their students and look to the research to guide them in their teaching of students with autism.

Finally, could you provide a personal anecdote that describes a success story, an example of a student who, through effective teacher and parent intervention, was able to make significant social and academic gains on the journey toward greater independence?

Only one? Yes, I have had many success stories, but one in particular stands out to me at this time. There is one student with ASD who I met when she was only 3 years old. She did not have the skills that her typical peers did, she did not engage in eye contact, she was not able to imitate simple actions, she did not play appropriately with toys, she was not speaking or imitating spoken language, and she also engaged in some challenging behaviors due to her lack of ability to communicate her needs.

We began a home-based program based on the principles of applied behavior analysis, and the child who seemed to not be able to learn was learning at a rapid speed. By the time she was 4 years old, we wanted her to have more structured opportunities with her peers, so in addition to the home-based services, she began attending a local preschool.

In preschool, we provided her with a supported inclusion program (a staff member trained in the principles of applied behavior analysis accompanied her to a general education class). While she was in the class, the shadow (staff member) provided her with reinforcers (including praise) for appropriate behavior and prompts as needed to interact with her teachers and peers.

Through the years and countless hours of hard work by her behavioral therapists and her parents, she began to gain a number of important skills. Slowly over the years, she began speaking, she was playing with toys, she began to initiate language for the first time. As the years passed, we stayed focused on her needs, and our focus changed often as she developed. She continued to attend inclusion classes with typical peers throughout her educational career.

She is now in high school, and she is able to have a conversation with me regarding just about any topic, she is very involved in her school and community as she acts in school plays, she sings in a singing group, and she attends dance class and performs in recitals.

This summer for the first time she is participating in an internship work program at a local aquarium (her future goal is to be an animal trainer at Sea World). She went on the interview (that in and of itself is an accomplishment) and she was awarded the internship. She was so excited about it that she called me to let me know that she had gotten the 'job.' I believe that she is an amazing person. I have learned so much from her and I am proud to know her. I hope teachers can feel that way about all their students and know what an impact you can make on someone's life.

Effective early intervention is crucial for children with ASD. I know she will continue to do great things in the future, and it is because of the foundation she was provided early on.

Summary

The focus of this chapter was autism spectrum disorder, with a focus on autistic disorder and higher functioning autism. An examination of the characteristics and etiology of these disorders revealed three key indicators (1) impairments in social interaction, (2) impairments in communication, and (3) restricted repetitive and stereotyped patterns of behavior. Both higher functioning autism and AD share all but one of these characteristics—impairments in communication. Children and youth who have higher functioning autism typically display precocious vocabulary development and are generally articulate and talkative.

Although experts agree that the diagnosis of ASD has increased dramatically in the last decade, the possible reasons for this exponential growth are controversial. Some researchers have suggested that the proliferation of environmental toxins and the use of biotic material in infant vaccinations might be a contributor, whereas others have maintained that the use of more sophisticated and discriminating diagnostic instruments and criteria helps to account for the drastic increase in diagnosis. Nevertheless, at present, the most promising etiological studies seem to point in the direction of genetic influences that affect neurological development.

One of the most reliable and best-documented instruments for assessment is the *Childhood Autism Rating Scale 2nd ed.* (CARS2; Schopler et al., 2010, 1988). This instrument is most effective for use with individuals 4 years of age or older. Another reliable assessment instrument, the *Gilliam Autism Rating Scale 3rd ed.* (GARS3; Gilliam, 2013) is useful in helping to identify autism spectrum disorders in persons aged 3 years and older.

Lastly, the *Children's Social Behavior Scale* (CSBQ; Luteijn et al., 2000), another relatively reliable screening instrument, can be useful in making a differential diagnosis. Diagnostic interviews and observation scales such as the *Autism*

Diagnostic Observation Schedule (ADOS2; Lord et al., 2012) can provide valuable information to help in the identification of autism spectrum disorder.

Effective interventions for students who have ASD include behavioral ones, such as discrete trial training (Lovaas, 1987) that reinforces behavioral approximations; naturalistic behavioral interventions, such as paradigm response training (PRT; Lei & Ventola, 2017; Vernon, 2017), which helps develop symbolic play (Stahmer, 1995); and joint attention (Whalen & Schreibman, 2003). Cognitive therapies, including video modeling (Zhang, S. et al., 2019) and social stories (Gray, 2022) via TEACCH (Alotaibi, 2017) can be used to teach social skills such as identifying affect, understanding the consequences of a particular behavior, understanding another's perspective, and, most important, recognizing socially inappropriate behaviors and replacing those with more appropriate, pro-social ones. Finally, there appears to be little evidence to support the efficacy of pharmacological interventions used to treat children and youth who have ASD.

Tips for Teachers

- Be sure to obtain and review the IEP for a student assigned to your classroom who has ASD, particularly the behavioral intervention plan. If you need clarification or guidance, contact your school psychologist or special education chairperson, and arrange to review the IEP together.
- Provide visual-pictorial reminders of students' schedules using picture exchange communication systems (PECS) for students who are nonverbal or unable to read; provide a written one for students who are literate and post the schedule near their desks or in a conspicuous spot that can be easily viewed as they come into the classroom.
- Try to avoid sudden changes in students' schedules; instead, introduce them gradually. Most students who have ASD find sudden changes in routine disconcerting and often react with displeasure and frustration, occasionally tantruming when faced with a change in schedule. If an unannounced change is necessary, have a contingency plan ready to help the agitated student cope with the anxiety and frustration imposed by the change. To the extent possible, ensure that all other activities in the student's schedule remain unaltered, and provide reminders of the schedule change throughout the day to help the student adapt to the new routine.

- Use a naturalistic behavioral intervention, such as PRT, to help increase intersubjectivity and improve joint attention, and use it consistently. Also, conscientiously record the number of approximations as well as the frequency in the student's achievement of the behavioral objective. Be sure that these successes receive positive reinforcement.
- Students who have higher functioning ASD often experience difficulty initiating and/or sustaining a dialogue with a social partner. You can use video instruction to provide nonthreatening modeling of successful behavior. Also, be sure that you comply with the strategies outlined in the student's BIP that address social and interpersonal skills issues.
- Be sure that you have a crisis intervention or crisis management plan established in the event of a serious behavioral incident and know and follow the prescribed procedures.
- Use prearranged cues to remind students who have higher functioning ASD when they are engaged in pedantic speech, are dominating a discussion, or fail to consider the perspective of a social partner.
- Become familiar with the triggers that incite a student who has ASD and diffuse the volatile situation by removing the affected student or antagonist or by redirecting the adversarial interaction.
- Use social stories when feasible in lessons or use the "teachable moment" to provide an opportunity to conduct a "social autopsy" on an ineffective or inappropriate social behavior, and then teach the correct behavioral response.
- Reduce self-stimulating behavior and stereotypy by providing differential reinforcement for other behaviors (DRO)—ones that are more appropriate substitutes for the target behaviors.

Focus Questions Revisited

Suppose you are going to be Stefan's classroom teacher next year. What would you want to know about his classroom performance and about his learning and behavioral needs as provided by his current teacher?

A Sample Response: I would need to have a copy of Stefan's current IEP, complete with a behavioral intervention plan that would help me understand his present level of performance in the academic curriculum as well as the strategies that are effective in helping him achieve his current goals. I would also ask to see samples of Stefan's academic work products in order to better understand how his academic strengths and weaknesses are manifest in the classroom. Finally, I would want to know the interpersonal strategies that facilitate Stefan's participation in the classroom as well as ones that elicit engagement in learning and social activities.

Similarly, imagine that you will be teaching Dylan next year. What would be important for you to know about Dylan's classroom performance to be fully prepared to help him learn and develop?

A Sample Response: Similar to Stefan, I would want to review Dylan's current IEP, noting especially his strengths and weaknesses as well as his current goals, both academic and behavioral. I would also study his behavioral intervention plan to learn effective strategies for helping Dylan cope with the social and behavioral challenges he experiences as a result of his higher functioning ASD. Furthermore, I would ask to see samples of his work both in the content areas in which he is successful and those in which he is struggling, so as to develop an effective academic support plan. Lastly, I would want to interview his current teachers to learn about the approaches they found helpful in improving Dylan's social skills as well as his academic performance.

Research the theory of mind and describe what insights it provides about the functional understanding of students who have autistic disorder.

A Sample Response: The theory of mind suggests that individuals who have autistic disorder experience difficulty in understanding the perspective of another because of a brain anomaly (Frith & Frith, 2005).

As Stefan's teacher, what are some important academic considerations to facilitate his acquisition of skills?

A Sample Response: Some important academic considerations might include the following.

- Be very clear and organized about everything you teach, especially when giving instructions. Any confusion will only create further anxiety, conflict, and tension for both you and the student.
- Establish routine patterns: Spatial routines associate specific locations with specific activities—for example, a pictorial chart used as a daily schedule. Temporal routines associate

time with an activity and make the beginning and ending of an activity visually apparent. Instructional routines associate specific social and communication behaviors.

- Initiate one-on-one interactions frequently throughout the day to help increase the student's eye contact.
- Break tasks down into simple parts. This will help the student achieve greater success while avoiding unnecessary frustration.
- Repeat, repeat, repeat instructions to help the child stay focused on the task at hand.
- Enhance the student's understanding of instructional and environmental structure by providing routines and visual aids in forms other than written language. For example, learn a few American Sign Language signs to signal transitions, such as the sign for snack or lunchtime.
- Minimize the time spent waiting to begin activities. Have all materials prepared and handy when starting a lesson. Teaching that is "scattered" and disorganized upsets a student who has autism or another form of pervasive developmental disorder.
- Teach appropriate social skills through modeling behavior role-playing, the use of social stories, and video instruction. Remember, however, to be patient, regularly taking time to help the child learn how to act in various situations. Extending this effort can be difficult, especially if the ASD is severe, but it will achieve positive results.
- Arrange for a peer to guide and cue the student through social situations. The affected student may be more willing to model her own behavior after that of a peer than that of a teacher.
- When the student is refraining from aggressive or inappropriate behavior, or employing a more appropriate alternative one, provide positive reinforcement that is both realistic and genuine.
- The student may not understand what may seem to you to be social common sense because of the ASD, or simply a lack of experience. Therefore, initially, take a more direct approach to teaching social skills rather than allowing the student to learn through trial and error. Specifically, the student may need help interpreting social situations and developing appropriate

responses; for example, you might help the student understand how to take turns with a toy (Adapted with permission from Pierangelo & Giuliani, 2008).

Suppose you have a student who has autistic spectrum disorder and a behavioral profile similar to Dylan's. This student has begun to dominate a discussion involving a controversial topic in current events: He is not allowing another student, with a different perspective, to express her views. A third classmate, frustrated by the lack of reciprocity on the part of the student who has higher functioning ASD, reproaches him, threatening him with physical violence. The student who has higher functioning ASD, feeling rejected, hurt, and afraid, abruptly runs from the classroom, hurling epithets at you and the other students while simultaneously throwing books, chalk, and an eraser at his adversary as he flees. What can you do to ensure the safety of this student and restore order to the classroom?

A Sample Response: You should have already established a crisis intervention plan for just such emergencies. Typically, without a plan, teachers either (a) allow the student in crisis to flee, unescorted, in order to maintain classroom control and then later address the student's departure with parents and administrators, or (b) chase after the fleeing student, leaving the other students to discuss the possible outcomes for the student in crisis or to take advantage of the lack of supervision to "act up."

An effective crisis intervention plan will let the teacher signal for assistance using a pre-arranged method—perhaps via a classroom telephone or intercom. This signal will alert a designated, trained emergency response or crisis intervention team to quickly converge on the location of the incident and either provide the necessary intervention there or gather information from the teacher who signaled for help about the antecedent events and probable location of the student or students in crisis. The teacher can then restore order to the classroom, write an eyewitness account of the incident using the designated form, and use the teachable moment to help the class understand the cause of the incident and help prevent its recurrence.

The teacher is also able, thereby, to avoid participating in a physical restraint, should that become necessary. This helps the child with higher functioning ASD continue to see the teacher as an ally, not an adversary, and preserves the therapeutic relationship between teacher and student.

Explain discrete trial training.

A Sample Response: In discrete trial training, the student who has ASD is taught skills presented in a logical sequence that builds on previously acquired ones. Concepts to be taught are identified and then broken into steps using task analysis. Each instructional session consists of a series of discrete trials. These trials involve a focus-step sequence: (a) instructional cue, (b) student response, (c) consequence (generally a positive reinforcer), and (d) pause. Information is "collected and analyzed to help monitor the student's progress and determine when a preset behavioral objective has been achieved" (Arick et al., 2005, p. 1004).

What is paradigm/pivotal response training (PRT), and why is it often preferred over more structured techniques such as discrete trial training?

A Sample Response: Like discrete trial training, PRT is based on a four-step sequence: (a) cue, (b) student response, (c) consequence, and (d) pause. The principal difference between the two behavioral approaches is that trials in PRT are incorporated into the environment in a functional context. For example, in PRT, the student selects the activity or object, and the reinforcer is a natural consequence to the behaviors being rewarded, making it possible to engage the student throughout all activities and locations in the course of the day (Lei & Ventola, 2017; Vernon, 2017).

Research comparing naturalistic techniques such as PRT and more structured ones such as DT has demonstrated that PRT resulted in more generalized and spontaneous use of skills (Lei & Ventola, 2017; Vernon, 2017). Furthermore, additional studies revealed that PRT helped reduce stress and increase a sense of well-being among both children with AD and their family members.

Describe video modeling and what its therapeutic implications are for children who have ASD?

A Sample Response: Video modeling, as opposed to in-vivo (live) modeling, refers to a therapeutic approach that involves the videotaping of "actors" or "role models," who demonstrate socially appropriate behaviors in conversational speech, verbal responding, daily living or adaptive behavior skills, and emotional empathy or understanding. Researchers have found that children who have AD acquire these skills with greater rapidity and generalize them to different contexts to a greater degree through video modeling than through in-vivo modeling, perhaps because the video characterizations are less intimidating and more visually stimulating (Zhang, S. et al., 2019).

In contrast, students who have high-functioning autism benefited more from in-vivo modeling (Schreibman & Ingersoll, 2005) and were able to use video-modeling to learn self-management techniques such as self-monitoring, self-delivery of reinforcement, and self-evaluation of performance (Thiemann & Goldstein, 2001).

What are social stories, and how are they used to help students who have higher-functioning autism (HFA) acquire strategies for appropriate social conversation and emotional regulation?

A Sample Response: Social stories are just that, stories that involve students similar to those with AS and HFA who are learning from them. These "stories" or "social scripts" depict a hypothetical social situation in which the protagonist makes ineffective choices. The teacher, parent, or therapist uses this safe hypothetical situation to teach the appropriate social response or choice and then allows the teacher and student to assume the role and read the script, choosing the correct behavioral response in a particular social context.

Social stories are designed to help those with HFA and AS understand their own social difficulties, pay careful attention to the social context, select the most important aspects of a social situation, identify appropriate behavioral responses, identify the social partner's perspective, and understand the consequences of a particular positive behavior (Alotaibi, 2017).

Suppose you are a classroom teacher in a public elementary school and because you are regarded as somewhat knowledgeable about autism spectrum disorder (having thoroughly read and understood this chapter), you are approached by some colleagues about the enigmatic behaviors exhibited by a new student for whom they share instruction. To help confirm their suspicions about the type of disorder that may be affecting this child, they ask you to assemble a list of behavioral characteristics typically observed in an individual who has autism spectrum disorder. What are some key characteristics you could provide?

A Sample Response: Some of the following characteristics may be evident in mild to severe forms of autism:

- Apparent insensitivity to pain
- Avoidance of touching others
- Unprovoked aggression
- Communication problems
- Difficulty relating to people
- Difficulty dealing with changes in routines

- Does not smile at familiar people
- Echolalia (repeats words or phrases instead of using normal language)
- Picky eating habits
- Hyper- or hyposensitivity (over-or under-sensitivity to sensory stimuli)
- Inappropriate attachment to objects
- Inappropriate emotional response to situations
- Lack of imagination or inability to pretend
- Limited, if any, eye contact
- Limited range of interests
- Little interest in making friends
- Perseverating behavior (excessive concentration on a single person, item, or idea)
- Disdain for physical contact (may seem cold and unaffectionate)
- Volatile temperament resulting in tantrums
- Apparent fearlessness
- Self-injurious behavior
- Unresponsive to verbal cues (seems deaf)
- Hyper- or hypoactivity
- Gesticulates instead of using speech
- Preference for being alone (isolation)
- Repetitive behavior patterns and body movements
- Self-stimulating behavior ("stimming")
- Sustained odd play
- Uneven gross and fine motor skills
- Unresponsiveness to standard teaching methods (Pierangelo & Giuliani, 2001)

Sam is a student who has autism. Using your knowledge of students who have disabilities, identify a grade level for Sam for which you are prepared to teach, then prepare a response in which you:

- ***Identify one other professional (e.g., general education teacher, specialist) who would typically provide services to Sam.***
- ***Recommend and describe one technique that a special educator and the professional you identified could use to prepare Sam to live harmoniously and productivity in a diverse society.***
- ***Describe how the special educator and the professional you identified could collaborate to implement the technique that you recommend.***
- ***Explain how this collaboration will meet Sam's needs and provide for effective monitoring of progress.***

A Sample Response: Sam is a 14-year-old boy with autism who attends general education classes for part of the day in an academic high school. Sam is relatively high functioning academically, but struggles with areas of socialization such as transitioning, pragmatic language, and social interaction with peers and adults. Sam has particular difficulty in the Earth Science Lab class, where he is expected to work cooperatively and independently with a lab partner. Specifically, he does not make eye contact and/or participate actively with his partner on assigned labs. The Earth Science teacher and the Special Education teacher have decided to work collaboratively to remediate Sam's deficits, since improving Sam's social skills would allow him to work more cooperatively with others and increase his social acceptance in the class. The technique chosen will be modeling and guided practice.

To implement the technique, care will be taken to choose a lab partner for Sam who is engaging, socially sophisticated, and willing to work with Sam. Initially, the Special Education Teacher will work with Sam on making and maintaining eye contact. A prompt card will be created which the Science teacher will place on Sam's lab table. It will serve as a reminder to Sam to continue to practice this skill. For example, the teacher or Sam's lab partner may point to the card to reinforce Sam's behavior. The acquisition of effective eye contact behavior will ultimately increase Sam's success in the class through increased social appropriateness.

To monitor the effectiveness of this technique, the Science teacher will complete a brief checklist, recording Sam's progress with respect to this skill, for each lab period. The Special Education teacher will complete a checklist for each resource period. In addition, Sam will collaborate with his teachers through self-monitoring on his own checklist.

(Source: NYSTCE Preparation Guide: Students with Disabilities CST (60) (2006) National Evaluation Systems, Inc., New York State Education Department, Office of Teaching Initiatives, Albany, NY).

Key Terms Used in the Chapter

Savant Skill:
A special brilliance, ability, or expertise in a particular area(s) that is in contrast to the individual's overall intelligence.

Sympathetic Nervous System:
The part of the nervous system that controls the fight-or-flight response.

Wernicke's Area:
A portion of the left posterior temporal lobe of the brain, involved in the ability to understand words.

Broca's Area:
A portion of the frontal lobe of the brain, usually of the left cerebral hemisphere, and associated with the motor control of speech.

Convergent Validity:
The degree to which a scale is similar to (converges on) other scale(s) that theoretically measure the same construct.

Discriminate Validity:
The degree to which a scale diverges from a scale(s) that theoretically measure a dissimilar construct.

Discrete Trial Training:
An intensive treatment designed to assist individuals who have developmental disabilities, such as autism. It involves directly training a variety of skills that individuals who have disabilities may not pick up naturally. Discrete trial training is conducted using intensive drills of selected materials. A specific behavior is prompted or guided, and children receive reinforcement for proper responses.

Social Stories:

A social story describes a situation, skill, or concept in terms of relevant social cues, perspectives, and common responses in a specifically defined style and format. The goal is to share accurate social information in a patient and reassuring manner that is easily understood by its audience.

Chapter 10

At-Risk Behaviors and Emotional Disturbance

Focus Questions

- *What are the four substances that are most commonly abused by children and adolescents, and why do they pose such a threat?*
- *The National Institute on Drug Abuse provides six guidelines in selecting an effective school-based drug-abuse prevention program: What are they?*
- *Identify the school professionals who serve as resources for teachers who have concerns about a student at risk for or engaged in substance abuse.*
- *What are two key factors that increase the risk of acquiring a sexually transmitted disease (STD) for adolescents who have emotional disturbances?*
- *Of the three sex education program types described in this chapter, identify the one that you consider to be most effective, and explain why you consider it so.*
- *As a new high school teacher, you notice that some of your students wear distinctive clothing and behave in ways that are unusual and a bit unsettling. What are some of the characteristics or warning signs that you might look for to confirm your suspicions of their gang affiliation?*
- *In developing a school-wide approach to prevent gang membership and gang activity, what are some critical elements to include?*

This chapter examines four behaviors (substance use, at-risk sexual activity, violence, and gang membership) in which those who have emotional disturbances have a higher risk of participation. The organization of this chapter is different than that of the preceding ones in that it does not pretend to give an in-depth overview of each of the problems, but rather enough information to sensitize school personnel to these at-risk behaviors and suggestions to access appropriate interventions.

Substance Use and Abuse

Case Example: Michael R.

Michael R., a high school senior, is completing his last academic course in summer school and looks forward to starting classes at a local community college in the fall. He eventually wants to become a meteorologist and has always enjoyed studying and observing weather. He is now poised to realize this life-long dream.

Two years ago, however, Michael's prospects looked very bleak. He was failing every subject in school and was drinking excessive amounts of alcohol, smoking marijuana, and using cocaine, Vicodin, OxyContin, and any other available substance to get 'high.' Michael's parents had divorced a year before he began using but were both very supportive of him and had tried, unsuccessfully, on two occasions to get him into rehab. The administration in his school was seeking to expel him because of his extensive truancy and absenteeism. Essentially, Michael was falling through the cracks. The final straw came late in his sophomore year when he overdosed on Vicodin and alcohol at a rave and would have died were it not for the quick and effective action of the detox-intensive care unit at a nearby hospital.

As it turned out, however, this near-death experience proved to be a turning point in Michael's life. While he was still recovering in the hospital, a clinical social worker found him a placement in a special residential treatment facility not too far from his home. Here, he could go to school and be enrolled in a reputable outpatient rehabilitation program. His progress on the road to 'clean and sober' would be carefully monitored by Alan G., the institution's drug awareness counselor. Alan, a clinical social worker with special certification in substance-abuse counseling, had worked successfully with several other students at the school, and he became Michael's lifeline and safety net. At any time during the day, Michael could call Alan at his confidential phone service and leave a message requesting a session; typically, within the hour, one was arranged. A similar contingency plan was established for night-time emergencies or struggles. After several months of halting gains and heart-breaking relapses, Michael was finally able to acquire the coping skills to enable him to remain drug- and alcohol-free.

That breakthrough occurred almost two years ago, and, thanks to the support network provided by school staff, Alan G., rehabilitation center counselors, and Michael's parents, he will be graduating with a high school diploma in only a few weeks.

Introduction

Adolescents who use substances have high rates of psychiatric disorders. Most experts, however, agree that substance use evolves into substance abuse and dependence through a complex interaction of multiple factors that include genetic, psychological, familial, and nonfamilial environments (Ahmed et al., 2020). Not all those who have emotional disturbances will abuse substances, yet it must be considered a significant factor. The more risk factors a student possesses, the greater is the risk for substance abuse. Specific groups of children have been identified as being at risk for substance abuse as evidenced in the list below.

Children at Risk for Substance Abuse

- Children engaged in early alcohol or drug experimentation
- Children of substance-dependent parents
- Children with substance-abusing siblings
- Children with conduct disorder
- Children with psychiatric disorders
- Children with deviant and substance-abusing peers
- Children temperamentally seeking high sensation
- Children with impulse and self-control problems
- Children under poor parental supervision
- Children living in heavy-drug-use neighborhoods
- Children with school problems
- Children with social skills deficits
- Children of parents with poor parenting skills
- Children who are victims of trauma, abuse, and neglect

From "Substance Use Disorders" by C.P. O'Brien, J.C. Anthony, K. Carroll, A.R. Childress, C. Dackis, G. Diamond et al. in Treating and Preventing Adolescent Mental Health Disorders (p. 416) by D.L. Evans, E.B. Foa, R.E. Gur, H. Hendin, C.P. O'Brien, M.E.P. Seligman et al., 2005, New York: Oxford University Press. Copyright 2005 by Oxford University Press. Reprinted with permission.

Youngsters who begin experimenting with tobacco and alcohol at a very young age (e.g., between 9 and 12 years) offer more cause for concern than those who experiment much later. One way of understanding and assessing drug use among adolescents is through the drug use continuum (Muisener, 1994) and the adolescent chemical use experience. In this model, there are four types of use along a continuum.

Experimental Use. Many adolescents will try a drug(s) as a result of peer pressure, wanting to belong, have fun or just plain curiosity. Experimenters who stay at his level do not develop a pattern of use and avoid dangerous situations involving drugs. They often limit themselves to the more 'acceptable' drugs, e.g., alcohol and marijuana.

Social Use. Social users develop a regular use of drugs on weekends, parties, etc. and seek the high experienced in the experimental stage. They can misuse and overindulge in drugs and are slowly learning to believe that there is no fun without drugs.

Operational Use. Synonymous with abuse, operational users turn to drugs to medicate themselves for unwanted feelings or painful stimulants. These compensatory users are more at-risk for developing a serious drug problem because they have learned early on that drugs are a coping mechanism that works well for them. They can also be constant pursuers of pleasure for which drugs are the best source.

Dependent Use. This stage is marked by an obsession and compulsion for a particular drug(s). There is significant interference in functioning as much time, energy, money is spent on accessing and consuming the drugs. One's identity is clearly linked to drugs use.

Although most adolescents will not progress beyond social use, those who do require help. With the help of the drug use continuum, teachers and other school personnel can make distinctions among the many types of adolescent substance users and intervene accordingly.

Drugs of Choice Among Adolescents

The four most common substances used and abused by children and adolescents are alcohol, nicotine, marijuana, and inhalants also known at the gateway drugs.

Alcohol

According to the 2020 *Monitoring the Future Study* (MFT) (Johnston et al., 2020), the lifetime prevalence rate for alcohol among 12th graders was 61.5 percent and among 8th graders it was 25.6 percent. Alcohol use among teenagers has actually been trending downward in recent years. Forty-five percent of children who start drinking before the age of 15 will become alcoholics at some point in their lives (Johnston et al., 2020). If the onset of drinking is delayed by five years, a child's risk of serious alcohol problems is significantly decreased (Newton-Howes et al., 2019). For many youth, what begins as experimental will develop later into uncontrollable drinking.

Nicotine

In the last ten years, the perceived risk of cigarette smoking among youth has increased and resulted in significant decreases in the rates of smoking among eighth, tenth, and twelfth graders (Johnston et al., 2020). In the last three years, cigarette use has held steady, around 23 percent for 12th graders; however, the use of nicotine through vaping has seen a huge increase in recent years (Johnston et al., 2020). In 2020, the prevalence rate for 12th graders who used nicotine through vaping was 44.3 percent, the second-highest to alcohol, and on par with marijuana at 43.7 percent (Johnston et al., 2020). Nicotine abuse is clearly a problem that begins in youth. Males are more likely to smoke than females, and American Indians and Alaska Natives are more likely to smoke than any other racial or ethnic group (Johnston et al., 2020).

Marijuana

Marijuana is the most widely used illicit drug in the United States and is usually the first illicit drug that adolescents use. With the advent of medical marijuana and the legalization of recreational marijuana in some states, the perception among adolescents often is that marijuana is less dangerous than alcohol and could even be good for you. There are many street names for marijuana, including "pot," "weed," "Mary Jane," "herb," and "boom," among others.

Research on the effects of marijuana is still in its early stages, and scientists have not been able to determine whether marijuana is physiologically addictive; however, the psychological addiction to marijuana is indisputable and very powerful (Colliver et al., 2006). More than 120,000 people per year seek treatment for their addiction to marijuana (Colliver et al., 2006). Consumption of marijuana both through vaping and cigarettes is on the rise. Vaping especially has seen a huge increase from 12 percent lifetime prevalence among 12th graders in 2017 to 30 percent in 2020 (National Institutes of Health, 2020).

Longitudinal research has also shown negative social consequences for heavy users of marijuana. For those below college age, marijuana use has been associated with lower achievement, high levels of delinquent and aggressive behavior, greater rebelliousness, poor relationships with parents, and having delinquent friends (Johnston et al., 2020)

Curbing marijuana use is a challenging task. Many adolescents experiment with marijuana and enjoy its perceived positive effects. It increases sensory perception; therefore, listening to music and smoking marijuana is a frequent combination for adolescents. Though still illegal on the federal level, the legalization of marijuana across most states is, for many, an eventual reality. Marijuana is readily available, and its use justified because it is less dangerous than other illicit drugs. These factors must be considered in trying to prevent marijuana abuse among adolescents.

Inhalants

Inhalants are "breathable chemical vapors that produce psychoactive (mind-altering) effects" (National Institute on Drug Abuse, 2020, p. 1) and they are the fourth most commonly used substance among youth and the most commonly used among eighth-grade students after alcohol, marijuana, and nicotine (National Institutes of Health, 2020). They are popular among young people because they are readily available, inexpensive, and can be used in a nonsuspicious fashion. Most adults are exposed daily to chemical vapors in homes and workplaces. As these substances are not meant to be inhaled, the average person may have difficulty considering these vapors as drugs. The different categories of inhalants are listed below.

Categories of Inhalants

Solvents

- Industrial or household solvents, including paint thinners, degreasers, gasoline, and glues
- Art or office supply solvents, including correction fluids, felt-tip marker fluid, and electronic contact cleaners

Gases

- Gases in household or commercial products, including butane lighters, propane tanks, whipping cream aerosols or dispensers, and refrigerant gases
- Household aerosol propellant, including solvents in spray paints, hair or deodorant sprays, and fabric protector sprays
- Medical anesthetic gases, including ether, chloroform, halothane, and nitrous oxide

Nitrates

- Aliphatic nitrites, including cyclohexyl nitrite, available to the general public; amyl nitrite, available by prescription; and butyl nitrite, now an illegal substance

Source: National Institute on Drug Abuse (2020). *Inhalants.* Retrieved from http://www.drugabuse.gov/inhalants/html

Summary

There is some good news for adolescent drug use. The 2021 Monitoring the Future showed continued lower levels of most substances and especially the low level of opioids that have ravaged the adult population (Sherburne, 2021). Although vaping leveled off in 2020, the tremendous rise in recent years is cause for concern. One cannot emphasize enough delaying the start of using a drug like alcohol to minimize the development of an addiction later in life.

Treatment of Substance Abuse

Treatment of substance abuse has been for the most part psychosocial in nature and consists of several different approaches: short-term (four to six weeks) inpatient, outpatient, therapeutic community, and Outward Bound-type or life skills training and 12-step programs. Most of the research on program evaluation and effectiveness, however, has been done with inpatient programs, and those that have been done on other programs often do not include comparison or control groups. Most adolescent substance abusers receive outpatient services for their problems; therefore, there is a serious need for more research into their effectiveness. Outpatient approaches typically have employed behavioral, cognitive-behavioral, family, and multisystemic approaches. Though relatively new and not so extensive, research into the effectiveness of treatment for adolescents with substance abuse has revealed the following:

- Well-defined structured approaches are better than no treatment at all.
- Treatments that focus on broad aspects of functioning seem to produce the best results.
- Those who complete treatment have the best results.
- Inclusion of family members increases retention and outcomes.
- Contingency management through behavioral therapy, which has been successful with adults, is beginning to show promise with adolescents.
- Cognitive-behavioral therapies also show promise, especially when used in conjunction with family therapy.
- Group approaches have produced mixed results, and there exists the possibility of deviant peers together escalating the problem (Winters et al., 2018).

Treatment of Comorbidities

High rates of comorbidity between substance abuse and emotional disturbance make it especially difficult to treat dually diagnosed adolescents. In general, these adolescents have poorer outcomes, and if the co-occurring disorder is left untreated, the probability of retention and completion in a drug intervention program is dramatically lessened (Brewer et al., 2017). Pharmacological treatment for dually diagnosed adolescents can be risky. Current research is investigating pharmacological agents with low abuse liability that can be used in substance-abusing adolescents with ADHD, bipolar disorder, depression, or anxiety disorders.

Prevention of Substance Abuse

Fortunately, much more research has been done on the effectiveness of drug prevention programs for children and adolescents. Programs that do not work include information-only programs, scare tactics, one-shot programs, and values-clarification programs. The National Institute on Drug Abuse (2020) has established the following principles as guides in adopting effective school-based prevention programs.

- School-based programs should extend from kindergarten through high school. At the very least, they should reach children in the critical middle school and high school years.
- Programs should employ well-tested, standardized interventions with detailed lesson plans and student materials.
- Programs should employ age-appropriate interactive teaching methods (e.g., modeling, role-playing, discussion, group feedback, reinforcement, and extended practice).
- Programs should foster pro-social bonding to both the school and the community.
- Program components should include teaching social competence (i.e., communication, self-efficacy, assertiveness) and drug resistance skills that are culturally and developmentally appropriate; promoting positive peer influence; promoting antidrug social norms; emphasizing skills training teaching methods; and include an adequate 'dosage' (ten to fifteen sessions in a year).
- Programs should be periodically evaluated to determine their effectiveness (National Institute on Drug Abuse, 2020).

Research has identified four goals associated with successful prevention programs: increasing students' self-esteem, social skills, decision-making/problem-solving skills, and ability to resist the influence of peers (World Health Organization, 2020). In addition, programs more recently have included alternative activities such as adventure recreation and education to substitute for the lure of risk-taking behaviors associated with drug use (McWhirter et al., 2016).

Numerous commercially driven, school-based programs exist for the prevention of adolescent substance abuse. It is not within the scope of this chapter to review these programs. School personnel who wish to implement a prevention program are cautioned to make an informed decision after reviewing the independent research regarding the effectiveness of such programs and their suitability for a particular school.

At-Risk Sexual Behaviors

A Study in Contrasts: Two Stories

Case Example: Miriam

Miriam, a 17-year-old high school senior and honor student, comes from an intact, middle-class family living in a comfortable home in suburban Minneapolis. Her father is the pastor of a local congregation, and her mother teaches in a school affiliated with the church. Miriam and her siblings, two older sisters and a younger brother, have always taken an active part in the church: Miriam teaches a Sunday school class for very young children, attends Wednesday night Bible study, and helps organize activities for the youth group that meets on Friday evenings.

In school, Miriam is a model student, active in the debating society and drama club, and participating as a soloist with the school chorale. In short, Miriam's free time is very limited, and her parents like it that way. They have extolled the virtues of serving others and staying viable through engagement in worthwhile pursuits, especially those relevant to her faith. To those around her, even those who know her well, Miriam is regarded in every way as an exemplary young woman: an ideal American teenager, the 'girl next door.' That is why it came as such a shock to her family, friends, and classmates when, quite unexpectedly, Miriam's school counselor informed her parents that she was two months pregnant!

Case Example: Elisha

In contrast to Miriam, Elisha comes from a poor family living in an economically depressed neighborhood near Seattle's busy marketplace. Surrounded by drug addicts and prostitutes, Elisha and her family members take risks every day just walking to school or the local grocery store. Elisha's father, an itinerant laborer, left their home when she was 2, and her mother, a recovering addict, has tried unsuccessfully to support the family through the tips and wages she receives as a waitress, supplemented by public assistance.

Elisha began to engage in risk-taking behaviors at an early age; for example, she began smoking cigarettes at age 7, drinking alcohol at 9, smoked her first joint at the age of 11, and eventually tried hard drugs a year or two later. Although she has never been to rehab and does not consider herself dependent on drugs or alcohol, she relishes life on the street, replete with its risks, dangers, and the ultimate perceived payoff: excitement!

Not surprisingly, she had her first sexual experience at the age of 12 with one of her mother's many short-term boyfriends, who subsequently violated her several more times. A few years later, after spending six months in 'juvey' (juvenile detention) for petty theft, vagrancy, and drug possession, one of her former 'boyfriends' confronted her about giving him the 'clap,' specifically, genital herpes. After weeks of prodding from a few concerned friends, Elisha went to an STD (sexually transmitted disease) clinic and discovered from the results of blood tests that she had not only contracted genital herpes but was also HIV positive. Upon receiving this news, Elisha felt as though she had just been given a death sentence.

Two young women, two different stories; however, their personal crises can be better appreciated both in nature and need after reading the following section.

Introduction

It is difficult to think of a topic that stimulates more interest and, at the same time, more controversy in schools than issues related to sexuality. Other than the most benign sex education done through health education classes, material about safer sex and pregnancy prevention is bound to cause a reaction in most school districts in the United States. Sexual development is an overwhelmingly important characteristic of adolescence; therefore, its presence in the school setting is unavoidable. And because sexual awakening brings with it a host of problems (romantic attachments and breakups, peer conflicts and jealousies, sexual harassment, unsafe sex, struggles with sexual orientation, and teenage pregnancy/motherhood), it is inconceivable that schools could be competent at their jobs without being knowledgeable about and feeling comfortable with sex-related matters.

Emotional disturbance is considered a risk factor for sexual victimization (Indias et al., 2019). Those with mental disability can be either victims or perpetrators of inappropriate sexual activity. This section, therefore, deals with at-risk sexual behaviors and covers such topics as HIV/AIDS, STDs, and teen pregnancy/parenthood.

Unprotected Sexual Activity: The Risk of HIV/AIDS

Adolescents, like any others who are sexually active, are at risk for acquiring sexually transmitted diseases, especially acquired immune deficiency syndrome (AIDS). Adolescent and young adults 15-24 account for over one quarter of the sexually active population but are responsible for half of the 20 million new sexually transmitted infections that occur in the United States each year (Shannon & Klaus, 2018). The most common STD in the United States is chlamydia, but gonorrhea, genital warts, herpes, and syphilis are also common (McWhirter et al., 2017). Youth aged 13 to 24 accounted for 21 percent of the 37,832 new HIV diagnoses in 2018 in the United States. They are the least likely to have sustained care and suppressed viral load. Adolescents need to have access to information and tools in order to make healthy decisions and reduce their risk for getting HIV, and to get treatment and stay in care if they have HIV (Centers for Disease Control and Prevention, 2013).

The most common routes for acquiring HIV are unprotected sexual contact with infected persons and sharing a needle with an infected person during intravenous drug use. School personnel should realize that all students, male or female, gay, straight, bisexual or trans, are at risk for contracting HIV if they engage in unprotected sexual behaviors that allow for the sharing of body fluids.

According to the 2019 Youth Behavior Survey (Szucs et al., 2020), 27.4 percent of high school students reported being sexually active. Most individuals, 89.7 percent, who had sexual contact with the opposite sex used a condom or another contraceptive method at last sexual intercourse (Szucs et al., 2020). Condoms were the most prevalent primary contraceptive method (43.9 percent versus 23.3 percent for birth control pills; 4.8 percent for intrauterine device [IUD] or implant; and 3.3 percent for shot, patch, or ring) (Szucs et al., 2020). No pregnancy prevention method was more common among non-Hispanic Black students (23.2 percent) and Hispanic (12.8 percent) students compared with non-Hispanic White students (6.8 percent) (Szucs et al., 2020). Prevalence of condom use was consistently lower among students with other sexual risk behaviors (Szucs et al., 2020).

One-quarter of sexually active high school students admitted to using alcohol or drugs during their most recent sexual encounter (Stinson, 2010).

Being under the influence of drugs or alcohol impairs judgment and increases the probability of engaging in risky sexual behaviors and the sharing of needles if drugs are used intravenously (Strandberg et al., 2019).

There is some positive news about the HIV/AIDS epidemic in that both knowledge and the practice of safer sex have increased among adolescents; however, they continue to be at risk for contracting HIV and other STDs. Research has shown that those who are most at risk (those adolescents who have multiple partners, abuse drugs and alcohol, and generally participate in delinquent behaviors) are the least likely to practice safer sex (Gillman et al., 2018). Among adolescents, HIV/AIDS occurs across race, socioeconomic status, gender, and sexual orientation; therefore, school personnel need to be very knowledgeable about HIV/AIDS and willing to initiate and support prevention efforts in their schools.

Helping Students Who are HIV-Positive

Everyone infected with HIV/AIDS is at increased risk for depression and suicide. They may manifest somatic complaints, anhedonia (the inability to experience pleasure), withdrawal, and irritability perhaps evidence of an underlying depression (Benton et al., 2019). Other emotional reactions can include sadness, confusion, anxiety, fear of isolation, rejection, loss of friends, and death (Chukwuorji et al., 2020).

A child's emotional difficulties may manifest more aggressively, such as fighting and classroom disruption (Webb et al., 2018). Most important, the school needs to provide the child with an opportunity to express any and all of the above emotions within an environment that is safe and nurturing. In addition, school personnel can focus on self-esteem building, problem-solving, conflict resolution, and the development of self-efficacy (Mahat & Scoloveno, 2018). Play therapy is a recommended modality for children suffering from HIV infection (Rubin, 2017). Because many providers will be involved in the life of an HIV-infected child, an important part of the school's job is environmental engineering—keeping track of the services the child receives, avoiding duplication of services, and advocating for the child whenever a needed service is lacking.

Many of the above guidelines for working with HIV-infected children are also applicable to working with HIV-infected adolescents. In addition, schools need to consider the formation of intimate meaningful relationships, issues of sexual orientation, safer sex practices, as well as other risky behaviors. Depression and suicide are very real threats for HIV-positive adolescents. The dynamics of loss have to be considered when working with HIV-positive adolescents, because they may perceive themselves as being unable to enjoy a life like their peers in terms of intimate relationships, physical ability, and so on. They may also suffer from guilt, especially if the disease was contracted through unprotected sex or intravenous drug use (Bhana et al., 2020). As with children, the emotional reactions can be quite varied. By showing empathy, support, and unconditional acceptance, teachers and other school personnel can play a vital role in the lives of HIV-infected adolescents.

Teenage Pregnancy and Motherhood

The good news is that the teen birth rate has declined dramatically in the last 10 years and has been on the decline since the early 1990s. In 2018, the birth rate among women ages 15-19 was 18 births per 1000 girls, the lowest it has ever been and half of what it was in 2008. The most dramatic decline has been among Asian (74 percent) followed by Hispanics (65 percent). For Blacks and Whites the rate fell by more than 50 percent in the last 10 years (Horowitz & Graf, 2019). Nevertheless, Black and Hispanic teens have birth rates double that of Whites and five times higher than Asians (Horowitz & Graf, 2019). Greater and more effective use of contraception along pregnancy prevention programs are thought to be a significant contributor to the decline in teenage birth rates (Pew Research Center, 2019).

A Typology of Adolescent Pregnancy

Adolescent pregnancy and motherhood are the result of a complex interplay of social, cultural, economic, family, and biological factors. To understand this complexity, it may be helpful to distinguish three categories of adolescent pregnancy to include intentional, accidental, and uninformed (MacFarlane, 1995).

Intentional Pregnancy

This group of adolescents wants to become pregnant. Within this group, there are two subtypes, those whose culture accepts and even rewards early pregnancy; the other whose psychological needs are fulfilled through having a baby. As an example of the first group, Sciarra & Ponterotto (1998) found that early pregnancy and motherhood restored a sense of balance and stability to low-income Hispanic families. These were families living in areas of urban blight, and many of the adolescents' mothers felt that by having a child, their daughter would remain off the street because of her duties and responsibilities to the newborn child. The psychological needs that adolescents among the second subtype may seek to fulfill through an intentional pregnancy are listed below. How accurately one can determine the number of intentional or desired pregnancies is difficult to know. Many adolescents will consider their pregnancy intended or desired after the fact rather than admit it was a mistake; others might covertly desire the pregnancy and overtly deny it. This may be especially true in cases in which the adolescent decides to bring the pregnancy to term.

Psychological Needs Fulfilled by an Intentional Pregnancy

Power: Teens may perceive that pregnancy will enhance their power to make choices in their lives by giving them "adult" status.

Control: Teens may use pregnancy to control other people. The adolescent may use the pregnancy to force a boyfriend to marry her or compel her parents to comply with her wishes or desires.

Intimacy: Teens may equate sex with intimacy. Instead of developing intimacy and then becoming sexually active, teenagers may have the misunderstanding that sexual involvement creates emotional intimacy. Teens often believe that having a baby will create more intimacy with their sexual partner. Likewise, adolescent girls may feel that their child will help meet their needs for intimacy.

Escape: Teens may view pregnancy as an avenue of escape. Adolescents who are experiencing difficulties at home or who want to move out of their parents' homes may believe that pregnancy will allow them to move into another household or to establish a household of their own. Pregnancy may also allow teenagers to escape the expectations others have for them concerning achievement and status.

Rebellion: Pregnancy may also be a means of rebelling against parental authority. If teenagers know that their parents dislike their sexual partners or are opposed to them being sexually active or becoming pregnant, a pregnancy is the ultimate "in your face" act for a teenager.

Purpose: Pregnancy can be an avenue to form a relationship with someone who will love them and give them a sense of purpose in life.

Procreation: Teens may see pregnancy as a way to pass on part of themselves to the next generation. The infant becomes a symbol of making a lasting legacy or contribution.

From *All About Sex: The School Counselor's role to Handling Tough Adolescent Problems* (pp. 43-44) by L.J. Bradley, E. Harchow, and B. Robinson, 1999, Thousand Oaks, CA: Corwin Press. Copyright by Corwin Press. Reprinted with permission.

Accidental Pregnancy

This appears to be the most common category of adolescent pregnancy. These adolescents know and understand the proper use of contraceptives but take risks by using them haphazardly or not at all (MacFarlane, 1995). Sometimes drugs or alcohol are involved, which cloud judgment, cause impulsiveness, and prevent the proper use of contraception.

Uninformed (Misinformed) Pregnancy

This group of pregnant teens reports that if proper contraception information had been provided to them, they would not have become pregnant (MacFarlane, 1995). This group may not even have thought about pregnancy, because their ignorance allows them to believe that it can't happen if they have sex only once, or if it's their first time. Their knowledge is limited and often inaccurate.

Risk Factors Associated with Adolescent Pregnancy and Motherhood

All of the following have been found to increase the risk of bearing children during adolescence:

- Having a parent who was also a teenage parent
- Having a sibling who is (was) a teenage parent
- Coming from a single-parent family
- Coming from a family marked by marital strife, instability, and poor communication
- Lower educational and career opportunities
- Poor school performance
- Ethnicity
- Low socioeconomic status

When several of these factors are present in a single individual, the risk for adolescent childbearing is significantly increased. No one can underestimate the influence of poverty on adolescent motherhood, because the overwhelming majority of adolescent mothers are from poor and low-income families. Those adolescents who choose to abort their pregnancy are more likely to come from higher socioeconomic environments, be more successful in school, have parents and friends with positive attitudes toward abortion, reside in communities that provide accessible publicly funded abortions, and tend to have fewer friends or relations who are adolescent parents (Espinoza et al., 2020).

Consequences of Early Childbearing

The factors associated with early childbearing can appear so cogent that one may wonder to what extent it is preventable; yet the consequences of early childbearing are so overwhelmingly negative that one cannot easily relinquish prevention efforts. Adolescent mothers suffer significant socioeconomic, educational, health-related, and family development consequences (McWhirter et al., 2016).

Socioeconomic Consequences

An adolescent mother is much more likely to live in poverty than her older counterpart. Adolescent mothers receive a disproportionate share of public assistance (Medicaid, food stamps, etc.) and are more likely to live in inadequate housing, suffer poor nutrition and health, be unemployed or underemployed, out of school, and have inadequate career training (Erfina et al., 2019; McWhirter, et al., 2017). If adolescent mothers come from poor and low-income backgrounds, their own childbearing will continue the cycle of poverty.

Educational Consequences

Teen mothers are three times more likely to drop out of school than those who delay childbearing until their 20s (McWhirter et al., 2016). Many schools have begun to provide alternative schools or programs for adolescent mothers. These initiatives are more than likely responsible for the increase in teen mothers who complete high school; however, only a small percentage attends college. The teen mother's lack of education has consequences for her children, who evidence more behavioral problems in school (Agnafors et al., 2019), poor attendance, low grade-point averages, lower scores on standardized tests, and lower expectations for attending college (Mollborn, 2017).

Health-Related Consequences

Pregnant teens have more prenatal, perinatal, and postnatal problems than older mothers (McWhirter et al., 2017). Only one in five pregnant teens under the age of 15 receives any prenatal care during the first trimester (Chambers & Erausquin, 2018). Teen mothers are more likely to have complications related to prematurity, which increases the likelihood of delivering a low-birth-weight child (under 5.5 pounds), and low-birth-weight children are two to ten times more likely to have academic or behavioral problems (Chambers & Erausquin, 2018). Children born to mothers under the age of 17 have higher rates of injury, illness, and sudden infant death syndrome (SIDS) (Mello et al., 2019). African American and Hispanic teen mothers are more likely to receive late or no prenatal care than their European American counterparts (McWhirter, et al., 2017).

Family Development

Close to 90 percent of adolescent child-bearers are not married (Morris et al., 2019). Many teenage fathers relinquish their responsibilities and do little to provide a secure emotional and financial environment for their children (Sciarra & Ponterotto, 1998). Single-mothers who do work are forced to work long hours at low-paying jobs because of their lack of education. The stress of trying to raise children and be the sole economic provider is overwhelming for many adolescent mothers and makes the potential for child abuse greater (Morris et al., 2019). In short, there is a great deal more likelihood that children born to teen mothers will grow up in families marked by greater conflict and instability.

Working with the Adolescent Mother-to-be

Listed below are suggestions for helping the pregnant teen who has made the decision to bring her pregnancy to term. With regard to continuing her education, one adolescent mom had this to say about her education:

> Well, you know, I thought, if I'm being bad like this and am pregnant and am gonna be a mother, I need to give example to other kids. I changed so I could be an example, a good example. Then when my baby be born, you know, she grows up, they could talk good things about me, not bad. When I wasn't pregnant, I used to not care. But now, you know, 'cause I have a baby, I have to give an example to her, you know, and to other kids, get an education for the baby, so when the baby asks her [the mother] something, she'll know what to answer. Or if not, if she don't finish school, she'll be a dropout, the baby's gonna be a dropout. She'll tell her mother, "You were a dropout. Why can't I be too? If you left school, why can't I leave too?" (Sciarra & Ponterotto, 1998, p. 759).

Suggestions for Working with the Adolescent Mother-to-Be

Assess the client's immediate needs. Many pregnant teens may be confused about prenatal care. School personnel can help them see the importance of such care and direct them to places where they can receive it. If the adolescent is afraid to tell her parents and/or boyfriend, school personnel can help her to work through these fears, because avoiding such disclosure is not going to improve the situation.

Decide whom to notify. Depending on state regulations and school polices, the teen's parent may have to be notified. If the student wants to tell her parents and/or boyfriend but does not know how, the teacher can offer to be part of the meeting with the parent. The teacher can also do some role-plays with the student to anticipate the reactions of the other party and strategize how to deal with such reactions.

Identify supportive relationships. A student who becomes pregnant may experience the rejection of her peers or feel isolated because of her situation. Many community agencies run support groups for pregnant teens, and the school can refer the student.

Consider long-term options. As the pregnancy advances, the school should help the adolescent plan her educational future. A decision should be made as to whether the pregnant teen will attend the same school or an alternative school. Childcare arrangements should also be discussed, so the adolescent can continue to attend school after birth. Many alternative schools provide daycare in the school building. Although the data regarding education and adolescent motherhood are not encouraging, schools should help the pregnant teen understand that she can have her baby and also continue her education. Schools can also help with other long-term needs by making sure the adolescent receives any public assistance for which she qualifies, especially from the Special Supplemental Food Program for Women Infants, and Children (WIC).

Note: Adapted from All About Sex: The School Counselor's Role to Handling Tough Adolescent Problems by J.J. Bradley, E. Harchow, and B. Robinson, 1999.

When suggesting services to a pregnant teen or adolescent mother, the school should consider the following issues to include transportation, application for health care and related services, necessary legal documents (birth certificate, social security card) and verification for related services (Smith-Battle et al., 2017). Many of these issues can and should be handled by the school social worker if there is one. If not, the student can be referred to local social services department.

Working with Teen Fathers

Often, the teenage father is forgotten about in the discussion of adolescent pregnancy and motherhood. Teenage fathers are sometimes susceptible to the couvade syndrome, the presence of physical symptoms that occur in male partners or husbands of pregnant women (Bakermans-Kranenburg et al., 2019). These symptoms can include indigestion, colic, gastritis, nausea, vomiting, increased or decreased appetite, diarrhea, constipation, headache, dizziness, and cramping.

In his research on teen fathers, Goodyear (2002) found that they clustered into two groups. One group was more predatory, less loving and committed to their partners, less responsible as fathers, and more likely to view the pregnancy as an indication of their masculinity. The other group was found to be the opposite: less predatory, more loving and committed, more responsible, and less inclined to view the pregnancy as a symbol of masculinity (Goodyear, 2002).

Cultural factors may also be involved in the teen father's seeming lack of involvement in the pregnancy and birth of his child (Sciarra & Ponterotto, 1998). School counselors are more likely to refer teen mothers than teen fathers for health and basic living services. If schools are reluctant to include teen fathers as part of their interventions with teen mothers, they perhaps exclude a source of support for the well-being of the adolescent mothers and their children, especially if these fathers belong to the less predatory group.

As part of the couvade syndrome, teen fathers may avoid the women they have impregnated. Schools can play a critical role in mitigating this avoidance, especially if the teen father is also a student at the school. Teen fathers should not be allowed to shirk their responsibility. Teachers and other school professionals can help them understand the consequences of their actions and the responsibility that accompanies fathering a child.

Approaches to Sex Education

In the literature, three basic programs in schools can be identified to promote safer sex and prevent pregnancy to include (1) abstinence-only programs (or delay of sexual activity) that do not discuss contraception, (2) programs that discuss abstinence and contraception, with concrete information about the different kinds of contraception, and (3) comprehensive programs that provide information about abstinence, contraception, clinical services, and reproductive health education topics (McWhirter et al., 2017).

Abstinence-Only Programs

Abstinence-only programs of sex education are usually provided as part of a health education curriculum that requires teaching about the physiological aspects of sex and reproduction. Normally, in these programs, abstinence is discussed as the only acceptable way of preventing pregnancy and STDs. These programs avoid dealing with controversial issues such as contraception and homosexuality, often because school personnel fear the reaction of parents and other members of the community. There is no research to support the effectiveness of abstinence-only programs in delaying first intercourse or preventing teen pregnancy; however, some abstinence-only programs have been found to promote stronger abstinence attitudes and do increase knowledge about reproduction and the biological aspects of sexuality (Heels, 2019).

Knowledge of and Access to Contraception

These programs provide all the information of traditional programs but also discuss contraception and how to get it. Research has been inconclusive about the effectiveness of such programs because knowledge alone is only weakly related to behavior. Some of these programs have been found to change both behavior and attitudes, whereas others have not. Neither knowledge alone nor access alone seems to be an effective approach in changing sexual behavior. On the other hand, there is no evidence to suggest that a contraception component in sex education programs increases sexual activity (Goldfarb et al., 2019).

Some evidence has supported school-based clinics that offer comprehensive family planning and health services, including the dispensation of contraception, as having succeeded in lowering pregnancy rates and delaying the initiation of intercourse (Denford et al., 2017). Although recent years have seen a great deal of controversy and consequential decreases in the number of programs that include access to contraceptives, their use among adolescents has increased significantly but not always with a correlated decrease in pregnancy or HIV infection (Love et al., 2019). It may be that simply providing access is not sufficient, but it must occur within a more comprehensive, multicomponent approach to preventing teenage pregnancy and HIV infection.

Life Skills/Life Options Approach

This category designates comprehensive prevention programs that include aspects of the other two programs along with attitude and skill-building themes intended to promote more responsible decisions about sexual activity. These programs encourage abstinence and/or delay of sexual activity, provide concrete knowledge about contraception, and deal with nonsexual factors such as self-esteem building, decision-making skills, assertiveness training, and delineating a clear vision of a successful and self-sufficient future (McWhirter et al., 2004, 2017). Much of the information imparted in these programs is applied to the student's personal situation through discussion, role plays, behavior simulation, and drama. These programs promote self-understanding through the examination of sexual attitudes and behaviors. Besides dealing with sexual matters, the life skills/life options programs also include a career component designed to help at-risk adolescents become more aware of job opportunities and promote a clearer vision of the future. Some programs even provide a part-time work experience along with remedial education in reading and math.

Many such programs exist, such as Youth Incentive Entitlement Employment Program (YIEPP), Teen Outreach Program (TOP), the American Youth and Conservation Corps, the Seattle Social Development Program, and the Quantum Opportunities Program. Comprehensive prevention programs are the most effective in reducing pregnancy and childbearing and promoting safer sex (Denford et al., 2017).

School Violence

Case Examples: Eric Harris and Dylan Klebold

The account by Cullen (2019), offers the most introspective reporting available. In Littleton, Colorado, April 20, 1999, promised to be just another day for the people of this Heartland community, one replete with good, law-abiding citizens, good schools, all American values, and good students. At 11:19 a.m., however, as many students in the local high school were in the cafeteria eating lunch, two young men, clothed in black trench coats and carrying a duffle bag and a backpack, but otherwise unremarkable, proceeded to create havoc for hundreds of innocent students and teachers and forever changed the notion that schools are a sanctuary - a safe place to learn and grow.

After the carnage, during which 188 rounds of ammunition and many small home-made bombs were expended or detonated, twelve students and one teacher lay dead, and twenty-five others had been wounded (Cullen, 2019). The perpetrators, two seniors, Eric Harris and Dylan Klebold, subsequently committed suicide. This seminal event in the annals of school violence represents a disturbing turning point. Whereas the incidence of school violence has declined over the last twenty years, the lethality of its consequences has sharply increased, as demonstrated by the carnage meted out by Harris and Klebold.

At first, school officials as well as the media portrayed these two young men as aberrations, misfits who seemed harmless enough. School officials, law enforcement officers, and parents defended themselves against assignations of blame by insisting they could never have predicted such a devastating outcome, based on the two boys' conduct and demeanor right up to their murderous spree (Cullen, 2019). These stakeholders maintained that the boys had played their parts very well and thus obscured their true feelings and intentions.

And yet, a closer examination of the facts reveals an entirely different profile of the two perpetrators. Both young men demonstrated a penchant for violence, had advocated and eagerly anticipated the annihilation of humankind in poetical and prosaic rants on the Internet, and had engaged in vandalizing homes as well as breaking and entering and theft (Cullen, 2019). The county record is available to the public and clearly details the nature of the offense for which both boys received ten months in the juvenile diversion program, which required that they perform community service and attend counseling sessions as well as anger-management training. In fact, Harris and Klebold had so thoroughly convinced the diversion officer assigned to them of their successful rehabilitation that on their release from the program, he noted optimistically that "Eric is a bright young man who is likely to succeed in life. Dylan is a very bright young man who has a great deal of potential." The juvenile justice system and the school, however, apparently missed the fact that the boys had been stockpiling weapons and constructing bombs in their own homes for months prior to the execution of their homicidal plan (Cullen, 2019). Likewise, they missed the fact that Harris had been in therapy and was taking Luvox to combat depression (Bai, 1999; Cullen, 2019).

It is our contention that both boys clearly displayed sociopathic tendencies that should, at minimum, have prompted teachers and administrators to recommend them for special education services under the classification of emotionally disturbed. The services provided to students who have been so diagnosed typically include counseling, which might have helped to avert this terrible tragedy. Sadly, this never happened.

In responding to incidents of school violence like that at Columbine and increasing concerns about the rising incidence of bullying in schools, teachers, and school professionals will benefit from the important information that follows.

Introduction

According to Villarreal (2004), the "Center for the Prevention of School Violence (CPSV) (2020), school violence is any behavior that violates a school's educational mission or climate of respect or jeopardizes the intent of the school to be free of aggression against person or property, drugs, weapons, disruptions, and disorder" (p. 2). One might rightly infer that within this definition bullying, sexual harassment, and abuse directed against LGBTQ students must be included.

This section is written from the perspective that any student behavior that creates a hostile school environment for another student is considered school violence. In one report, 12 percent of teens said the behavior of students in their school was a positive influence, while 40 percent said it interfered with their performance, and almost one in five students reported being threatened with a beating (U.S. Departments of Education and Justice, 2020). Summarized below is important data on school violence and safety.

Summary of Data on School Violence

Crime at School	• The most common criminal incidents in school are theft, larceny, and physical attack/fight without a weapon • Younger students (ages 12-14) are more likely than older students to be victims of crime at school • The percentage of students reporting any criminal victimization declined from 4 percent in 2009 to 2 percent in 2019
Teacher Victimization	• Secondary school teachers were more likely than elementary school teachers to have been threatened with injury by a student. However, elementary school teachers were more likely than secondary school teachers to report having been physically attacked • Approximately, 80 percent of the crimes against teacher are neither violent nor serious; 66 percent of the crimes are theft. • More male than female teachers report having been threatened with injury, but female teachers were more likely than their male counterparts to have been physically attacked. • Central city teachers are more likely to be victims of violent crime than urban fringe, suburban and rural teachers
School Environment	• The percentage of public schools experiencing one or more violent incidents was 81 percent. • An estimated 160,00 students skip school daily for fear of physical harm • Black and Hispanic students fear more for their safety than White students

- The percentage of students who reported that street gangs were present at their schools was 24 percent
- In recent years, the percentage of students carrying a weapon such as a gun, knife or club to school has been about 10 percent
- Bullying and sexual harassment are by far the most common forms of school violence reported by students. Seventy-five percent of students report having been bullied at some point in their schooling, and 81 percent of female students report some form of sexual harassment in school or on school grounds
- Gay students are the most frequent victims of hate crimes occurring at school and skip school at a rate of five times more than heterosexual students because of personal safety concerns
- About 13 percent of students experience hate-related words in school, and 38 percent report having seen hate-related graffiti in school

---

Source: U.S. Departments of Education and Justice (2020). *Indicators of school crime and safety, 2020.* Retrieved from https://nces.ed.gov/programs/crimeindicators/2020.

The chapter on CD (Chapter 2) discussed at length the many factors that research has implicated in the etiology of violence and aggression. Recent research allows us to conclude that certain factors are stronger predictors than others, and a factor's strength depends on the age of the child. To reiterate, risk factors involved in youth violence create a complicated picture. Some factors are stronger predictors at a certain age than at another age. The most significant factors appear to be

- Parental attitudes that are favorable towards violence
- Parental criminality
- Poor family management practices
- Low commitment to schooling
- Having delinquent friends
- Sensation seeking and involvement in drug selling
- Gang membership
- Hyperactivity or attention deficits

The more risk factors a student possesses, the greater is the potential for violent behavior.

Early Warning Signs

In 1998, the U.S. Department of Education and the U.S. Department of Justice published a well-received document entitled, *Early Warning, Timely Response: A Guide to Safe Schools* (Dwyer et al., 1998). The document began by listing sixteen early warning signs of aggressive and violent behavior. Schools might consider posting these warning signs on the walls of offices or creating a handout to be available to students, teachers, and parents in the literature rack of the counseling office. The sixteen early warning signs of violent behavior are listed below.

The Sixteen Early Warning Signs of Aggressive and Violent Behavior

1. Social withdrawal
2. Excessive feelings of isolation and being alone
3. Excessive feelings of rejection
4. Being a victim of violence
5. Feeling picked on and persecuted
6. Low school interest and poor academic performance
7. Expression of violence in writings and drawings
8. Uncontrolled anger
9. Patterns of impulsive and chronic hitting, intimidating, and bullying behaviors
10. History of discipline problems
11. History of violent and aggressive behaviors
12. Intolerance for differences and prejudicial attitudes
13. Drug use and alcohol use
14. Affiliation with a gang
15. Inappropriate access to, possession of, and use of firearms
16. Serious threats of violence

Source: Dwyer, K., Osher, D., & Warger, C. (1998). *Early warning, timely response: A guide to safe schools* (pp. 14–17). Washington, DC: U.S. Department of Education.

Imminent Warning Signs

Imminent warning signs mean that a student is close to behavior that is dangerous to himself or herself and others (Dwyer et al. 2000). These signs require an immediate response on the part of the school and the student's family. Imminent warning signs include:

- Serious physical fighting with peers or family members
- Severe destruction of property
- Severe rage for seemingly minor reasons
- Detailed threats of lethal violence
- Possession and/or use of firearms and other weapons
- Other self-injurious behaviors or threats of suicide (Dwyer et al., 1998)

Law enforcement should be called to the school when a student is carrying a weapon and has threatened to use it, and/or has presented a detailed plan (i.e., a designated time, place, and method) to harm or kill others. If imminent signs other than these two are present, school personnel should immediately inform the parents and help arrange for assistance from appropriate agencies, such as child and family services and community mental health. The National School Safety Center (1998) provides a comprehensive checklist to help schools assess a student's potential for violence.

Checklist of Characteristics of Youth Who Have Caused School-Associated Violent Deaths

1. Has a history of tantrums and uncontrollable angry outbursts
2. Characteristically resorts to name-calling, cursing, or abusive language
3. Habitually makes violent threats when angry
4. Has previously brought a weapon to school
5. Has a background of serious disciplinary problems at school and in the community
6. Has a background of drug, alcohol, or other substance abuse or dependency
7. Is on the fringe of his or her peer group, with few or no close friends
8. Is preoccupied with weapons, explosives, or other incendiary devices
9. Has previously been truant, suspended, or expelled from school
10. Displays cruelty to animals
11. Has little or no supervision and support from parents or a caring adult
12. Has witnessed or been a victim of abuse or neglect in the home
13. Has been bullied and/or bullies or intimidates peers or younger children
14. Tends to blame others for difficulties and problems that he causes himself
15. Consistently prefers TV shows, movies, or music that expresses violent themes and acts
16. Prefers reading materials that deal with violent themes, rituals, and abuse
17. Reflects anger, frustration, and the dark side of life in school essays or writing projects
18. Is involved with a gang or an antisocial group on the fringe of peer acceptance

19. Is often depressed and/or has significant mood swings
20. Has threatened or attempted suicide

Source: National School Safety Center (1998). *Checklist of characteristics of youth who have caused school-associated violent deaths.* Retrieved from http://www.schoolsafety.us/Checklist-of-Characteristics-of-Youth-Who-Have-Caused-School-Associated-Violent-Deaths-p-7.html.

Evaluating and Responding to Threats of Violence

In schools, the number of threats of violence far surpasses the number of violent incidents. On the one hand, this is fortunate, because the risk of lethal violence in schools is very low; on the other hand, threats of violence are quite common and are potentially a problem in any school. Therefore, schools need an informed way of dealing with threats. Much of what follows in this section is based on *The School Shooter: A Threat Assessment Perspective* (National Center for the Analysis of Violent Crime [NCAVC], 2001). The document is the result of studying eighteen schools throughout the country. At fourteen of these schools, actual shootings occurred; at the other four, a student(s) made significant preparations but was detected and preempted by law enforcement officers. The NCAVC defines a threat as "an expression of intent to do harm or act out violently against someone or something. A threat can be spoken, written, or symbolic—for example, motioning with one's hands as though shooting another person" (p. 6). Much like those who threaten suicide, those who threaten violence are not all equal and therefore each threat must be assessed for its own seriousness.

Threats can be direct ("I'm going to place a bomb on the top shelf in the reference section of the library"), indirect ("If I wanted to, I could blow this place up"), veiled ("This place would be much better off if you weren't a teacher here"), or conditional ("If you call my parents, I'm gonna shoot you"). Threats are more serious if they contain specific plausible detail, the emotional state of the threatener is questionable, and there are identifiable precipitating stressors.

According to the NCAVC (2001), threats can be divided into three levels of risk to include low (threat poses minimal risk to the victim and public safety), medium (a threat that could be carried out), and high (a threat that poses an imminent and serious danger to the safety of others. An example of a high level of threat would be "Tomorrow at 7:30 in the morning, I'm going to shoot Mrs. Wilson because at that time she is always in her homeroom by herself. I have a 9-mm. Believe me, I'm gonna do it. I'm sick and tired of the way she treats me." The parallels to the assessment process for suicide risk are obvious

- The more direct and detailed the plan, the more serious is the risk. Personality, family, school, and social factors (as outlined earlier in this chapter) need to be considered in order to properly assess the student making the threat and to better judge its seriousness. The characteristics for each level of risk are listed below.

Characteristics of Low, Medium, and High Levels of Threat

Low Level of Threat

- The threat is vague and indirect.
- Information in the threat is inconsistent, implausible, or lacks detail.
- The threat lacks realism.
- The content of the threat suggests the person is unlikely to carry it out.

Medium Level of Threat

- The threat is more direct and more concrete than a low-level threat.
- The wording of the threat suggests that the threatener has given some thought to carrying out the act.
- There may be a general indication of a possible place and time.
- There is no strong indication that the threatener has taken preparatory steps, although there may be some veiled reference or ambiguous or inconclusive evidence pointing to that possibility—an allusion to a book or movie that shows the planning of a violent act, or a value, general statement about the availability of weapons.
- There may be a specific statement seeking to convey that the threat is not empty: "I'm serious" or "I really mean this."

High Level of Threat

- The threat is direct, specific, and plausible.
- The threat suggests that concrete steps have been taken toward carrying it out—for example, a statement indicating that the threatener has acquired or practiced with a weapon or has had the victim under surveillance.

Source: National Center for the Analysis of Violent Crime (2001). *The school shooter: A threat assessment perspective* (pp. 8–9). Retrieved from www.fbi.gov/library/schools/school2.

Threat Management in Schools

To properly manage threats in a school, the NCACV (2001) recommended the following guidelines.

- **Inform students and parents of school policies.** Schools should publicize a threat response and intervention policy at the beginning of each school year. The school's policy should detail how the school evaluates threats and responds to them. Students and parents should receive a clear message that any threat will be reported, investigated, and dealt with in an efficient and uncompromising fashion.

- **Designate a threat assessment coordinator.** This person, having received appropriate threat assessment training, should oversee and coordinate the school's response to all threats. Any student who makes a threat should be referred to the coordinator, who will assess the level of threat, evaluate the threatener, plan and monitor interventions, and maintain close relationships with community resources, especially in terms of getting help with a high-level threat that requires the involvement of law enforcement officers.

- **Facilitate leakage**. "Leakage" refers to students who reveal threats made by another student to the proper authorities. Students are in the best position to see and hear signs of potential violence, and schools must help and support them in breaking the "code of silence." In the same way that students are taught to reveal their friends who are in trouble (thinking of suicide, suffering physical or sexual abuse, etc.), they should understand the importance of revealing threats. A common strategy is for students to imagine the threatened scenario taking place: "If so and so really did such and such, you knew about it and didn't tell anyone, think for a minute the burden you would carry for the rest of your life. True friends help and protect other friends from endangering themselves and others."

- **Consider forming a multidisciplinary team**. In addition to the threat assessment coordinator, schools can form teams drawn from school staff and other professionals in mental health and law enforcement. The team can review threats, consult with experts, and provide recommendations and advice to the coordinator and/or school administration. These functions can be part of a general crisis response team that deals with other problems such as suicide. Proper intervention must go beyond disciplinary action to deal with the emotional turmoil that causes a student to make threats.

The NCACV (2001) described succinctly the role of disciplinary action:

> It is especially important that a school not deal with threats by simply kicking the problem out the door. Expelling or suspending a student for making a threat must not be a substitute for careful threat assessment and a considered, consistent policy of intervention. Disciplinary action alone, unaccompanied by any effort to evaluate the threat or the student's intent, may actually exacerbate the danger—for example, if a student feels unfairly or arbitrarily treated and becomes even angrier and more bent on carrying out a violent act (n.p.).

Ineffective Approaches to School Violence

Zero Tolerance Policies and Students with Disabilities

Currently, little research has supported the effectiveness of zero-tolerance policies in preventing school violence (Kyere et al., 2020; McAndrews, 2001; Skiba & Peterson, 1999; Smothers, 2000). In the case of students who have disabilities who transgress school discipline policies and are removed from school, there is a required course of action that involves the development of a functional behavioral assessment (FBA) from which a positive behavioral intervention plan or positive behavior supports (PBS) plan is implemented, regardless of the cause of the removal. Such a plan should ideally include multiple strategies that include teaching pro-social behaviors and do not rely on coercion and punishment to affect such change (Kyere et al., 2020). Moreover, behavioral plans that simply describe the misconduct and its consequences are out of compliance with the federal Individuals with Disabilities Education Act (IDEA, 2004). In addition, the IDEA (2004) further legislates that school personnel responsible for the education of students displaying problem behaviors receive adequate training in both the development of an FBA as well as the implementation of effective behavioral interventions (Kyere et al., 2020). Such a shift in focus from intolerance to intervention should obviate the need for a school culture based on consequences. What the literature has recommended, in contrast to ineffective zero-tolerance policies, are programs that seek to provide an understanding of the conditions that incubate school violence and thus preempt their development at the very earliest stages. The following is a synthesis of some of the best practices endorsed by research as being effective in helping prevent school violence.

Effective Approaches to School Violence

A comprehensive examination of the research that supports the most effective practices in preventing violence in schools revealed that most could be organized according to discrete categories, including (1) the effective use of functional behavioral analysis and behavioral intervention plans, (2) screening for risk factors, (3) teaching acceptance of diversity, (4) self-esteem building and social skills training, (5) conflict resolution through peer mediation, (6) the importance of family and community involvement, and (7) the classroom as community. Ideally, schools should incorporate as many of these components as possible in the development of their school-wide violence prevention programs. An overview of each of the recommended components follows.

Effective Use of Functional Behavioral Assessment

First, in accordance with IDEA (2004), students who show a tendency toward the commission of violent acts should be prescribed a functional behavioral analysis (FBA) to determine the various antecedents that may have some bearing on the cause as well as the purpose of the behavior. Once a cause or purpose has been identified, then an appropriate behavioral intervention plan (BIP) must be developed to help the student learn an alternate and pro-social means of obtaining his or her goal. The BIP must be effectively implemented and monitored by all stakeholders, which presumes that school personnel has received training in both the creation and use of this behavior-change technique (Kyere et al., 2020).

Screening for Risk Factors

Effective prevention through screening for various predisposing factors that suggest the potential for violent behavior has also been recommended in the literature (Welsh et al., 2008). Research has led to the recommendation of several approaches that have shown some predictive reliability in identifying students who are most likely to commit violent acts (Burns et al., 2001). The most promising of these include

- Informal early-warning checklists and profiling characteristics and conditions (Hazler & Carney, 2000; Spivak & Prothrow-Stith, 2001);
- The *Systematic Screening for Behavior Disorders* (SSBD) checklist (Caldarella et al., 2014);

- The *My Worst School Experience Scale* (MWSES; Albuquerque & Williams, 2018); and
- The *Pathways of Ideas and Behaviors* approach (Borum et al., as cited in Burns et al., 2001).

The goal of the first two of these predictive instruments, informal checklists, and profiling characteristics of the SSBD (Caldarella et al., 2014), is to identify students who may engage in violent behaviors for the purpose of providing primary intervention. The limitation inherent in assembling a checklist or profile is always the tendency to overidentify relative to the rather generalized quality of the characteristics. Further, it is difficult to establish predictive validity for checklists based on characteristics apparent in violent students. Nevertheless, the SSBD (Caldarella et al., 2014) shows promise as a predictive instrument, principally because it is based on the antecedent behaviors of at-risk students.

Research has suggested that previous behavior is the most reliable predictor of future behavior (Burns et al., 2001). The MWSES (Albuquerque & Williams, 2018) is derived from scales that assess educator-induced posttraumatic stress disorder. While reliability levels are reported as being relatively high, the newness of the scale has resulted in limited data from which to assess construct validity; however, researchers are optimistic about its usefulness in the early identification of students who are at risk for violent behavior. The concept of a "threat assessment" approach, which bypasses profiling characteristics in favor of the determination of a behavioral "process" leading to violence, represents a promising preventative measure. One version of this approach employs a ten-question survey, which helps the assessor determine whether the student has sufficient predisposing factors for the commission of a violent act as well as the means to do so (access to a weapon, a viable plan, a support system, etc.).

Other predictive systems involve reconceptualizing threat assessment as "risk management" (Mulvey & Cauffman, 2001). This perspective acknowledges that risk for violent behavior is a dynamic process requiring an ongoing evaluation of the factors that increase such risk for children and youth who have been categorized as high-risk. Thus, the process starts with a risk assessment of the individual, which identifies high- or low-risk status, followed by close monitoring of changes that might signal a violent episode.

Some researchers caution that no one method of risk assessment for the commission of violence is defensibly superior because of the low base rate of violent acts committed in schools; however, an array of effective risk assessment and management strategies is clearly recommended as a preemptive measure (Monahan et al., 2001). In addition, any risk screening instrument used by schools should meet two criteria. First, it must produce reliable assessment; and second, it must provide quality data that facilitate the development of an effective intervention. Finally, effective risk assessment should consider the effect of a school's ability to provide early intervention as well as the existing climate and discipline policy in the school.

Violence prevention programs are proliferating in schools across the United States; however, more valuable to the practitioner than specific program descriptions is a delineation of the components that make them effective. The following is a discussion and synthesis of some of the more promising themes repeated in many of the programs.

Teaching Acceptance of Diversity

An important aspect of any violence prevention program is helping students to appreciate diversity across the spectrum of difference that encompasses race, ethnicity, learning, and gender (Banks, 2004). This can be accomplished best by teaching children at an early age to celebrate and understand diversity. The current trend toward inclusive education represents a positive move in that direction. Similarly, placing diverse students in learning groups helps to reduce stigmatization and prejudice, which are especially prevalent among very young students. Finally, teaching students social and self-management skills as well as providing them with a vocabulary that facilitates a meaningful discussion of diversity issues is critical to this process (Banks, 2004).

Self-Esteem Building and Social Skills Training

The Resolving Conflict Creatively Program (RCCP) prescribes a K–12 classroom curriculum that incorporates the skills of empathy, active listening, assertiveness, the expression of feeling in appropriate ways, perspective-taking, cooperation, and negotiation (Brown et al., 2004). In a related study, students who had emotional disorders (ED) acted as student trainers to teach appropriate social interactions to peers who had ED. The results showed that both peer trainers and student trainees derived benefit from such a program, displaying improved social skills that were maintained and generalized across settings. Similar programmatic research has suggested that effective anti-violence interventions involve teaching students alternative ways to express anger and frustration, how to make effective nonviolent choices rather than simply reacting to emotional stimuli, and, through modeling, how to deal proactively with feelings of anger, frustration, and impatience (Chalamandaris & Piette, 2015).

As noted by Speaker and Petersen (2000), the five-factor model for violence and suicide reduction requires the important step of creating a student success identity that flows from a sense of responsibility for oneself and one's environment. A sense of self-esteem and self-worth is linked to the development of the awareness of one's potential for success and contributes significantly to reduced participation in violent acts (Speaker & Petersen, 2000).

Similarly, Edwards (2001) stated that children should be provided opportunities to develop resilience within the school curriculum. Resilience has been shown to help students deal positively with disruptive circumstances at home or in school that might otherwise result in misbehavior and violence. A further benefit of resilience is its correlation to the development of ancillary strengths such as social competence, problem-solving skills, a critical consciousness, responsible autonomy, and a sense of purpose (Masten & Barnes, 2018).

Likewise, embedded in social competence are empathy, communication skills, flexibility, responsiveness, and a sense of humor. Problem-solving skills refer to the ability to make meaningful plans, be resourceful, and think creatively. A critical consciousness involves the intrinsic awareness of the sources of oppression in one's life such as abusive parents, unreasonable teachers, and an elitist student culture. Students who are autonomous have succeeded in developing an internal locus of control and, ultimately, a sense of self-efficacy; therefore, resilient students are not influenced by destructive criticism, nor are they victims of pathological relationships (Masten & Barnes, 2018). For this reason, they are less likely to engage in violent or antisocial behaviors as a means of retaliation.

Conflict Resolution Through Peer Mediation

A significant component of many violence prevention programs is conflict resolution, most typically accomplished using some form of peer mediation (Schellenberg et al., 2007; Sellman, 2011). Peer mediation is described in both the RCCP (Lantieri, 1998) and the *S.T.O.P. the Violence* (Lovell & Richardson, 2001) programs. The rationale that supports the value of peer mediation has evolved from a growing belief that students should be included in the school as participants in policymaking and community building. As such, they should have a role in the development of a nonviolent inclusive atmosphere (Schellenberg et al., 2007; Sellman, 2011).

The function of a peer mediator is simply to provide fair and impartial arbitration in an atmosphere that requires a civil and nonviolent presentation of both sides of a disputed issue. The value of this student-chaired mediation is that it facilitates an open and unabridged meeting of the two disputants without the fear of disciplinary repercussions, provided the rules of mediation are followed. The success rate of this intervention in defusing potentially violent student confrontations is remarkably good (Schellenberg et al., 2007; Sellman, 2011).

The Importance of Family and Community Involvement

Two of the five critical factors identified in one study as the principal causes of school violence were (1) a decline in family structure and (2) family violence and drug use (Speaker & Petersen, 2000). If the family is a catalyst of violence that can generalize to the school, it seems prudent to include its constituents in any prevention program. Further, besides acting as a clearinghouse for essential family services such as health care and family counseling, schools should provide opportunities for families to be involved during instructional time as well as in after-school activities such as parent volunteers for various in-school duties and after-school tutoring, and as chaperones for special events.

Violence prevention plans are most effective when they involve all the key stakeholders: families, administrators, teachers, and students, as well as the community. Because research has suggested a correlation between violence committed by youth in the community as well as in the school, students who commit violent acts in the community are more likely to do the same in school and vice versa (Lesneskie & Block, 2017). Partnerships, therefore, between local law enforcement, business, social service agencies, teachers, administrators, and families create a sense of shared purpose and collaboration in reducing both school and community violence.

The Classroom as Community

Finally, an essential component of any violence prevention program is *community building*. Earlier studies have supported the notion of the importance of developing a positive school climate; one that honors diversity, provides a forum for dissidence, and values the contributions of every student (Church, 2015). Similarly, educators need to address the purpose of classroom management. In an innovative approach to this issue, Kohn (2006) has suggested that teachers determine whether their goal is to inculcate compliance or encourage democratic skills engendered through partnership with and empowerment of their students.

The principles espoused by Dewey (1899) are not out of step with the issues of violence prevention facing schools at the dawn of the twenty-first century. Nor is it anachronistic to describe schools as moral communities in which the constituents care for each other, where acceptance is unconditional, and where the struggles of the individual member become the concerns of all. Indeed, according to Dewey (1899) and others, schools should have the same imperatives as a democratic society, where individual freedoms are safeguarded, and the rights of the majority of students and faculty are protected. Similarly, students who feel that they are valued members of a community of learners may experience the power of choice derived from an internal locus of control and thus will be more likely to eschew violence and antisocial behavior (Austin, 2003; Church, 2015; Kent & Simpson, 2012; Kohn, 1996).

Bullying

One of the leading researchers on bullying is the Norwegian Dan Olweus. According to Olweus (1992), a student is bullied or victimized "when he or she is exposed, repeatedly and over time to negative actions on the part of one of more other persons" (p. 101). These negative actions are understood as intentionally inflicting or attempting to inflict injury or discomfort on another. Behaviors perpetrated toward the victim may be physical (e.g., hitting, kicking, pushing, choking), verbal (e.g., name calling, taunting, malicious teasing, threatening, spreading nasty rumors), or other types, such as obscene gestures, making faces, or keeping someone isolated from a group (Olweus, 2004). These latter, more subtle forms are referred to as *indirect bullying*, in contrast to *direct bullying*, which denotes more active attacks on the victim. Bullying is found among both boys and girls, although among girls the forms of bullying tend to be more subtle.

It may be difficult for parents and school personnel to distinguish between normal teasing and bullying. A series of questions to help educators make this distinction is listed below. If the agent's behavior is in the direction of age-inappropriate, negative, intense, and frequent, then it is better understood as bullying rather than teasing.

The effects of bullying on the victim are both short- and long-term. The short-term effects include unhappiness, pain and humiliation, confusion, distress, loss of self-esteem, anxiety, insecurity, loss of concentration, and refusal to go to school. Some victims develop psychosomatic complaints such as headaches and stomachaches. The psychological consequences of being bullied are serious, as victims begin to feel stupid, ashamed, and unattractive, and see themselves as failures (Olweus, 2004). Regarding long-term effects, Olweus (1993) found that young adults at the age of 23 who had been bullied in grades 6 through 9 were more depressed and suffered lower self-esteem than their nonvictim counterparts.

How to Distinguish Bullying from Normal Teasing

1. What is the nature of the behavior in question? Is it age-appropriate? To whom is it directed? Is it specific to one gender or both? Is it directed toward vicinity-aged peers or those younger or older in age? What is the content of the behavior?
2. What is the level of intensity of the behavior? What are the specifics of the behavior? Is the behavior verbal, physical, or psychological? Is the behavior seemingly done in a humorous fashion or with anger, harshness, or malicious intent by the agent?
3. How often does the behavior occur? Is this a frequent occurrence or an isolated incident? Are there times when the behavior occurs more often?
4. How does the target of the agent's behavior respond? Is the target upset or offended by the behavior? Does the target understand the behavior? Does the target reciprocate in kind to the agent? How does the agent respond to the target's attempts at self-defense against the behavior?

Source: Roberts, W. B., Jr., & Morotti, A. A. (2000). The bully as victim: Understanding bully behaviors to increase the effectiveness of interventions in the bully-victim dyad. *Professional School Counseling, 4*(2), 150. Copyright by the American School Counselor Association.

Who Bullies and Why

Bullies tend to possess certain characteristics. However, the seriousness and pervasiveness of their bullying depends on environmental factors such as the school's tolerance for such behaviors, teacher attitudes, the arrangement of break periods, and so on. As indicated in the previous section on predictors of violence, the influence of the early home environment cannot be underestimated. Bullies learn their behaviors early in life and tend to come from home environments that are quite harsh (Fekkes et al., 2005; Frisén et al., 2007), where punishment is usually physical and capricious. The home environment is filled with criticism, sarcasm, and put-downs (Fekkes et al., 2005; Frisén et al., 2007), and there is a general absence of warmth and nurturing. As a result, a personality is formed around the belief and justification that intimidation and force are the ways to deal with life's challenges (Roberts & Morotti, 2000). Through the dynamics of projective identification, the bully tends to prey on the less powerful, who remind the bully of his or her own vulnerability. "Bullies, through attacking the weaknesses of others, are striking out against the shame and humiliation they feel for their own inability to defend themselves against their abusers" (Roberts & Morotti, 2000, p. 151).

Unfortunately, the bully's behavior is often reinforced by parents, peers, and the media. The bully's parents often defend their child's behaviors as sticking up for himself. The parents themselves have modeled such behaviors; therefore, they find it hard to disapprove of it. Some of the bully's peers may take delight in seeing another student victimized and encourage the bully to continue the victimization. The media is also guilty of portraying behaviors common to the bully as appropriate ways to deal with difficult and challenging situations.

Who Gets Bullied and Why

Because bullying affects many students, it is somewhat difficult to profile the typical victim. Hanish and Guerra (2000) examined the variables of children at risk for victimization along four dimensions: demographic characteristics, behavioral characteristics, peer group dynamics, and school structure influences.

Demographic Characteristics

Younger children are more vulnerable to peer victimization than older children, because younger children are less apt to have developed protection skills. Bullying in elementary school, however, is generally transient and relatively untargeted. Fewer older children are victimized, but when bullying does occur, it remains more stable over time (Fekkes et al., 2005; Frisén et al., 2007). There are also gender differences in the type of victimization experienced. Boys are more likely to be physically victimized, whereas girls are more likely to be sexually and relationally victimized (i.e., gossiped about, excluded from activities, and sexually harassed) (Fekkes et al., 2005; Frisén et al., 2007). In terms of race and ethnicity, Xu et al. (2020) found that more research is needed to determine to what degree race and ethnicity are significant variables in school victimization.

Behavioral Characteristics

Some children are victimized because they are perceived as being unable to defend themselves. They may be physically weak, submit easily to peer demands, be rejected by peers, and have few friends (Fekkes et al., 2005; Frisén et al., 2007; Olweus, 1993). Also, aggressiveness has been found to increase the likelihood of being victimized (Fekkes et al., 2005; Frisén et al., 2007). Aggressive behaviors can annoy and alienate others, leaving the student without support and therefore vulnerable to bullies. Students who are socially withdrawn, shy, or unsure of themselves are also at risk of being victimized. Social withdrawal is a stronger risk factor among older children (Fekkes et al., 2005; Frisén et al., 2007). Contrary to popular belief, there is little empirical support that students who are fat, wear glasses, speak with an unusual dialect, or have a different ethnic background are more likely to be bullied (Olweus et al., 1999).

Peer Group Dynamics. As mentioned earlier, peers can display a spectrum of reactions to bullying. Estimates are that peer protection occurs in less than 15 percent of bullying incidents (Salmivalli, 2014). Peers may be distressed by the bullying, but active defense against the bully is relatively uncommon. On the contrary, peers may encourage the bullying. Bullying can be the result of wanting to attain or maintain a position of influence and power among peers in the school (Salmivalli, 2014). If the bullied one does not have an active support group, the victimization will remain more stable over time; therefore, have more significant consequences for the victim.

School Structure Influences

Unfortunately, schools provide environmental influences that can sometimes be conducive to bullying. Unsupervised time allows the bully opportunities to prey on victims and causes most incidents to happen in hallways, during change of classes, and on the playground (Salmivalli, 2014). In addition, victims are reluctant to report the bully's behavior for fear of reprisal (Salmivalli, 2014). Bullying, therefore, can occur even on a large scale without the knowledge of school officials.

The Victim-Turned-Aggressor

By its very definition, bullying is intense and sustained; therefore, the victim finds it impossible to be indifferent to the harassment. Although many victims will manifest negative symptoms (withdrawal, depression, truancy, dropping out of school, and even suicide), some will turn aggressor and, in some rare instances, commit deadly school violence. A significant number of school shooters have had a history of being bullied; therefore, the victim-turned-aggressor has become a concern in many schools.

Several experts on violence have suggested that suicide and deadly revenge are the result of the same psychodynamics operating within the victim (Hazler & Carney, 2000; Jordan & Austin, 2012). In other words, the risk factors for the level of aggression against the self and others are the same. Hazler and Carney (2000) have categorized these risk factors as biological, psychological, cognitive, and environmental.

Biological Risk

Reaching the age of puberty increases the risk level for victims turned aggressors. Hormonal fluctuations along with rapid physical and psychological changes can increase the individual's level of hostility and desire for revenge.

Psychological/Cognitive Risk

If the victim is severely depressed, a sense of hopelessness and negative self-evaluation increases the risk level for serious aggression. The victim may reason that if life is not worth living, what's the difference if they were to kill themself as well as those who have been tormenting them. Often, an accompaniment to depression is cognitive rigidity, an example of which is seeing revenge as the only option, and which can lead a victim to serious aggression against others. Michael Carneal, after killing three of his fellow students in Paducah, Kentucky, cried out "Kill me now. Shoot me." (Hazler & Carney, 2000).

Environmental Risk

Both family factors and poor peer relationships can elevate the risk of violent aggression. Families with poor problem-solving skills that do not encourage assertiveness make it hard for the victim to learn alternative ways of dealing with conflict (Hazler & Carney, 2000). Isolation from peers also increases the risk of perpetrating deadly violence (Hazler, 1996; Jordan & Austin, 2012). Many school shooters could not rely even on one friend to provide a safety net and prevent tragedy from occurring.

Bullying And Students Who Have Disabilities

Students who have disabilities, particularly those who have emotional or behavioral disorders, appear more likely to be either bullies or victims of bullying than the normal student population. Although this is a logical inference, we support this contention with the findings of several studies; for example, Maag and Katsiyannis (2012) found that bullies typically engaged in higher rates of substance abuse, negative peer interactions, delinquency, gang involvement, depression, and suicidal ideation than the normal population. In addition, they were found to be much more predisposed to committing criminal acts as well as participating in domestic violence (Maag & Katsiyannis 2012). In further support of these findings, Olweus (1993) found that approximately 60 percent of boys identified as bullies in grades 6 through 9 had one criminal conviction by the time they reached 24 years of age.

Similarly, targets of bullying were found to experience higher rates of anxiety, depression, withdrawal, suicide, and aggression, as well as physical health problems. Individuals who exhibited both behavioral characteristics seemed to be most affected and were, consequently, the most rejected by peers (Maag & Katsiyannis, 2012). Clearly, these behavioral outcomes represent characteristics present in many students who are diagnosed with emotional or behavioral disorders.

As noted earlier in the chapter, students engage in bullying for a variety of reasons, and their targets, either excessively vulnerable or aggressive and proactive, have psychosocial characteristics that mark them as such and define their roles in school. Similarly, the role of the bystander witness clearly influences the bullying process. In addition, teachers, administrators, and parents significantly affect the dynamic and pathological relationship between bully and target. It is essential, therefore, that any effective intervention plan addresses the influences of these actors in its development and design.

Interventions To Reduce Bullying in Schools

Thanks to the work of investigators such as Olweus (1993), as well as others in the field, several effective approaches have been established and represent helpful options in addressing bullying as a school-wide issue. We will describe a few of the more promising approaches later in this section, but these programmatic solutions share some basic characteristics:

- Enlist the school principal's commitment and involvement.
- Have ongoing educational teacher discussions.
- Use a multifaceted, comprehensive approach that includes establishing a school-wide policy, which addresses indirect bullying (e.g., social exclusion) as well as direct bullying (e.g., physical aggression); provide guidelines for actions that teachers, other staff, and students should take if bullying is observed; educate and involve parents; adopt specific intervention strategies to deal with bullies, their targets, and bystanders; develop strategies to deal with bullying that occurs in specific settings by providing increased supervision, and conduct postintervention surveys to assess the efficacy of the strategy in reducing bullying.
- Create a positive, school-wide, "violence-free" environment.
- Establish class rules and conduct meetings on a weekly basis to review the effects of these rules (explicit in these class rules is one that specifically repudiates bullying and enlists the help of all students in eliminating it and helping defend the target).
- Implement formative consequences that take away a desired activity and replace it with one that is restorative and promotes awareness and empathy (e.g., the bully must come up with a way to provide assistance or support to the target).

- Train targets and bullies in social skills (e.g., empathy, self-regulation, anger management and awareness, tolerance, respect for others, initiating and maintaining a conversation, as well as understanding the hidden curriculum.
- Involve parents (e.g., inform the parents of both the bully and the target of the bullying and make them aware of bullying prevention policies as well as the consequences associated with the behavior). (Heinrichs, 2003; Raskauskas & Modell, 2011; Sampson, 2002)

Four research-based interventions that have demonstrated success in reducing bullying in schools are (1) the Olweus Bullying Prevention Program, (2) A General Semantics Approach to School-Age Bullying, (3) A Human Rights Approach to Bullying Prevention, and (4) A Change the School Approach (Employing the Peace-Able Place Program, currently known as the Too Good for Violence Program). We will, in turn, briefly outline the important characteristics of each of these programs.

The Olweus Bullying Prevention Program

First, the Olweus Bullying Prevention Program (Olweus, 1993, Olweus et al., 1999) is widely considered one of the most effective and comprehensive interventions for use in schools. The program operates with interventions targeting three levels (1) the school, (2) the classroom, and (3) the individual (including the bully, the target, and the parents of both). At the school-level, the program is initiated with the administration of a questionnaire that anonymously assesses students' perceptions of bullying in their school.

Next, a bully prevention coordinating committee is established that consists of teachers, parents, and school administrators. In-service training is provided to staff on a systematic basis, and school-wide rules against bullying are developed and posted conspicuously throughout the school. Finally, staff members are posted strategically throughout the school to increase effective student supervision during break periods.

Classroom-level interventions involve regular teacher-led classroom meetings about bullying and peer relations as well as class parent meetings.

Lastly, individual-level interventions include individual meetings with children who bully, meetings with children who are targets of bullying, and meetings with affected parents (Limber, 2011).

The General Semantic Approach to School-Age Bullying

This approach to bullying prevention focuses on specifics rather than generalities (e.g., encouraging students, teachers, administrators, and other school staff to describe their personal bullying experiences), grounding them in real-life issues and solutions. In so doing, it reminds us that we are all complex, multifaceted individuals who operate within the world, creating experiences that are unique to each of us. Another aspect of this approach is the "indexing" of types of bullying (e.g., physical abuse differs from relational abuse), which helps to target the intervention to the context of the behavior.

The next step in this approach is to use the imperative "No!" as a consistent countermeasure when confronted with or observing an act of bullying. Consistently applied, this sends a message to the individual who bullies that his or her behavior is unacceptable and will not accomplish whatever function is intended. Furthermore, the authors exhort students and adults to refrain from intentional responses to the bully that can become too personal and exacerbate the situation, actually encouraging further retaliation. Instead, students and teachers should keep statements neutral and factual; for example, an extensional response to someone who engages in bullying behavior might be to say, "Bullying causes problems for everyone, including you—stop it now so we can work things out." Confrontations like this, however, should only be conducted with the support of a group, to minimize risk to the speaker.

Step three of this approach involves training in self- or anger management techniques to students and teachers. The rationale for this is that if individuals, target or bystander, who are affected by bullying can leave to delay their reactions and manage their emotions and behavior, they can effectively neutralize the intended effect of the bully—that is, a "knee-jerk reaction" to the bullying. To accomplish this, the program teaches participants Ellis's "ABC's" of "Rational-Emotive-Behavior Therapy," in which the A represents an Activating event, the B, Beliefs" or thoughts about an event, and the C, the emotional Consequences of one's beliefs. The idea here is that if teachers and students can learn to use self-talk to help process the experience, they can defuse their emotional response to a situation. The key to its effective use is the ability to replace absolutes or "allness" statements with more general ones. For example, in a situation in which a bully has called a child a bad name, the child might be tempted to react with, "I won't let him talk to me that way. It makes me feel hurt and angry!" According to the ABC approach, a better response is to replace the absolutes with generalities, that is, "I'd rather he didn't talk to me that way. It's unpleasant and annoying!"

The final step in the general semantic approach is the use of empathy. The authors contend that, when dealing with a bully, before administering correction or discipline, it is best to offer empathy first. For example, using the words "I understand" or "I think I can understand," followed by an appraisal of what might have provoked or initiated the bullying behavior, leads the child who bullies to feel understood or acknowledged; this feeling will predispose him to accept the corrective action and listen to your admonition, as opposed to becoming hostile and unreceptive (Liepe-Levinson & Levinson, 2005).

A Human Rights Approach to Bullying Prevention

As Michael Greene (2006) noted, the most important step in developing a school-based bullying prevention program involves "gaining the support of administrators, teachers, parents, auxiliary school staff, and partners in establishing intervention and prevention programs and policies" (p. 73).

Some states, such as Idaho, have adopted a K–12 Human Rights curriculum that is an integral part of the social studies curriculum. Michael Greene (2006) pointed out that the strength of these curricula rests on their emphasis on "creating a classroom and school-wide dialogue about what constitutes bullying and harassment and what the rights and expectations of every student should be vis-à-vis respect and civil treatment" (p. 75).

Furthermore, to educate students about human rights and human rights infractions, teachers provide assignments that require them to investigate instances of human rights abuses and develop meaningful ways to address them. Similarly, teachers and administrators should be provided ongoing professional development in the area of bullying identification and prevention techniques. Moreover, research supports that teachers who express caring attitudes towards their students are confident in their craft, monitor academic work and social behavior, and intervene swiftly when problems occur tend to have fewer problems of bullying (Kolstrein & Jofré, 2013).

A Change in the School Approach to Bullying

In accordance with the recommendations provided by many researchers, the first step in this, and any effective bullying prevention program, is to establish a school-wide committee to determine the prevalence of bullying in the school. Next, based on the results of this investigation, the committee disseminates these findings to the school faculty and administration, identifying key goals for helping to prevent bullying. These goals then serve as the focus of any preventative approach. Inherent in any good prevention plan are core values, acknowledged schoolwide. Any viable plan should endeavor to reinforce these desirable values or traits in students, while eliminating interventions or approaches that are not compatible with them; for example, one school identified verbal aggression as a frequent antecedent to bullying and consequently established it as a primary goal to be addressed by its prevention program.

The "change the school" approach to reducing or eliminating bullying and other forms of school violence involves three components (1) modify the school norms and policies to create a positive school environment, (2) educate the students, and (3) train teachers who are not compatible with these values. Accordingly, we will briefly discuss each of these (Orpinas & Horne, 2006).

- **Create a Positive Environment**. Schools are encouraged to follow Curwin, Mendler, and Mendler's (2018) four steps to create a positive environment that is free of violence and bullying: (a) identify the school's core values, (b) create rules and consequences based on these values, (c) model these values, and (d) eliminate behaviors and interventions that are not synchronous with these values.

- **Educate Students**. One recommended program that teaches students skills that militate against violence and bullying is "Too Good for Violence" (Mendez Foundation, 2022). Essentially, this program provides students with training in anger management, conflict resolution, respect for self and others, and effective communication. The training format for each of these skill areas typically consists of experiential learning, cooperative groups, and role-playing. The keys to the success of this program are twofold: the quality of the training, and time commitment.

- **Train Teachers**. Teacher training incorporates school-wide strategies for bullying and aggression prevention, including conflict-resolution strategies, character education, and behavior management approaches. In addition, such training should be flexible enough to permit adaptations and modifications as required by the teacher and the relevant contexts.

To conclude, although the occurrence of school violence has declined in recent years, incidents of bullying, in contrast, continue to rise. For example, according to the U.S. Department of Justice, one out of every four children are bullied by a peer in school each month (Finkelhor, 2014), and approximately

1.6 million students in grades 6 through 10 in the United States are bullied at least once a week (Lebrun-Harris et al., 2019; Seldin & Yanez, 2019).

The effects of bullying are profound for both the bully and the target of the bullying behavior. Targets of bullying experience loneliness, have difficulty making social and emotional adjustments, and suffer humiliation, insecurity, and a loss of self-esteem. As adults they are at greater risk of experiencing depression as well as other mental disorders, including schizophrenia, and they are more likely to commit suicide.

Bullies, on the other hand, typically engage in other forms of antisocial behavior, including the destruction of property, theft, truancy, fighting, dropping out of school, and substance abuse. Furthermore, bullies are more likely to participate in criminal activities as adults and, similarly, to be convicted of at least one crime (Lebrun-Harris et al., 2019; Seldin & Yanez, 2019). Fortunately, there are things that schools and school personnel can do to reduce the incidence of bullying. The following are the key elements that should be included in any effective preventive program

- enlist the involvement and commitment of school administrators
- schedule ongoing teacher discussions
- develop a multifaceted, comprehensive approach that includes establishing a school-wide policy and provide guidelines for teachers and administrators
- create a positive school environment
- establish class rules regarding bullying
- develop and implement specific consequences for bullying behavior
- provide students with social skills training and self-awareness/ self-regulation strategies
- involve parents in the bullying prevention plan as well as enforcement procedures (Orpinas & Horne, 2006).

Lastly, there are a variety of effective, research-based programs that are designed to reduce and, ideally, prevent bullying in schools. The following represent a few of the most recommended of these that have been described in greater detail earlier in this section (1) The Olweus Bullying Prevention Program, (2) A General Semantic Approach to School-Age Bullying, (3) A

Human Rights Approach to Bullying Prevention, and (4) A "Change the School" Approach to Bullying.

It is our hope that the preceding information will help teachers become actively engaged in one of these vital preventive programs; the consequences of bullying are simply too damaging to the affected students and their families for teachers to remain uninformed and uninvolved.

Gang Membership and Related Activities

Case Example: Matteo

Matteo (not his real name) was 16 years old and had been living in the Fordham section of the Bronx before being referred to a school for children and youth who have emotional or behavioral disorders. As the teacher read his case file, he realized that this was a young man who had never received a break and was long overdue for one. The teacher was eager to do whatever he could to make a difference in this young man's life and had visions, as do most young teachers, of being instrumental in his redemption and future success.

As the days and weeks passed, the teacher began to understand that it would take a good deal more than the best intentions of a young white teacher from Canada to provide Matteo with an epiphany. The teacher frequently drove to town to "retrieve" Matteo from the streets, ran interference for him when he ran afoul of other teachers, community members, and the local police, and tried to provide him with the "fatherly" advice and attention, which the teacher perceived he was sorely missing and which, he was convinced, was the key to his reformation. The teacher soon realized he was so wrong.

First of all, as Matteo firmly pointed out one day after the teacher once again intervened in an altercation involving another teacher, he was beyond redemption and certainly did not want to be 'saved' if it meant becoming 'white' or 'establishment' like him. Although he was respectful to the teacher and appreciated all that he was trying to do to help him, he made it clear that the teacher was neither his father nor a member of his neighborhood family.

Undaunted, the teacher set about, more fervently than ever, to prove him wrong. He accompanied him to his cottage after school and provided an hour of extra tutoring, he prepared review materials to help him prepare for the state comprehensive exams, and he continued to be an advocate in both the school and the community. The teacher even went as far as to obtain special permission to bring Matteo to my home for Thanksgiving dinner. Matteo genuinely appreciated this opportunity and thoughtfully presented and my wife and me with a box of chocolates to show it.

In the teacher's naiveté, he thought he was making progress, winning Matteo over, transforming a life, yet he had much to learn about Matteo and Matteo's world. His enlightenment, however, was swiftly approaching. In May of that year, the teacher had an epiphany. He had just returned from lunch and was preparing to teach a lesson about, interestingly, the themes of war, power, and human conflict represented in Henry V, when he heard what sounded like a riot just outside the classroom window. The students and teacher ran to the window just in time to see Matteo swinging a baseball bat at five older boys—on further investigation, these boys were armed with 'shivs' (knives) and handguns. Someone from the principal's office had already called the police, and before the teacher could run outside, foolishly, to intervene, they had the five other boys and Matteo in custody.

After school, the teacher drove to the police headquarters where Matteo and the other boys were confined and learned the full story from Matteo. According to Matteo, these five young men were from his 'hood' but were members of a rival gang. They claimed that Matteo had been implicated in a beating inflicted on one of their members that was so severe, he was left seriously injured and would be maimed for life. Matteo denied taking part in the beating, but admitted that he was a member of a rival gang, the Black Aces, and was subsequently taken to the Juvenile Offenders wing of Rikers' Island Detention Center to await trial (the police found a gun and a bag of "ice" [crystal methamphetamine] on him during their body search).

The teacher did not know about gangs and gang behavior before working with Matteo. The only gangs he had knowledge of were the Sharks and the Jets from West Side Story. After this experience, the teacher researched as much information about gangs as he could find and discovered two glaring oversights in his dealings with Matteo. First, Matteo was trying to explain that he had a family that was his neighborhood, a code or euphemism for the gang, and that this 'family' gave him everything he needed. Second, he had been initiated into the Black Aces at the age of 13, a rite of passage that was typical for many young men in his community. His biological father was a member of the gang and even presided over his initiation, which involved participation in a brazen, premeditated attack on members of a rival gang.

Third, the teacher had missed the telltale signs and signals that are very clearly displayed by gang members; for example, Matteo always wore a black-and-white bandanna, which he carefully stuffed in a back pocket of his jeans, allowing a corner to hang, obtrusively, from it. The teacher had noticed that he wore the bandanna around his head occasionally when he was off school grounds. Finally, Matteo showed the teacher a 'tag' (gang graffiti) that he used to mark books, notebooks, and even the stalls in the boys' bathroom at school.

The teacher learned that this 'tag' was used by gang members to mark their turf, or as a challenge to a rival gang.

Youth Gangs in the United States: Current Data

According to a survey conducted in 2000 by the National Youth Gang Center (NYGC), an affiliate of the federal Office of Juvenile Justice and Delinquency Prevention (OJJDP), there are more than 24,000 active gangs in the United States. The overall membership in these gangs exceeded 760,800 in 2004 (Howell, 2010; Howell, 2019b). Whereas this number represents a decline of 5 percent from the previous year, in cities with a population of 25,000 or more, the number of gang members actually increased by 2 percent (Howell, 2019). Similarly, 91 percent of cities with a population of more than 25,000 reported at least one gang-related homicide from 1999 to 2000 (Howell, 2019). This statistic represents an increase in the number of gang-related homicides for 47 percent of these cities. In addition, researchers have noted that gang-related homicides account for approximately one-fourth of all homicides in the 173 U.S. cities that have a population of 100,000 or more (Howell, 2019). In two of these cities, Los Angeles and Chicago, the number of gang-related homicides exceeded 50 percent of the total number of homicides (Coid et al., 2013).

Furthermore, researchers noted that as many as 48 percent of the youth involved in gangs arguably could be considered emotionally disturbed (Coid et al., 2013). Similarly, Gray et al. (2011) acknowledged a significant link between emotional or behavioral disorders and at-risk behaviors, particularly school violence and gang membership.

Another study of youth in detention, in which a majority met the diagnostic criteria for one or more psychiatric disorders—most commonly, conduct disorder—revealed that nearly 60 percent of males and 75 percent of females were involved in or affiliated with a gang (Teplin et al., 2005). Delinquency, which correlates with conduct disorder, is highly represented in youth who are gang members. Moreover, depression is also more prevalent in youthful gang members than in same-age peers who are not affiliated with gangs (Teplin et al., 2005).

These and other studies support our contention that youth who have emotional or behavioral disorders are at risk for gang involvement at a rate that is significantly higher than the normal population. Such findings highlight the need for teachers to be knowledgeable about the characteristics of gang membership and behavior, the functions served by gang membership, typical gang-related activities, the impact of gang membership on schools, and interventions that may help reduce gang membership and its potentially devastating consequences.

Gang Impact in Schools

Seldin and Yanez (2019) identified a strong correlation between the presence of gangs in schools and an increase in the prevalence of guns and drugs. Evidence has also supported the significant role that gangs have played in the widespread increase in school violence (Carson & Esbensen, 2019). Rates of violence are significantly higher in schools where gangs are present and, conversely, the victimization rate in schools that do not report the presence of gangs is lower (Yanez & Seldin, 2019).

Furthermore, although gangs may not be directly responsible for all school violence, their very presence can create a toxic environment that incubates it. In response to the perceived presence of gangs, many youths are arming themselves, which increases the potential for shootings—either offensive, in connection with criminal activity, or in defense against or revenge for such acts. Several studies have revealed that because gangs frequently engage in drug trafficking and weapons sales, their presence in schools invariably means that these undesirable commodities will be more prevalent and available (Seldin & Yanez, 2019; Yenez & Seldin, 2019). In addition, students in schools that have gangs are twice as likely to report that they fear being a victim of violence as their peers at schools without gangs (Yenez & Seldin, 2019).

Another unanticipated and insidious effect of gangs in schools is their use of schools as sites for gang recruitment and socialization (Gray et al., 2011; Gallupe & Gravel, 2018). One study even found that gang members who had dropped out or been expelled from school often returned to it clandestinely in order to socialize with gang members who were still attending the school (Gallupe & Gravel, 2018).

Characteristics of Gangs in Schools

Howell and Lynch (2000) surveyed high school students to determine their awareness of the characteristics of gangs and gang members in their schools. Through the results of this survey, they were able to identify five indicators of gang presence (1) a recognized name of the gang, (2) "tagging" or marking turf with graffiti, (3) time spent with other gang members, (4) violence, and (5) clothing or other identifying items. This study further determined that gang presence in schools appeared to be correlated with several factors, especially:

- The size of the community (increased presence in schools in communities of up to 50,000 population).
- Drug availability: As expected, gangs were more prolific where drugs were more accessible.

- Security steps: Schools with more elaborate and extensive security procedures were more likely to have gangs.
- The level of victimization at school: The higher the frequency of victimization, the greater was the prevalence of gangs in the school (Howell et al., 2011; Howell & Lynch, 2000; Naber et al., 2006).

These factors might be explained as follows.

- First, the size of communities reporting increased gang presence is becoming progressively smaller, apparently because gangs are now becoming very much a part of small cities and suburbs as the population in large cities migrates to less expensive metropolitan areas, such as the boroughs, suburbs, and surrounding small communities.
- Drugs have traditionally been associated with criminal activity, given the demand, their illicit nature, and, consequently, the opportunity to make a huge profit very quickly. Gangs, by their very nature and organizational structure, are uniquely positioned to benefit from the drug trade, and they can achieve a monopoly in schools as a result of their willingness to use violence to intimidate competitors and control the market.
- Heightened security procedures in schools are an indirect predictor of increased gang presence because these measures are usually implemented in urban schools located in high-crime neighborhoods, and gangs tend to incubate in these conditions.

Similarly, although victimization at school may not be related directly to the presence of gangs, schools in which victimization rates are high are typically located in high-crime neighborhoods in which gangs flourish. Students in these schools tend to associate gangs either directly or indirectly with increased victimization, whether such association is justified or not. It seems fair to assume that at least some of the school-related victimization and violence can be attributed to gangs, because analyses of gang arrests show that violent gang crimes begin to escalate early in the school day and peak in the early afternoon (Howell & Lynch, 2000; Naber et al., 2006).

Purpose Served by Gang Membership

The two key predictors of gang membership are residence in a gang-infested neighborhood and having an older sibling who is a member of a gang (Hixon, 1999). According to Spergel (1995), there is no specific personality type that predisposes youth to gang membership.

Sanchez-Jankowski (1991) suggested several reasons for joining a gang, after systematically debunking some popular misperceptions such as the deleterious effect of a broken home; the untenable nature of a dysfunctional family that leads the child to seek out a more stable, safe, accepting environment; the constraints on employment options based on dropping out of school; and finally, the "Pied Piper" effect—that is, succumbing to the seduction of the romanticized gang life represented by high-status older peers.

In contrast to these unsubstantiated reasons, Sanchez-Jankowski (1991) and Molidor (1996) proposed several empirically supported ones to include (1) material incentives, (2) recreation, (3) a place of refuge and camouflage, (4) physical protection, (5) an opportunity to resist living lives like one's parents, and (6) commitment to one's community.

Relative to the school, Parks (1995) advanced several possible incentives. The first is the notion that in some cases negative teachers may help turn some children and youth to seek acceptance and values in a gang (Padilla, 1992). Likewise, school administrators who establish arbitrary and oppressive rules, exact capricious punishments, and enforce them inconsistently may inadvertently contribute to a student's decision to turn to a gang for succor (Miller, 1992).

Finally, the structure of the school may also contribute to gang membership. Huff (1996) reported the alienating effect of harsh disciplinary measures, consistent academic failure, unresponsive teachers, and an irrelevant curriculum. Similarly, Harootunian (1986) noted that labeling, stereotyping, tracking, and other discriminatory practices of school staff may also help to make gang membership more appealing.

In addition, according to Sanchez-Jankowski (1991; 2003), several key factors are integral to the formation of youth gangs:

- Youth experience a sense of alienation and helplessness because traditional supports (family, school) are missing, and a gang fills this void.
- Gangs provide a sense of identity, power, and control, and serve as an outlet for anger.

- The control of 'turf' is critical to the survival and well-being of the gang and is therefore zealously defended.
- Finally, the gang must recruit successfully, filling its ranks with willing and unwilling members, in order to survive and be relevant in the school and community.

Profile of an Adolescent Gang Member

In the United States, the typical gang member tends to be a young man of color, 13 to 24 years of age, from the urban underclass (Parks, 1995). Although there are exceptions, gangs tend to be composed of individuals from the same race or ethnicity and often display their membership through distinctive styles of dress, referred to as 'colors,' and through specific activities and patterns of behavior. Furthermore, gang members typically show great loyalty to their community or neighborhood and often demarcate their 'turf' with representative graffiti, referred to as 'tagging.' This graffiti is also displayed on school walls, usually in the bathrooms, as well as on exterior walls and windows (Sanchez-Jankowski, 1991; 2003).

As noted earlier, gang members are usually youth who feel particularly vulnerable as a result of living in a dangerous, gang-infested neighborhood, or who seek the family they do not have, or who look for the power and prestige that has eluded them often because of prejudice and discrimination.

Female gang members, while fewer than their male counterparts, make up about 10 percent of gangs and share some characteristics similar to those of male members. Their ages range from 13 to 18, and they are becoming more like their male counterparts in the level and type of violent acts and crimes that they commit. Female gang members, like male members, tend to be individuals who have grown up in gang-infested and impoverished neighborhoods. They also reflect a pattern of failure in school and have frequently been suspended from school for fighting or drug or weapon possession. Unlike the young male gang members, however, they typically have been and continue to be victims of sexual abuse. Usually, after they have been suspended, these girls drop out of school or are truant so often that they fail. Furthermore, there appears to be little, if any, school, or parent follow-up once these girls stop attending school. While they were attending, the majority of gang-involved females carried a knife or a gun for a 'boyfriend,' because women are less frequently and thoroughly searched by school security personnel. Finally, like the boys in gangs, female members are most frequently African American or Latina and come from lower-socioeconomic households in neighborhoods defined as 'urban poor' (Molidor, 1996).

Combatting Gang Activities in Schools

After reviewing the literature about preventing or reducing gang-related behavior in schools, three themes become apparent (1) the need for pro-social and constructive alternatives to supplant the benefits provided by gang membership; (2) finding positive ways to address students' needs for validation and self-esteem; and (3) instituting these measures in elementary and middle schools, because research has indicated that gangs begin recruiting future members at these early levels (Gallupe & Gravel, 2018). These themes are discussed in this section.

Wallach (1994), Gallupe and Gravel (2018) and others have identified several approaches that have been shown to be effective strategies in themselves, or combined in various ways, can form the basis for a school-wide approach:

- Target students who are vulnerable to gang recruitment for special assistance, particularly through the use of peer counselors and support groups.
- Establish moral and ethical education, values clarification, and conflict resolution as important components of the school curriculum.
- Create an inviting school climate in which every student feels valued.
- Educate all school staff, including support staff, about how gangs develop and how to respond to them.
- Using a culturally sensitive approach, offer special programs for parents about gangs and how to deal with them as parents.
- Monitor youths who are at risk for gang involvement, such as those who have been diagnosed with emotional or behavioral disorders and offer educational programs that provide information about the destructiveness of gang involvement.
- Monitor youths who are not enrolled in the school but who loiter around the school during the daytime.
- Provide opportunities for students to discuss their school experiences as well as constructive and productive plans for the future.

Taylor et al. (2016) and Veliz and Shakib (2012) reported that the development and promotion of intramural sports has proved to be a very effective alternative to the need for competition and physical interaction that gang membership provides. Such involvement has deterred many at-risk youth from joining gangs. Involvement in intramural sports and other extracurricular groups encourages new friendships and loyalties, increases an individual's attachment to the school while simultaneously helping to improve academic performance as well as opportunities for success both within the classroom setting and beyond.

Further, engaging gang leaders in peer mediation helps them to learn to use their leadership skills to serve peers in a pro-social, constructive way. Veliz and Shakib (2012) also suggested that schools provide alternative outreach programs to educate gang members in more accessible venues and at times that accommodate conflicting work schedules. In another vein, in schools in which rival gangs are feuding, school officials are encouraged to communicate with both groups and negotiate a truce to ensure that the educational process is neither threatened nor disrupted (Veliz & Shakib, 2012).

Another relevant study, conducted by Wood and Huffman (1999), identified some key implications for schools, administrators, and teachers regarding the prevention of gang activities in the school. Most noteworthy among them is the need for staff and administrator training in developing a school safety management plan. In conjunction with the development of this plan, the authors stress the importance of staff development for teachers and the community, including police officers, probation officers, and staff members, and addressing school safety, gang activity, and violence.

All students should be made aware of policies and rules as well as the rationale behind their implementation. In addition, teachers should be selected for their concern for individual students, their willingness to mentor students, and their ability to work as part of a team beyond their command of the subject matter. Furthermore, teachers should receive training in crisis intervention and classroom management techniques, both as an integral part of the teacher preparation program and in ongoing staff development.

One very effective program, called *therapeutic crisis intervention* (TCI), has been widely used to train school and residential treatment staff to defuse potentially violent situations and intervene using minimal and well-orchestrated restraints. The goal of TCI and similar crisis intervention training is to help staff establish a solid rapport and mutually respectful relationship with students. Parents should also be included, where possible, in student activities, staff development, and behavior management training with their students. Research has supported the importance of including even estranged and dysfunctional parents in these processes, with the understanding that stronger family systems can help reduce the attraction of gangs, which often serve as surrogate families (Bitton & Rajpurkar, 2015; Wood & Hufman, 1999).

Research has supported the need for a comprehensive approach to the prevention of gang-related activities in schools (Miller, 1992); therefore, schools might consider the model proposed by Green and Kreuter (1992), called "Pre-cede-Proceed." This model proposes that three types of factors influence the growth and development of gangs: predisposing factors, enabling factors, and reinforcing or support factors.

These authors suggested that any effective intervention/prevention approach should address each of these three factors

- **Predisposing Factors.** Research has identified teen-aged African American and Hispanic males as the most-represented racial/ethnic group among gang members. Because many of these young men come from single-parent homes in which that parent is most often the mother, it is reasonable to hypothesize that strong male mentoring might be effective, such as that provided by male teachers. Similarly, because these at-risk young men look to gangs to provide honor, respect, and power as well as to instill courage, after-school intramural sports programs might help to satisfy these needs in a pro-social way.

- **Enabling Factors**. According to Green and Kreuter (1992), the major factors that must be addressed to prevent school gang violence are the school, the community, and racism. For many children, especially those of color, schools are irrelevant and discriminatory institutions. This perception is furthered by the dearth of teachers and administrators of color, the lack of culturally relevant curricula, and distinctly lower expectations for minority children. Such awareness can be discouraging for at-risk youth and may, consequently, predispose them to gang influence and membership (Miller, 1992; Parks, 1995). In response, schools must begin to actively recruit male teachers of color, develop curricula that incorporate and value a multicultural perspective, provide viable after-school programs, and train teachers to be more culturally sensitive and inclusive as they plan and implement units and lessons.
  Furthermore, other investigators believe that in-school gang mediation is effective in helping to prevent and significantly reduce the incidence of gang-related violence (Roman et al., 2017). This approach solicits the participation of gang leaders, trains them in effective peer mediation techniques, and then involves them as mediators in gang-related

disputes. Participants in the mediation process must do so voluntarily and submit to very explicit rules of conduct and procedures laid out by the mediator. The keys to successful mediation are respect for the mediator and the mediator's ability to facilitate and sustain open and productive dialogue between the disputants (Roman et al., 2017).

Perhaps the most subtle yet significant factor in the perpetuation of gang-related violence is racism. Schools, as noted earlier, can inadvertently contribute to this problem through the perpetuation of racial stereotyping relative to learning and academic success (e.g., African American, and Latinx students typically perform less well than white and Asian American students). Teachers and administrators must guard against subtle and sometimes unconscious attitudes and behaviors that might be perceived as racist or discriminatory by their students. One way to counter these unhealthy attitudes and prejudices is to celebrate diversity and multicultural identity in the classroom and the school through a multicultural fair, or by observing a specific national or ethnic holiday (Kwanzaa, Chinese New Year, Cinco de Mayo, Puerto Rican Day, Martin Luther King Day, Black History Month, etc.)

- **Reinforcing or Support Factors.** Family, friends, peers, employers, teachers, administrators, and other stakeholders can have a powerful influence on the perpetuation or suppression of gang violence. Preeminent among them are parents, families, and teachers (Lenzi et al., 2015; Shute, 2013). According to Arthur and Erickson (1992), teachers need to strive to acquire the following skills, through either in-service or preservice training programs: (a) how to connect with "tough" inner-city youth, (b) knowledge of students' cultures, (c) effective interpersonal skills, (d) active (and sincere) listening, and (e) cross-cultural communication.

An Example of a Successful Prevention Program

One very effective program in helping curb gang membership is called *Gang Resistance Is Paramount* ([G.R.I.P.] National Gang Center, n.d.). The success of this program is due to the combined effect of its three major components (1) neighborhood meetings that provide parents with support, resources, and tangible assistance as they work to keep their children out of gangs; (2) a fifteen-week course for fifth-grade students and a ten-week program for second-grade students that addresses everything from 'tagging' to 'tattoos' and includes discussions about drug abuse, the effect of gang involvement on the family, and peer pressure, as well as attractive, pro-social activities and opportunities; and (3) a school-based follow-up program for ninth-graders that helps build self-esteem, takes an unequivocal look at the consequences of a criminal lifestyle, and examines the undeniable benefits of an education and the career opportunities that it provides. An exit survey determined that of 3,612 former program participants, all of whom were considered at risk for gang membership, 96 percent were not identified as gang members (Cooper & Ward, 2012; Thomas, 2010).

Conclusion

The case of the young man profiled at the beginning of this section is, unfortunately, not unique. Matteo's story is far from over, but he will need extensive help and support once he is released from detention to stay free of the gang life. Unfortunately, without the intensive intervention of teachers, family members, and community stakeholders, it will be almost impossible for Matteo to break his connection to the Black Aces.

In this section, we have examined the structure and characteristics of gangs and their connection with the school. We have also examined their detrimental effects on the school and its constituents. To understand better the pressures exerted on young men like Matteo, we also considered the purpose that gang membership serves as well as its seductive effect on young men of color living in poor urban neighborhoods.

Finally, in a more optimistic vein, various effective, field-tested interventions were discussed that help students who are at risk for gang involvement to resist their allure and thus avoid becoming perpetrators of gang violence in the school. It is our hope that this information may help teachers become effective agents of intervention to help save a young man or woman from a life of crime.

From the Field

Bryan Mulvihill, LCSW

Bryan Mulvihill is a drug awareness counselor at The Summit School, a residential program and day school for adolescents who have learning and adjustment difficulties.

Tell us about the students you typically work with.

The students that I work with come from all over the New York City metro area and as far away as upstate New York. The students are referred by their home school district, usually because of emotional or behavioral problems. These problems can range from depression, bipolar disorder, and pervasive developmental disorders to truancy, conduct, and oppositional problems. The students end up at The Summit School because their home district can no longer provide the appropriate level of education. By the time students arrive at The Summit School, most, but not all, have been through psychiatric hospitalizations, some form of drug treatment, other residential or day school programs, and/or homeschooling provided by the district. Inherent with students like this is substance abuse. The level of substance use can range from experimentation to abuse to dependence. The students that I work with are generally good kids that just happen to have a long list of unfortunate circumstances. Some have difficult family lives. Some get mixed up on the streets, and some have organic predisposition to substance use and/or psychiatric disorders. Most of the substance abuse students that I work with have co-occurring disorders, meaning that they have a psychiatric disorder as well as a substance use disorder. Substance use is often their attempt to manage their problems.

What approach or approaches have you used that have proven effective in connecting with or "getting through" to your students?

Be honest and direct with the students. You don't have to disclose personal information in an attempt to relate or connect with them. If you do, chances are that they will still say, "You don't know what it's like." If you are honest and direct with them, they will see you for who you are and that's where the connection is made. Avoid falling into the trap of asking twenty questions or accusatory questions. Students will immediately get suspicious and shut down. Start with a normal conversation or with a check-in type of conversation. This will help promote a relaxed environment and not the sense that they are in trouble. Try to avoid jumping right into the topic or incident at hand. In most cases, the student will bring up the incident at some point during the conversation. Allowing the students to bring it up on their terms helps to put you in a more supportive role rather than an authoritative role. Also, avoid taking sides. The more you argue or try to convince them that what they are doing is wrong, the more they will try to defend their actions.

What practical advice would you offer a teacher who suspects that one of her students is coming to class "high?"

Speak with the student one-on-one. Let them know your concerns and that you will have to speak with the appropriate school staff. The student will more than likely be upset, but you will be doing them a greater service in the long run. Ignoring the behavior will only enable it and the student will look at their behavior as okay or that you don't mind. How to confront the student and who to tell will all depend on the student and their family. I would be cautious about reaching out to the family unless you have a working relationship with them. You never know how a family will react. Some could appreciate your call, while another could be angry with you for meddling in their business.

Tell us some of the not-so-effective ways in which you or other school professionals you know have been inclined to address the issue of a student coming to school under the influence. Why did they seem like good approaches at the time? Why were they not as effective as you or others had hoped?

I think one of the more common mistakes that someone can make is to keep it between the student and themselves. I think at the time, it might seem like a good approach because they don't want to betray the student's trust or maybe they feel the student has enough problems in their life and they don't want to add to them by getting them in trouble. Clearly, approaching it this way does nothing to address or resolve the problem. Therefore, the problem will continue. Another mistake is not involving the student and telling them what is happening. The student needs to be part of the process, whether they are happy with it or not. In some cases, this may not be appropriate (i.e., the student needs to be sent to the emergency room). I think some people avoid involving the student because they don't want to confront the student for fear of how they may react. The reality is that if a student is coming to school under the influence, then they need to be confronted. They need to understand that coming to school under the influence is not an acceptable behavior. This kind of situation is a big opportunity to have a successful intervention. Some students will learn their lesson, while others will blow it off and continue to do what they want. In these kinds of situations, you can only reach the ones that want to be reached. By not involving the student you miss the opportunity for them to take responsibility for their actions.

How about a brief anecdote about a successful experience you have had "reaching" a student who was abusing?

First, you have to decide how you would define success. Success for each student will be different. For one student, it might be them reducing the amount of their use. For another, it might be them becoming sober. A successful experience that I had working with a student was with a student named Elan. Elan was referred to our program by her local school district after long-term school difficulties, ongoing conflictual relationships with her family, and extensive drug use. Her drug of choice was marijuana, which she was using on a daily basis. She had also experimented with cocaine, ecstasy, mushrooms, and Special K [ketamine hydrochloride, an anesthetic]. Elan had a history of two hospitalizations. One related to drug use and the other related to her mood swings. She was later diagnosed as having bipolar disorder. Upon her arrival at The Summit School Elan continued to use drugs despite repeated consequences. Her drug use was affecting her personal life, her family, socially, and academically. Elan's drug use only made her more anxious and her moods more volatile. Eventually, she was referred to an outpatient drug treatment program. After three months, she signed herself out of that program. I continued to see her for individual drug counseling and in a drug group on campus. One day she just decided to stop completely. She made her mind up that she had had enough. She no longer liked the high or the feeling of being out of control. By the time she graduated from The Summit School, she was three years sober. I think what helped me reach her was that I listened to her and didn't pass judgment about what she said. She was the kind of student that you couldn't tell her what she should or shouldn't do. Instead, she needed to find her own way. My role was just to guide her in the more positive direction.

Summary

There is significant evidence that students who have emotional or behavioral disorders, especially disruptive behaviors such as those associated with ADHD and conduct disorder, are at greater risk of engaging in certain destructive behaviors. The most common and pernicious of these are substance use and abuse, risky sexual behaviors, school violence, and gang membership and related activities.

Substance abuse among children and youth with emotional or behavioral disorders continues to proliferate, despite the best attempts to intervene and slow the process. This risk-taking behavior is particularly onerous because of the volatile interaction of abused drugs with prescribed ones, as well as the unpredictable effects of nonprescribed drugs on individuals with serious psychiatric disorders. Intervention and effective rehabilitation are critical to help affected young people who have emotional or behavioral disorders continue to comply with their behavioral intervention plans.

Risky sexual behaviors are more frequent among students who have emotional or behavioral disorders because of the impulsivity of many of these individuals, their apparent lack of concern for the consequences of their actions, and their tendency toward narcissism. The risk of detrimental outcomes for these behaviors has increased today as a result of the prevalence of sexually transmitted diseases, the most serious of which is HIV/AIDS. Another related issue is the increased likelihood of accidental, intentional, and uninformed pregnancy, which carries significant health and emotional consequences as well as socioeconomic implications. Key interventions used to counter risky, impulsive, and irresponsible sexual behavior include abstinence-only programs, knowledge of and access to contraception, and life skills/life options approaches such as that provided by the Teen Outreach Program and Quantum Opportunities Program, to name two.

Despite its drop in the last decade or so, the severity of school violence and its sometimes-lethal results have generated much attention. Schools should have clear and comprehensive plans for responding to these rare, but frequently catastrophic, events, and teachers, students, and administrators must be proactive in recognizing the early warning signs and following crisis intervention protocols. One form of school violence, however, continues to increase - the ubiquitous bullying phenomenon. Many studies have been conducted in the course of the last decade that have examined the etiology of bullying, the characteristics of the bully and the target of bullying, the possible repercussions if the bullying is not addressed, and programs that have shown progress in reducing and preventing bullying and its potentially devastating consequences.

Finally, in this chapter, we examined youth gangs and their effects on schools. Our investigation revealed the characteristics of youth gangs, the typical profile of a gang member, the effects of gangs on schools and their constituents, as well as some effective prevention and intervention strategies.

We hope that the information in this chapter will be both illuminating and helpful to teachers working with students who have emotional and behavioral disorders, who, by the very nature of these disorders, are at greater risk for engaging in drug abuse, sexually promiscuous behaviors, school violence, bullying, and gang membership.

Tips for Teachers

For Students Who Are Substance Abusers

- Substance abuse, if it involves a controlled substance, involves the potential for criminal prosecution; therefore, teachers may want to refer students of concern to the appropriate school counselor (e.g., the drug awareness counselor), with whom they have a level of confidentiality and privilege. Teachers should avoid accusing any student specifically of abusing drugs and/or alcohol or speaking publicly or privately about the problem with the student because of lack of professional qualification and potential legal implications.

- Students who come to school “high” or intoxicated should be intercepted at the door or in homeroom and parents or caregivers contacted to take the individual home.
- Students who abuse drugs or alcohol during the school day and are suspected of being “high” or intoxicated in class should be escorted to the nurse’s office for evaluation, and both school administration and the student’s parents or caregivers should be notified and asked to take the individual home for further evaluation.
- Students who voluntarily share a concern about a personal struggle with abuse or that of another student should be referred to the appropriate school counselor or drug awareness counselor for assistance and follow-up.
- It is the job of the drug awareness counselor or psychologist, in conjunction with the parents and the affected student, to discuss the need for and options regarding effective rehabilitation programs. It is beyond the purview of teachers to engage in these conversations with the student, and such unwarranted discussion can have serious legal implications. Simply put, teachers should always act as referents for students suspected of substance abuse or who voluntarily disclose substance abuse. Therefore, teachers need to know the referral procedures: who to contact, and how to follow up to ensure the student receives the help he or she needs.

For Students Who Engage in Risky Sexual Behaviors

- Clearly, teachers are not trained to deal with the issues surrounding teen pregnancy or sexually promiscuous behaviors that occur outside the school; however, as with substance abusers, they should refer an affected student to the school counselor or health professional, who can then provide the individual with helpful resources.
- Although teachers should not engage in discussion about sexual or reproductive issues, they should be supportive of students’ concerns and encourage students to speak with their parents, medical practitioner, school counselor, or health care professional about their concerns.

- Teachers should avoid sharing a particular philosophy about sexual behavior, whether they favor abstinence or safe sex. Teachers should ensure that students receive appropriate sex education as part of the health curriculum and that student issues or concerns are treated confidentially and respectfully and are addressed quickly by appropriate school personnel.

- Teachers' primary concerns in matters involving student sexual behaviors should be for the health and safety of the student and the prevention of unwanted pregnancy and sexually transmitted disease.

For Students Who Perpetrate School Violence and Engage in Bullying

- Do not tolerate bullying: allowing seemingly harmless behavior to continue unaddressed can be viewed by children who bully as an indication of tolerance or acceptance.

- Set rules for behavior in your classroom and ensure that students share in their development and enforcement as well as specific consequences and restitutions for breaking them.

- Learn and teach both conflict-resolution and anger-management skills. An example of a free online training program that teaches these skills is the New Jersey Education Association (NJEA) program called *Peer Mediation and Conflict Resolution Program* (available online at: www.njsbf.com/njsbf/ student/conflictres/conflictres.cfm).

- Learn and watch for the warning signs of violence: these include social withdrawal, feelings of rejection, rage, expressions of violence in writings or drawings, gang affiliation, and making serious threats of violence.

- Know your school resources for dealing with students who engage in threats or in violent behavior (e.g., school counselor, school psychologist, crisis intervention team and plan).

- Enforce school policies that seek to reduce the risk of violence (e.g., keep an eye on hallways between periods, check on students in recess areas or the school cafeteria during recess or lunch breaks).

- Help implement a safe school plan. If one doesn't exist, organize other concerned teachers, and approach the administration about establishing one.
- Report safety threats or legitimate concerns about potential violence to the school administration, immediately.
- Encourage and support student-led violence prevention programs. Examples of these programs include peer mediation, teen courts, and violence prevention training.
- Take time to get to know your students' parents or caregivers. It is possible that many of the more recent and lethal episodes of school violence might have been averted had teachers been alerted to the possibility by family members. (Adapted from Druck & Kaplowitz, 2005)

For Students Who Are Involved in Gangs and Gang Violence

Seven Warning Signs of Gang Involvement

1. The student suddenly has a new group of friends.
2. The student has a new nickname.
3. The student shows a lack of interest in studies and school activities.
4. The student has truancy problems and performs poorly in school.
5. The student is frequently late or is unaccounted for at times during the school day.
6. The student wears specific theme colors or has a particular style of dress.
7. This student has tattoos and wears clothing with distinctive logos or insignias. (Adapted from Hixon, 1999)

What Teachers Can Do to Help

1. Learn the characteristics of local gangs.
2. Heed the preceding seven warning signs of gang involvement.
3. Listen to the concerns of your students. Discuss gangs, drug use, and the criminal justice system with them, and, when

possible, invite community experts, such as representatives of the local police, to share in the discussion of these issues.

4. Build self-esteem in your students.
5. Encourage membership in school-sponsored teams and clubs.
6. Supervise your students and routinely check both isolated and obscure school locations as well as the activities of large gatherings of students (during school breaks or lunch time).
7. Work hard to prevent students from dropping out of school.
8. Report suspected gang activity to the school administration.
9. Promote gun safety programs.
10. Organize a gang task force in the school. (Adapted from Hixon, 1999)

Focus Questions Revisited

What are the four substances that are most commonly abused by children and adolescents, and why do they pose such a threat?

A Sample Response: The four most commonly abused substances are alcohol, nicotine, marijuana, and inhalants (solvents, gases, and nitrates). They present a real problem for youth and those who wish to prevent substance use and abuse because three of them are sold "over the counter" and are therefore readily available to children and youth. The fourth, marijuana, though it is a controlled substance, is nonetheless ubiquitous and is easily obtained from sources in the community.

The National Institute on Drug Abuse provides six guidelines in selecting an effective school-based drug-abuse prevention program: What are they?

A Sample Response:

1. School-based programs should extend from kindergarten through high school. At the very least, they should reach children in the critical middle school and high school years.
2. Programs should employ well-tested, standardized interventions with detailed lesson plans and student materials.
3. Programs should employ age-appropriate interactive teaching methods (e.g., modeling, role playing, discussion, group feedback, reinforcement, and extended practice).

4. Programs should foster pro-social bonding to both the school and the community.

5. Program components should include (a) teaching social competence (i.e., communication, self-efficacy, assertiveness) and drug resistance skills that are culturally and developmentally appropriate; (b) promoting positive peer influence; (c) promoting antidrug social norms; (d) emphasizing skills training teaching methods; and (e) include an adequate "dosage" (ten to fifteen sessions in a year).

Programs should be evaluated periodically to determine their effectiveness. (Compton et al., 2005)

Identify the school professionals who serve as resources for teachers who have concerns about a student at risk for or engaged in substance abuse.

A Sample Response: Teachers should know that most schools now employ a drug awareness counselor or assign a school counselor with appropriate training to that position.

What are two key factors that increase the risk of acquiring an STD for adolescents who have emotional disturbances?

A Sample Response: There are two key risk factors that predispose adolescents who have emotional disturbances to the acquisition of an STD: (a) the higher incidence of substance abuse, including intravenous use, in youth who have emotional disturbances, and (b) the behavioral tendency toward risk-taking, impulsive behaviors that is characteristic of many individuals who have emotional disturbances. Note: Although the most commonly abused substances are not taken intravenously, the altered state produced by these substances, i.e., alcohol and marijuana, can impair judgment regarding safe sex practices.

Of the three sex education program types described in this chapter, identify the one that you consider to be most effective, and explain why you consider it so.

A Sample Response: In my opinion, the most effective type of sex education program is a comprehensive approach. For example, the Life Skills/Life Options Approach combines, in my opinion, the critical elements of the other major approaches, including encouraging abstinence or delay of sexual activity, providing concrete knowledge about contraception, and offering strategies for building self-esteem, decision-making skills, and developing a clear vision of a successful and independent future (McWhirter, 2004).

For each of the following scenarios involving instances of school bullying and violence or the potential for violence, provide a viable intervention that could be employed by a classroom teacher to mitigate the problem. (Hint: Use this chapter as a source for possible research-based solutions.)

a. Devon is a new student in your grade 8 class. He exhibits very oppositional and defiant behavior toward you and other authority figures. He refuses to comply with any of your requests, preferring to respond with barely audible insults or threats. The class is really becoming affected by his inappropriate remarks and intimidating gestures. He has begun to threaten other students who complain about his behavior. You are at your wits' end and notice that you are beginning to avoid him. Learning is seriously jeopardized by his behavior. What should you do short of removing him from class?

b. John has borrowed money from a classmate and is overdue in repaying the loan. John has assured Dustin, the classmate, several times that he would repay the money on a specific date; each time John has had a different excuse for not having the money. This most recent excuse was, for Dustin, the "last straw." You observe Dustin approach John as your students enter the classroom, witness a brief verbal exchange, and see Dustin punch John in the mouth, which precipitates a fistfight. Several members of the class begin to shout encouragement for one combatant or the other, while the rest of the class are shocked spectators frozen into inaction. Blood has begun to flow from John's mouth and nose as well as from a cut above Dustin's right eye. Two of the larger boys are holding back students who seem intent on helping to break up the fight. What do you do and what resources do you employ to regain control, stop the fight, and give appropriate consequences to the students involved in the melee?

c. Maria and Chantelle are attending the seventh-grade dance. The girls used to be "best friends," but they have been at odds over the attentions of a certain boy. You are a chaperone for the dance and have been assigned hallway patrol outside the boys' and girls' bathrooms. As you pass the girls' lavatory, you hear an animated conversation between Maria and Chantelle. The volume and intensity escalates until you observe Maria run out into the hallway pursued by Chantelle, who says, "Listen b—-, if I see you anywhere near Marcus I will f—- you up, you hear me!" When you try to ask Chantelle to explain the reason for her inappropriate outburst, she turns to you and says loudly and in front of a group of students attracted by the commotion, "Why don't you stay out of my business? Nobody asked you to butt in, b—-!" What is your response?

d. Evan, a quiet, gifted student in your fifth-grade homeroom, has become rather morose of late, ever since the transfer in of Billy, a new student who has a reputation as a "tough guy." You have observed the change in Evan's demeanor whenever Billy enters the room or passes by Evan's desk. Evan avoids eye contact with Billy and appears to be intimidated by Billy's size and aggressive behaviors. One day you overhear a conversation between the two boys in which Billy threatens Evan if he does not agree to share his answers to an important homework assignment. When you confront Billy and Evan about the incident, Billy laughs and says he was just "playing" with Evan. Evan, glancing quickly at Billy, agrees. Shortly after this incident, however, two of your most conscientious students approach you and report that Billy is constantly threatening Evan, occasionally punching him in the chest or arm or tackling him in the schoolyard. Evan is really afraid of Billy. . . too afraid to tell his teachers or parents for fear of retaliation. What do you do to help Evan, deal effectively with Billy, and address the bullying?

e. Ten-year-old Mandy passes Urdu's desk and hold her nose. "Someone smells bad around here," she announces to the class. The classroom erupts in laughter. Another classmate, Bryan, chimes in, "It's all the curry and stuff they eat—they all stink! Get some air fresheners, quick!" Again, the class roars. After speaking privately to Bryan and Mandy about their hurtful behavior, you notice that Urdu is silent, using her textbook to hide the tears that she is unable to suppress. What do you do to help Urdu become more accepted by the class? What are the appropriate consequences for Mandy, Bryan, and the rest of the class? How can such prejudice and rejection be prevented in the future?

f. You are asked by the principal of your school to cover a grade 8 class that has a particularly ominous reputation for misbehavior. As the substitute, you want to do things right and, with your background in special education, you feel confident that you can "handle' the assignment. During the morning's math lesson, you notice a brief exchange between two of the boys in the back of the class. You observe a large, surly boy toss a crumpled piece of looseleaf paper onto the desk of a small, frail-looking boy, who seems clearly fearful and intimidated. In order to avoid an embarrassing confrontation, you say nothing, but you pick up the discarded paper after the class is dismissed. A note scribbled on the paper reads:

> "Jeff you —! If you don't want to get beat you better have my money for me after school. Meet me out back by the maintenance shed before the buses come. You better show up with the money or u no what will happen! P.S. Don't tell anyone or yore ded!!!"

You toss the note in your desk drawer and contemplate your next move. You must think fast, because the class will return from gym in ten minutes and then will be dismissed for the day. What are your options? What is your best course of action?

As a new high school teacher, you notice that some of your students wear distinctive clothing and behave in ways that are unusual and a bit unsettling. What are some of the characteristics or warning signs that you might look for to confirm your suspicions of their gang affiliation?

A Sample Response: There are several characteristics that I would look for to help confirm my suspicions about the students' gang involvement and prompt me to report my concerns to the appropriate administrator and/or to law enforcement officials. The following are highly correlated ones: (a) the students have new "nicknames," (b) the students show a lack of interest in studies and school activities, (c) the students have developed chronic truancy problems and are performing poorly in school, (d) the students are frequently late for class or are unaccounted for during the school day, (e) the students wear specific theme colors and have a particular style of dress, and (f) the students have tattoos and wear clothing with distinctive logos or insignias (Hixon, 1999).

In developing a school-wide approach to prevent gang membership and gang activity, what are some critical elements to include?

A Sample Response: The following are eight critical elements for inclusion in any effective school-wide gang prevention program:

a. Target students who are vulnerable to gang recruitment for special assistance.

b. Establish values clarification and character education as part of the school curriculum.

c. Create an inviting school climate in which every student feels valued.

d. Educate all school staff, including support staff, about how gangs recruit and develop and how to respond to them.

e. Offer special programs for parents about gangs and how to deal with their influence on their children.

f. Monitor youths who have been identified as being at risk for gang involvement.

g. Monitor youths who are not enrolled in the school, but who loiter around the school while it is in session.

h. Provide opportunities for students to engage in after-school activities, such as clubs and intramural sports teams.

Key Terms Used in the Chapter

Resilience:
The positive capacity of people to cope with stress and catastrophe. It is also used to indicate a characteristic of resistance to future negative events. In this sense, resilience corresponds to cumulative protective factors and is used in opposition to cumulative risk factors.

Self-Efficacy:
People's beliefs about their capabilities to produce designated levels of performance that exercise influence over events that affect their lives. Self-efficacy beliefs determine how people feel, think, motivate themselves, and behave. Such beliefs produce these diverse effects through four major processes: cognition, motivation, affect, and selection.

Gangs:
Groups of individuals, juvenile and/or adult, who associate on a continuing basis, form an allegiance for a common purpose, and participate in delinquent or criminal activities. Gangs may range from a loose-knit group of individuals who associate and commit crimes together to a formal organization with a leader or ruling council, gang colors, gang identifiers, and a gang name.

Chapter 11

Conclusion

Focus Questions

- *What are some of the variables that contribute to maladaptive behaviors in children and youth?*
- *List three important contributions that teachers can make to students who have emotional and behavioral disorders.*
- *In preparing to work effectively with students who exhibit maladaptive behaviors, the teacher must understand three things about them and the undesirable behaviors. What are they?*
- *Identify the key implications of IDEA (2004) for students who have emotional and behavioral disorders.*
- *How would you define meaningful learning as it relates to students who have emotional and behavioral disorders? What can a teacher do to ensure that these students are learning meaningful and relevant skills in the classroom?*
- *How important is developing a positive relationship with students who have emotional and behavioral disorders, and how is this best accomplished?*
- *What are the dangers of stereotyping in working with students who misbehave? How can we avoid the pitfalls of misperception and subsequent misidentification that are frequently based on our own prejudices and cultural ignorance?*
- *How can we work collaboratively with caregivers and family members to improve the classroom and social performance of children who have emotional and behavioral disorders?*

Retrospective And Overview

When the present authors were students, eons ago, teaching was a very explicit, well-defined task: Disperse knowledge, test to evaluate, and promote or retain. There was nothing in the teacher's job description that involved social skills instruction or, for that matter, any involvement or concern with the student's social-emotional state or with life outside the classroom. In many cases, even today, there are teachers, administrators, and parents who prefer this view of the teacher's job description. One teacher I spoke with a few years ago reflected this perception when he basically told me that he was being paid to teach and was not a social worker or a psychologist. If teaching was well executed, he contended, there would be little time for anything else; and if students were alone held accountable for their performance, many of the behavior problems currently encountered in the classroom would simply disappear.

Although I believe my friend shared a popularly held view that has some merit, I do not think it is a very realistic one. I compare this view to the one held about drug and alcohol addiction by many in society today. For them, addiction represents narcissism at its worst and is simply caused by a series of poor choices made by very lazy, weak, or undisciplined people. Some are very skeptical of the 'disease model' used to understand and treat the disorder and consequently consider rehabilitation treatments or the twelve-step programs originally associated with alcoholics anonymous to be essentially flawed. They support this belief with examples of persons who have been in and out of rehabilitation programs for years and have never been successful at living entirely independent of drugs or alcohol.

Similarly, many parents, teachers, and administrators consider the majority of students who have chronic behavior problems to simply need "a firm hand" at home and in school. They attribute the maintenance of these misbehaviors to a permissive social culture, one that is quick to 'pathologize' laziness, irresponsibility, and bad behavior, thereby excusing the action. For many, zero-tolerance policies and strictly enforced disciplinary procedures represent the best approach to dealing with chronic misbehavior. Those students who display more serious emotional or behavioral disorders (EBD) are the purview of the school psychologist or outside professionals, and if they cannot be sustained by these measures, many believe that these children should be placed in a more intensive treatment facility.

Clearly, the authors of this book do not subscribe to that perspective. We believe, after more than fifty years of experience between us, that, much like physical diseases, emotional and behavioral disorders have defining characteristics that facilitate treatment and intervention. The purpose of these varied diagnostic categories is not to stigmatize or stereotype an individual, but actually to help caregivers and professionals provide more effective interventions—ones that are ultimately individualized to serve the specific needs of a child.

Our intention, in developing each chapter, was to provide exemplary cases, based on the experiences of actual children and youth. These cases were then used to provide a systematic approach to identifying and treating the behavioral problems displayed by a child who exhibits a set of characteristics that correlate to a particular disorder, however, we have tried to be clear, even in our discussion of these case examples, that each child is unique, with problems that are very individual and, consequently, must the interventions be. Furthermore, we remind the reader that every child's behavioral problems are a function of several critical and intersecting variables that include, but are not limited to, (1) environment, (2) antecedent events, (3) personological variables, (4) the function a behavior serves, and (5) the factors that contribute to and sustain it.

The reader will have noticed that we recommend a multisystemic approach in the treatment of the disorders we address. This multisystemic method is the approach that has been most often recommended in the literature and, we believe, offers the student the best chance for successful remediation of the problem. Many behavioral disorders are simply manifestations of years of physical, psychological, or emotional abuse, ineffective parenting, and pathological family systems. The affected children growing up in these circumstances may either "learn" or acquire the destructive behaviors of the caregivers, or they may develop coping skills that manifest as antisocial or disruptive behaviors. These undesirable behaviors are then transferred to the classroom, with the result that the teacher is often substituted for the parent. In these cases, teachers can implement behavioral interventions that involve a positive reinforcement system to help reduce the undesired behaviors while reinforcing and encouraging more pro-social ones. It is dangerous to assume; however, that children learn, by osmosis, these more appropriate replacement behaviors—it is therefore incumbent on the teacher to "teach" these skills.

For most students who misbehave or who are experiencing emotional problems, it is not sufficient simply to teach reactive responses to various behavioral stimuli. If we want these behaviors to generalize to other social contexts and settings, we must also teach these students more pro-social and effective ways of thinking about and approaching a problem (problem-solving skills); therefore, for students who engage in defiant, aggressive, or destructive behaviors, teaching some sort of cognitive-behavioral response is highly recommended.

For students who have EBD and who are not cognitively intact (e.g., those with low-functioning autism), interventions that are exclusively behavioral, such as discrete trial training, appear to be the most effective.

To return to a point discussed earlier, namely, that teachers should not be expected to engage in professional activities other than teaching, we remind the reader that, in many cases, teachers have more sustained contact with students during the course of a typical day than parents do (Cavin, 1998). It is imperative, therefore, that teachers use that opportunity to effect positive change in their students, both academic and social. In a similar vein, studies of "resilience" have revealed that children who grow up in abusive, disruptive households and dangerous communities and who do not succumb to these destructive influences do so for two reasons (1) a higher level of innate resilience and (2) someone in their lives who believes in them and provides support (Rosenberg et al., 2004; Wickes-Nelson & Israel, 2006). In many cases, the role of 'supporter' falls to the teacher.

Indeed, our students notice everything we say but do not do and idealize but fail to live out. As teachers, we have a profound influence on our students' lives and, as a result, we are obliged to use our influence to help students develop as learners as well as members of a civil society. In the preceding chapters in this book, we have provided examples of how teachers may help their students develop social skills and acquire more pro-social behaviors, in conjunction with the support of parents and professionals such as the school psychologist or school counselor. These approaches have demonstrated success, but not without the key initiatives on the part of the teacher of (genuine) empathy, reality, and support. We refer to empathy as the feeling of genuine compassion for the welfare of another or the act of sharing another's feelings; reality is used here to mean that, like a mirror, we reflect back to the student the real effects of her behavior on herself and others; and by support we imply the extent to which a teacher, given her resources and opportunities, provides emotional and physical help to a student in trouble. Psychologists have acknowledged that, ultimately, these three contributions are all we can really give anyone, but they are essential in the development of a positive rapport with students who have EBD (Cornelius-White & Harbaugh, 2009).

Another important characteristic of many children who have EBD is their tendency to feel that they are not and cannot be protected. The role of the teacher in combatting this misperception is as a 'protector'-though this is not to suggest that the teacher is a superhero who can protect the child from all the forces of evil that threaten the child (including the child himself), but that the teacher can model ways in which a healthy, resilient individual protects himself; sometimes with words, sometimes with actions, and sometimes through intentionally avoiding and ignoring or 'running away.'

Nevertheless, neither teachers nor caregivers can provide the interventions and support that a child needs unless they fully appreciate the history, context, and functions of the child's problem behavior. This book has highlighted these aspects in each chapter and provided concrete examples of how teachers can ascertain these factors. Thus, once again, truly effective intervention is wholly dependent on accurate and thorough assessment of the child and the problem behavior.

Whether prepared or unprepared, willing, or unwilling, today's classroom teachers are as much players in a child's social-emotional development as they are in the child's academic growth. Not being prepared to provide empathy, reality, and support is abdicating both a teacher's principal responsibility and privilege. Refusing to understand the student's social milieu and accept the multivariate roles of teachers in working with students is to miss a wonderful opportunity to make a difference in the lives of children.

Next, we examine the impact of the newly reauthorized federal Individuals with Disabilities Education Act (IDEA, 2004) on students who have emotional or behavioral disorders and their parents.

Implications of IDEA (2004) Regulations for Students Who Have Emotional or Behavioral Disorders

First, the provisions of IDEA that require a functional behavioral assessment and a behavioral intervention plan that were established in the 1997 reauthorization of the act continue to be mandated in IDEA 2004; however, there have been a few changes to the 1997 regulations regarding discipline that could have a profound impact on the educational and, consequently, the social outcomes for students who have EBD.

The first of these relates to the 'stay put' provision, which previously was denied only to students with disabilities who are involved in drug sales or possession, the possession of weapons, or engagement in dangerous behavior, specifically regarded as the commission of violent acts. Under the new regulations, the right of a student who has a disability to 'stay put' in his or her current educational placement pending an appeal is eliminated.

The ramifications of this change for students who have EBD and their families are grave; for example, one immediate effect is the threat to such a child's assurance of a free and appropriate public education in the least restrictive environment, two of the key principles of IDEA. We have learned in this book that, for most students who have EBD, predictability with minimal disruption to routine are critical to academic success. Furthermore, under the Every Student Succeeds Act (U. S. Department of Education, 2015), children who are transferred to alternative settings during the course of the school year are not required to be included in the reporting of Adjusted Yearly Progress (AYP). This exclusion of challenging students by removing them to alternative settings might provide school administrators with a convenient solution to the deleterious effect of students who have EBD on AYP reports. Ostensibly, such an option might encourage the proliferation of disciplinary actions against these and other students who have disabilities.

Prior to the recent reauthorization, the burden of proof in determining that a student's behavior was not a manifestation of the child's disability, before standard sanctions could be imposed, fell on the school district. Under IDEA 2004, the burden of proof rests squarely with the child's parents. This is often a lop-sided battle because, without expert council or familiarity with the law, most parents do not know the procedures for collecting and presenting appropriate supporting data. Furthermore, the language requiring the Individualized Education Plan (IEP) team to consider whether the child's disorder impaired his ability to control or fully understand the consequences of his misbehavior has been deleted. Similarly, the language that required the multidisciplinary or IEP team to consider whether the IEP was appropriate has also been deleted. The possible implications of these omissions should be apparent to the reader.

In addition, a very important change affecting teachers is the revised standard for a basis of knowledge for children who are not yet eligible for special education and related services. Essentially, a local education agency (LEA) should be considered to have knowledge that a child has a bona-fide disability if, before the behavior that precipitated the disciplinary action occurred, a teacher of that child expressed concern in writing directly to either a school administrator or the director of special education that she "has specific concerns about a pattern of behavior demonstrated by the child" (U.S. Department of Education, 2004).

A minor change involves the forty-five-calendar-day limit on the removal of a student for school code violations. Effective in 2005, this removal limit has been extended to forty-five school days, which translates to nine weeks without participation in the school curriculum—a further impediment for students who are already struggling academically.

What are the implications of these changes for students who have emotional and behavioral disorders? These changes reflect a growing intolerance for acting out or dangerous behaviors on the part of society in general. Recent school shootings and the lingering war in Iraq, Afghanistan, and Ukraine as publicized in the media have helped to sensitize the American public to acts perceived as violent or antisocial. Adults and even children who engage in such behaviors receive little compassion these days, and tolerance for defiance and aggression is extremely low. If you were careful in your reading of the previous few pages, you will have noticed that this growing intolerance of antisocial acts among the general public is reflected in the amendments to the disciplinary statutes that once protected the rights of students who have EBD and their parents, placing the burden of proof for manifestation on school district officials. In 2004, however, that burden was removed from the school and placed squarely on the shoulders of the child's parents. The problem with such a transfer is that parents typically lack the data and legal expertise to argue effectively in support of their child's right to remain in the school.

Furthermore, we know from research that change is exceptionally difficult for students who have EBD and can simply exacerbate their behavior problems (Alhuzimi, 2020). This modification to IDEA will most assuredly aggravate these problems by increasing the likelihood that more students who have EBD will remain in alternative placements.

Similarly, the 2004 change in the language relative to the forty-five-day removal policy from calendar days to school days means that students awaiting a manifestation determination will be out of their home school for an additional two weeks. The possible negative effects of this extension are the same as those previously discussed.

What can we do, in light of these changes to IDEA, to ensure that we continue to serve as advocates for our students who have disabilities and their parents? First, we need to ensure that we employ behavioral interventions that are effective in helping to decrease the misbehavior of our students who have EBD. Second, we must ensure that the parents of these children understand their rights and responsibilities under IDEA 2004 and its changes regarding disciplinary procedures. This requires that we provide them with not only access to this information, but also that we explain some of the more technical aspects in a way that facilitates their understanding of the act as well as its implications for their child. Third, we have to convey these changes to the students they might affect in a way that is clear and concise. It is important that the students understand the consequences of violations of school rules and policies in light of the changes that have been made to the discipline provisions of IDEA (U.S. Department of Education, 2004).

Finally, there is one modification that is supportive of the implication of a child's disability relative to a misbehavior or act that results in disciplinary intervention or punishment, namely, that parents and teachers can establish a 'basis for knowledge' that a child committing a school code violation does or can be construed to have a disability as long as the parents or teachers have expressed "specific concern in writing about a pattern of behavior demonstrated by the child" or that the child is in need of special education services to the appropriate administrative personnel of the school or agency" (U.S. Department of Education, 2004). As long as a parent or teacher of the affected child has done this, then the school has a basis of knowledge for suggesting that the misbehavior is a manifestation of an existing disorder, that is, an emotional or behavioral disorder and, providing the child did not engage in dangerous behavior that includes the sale or possession of drugs or weapons, or has not inflicted serious bodily injury to himself or others, the school must provide a valid rationale for the removal of the child for more than ten consecutive days from his current educational placement.

Positive Effect of Technology and Meaningful Learning Experiences

Research has supported the benefit of meaningful learning experiences for students who have emotional and behavioral disorders (Smith et al. 2011). By *meaningful* we mean the teaching of skills that the student perceives as useful. If a student, or without a behavior disorder, asks you, "Why do I have to learn that?" and you cannot provide a valid rationale, perhaps the skill isn't worth learning. Clearly, as teachers, we must address the skills and topics mandated by the curriculum and prepare our students to take standardized tests; however, it is incumbent upon us to ensure that all of our students are engaged in some purposeful learning activity that prepares them for life and not just to be able to successfully complete tests (Popham, 2007).

The definition of *meaningful learning* is just that: skills and knowledge that prepare our students to live successful and independent lives, not simply as voyeurs or consumers of services, but also as participants and contributors. Is this an overly ambitious goal for teachers? We don't think so, because we know that self-efficacy is a critical component of self-esteem, and self-esteem correlates with ownership, value, and self-worth. When individuals feel that they have a stake in the outcome of things as well as in the rewards, they tend to develop a sense of ownership and are less likely to engage in behavior that jeopardizes its success; therefore, they are less inclined to act out, misbehave, steal, fight, vandalize, or engage in the destructive behaviors that society abhors.

That is not to say that providing meaningful learning activities will serve as a panacea for behavioral disorders. On the contrary, there will continue to be students who have been so affected by their unwholesome environment that they simply cannot integrate or use the skills learned in the classroom in productive ways and may continue to practice destructive behavior patterns. However, there is evidence that much of the antisocial behavior observed in schools can be significantly reduced by engaging the students in meaningful learning activities.

A Word on the Use of Computers

The proliferation of computers in schools and in society at large is no longer a phenomenon but an expectation. Given the versatility of computers, combined with access to the Internet and all the resources that such a connection provides, the usefulness of computers as an educational resource is unmatched. Furthermore, as a result of the larger class sizes in today's schools, the personal computer can often provide individualized instruction that the harried teacher cannot.

The advent of learner-centered software represents a paradigm shift in the pedagogical use of the computer. The unique benefits of this innovative software include (1) offering students a choice in selecting the goal of the activity, thus empowering students who have emotional or behavioral disorders, who typically feel disenfranchised in the learning process (2) providing feedback that is informational and nonjudgmental; and (3) encouraging estimation and approximation, which reinforce the importance of understanding the process whereby a solution is achieved and not focusing solely on providing the correct response (Quintana et al., 2013). Similarly, word processing software encourages students to write more and, ultimately, better, because typewritten drafts are easier to edit and thus facilitate revision, as well as compensating for some students' illegible handwriting.

Regardless of which academic interventions we use to help improve the educational performance of students who have EBD, the fact remains that we must acknowledge the recursive relationship between a child's learning set and misbehavior that impedes it. Academic achievement is highly correlated with engagement, so interventions that increase the latter have a higher probability of success. An example of one such approach is direct instruction (Winarno et al., 2018), which emphasizes the structure, sequencing, and pacing of instruction as well as the opportunity to receive feedback and practice.

Other effective practices include class-wide peer tutoring (CWPT) (Maheady, & Gard, 2010) and reciprocal peer tutoring (RPT) (Dufrene et al., 2005; Moliner & Alegre, 2020). Both of these approaches have been shown to increase students' academic engagement and rates of responding. The success realized as a result of employing either of these tutoring formats is attributed to the effects of group-oriented contingencies. In both programs, the student is reinforced through the praise and encouragement generated by a more skilled peer as well as by the opportunity for immediate error correction and reinforcement.

Yet another effective academic learning intervention that we have acknowledged several times throughout this book is self-monitoring, also frequently referred to as self-management or self-recording (Menzies et al., 2009). This strategy improves the academic performance of students who have EBD by teaching these students systematic procedures for observing, evaluating, and recording their own behavior at specific times during the school day. The benefit of this practice for the student is the improvement in his rate of on-task behavior and, consequently, an increase in academic productivity. Similarly, continuous monitoring of student performance is a very effective practice in improving academic performance. This is especially true in conjunction with curriculum-based measurement (CBM), which uses performance scores on criterion-referenced tests to inform instructional decisions (Hosp et al., 2016).

Next, we turn our attention to the pragmatics of classroom management and how to teach those students who are the most personally challenging. We informally refer to them as 'trigger children' because they seem so adept at finding and exploiting our vulnerabilities.

How to Work Effectively with Children that Provoke Confrontation

These are children who seem to have a real capacity for inciting anger and outrage and provoking nontherapeutic responses from teachers and other caregivers. These children typically manifest the disruptive disorders we described in Chapters 2 and 3, conduct disorder and oppositional defiance disorder; however, children who have anxiety disorders such as obsessive-compulsive disorder (see Chapter 6) can also fall in this category. In truth, any child whose behaviors cause professional educators, caregivers, or parents to respond in kind—that is, in an unprofessional manner—constitutes, for that individual, a 'trigger child.'

First, as we discussed earlier, it is important to find a reason to like the trigger child. Sometimes this can be accomplished through conscientious effort on the teacher's part; for example, initiating conversation with the child on a topic in which he is interested, praising the child for some small accomplishment, or asking about her well-being can foster compassion. Learning about the child's history, engaging the parents in a collaborative discussion about the child's school experience as well as behavior displayed at home, recreational preferences, likes and dislikes, can provide the teacher with valuable insights into the child and his behavioral repertoire.

A Word About Relationships

In our experience, there is no single intervention that surpasses the benefit of relationship. Establishing one with a child who has an emotional or behavioral disorder is not a guarantee that the undesired behavior will disappear or even diminish, but without one, the behaviors will probably continue and likely escalate, at least in your classroom. By relationship we do not imply that the teacher need compete with parents, relatives, or best friends. We are instead referring to a healthy, affirming pro-social human connection. Most children who have EBD experience a real challenge in making friends with peers, let alone establishing relationships with authority figures. Your efforts in that endeavor will improve your classroom climate, make interactions with the child more positive, preclude or reduce defiant and confrontational behaviors while simultaneously providing the affected individual with a wonderful model for establishing and sustaining relationships in the future.

Developing relationships with these students is a risky business because, many times, the child's disorder almost compels him to try to destroy or scuttle relationships. Children who have EBD are generally so used to rejection and isolation that they simply do not have any experience in establishing and maintaining relationships. Likewise, they often do not have any examples of healthy, reciprocal relationships to draw on. Establishing a relationship with one of these children requires a leap of faith on the part of the teacher, because one cannot truly enter into a relationship with another individual without trust, and trust requires a certain level of self-disclosure. Relationship, like dialogue, is a shared experience, one that demands reciprocity.

The best way to start developing a relationship with one of your affected students is simply to be yourself. That is sometimes more difficult than it sounds because, as teachers, we often play an expected role, one that was modeled for us by our mentor-teachers and was typically devoid of relationship—except for those few special teachers who made a difference in our appreciation of school and, subsequently, of life. If we were able to analyze the interpersonal skills employed by our favorite teachers, we would find, invariably, that they were just being themselves and generously shared the best of who they were with us, their students. Why take such risks, you might ask; isn't such behavior crossing the line demarcating professionalism? The answer is an unqualified NO. How else can children learn to connect with the world and enjoy interacting in a positive and prosocial way with others?

Knowing others and being known by them is beneficial to students who have EBD on three levels: first, by simply sharing feelings or experiences or personal anecdotes, we bring our students closer and let them know that personal sharing is welcome; second, opportunities to engage in polite discourse such as those teachers provide may not be possible in other aspects of the students' lives and can enable them to engage in the kind of reciprocal communication that will be helpful to them in life; third, the process of unpacking, that is, letting oneself be known and, likewise, learning about others, is a step toward better mental health, a deeper sense of connectedness or belongingness (Kohn, 2006) and an enrichment of one's self-esteem.

Another strategy that has potential in changing defiant, disruptive student behaviors is simply to avoid reacting to such behavior and meeting anger and hostility with kindness. There is an aphorism in the Bible that states, "A soft answer turns away wrath," and this is a very poignant maxim for teachers working with a difficult child. This does not mean we do not impose consequences for rule-breaking and insubordinate behavior; it simply means that our demeanor and behavioral response is not influenced by the child's maladaptive behavior. By avoiding the temptation to react in kind, we free ourselves to try alternatives that avoid the struggle for power and teach the student ways of resolving conflict appropriately, without 'losing face.'

Likewise, humor, if appropriate to the circumstances, can help defuse a potentially explosive situation. Also, a humorous anecdote, strategically interjected, can be a wonderful stress reliever. It can also teach a lesson in a way that is nonthreatening and far more palatable than an exposition about right versus wrong. In this vein, we are reminded of the teacher who, noticing one of her newest students standing alone at one end of the soccer field while her classmates frolicked farther down the field, asked how she was feeling. The student, appearing rather distracted, shot back a terse, "Fine, thank you, Ma'am." This raised the level of concern of the teacher, a special educator, who was nonplussed and emboldened to inquire further: "Do you have any friends?" The student, once again, responded cryptically, "Lots!" Finally, the teacher, inspired to take action, sidled up to the alienated child and asked sincerely, "Would you like me to be your friend?" Exasperated, the young girl looked at the teacher and said, "Yes, Ma'am, but could you please get off the soccer field, we're playing a game here and I'm the goalie!" In recounting this humorous anecdote, we are reminded of the old adage, "Laughter is the best medicine," and often when working through crises in the classroom, so it is!

Another important strategy in working with the difficult child is engaging in nonjudgmental conversation, what can also be referred to as active listening. Often, as teachers, we are so used to providing solutions that we feel we must do so even when our most troubled students express a concern, fear, or problem; however, many times this is not what the student wants or needs; she just needs a sympathetic ear, someone who will not judge her disclosure.

"Confession is good for the soul," the saying goes, and sharing sensitive or troubling issues is cathartic and requires great courage and trust; being able to just listen and not offer rebuke or unsolicited advice builds such trust. Children who have EBD often have real issues about trusting adults, and by engaging in non-judgmental conversation, teachers demonstrate that some adults are trustworthy, thus increasing the likelihood that these children will confide in them in the future.

Avoiding the Pitfalls of Stereotyping

While we acknowledge that, as special educators, we work within the framework of IDEA and the thirteen categories of disability that are encompassed therein; nevertheless, we do not advocate the arbitrary classification of students who have emotional or behavioral issues without applying early and prereferral interventions to mitigate the stigma of the emotional disturbance diagnosis. It is our conviction, however, that students who truly meet the criteria and do not respond to prereferral intervention should be appropriately classified in order to receive the benefit of the full array of special education services available to them.

We contend that often, a far more destructive outcome of the classification of emotional disturbance (ED) is represented in the rush to judgment and the misperceptions and outright fallacies it engenders in the unenlightened. Too often, children who have been classified as ED are assumed to be defiant, antisocial, violent, or disruptive. This assumption is frequently incorrect because, as we know from reading this book, many students receive this classification because of an anxiety or mood disorder, and these children rarely display the types of behaviors that teachers find either threatening or disruptive. It is, therefore, incumbent on teachers to help reduce the stigma that is associated with the classification of emotional disturbance by educating their students and their parents about the nature of ED and its various typologies. Books such as this one help teachers do just that by providing current and complete information about the various disorders encompassed within this broad category.

Understanding Diversity and Its Relevance to Identification and Intervention

First, we want to remind teachers of the significant studies conducted in the latter half of the 1990s and continuing today that establish the disproportionate identification of children and youth of color as recipients of special education. Whereas African Americans make up about 12 percent of the U.S. population, they constitute a disproportionate 24 percent of children receiving special education services (U.S. Department of Education, 2017). Research has revealed that much of this overidentification is related to racial stereotyping and discriminatory practices (Blanchette, 2014). In addition to African Americans, research has also demonstrated a similar disproportionate representation of Latino and Native American children (U.S. Department of Education, 2017). In fact, over the past three decades, research has continued to reveal a pattern of overrepresentation of all three ethnic groups, particularly in the more stigmatizing categories of mental retardation, emotional disturbance, and communication disorder (Blanchett, 2006; Blanchett, 2014; Fish, 2019). Furthermore, to dispel another misperception that is frequently held by the majority culture, poverty is not a significant contribution to disproportionality in special education—in fact, recent studies have demonstrated that race continues to be the single most significant correlate (Skiba & Peterson, 2000).

In response to this patent inequity, IDEA (U.S. Department of Education, 2004) required, effective July 1, 2005, the collection and examination of data from each state to determine if significant disproportionality based on race and ethnicity is occurring within state and local education agencies (LEAs) with respect to (1) the identification of children as children who have disabilities in accordance with a particular impairment as described in Section 602 (3), (2) the placement in a particular educational setting of such children; and (3) the incidence, duration, and type of disciplinary actions, including suspensions and expulsions.

The reauthorization of IDEA has established specific requirements that must be followed when reviewing policies and procedures of states or LEAs in the case of a determination of significant disproportionality with respect to the identification of children as children who have disabilities.

In such cases, the state must provide for review and, if appropriate, revision of policies, procedures, and practices that may have caused the overrepresentation, require any such LEA to provide comprehensive early intervention services to serve all children in the LEA, particularly children from overidentified groups, and require the LEA to report on the revised policies, practices, and procedures (U.S. Department of Education, 2017). Relative to the disproportionate representation of minority populations, particularly in the category of emotional disturbance, teachers should implement a solution-focused approach to early intervention (Green et al., 2019; Raines et al., 2012). Such an approach addresses the potential for prejudice among the students' teachers and related services personnel, helping them to be more understanding and supportive, focusing on the affected child's behavioral strengths rather than his shortcomings (i.e., non-pathologizing versus problem-saturated perspective). Integral to this solution-focused approach is allowing the student to be the 'expert' in developing solutions to his behavior issues rather than viewing the child as 'the problem.' Examples of questions that a teacher can use to help the student who is at risk for referral become the 'expert' in developing some effective solutions include the following:

- "Tell me about a time when you could have easily blown up, but instead, you kept your cool."
- "How did you deal with the urge to blow up?"
- "What advice would you give to someone your age who's having a hard time controlling their temper?"

A second phase of the solution-focused approach is to create a portfolio or book with the at-risk student that documents the individual's strengths and improvements and also contains a classroom-based contingency management plan that is based on a points reward system.

Another way that teachers can help to reduce the incidence of misidentification or overidentification of 'minority-categorized' children is by learning to appreciate the different ways that parents from diverse cultures interact with school personnel and the traditions of the school. This knowledge or cultural competence may help teachers appreciate the various ways that their students approach the school and its teachers, which may reflect cultural norms that differ from those of the dominant society. In other words, teachers need to ask themselves, "Is the child's behavior truly maladaptive, or am I simply reacting to behavioral norms that are different from mine and projecting my cultural expectations on this child?"

Teachers are the primary source of referral for special education services, and 75 to 80 percent of children who are referred for evaluation are classified; therefore, it is critical these teachers ensure that their reasons for referral are based on scientific evidence and are not influenced by cultural or ethnic bias. This requires honest self-reflection and thoughtful consideration of a holistic evaluation of the child's problem behaviors and their context—in other words, a conscientiously applied functional behavioral assessment (Cavendish et al., 2014; Harry & Klingner, 2014). In short, if a student from an ethnic minority group (e.g., African American, Latino, or Native American) is legitimately identified as needing special education services, the interventions, provided they are based on a sound and thorough FBA and are research-based, should prove as successful as they would for a similarly identified child from the majority cultural group.

The real challenge is ensuring that teachers strive to provide effective early intervention that is scientifically based and appropriate for the individual before referring the child for formal evaluation by the multidisciplinary team (MDT). Likewise, it is important that teachers examine their own cultural biases when working with a child from another ethnicity or culture who presents behavior problems to ensure that, to the extent possible, these inherent or unconscious biases do not influence their perception of the child and her behavioral purposes (Cavendish et al., 2014; Harry & Klingner, 2014).

Working Collaboratively with the Families of Students who Have Emotional/Behavioral Disorders

IDEA (U.S. Department of Education, 2004; 2017usdoe) requires that parents receive notification and are included in all aspects of their child's special education experience; nonetheless, the benefits of parent involvement appear to be self-evident (Hara & Burke, 1998). Christenson and Cleary (1990) provide a list of some of the most frequently identified benefits of parent involvement (1) students' grade and test scores improve, they complete more homework, and they are more involved in classroom activities; (2) teachers are perceived as having better interpersonal and teaching skills, are given higher teacher evaluation scores by principals, and report greater job satisfaction; (3) parents show better understanding of school functions, enjoy better communication with their children and teachers relative to school work, and are more involved in their children's homework; and (4) parents regard school as more effective in providing successful school programs.

Schultz et al. (2016) noted that parent-teacher collaboration produces significant beneficial effects for teachers as well. Specifically, research has determined that teachers' self-efficacy is positively correlated with parent involvement in conferences, volunteering, and home tutoring. Likewise, teachers with high self-efficacy tend to see parents as significant contributors to the academic success of their students (Topor et al., 2010). Based on these and other findings, it seems to be to the school's advantage to develop greater parent involvement through approaches that facilitate increased parent participation in the education of their children.

Barriers to the collaborative process between parents and teachers include: (1) lack of consistent and personal contact, e.g., via weekly newsletters, bulletins, or notes; (2) the tendency to use disprivileging speech that alienates parents, such as when teachers employ professional jargon or acronyms such as IEP, CSE, IDEA, or LRE without explanation; (3) patronizing speech that places parents in a 'one-down' or subservient role to teachers; (4) planning IEP meetings, annual reviews, or parent-teacher conferences at times that accommodate the teachers but represent a scheduling challenge for working parents; and (5) failure to make the parent feel valued and important to the process; as well as (6) not recognizing that parental resistance or hostility may represent a historic distrust of schools and the school system (Bang, 2018; Murray et al., 2014). Similarly, Bang (2018) noted that "...being passive, unreasonably demanding, and going directly to a director to protest were considered to hinder parent-teacher collaborations... that there is a perceptional gap and limited understanding between teachers and parents regarding the types of behavior needed for effective collaboration" (p. 1787).

These barriers can be removed, according to Fine (1991), by (1) including parents in the decision-making process for their child; (2) educating these parents regarding their rights under IDEA and as bona-fide members of the decision-making team; and (3) empowering them through the development of trust and mutual respect. In a similar vein, Bang (2018) states that "[parents and teachers] should develop an understanding based on their views and experiences, which necessitates more opportunities to communicate with frankness and authenticity" (p.1787). In short, parents should feel that they share a mandate with the multidisciplinary team, that is, to make educational decisions and design effective interventions that are in the best interests of their child.

The following represent some of the ways that teachers can facilitate the involvement of parents as collaborators in their child's treatment. First, teachers can help to educate parents about child and adolescent developmental characteristics so that parents will have reasonable expectations for child behavior and learning across grade levels. Second, teachers can use a variety of means to communicate with parents on a routine basis; for example, they can send progress reports home, call parents to remind them about upcoming classroom activities and parent-teacher meetings and workshops, and, where appropriate, schedule meetings with parents not just in the school but, where feasible, in a variety of conducive locations. Third, parents can be encouraged to volunteer in the school. As volunteers, they can assist with class trips, help with individual tutoring, assist with projects and crafts, and read aloud to small groups. Fourth, parents can provide valuable oversight for homework. To facilitate this, some schools provide "college in the classroom" workshops after school in which the children's teachers instruct parents about the content skills currently taught in the classroom, thus providing parents with the knowledge necessary to be a valuable at-home tutor. Fifth, parents can and should be involved in decision-making, governance, and advocacy through membership in one or more parent-teacher organizations and committees such as a Parent-Teacher Association-PTA or Special Education Parent Teacher Association-SEPTA.

Finally, parents should be informed by the school about various community support groups that can provide outside resources in support of their frame of reference, that is, the individual's knowledge of the issues as well as any prejudices or orientations in conjunction with that person's emotional investment in the outcomes; introducing ideas noncompetitively—avoiding their win-lose quality; for example, present ideas as suggestions, not mandates; and avoid off-topic conversations that prove a distraction rather than a solution; instead, approach any parent-teacher conflict using a solution-oriented process whereby both stakeholders reach agreement on what they want to happen, relative to the affected child, and what needs to occur to realize that goal.

Research conducted within the last twenty years has also produced recommendations for both the preservice and in-service teacher (Ratcliff & Hunt, 2009). In the case of preservice teachers, the research asks them to (1) consider their own perceptions and beliefs about parents and parent involvement, (2) understand the parents' perspective relative to their support for the teacher's educational goals, (3) investigate parent-school practices, (4) review studies on parent-teacher interaction, (5) participate in role-playing activities to help prepare for actual communication with parents, (6) engage in actual parent conferences as an integral part of field experience, (7) candidly assess the quality of communication with parents, and (8) develop a parent collaboration plan that complements the teacher's personality, experience, and teaching goals (Ratcliff & Hunt, 2009).

Ratcliff and Hunt (2009) and others urged schools to provide workshops in which real teachers share their successful collaborative experiences with parents. They proposed that these workshops also specifically address the development of teacher-parent collaboration skills, effective communication techniques, and shared governance with parents. Finally, they contended that teachers need opportunities to employ collaborative practices involving parents and then assess these practices to determine the most effective ones.

Final Thoughts

We hope that the reader will appreciate the importance we place on conducting good assessment in the case of students who misbehave and demonstrate emotional and behavioral disorders. Target behaviors must be carefully identified and measured for two reasons: first, to establish a baseline on which to base intervention goals; and second, to assess the effectiveness of interventions with an eye to achieving the maximum benefit for the student. Simply put, teachers cannot provide effective interventions that produce meaningful and lasting improvements without conducting sound, measurable assessment using reliable and valid instruments. That is not to say that every aspect of the child's maladaptive behavior can be measured using a schedule or checklist; some of the elements that form pathological behavior patterns, such as personological variables like temperament, are affective and are not easily quantified. In acknowledgement of this, Kauffman (2005) noted, "Teaching is much more than measurement. A mechanical approach to teaching that excludes affective concerns is no more justifiable than an approach that neglects cognitive and behavioral goals" (p. 440). He added, "If the student's most important behavioral characteristics are not monitored, however, then it will be almost impossible for the teacher to communicate anything of substance about the student's progress to the youngster or to anyone else" (p. 440).

It is important that teachers understand that, despite all the rhetoric about one size fits all programs and new research-based interventions, there are truly only four things they can provide a student who has an emotional or behavioral disorder: caring (empathy), honesty (reality), support (academic and emotional), and consistency. It is essential that teachers find a reason to *care* for each of their students, and the reason must be founded. We can all do that! Caring does not mean that we do not provide relevant consequences, and it does not imply that we should allow students to dodge accountability through excuses. What it does mean is that we recognize the capacity for kindness and civility that is inherent in every human being and nurture the humanity in every student we teach.

Furthermore, we must be *honest* with our students and with ourselves. Our students are constantly observing us and unconsciously measuring the degree to which our actions support our words. Does their scrutiny disclose our hypocrisy or our integrity? Children and youth who have EBD need us to be honest in our communications about both their deficiencies and their strengths. Compliments need to be founded on real accomplishments, not on empty pronouncements about future achievement. The child in our class who has conduct disorder may never be the CEO of a major corporation, but he can achieve a quality of life that includes happy times with family and friends, satisfying work, and financial stability.

Support is the one thing that most teachers are eager and willing to provide to each of their students. However, support for a child with an emotional or behavioral disorder does not include watering down the curriculum, extending a due date because the student made excuses, or holding that student to an inferior standard. On the contrary, research has supported that all students, particularly those with emotional and behavioral disorders, respond to higher standards in kind (Kohn, 2006). Thus, academic support and, for the most part, emotional support, needs to be scaffolded and follow the notion of proximal development espoused by Vygotsky (1978) and others. To borrow an aphorism attributed to Thomas Jefferson, "[Teachers] should not do for students what they can do for themselves." Struggle is good, as Kauffman (2005) observed "The teacher's task is to choose at first just manageable tasks for students and then gradually allow them to set their own goals as they become attuned to their true capabilities and desires" (p. 442).

Teachers need to provide consistency for their students who have emotional or behavioral challenges. If you establish a classroom rule, you must enforce it and provide the stated consequences every time it is broken. Be very careful about making promises and threats; whatever you promise must be actualized, because your credibility is at stake. As we have learned, students who have emotional and behavioral disorders thrive on consistency; they typically have been exposed to models of inconsistency and whimsy at home and thus frequently look to teachers to provide stability and predictability.

We offer the following anecdote to highlight the importance of this characteristic. As a weekly behavioral incentive, one of the authors typically provided his high school students with a breakfast of bagels and cream cheese every Friday morning. On one such Friday, he was running late and decided not to stop at the bagel shop on his way to school. When he got to school, however, he discovered that his students had not forgotten, and they were clearly disappointed; some even said that they counted on their Friday bagel as breakfast for the day. Seeing how important this ritual was to the students, the author requisitioned a van and took them to the bagel shop, after which they resumed normal classroom activities, appeased and gratified that an important expectation had been met. To the extent possible, teachers must be dependable and model consistent behaviors.

One of the characteristics of many of our children and youth who have EBD that we have not stressed in this book is the need to feel and be safe. This is not exclusive to these children; it is, of course, an essential human need identified by Maslow (McLeod, 2014) and others. Nevertheless, many of these children are extremely vulnerable individuals and do not know how to be or feel safe. Often, their homes and communities are fearful places in which they are neither physically nor emotionally safe. Teachers can help these children feel secure by modeling safe behaviors.

Safe behaviors are the antithesis of risk-taking ones; students who have EBD are frequently consummate risk takers, but they seldom know how to avoid dangers and reduce the risks that imperil their young lives on many levels. The modeling of safe behavior can be accomplished when teachers make choices that are healthy, such as pursuing a hobby, playing a team sport, eating a salad instead of a hamburger, and avoiding unhealthy behaviors such as smoking, drinking excessively, and not using epithets or slurs to denigrate a colleague or student.

Teachers also model safe behavior when they avoid provocation and remain calm in a crisis. Lastly, teachers model safe behavior when they follow the rules they espouse and adhere to a personal philosophy that values integrity and honesty but does not neglect fun and sharing a good laugh with others. Ironically, many times, students who have EBD engage in risk-taking behavior either consciously or unconsciously to prove to us that we cannot keep them safe, and they are usually right! However, we can help them learn to make the kinds of choices that will, in time, ensure that they can take responsibility for their own well-being.

We close this chapter and the book with a passage written by Clark Cavin (1998), a very committed special educator; from his article, *Maintaining Sanity in an Insane Classroom*:

> Above all, remember that these kids with all of their problems, their criminal records, their probation officers, their idiosyncrasies, their unlovable characteristics, and their strange families are still kids. They

> need someone to care. They need someone to accept them. They need to know they are somebody. If you are willing to provide these ideals, you can be the connection that bridges the gap from dropout to diploma.
>
> Working with students who have behavioral disorders and emotional disturbances is the most challenging undertaking in education. If you are searching for rewards and accolades, teach gifted and talented or one of the fine arts. If you teach because you love the subject matter, choose English, history, Spanish, math, or whatever subject excites you. If you want to work with neat kids who really care and want to better themselves, work in honors, athletics, or student government. But, if you want to set up camp a few feet outside the gates of hell and try to rescue a few just before they tumble in, join me in this place. Few will praise you. Colleagues may look on you as a second-class citizen. Most of the kids will not appreciate you. You won't get Christmas gifts or thank-you letters. Your deepest satisfaction comes from knowing that Chris and Nick would not have graduated without you, that Marvin would have been expelled without you, that Eric ran away from home and would not give his new phone number to anyone but you. With a whole lot of love, prayer, and hard work, you did the impossible. And, tomorrow morning, when the bell rings at 8:00, you will have the opportunity to do the impossible again (p. 384).

We sincerely hope that tomorrow morning, when the bell rings, you will be there, in your classroom, ready to teach these challenged and challenging students who desperately need you, whether they know it or not.

From the Field

Nina Zaragoza, Ph.D.

From the beginning of her career to the present, Nina Zaragoza has worked in urban environments as an early childhood teacher, elementary school teacher, special education teacher, English teacher, professor of education, and director of education for a nonprofit organization focused on children. Her professional journey has taken her from Buffalo to Miami, to Vladimir, Russia, to Brooklyn, and the South Bronx, and has enabled her to work with children, youth, teachers, and community youth workers of varying ethnicities and backgrounds. In the past few years, she served as a special education teacher in Brooklyn, an adjunct professor at local colleges, and a consultant with children, teachers, community workers, and families in New York City and abroad. Dr. Zaragoza is presently the president of Creative Curriculum Connections, Inc.

As someone who has been a classroom teacher as well as a researcher, author, and college professor, you have had the benefit of several vantage points from which to view and "experience" the development of the field of special education. Because this book is primarily concerned with students who have emotional and behavioral disorders, can you share your insights and a personal experience or two relative to IDEA (2004) and its implications for them?

The IDEA's emphasis on high expectations and its focus on ensuring all students the foundation and opportunity to pursue further education have powerful implications for students and teachers. Because of IDEA, teachers now have the privilege of looking beyond traditional assumptions about academic proficiency and access because of behavioral and emotional difficulties. IDEA supports all students' right to receive the dignity and respect they deserve, no matter what their label. Now, with the support of IDEA, teachers must provide purposeful, relevant work which enables all students to progress and strive toward continued and life-long learning. In fact, IDEA helps teachers and students break the debilitating chains of low-expectations and look beyond to healthy work and relationships.

As a classroom teacher of children labeled "special education," I often notice that my students do much more than expected by the administration and their other teachers. These low expectations deeply sadden me, but I hope that the work of my students will inspire others to look beyond the labels. Indeed, my students' performances of poetry, self-authored drama productions, and purposeful work in the community (i.e., visiting senior homes, contributing writing to local libraries, etc.) confirm the belief that all students can and want to learn.

I saw this same confirmation in the glowing faces of twelve high schoolers with emotional and behavioral difficulties when they read their own stories to children at a neighboring elementary school. These high school students worked through feelings of helplessness, anxiety, and fear of public speaking to serve as reading models to the younger children. Yes, there were difficulties for the teacher and students during the writing, finding pictures to the text, and bookbinding. And it was even more difficult to convince these students, who have already met with so much failure academically, emotionally, and behaviorally, to step out and share. But because we persevered with diligence and faith, we will always remember the success symbolized by Andre, a 15-year-old who, upon leaving the elementary school, kissed his book and said, "I won't ever forget this!"

Based on your professional experiences and insights, how has the proliferation of technology improved learning and achievement for students who have emotional and behavioral disorders, among others with disabilities?

I think that technology in these classrooms can have varying effects depending on how and when the teacher encourages its use. Technology used as a part of purposeful work, i.e., writing, publication, and some electronic communication, serves to ease some of the obstacles that have previously hindered many of our students. For example, difficulties with spelling and grammar can be eased with the various spell and grammar check programs available. I often see, though, that excessive use of computer-assisted instruction and assessment has negative effects on academic and social growth. Learning happens within relationships, and the necessary time needed to form and strengthen these teaching and learning relationships should be paramount. When children are placed in front of computers to learn concepts that can be done within relationships, valuable lessons of community and connections are lost.

I also think that technology such as television, computers, and handheld games permeate many of the homes of our students. Too often parents place their children in front of the TV to manage and control them. Too often children sit before the computer screen for hours playing games, interacting with WebKins, My Space, etc. I do not support any justification of this excessive use and, in fact, because of the prominent place of television/computer programs in the home, we as teachers must limit such use in the classroom. Whether television/computer programs exhibit educational value, this is not justification enough to deny children the real social interaction so necessary for academic and emotional growth.

Before I discuss concrete examples and specific suggestions, I'd like to note that my suggestions focus on teacher thinking and behavior. We can complain endlessly about student behavior, lack of administrative support, lack of parental concern, poor living conditions, etc., etc., and while we might want to address these areas in different ways at different times, we often do not have control over them. So we can either choose to allow these factors to block us and paralyze us to bitter inaction or we can decide to look at what we can do and what we can change within our own area of influence. We each have the power to look at the underlying reasons for our responses toward these "difficult" children. We, indeed, have the power to not react negatively and decide to change our perceptions of the student and of the behavior. Let's get on to some real scenarios for clarity.

As an educational consultant, many schools call me to work in classrooms to help support teachers and students. I am sometimes asked to follow students seen as troublesome and disruptive so that I can give suggestions to help improve the situation. These are the students seen loitering in high school hallways because they don't care to enter the classroom, or they have been sent out of the classroom because of inappropriate behavior. While some variation in behavior occurs depending on the teacher, some common teacher behaviors/practices are usually evident across classrooms. For example, because teachers expect negative, disruptive behavior from these students, they notice every little movement made. I saw this recently in one high school English classroom. When John called out or turned to his friend to talk, an immediate reprimand followed. When another student exhibited the same disruptive behavior, it was ignored. In every class, teachers were either hypervigilant in regard to John or totally ignored him for the entire period and allowed him to come and go as he pleased. These extremes came from good intentions but need to be examined more deeply.

Let's think about the messages we send John and his classmates through these behaviors. Of course, everyone knows, John included, that John is a "marked" man, i.e., a "trigger child." This already colors the messages that teachers send. Therefore, everyone expects John to be either negatively signaled out or allowed to get away with murder. Whether one or the other happens usually depends on the mood and energy of the teacher. This unpredictability wreaks havoc in any classroom and actually does the same internally to the students and teachers involved. We all need to feel emotionally safe and secure before any learning happens.

While ignoring inappropriate behavior definitely has its place, it must occur within a context of positive recognition. Therefore, while I often suggest ignoring a behavior until it is extinguished, this technique will be totally ineffective and actually harmful if the student does not also receive recognition for positive work and interactions. Yes, I can already hear some of you thinking, "But he/she never does anything positive!" You know what? I don't believe this. I believe that you have allowed this child to drain you so that you cannot see the small, positive interactions that happen right before your eyes. He/she sits and waits patiently for five minutes before class begins. He turns to the right page. He raises his hand without calling out. He enters the room and says, "Hello, Miss." Do you say hello back, or do you answer with something sarcastic (also mislabeled "humor"). Can you say, "Thank you, John, I see you raised your hand and haven't called out." Or "I'm sorry we didn't start right away but I noticed, John, you were waiting patiently for us to begin." This kind of recognition and appreciation needs to be part of our classroom culture. But sadly, in almost every classroom I visit, it is not. (For more details, see Shanika's story in Zaragoza [2002]). Let me point out, though, ignoring doesn't mean that we allow a student to sit and not complete the required work because, "at least he/she is quiet." These low expectations send the clear message, whether intentional or not, that you do not care about this student's progress. The message sent, whether intentional or not, clearly states that this student means less to you than the others. The message states that you do not have faith in this student and that you do not care. Yes, I know these words sound harsh, but think about the harshness of the messages you inadvertently send. Teaching is a high calling and a serious responsibility. Do we need to be perfect? Of course not. Must we reflect continually on our words and actions? Most definitely.

Clear, appropriate consequences need to be in place for all students to address incomplete or missing work. But it actually isn't difficult to understand why so many of our students do not complete the work given. For a minute, let's put ourselves in their places. Look at the actual tasks you require. Would you like to complete them? Do they really hold any value in the big picture? Answer the questions after the passage, write a summary, color in the right bubble. Why? If you answer, "Because that's what we're told to do," then I beseech you to rethink what you are doing and why. Did you become a teacher to push papers or to have a positive impact on the next generation? If you answer the latter, then you know teaching and learning is much more than filling in the blank and test prep. You know that it is about purpose, joy, and service to others. Students involved in work that has a purpose and impact on an audience (i.e., drama, poetry, community project) will complete it. (For more details, see "Project Orientation" at www.ninazaragoza.com.)

Finally, let me encourage you as you reflect upon your responses to your students to take care of your own emotional health. We all have issues that in certain contexts negatively color our thoughts and interactions. For example, if we have a psychological need to be in a position of authority, this might hinder us from enabling our students to have authority and ownership over their own work and choices. If we have a tendency to note what we lack instead of acknowledging our own strengths, then we will more times than not first see the deficits in others before seeking to understand their strengths. I ask that you open your heart to yourself and your students. For in the end, real teaching and learning happens within caring, connected relationships.

In your books and publications, you discuss the importance of appreciating diversity in its many connotations. Based on your experience, how can teachers ensure that they consider cultural, language, and learning differences when working with students who engage in maladaptive and/or disruptive behaviors?

To ensure that all students in our classes are appreciated and honored for who they are, we need to set up a noncompetitive, nurturing classroom community so that all members feel safe to be who they are and who they are becoming. Appreciating diversity is not about designating a special month for this or that culture but about giving voice to the personal story of each student and teacher. Therefore, in my classrooms, Langston Hughes' poetry permeates the curriculum all year—not just in February. We study Jose Marti, Nikki Giovanni, Toni Morrison over the year as students are enabled to make choices to connect to a variety of authors. I also encourage and enable (through library, museum visits, guest speakers, etc.) my students and families to share aspects of their cultures so that we continue classroom and cultural connections throughout the year.

Curriculum decisions also honor diversity. For example, when students have some choice about their reading material, writing topics, long-term projects, and response to material covered, we continue to learn about who they are and what they care about. Indeed, we begin to know each other, and what better way to show honor but to know and deeply care about each individual heart.

Another theme in this chapter that is addressed in your writing relates to working collaboratively with parents and families of students who have disabilities. Because, frequently, the parents of students who have emotional and behavioral disorders as well as those of children who have other disabilities feel a sense of alienation from the school and are, consequently, reluctant to approach teachers for help. Could you share some ways that you have engaged them as collaborators in their child's learning?

Again, in the end (and the beginning!), it's a matter of the heart. When families begin to understand that you care about their children, they themselves begin to feel cared for. So we, as teachers, must grow to care about each and every child. If we do not care about our students, then we have already lost our families. Why would a parent want to connect to a teacher who either openly or subtly dislikes their child? I ask you to put yourself in their place. I ask that you do whatever inner work necessary to build love and compassion for each one of your students no matter how difficult they may be and no matter how many you have. Yes, this is deep, serious, and difficult. But it must be part of the teaching and learning process.

I hear from many teachers that it is difficult to care about certain children, that some children are unlikeable. This grieves me. Perhaps we dislike the behavior of a student, but the student's behavior is not the student. Sadly, so many forget to keep the label separated from the child and have children designated as "favorites." I hear, "But it's normal to have favorites. That's just human nature." I do not accept this dangerous belief that divides students against students. We have a duty to view each and every one of our students with eyes of compassion, eyes that look beyond labels, culture, socioeconomic status, and, yes, beyond behavior. We have the duty to, indeed, see a positive, healthy vision for this student and set up respectful classroom environments that support this vision.

How will families know that you care? They will know because you:

- Smile when you see them
- Respect their knowledge by asking for suggestions and insight about their child
- Write consistent notes with positive news about their child
- Translate all written material, workshop information, etc., into their first language
- Send appropriate homework that exhibits that you have taken the time to teach the homework concepts
- Give appropriate notice and sufficient guidance for long-term projects so as not to add stress to family
- Make regular phone calls (even in middle school and high school) to report on progress
- Arrange workshops at various times to allow for different work schedules and younger siblings

Finally, I ask that you have compassion for your families. Perhaps they do things that you totally disagree with. Perhaps these behaviors negatively influence their children's progress. Perhaps you're right. But remember, parents love their children and do the best they can with what they know and what they have. Show compassion and treat their children the way that you would want your own treated. (See Zaragoza [2005] for more detail.)

Is there a success story from your considerable experience in the field relative to a student who has an emotional or behavioral disorder that negatively affects his or her learning that you could share with our readers, which might provide them with an additional insight or intervention strategy?

I will always hold dear the story I shared above about the twelve high schoolers who worked through writing and publication to read their own stories to elementary school children. I will never forget their faces that showed confidence and satisfaction in an important job finished and well done. The following day the teacher sent me an email saying, "That was amazing. Best part of the year for myself and my students. Thank you so much for everything!"

In fact, part of this success story includes this teacher who, throughout the year, voiced discouragement about his students' extremely disruptive behavior and language, poor attitude, and lack of motivation. This teacher, too, doubted his ability to handle it all. But with consistent coaching about noting the small improvements, setting up a positive classroom structure, allowing students more academic choice, and striving toward more project-oriented work, the classroom environment slowly changed for the better. (See "Suggestions for Teachers" at www.ninazara goza.com for more detail.)

As you can probably tell even from these few responses, I do not believe that decontextualized strategies or recipes have a place in the teaching and learning process. Decisions need to be made within the context of a philosophy of education that honors the strengths and abilities of all classroom members. We all have varying abilities and emotional profiles, but we also all have similar needs that when filled will enable us to grow optimally. We all need to feel safe, respected, cared for, and given opportunities to care for others. We need to know that our life matters. We need to engage in productive, purposeful work that impacts ourselves and others in a deep and meaningful way. To enable a community that will address these needs requires deep, ongoing reflection, conversation, and support. It is serious work that will impact the hearts of a generation.

Focus Questions Revisited

What are some of the variables that contribute to maladaptive behaviors in children and youth?

A Sample Response: Some of the critical and intersecting variables that foster and sustain maladaptive behaviors in children and youth include but are not limited to: (a) environment, (b) antecedent events, (c) personological variables, (d) the function a behavior serves, and (e) the factors that contribute to and sustain it. Many behavioral disorders are simply manifestations of years of physical, psychological, or emotional abuse, ineffective parenting, and pathological family systems. The affected children growing up in these circumstances may either "learn" or acquire the destructive behaviors of the caregivers or may develop coping skills that manifest as antisocial or disruptive behaviors. These undesirable behaviors are then transferred to the classroom, with the result that the teacher is often substituted for the parent.

List three important contributions that teachers can make to students who have emotional and/or behavioral disorders.

A Sample Response: Three important contributions a teacher can make to students who have emotional and behavioral disorders are (genuine) empathy, reality, and support. Empathy is feeling genuine compassion for the welfare of another or sharing another's feelings; reality can be understood as a mirror, by which the teacher reflects back to the student the real effects of her behavior on both herself and others; support refers to the extent to which a teacher, given her resources and opportunities, provides emotional and physical help to a student who is in trouble. Psychologists have acknowledged that, ultimately, these three contributions are all we can really give anyone, but they are essential in the development of a positive rapport with students who have emotional and behavioral disorders (Connolly, 2006).

In preparing to work effectively with students that exhibit maladaptive behaviors, the teacher must understand three things about them and the undesirable behaviors. What are they?

A Sample Response: Three things that teachers must understand about students who have emotional and behavioral disorders with whom they work are the history, context, and functions of the child's problem behavior.

Identify the key implications of IDEA (2004) for students who have emotional and behavioral disorders.

A Sample Response: The first key implication relates to the 'stay put' provision, which previously was denied only to students with disabilities who are involved in drug sales or possession, the possession of weapons, or engagement in dangerous behavior, specifically regarded as committing violent acts. Under the new regulations, the right of a student who has a disability to 'stay put' in his or her current educational placement pending an appeal is eliminated.

In addition, under IDEA 2004, the burden of proof relative to the manifestation determination rests squarely with the child's parents. This is often a lop-sided battle because, without expert council or familiarity with the law, most parents do not know the procedures for collecting and presenting such supporting data. Furthermore, the language requiring the IEP team to consider whether the child's disorder impaired his ability to control or fully understand the consequences of his misbehavior has been deleted. The possible implications of these omissions should be apparent. Even more disturbing is the determination that a local education agency (LEA) should be considered to have knowledge that a child has a bona-fide disability if, before the behavior that precipitated the disciplinary action occurred, a teacher of that child expressed concern in writing directly to either a school administrator or the director of special education that she "has specific concerns about a pattern of behavior demonstrated by the child" (U.S. Department of Education, 2017). Finally, the 2004 change in the language relative to the forty-five-day removal policy from calendar days to school days means that students awaiting a manifestation determination will be out of their home school for an additional two weeks. Similarly, effective in 2005, this removal limit has been extended to forty-five school days, which translates to nine weeks without participation in the school curriculum, a further impediment for students who are already struggling academically.

How would you define <u>meaningful learning</u> as it relates to students who have emotional and behavioral disorders? What can a teacher do to ensure that these students are learning meaningful and relevant skills in the classroom?

A Sample Response: *Meaningful learning* refers to the teaching of knowledge and skills that the student perceives as useful. If a student, with or without a behavior disorder, asks you, "Why do I have to learn that?" and you can't provide a valid justification, perhaps the skill *isn't* worth learning. Clearly, as teachers, we must address the skills and topics mandated by the curriculum and prepare our students to take standardized tests; however, it is incumbent upon us to ensure that all of our students are engaged in some purposeful learning activity that prepares them for life and not just to be able to successfully complete tests (Popham, 2001). The definition of meaningful learning is just that: skills and knowledge that prepare our students to live successful and independent lives, not simply as voyeurs or consumers of services, but also as participants and contributors.

How important is developing a positive relationship with students who have emotional and behavior disorders, and how is this best accomplished?

A Sample Response: By "relationship," the inference is to a healthy, affirming pro-social human connection. Most children who have emotional or behavioral disorders experience a real challenge in making friends with peers, let alone establishing relationships with authority figures. Teachers' efforts in that endeavor will improve their classroom climate, make interactions with the child more positive, preclude or reduce defiant and confrontational behaviors while simultaneously providing the affected individual with a model for establishing and sustaining relationships in the future.

What are the dangers of stereotyping in working with students who misbehave? How can we avoid the pitfalls of misperception and subsequent misidentification that are frequently based on our own prejudices and cultural ignorance?

A Sample Response: Too often, children who are classified as emotionally disturbed are assumed to be defiant, antisocial, violent, or disruptive. This assumption is frequently incorrect, because many students receive this classification because of an anxiety or mood disorder, and these children rarely display the types of behaviors that teachers find either threatening or disruptive. It is therefore incumbent on teachers to help reduce the stigma that is associated with the classification of emotionally disturbed by educating their students and their parents about the nature of the disorder and its various typologies. Books such as this one help teachers do just that, by providing current and complete information about the various disorders encompassed within this broad category.

How can we work collaboratively with caregivers and family members to improve the classroom and social performance of their children who have emotional and behavioral disorders?

A Sample Response: The following are some of the ways that teachers can facilitate the involvement of parents as collaborators in their child's treatment.

- Teachers can help to educate parents about child and adolescent developmental characteristics so that parents will have reasonable expectations for child behavior and learning across grade levels.
- Teachers can use a variety of means to communicate with parents on a routine basis; for example, they can send progress reports home, call parents to remind them about upcoming classroom activities and parent-teacher meetings and workshops, and, where appropriate, schedule meetings with parents not just in the school but, where feasible, in a variety of conducive locations.
- Parents can be encouraged to volunteer in the school. As volunteers, they can assist with class trips, help with individual tutoring, assist with projects and crafts, and read aloud to small groups.
- Parents can provide valuable oversight for homework. To facilitate this, some schools provide "college in the classroom"

workshops after school in which the children's teachers instruct parents about the content skills currently taught in the classroom, thus providing parents with the knowledge necessary to be a valuable at-home tutor.

- Parents can and should be involved in decision-making, governance, and advocacy through membership in one or more parent-teacher organizations and committees (e.g., PTA, SEPTA).
- Parents should be informed by the school about various community support groups that can provide outside resources in support of their child (i.e., childcare, health care, and cultural activities).

Key Terms Used in the Chapter

Multisystemic Approach:
A multiple-system treatment approach to many emotional and behavioral disorders that typically combines family therapy with individual and peer-oriented therapies, acknowledging the importance of affecting behavior change in all these important milieus.

Stay Put Provision:
The former right of a student who has a disability to "stay put" in his or her current educational placement pending an appeal, which was eliminated in IDEA (2004).

Forty-Five-Day Removal Policy:
Refers, effective 2004, to the IDEA regulation that students awaiting a manifestation determination may be removed from their home school for forty-five school days (the regulation previously specified forty-five calendar days).

Direct Instruction:
A general term for the explicit teaching of a skill set using lectures or demonstrations of the material rather than exploratory models such as inquiry-based learning. Emphasizes the structure, sequencing, and pacing of instruction as well as the opportunity to receive feedback and practice.

Class-Wide Peer Tutoring (CWPT):
A peer-assisted instructional strategy designed to be integrated with most existing reading curricula. This approach provides students with increased opportunities to practice reading skills by asking questions and receiving

immediate feedback from a peer tutor. Pairs of students take turns tutoring each other to reinforce concepts and skills initially taught by the teacher. The teacher creates age-appropriate peer teaching materials for the peer tutors; these materials take into account tutees' language skills and disabilities.

Reciprocal Peer Tutoring (RPT):
A collaborative approach that embeds assessment in a formalized learning process to facilitate student involvement with course content and improve achievement. Students engaging in RPT are paired and given explicit instruction on how to construct multiple-choice questions for different types of statistical content knowledge.

Self-Monitoring:
A strategy for improving the academic performance of students who have emotional or behavioral disorders by teaching these students systematic procedures for observing, evaluating, and recording their own behavior at specific times during the school day. The benefit for the student is an improvement in his or her rate of on-task behavior and, consequently, an increase in academic productivity.

Curricular-Based Measurement (CBM):
A method of monitoring student educational progress through direct assessment of academic skills. CBM can be used to measure basic skills in reading, mathematics, spelling, and written expression. It can also be used to monitor readiness skills. When using CBM, the instructor gives the student brief, timed samples, or "probes," made up of academic material taken from the child's school curriculum.

Belongingness:
Being a part or member of a group, whether it is family, friends, career, or sports affiliations. People have a desire to belong and be an important part of something. A motive to belong is the need for strong, stable relationships with other people.

Active Listening:
An intent to "listen for meaning", in which the listener checks with the speaker to see that a statement has been correctly heard and understood. The goal of active listening is to improve mutual understanding.

Disproportionality:
The disproportionate representation of minority students in special education.

Disprivileging Speech:
The intended or unintended effects of using technical or professional terminology to effectively disenfranchise a nonaffiliated or individual or group unfamiliar with such language

Personological Variables:
Inherent or inborn traits and behavioral characteristics that help define the "personality" of an individual.

Author Bios

Vance Austin, PhD, has worked for over 40 years with children, adolescents, and young adults who have learning disabilities, various emotional and behavioral disorders, and autism, as a child-care counselor, program coordinator, and teacher. He currently teaches part-time in a school for adolescents with emotional/behavioral disorders in Nyack, NY.

In addition, Vance has been a college professor at five universities and colleges and is currently a Professor and Chairperson of the Department of Special Education at Manhattanville College, in Purchase, NY. He has authored numerous articles and book chapters and has co-authored two popular textbooks on topics related to working effectively with students that have learning and behavior problems as well as co-authored two books with Daniel Sciarra: *Difficult students and disruptive behavior in the classroom: Teacher responses that work* (W.W. Norton, 2016) and *Children and adolescents with emotional and behavioral disorders* (Pearson Education, 2010) and has presented his research at national and international conferences. In addition, Vance is an editor for Insights on Learning Disabilities: From Prevailing Theories to Validated Practices and is on the editorial board for the Journal of the American Academy of Special Education Professionals.

Dan Sciarra, PhD, is Professor of Counselor Education and Chairperson of the Department of Counseling, Research, Special Education, and Rehabilitation at Hofstra University. He is both a licensed psychologist and a certified school counselor at the secondary level. Dr. Sciarra has worked for over 20 years with children and adolescent in school and community/clinical settings. He currently practices at the Child Guidance Center in Stamford, Ct where he provides bilingual (Spanish) counseling services to children, adolescents, and their families many of whom have a member(s) with a disability.

At Hofstra, Dr. Sciarra supervises practicum counseling students and teaches a course, among others, entitled "Contemporary Issues in School Counseling." Dr. Sciarra is the sole author of two books, Multiculturalism in Counseling (Peacock, 1999) and School Counseling: Foundations and Contemporary Issues (Thompson/Wadsworth, 2004) as well as two books: Difficult students and disruptive behavior in the classroom: Teacher responses that work (W.W. Norton, 2016) and Children and adolescents with emotional and behavioral disorders (Pearson Education, 2010) co-authored with Vance Austin. He has published numerous journal articles and book chapters in the field of multicultural counseling. His current research involves the study of predictive factors in the post-secondary education status of Latinos.

Elizabeth J. Bienia, EdD, has served as an elementary school administrator and educator in various rural and urban settings in Massachusetts for more than 30 years, where she has worked to create positive learning environments for all students. As a building administrator, she has fostered partnerships with staff, families, various local businesses, and higher education institutions. Dr. Bienia has previously been a graduate adjunct professor at the Van Loan School of Education, Endicott College and the College of Our Lady of the Elms.

Dr. Bienia is a primary author on *Masculinity in the Making: Managing the Transition to Manhood* (2020); *The Burden of Being a Boy: Bolstering Educational and Emotional Well-Being in Young Males* (2020); *Acceptance, Understanding, and the Moral Imperative of Promoting Social Justice Education in the Schoolhouse* (2019); *The Empathic Teacher: Learning and Applying the Principles of Social Justice Education to the Classroom* (2019); *From Cradle to Classroom: A Guide to Special Education for Young Children* (2019); *The Potency of the Principalship: Action-Oriented Leadership at the Heart of School Improvement* (2018); *Dog Tags to Diploma: Understanding and Addressing the Educational Needs of Veterans, Servicemembers and their Families* (2018); *Stars in the Schoolhouse: Teaching Practices and Approaches that Make a Difference* (2018); *From Head to Heart: High Quality Teaching Practices in the Spotlight* (2018); *From Lecture Hall to Laptop: Opportunities, Challenges and the Continuing Evolution of Virtual Learning in Higher Education* (2017). She has also written book chapters on such topics as emotional well-being for students with learning disabilities, post-secondary campus supports for emerging adults, parental support for students with learning disabilities, home-school partnerships, virtual education, public and private partnerships in public education, professorial pursuits, technology partnerships between P-12 and higher education, developing a strategic mindset for LD students, the importance of skill and will in developing reading habits for young children, and middle school reading interventions to name a few. Additionally, she has co-authored and illustrated several children's books to include *Yes, Mama* (2018), *The Adventures of Scotty the Skunk: What's that Smell?* (2014), and many of the *I am Full of Possibilities* Series for Learning Disabilities Worldwide.

References

Abraham, I. (2018). The continuum hypothesis of eating disorders, the evolution of a model from 1970's to the present. *Official Journal of the Hungarian Association of Psychopharmacology, 20*(4), 131–139.

Achenbach, T. M. (2000). Child behavior checklist. In A. E. Kazdin (Ed.), *Encyclopedia of psychology: Vol. 2.* (pp. 69–70). American Psychological Association. https://doi.org/10.1037/10517-028

Achenbach, T. M. & Edelbrock, C. S. (1991). *Child behavior checklist and youth self-report.* University of Vermont. Department of Psychiatry.

Achenbach, T. M. & Rescorla, L. A. (2004). The Achenbach System of Empirically Based Assessment (ASEBA) for ages 15 to 18 years. In M. E. Maruish (Ed.), *The use of psychological testing for treatment planning and outcomes assessment: Instruments for children and adolescents: Vol 2.* (3rd ed., pp. 179–213). Lawrence Erlbaum Associates.

Aebi, M., Müller, U. C., Asherson, P., Banaschewski, T., Buitelaar, J., Ebstein, R., Eisenberg, J., Gill, M., Manor, I., Miranda, A., Oades, R. D., Roeyers, H., Rothenberger, A., Sergeant, J., Sonuga-Barke, E., Thompson, M., Taylor, E., Faraone, S. V. & Steinhausen, H. C. (2010). Predictability of oppositional defiant disorder and symptom dimensions in children and adolescents with ADHD combined type. *Psychological Medicine, 40*(12), 2089–2100. https://doi.org/10.1017/S0033291710000590

Agnafors, S., Bladh, M., Svedin, C. G. & Sydsjö, G. (2019). Mental health in young mothers, single mothers and their children. *BMC Psychiatry, 19*(1). Article 112. https://doi.org/10.1186/s12888-019-2082-

Agras, W. S., Fitzsimmons-Craft, E. E. & Wilfley, D. E. (2017). Evolution of cognitive-behavioral therapy for eating disorders. *Behaviour Research and Therapy, 88,* 26–36.

Ahmed, S. H., Badiani, A., Miczek, K. A. & Müller, C. P. (2020). Non-pharmacological factors that determine drug use and addiction. *Neuroscience & Biobehavioral Reviews, 110,* 3–27.

Ainsworth, M. S. (1969). Object relations, dependency, and attachment: A theoretical review of the infant-mother relationship. *Child Development, 40*(4), 969-1025.

Albano, A. M., Marten, P. A., Holt, C. S., Heimberg, R. G. & Barlow, D. H. (1995). Cognitive-behavioral group treatment for social phobia in adolescents: A preliminary study. *Journal of Nervous and Mental Disease, 183*(10), 649–656.

Albano, A. M. & Silverman, W. K. (2016). *Anxiety disorders interview schedule for DSM-5, child version, child and parent interview schedules.* Oxford University Press.

Albuquerque, P. P. D. & Williams, L. C. D. A. (2018). My worst school experience: A retrospective characterization of student's victimization. *Estudos de Psicologia (Natal), 23*(2), 133-144.

Alhussien, B. H., Alshammari, S. & Anza, S. A. (2019.). Association between depression and anorexia nervosa. *International Journal of Medicine in Developing Countries, 3*(5), 435–440.

Alhuzimi, T. (2020). Stress and emotional wellbeing of parents due to change in routine for children with autism spectrum disorder (ASD) at home during COVID-19 pandemic in Saudi Arabia. *Research in Developmental Disabilities, 108*, e103822.

Ali, K., Farrer, L., Fassnacht, D. B., Gulliver, A., Bauer, S. & Griffiths, K. M. (2017). Perceived barriers and facilitators towards help-seeking for eating disorders: A systematic review. *International Journal of Eating Disorders, 50*(1), 9–21.

Aljehany, M. S. & Bennett, K. D. (2019). Meta-analysis of video prompting to teach daily living skills to individuals with autism spectrum disorder. *Journal of Special Education Technology, 34*(1), 17–26.

Alotaibi, F. E. (2017). *Teachers' perceptions of the use and effectiveness of social stories™ in the development of social skills for children with autism spectrum disorder (ASD) in Saudi Arabia* [Unpublished doctoral dissertation]. University of Reading.

Ambrosini, P. J. (2000). Historical development and present status of the schedule for affective disorders and schizophrenia for school-age children (K-SADS). *Journal of the American Academy of Child & Adolescent Psychiatry, 39*(1), 49–58. https://doi.org/10.1097/00004583-200001000-00016

American Foundation for Suicide Prevention. (2022). *Suicide statistics.* https://afsp.org/suicide-statistics/

American Psychiatric Association. (2013*). Diagnostic and statistical manual of mental disorders* (5th ed.).

American Psychological Association. (2020). *APA dictionary of psychology: parallel processing.* https://dictionary.apa.org/parallel-processing

Anand, S., Tong, H., Besag, F., Chan, E., Cortese, S. & Wong, I. (2017). Safety, tolerability, and efficacy of drugs for treating behavioural insomnia in children with attention-deficit/hyperactivity disorder: A systematic review with methodological quality assessment. *Pediatric Drugs, 19*(3), 235–250. https://doi.org/10.1007/s40272-017-02246.

Anderson, D.L., Watt, S.E., Noble, W. & Shanley, D.C. (2012), Knowledge of attention deficit hyperactivity disorder (ADHD) and attitudes toward teaching children with ADHD: The role of teaching experience. *Psychology in Schools, 49*, 511-525. doi:10.1002/pits.21617.

Andersson, M., Tangen, Ä., Farde, L., Bölte, S., Halldin, C., Borg, J. & Lundberg, J. (2020). Serotonin transporter availability in adults with autism—A positron emission tomography study. *Molecular Psychiatry.* https://doi.org/10.1038/s41380-020-00868-3

Andreou, M. & Skrimpa, V. (2020). Theory of mind deficits and neurophysiological operations in autism spectrum disorders: A review. *Brain Sciences, 10*(6), 393. https://doi.org/10.3390/brainsci10060393

Angold, A. & Costello, E. J. (2000). The Child and Adolescent Psychiatric Assessment (CAPA). *Journal of the American Academy of Child & Adolescent Psychiatry, 39*(1), 39–48. https://doi.org/10.1097/00004583-200001000-00015

Anxiety & Depression Association of America [ADAA]. (2019). *Understanding anxiety & depression: Facts & statistics.* https://adaa.org/understanding-anxiety/facts-statistics

Arick, J. R., Krug, D. A., Fullerton, A., Loos, L. & Falco, R. (2005). School-based programs. *Handbook of autism and pervasive developmental disorders* (2nd ed.), 1003–1028.

Arthur, R. & Erickson, E. (2000). *Gangs and schools.* Learning Publications, Inc.

Asbrand, J., Svaldi, J., Krämer, M., Breuninger, C. & Tuschen-Caffier, B. (2016). Familial accumulation of social anxiety symptoms and maladaptive emotion regulation. *PloS One, 11*(4). https://doi.org/10.1371/journal.pone.0153153

Aupperle, R. L., Melrose, A. J., Stein, M. B. & Paulus, M. P. (2012). Executive function and PTSD: disengaging from trauma. *Neuropharmacology, 62*(2), 686–694. https://doi.org/10.1016/j.neuropharm.2011.02.008

Austin, V. L. (2001). Teachers' beliefs about co-teaching. *Remedial and Special Education, 22* (4), 245–255.

Austin, V. L. (2003). Pharmacological interventions for students with ADD. *Intervention in School and Clinic, 38* (5), 289–296. https://doi.org/10.1177/10534512030380050401

Austin, V. & Sciarra, D. (2016). *Difficult students and disruptive behavior in the classroom: Teacher responses that work.* WW Norton & Company.

Bai, M. (1999, May 3). Anatomy of a massacre. *Newsweek,* 24–31.

Bailer, U. F., Price, J. C., Meltzer, C. C., Wagner, A., Mathis, C. A., Gamst, A. & Kaye, W. H. (2017). Dopaminergic activity and altered reward modulation in anorexia nervosa—Insight from multimodal imaging. *International Journal of Eating Disorders, 50*(5), 593–596.

Baixauli, I., Colomer, C., Roselló, B. & Miranda, A. (2016). Narratives of children with high-functioning autism spectrum disorder: A meta-analysis. *Research in Developmental Disabilities, 59,* 234–254.

Baker, P. H. (2005). Managing student behavior: How ready are teachers to meet the challenge? American Secondary Education, *33*(3), 51–64.

Bakermans-Kranenburg, M. J., Lotz, A., Alyousefi-van Dijk, K. & van IJzendoorn, M. (2019). Birth of a father: Fathering in the first 1,000 days. *Child Development Perspectives, 13*(4), 247–253.

Bakker, M. J., Greven, C. U., Buitelaar, J. K. & Glennon, J. C. (2017). Practitioner review: Psychological treatments for children and adolescents with conduct disorder problems–A systematic review and meta-analysis. *Journal of Child Psychology and Psychiatry, 58*(1), 4–18.

Bakker-Huvenaars, M. J., Greven, C. U., Herpers, P., Wiegers, E., Jansen, A., Van Der Steen, R., van Herwaarden, A. E., Baanders, A. N., Nijhof, K. S. & Scheepers, F. (2020). Saliva oxytocin, cortisol, and testosterone levels in adolescent boys with autism spectrum disorder, oppositional defiant disorder/conduct disorder and typically developing individuals. *European Neuropsychopharmacology, 30,* 87–101.

Bandelow, B., Baldwin, D., Abelli, M., Altamura, C., Dell'Osso, B., Domschke, K., Fineberg, N. A., Grünblatt, E., Jarema, M. & Maron, E. (2016). Biological markers for anxiety disorders, OCD and PTSD–a consensus statement. Part

I: Neuroimaging and genetics. *The World Journal of Biological Psychiatry, 17*(5), 321–365.

Bandura, A. (1973). *Aggression: A social learning analysis.* Prentice-Hall.

Bandura, A. (1977). *Social learning theory.* General Learning Press.

Bandura, A. (1986). *Social foundations of thought and action: A social cognitive theory.* Prentice Hall.

Banerjee, E. & Nandagopal, K. (2015). Does serotonin deficit mediate susceptibility to ADHD? *Neurochemistry International, 82,* 52–68. https://doi.org/10.1016/j.neuint.2015.02.001.

Bang, Y. S. (2018). Parents' perspectives on how their behaviors impede parent-teacher collaboration. *Social Behavior and Personality: An International Journal, 46*(11), 1787-1799.

Banks, J. A. (2004, December). Teaching for social justice, diversity, and citizenship in a global world. *The Educational Forum, 68*(4), 296-305.

Barajas-Iglesias, B., Jáuregui-Lobera, I., Laporta-Herrero, I. & Santed-Germán, M. Á. (2017). Eating disorders during the adolescence: Personality characteristics associated with anorexia and bulimia nervosa. *Nutrición Hospitalaria, 34*(5), 1178–1184.

Barbano, A. C., van der Mei, W. F., deRoon-Cassini, T. A., Grauer, E., Lowe, S. R., Matsuoka, Y. J., O'Donnell, M., Olff, M., Qi, W. & Ratanatharathorn, A. (2019). Differentiating PTSD from anxiety and depression: Lessons from the ICD-11 PTSD diagnostic criteria. *Depression and Anxiety, 36*(6), 490–498.

Barker, E. D., Cecil, C. A., Walton, E. & Meehan, A. J. (2017). Genetic and gene-environment influences on disruptive behavior disorders. In J.E. Lochman & W. Mathys (Eds.), *The Wiley handbook of disruptive and impulse-control disorders* (pp.127-141). Wiley.

Barkley, R. A. (2003). Issues in the diagnosis of attention-deficit/hyperactivity disorder in children. *Brain and Development,* 25(2), 77-83.

Barkley, R. A. & Murphy, K. R. (1998). *Attention-deficit hyperactivity disorder: A clinical workbook.* Guilford Press.

Barnes, S. A., Iovannone, R., Blair, K-S, Crosland, K. & Peshak George, H. (2020). Evaluating the prevent-teach-reinforce (PTR) model in general education settings. *Preventing School Failure: Alternative Education for Children and Youth, 64*(2), 128-141. doi.10.1080/1045988X.2019.1688228

Barnett, D.A. (2010). *Constructing new theory for identifying students with emotional disturbance: A grounded theory approach.* California State University: Fullerton. ProQuest.

Barrett, P., Games, N., Fisak, B., Stallard, P. & Phillips, L. (2019). The treatment of anxiety disorders in preschool-aged children. In B. Fisak & P. Barrett (Eds.), *Anxiety in Preschool Children: Assessment, Treatment, and Prevention* (pp. 114–141). Routledge/Taylor & Francis Group. https://doi.org/10.4324/9781315213828-6

Barnhill, G. P. (2005). Functional behavioral assessment in schools. *Intervention in School and Clinic, 40*(3), 131-144.

Baron-Cohen, S. (2000). Theory of mind and autism: A fifteen-year review. *Understanding Other Minds: Perspectives from Developmental Cognitive Neuroscience, 2*(3-20), 102.

Bartholdy, S., Campbell, I. C., Schmidt, U. & O'Daly, O. G. (2016). Proactive inhibition: An element of inhibitory control in eating disorders. *Neuroscience & Biobehavioral Reviews, 71*, 1–6.

Bartholdy, S., Rennalls, S. J., Jacques, C., Danby, H., Campbell, I. C., Schmidt, U., & O'Daly, O. G. (2017). Proactive and reactive inhibitory control in eating disorders. *Psychiatry Research, 255*, 432–440.

Bauer, A.M. (1987). A teacher's introduction to childhood depression. *Clearing House, 61*, 81-84.

Beck, A. T. (1967). *Depression.* Harper and Row.

Beck, A.T., Rush, A.G., Shaw, B.F. & Emery, G. (1979). *Cognitive therapy for depression.* Guilford Press.

Beck, A.T., Steer, R.A. & Brown, G.K. (1996). *Manual for the Beck depression inventory-II.* San Antonio, TX: Psychological Corporation.

Becker, M., & Correll, C. U. (2020). Suicidality in childhood and adolescence. *Deutsches Arzteblatt International, 117*(15), 261–267. https://doi.org/10.3238/arztebl.2020.0261

Beidel, D. C., Alfano, C. A., Kofler, M. J., Rao, P. A., Scharfstein, L. & Sarver, N. W. (2014). The impact of social skills training for social anxiety disorder: A randomized controlled trial. *Journal of Anxiety Disorders, 28*(8), 908–918. https://doi.org/10.1016/j.janxdis.2014.09.016

Beidel, D. C. & Turner, S. M. (2007). Prevalence of Social Anxiety Disorder. In D. C. Beidel & S.M. Turner (Eds.), *Shy Children, Phobic Adults: Nature and Treatment of Social Anxiety Disorders* (2nd ed., pp. 81–89). American Psychological Association. https://doi.org/10.1037/11533-003

Beidel, D. C., Turner, S. M. & Morris, T. L. (1999). Psychopathology of childhood social phobia. *Journal of the American Academy of Child & Adolescent Psychiatry, 38* (6), 643–650.

Beijers, L., Wardenaar, K. J., van Loo, H. M. & Schoevers, R. A. (2019). Data-driven biological subtypes of depression: Systematic review of biological approaches to depression subtyping. *Molecular Psychiatry, 24*(6), 888–900.

Benton, T. D., Ng, W. Y. K., Leung, D., Canetti, A. & Karnik, N. (2019). Depression among youth living with HIV/AIDS. *Child and Adolescent Psychiatric Clinics, 28*(3), 447–459.

Berends, T., van de Lagemaat, M., van Meijel, B., Coenen, J., Hoek, H. W. & van Elburg, A. A. (2018). Relapse prevention in anorexia nervosa: Experiences of patients and parents. *International Journal of Mental Health Nursing, 27*(5), 1546–1555.

Bergin, C., & Bergin, D. (2009). Attachment in the classroom. *Educational Psychology Review, 21*(2), 141–170. https://doi.org/10.1007/s10648-009-9104-0

Bernaras, E., Jaureguizar, J. & Garaigordobil, M. (2019). Child and adolescent depression: A review of theories, evaluation instruments, prevention programs, and treatments. *Frontiers in Psychology, 10*, 543. https://doi.org/10.3389/fpsyg.2019.00543

Bernstein, G. A., Crosby, R. D., Perwien, A. R. & Borchardt, C. M. (1996). Anxiety rating for children-Revised: Reliability and validity. *Journal of Anxiety Disorders, 10*(2), 97–114. https://doi.org/10.1016/0887-6185(95)00039-9

Bertollo, J. R., Strang, J. F., Anthony, L. G., Kenworthy, L., Wallace, G. L. & Yerys, B. E. (2020). Adaptive behavior in youth with autism spectrum disorder: The role of flexibility. *Journal of Autism and Developmental Disorders, 50*(1), 42–50.

Bhana, A., Abas, M. A., Kelly, J., van Pinxteren, M., Mudekunye, L. A. & Pantelic, M. (2020). Mental health interventions for adolescents living with HIV or affected by HIV in low-and middle-income countries: Systematic review. *BJPsych Open, 6*(5), 1-15.

Bi, T. & Fang, F. (2017). Impaired face perception in individuals with autism spectrum disorder: Insights on diagnosis and treatment. *Neuroscience Bulletin, 33*(6), 757–759.

Birmaher, B., Ehmann, M., Axelson, D. A., Goldstein, B. I., Monk, K., Kalas, C., Kupfer, D., Gill, M. K., Leibenluft, E. & Bridge, J. (2009). Schedule for affective disorders and schizophrenia for school-age children (K-SADS-PL) for the assessment of preschool children–a preliminary psychometric study. *Journal of Psychiatric Research, 43*(7), 680–686.

Birmaher, B., Khetarpal, S., Brent, D., Cully, M., Balach, L., Kaufman, J. & Neer, S. M. (1997). The Screen for Child Anxiety Related Emotional Disorders (SCARED): Scale construction and psychometric characteristics. *Journal of the American Academy of Child & Adolescent Psychiatry, 36*(4), 545–553. https://doi.org/10.1097/00004583-199704000-00018

Bishop, S. R., Lau, M., Shapiro, S., Carlson, L., Anderson, N. D., Carmody, J., Segal, Z. V., Abbey, S., Speca, M., Velting, D. & Devins, G. (2004). Mindfulness: A proposed operational definition. *Clinical Psychology: Science and Practice, 11*(3), 230–241. https://doi.org/10.1093/clipsy.bph077

Bitton, M. S. & Rajpurkar, S. (2015). Therapeutic crisis intervention system in residential care for children and youth: Staff knowledge, attitudes, and coping styles. *Children and Youth Services Review, 56*, 1-6.

Bjørklund, G., Meguid, N. A., El-Ansary, A., El-Bana, M. A., Dadar, M., Aaseth, J., Hemimi, M., Osredkar, J. & Chirumbolo, S. (2018). Diagnostic and severity-tracking biomarkers for autism spectrum disorder. *Journal of Molecular Neuroscience, 66*(4), 492–511.

Bjornsson, A. S., Hardarson, J. P., Valdimarsdottir, A. G., Guðmundsdottir, K., Tryggvadottir, A., Thorarinsdottir, K., Wessman, I., Sigurjonsdottir, Ó., Davidsdottir, S. & Thorisdottir, A. S. (2020). Social trauma and its association with post-traumatic stress disorder and social anxiety disorder. *Journal of Anxiety Disorders, 72*, 1-9.

Blanchett, W. J. (2006). Disproportionate representation of African American students in special education: Acknowledging the role of white privilege and racism. *Educational Researcher, 35*(6), 24-28.

Blanchett, W. J. (2014). African American students and other students of color in special education. In H. R. Milner & K. Lomotey (Eds.), *Handbook of urban education* (pp. 271–284). New York: Taylor & Francis

Bonnet-Brilhault, F., Rajerison, T. A., Paillet, C., Guimard-Brunault, M., Saby, A., Ponson, L., Tripi, G., Malvy, J. & Roux, S. (2018). Autism is a prenatal disorder: Evidence from late gestation brain overgrowth. *Autism Research, 11*(12), 1635–1642.

Borduin, C. M., Brown, C. E. & Sheerin, K. M. (2018). Multisystemic therapy for serious juvenile offenders: From development to dissemination. In E.L. Jeglic & C. Calkins (Eds.) *New frontiers in offender treatment* (pp. 251–267). Springer.

Borduin, C. M., Dopp, A. R., Quetsch, L. B. & Johnides, B. D. (2017). Multisystemic therapy for violent and aggressive youths. In P. Sturney (Ed.) *The Wiley handbook of violence and aggression*, 1–14. Wiley.

Borys, C., Lutz, J., Strauss, B. & Altmann, U. (2015). Effectiveness of a multimodal therapy for patients with chronic low back pain regarding pre-admission healthcare utilization. *PloS one*, *10*(11), e0143139. https://doi.org/10.1371/journal.pone.0143139

Borza, L. (2017). Cognitive-behavioral therapy for generalized anxiety. *Dialogues in Clinical Neuroscience, 19*(2), 203-208.

Boston Children's Hospital. (2022). *General Anxiety Disorder.* https://www.childrenshospital.org/conditions-and-treatments/conditions/g/generalized-anxiety-disorder-gad

Bowlby, J. (1969*). Attachment and loss.* Random House.

Bowlby, J. (1980). *Attachment and loss.* Basic Books.

Boxer, P., Docherty, M., Ostermann, M., Kubik, J. & Veysey, B. (2017). Effectiveness of multisystemic therapy for gang-involved youth offenders: One year follow-up analysis of recidivism outcomes. *Children and Youth Services Review, 73*, 107–112.

Braaten, E. (2016). *ADHD medication for kids: Is it safe? Does it help?* https://www.health.harvard.edu/blog/adhd-medication-for-kids-is-it-safe-does-it-help-201603049235

Brewer, S., Godley, M. D. & Hulvershorn, L. A. (2017). Treating mental health and substance use disorders in adolescents: What is on the menu? *Current Psychiatry Reports, 19*(1), Article 5. https://doi.org/10.1007/s11920-017-0755-0

Bright, G. M. (2008). Abuse of medications employed for the treatment of ADHD: Results from a large-scale community survey. *The Medscape Journal of Medicine, 10*(5), 111.

Broderick, P. (2019). *Learning to breathe.* https://learning2breathe.org/

Brown, J. L., Roderick, T., Lantieri, L. & Aber, J. L. (2004). The resolving conflict creatively program: A school-based social and emotional learning program. In J. E. Zins, R. P. Weissberg, M. C. Wang, & H. J. Walberg (Eds.), *Building academic success on social and emotional learning: What does the research say?* (pp. 151–169). Teachers College Press.

Brown, M. B. (2000). Diagnosis and treatment of children and adolescents with attention-deficit/hyperactivity disorder. *Journal of Counseling and Development, 78*(2), 195–203.

Brown, T. E. (1996). *Brown attention deficit disorder scales manual.* Psychological Corporation.

Buck, G. H., Polloway, E. A., Kirkpatrick, M. A., Patton, J. R. & McConnell Fad, K. (2000). Developing behavioral intervention plans: A sequential approach. *Intervention in School and Clinic, 36*(1), 3. Wilson Education Abstracts database (Document ID: 59160207).

Bulik, C. M., Kleiman, S. C. & Yilmaz, Z. (2016). Genetic epidemiology of eating disorders. *Current Opinion in Psychiatry, 29*(6), 383-388.

Burke, J. D. & Loeber, R. (2017). Evidence based interventions for oppositional defiant disorder in children and adolescents. In L.A. Theodore (Ed.) *Handbook of evidence-based interventions for children and adolescents* (pp. 181-191). Springer.

Burke, J. D., Loeber, R. & Birmaher, B. (2002). Oppositional defiant disorder and conduct disorder: A review of the past 10 years, part II. *Journal of the American Academy of Child & Adolescent Psychiatry, 41*(11), 1275–1293. https://doi.org/10.1097/00004583-200211000-00009

Burke, J. D. & Romano-Verthelyi, A. M. (2018). Oppositional defiant disorder. In M.M. Martel (Ed.), *Developmental pathways to disruptive, impulse-control and conduct disorders* (pp. 21–52). Elsevier.

Burns, M. K., Dean, V. J. & Jacob-Timm, S. (2001). Assessment of violence potential among school children: Beyond profiling. *Psychology in Schools,* 38, 239–246.

Burton, C. L., Barta, C., Cath, D., Geller, D., van den Heuvel, O. A., Yao, Y., Disorder, O. C., Eapen, V., Grünblatt, E. & Zai, G. (2020). Genetics of obsessive-compulsive disorder and Tourette disorder. In B.T. Baune (Ed.) *Personalized psychiatry* (pp. 239–252). Elsevier.

Butler, T., Harvey, P., Cardozo, L., Zhu, Y.-S., Mosa, A., Tanzi, E. & Pervez, F. (2019). Epilepsy, depression, and growth hormone. *Epilepsy & Behavior, 94,* 297–300.

Caldarella, P., Hallam, P. R., Christensen, L. & Wall, G. (2014). Systematic screening for behavior disorders in professional development schools: A social validity study. *School-University Partnerships, 7*(2), 19-33.

Calix, S. I. & Fine, M. A. (2018). Evidence-based family treatment of adolescent substance-related disorders. In C.G. Leukefled, T.P. Gullota, & M. Staton-Tindall (Eds.) *Adolescent substance abuse* (pp. 173–190). Springer.

Calles Jr, J. L. (2016). Major depressive and dysthymic disorders: A review. *Journal of Alternative Medicine Research, 8*(4), 393-404.

Capriola-Hall, N. N., Booker, J. A. & Ollendick, T. H. (2020). Parent-and child-factors in specific phobias: The Interplay of overprotection and negative affectivity. *Journal of Abnormal Child Psychology, 48,* 1291-1302.

Caputo, A. A., Frick, P. J. & Brodscky, S. L (1999). Family violence and juvenile sex offending: Potential mediating roles of psychopathic traits and negative attitudes toward women. *Criminal Justice and Behavior,* 26, 338–356.

Capuzzi, D. & Gross, D. R. (2019). "I don't want to live": The adolescent at risk for suicidal behavior. In D. Capuzzi & D. R. Gross (Eds.), *Youth at risk: A prevention resource for counselors, teachers, and parents* (7th ed., pp. 229–263). American Counseling Association.

Cardon, T., Wangsgard, N. & Dobson, N. (2019). Video modeling using classroom peers as models to increase social communication skills in children with ASD in an integrated preschool. *Education and Treatment of Children, 42*(4), 515–536.

Carlisi, C. O., Norman, L., Murphy, C. M., Christakou, A., Chantiluke, K., Giampietro, V., Simmons, A., Brammer, M., Murphy, D. G. & Mataix-Cols, D. (2017). Shared and disorder-specific neurocomputational mechanisms of decision-making in autism spectrum disorder and obsessive-compulsive disorder. *Cerebral Cortex, 27*(12), 5804–5816.

Carlton, C. N., Sullivan-Toole, H., Strege, M. V., Ollendick, T. H. & Richey, J.A. (2020). Mindfulness-Based Interventions for Adolescent Social Anxiety: A Unique Convergence of Factors. *Frontiers in Psychology, 11*(1783). doi: 10.3389/fpsyg.2020.01783

Carson, D. C. & Esbensen, F. A. (2019). Gangs in school: Exploring the experiences of gang-involved youth. *Youth Violence and Juvenile Justice, 17*(1), 3-23.

Carter, A. S., Davis, N. O., Klin, A., & Volkmar, F. R. (2005). Social development in autism. In F. R. Volkmar, R. Paul, A. Klin, & D. Cohen (Eds.), *Handbook of autism and pervasive developmental disorders: Diagnosis, development, neurobiology, and behavior* (p. 312–334). Wiley.

Carter, E. W., Dykstra Steinbrenner, J. R. & Hall, L. J. (2019). Exploring feasibility and fit: Peer-mediated interventions for high school students with autism spectrum disorders. *School Psychology Review, 48*(2), 157–169.

Carter, E. W., Gustafson, J. R., Sreckovic, M. A., Dykstra Steinbrenner, J. R., Pierce, N. P., Bord, A., Stabel, A., Rogers, S., Czerw, A. & Mullins, T. (2017). Efficacy of peer support interventions in general education classrooms for high school students with autism spectrum disorder. *Remedial and Special Education, 38*(4), 207–221.

Case, S. M., Sawhney, M. & Stewart, J. C. (2018). Atypical depression and double depression predict new-onset cardiovascular disease in US adults. *Depression and Anxiety, 35*(1), 10–17.

Collaborative for Academic, Social, and Emotional Learning [CASEL]. (2022). CASEL Program Guide. https://pg.casel.org/

Castagna, P. J., Davis, T. E. & Lilly, M. E. (2017). The behavioral avoidance task with anxious youth: A review of procedures, properties, and criticisms. *Clinical Child and Family Psychology Review, 20*(2), 162–184.

Catalá-López, F., Hutton, B., Núñez-Beltrán, A., Page, M. J., Ridao, M., Macías Saint-Gerons, D., Catalá, M. A., Tabarés-Seisdedos, R. & Moher, D. (2017). The pharmacological and non-pharmacological treatment of attention deficit hyperactivity disorder in children and adolescents: A systematic review with network meta-analyses of randomised trials. *PloS one, 12*(7), e0180355. https://doi.org/10.1371/journal.pone.0180355

Cautela, J. R., Cautela, J., & Esonis, S. (1983). *Forms for behavior analysis with children.* Research Press.

Cavendish, W., Artiles, A. J. & Harry, B. (2014). Tracking inequality 60 years after Brown: Does policy legitimize the racialization of disability? *Multiple Voices for Ethnically Diverse Exceptional Learners, 14*(2), 30-40.

Cederlöf, M., Maughan, B., Larsson, H., D'Onofrio, B. M., & Plomin, R. (2017). Reading problems and major mental disorders-co-occurrences and familial overlaps in a Swedish nationwide cohort. *Journal of Psychiatric Research, 91*, 124–129.

Centers for Disease Control and Prevention. (2003). *HIV/AIDS surveillance report, volume 15.* https://www.cdc.gov/hiv/library/reports/hiv-surveillance.html

Centers for Disease Control and Prevention. (2016). *WISQARS leading causes of death reports, 1981–2018.* https://webappa.cdc.gov/sasweb/ncipc/leadcause.html

Centers for Disease Control and Prevention. (2019). *Youth risk behaviors survey: United States 2019 results.* https://www.cdc.gov/healthyyouth/data/yrbs/index.htm

Centers for Disease Control and Prevention. (2020). *What is ADHD?* https://www.cdc.gov/ncbddd/adhd/facts.html

Centers for Disease Control and Prevention. (2021). *Autism prevalence higher in CDC's ADDM network.* https://www.cdc.gov/media/releases/2021/p1202-autism.html

Cerniglia, L., Cimino, S., Tafà, M., Marzilli, E., Ballarotto, G. & Bracaglia, F. (2017). Family profiles in eating disorders: Family functioning and psychopathology. *Psychology Research and Behavior Management, 10,* 305-312.

Çetin, F. H., Torun, Y. T. & Güney, E. (2017). The role of serotonin in aggression and impulsiveness. In F. S. Kaneez (Ed.), *Serotonin: A chemical messenger between all types of living cells* (pp. 242-251). Avesis.

CHADD. (2022). *ADHD fact sheets.* https://chadd.org/understanding-adhd/adhd-fact-sheets/

Chalamandaris, A. G. & Piette, D. (2015). School-based anti-bullying interventions: Systematic review of the methodology to assess their effectiveness. *Aggression and Violent Behavior, 24,* 131-174.

Chamberlain, P. & Patterson, G. R. (2002). Discipline and child compliance in parenting. In M. H. Bornstein (Ed.), *Handbook of parenting, Vol. 4: Applied and practical parenting.* (pp. 205–225). Lawrence Erlbaum.

Chambers, B. D., & Erausquin, J. T. (2018). Reframing the way we think about teenage motherhood. In S. Choudary, J.T. Erasquin & M. Withers (Eds.) *Global Perspectives on Women's Sexual and Reproductive Health Across the Life Course* (pp. 59–71). Springer.

Chan, W., Smith, L. E., Hong, J., Greenberg, J. S. & Mailick, M. R. (2017). Validating the social responsiveness scale for adults with autism. *Autism Research, 10*(10), 1663–1671.

Chartier, M. J., Walker, J. R. & Stein, M. B. (2003). Considering comorbidity in social phobia. *Social Psychiatry and Psychiatric Epidemiology: The International Journal for Research in Social and Genetic Epidemiology and Mental Health Services, 38*(12), 728–734. https://doi.org/10.1007/s00127-003-0720-6

Chatfield, J. (2002). AAP guideline on treatment of children with ADHD. *American Family Physician, 65,* 726-728.

Chawarska, K. & Volkmar, F. R. (2020). *Autism spectrum disorder in the first years of life.* Guilford Press.

Chia, G. L. C., Anderson, A. & McLean, L. A. (2018). Use of technology to support self-management in individuals with autism: Systematic review. *Review Journal of Autism and Developmental Disorders, 5*(2), 142–155.

Chia, M. F., Cotton, S., Filia, K., Phelan, M., Conus, P., Jauhar, S., Marwaha, S., McGorry, P. D., Davey, C. & Berk, M. (2019). Early intervention for bipolar disorder–Do current treatment guidelines provide recommendations for the early stages of the disorder? *Journal of Affective Disorders, 257,* 669–677.

Chiarotti, F. & Venerosi, A. (2020). Epidemiology of autism spectrum disorders: A review of worldwide prevalence estimates since 2014. *Brain Sciences, 10*(5), 274. https://doi.org/10.3390/brainsci10050274

Chien, Y. L., Chou, M.C., Chou, W.J., Wu, Y.Y., Tsai, W.C., Chiu, Y.N. & Gau, S. S.F. (2019). Prenatal and perinatal risk factors and the clinical implications on autism spectrum disorder. *Autism, 23*(3), 783–791.

Choi, K. R., Stewart, T., Fein, E., McCreary, M., Kenan, K. N., Davies, J. D., Naureckas, S. & Zima, B. T. (2020). The impact of attachment-disrupting adverse childhood experiences on child behavioral health. *The Journal of Pediatrics, 221*, 224–229.

Chukwuorji, J. C., Uzuegbu, C. N., Chukwu, C. V., Ifeagwazi, C. M. & Ugwu, C. (2020). Social support serves emotion regulation function in death anxiety among people living with HIV/AIDS. *South African Journal of Psychology, 50*(3), 395–410.

Church, E. B. (2015). Building community in the classroom. *Scholastic.* Retrieved from http://www.scholastic.com/teachers/article/building-community-classroom

Cividini-Motta, C., Garcia, A. R., Livingston, C. & MacNaul, H. L. (2019). The effect of response interruption and redirection with and without a differential reinforcement of alternative behavior component on stereotypy and appropriate responses. *Behavioral Interventions, 34*(1), 3–18.

Clanton, R. L., Baker, R. H., Rogers, J. C. & De Brito, S. A. (2017). Conduct disorder. In S. Goldstein & M. DeVries (Eds.), *Handbook of DSM-5 disorders in children and adolescents* (pp. 499–527). Springer.

Clarke, G. N., DeBar, L. L. & Lewinsohn, P. M. (2003). Cognitive-behavioral group treatment for adolescent depression. In A. E. Kazdin & J. R. Weisz (Eds.), *Evidence-based psychotherapies for children and adolescents* (pp. 120–134). Guilford.

Cleveland Clinic. (2019). *Bulimia nervosa.* https://my.clevelandclinic.org/health/diseases/9795-bulimia-nervosa

Cloth, A. H., Evans, S. W., Becker, S. P. & Paternite, C. E. (2014). Social maladjustment and special education: State regulations and continued controversy. *Journal of Emotional and Behavioral Disorders, 22*(4), 214-224.

Coelho, C. M., Gonçalves-Bradley, D. & Zsido, A. N. (2020). Who worries about specific phobias? A population-based study of risk factors. *Journal of Psychiatric Research,* 126, 67-72.

Cohen, J. A. & Mannarino, A. P. (2004). Posttraumatic stress disorder. In T. H. Ollendick & J. S. March (Eds.), *Phobic and anxiety disorders in children and adolescents: A clinician's guide to effective psychosocial and pharmacological interventions* (pp. 405–432). Oxford University Press.

Cohen, J.A, Mannarino A. P. & Deblinger E. (2017). *Treating trauma and traumatic grief in children and adolescents.* Taylor & Francis.

Coid, J. W., Ullrich, S., Keers, R., Bebbington, P., Destavola, B. L., Kallis, C., Yang, M., Reiss, D., Jenkins, R. & Donnelly, P. (2013). Gang membership, violence, and psychiatric morbidity. *American Journal of Psychiatry, 170*(9), 985-993.

Colalillo, S. & Johnston, C. (2016). Parenting cognition and affective outcomes following parent management training: A systematic review. *Clinical Child and Family Psychology Review, 19*(3), 216–235.

Coleman, M. C. & Webber, J. (2002). *Emotional and behavioral disorders: Theory and practice.* Allyn and Bacon.

Colliver, J. D., Compton, W. M., Gfroerer, J. C., & Condon, T. (2006). Projecting drug use among aging baby boomers in 2020. *Annals of epidemiology, 16*(4), 257-265.

Comings, D. E., & Blum, K. (2000). Reward deficiency syndrome: Genetic aspects of behavioral disorders. *Progress in Brain Research, 126,* 325–341.

Compton, W. M., Stein, J. B., Robertson, E. B., Pintello, D., Pringle, B., & Volkow, N. D. (2005). Charting a course for health services research at the National Institute on Drug Abuse. *Journal of Substance Abuse Treatment, 29*(3), 167–172. https://doi.org/10.1016/j.jsat.2005.05.008

Conners, C. K., Wells, K. C., Parker, J. D. A., Sitarenios, G., Diamond, J. M. & Powell, J. W. (1997). A new self-report scale for assessment of adolescent psychopathology: Factor structure, reliability, validity, and diagnostic sensitivity. *Journal of Abnormal Child Psychology, 25*(6), pp. 487-497.

Conners, C. K. (2008). *Conners rating scale* (3rd ed.). https://www.pearson clinical.com.au/files/744501471228127.pdf

Constantino, J.N. (2012). *The Social Responsiveness Scale.* Western Psychological Services.

Cook, C. R., Mayer, G. R., Wright, D. B., Kraemer, B., Wallace, M. D., Dart, E., Collins, T. & Restori, A. (2012). Exploring the link among behavior intervention plans, treatment integrity, and student outcomes under natural educational conditions. *The Journal of Special Education, 46*(1), 3-16.

Cooney, M., Lieberman, M., Guimond, T. & Katzman, D. K. (2018). Clinical and psychological features of children and adolescents diagnosed with avoidant/restrictive food intake disorder in a pediatric tertiary care eating disorder program: A descriptive study. *Journal of Eating Disorders, 6*(1), 1–8.

Cooper A. & Ward, C. L. (2012). Intervening with youth in gangs. In W. C. van der Merwe & A. Dawes (Eds.), *Youth violence: Sources and solutions in South Africa* (pp. 258-272). UCT Press.

Coplan, R. J., Schneider, B. H., Ooi, L. L. & Hipson, W. E. (2018). Peer-based interventions for behaviorally inhibited, socially withdrawn, and socially anxious children. In W.M. Bukowski, B. Laursen, & K.H. Rubin (Eds.), *Handbook of peer interactions, relationships, and groups* (pp.657-675). Guilford Press.

Cornacchio, D., Bry, L. J., Sanchez, A. L., Poznanski, B. & Comer, J. S. (2018). Psychosocial treatment and prevention of conduct problems in early childhood. In J. E. Lochman & W. Matthys (Eds.), *The Wiley handbook of disruptive and impulse-control disorders* (pp.433–449). Wiley.

Cornelius-White, J. H. & Harbaugh, A. P. (2009). *Learner-centered instruction: Building relationships for student success.* Sage.

Corrado, R. R., Peters, A. M. & Mathesius, J. (2019). The serious and violent young offender: Examining the multi-domain risk profile, mental health, and treatment intervention strategies. In D.L. Polaschek, A. Day, & C.R.

Hollin (Eds.), *The Wiley international handbook of correctional psychology* (pp. 221–234). Wiley.

Couturier, J. & Lock, J. (2006). Eating disorders: Anorexia nervosa, bulimia nervosa, and binge eating disorder. In T. G. Plante (Ed.), *Mental disorders of the new millennium: Biology and function, Vol. 3.* (pp. 135–156). Praeger.

Crane, M. E. & Kendall, P. C. (2020). Psychometric evaluation of the child and parent versions of the coping questionnaire. *Child Psychiatry and Human Development, 51,* 709-720.

Cresswell, L., Hinch, R. & Cage, E. (2019). The experiences of peer relationships amongst autistic adolescents: A systematic review of the qualitative evidence. *Research in Autism Spectrum Disorders, 61,* 45–60.

Crone, D. A., Hawken, L. S. & Horner, R. H. (2015). *Building positive behavior support systems in schools: Functional behavioral assessment.* Guilford Press.

Crosby, S. D., Howell, P. & Thomas, S. (2018). Social justice education through trauma-informed teaching. *Middle School Journal, 49*(4), 15–23. https://doi.org/10.1080/00940771.2018.1488470

Crowell, J. A., Keluskar, J. & Gorecki, A. (2019). Parenting behavior and the development of children with autism spectrum disorder. *Comprehensive Psychiatry, 90,* 21–29.

Cuijpers, P., Muñoz, R. F., Clarke, G. N. & Lewinsohn, P. M. (2009). Psychoeducational treatment and prevention of depression: The "coping with depression" course thirty years later. *Clinical Psychology Review, 29*(5), 449–458. https://doi.org/10.1016/j.cpr.2009.04.005

Cukier, H. N., Griswold, A. J., Hofmann, N. K., Gomez, L., Whitehead, P. L., Abramson, R. K., Gilbert, J. R., Cuccaro, M. L., Dykxhoorn, D. M. & Pericak-Vance, M. A. (2020). Three brothers with autism carry a stop-gain mutation in the HPA-Axis Gene NR3C2. *Autism Research, 13*(4), 523–531.

Culatta, R. A., Tompkins, J. R. & Werts, M. G. (2003). *Fundamentals of special education: What every teacher needs to know* (2nd ed.). Upper Saddle River, NJ: Merrill/Prentice Hall.

Cullen, D. (2019). *Columbine.* RiverRun.

Cullinan, D. (2002). *Students with emotional and behavioral disorders: An introduction for teachers and other helping professionals.* Merrill/Prentice Hall.

Cunningham, M. W. & Cox, C. J. (2016). Autoimmunity against dopamine receptors in neuropsychiatric and movement disorders: A review of Sydenham chorea and beyond. *Acta Physiologica, 216*(1), 90–100.

Cunningham, N.R., Wolff, J.C. & Jarrett, M.A. (2013). Assessment of disruptive behavior disorders in anxiety. In D. McKay & E. A. Storch (Eds.), *Handbook of assessing variants and complications in anxiety disorders* (pp. 231-242). Springer.

Cunningham, P. B., Randall, J., Ryan, S. R. & Fleming, B. D. (2016). Conduct disorder and oppositional defiant disorder. In A. Breland-Noble, C. S. Al-Mateen, & N. N. Singh (Eds.), *Handbook of mental health in African American youth* (pp. 143–162). Springer.

Curwin, R. L., Mendler, A. N. & Mendler, B. D. (2018). *Discipline with dignity: How to build responsibility, relationships, and respect in your classroom.* ASCD.

da Cunha-Bang, S., Mc Mahon, B., MacDonald Fisher, P., Jensen, P. S., Svarer, C. & Moos Knudsen, G. (2016). High trait aggression in men is associated with low 5-HT levels, as indexed by 5-HT 4 receptor binding. *Social Cognitive and Affective Neuroscience, 11*(4), 548–555.

Daly, B. P., DeMatteo, D., Hildenbrand, A., Baker, C. N. & Fisher, J. H. (2018). Psychosocial treatment and prevention in the adolescent years for ODD and CD. In J. E. Lochman & W. Matthys (Eds.), *The Wiley handbook of disruptive and impulse-control disorders* (pp. 467-483). Wiley.

Daly, B. P., Hildenbrand, A. K. & Brown, R. T. (2016). *Attention-deficit hyperactivity disorder in children and adolescents.* Hogrefe Publishing Corp.

Danielson, M. L., Bitsko, R. H., Ghandour, R. M., Holbrook, J. R., Kogan, M. D. & Blumberg, S. J. (2018). Prevalence of parent-reported ADHD diagnosis and associated treatment among U.S. children and adolescents, 2016. *Journal of clinical child and adolescent psychology: the official journal for the Society of Clinical Child and Adolescent Psychology, American Psychological Association, Division 53, 47*(2), 199–212. https://doi.org/10.1080/15374416.2017.1417860

Darby, R. R. (2018). Neuroimaging abnormalities in neurological patients with criminal behavior. *Current Neurology and Neuroscience Reports, 18*(8). Article 47. https://doi.org/10.1007/s11910-018-0853-3

Dardas, L. A., van de Water, B. & Simmons, L. A. (2018). Parental involvement in adolescent depression interventions: A systematic review of randomized clinical trials. *International Journal of Mental Health Nursing, 27*(2), 555–570.

Dark-Freudeman, A., Greskovich, L. & Terry, C. (2016). The relationship between attachment style, depressive symptoms, and social support: A survey of caregivers. *Educational Gerontology, 42*(2), 89–99.

Darwall, S. (2004, November). Respect and the second-person standpoint. In *Proceedings and Addresses of the American Philosophical Association, 78*(2), 43-59. American Philosophical Association.

Davidson, A. (2016). *Adult attachment and generalized social anxiety disorder: Implications for affective functioning, interpersonal schemas, and functional impairment.* Dissertation Abstracts International: Section B: The Sciences and Engineering, Vol 76(8-B) (E). ProQuest Information & Learning.

de Bildt, A., Mulder, E. J., Hoekstra, P. J., van Lang, N. D., Minderaa, R. B. & Hartman, C. A. (2009). Validity of the Children's Social Behavior Questionnaire (CSBQ) in children with intellectual disability: Comparing the CSBQ with ADI-R, ADOS, and clinical DSM-IV-TR classification. *Journal of Autism and Developmental Disorders, 39*(10), 1464–1470.

De Crescenzo, F., Cortese, S., Adamo, N. & Janiri, L. (2017). Pharmacological and non-pharmacological treatment of adults with ADHD: a meta-review. *Evidence-Based Mental Health, 20*(1), 4-11.

de la Vega, R., Racine, M., Sánchez-Rodríguez, E., Solé, E., Castarlenas, E., Jensen, M. P., Engel, J. & Miró, J. (2016). Psychometric properties of the short form of the Children's Depression Inventory (CDI-S) in young people with physical disabilities. *Journal of Psychosomatic Research, 90,* 57–61.

de Oliveira Gonzalez, M., Salzano, F. T., Azevedo, A., Lopes, A. C., Baise, M. & Táki, A. C. (2020). Eating disorders and personality disorders in women. In J. Rennó, G. Valadares, A. Cantilino, J. Mendes-Ribeiro, R. Rocha, & A. Geraldo da Silva (Eds.), *Women's mental health* (pp. 175-189). Springer.

de Souza Duarte, N., de Almeida Corrêa, L. M., Assunção, L. R., de Menezes, A. A., de Castro, O. B. & Teixeira, L. F. (2017). Relation between depression and hormonal dysregulation. *Open Journal of Depression, 6*(3), 69–78.

Denford, S., Abraham, C., Campbell, R. & Busse, H. (2017). A comprehensive review of reviews of school-based interventions to improve sexual-health. *Health Psychology Review, 11*(1), 33–52.

Depue, R. A., Krauss, S., Spoont, M. R. & Arbisi, P. (1989). General Behavior Inventory identification of unipolar and bipolar affective conditions in a nonclinical university population. *Journal of Abnormal Psychology, 98*(2), 117-126.

DeSole, L. M., Nelson, A. & Young, L. L. (2016). *Making contact: The therapist's guide to conducting a successful first interview.* Pearson.

Deveci Şirin, H. (2019). Parental acceptance–rejection and adult separation anxiety: The mediation of adult attachment insecurity. *SAGE Open, 9*(4), 1-9. https://doi.org/10.1177/2158244019885138

Dewey, J. (1899). *The school and society: Being three lectures.* The University of Chicago Press.

Dieke, J. S. (2012). *A quiet transformation.* http://blog.sfusd.edu/2012/09/a-quiet-transformation.html

Dobrescu, S. R., Dinkler, L., Gillberg, C., Raastam, M., Gillberg, C. & Wentz, E. (2020). Anorexia nervosa: 30-year outcome. *The British Journal of Psychiatry, 216*(2), 97–104.

Dobson, E. T., Bloch, M. H. & Strawn, J. R. (2019). Efficacy and tolerability of pharmacotherapy for pediatric anxiety disorders: A network meta-analysis. *Journal of Clinical Psychiatry,80*(1). doi.10.4088/JCP17r12064

Docherty, M., Beardslee, J., Byrd, A. L., Yang, V. J. & Pardini, D. (2019). Developmental trajectories of interpersonal callousness from childhood to adolescence as predictors of antisocial behavior and psychopathic features in young adulthood. *Journal of Abnormal Psychology, 80,* 700-709.

Döpfner, M., Breuer, D., Schürmann, S., Wolff Metternich, T., Rademacher, C. & Lehmkuhl, G. (2004). Effectiveness of an adaptive multimodal treatment in children with Attention–Deficit Hyperactivity Disorder – global outcome. *European Child & Adolescent Psychiatry, 13,* 117–129. https://doi.org/10.1007/s00787-004-1011-9.

Druck, K. & Kaplowitz, M. (2005). Setting up a no-bully zone. *Virginia Journal of Education, 98*(4), 6-10.

Dryfoos, J. G. (1990). *Adolescents at risk: Prevalence and prevention.* Oxford University Press.

Dudley, M. Z., Salmon, D. A., Halsey, N. A., Orenstein, W. A., Limaye, R. J., O'Leary, S. T. & Omer, S. B. (2018). Do vaccines cause autism? In M.Z. Dudley, D.A. Salmon, N.A. Halsey, W.A. Orenstein, R.J. Limaye, S.T. O'Leary, & S.B. Omer (Eds.), *The clinician's vaccine safety resource guide* (pp. 197–204). Springer.

Dueñas, A. D., Plavnick, J. B. & Goldstein, H. (2020). Effects of a multicomponent peer mediated intervention on social communication of preschoolers with autism spectrum disorder. *Exceptional Children, 87,* 236-257.

Duffy, F., Sharpe, H. & Schwannauer, M. (2019). The effectiveness of interpersonal psychotherapy for adolescents with depression–a systematic review and meta-analysis. *Child and Adolescent Mental Health, 24*(4), 307–317.

Dufrene, B. A., Noell, G. H., Gilbertson, D. N. & Duhon, G. J. (2005). Monitoring implementation of reciprocal peer tutoring: Identifying and intervening with students who do not maintain accurate implementation. *School Psychology Review, 34*(1), 74-86.

Duggal, N. (2020). *Attention deficit hyperactivity disorder (ADHD): The role of dopamine.* https://www.healthline.com/health/adhd/adhd-dopamine

DuPaul, G. J., Power, T. J., Anastopoulos, A. D. & Reid, R. (1999). *The ADHD rating scale–IV: Checklists, norms, and clinical interpretation.* Guilford Press.

Dwyer, K. P., Osher, D. & Hoffman, C. C. (2000). Creating responsive schools: Contextualizing early warning, timely response. *Exceptional Children, 66*(3), 347–365. https://doi.org/10.1177/001440290006600306

Dwyer, K., Osher, D. & Warger, C. (1998). *Early warning, timely response: A guide to safe schools.* U.S. Department of Education.

Eddy, K. T., Tabri, N., Thomas, J. J., Murray, H. B., Keshaviah, A., Hastings, E., Edkins, K., Krishna, M., Herzog, D. B. & Keel, P. K. (2017). Recovery from anorexia nervosa and bulimia nervosa at 22-year follow-up. *The Journal of Clinical Psychiatry, 78*(2), 184–189.

Eddy, K. T. & Thomas, J. J. (2019). Introduction to a special issue on child and adolescent feeding and eating disorders and avoidant/restrictive food intake disorder. *International Journal of Eating Disorders, 52*(4), 327–330.

Edmiston, E. K., Blain, S. D. & Corbett, B. A. (2017). Salivary cortisol and behavioral response to social evaluative threat in adolescents with autism spectrum disorder. *Autism Research, 10*(2), 346–358.

Edwards, C. H. (2001). Student violence and the moral dimensions of education. *Psychology in the Schools, 38,* 249–257.

Efferson, L. M. & Glenn, A. L. (2018). The neurobiology of oppositional defiant disorder and conduct disorder. In J. E. Lochman & W. Matthys (Eds.), *The Wiley handbook of disruptive and impulse-control disorders* (p. 143–158). Wiley.

El Ouardani, C. N. (2017). Innocent or intentional?: Interpreting oppositional defiant disorder in a preschool mental health clinic. *Culture, Medicine, and Psychiatry, 41*(1), 94–110.

Elflein, J. (2020). *Total number of deaths in the United States due to eating disorders from 2018-2019, by condition.* Statista. https://www.statista.com/statistics/1230552/us-deaths-due-to-eating-disorders-by-condition/

Elias, M. J. (2016). *4 approaches to building positive community in any classroom.* https://www.edutopia.org/blog/4-approaches-building-positive-community-any-classroom-maurice-elias

Elias, M. J., & Leverett, L. (2011). Consultation to urban schools for improvements in academics and behavior: No alibis. No excuses. No exceptions. *Journal of Educational & Psychological Consultation, 21*(1), 28–45. https://doi.org/10.1080/10474412.2010.522877

Elliott, J. G. & Place, M. (2019). Practitioner review: School refusal: developments in conceptualization and treatment since 2000. *Journal of Child Psychology and Psychiatry, 60*(1), 4–15.

Elliott, S. N., Witt, J. C., Kratochwill, T. R. & Stoiber, K. C. (2002). Selecting and evaluating classroom interventions. In M. R. Shinn, H. M. Walker, and G. Stoner (Eds.), *Interventions for academic and behavior problems II: Preventive and remedial approaches* (pp. 275–294). National Association of School Psychologists.

Enache, R. G. (2017). Body image and eating disorders in adolescence. *Agora Psycho-Pragmatica, 11*(1), 24–31.

Erfina, E., Widyawati, W., McKenna, L., Reisenhofer, S. & Ismail, D. (2019). Adolescent mothers' experiences of the transition to motherhood: An integrative review. *International Journal of Nursing Sciences, 6*(2), 221–228.

Ericsson, M., Poston, W. S. C. & Foreyt, J. P. (1996). Common biological pathways in eating disorders and obesity. *Addictive Behaviors, 21*(6), 733-743.

Ernst, M., Cookus, B. A. & Moravec, B. C. (2000). Pictorial Instrument for Children and Adolescents (PICA-III-R). *Journal of the American Academy of Child & Adolescent Psychiatry, 39*(1), 94–99. https://doi.org/10.1097/00004583-200001000-00021

Erskine, H. E., Norman, R. E., Ferrari, A. J., Chan, G. C., Copeland, W. E., Whiteford, H. A., & Scott, J. G. (2016). Long-term outcomes of attention-deficit/hyperactivity disorder and conduct disorder: A systematic review and meta-analysis. *Journal of the American Academy of Child & Adolescent Psychiatry, 55*(10), 841–850.

Espinoza, C., Samandari, G. & Andersen, K. (2020). Abortion knowledge, attitudes and experiences among adolescent girls: A review of the literature. *Sexual and Reproductive Health Matters, 28*(1). Article 1744225. https://doi.org/10.1080/26410397.2020.1744225

Essayli, J. H., & Vitousek, K. M. (2020). Cognitive behavioral therapy with eating disordered youth. In R.D. Friedberg & B.J. Nakamura (Eds.), *Cognitive behavioral therapy in youth: Tradition and innovation* (pp. 163–187). Springer.

Evans B. (2014). The foundations of autism: the law concerning psychotic, schizophrenic, and autistic children in 1950s and 1960s Britain. *Bulletin of the History of Medicine, 88*(2), 253–285. https://doi.org/10.1353/bhm.2014.0033

Eyberg, S. & Pincus, D. (2022). *Eyberg child behavior inventory & Sutter-Eyberg student behavior inventory-revised: Professional manual.* Psychological Assessment Resources. https://www.parinc.com/products/pkey/97

Fad, K. M., Patton, J. R. & Polloway, E. A. (1998). *Behavioral intervention planning: Completing a functional behavioral assessment and developing a behavioral intervention plan.* Pro-Ed.

Fairchild, G., Hawes, D. J., Frick, P. J., Copeland, W. E., Odgers, C. L., Franke, B., Freitag, C. M. & De Brito, S. A. (2019). Conduct disorder. *Nature Reviews Disease Primers, 5*(1), 1–25.

Fallah, M. S., Shaikh, M. R., Neupane, B., Rusiecki, D., Bennett, T. A. & Beyene, J. (2019). Atypical antipsychotics for irritability in pediatric autism: A systematic review and network meta-analysis. *Journal of Child and Adolescent Psychopharmacology, 29*(3), 168–180.

Farmer, T. W., Dawes, M., Hamm, J. V., Lee, D., Mehtaji, M., Hoffman, A. S. & Brooks, D. S. (2018). Classroom social dynamics management: Why the invisible hand of the teacher matters for special education. *Remedial and Special Education, 39*(3), 177-192.

Farrington, C. P., Miller, E., & Taylor, B. (2001). MMR and autism: Further evidence against a causal association. *Vaccine, 19*(27), 3632–3635.

Farrington, D. P., Gaffney, H. & Ttofi, M. M. (2017). Systematic reviews of explanatory risk factors for violence, offending, and delinquency. *Aggression and Violent Behavior, 33*, 24–36.

Farstad, S. M., McGeown, L. M. & von Ranson, K. M. (2016). Eating disorders and personality, 2004–2016: A systematic review and meta-analysis. *Clinical Psychology Review, 46*, 91–105.

Fatt, S. J., Mond, J., Bussey, K., Griffiths, S., Murray, S. B., Lonergan, A., Hay, P., Pike, K., Trompeter, N. & Mitchison, D. (2020). Seeing yourself clearly: Self-identification of a body image problem in adolescents with an eating disorder. *Early Intervention in Psychiatry.* Wiley Online Library. https://doi.org/10.1111/eip.12987

Feingold, B. F. (1975). Hyperkinesis and learning disabilities linked to artificial food flavors and colors. *The American Journal of Nursing*, 75(5), 797-803.

Fekkes, M., Pijpers, F. I. & Verloove-Vanhorick, S. P. (2005). Bullying: Who does what, when and where? Involvement of children, teachers, and parents in bullying behavior. *Health Education Research, 20*(1), 81-91.

Fernandes, J. M., Cajão, R., Lopes, R., Jerónimo, R. & Barahona-Corrêa, J. B. (2018). Social cognition in schizophrenia and autism spectrum disorders: A systematic review and meta-analysis of direct comparisons. *Frontiers in Psychiatry, 9.* Article 504. http://dx.doi.org.ezproxy.hofstra.edu/10.3389/fpsyt.2018.00504

Ferri, S. L., Abel, T. & Brodkin, E. S. (2018). Sex differences in autism spectrum disorder: A review. *Current Psychiatry Reports, 20*(2), 9. https://doi.org/10.1007/s11920-018-0874-2

Feshbach, N. (1983) Learning to care: A positive approach to child training and discipline. *Journal of Clinical Child Psychology, 12*, 266-271.

Findling, R. L., Stepanova, E., Youngstrom, E. A. & Young, A. S. (2018). Progress in diagnosis and treatment of bipolar disorder among children and adolescents: An international perspective. *Evidence-Based Mental Health, 21*(4), 177–181.

Findling, R. L., Wigal, S. B., Bukstein, O. G., Boellner, S. W., Abikoff, H. B., Turnbow, J. M. & Civil, R. (2009). Long-term tolerability of the methylphenidate transdermal system in pediatric attention-deficit/hyperactivity disorder: a multicenter, prospective, 12-month, open-label, uncontrolled, phase III extension of four clinical trials. *Clinical Therapeutics,31*(8), 1844-1855.

Finkelhor, D. (2014). *Trends in bullying and peer victimization.* Crimes Against Children ResearchCenter.

Fischer, M. & Newby, R. F. (1998). Use of the restricted academic task in ADHD dose-response relationships. *Journal of Learning Disabilities, 31*(6), 608-612.

Fish, R. E. (2019). Teacher race and racial disparities in special education. *Remedial and Special Education, 40*(4), 213-224.

Flannery-Schroeder, E. C. & Kendall, P. C. (2000). Group and individual cognitive-behavioral treatments for youth with anxiety disorders: A randomized clinical trial. *Cognitive Therapy and Research, 24*(3), 251–278.

Flook, L., Goldberg, S. B., Pinger, L. & Davidson, R. J. (2015). Promoting prosocial behavior and self-regulatory skills in preschool children through a mindfulness-based Kindness Curriculum. *Developmental psychology, 51*(1), 44–51. https://doi.org/10.1037/a0038256

Foa, E. B., Johnson, K. M., Feeny, N. C. & Treadwell, K. R. (2001). The Child PTSD Symptom Scale: A preliminary examination of its psychometric properties. *Journal of Clinical Child Psychology, 30*(3), 376–384.

Franklin, M., Foa, E. & March, J. S. (2003). The pediatric obsessive-compulsive disorder treatment study: Rationale, design, and methods. *Journal of Child and Adolescent Psychopharmacology, 13* (2), 39–51.

Freeman, K. A. & Hogansen, J. M. (2006). Conduct disorders. In M. Hersen (Ed.), *Clinician's handbook of child behavioral assessment* (pp. 477–501). Elsevier. https://doi.org/10.1016/B978-012343014-4/50020-4

Frick, A., Engman, J., Alaie, I., Björkstrand, J., Gingnell, M., Larsson, E.-M., Eriksson, E., Wahlstedt, K., Fredrikson, M. & Furmark, T. (2020). Neuroimaging, genetic, clinical, and demographic predictors of treatment response in patients with social anxiety disorder. *Journal of Affective Disorders, 261*, 230–237.

Frick, A., Engman, J., Wahlstedt, K., Gingnell, M., Fredrikson, M. & Furmark, T. (2018). Anterior cingulate cortex activity as a candidate biomarker for treatment selection in social anxiety disorder. *BJPsych Open, 4*(3), 157–159.

Frick, M. A. & Brocki, K. C. (2019). A multi-factorial perspective on ADHD and ODD in school-aged children: What is the role of cognitive regulation, temperament, and parental support? *Journal of Clinical and Experimental Neuropsychology, 41*(9), 933–945.

Frick, P. J., Cornell, A. H., Bodin, S. D., Dane, H. A., Barry, C. T. & Loney, B. R. (2003). Callousunemotional traits and developmental pathways to severe conduct problems. *Developmental Psychology, 39,* 246–260.

Frisén, A., Jonsson, A. K. & Persson, C. (2007). Adolescents' perception of bullying: who is the victim? who is the bully? what can be done to stop bullying? *Adolescence, 42*(168), 750-761.

Frith, C. & Frith, U. (2005). Theory of mind. *Current biology, 15*(17), R644-R645. doi:10.1016/j.cub.2005.08.041

Froehlich, T. E., Anixt, J. S., Loe, I. M., Chirdkiatgumchai, V., Kuan, L. & Gilman, R. C. (2011). Update on environmental risk factors for attention-deficit/ hyperactivity disorder. *Current Psychiatry Reports, 13*(5), 333. doi.org/10.1007/s11920-011-0221-3

Frost, R., Hyland, P., Shevlin, M. & Murphy, J. (2020). Distinguishing Complex PTSD from Borderline Personality Disorder among individuals with a history of sexual trauma: A latent class analysis. *European Journal of Trauma & Dissociation, 4*(1). Article 100080. https://doi.org/10.1016/j.ejtd.2018.08.004

Fu, C. P., Chen, K. L., Tseng, M. H., Chiang, F. M., & Hsieh, C. L. (2012). Reliability and validity of the psychoeducational profile-third edition caregiver report in children with autism spectrum disorders. *Research in Autism Spectrum Disorders, 6*(1), 115–122. https://doi.org/10.1016/j.rasd. 2011.03.011

Furman, L. (2005). What is attention-deficit hyperactivity disorder (ADHD)? *Journal of Child Neurology*, 20, 994-1002.

Furniss, F. & Biswas, A. B. (2020). Self-injurious behavior in persons with autism spectrum conditions. In F. Furniss & A. B. Biswas (Eds.), *Self-injurious behavior in individuals with neurodevelopmental conditions* (pp. 281–311). Springer.

Gallupe, O. & Gravel, J. (2018). Social network position of gang members in schools: Implications for recruitment and gang prevention. *Justice Quarterly, 35*(3), 505-525.

Garaigordobil, M., Jaureguizar, J. & Bernarás, E. (2019). Evaluation of the effects of a childhood depression prevention program. *The Journal of Psychology, 153*(2), 127–140.

Garber, J. & Kaminski, K. M. (2000). Laboratory and performance-based measures of depression in children and adolescents. *Journal of Clinical Child Psychology, 29*(4), 509–525. https://doi.org/10.1207/S15374424JCCP2 904_5

Gatti, U., Grattagliano, I. & Rocca, G. (2019). Evidence-based psychosocial treatments of conduct problems in children and adolescents: An overview. *Psychiatry, Psychology and Law, 26*(2), 171–193.

Geller, B. (2004). Hypersexuality in children with mania: Differential diagnosis and clinical presentation. *Psychiatric Times, 21*(12). https://www.psychiatric times.com/view/hypersexuality-children-mania-differential-diagnosis-and-clinical-presentation

Geller, B., Zimerman, B., Williams, M., Bolhofner, K. & Craney, J. L. (2001). Bipolar disorder at prospective follow-up of adults who had prepubertal major depressive disorder. *The American Journal of Psychiatry, 158*(1), 125-7.

Gervais, H., Belin, P., Boddaert, N., Leboyer, M., Coez, A., Barthelemy, C., Samson, Y. & Zilbovicius, M. (2004). Abnormal voice processing in autism: A fMRI study. *Nature Neuroscience, 7*, 801–802.

Getahun, D., Jacobsen, S. J., Fassett, M. J., Wing, D. A., Xiang, A. H., Chiu, V. Y. & Peltier, M. R. (2018). Association between maternal hypothyroidism and autism spectrum disorders in children. *Pediatric Research, 83*(3), 580–588.

Gibbons, B. (2020). *Using child-centered play therapy as an intervention to reassess ADHD diagnoses and trauma in children: A literature review.* [*Expressive Therapies Capstone Theses*]. Lesley University. https://digitalcommons.lesley. edu/expressive_theses/358

Gilliam, J. E. (2013). *GARS-3: Gilliam Autism Rating Scale* (3rd ed.). Pro-Ed.

Gillman, A. S., Yeater, E. A., Ewing, S. W. F., Kong, A. S. & Bryan, A. D. (2018). Risky sex in high-risk adolescents: Associations with alcohol use, marijuana use, and co-occurring use. *AIDS and Behavior, 22*(4), 1352–1362.

Giordano, K., Eastin, S., Calcagno, B., Wilhelm, S. & Gil, A. (2020). Examining the effects of internal versus external coaching on preschool teachers' implementation of a framework of evidence-based social-emotional practices. *Journal of Early Childhood Teacher Education*, 1-14. https://doi.org/10.1080/10901027.2020.1782545

Gladding, S. T. (2018). *The counseling dictionary* (4th ed.). American Counseling Association.

Glasser, W. (1965). *Reality therapy: A new approach to psychiatry*. Harper and Row.

Gnanavel, S., Sharma, P., Kaushal, P. & Hussain, S. (2019). Attention deficit hyperactivity disorder and comorbidity: A review of literature. *World Journal of Clinical Cases, 7*(17), 2420–2426. https://doi.org/10.12998/wjcc.v7.i17.2420

Gold, M. S., Blum, K., Oscar-Berman, M. & Braverman, E. R. (2014). Low dopamine function in attention deficit/hyperactivity disorder: Should genotyping signify early diagnosis in children? *Postgraduate Medicine, 126*(1), 153–177. https://doi.org/10.3810/pgm.2014.01.2735

Goldfarb, E. S., Lieberman, L., Opthof, E., Mauro, K. & Strucinski, N. (2019). Evidence for affirmative approaches to sex education: Uncovering the "missing pieces" of a systematic literature review of three decades of school-based sex education. *APHA's 2019 Annual Meeting and Expo* (Nov. 2-Nov. 6).

Goodyear, R. K. (2002). A concept map of male partners in teenage pregnancy: Implications for school counselors. *Professional School Counseling, 5*(3), 186–193.

Gorrell, S., Matheson, B. E., Lock, J. & Le Grange, D. (2020). Remission in adolescents with bulimia nervosa: Empirical evaluation of current conceptual models. *European Eating Disorders Review,28(4),* 445-453

Gosch, E. A., Brookland, R. & Wolensky, M. (2018). Treatment of generalized anxiety disorder. In P.C. Kendall (Ed.), *Cognitive therapy with children and adolescents: A casebook for clinical practice* (3rd ed., pp.70-93). Guilford.

Gotestam, K.G. & Agras, W. S. (1995). General population-based epidemiological study of eating disorders in Norway. *International Journal of Eating Disorders, 18*, 119-126.

Gottfredson, D. C., Kearley, B., Thornberry, T. P., Slothower, M., Devlin, D. & Fader, J. J. (2018). Scaling-up evidence-based programs using a public funding stream: A randomized trial of functional family therapy for court-involved youth. *Prevention Science, 19*(7), 939–953.

Grant, J. E. & Chamberlain, S. R. (2020, March 2). Exploring the neurobiology of OCD: Clinical implications. *The Psychiatric Times*, pp. 1-7.

Grant, J., Indermaur, D., Thornton, J., Stevens, G., Chamarette, C. & Halse, A. (2009). Intrafamilial adolescent sex offenders: Psychological profile and treatment. *Trend and Issues in Crime and Criminal Justice, 375*, pp. 1-6. https://search.informit.org/doi/10.3316/agispt.20094117

Gray, C. (2022). *What is a social story?* https://carolgraysocialstories.com/social-stories/what-is-it/

Gray, K. M., Piccinin, A. M., Hofer, S. M., Mackinnon, A., Bontempo, D. E., Einfeld, S. L., Parmenter, T. & Tonge, B. J. (2011). The longitudinal relationship between behavior and emotional disturbance in young people with intellectual disability and maternal mental health. *Research in Developmental Disabilities, 32*(3), 1194-1204.

Green, A. L., Cohen, D. R. & Stormont, M. (2019). Addressing and preventing disproportionality in exclusionary discipline practices for students of color with disabilities. *Intervention in School and Clinic, 54*(4), 241-245.

Green, L. W. & Kreuter, M. W. (1992). CDC's planned approach to community health as an application of PRECEDE and an inspiration for PROCEED. *Journal of Health Education, 23,* 140–147.

Greene, M. B. (2006). Bullying in schools: A plea for measure of human rights. *Journal of Social Issues, 62*(1), pp.63.79. https://doi.org/10.1111/j.1540-4560.2006.00439.x

Greene, R. W. (2006). Oppositional defiant disorder. In R. T. Ammerman (Ed.), *Comprehensive handbook of personality and psychopathology, Vol. 3.* (pp. 285–298). Wiley.

Greenhill, L., Kollins, S., Abikoff, H., McCracken, J., Riddle, M., Swanson, J., McGough, J., Wigal, S., Wigal, T., Vitiello, B., Skrobala, A., Posner, K., Ghuman, J., Cunningham, C., Davies, M., Chuang, S. & Cooper, T. (2006). Efficacy and safety of immediate-release methylphenidate treatment for preschoolers with ADHD. *Journal of the American Academy of Child & Adolescent Psychiatry, 45*(11), 1284-1293.

Greenhill, L. L., Halperin, J. M. & Abikoff, H. (1999). Stimulant medications. *Journal of the American Academy of Child and Adolescent* Psychiatry, 38, 503-512.

Grenon, R., Tasca, G. A., Maxwell, H., Balfour, L., Proulx, G. & Bissada, H. (2016). Parental bonds and body dissatisfaction in a clinical sample: The mediating roles of attachment anxiety and media internalization. *Body Image, 19,* 49–56.

Gresham, F. M. (2004). Current status and future directions of school-based behavioral interventions. *School Psychology Review, 33,* 326-343.

Gresham, F. M. (2005). Response to intervention: An alternative means of identifying students as emotionally disturbed. *Education & Treatment of Children, 28*(4), 328-344. Wilson Education Abstracts database.

Gresham, F. M. (2007). Response to intervention and emotional and behavioral disorders. *Assessment for Effective Interventions, 32*(4), 214–222.

Gresham, F. M. (2011). Social behavioral assessment and intervention: Observations and Impressions. *School Psychology Review, 40*(2), 275–283.

Gresham, F. M., Watson, T. S., & Skinner, C. H. (2001). Functional behavioral assessment: Principles, procedures, and future directions. *School Psychology Review, 30*(2), 156–172.

Griffith, S. F., Arnold, D. H., Rolon-Arroyo, B. & Harvey, E. A. (2019). Neuropsychological predictors of ODD symptom dimensions in young children. *Journal of Clinical Child & Adolescent Psychology, 48*(1), 80–92.

Groth, T., Hilsenroth, M., Boccio, D. & Gold, J. (2019). Relationship between trauma history and eating disorders in adolescents. *Journal of Child & Adolescent Trauma, 13,* 443-453.

Grover, S. & Avasthi, A. (2019). Clinical practice guidelines for the management of depression in children and adolescents. *Indian Journal of Psychiatry, 61*(Supplement 2), 226-240.

Gullone, E. & King, N. J. (1992). Psychometric evaluation of a revised fear survey schedule for children and adolescents. *Child Psychology & Psychiatry & Allied Disciplines, 33*(6), 987–998.

Gushue, G. V. (2004). Race, color-blind racial attitudes, and judgments about mental health: A shifting standards perspective. *Journal of Counseling Psychology, 51*(4), 398–407.

Gushue, G. V., Constantine, M. G. & Sciarra, D. T. (2008). The influence of culture, self-reported multicultural counseling competence, and shifting standards of judgment on perceptions of family functioning of White family counselors. *Journal of Counseling & Development, 86*(1), 85–94.

Ha, S., Sohn, I. J., Kim, N., Sim, H. J. & Cheon, K. A. (2015). Characteristics of brains in autism spectrum disorder: Structure, function and connectivity across the lifespan. *Experimental Neurobiology, 24*(4), 273–284. https://doi.org/10.5607/en.2015.24.4.273

Hale, M. D. & Logomarsino, J. V. (2019). The use of enteral nutrition in the treatment of eating disorders: A systematic review. *Eating and Weight Disorders-Studies on Anorexia, Bulimia and Obesity, 24*(2), 179–198.

Haleem, D. J. (2017). Improving therapeutics in anorexia nervosa with tryptophan. *Life Sciences, 178*, 87–93.

Hallahan, D. P., Lloyd, J. W., Kauffman, J. M., Weiss, M. & Martinez, E. A. (2005). *Learning disabilities: Foundations, characteristics, and effective teaching* (3rd ed.). Pearson Education.

Hallahan, D., Pullen, P., Kauffman, J. & Badar, J. (2020, February 28). Exceptional learners. *Oxford Research Encyclopedia of Education*. https://oxfordre.com/education/view/10.1093/acrefore/9780190264093.001.0001/acrefore-9780190264093-e-926.

Hanish, L. D. & Guerra, N. G. (2000). Children who get victimized at school: What is known? What can be done? *Professional School Counseling, 4*(2), 113.

Hara, S. R. & Burke, D. J. (1998). Parent involvement: The key to improved student achievement. *School Community Journal, 8*(2), 9-19.

Haraway, D. L. (2012). Monitoring students with ADHD within the RTI framework. *The Behavior Analyst Today, 13*(2), 17.

Harris, J. (2019). *Treating conduct disorder using cognitive behavioral therapy for anger and aggression in children: A case study of a male juvenile offender* [Unpublished doctoral dissertation]. Washburn University.

Harris, M. L., Schumaker, J. B. & Deshler, D. D. (2011). The effects of strategic morphological analysis instruction on the vocabulary performance of secondary students with and without disabilities. *Learning Disability Quarterly, 34*(1), 17-33.

Harry, B. & Klingner, J. (2014). *Why are so many minority students in special education?* Teachers College Press.

Hart, B. M. & Risley, T. R. (1968). Establishing use of descriptive adjectives in the spontaneous speech of disadvantaged preschool children. *Journal of Applied Behavior Analysis, 1*(2), 109–120.

Hart, R., Ivtzan, I. & Hart, D. (2013). Mind the gap in mindfulness research: A comparative account of the leading schools of thought. *Review of General Psychology, 17*(4), 453–466. https://doi.org/10.1037/a0035212

Hartmann, D., Ueno, K. & Schwenck, C. (2020). Attributional and attentional bias in children with conduct problems and callous-unemotional traits: A case–control study. *Child and Adolescent Psychiatry and Mental Health, 14*(1), 1–11.

Harvey, E. A., Breaux, R. P. & Lugo-Candelas, C. I. (2016). Early development of comorbidity between symptoms of attention-deficit/hyperactivity disorder (ADHD) and oppositional defiant disorder (ODD). *Journal of Abnormal Psychology, 125*(2), 154–167. https://doi.org/10.1037/abn0000090

Hayden, B. M. & Patterson, B. R. (2018). Oppositional defiant disorder (ODD). In A. Marakakis & W.T. O'Donohue (Eds.), *Principle-based stepped care and brief psychotherapy for integrated care settings* (pp. 289–302). Springer.

Hazler, R. J. (1996). *Breaking the cycle of violence: Interventions for bullying and victimization.* Accelerated Development.

Hazler, R. J. & Carney, J. V. (2000). When victims turn aggressors: Factors in the development of deadly school violence. *Professional School Counseling,* 4(2), 105-112.

Hazlett, H. C., Gu, H., Munsell, B. C., Kim, S. H., Styner, M., Wolff, J. J., Elison, J. T., Swanson, M. R., Zhu, H. & Botteron, K. N. (2017). Early brain development in infants at high risk for autism spectrum disorder. *Nature, 542*(7641), 348–351.

Healy, O., Lydon, S., Brady, T., Rispoli, M., Holloway, J., Neely, L. & Grey, I. (2019). The use of differential reinforcement of other behaviours to establish inhibitory stimulus control for the management of vocal stereotypy in children with autism. *Developmental Neurorehabilitation, 22*(3), 192–202.

Heatly, M. C. & Lee, P. (2018). Conduct disorder. In A. Marakakis & W.T. O'Donohue (Eds.), *Principle-based stepped care and brief psychotherapy for integrated care settings* (pp. 143–154). Springer.

Heels, S. W. (2019). The impact of abstinence-only sex education programs in the United States on adolescent sexual outcomes. *Perspectives, 11*(1). Article 3.

Heinrichs, R. (2003). A whole-school approach to bullying: Special considerations for children with exceptionalities. *Intervention in School and Clinic, 38* (4), p. 195-204.

Heiser, N. A., Turner, S. M., Beidel, D. C. & Roberson-Nay, R. (2009). Differentiating social phobia from shyness. *Journal of Anxiety Disorders, 23*(4), 469–476. https://doi.org/10.1016/j.janxdis.2008.10.002

Hendren, R. L. & Mullen, D. J. (2006). Conduct disorder and oppositional defiant disorder. In M. K. Dulcan & J. M. Wiener (Eds.), *Essentials of child and adolescent psychiatry* (pp. 357–387). American Psychiatric Publishing.

Henggeler, S. W. (2017). Multisystemic therapy. In C. J. Schreck, M. J. Leiber, H. V. Miller and K. Welch (Eds.), *The encyclopedia of juvenile delinquency and justice* (pp.1-5). Wiley.

Herman, K. C., Hickmon-Rosa, J. E. & Reinke, W. M. (2018). Empirically derived profiles of teacher stress, burnout, self-efficacy, and coping and associated student outcomes. *Journal of Positive Behavior Interventions, 20*(2), 90-100.

Herren, J. & Berryhill, J. (2018). Working with young children with OCD. In E. A. Storch, J. F. McGuire, & D. McKay (Eds.), *The Clinician's Guide to Cognitive-*

Behavioral Therapy for Childhood Obsessive-Compulsive Disorder (pp. 289–307). Elsevier.

Hesse, E., & Main, M. (2000). Disorganized infant, child, and adult attachment: Collapse in behavioral and attentional strategies. *Journal of the American Psychoanalytic Association, 48*(4), 1097–1127. https://doi.org/10.1177/00030651000480041101

Higa-McMillan, C. K., Francis, S. E., Rith-Najarian, L., & Chorpita, B. F. (2016). Evidence base update: 50 years of research on treatment for child and adolescent anxiety. *Journal of Clinical Child & Adolescent Psychology, 45*(2), 91–113.

Hilbert, A., Herpertz, S., Zipfel, S., Tuschen-Caffier, B., Friederich, H. C., Mayr, A. & de Zwaan, M. (2020). Psychopathological networks in cognitive-behavioral treatments for binge-eating disorder. *Psychotherapy and Psychosomatics, 89*(6), 379–385.

Hilbert, A., Hoek, H. W. & Schmidt, R. (2017). Evidence-based clinical guidelines for eating disorders: International comparison. *Current Opinion in Psychiatry, 30*(6), 423-437.

Hilbert, A., Petroff, D., Herpertz, S., Pietrowsky, R., Tuschen-Caffier, B., Vocks, S. & Schmidt, R. (2020). Meta-analysis on the long-term effectiveness of psychological and medical treatments for binge-eating disorder. *International Journal of Eating Disorders, 53*(9), 1353–1376.

Hilbert, A., Saelens, B. E., Stein, R. I., Mockus, D. S., Welch, R. R., Matt, G. E. & Wilfley, D. E. (2007). Pretreatment and process predictors of outcome in interpersonal and cognitive behavioral psychotherapy for binge eating disorder. *Journal of Consulting and Clinical Psychology, 75*(4), 645-651.

Himmerich, H., Kan, C., Au, K. & Treasure, J. (2020). Pharmacological treatment of eating disorders, comorbid mental health problems, malnutrition and physical health consequences. *Pharmacology & Therapeutics, 217.* Article 107667. https://doi.org/10.1016/j.pharmthera.2020.107667

Hirota, T., Veenstra-VanderWeele, J., Hollander, E. & Kishi, T. (2014). Antiepileptic medications in autism spectrum disorder: A systematic review and meta-analysis. *Journal of Autism and Developmental Disorders, 44*(4), 948–957. https://doi.org/10.1007/s10803-013-1952-2

Hixon, A.L. (1999). Preventing street gang violence. *American Family Physician, 59(*8), 2121-2123.

Hodges, K., Kline, J., Stern, L., Cytryn, L. & McKnew, D. (1982). The development of the child assessment interview for research and clinical use. *Journal of Abnormal Child Psychology, 10,* 173–189.

Hodgkins, P., Shaw, M., McCarthy, S. & Sallee, F. R. (2012). The pharmacology and clinical outcomes of amphetamines to treat ADHD. *CNS Drugs 26,* 245–268. https://doi.org/10.2165/11599630-000000000-00000

Hoek H. W. (2006). Incidence, prevalence and mortality of anorexia nervosa and other eating disorders. *Current Opinion in Psychiatry, 19*(4), 389–394. https://doi.org/10.1097/01.yco.0000228759.95237.78

Holz, N. E., Zohsel, K., Laucht, M., Banaschewski, T., Hohmann, S. & Brandeis, D. (2018). Gene x environment interactions in conduct disorder: Implications for future treatments. *Neuroscience & Biobehavioral Reviews, 91,* 239–258.

Horner, R. H. & Sugai, G. (2015). School-wide PBIS: An example of applied behavior analysis implemented at a scale of social importance. *Behavior Analysis in Practice, 8*(1), 80-85.

Horner, R. H. Sugai, G., Todd, A. W., & Lewis-Palmer, T. (2000). Elements of behavior support plans: A technical brief. *Exceptionality, 8*(3), 205–215.

Hornstra, R., Bosmans, G., van den Hoofdakker, B. J., De Meyer, H. & Van der Oord, S. (2019). Self-reported attachment styles in children with and without attention-deficit/hyperactivity disorder (ADHD). *European Child & Adolescent Psychiatry, 28*(9), 1277–1280.

Horowitz, J. M. & Graf, N. (2019). *Most US teens see anxiety and depression as a major problem among their peers.* Pew Research Center.

Hosp, M. K., Hosp, J. L. & Howell, K. W. (2016). *The ABCs of CBM: A practical guide to curriculum-based measurement.* Guilford Publications.

Howell, J. C. (2010). Gang prevention: An overview of current research and programs (Document No. 253165). National Criminal Justice Reference Service. http://www.ncjrs.gov/App/publications/abstract.aspx?ID=253165

Howell, J. C. (2019). Youth gangs: Nationwide impacts of research on public policy. *American Journal of Criminal Justice, 44*(4), 628-644.

Howell, J. C., Egley, A., Tita, G.E. & Griffiths, E. (2011). U.S. gang problem trends and seriousness, 1996-2009. National Gang Centre USA. https://www.nationalgangcenter.gov/Content/Documents/Bulletin-6.pdf

Howell, J. C. & Lynch, J. P. (2000). Youth gangs in schools. Youth Gang Series. *Juvenile Justice Bulletin.* https://ojjdp.ojp.gov/library/publications/youth-gangs-schools

Howes, C. & Ritchie, S. (1999). Attachment organizations in children with difficult life circumstances. *Development and Psychopathology, 11*(2), 251–268. https://doi.org/10.1017/S0954579499002047

Howes, O. D., Rogdaki, M., Findon, J. L., Wichers, R. H., Charman, T., King, B. H., Loth, E., McAlonan, G. M., McCracken, J. T., & Parr, J. R. (2018). Autism spectrum disorder: Consensus guidelines on assessment, treatment and research from the British Association for Psychopharmacology. *Journal of Psychopharmacology, 32*(1), 3–29.

Hübel, C., Leppä, V., Breen, G. & Bulik, C. M. (2018). Rigor and reproducibility in genetic research on eating disorders. *International Journal of Eating Disorders, 51*(7), 593–607.

Hudec, K. L. & Mikami, A. Y. (2018). Diagnostic issues for ODD/CD with ADHD comorbidity. In J.E. Lochman & W. Matthys (Eds.), *The Wiley handbook of disruptive and impulse-control disorders* (pp. 55-71). Wiley.

Huemer, J., Greenberg, M. & Steiner, H. (2017). Pharmacological treatment for children and adolescents with trauma-related disorders. In M.A. Landolt, M. Cloitre, & U. Schnyder (Eds.), *Evidence-based treatments for trauma related disorders in children and adolescents* (pp. 385–401). Springer.

Huff, C.R. 1996. The criminal behavior of gang members and nongang at-risk youth. In C.R. Huff (Ed.) *Gangs in America* (2d ed., pp.75-102). Sage.

Humayun, S., Herlitz, L., Chesnokov, M., Doolan, M., Landau, S. & Scott, S. (2017). Randomized controlled trial of Functional Family Therapy for offending and antisocial behavior in UK youth. *Journal of Child Psychology and Psychiatry, 58*(9), 1023–1032.

Husarić, M., Selimović, L. T. & Emić, E. (2018). The role of family factors in the development of eating pathology. *Društvene i Humanističke Studije, 3*(4), 325–340.

Husby, S. M. & Wichstrøm, L. (2017). Interrelationships and continuities in symptoms of oppositional defiant and conduct disorders from age 4 to 10 in the community. *Journal of Abnormal Child Psychology, 45*(5), 947–958.

Hussain, F. S., Dobson, E. T. & Strawn, J. R. (2016). Pharmacologic treatment of pediatric anxiety disorders. *Current Treatment Options in Psychiatry, 3*(2), 151–160.

Hussain, H., Dubicka, B. & Wilkinson, P. (2018). Recent developments in the treatment of major depressive disorder in children and adolescents. *Evidence-Based Mental Health, 21*(3), 101–106.

Ibrahim, K., Eilbott, J. A., Ventola, P., He, G., Pelphrey, K. A., McCarthy, G. & Sukhodolsky, D. G. (2019). Reduced amygdala–prefrontal functional connectivity in children with autism spectrum disorder and co-occurring disruptive behavior. *Biological Psychiatry: Cognitive Neuroscience and Neuroimaging, 4*(12), 1031–1041.

Indias, S., Arruabarrena, I. & De Paúl, J. (2019). Child maltreatment, sexual and peer victimization experiences among adolescents in residential care. *Children and Youth Services Review, 100*, 267–273.

Ingram, K., Lewis-Palmer, T. & Sugai, G. (2005). Function-based intervention planning: Comparing the effectiveness of FBA indicated and contraindicated intervention plans. *Journal of Positive Behavior Interventions*, 7, 224–236.

Isserlin, L., Spettigue, W., Norris, M. & Couturier, J. (2020). Outcomes of inpatient psychological treatments for children and adolescents with eating disorders at time of discharge: A systematic review. *Journal of Eating Disorders, 8*(1), 1–17.

Izydorczyk, B. & Sitnik-Warchulska, K. (2018). Sociocultural appearance standards and risk factors for eating disorders in adolescents and women of various ages. *Frontiers in Psychology, 9*, Article 429. http://dx.doi.org.ezproxy.hofstra.edu/10.3389/fpsyg.2018.00429

Jackson, D. B., Newsome, J. & Lynch, K. R. (2017). Adverse housing conditions and early-onset delinquency. *American Journal of Community Psychology, 60*(1–2), 160–174.

Jacobson, L., Crocetti, D., Dirlikov, B., Slifer, K., Denckla, M., Mostofsky, S. & Mahone, E. (2018). Anomalous brain development is evident in preschoolers with attention-deficit/hyperactivity disorder. *Journal of the International Neuropsychological Society, 24*(6), 531-539. doi:10.1017/S1355617718000103.

Jacoby, R. J. & Abramowitz, J. S. (2016). Inhibitory learning approaches to exposure therapy: A critical review and translation to obsessive-compulsive disorder. *Clinical Psychology Review, 49*, 28–40.

Jakubovski, E., Johnson, J. A., Nasir, M., Müller-Vahl, K. & Bloch, M. H. (2019). Systematic review and meta-analysis: Dose–response curve of SSRIs and SNRIs in anxiety disorders. *Depression and Anxiety, 36*(3), 198–212.

James, S. C., Farrell, L. J. & Zimmer-Gembeck, M. J. (2017). Description and prevalence of OCD in children and adolescents. In J.S. Abramowitz, D. McKay, & A. E. Storch (Eds.), *The Wiley handbook of obsessive-compulsive disorders, Vols 1-2* (pp. 5-23). Wiley.

Jennings, W. G., Perez, N. M. & Reingle Gonzalez, J. M. (2018). Conduct disorder and neighborhood effects. *Annual Review of Clinical Psychology, 14*, 317–341.

Jensen, M. M. (2005). *Introduction to emotional and behavioral disorders: Recognizing and managing problems in the classroom.* Pearson.

Jeong, S., Lee, B. H. & Martin, J. H. (2014). Evaluating the effectiveness of a special needs diversionary program in reducing reoffending among mentally ill youthful offenders. *International Journal of Offender Therapy and Comparative Criminology, 58*(9), 1058-1080.

Jewell, T., Blessitt, E., Stewart, C., Simic, M. & Eisler, I. (2016). Family therapy for child and adolescent eating disorders: A critical review. *Family Process, 55*(3), 577–594.

Jiang, M. Y. & Vartanian, L. R. (2018). A review of existing measures of attentional biases in body image and eating disorders research. *Australian Journal of Psychology, 70*(1), 3–17.

Johnco, C., Lewin, A. B., Salloum, A., Murphy, T. K., Crawford, E. A., Dane, B. F., McBride, N. M. & Storch, E. A. (2016). Adverse prenatal, perinatal and neonatal experiences in children with anxiety disorders. *Child Psychiatry & Human Development, 47*(2), 317–325.

Johnson, S. M. (2008). Couple and family therapy: An attachment perspective. In J. Cassidy & P. R. Shaver (Eds.), *Handbook of attachment: Theory, research, and clinical applications* (2nd ed., pp. 811–829). Guilford.

Johnston, L.D., O'Malley, P.M., Bachman, J.G. & Schulenberg, J.E. (2020). *Monitoring the future: National results on adolescents drug use.* National Institute on Drug Abuse.

Jones, E. A., Feeley, K. M., & Takacs, J. (2007). Teaching spontaneous responses to young children with autism. *Journal of Applied Behavior Analysis, 40*(3), 565-570.

Jones, R. B., Thapar, A., Stone, Z., Thapar, A., Jones, I., Smith, D. & Simpson, S. (2018). Psychoeducational interventions in adolescent depression: A systematic review. *Patient Education and Counseling, 101*(5), 804–816.

Jones, S. M. & Bouffard, S. M. (2012). *Social and emotional learning in schools: From programs to strategies and commentaries.* https://doi.org/10.1002/j.2379-3988.2012.tb00073.x

Jones, V., Dohrn, E. & Dunn, C. (2004). *Creating effective programs for students with emotional and behavior disorders: Interdisciplinary approaches for adding meaning and hope to behavior change interventions.* Pearson.

Jones, V. F. & Jones, L. S. (2017). *Comprehensive classroom management: Creating communities of support and solving problems,* (6th ed.) Pearson Education.

Jordan, K. & Austin, J. (2012). A review of the literature on bullying in US schools and how a parent–educator partnership can be an effective way to handle bullying. *Journal of Aggression, Maltreatment & Trauma, 21*(4), 440-458.

Joseph, H., Walker, C., McDermott, C., Song, Y., Simpson, M. & Khan, S. (2019). Effective medications for treating externalizing disorders. In J. S. Carlson & J. A. Barterian (Eds.), *School psychopharmacology* (pp. 51–68). Springer.

Just, M. A., Cherkassky, V. L., Keller, T. A. & Minshew, N. J. (2004). Cortical activation and synchronization during sentence comprehension in high-functioning autism: Evidence of underconnectivity. *Brain, 127*(8), 1811–1821.

Justice Policy Institute. (2021). *Sticker Shock: The cost of youth incarceration.* https://justicepolicy.org/research/policy-brief-2020-sticker-shock-the-cost-of-youth-incarceration/

Kabat-Zinn, J. (2005). *Coming to our senses: Healing ourselves and the world through mindfulness.* Hyperion.

Kagan, D. M. (1990). How schools alienate students at risk: A model for examining proximal classroom variables. *Educational Psychologist, 25*(2), 105-125.

Kagan, J., Reznick, J. S. & Gibbons, J. (1989). Inhibited and uninhibited types of children. *Child Development, 60*(4), 838–845.

Kang, E., Gadow, K. D. & Lerner, M. D. (2020). Atypical communication characteristics, differential diagnosis, and the autism spectrum disorder phenotype in youth. *Journal of Clinical Child & Adolescent Psychology, 49*(2), 251–263.

Kapalka, G., Brown, R. T., Curtis, D. F., Wu, T. C. & Marquez, M. (2018). Childhood and adolescent disorders: Evidence-Based integrated biopsychosocial treatment of ADHD and disruptive disorders. In M. Muse (Ed.) *Cognitive Behavioral Psychopharmacology: The clinical practice of evidence based biopsychosocial integration,* (pp 243-281). Wiley Blackwell.

Kaplow, J. B., Rolon-Arroyo, B., Layne, C. M., Rooney, E., Oosterhoff, B., Hill, R., Steinberg, A. M., Lotterman, J., Gallagher, K. A. & Pynoos, R. S. (2020). Validation of the UCLA PTSD Reaction Index for DSM-5: A developmentally informed assessment tool for youth. *Journal of the American Academy of Child & Adolescent Psychiatry, 59*(1), 186–194.

Karam, A. M., Fitzsimmons-Craft, E. E., Tanofsky-Kraff, M. & Wilfley, D. E. (2019). Interpersonal psychotherapy and the treatment of eating disorders. *Psychiatric Clinics, 42*(2), 205–218.

Karama, S., Ben Amor, L., Grizenko, N., Ciampi, A., Mbekou, V., Ter-Stepanian, M., Lageix, P., Baron, C., Schwartz, G. & Joober, R. (2009). Factor structure of the restricted academic situation scale: implications for ADHD. *Journal of Attention Disorders, 12*(5), 442-448.

Karoff, M., Tucker, A. R., Alvarez, T. & Kovacs, P. (2017). Infusing a peer-to-peer support program with adventure therapy for adolescent students with autism spectrum disorder. *Journal of Experiential Education, 40*(4), 394–408.

Kashdan, T., Jacob, R. G., Pelham, W. E., Lang, A. R., Hoza, B., Blumenthal, J. D. & Gnagy, E. M. (2004). Depression and anxiety in parents of children with ADHD and varying levels of oppositional defiant behaviors: Modeling relationships with family functioning. *Journal of Clinical Child & Adolescent Psychology, 33*(1), 169-181 doi:10.1207/S15374424JCCP3301_16.

Kauffman, J. M. (2005). *Characteristics of emotional and behavioral disorders of children and youth* (8th ed.). Pearson.

Kauffman, J. M. (2015). Opinion on recent developments and the future of special education. *Remedial & Special Education, 36*(1), 9–13. https://doi.org/10.1177/0741932514543653

Kauffman, J. M. & Badar, J. (2013). How we might make special education for students with emotional or behavioral disorders less stigmatizing. *Behavioral Disorders,* 39(1), 16–27. https://doi.org/10.1177/019874291303900103

Kauffman, J. M. & Landrum, T. J. (2018). *Characteristics of emotional and behavioral disorders of children and youth* (11th ed). Pearson.

Kavale, K. A. & Mostert, M. P. (2004). *Social skills interventions for individuals with learning disabilities.* https://files.eric.ed.gov/fulltext/EJ704971.pdf

Kawashima, M., & Maynard, D. W. (2019). The social organization of echolalia in clinical encounters involving a child diagnosed with autism spectrum disorder. In J. Lamerichs, S. J. Danby, A. Bateman, & S. Ekberg (Eds.), *Children and mental health talk* (pp. 49–72). Springer.

Kazdin, A. E. (2017). Parent management training and problem-solving skills training for child and adolescent conduct problems. In J. R. Weisz & A. E. Kazdin (Eds.), *Evidence-Based Psychotherapies for Children and Adolescents* (3rd ed., pp.142–158). Guilford.

Kazdin, A. E., Glick, A., Pope, J., Kaptchuk, T. J., Lecza, B., Carrubba, E., McWhinney, E. & Hamilton, N. (2018). Parent management training for conduct problems in children: Enhancing treatment to improve therapeutic change. *International Journal of Clinical and Health Psychology, 18*(2), 91–101.

Keles, S. & Idsoe, T. (2018). A meta-analysis of group cognitive behavioral therapy (CBT) interventions for adolescents with depression. *Journal of Adolescence, 67,* 129–139.

Kelley, S. E., Balsis, S., Smith, S. T., Edens, J. F., Douglas, K. S. & Poythress Jr, N. G. (2016). A dimensional comparison of a self-report and a structured interview measure of conduct disorder. *Journal of Personality Disorders, 30*(2), 232–241.

Kendall, P. C. (1992). *Copycat workbook.* Workbook Publishing.

Kendall, P. C., Pimentel, S., Rynn, M. A., Angelosante, A. & Webb, A. (2004). Generalized anxiety disorder. In T. H. Ollendick & J. S. March (Eds.), *Phobic and anxiety disorders in children and adolescents: A clinician's guide to effective psychosocial and pharmacological interventions* (pp. 334–380). Oxford University Press.

Kennedy, C. H. & Itkonen, T. (1993). Effects of setting events on the problem behavior of students with severe disabilities. *Journal of Applied Behavior Analysis, 26*(3), 321–327.

Kennedy, J. H. & Kennedy, C. E. (2007). Applications of attachment theory in school psychology. *Journal of Early Childhood and Infant Psychology, 3,* 7–25.

Kent, A. & Simpson, J. (2012). The power of literature: establishing and enhancing the young adolescent classroom community. *Reading Improvement, 49*(1), 28-34.

Kenworthy, L., Yerys, B. E., Anthony, L. G. & Wallace, G. L. (2008). Understanding executive control in autism spectrum disorders in the lab and in the real world. *Neuropsychology Review, 18*(4), 320-338.

Kessler, R. C., Aguilar-Gaxiola, S., Alonso, J., Bromet, E. J., Gureje, O., Karam, E. G., Koenen, K. C., Lee, S., Liu, H. & Pennell, B. E. (2018). The associations of earlier trauma exposures and history of mental disorders with PTSD after subsequent traumas. *Molecular Psychiatry, 23*(9), 1892–1899.

Khanjani, Z., Mohammadi, E. & Shadbafi, M. (2020). The prediction of children's accident proneness based on attention deficit hyperactivity disorder and sluggish cognitive tempo symptoms: the mediating role of sensitivity to reward and punishment. *Quarterly Journal of Child Mental Health, 7*(1), 44-56. http://dx.doi.org/10.29252/jcmh.7.1.5

Killu, K. (2008). Developing effective behavior intervention plans: Suggestions for school personnel. *Intervention in School and Clinic, 43*(3), 140–149. https://doi.org/10.1177/1053451207311610

Kimonis, E. R. & Frick, P. J. (2006). Conduct disorder. In R. T. Ammerman (Ed.), *Comprehensive handbook of personality and psychopathology: Vol 3. Child psychopathology* (pp. 299–315). Wiley.

Kimonis, E. R., Frick, P. J. & McMahon, R. J. (2014). Conduct and oppositional defiant disorders. In E. J. Mash & R. A. Barkley (Eds.), *Child Psychopathology* (3rd ed., pp. 145–179). Guilford.

King, N. J., Muris, P. & Ollendick, T. H. (2005). Childhood fears and phobias: Assessment and treatment. *Child and Adolescent Mental Health, 10*(2), 50–56. https://doi.org/10.1111/j.1475-3588.2005.00118.x

Klin, A., Jones, W., Schultz, R. & Volkmar, F. (2003). The enactive mind, or from actions to cognition: Lessons from autism. *Philosophical Transactions of the Royal Society of London. Series B: Biological Sciences, 358*(1430), 345-360.

Kobak, R. & Madsen, S. (2008). Disruptions in attachment bonds: Implications for theory, research, and clinical intervention. In J. Cassidy & P. R. Shaver (Eds.), *Handbook of attachment: Theory, Research, and Clinical Applications* (2nd ed., pp. 23–47). Guilford.

Kodal, A., Fjermestad, K., Bjelland, I., Gjestad, R., Öst, L.-G., Bjaastad, J. F., Haugland, B. S., Havik, O. E., Heiervang, E. & Wergeland, G. J. (2018). Long-term effectiveness of cognitive behavioral therapy for youth with anxiety disorders. *Journal of Anxiety Disorders, 53,* 58–67.

Koegel, R. L. & Koegel, L.K. (2019). *Pivotal response treatment for autism spectrum disorders* (2nd ed.). Paul H. Brookes.

Kohn, A. (2006). *Beyond discipline: From compliance to community.* Association for Supervision and Curriculum Development.

Kohn, A. (1996). *Beyond discipline: From compliance to community.* Association for Supervision and Curriculum Development.

Kollins, S. H., Barkley, R. A. & DuPaul, G. J. (2001). Use and management of medications for children diagnosed with attention deficit hyperactivity disorder (ADHD). *Focus on Exceptional Children,* 33(5), 1-23.

Kolstrein, A. M. & Jofré, M. I. T. (2013). Bullying: An analysis from the perspective of human rights, target groups and interventions. *The International Journal of Children's Rights, 21*(1), 46-58.

Korkiakangas, T. (2018). *Communication, gaze and autism: A multimodal interaction perspective.* Routledge.

Kowatch, R.A., Emslie, G.J., Wilkaitis, J. & Dingle, A.D. (2005). Mood disorders. In S. B. Sexson & R. B. David (Ed.), *Child and adolescent psychiatry* (pp. 132-153). Blackwell.

Krain, A. L. & Castellanos, F. X. (2006). Brain development and ADHD. *Clinical Psychology Review, 26*(4), 433-444.

Krug, D. A., Arick, J. R. & Almond, P. (2008). *Autism screening instrument for educational planning.* Pro-ed.

Krzystanek, M. & Palasz, A. (2020). The role of blocking serotonin 2C receptor by fluoxetine in the treatment of bulimia. *Farmakoterapia w Psychiatrii i Neurologii* 2020. https://doi.org/10.33450/fpn.2020.07.001

Kuhfeld, M. & Sturm, A. (2018). An examination of the precision of the Autism Diagnostic Observation Schedule using item response theory. *Psychological Assessment, 30*(5), 656–668. https://doi.org/10.1037/pas0000512

Kujanpää, T. S., Jokelainen, J., Auvinen, J. P. & Timonen, M. J. (2017). The association of generalized anxiety disorder and somatic symptoms with frequent attendance to health care services: A cross-sectional study from the Northern Finland Birth Cohort 1966. *The International Journal of Psychiatry in Medicine, 52*(2), 147–159.

Kurth, W. (2013). Attachment theory and psychohistory: Overview. *The Journal of Psychohistory, 41*(1), 14–38.

Kyere, E., Joseph, A. & Wei, K. (2020). Alternative to zero-tolerance policies and out-of-school suspensions: A multitiered centered perspective, *Journal of Ethnic & Cultural Diversity in Social Work, 29*(5), 421-436, DOI: 10.1080/15313204.2018.1528914

Kyranides, M. N., Fanti, K. A., Katsimicha, E. & Georgiou, G. (2018). Preventing conduct disorder and callous unemotional traits: Preliminary results of a school-based pilot training program. *Journal of Abnormal Child Psychology, 46*(2), 291–303.

Lakhan, S. E. & Kirchgessner, A. (2012). Prescription stimulants in individuals with and without attention deficit hyperactivity disorder: misuse, cognitive impact, and adverse effects. *Brain and Behavior, 2*(5), 661-677.

Land, M. K. (2011) *Five simple techniques to incorporate social emotional learning.* https://www.edutopia.org/blog/social-emotional-learning-education-sel-mary-kate-land

Lane, K.L., Gresham, F.M. & O'Shaughnessy, T. E. (2002). Serving students with or at-risk for emotional and behavior disorders: Future challenges. *Education and Treatment of Children, 25*, 507-521.

Lantieri, L. & Patti, J. (1998). Waging peace in our schools. *Journal of Negro Education, 65*, 356–368.

Laporta-Herrero, I., Jáuregui-Lobera, I., Barajas-Iglesias, B. & Santed-Germán, M. Á. (2018). Body dissatisfaction in adolescents with eating disorders. *Eating and Weight Disorders-Studies on Anorexia, Bulimia and Obesity, 23*(3), 339–347.

Larsson, H., Chang, Z., D'Onofrio, B. M. & Lichtenstein, P. (2014). The heritability of clinically diagnosed attention deficit hyperactivity disorder across the lifespan. *Psychological Medicine, 44*(10), 2223–2229. https://doi.org/10.1017/S0033291713002493

Latson, J. (2016). *How Karen Carpenter's death changed the way we talk about anorexia.* https://time.com/3685894/karen-carpenter-anorexia-death/

Lavallee, K. L. & Schneider, S. (2019). Separation anxiety disorder. In S. N. Compton, M. A. Villabo & H. Kristensen (Eds.), *Pediatric Anxiety Disorders* (pp. 151–176). Elsevier.

LaVoie, R. (2005). *It's so much work to be your friend: Helping the child with learning disabilities find social success.* Simon & Schuster.

Lawrence, H. R., Nangle, D. W., Schwartz-Mette, R. A. & Erdley, C. A. (2017). Medication for child and adolescent depression: Questions, answers, clarifications, and caveats. *Practice Innovations, 2*(1), 39.

Lawrence, K., Estrada, R. D. & McCormick, J. (2017). Teachers' experiences with and perceptions of students with attention deficit/hyperactivity disorder. *Journal of Pediatric Nursing, 36*, 141-148.

Leaf, J. B., Townley-Cochran, D., Cihon, J. H., Mitchell, E., Leaf, R., Taubman, M., & McEachin, J. (2019). Descriptive analysis of the use of punishment-based techniques with children diagnosed with autism spectrum disorder. *Education and Training in Autism and Developmental Disabilities, 54*(2), 107–118.

Lebel, C. A., McMorris, C. A., Kar, P., Ritter, C., Andre, Q., Tortorelli, C., & Gibbard, W. B. (2019). Characterizing adverse prenatal and postnatal experiences in children. *Birth Defects Research, 111*(12), 848–858.

Lebrun-Harris, L. A., Sherman, L. J., Limber, S. P., Miller, B. D. & Edgerton, E. A. (2019). Bullying victimization and perpetration among US children and adolescents: 2016 national survey of children's health. *Journal of Child and Family Studies, 28*(9), 2543-2557.

Le Couteur, A., Rutter, M., Lord, C. & Rios, P. (1994). Autism Diagnostic Interview: A standardized investigator-based instrument. *Journal of Autism and Developmental Disorders, 19*(3), 363-387.

Ledford, J. R., King, S., Harbin, E. R. & Zimmerman, K. N. (2018). Antecedent social skills interventions for individuals with ASD: What works, for whom, and under what conditions? *Focus on Autism and Other Developmental Disabilities, 33*(1), 3–13.

Leekam, S. R., Libby, S. J., Wing, L., Gould, J. & Taylor, C. (2002). The Diagnostic Interview for Social and Communication Disorders: Algorithms for ICD-10 childhood autism and Wing and Gould autistic spectrum disorder. *Journal of Child Psychology and Psychiatry, 43*(3), 327–342.

Lefkowitz, M. M. & Tesiny, E. P. (1980). Assessment of childhood depression. *Journal of Consulting and Clinical Psychology, 48*(1), 43–50. https://doi.org/10.1037/0022-006X.48.1.43

Legato, L. J. (2011). *Effects of teacher factors on expectations of students with ADHD.* [Doctoral Dissertation, College of Liberal Arts & Social Sciences Theses and Dissertations] https://via.library.depaul.edu/etd/66.

Lei, J. & Ventola, P. (2017). Pivotal response treatment for autism spectrum disorder: Current perspectives. *Neuropsychiatric Disease and Treatment, 13*, 1613-1626.

Lenz, B. K. & Hughes, C. A. (1990). A word identification strategy for adolescents with learning disabilities. *Journal of Learning Disabilities, 23(3)*, 149–158.

Lenzi, M., Sharkey, J., Vieno, A., Mayworm, A., Dougherty, D. & Nylund-Gibson, K. (2015). Adolescent gang involvement: The role of individual, family, peer, and school factors in a multilevel perspective. *Aggressive Behavior, 41*(4), 386-397.

Leslie, L.K., Weckerly J., Plemmons D, Landsverk J. & Eastman S. (2004). Implementing the American Academy of Pediatrics Attention-Deficit/Hyperactivity Disorder Diagnostic Guidelines in primary care settings. *Pediatrics, 114*(1) 129-140. doi.10.1542/peds.114.1.129.

Lesneskie, E. & Block, S. (2017). School violence: The role of parental and community involvement. *Journal of School Violence, 16*(4), 426-444.

Levine, M. P. (2019). Prevention of eating disorders: 2018 in review. *Eating Disorders, 27*(1), 18–33.

Levine, M. P. & Smolak, L. (2020). *The prevention of eating problems and eating disorders: Theories, research, and applications.* Routledge.

Levinson, C. A., Zerwas, S., Calebs, B., Forbush, K., Kordy, H., Watson, H., Hofmeier, S., Levine, M., Crosby, R. D. & Peat, C. (2017). The core symptoms of bulimia nervosa, anxiety, and depression: A network analysis. *Journal of Abnormal Psychology, 126*(3), 340-354.

Lewinsohn, P. M., Clarke, G. N., Rohde, P., Hops, H., Hibbs, E. D. & Jensen, P. S. (1996). A course in coping: A cognitive-behavioral approach to the treatment of adolescent depression. In E. D. Hibbs & P. S. Jensen (Eds.), *Psychosocial treatments for child and adolescent disorders: Empirically based strategies for clinical practice.* (pp. 109-135). American Psychological Association.

Lewis, T. J., Jones, S. E., Horner, R. H., & Sugai, G. (2010). School-wide positive behavior support and students with emotional/behavioral disorders: Implications for prevention, identification, and intervention. *Exceptionality, 18*(2), 82-93.

Lewis, T. J., Mitchell, B. S., Bruntmeyer, D. T., & Sugai, G. (2016). School-wide positive behavior support and response to intervention: System similarities, distinctions, and research to date at the universal level of support. In S.R. Jimerson, M.K. Burns, & A.M. VanDerHeyden (Eds.), *Handbook of response to intervention* (pp. 703-717). Springer.

Li, A., Cunich, M., Miskovic-Wheatley, J., Maloney, D., Madden, S., Wallis, A. & Maguire, S. (2020). Factors related to length of stay, referral on discharge and hospital readmission for children and adolescents with anorexia nervosa. *International Journal of Eating Disorders 54,* 409-421.

Li, J., Zhu, L. & Chen, Z. (2018). The association between punishment and cooperation in children with high-functioning autism. *Journal of Experimental Child Psychology, 171,* 1–13.

Liberman, L. C. & Öst, L.-G. (2016). The relation between fears and anxiety in children with specific phobia and parental fears and anxiety. *Journal of Child and Family Studies, 25*(2), 598–606.

Liepe-Levinson, K. & Levinson, M.H. (2005). A general semantics approach to school-age bullying. *A Review of General Semantics, 62*(1), 4-17.

Limber, S. P. (2011). Development, evaluation, and future directions of the Olweus Bullying Prevention Program. *Journal of School Violence, 10*(1), 71-87.

Linardon, J., Phillipou, A., Newton, R., Fuller-Tyszkiewicz, M., Jenkins, Z., Cistullo, L. L. & Castle, D. (2018). Testing the relative associations of different components of dietary restraint on psychological functioning in anorexia nervosa and bulimia nervosa. *Appetite, 128,* 1–6.

Linardon, J., Wade, T. D., De la Piedad Garcia, X., & Brennan, L. (2017). The efficacy of cognitive-behavioral therapy for eating disorders: A systematic review and meta-analysis. *Journal of Consulting and Clinical Psychology, 85*(11), 1080.

Lindblad-Goldberg, M. & Northey, W.F. (2013). Ecosystemic structural family therapy: Theoretical and clinical foundations. *Contemporary Family Therapy, 35,* 147-160. https://doi.org/10.1007/s10591-012-9224-4

Lindgreen, P., Lomborg, K., & Clausen, L. (2018). Patient experiences using a self-monitoring app in eating disorder treatment: Qualitative study. *JMIR MHealth and UHealth, 6*(6). Article 10253. doi:10.2196/10253

Liu J. (2004). Childhood externalizing behavior: theory and implications. *Journal of Child and Adolescent Psychiatric Nursing: Official Publication of the Association of Child and Adolescent Psychiatric Nurses, Inc., 17*(3), 93–103. https://doi.org/10.1111/j.1744-6171.2004.tb00003.x

Liu, J., Chen, X. & Lewis, G. (2011). Childhood internalizing behaviour: analysis and implications. *Journal of Psychiatric and Mental Health Nursing, 18*(10), 884–894. https://doi.org/10.1111/j.1365-2850.2011.01743.x

Lloyd, E. C., Haase, A. M., Foster, C. E. & Verplanken, B. (2019). A systematic review of studies probing longitudinal associations between anxiety and anorexia nervosa. *Psychiatry Research, 276,* 175–185.

Lock, J. (2019). Updates on treatments for adolescent Anorexia Nervosa. *Child and Adolescent Psychiatric Clinics of North America, 28*(4), 523–535.

Lock, J., Fitzpatrick, K. K., Vierhile, M. & Sadeh-Sharvit, S. (2017). Parental guided self-help family-based treatment for adolescents with anorexia nervosa: A feasibility study. *International Journal of Eating Disorders, 50*(9), 1104–1108.

Lock, J. & Le Grange, D. (2006). Eating disorders. In D. A. Wolf & E. J. Mash (Eds.) *Behavioral and emotional disorders in adolescents: Nature, assessment, and treatment* (pp. 485–504). Guilford.

Lock, J. & Le Grange, D. (2019). Family-based treatment: Where are we and where should we be going to improve recovery in child and adolescent eating disorders. *International Journal of Eating Disorders, 52*(4), 481–487.

Loe, I. M. & Feldman, H. M. (2007). Academic and educational outcomes of children with ADHD. *Journal of Pediatric Psychology, 32*(6), 643–654. https://doi.org/10.1093/jpepsy/jsl054.

Loney, B. R. & Lima, E. N. (2003). Classification and assessment. In C. A. Essau (Ed.), *Conduct and oppositional defiant disorders: Epidemiology, risk factors, and treatment* (pp. 3–31). Lawrence Erlbaum Associates.

Long, N. J., Wood, M. M. & Fecser, F. A. (2001). *Life space crisis intervention: Talking with students in conflict.* Pro-Ed.

Looney, K., DeQuinzio, J. A. & Taylor, B. A. (2018). Using self-monitoring and differential reinforcement of low rates of behavior to decrease repetitive behaviors: A case study. *Behavioral Interventions, 33*(3), 251–259.

Lord, C., Rutter, M., DiLavore, P., Risi, S., Gotham, K. & Bishop, S. (2012). *Autism diagnostic observation schedule–2nd edition (ADOS-2).* Western Psychological Corporation.

Losinski, M., Cook, K., Hirsch, S. & Sanders, S. (2017). The effects of deep pressure therapies and antecedent exercise on stereotypical behaviors of students with autism spectrum disorders. *Behavioral Disorders, 42*(4), 196–208.

Lovaas, O. I. (1987). Behavioral treatment and normal educational and intellectual functioning in young autistic children. *Journal of Consulting and Clinical Psychology, 55*(1), 3-9.

Love, H. E., Schlitt, J., Soleimanpour, S., Panchal, N. & Behr, C. (2019). Twenty years of school-based health care growth and expansion. *Health Affairs, 38*(5), 755–764.

Lovell, M. K. & Richardson, B. (2001). Family and consumer sciences educators can play significant roles in curbing school violence. *Journal of Family and Consumer Sciences, 93*(1), 24–29.

Luis-Joaquin, G. L., Lourdes, E. F. & José A. M. M. (2020). Behavioral inhibition in childhood as a risk factor for development of social anxiety disorder: A longitudinal study. *International Journal of Environmental Research and Public Health, 17*(11). Article 3941. https://doi.org/10.3390/ijerph17113941

Luteijn, E., Luteijn, F., Jackson, S. Volkmar, F., & Minderaa, R. (2000). The Children's Social Behavior Questionnaire for milder variants of PDD problems: Evaluation of the psychometric characteristics. *Journal of Autism and Developmental Disorders, 30*(4), 317–330.

Maag, J. W. & Katsiyannis, A. (2012). Bullying and students with disabilities: Legal and practice considerations. *Behavioral Disorders, 37*(2), 78-86.

MacFarlane, R. M. (1995). Adolescent pregnancy. *Psychological Aspects of Women's Reproductive Health,* 248–264.

Madjar, N., Mansbach-Kleinfeld, I., Daeem, R., Farbstein, I., Apter, A., Fennig, S., Elias, R. & Shoval, G. (2020). Discrepancies in adolescent-mother dyads' reports of core depression symptoms: Association with adolescents' help-seeking in school and their somatic complaints. *Journal of Psychosomatic Research, 137,* Article 110222. http://dx.doi.org.ezproxy.hofstra.edu/10.1016/j.jpsychores.2020.110222

Magson, N. R., Handford, C. M. & Norberg, M. M. (2020). The empirical status of cue exposure and response prevention treatment for binge eating: A systematic review. *Behavior Therapy,* 52, 442-454.

Mahat, G. & Scoloveno, M. A. (2018). Effectiveness of adolescent peer education programs on reducing HIV/STI risk: An integrated review. *Research and Theory for Nursing Practice, 32*(2), 168–198.

Maheady, L. & Gard, J. (2010). Classwide peer tutoring: Practice, theory, research, and personal narrative. *Intervention in School and Clinic, 46*(2), 71-78.

Main, M. & Solomon, J. (1990). Procedures for identifying infants as disorganized/disoriented during the Ainsworth Strange Situation. In M. T. Greenberg, D. Cicchetti, & E. M. Cummings (Eds.), *Attachment in the preschool years: Theory, research, and intervention* (pp. 121–160). University of Chicago Press.

Mairs, R. & Nicholls, D. (2016). Assessment and treatment of eating disorders in children and adolescents. *Archives of Disease in Childhood, 101*(12), 1168–1175.

Mangold, A. C. & King, A. R. (2020). Relationships between experiences of sibling physical aggression and lifetime aggression using statistical controls for poly-victimization. *Journal of Family Violence, 36*, 235-247.

Mangweth-Matzek, B. & Hoek, H. W. (2017). Epidemiology and treatment of eating disorders in men and women of middle and older age. *Current Opinion in Psychiatry, 30*(6), 446-451.

Marans, W. D., Rubin, E. & Laurent, A. (2005). Addressing social communication skills in individuals with high-functioning autism and Asperger syndrome: Critical priorities in educational programming. In F. R. Volkmar, R. Paul, A Klin, & D. Cohen (Eds.), *Handbook of autism and pervasive developmental disorders Vol 2.* (3rd ed., pp. 977–1002). Wiley.

March, J. S., Amaya-Jackson, L., Murray, M. C. & Schulte, A. (1998). Cognitive-behavioral psychotherapy for children and adolescents with posttraumatic stress disorder after a single-incident stressor. *Journal of the American Academy of Child & Adolescent Psychiatry, 37*(6), 585–593. https://doi.org/10.1097/00004583-199806000-00008

March, J. S., Parker, J. D. A., Sullivan, K., Stallings, P. & Conners, C. K. (1997). The Multidimensional Anxiety Scale for Children (MASC): Factor structure, reliability, and validity. *Journal of the American Academy of Child & Adolescent Psychiatry, 36*(4), 554–565. https://doi.org/10.1097/00004583-199704000-00019

March, J. S., Silva, S., Petrycki, S., Curry, J., Wells, K., Fairbank, J., Burns, B., Domino, M., McNulty, S. & Vitiello, B. (2007). The treatment for adolescents with depression study (TADS): Long-term effectiveness and safety outcomes. *Archives of General Psychiatry, 64*(10), 1132–1144.

Marks, I. M. (1969). *Fears and phobias.* Academic Press.

Martin, G. & Pear, J. J. (2019). *Behavior modification: What it is and how to do it.* Routledge.

Marucci, S., Ragione, L. D., De Iaco, G., Mococci, T., Vicini, M., Guastamacchia, E. & Triggiani, V. (2018). Anorexia nervosa and comorbid psychopathology. *Endocrine, Metabolic & Immune Disorders-Drug Targets (Formerly Current Drug Targets-Immune, Endocrine & Metabolic Disorders), 18*(4), 316–324.

Marzola, E., Cavallo, F., Panero, M., Porliod, A., Amodeo, L. & Abbate-Daga, G. (2020). The role of prenatal and perinatal factors in eating disorders: A systematic review. *Archives of Women's Mental Health.* Article 32767123. http://dx.doi.org.ezproxy.hofstra.edu/10.1007/s00737-020-01057-5

Masten, A. S. & Barnes, A. J. (2018). Resilience in children: Developmental perspectives. *Children, 5*(7), 98. https://doi.org/10.3390/children5070098

Matherly, S. M., Klusek, J., Thurman, A. J., McDuffie, A., Abbeduto, L. & Roberts, J. E. (2018). Cortisol profiles differentiated in adolescents and young adult males with fragile X syndrome versus autism spectrum disorder. *Developmental Psychobiology, 60*(1), 78–89.

Matthys, W. & Schutter, D.J.L.G. (2021). Increasing effectiveness of cognitive behavioral therapy for conduct problems in children and adolescents: What can we learn from neuroimaging studies? *Clinical Child & Family*

Psychological Review. 24, 484-499. https://doi.org/10.1007/s10567-021-00346-4

Maximova, A. A. (2020). Effects of thyroid dysfunction and cortisol imbalance on the cognitive and mental development of children with autism spectrum disorder. *Международный Научно-Исследовательский Журнал, 11,* 30-38. https://doi.org/10.23670/IRJ.2020.101.11.038

Mayes, S. D., Waxmonsky, J. G., Baweja, R., Mattison, R. E., Memon, H., Klein, M., Hameed, U. & Waschbusch, D. (2020). Symptom scores and medication treatment patterns in children with ADHD versus autism. *Psychiatry Research, 228.* Article 112937. https://doi.org/10.1016/j.psychres.2020.112937

McAndrews, T. (2001). *Zero tolerance policies.* (ERIC Digest No. 146, Report No. EDO-EA-01-03). ERIC Clearinghouse on Educational Management. ERIC Document Reproduction Service No. ED451579.

McCabe, M., Tatangelo, G., Watson, B., Fuller-Tyszkiewicz, M., Rodgers, R. F., Aimé, A., Mellor, D., Granero-Gallegos, A., Strodl, E. & Caltabiano, M. (2019). Development and testing of a model for risk and protective factors for eating disorders and higher weight among emerging adults: A study protocol. *Body Image, 31,* 139–149.

McCarney, S. B., & House, S. N. (2019). *Attention deficit disorder evaluation scale-fifth edition (ADDES-5).* Hawthorne Educational Services, Inc. https://www.hawthorne-ed.com/attention-deficit-disorder-evaluation-scale-fifth-edition-complete-kit-details.html

McCart, M. R., Schaeffer, C. & Henggeler, S. W. (2014). Conduct disorder and delinquency. In S. G. Hofmann, D. J. A. Dozois, W. Rief, & J. A. J. Smits (Eds.), *The Wiley handbook of cognitive behavioral therapy., Vols. 1-3.* (pp. 797–819). Wiley-Blackwell.

McClafferty, H. (2017). *Integrative pediatrics.* Routledge.

McCluskey, K. & McCluskey, A. (1999). The agony and the empathy: A hyperactive child's journey from despair to achievement. *Reclaiming Children and Youth, 7,* 205-212.

McDonald, K. L. & Gibson, C. E. (2017). Peer rejection and disruptive behavioral disorders. In J. E. Lochman & W. Matthys (Eds.), *The Wiley handbook of disruptive and impulse-control disorders* (pp. 325–338). Wiley.

McIntyre, N. S., Solari, E. J., Gonzales, J. E., Solomon, M., Lerro, L. E., Novotny, S., Oswald, T. M. & Mundy, P. C. (2017). The scope and nature of reading comprehension impairments in school-aged children with higher-functioning autism spectrum disorder. *Journal of Autism and Developmental Disorders, 47*(9), 2838–2860.

McLeod, S. (2014). *Maslow's hierarchy of needs.* https://2.files.edl.io/NghLRUHA09ycRFi190Zws5youGeihn81UYVGpHLCukqjXEs1.pdf

McNeilis, J., Maughan, B., Goodman, R. & Rowe, R. (2018). Comparing the characteristics and outcomes of parent-and teacher-reported oppositional defiant disorder: Findings from a national sample. *Journal of Child Psychology and Psychiatry, 59*(6), 659–666.

McWhirter, J.J. (2004). Teenage pregnancy and risky sexual behavior. In J.J. McWhirter, B.T. McWhirter, E.H. McWhirter, & R.J. McWhirter (Eds.), *At-risk youth: A comprehensive response* (3rd ed., pp. 133-155). Brooks/Cole.

McWhirter, B. T., McWhirter, J. J., Hart, R. S., & Gat, I. (2000). Preventing and treating depression in children and adolescents. In D. Capuzzi & D. R. Gross (Eds.), *Youth risk: A prevention resource for counselors, teachers, and parents* (3rd ed., pp. 137–165). American Counseling Association.

McWhirter, J. J., McWhirter, B. T., McWhirter, E. H., & McWhirter, A. C. (2016). *At risk youth.* Cengage Learning.

Mehler, P. S. (2017a). *Eating disorders: A guide to medical care and complications.* John Hopkins.

Mehler, P. S. (2017b). General endocrinology. In P.S. Mehler (Ed.), *Eating disorders: A guide to medical care and complications* (3rd ed., pp. 173-180). John Hopkins.

Mello, M. J., Gilbard, Z., Burstein, D., Baird, J., Zonfrillo, M. R., Flanagan, P., Linakis, J. G., Hackman, H. & Howland, J. (2019). Formative research to underpin a text messaging home safety intervention for young mothers. *Health Education Journal, 78*(3), 266–272.

Mendez Foundation. (2022). *Mendez Foundation: A comprehensive approach.* https://mendezfoundation.org/a-comprehensive-approach/

Mendlowitz, S. L., Manassis, K., Bradley, S., Scapillato, D., Miezitis, S. & Shaw, B. F. (1999). Cognitive-behavioral group treatments in childhood anxiety disorders: The role of parental involvement. *Journal of the American Academy of Child & Adolescent Psychiatry, 38*(10), 1223–1229. https://doi.org/10.1097/00004583-199910000-00010

Menzies, H. M., Lane, K. L., & Lee, J. M. (2009). Self-monitoring strategies for use in the classroom: A promising practice to support productive behavior for students with emotional or behavioral disorders. *Beyond Behavior, 18*(2), 27-35.

Menzies, R. G. & Clarke, J. C. (1993). The etiology of childhood water phobia. *Behaviour Research and Therapy, 31*(5), 499–501.

Miller, L. C., Barrett, C. L. & Hampe, E. (1974). Phobias of childhood in a prescientific era. In A. Davids (Ed.), *Child personality and psychopathology: current topics.* Oxford.

Miller, W. B. (1992). *Crime by youth gangs and groups in the United States.* Office of Juvenile Justice and Delinquency Prevention.

Minaei, A. & Nazeri, S. (2018). Psychometric properties of the Gilliam Autism Rating Scale–Third Edition (GARS-3) in individuals with autism: A pilot study. *Journal of Exceptional Children, 18*(2), 113–122.

Minihan, J. (2019). *Trauma-informed teaching strategies.* https://www.ascd.org/el/articles/trauma-informed-teaching-strategies

Minino, A. M., Arias, E., Kochanek, K. D., Murphy, S. L. & Smith, B. L. (2002). Deaths: Final data for 2000. *National Vital Statistics Report, 50*(15), 1-15.

Minuchin, S. (1974). *Families and family therapy.* Harvard University Press.

Mohammadi, M. R., Badrfam, R., Khaleghi, A., Hooshyari, Z., Ahmadi, N. & Zandifar, A. (2020). Prevalence, comorbidity and predictor of Separation Anxiety Disorder in children and adolescents. *The Psychiatric Quarterly, 91,* 1415-1429.

Mohammadi, M. R., Salmanian, M., Hooshyari, Z., Shakiba, A., Alavi, S. S., Ahmadi, A., Khaleghi, A., Zarafshan, H., Mostafavi, S. A. & Alaghmand, A.

(2020). Lifetime prevalence, sociodemographic predictors, and comorbidities of oppositional defiant disorder: The national epidemiology of Iranian child and adolescent psychiatric disorders (IRCAP). *Brazilian Journal of Psychiatry, 42*(2), 162–167.

Mohan, L., Yilanli, M. & Sagarika, R. (2021). *Conduct disorder.* https://www.ncbi.nlm.nih.gov/books/NBK470238/

Moldavsky, M. & Sayal, K. (2013). Knowledge and attitudes about attention-deficit/hyperactivity disorder (ADHD) and its treatment: The views of children, adolescents, parents, teachers and healthcare professionals. *Current Psychiatry Reports 15*(377). https://doi.org/10.1007/s11920-013-0377-0.

Molidor, C. E. (1996). *Female gang members: A profile of aggression and victimization.* Social Work, 41(3), 251-260.

Moliner, L. & Alegre, F. (2020). Peer tutoring effects on students' mathematics anxiety: A middle school experience. *Frontiers in Psychology, 11,* 1610. https://doi.org/10.3389/fpsyg.2020.01610

Mollborn, S. (2017). Teenage mothers today: What we know and how it matters. *Child Development Perspectives, 11*(1), 63–69.

Monahan, J., Steadman, H. J., Silver, E., Appelbaum, P. S., Robbins, P. C., Mulvey, E. P., Roth, L. H., Grisso, T. & Banks, S. (2001). *Rethinking risk assessment: The MacArthur study of mental disorder and violence.* Oxford University Press.

Moon, S. J., Hwang, J. S., Shin, A. L., Kim, J. Y., Bae, S. M., Sheehy-Knight, J. & Kim, J. W. (2019). Accuracy of the Childhood Autism Rating Scale: A systematic review and meta-analysis. *Developmental Medicine & Child Neurology, 61*(9), 1030–1038.

Moore, A. A., Lapato, D. M., Brotman, M. A., Leibenluft, E., Aggen, S. H., Hettema, J. M., York, T. P., Silberg, J. L. & Roberson-Nay, R. (2019). Heritability, stability, and prevalence of tonic and phasic irritability as indicators of disruptive mood dysregulation disorder. *Journal of Child Psychology and Psychiatry, 60*(9), 1032–1041.

Moore, A. A., Silberg, J. L., Roberson-Nay, R. & Mezuk, B. (2017). Life course persistent and adolescence limited conduct disorder in a nationally representative US sample: Prevalence, predictors, and outcomes. *Social Psychiatry and Psychiatric Epidemiology, 52*(4), 435–443.

Morales, S., Taber-Thomas, B. C. & Pérez-Edgar, K. E. (2017). Patterns of attention to threat across tasks in behaviorally inhibited children at risk for anxiety. *Developmental Science, 20*(2). Article 12391. https://doi.org/10.1111/desc.12391

Moreno-García, I., Meneres-Sancho, S., Camacho-Vara de Rey, C. & Servera, M. (2019). A randomized controlled trial to examine the posttreatment efficacy of neurofeedback, behavior therapy, and pharmacology on ADHD measures. *Journal of Attention Disorders, 23*(4), 374–383. https://doi.org/10.1177/1087054717693371.

Morris, M. C., Marco, M., Maguire-Jack, K., Kouros, C. D., Im, W., White, C., Bailey, B., Rao, U. & Garber, J. (2019). County-level socioeconomic and crime risk factors for substantiated child abuse and neglect. *Child Abuse & Neglect, 90,* 127–138.

Moscati, A., Flint, J. & Kendler, K. S. (2016). Classification of anxiety disorders comorbid with major depression: Common or distinct influences on risk? *Depression and Anxiety, 33*(2), 120–127.

Moss, E., St-Laurent, D., Dubois-Comtois, K. & Cyr, C. (2005). Quality of attachment at school age: Relations between child attachment behavior, psychosocial functioning, and school performance. In K. A. Kerns & R. A. Richardson (Eds.), *Attachment in middle childhood* (pp. 189–211). Guilford.

Motavalli Pour, A., Beh-Pajooh, A., Shokoohi-Yekta, M., Sorbi, M. H. & Farahzadi, M. H. (2018). The relationship between cognitive-behavioral skills and mother-child interaction with conduct disorder symptoms and Oppositional Defiant Disorder in children with ADHD. *Journal of Community Health Research, 7*(4), 231–241.

Mouton, B., Loop, L., Stievenart, M. & Roskam, I. (2018). Parenting programs to reduce young children's externalizing behavior: A meta-analytic review of their behavioral or cognitive orientation. *Child & Family Behavior Therapy, 40*(2), 115–147.

MTA Cooperative Group. (2004). National Institute of Mental Health Multimodal Treatment Study of ADHD follow-up: 24-month outcomes of treatment strategies for attention-deficit/hyperactivity disorder. *Pediatrics, 113*(4), 754-761.

Muisener, P. P. (1994). *Understanding and treating adolescent substance abuse.* Thousand Oaks, CA, US: Sage Publications, Inc.

Mullen S. (2018). Major depressive disorder in children and adolescents. *The mental health clinician, 8*(6), 275–283. https://doi.org/10.9740/mhc.2018.11.275

Mullet, J. H. (2014). Restorative discipline: From getting even to getting well. *Children & Schools, 36*(3), 157–162. https://doi.org/10.1093/cs/cdu011

Mulvey, E. P. & Cauffman, E. (2001). The inherent limits of predicting school violence. *American Psychologist,* 56, 797–802.

Mundy, P. (2018). A review of joint attention and social-cognitive brain systems in typical development and autism spectrum disorder. *European Journal of Neuroscience, 47*(6), 497–514.

Munene, A. & James, N. (2017). Conduct Disorder and distressful situations experienced by juvenile delinquents in Kenya. *African Journal of Clinical Psychology, 1(3),* 1- 19.

Munro, K. (2018, July 31). How safe is flying? Here's what the statistics say. *SBS News.* https://www.sbs.com.au/news/how-safe-is-flying-here-s-what-the-statistics-say.

Muris, P. (2017). Specific phobias. In B. O. Olatungi (Ed.) *Handbook of childhood psychopathology and developmental disabilities treatment* (pp. 207–219). Springer.

Muris, P., Ollendick, T. H., Roelofs, J. & Austin, K. (2014). The short form of the Fear Survey Schedule for Children-Revised (FSSC-R-SF): An efficient, reliable, and valid scale for measuring fear in children and adolescents. *Journal of Anxiety Disorders, 28*(8), 957–965. https://doi.org/10.1016/j.janxdis.2014.09.020

Murray, K. W., Finigan-Carr, N., Jones, V., Copeland-Linder, N., Haynie, D. L. & Cheng, T. L. (2014). Barriers and facilitators to school-based parent involvement for parents of urban public middle school students. *SAGE open, 4*(4), 10.1177/2158244014558030. https://doi.org/10.1177/2158244014558030

Murray, S. B. (2019). Updates in the treatment of eating disorders in 2018: A year in review in eating disorders: The journal of treatment & prevention. *Eating Disorders, 27*(1), 6–17.

Murrihy, R. C., Burns, J. R., Reinke, W. M., Herman, K. C. & King, K. R. (2017). Evidence-based assessment and intervention for oppositional defiant disorder and conduct disorder in school psychology. In M. Thielking & M. D. Terjesen (Eds.) *Handbook of australian school psychology* (pp. 331–347). Springer.

Musu, L., Zhang, A., Wang, K., Zhang, J. & Oudekerk, B. (2019). *Indicators of school crime and safety: 2018.* https://www.bjs.gov/content/pub/pdf/iscs18.pdf.

Naber, P. A., May, D. C., Decker, S. H., Minor, K. I. & Wells, J. B. (2006). Are there gangs in schools? It depends upon whom you ask. *Journal of School Violence, 5*(2), 53-72.

Naigles, L. (2016). *Innovative investigations of language in autism spectrum disorder.* Walter de Gruyter GmbH & Co KG.

Naigles, L. R., Cheng, M., Rattanasone, N. X., Tek, S., Khetrapal, N., Fein, D., & Demuth, K. (2016). "You're telling me!" The prevalence and predictors of pronoun reversals in children with autism spectrum disorders and typical development. *Research in Autism Spectrum Disorders, 27,* 11–20.

National Center for Education Statistics (2020). *Graduation and dropout rates 2017-2018 school year,* https://nces.ed.gov/programs/coe/indicator_coi.asp

National Center for Education Statistics. (2021). Students with disabilities. *Condition of Education.* U.S. Department of Education, Institute of Education Sciences. https://nces.ed.gov/programs/coe/indicator/cgg.

National Center for Health Statistics (2007). *ASD growth rate.* http://www.cdc.gov/nchs/

National Center for Learning Disabilities [NCLD]. (2017). *Social, emotional and behavioral challenges.* https://www.ncld.org/research/state-of-learning-disabilities/social-emotional-and-behavioral-challenges/

National Center for the Analysis of Violent Crime (2001). *The school shooter: A threat assessment perspective* (pp. 8–9). www.fbi.gov/library/schools/ school2.

National Center for PTSD (n.d.). *How common is PTSD in adults?* https://www.ptsd.va.gov/understand/common/common_adults.asp

National Child Traumatic Stress Network. (2017). Creating, supporting, and sustaining trauma-informed schools: A system framework. Los Angeles, CA, and Durham, NC: National Center for Child Traumatic Stress. https://www.nctsn.org/sites/default/files/resources/creating_supporting_sustaining_trauma_informed_schools_a_systems_framework.pdf

National Gang Center. (n.d.). *Gang resistance is paramount [G.R.I.P.].* https://nationalgangcenter.ojp.gov/spt/Programs/69

National Institute on Drug Abuse (2020). *Cannabis (marijuana) research report.* https://www.drugabuse.gov/download/1380/marijuana-research-report.pdf?v=d9e67cbd412ae5f340206c1a0d9c2bfd

National Institute of Mental Health. (2021). *Eating disorders: About more than food.* https://www.nimh.nih.gov/sites/default/files/documents/health/publications/eating-disorders/21-MH-4901-EatingDisorders_0.pdf

National Institutes of Health. (2020). *Study finds surge of teen vaping levels off but remains high in early 2020.* https://www.nih.gov/news-events/news-releases/study-finds-surge-teen-vaping-levels-remains-high-early-2020

Nelson, M. M. & Olsen, B. (2018). Dyadic parent–child interaction coding system (DPICS): An adaptable measure of parent and child behavior during dyadic interactions. In L. N. Niec (Ed.), *Handbook of parent-child interaction therapy: innovations and applications for research and practice* (pp. 285–302). Springer.

New York State Division of Criminal Justice Services (2003). *2002–2004 New York State comprehensive juvenile justice plan.* Retrieved March 4, 2008, from www.criminaljustice.state.ny.us/ofpa/pdfdocs/jj3yrplan.pdf

New York State Education Department. (2017). *The New York State dignity for all act: A resource and promising practices guide for school administrators & faculty.* https://www.p12.nysed.gov//dignityact/documents/FINALDignityForAllStudentsActGuidanceDec2017.pdf

New York State Education Department. (2018). *New York State social emotional learning benchmarks.* https://www.p12.nysed.gov//sss/documents/NYSSELBenchmarks.pdf

New York State Education Department. (2021). *School safety.* https://www.p12.nysed.gov/sss/ssae/schoolsafety/

Newman, M. G., Shin, K. E. & Zuellig, A. R. (2016). Developmental risk factors in generalized anxiety disorder and panic disorder. *Journal of Affective Disorders, 206*, 94–102.

Newton-Howes, G., Cook, S., Martin, G., Foulds, J. A. & Boden, J. M. (2019). Comparison of age of first drink and age of first intoxication as predictors of substance use and mental health problems in adulthood. *Drug and Alcohol Dependence, 194*, 238–243.

Nigar, A. & Naqvi, I. (2019). Body dissatisfaction, perfectionism, and media exposure among adolescents. *Pakistan Journal of Psychological Research, 34*, 57–77.

Ninivaggi, F. J. (2017). *Making sense of emotion: Innovating emotional intelligence.* Rowman & Littlefield.

Nogales, V. (2007). Family Adaptability and Cohesion Evaluation Scales-IV (FACES IV). *Revista Deficiencias Psicológicas.* http://Pepsic. Bvsalud. Org/Pdf/Cpsi/V1n2/V1n2a07. Pdf.

Nordahl, H. M., Vogel, P. A., Morken, G., Stiles, T. C., Sandvik, P. & Wells, A. (2016). Paroxetine, cognitive therapy, or their combination in the treatment of social anxiety disorder with and without avoidant personality disorder: A randomized clinical trial. *Psychotherapy and Psychosomatics, 85*(6), 346–356.

Norton, A. R. & Abbott, M. J. (2017). The role of environmental factors in the etiology of social anxiety disorder: A review of the theoretical and empirical literature. *Behaviour Change, 34*(2), 76–97.

Nota, J. A., Potluri, S., Kelley, K. N., Elias, J. A. & Krompinger, J. W. (2020). Delayed bedtimes are associated with more severe obsessive-compulsive symptoms in intensive residential treatment. *Behavior Therapy, 51*(4), 559–571.

Nygaard, K. (2019). *The causes of teacher burnout and attrition* (Thesis, Concordia University, St. Paul).

Oar, E. L., Farrell, L. J. & Ollendick, T. H. (2019). Specific phobia. In In S. N. Compton, M.A. Villabo & H. Kristensen (Eds.) *Pediatric anxiety disorders* (pp. 127–150). Elsevier.

O'Brien, K. M., Whelan, D. R., Sandler, D. P., Hall, J. E. & Weinberg, C. R. (2017). Predictors and long-term health outcomes of eating disorders. *PloS One, 12*(7) Article 0181104. https://doi.org/10.1371/journal.pone.0181104

Okabe-Miyamoto, K. (2021). *Social connection and well-being during COVID-19.* https://worldhappiness.report/ed/2021/social-connection-and-well-being-during-covid-19/

O'Kearney, R., Salmon, K., Liwag, M., Fortune, C.-A. & Dawel, A. (2017). Emotional abilities in children with oppositional defiant disorder (ODD): Impairments in perspective-taking and understanding mixed emotions are associated with high callous–unemotional traits. *Child Psychiatry & Human Development, 48*(2), 346–357.

O'Leary, K. D., & Solano, I. (2018). Relationship discord, intimate partner physical aggression, and externalizing problems of children. In J.E. Lochman & W. Matthys (Eds.) *The Wiley handbook of disruptive and impulse-control disorders* (pp. 291-305). Wiley.

Ollendick, T. H. (2017). Fear reduction techniques. *Progress in Behavior Modification, 8*(8) 127-164.

Ollendick, T. H., Greene, R. W., Austin, K. E., Fraire, M. G., Halldorsdottir, T., Allen, K. B., Jarrett, M. A., Lewis, K. M., Whitmore Smith, M., & Cunningham, N. R. (2016). Parent management training and collaborative & proactive solutions: A randomized control trial for oppositional youth. *Journal of Clinical Child & Adolescent Psychology, 45*(5), 591–604.

Ollendick, T. H., & King, N. J. (1991). Origins of childhood fears: An evaluation of Rachman's theory of fear acquisition. *Behaviour Research and Therapy, 29(*2), 117–123.

Ollendick, T. H., King, N. J., & Chorpita, B. F. (2006). Empirically supported treatments for children and adolescents. In P. C. Kendall (Ed.), *Child and adolescent therapy: Cognitive-behavioral procedures* (pp. 492–520). Guilford Press.

Olson, K. M. (2016). *Unidentified language deficits in students with emotional and behavioral disorders.* Thesis. [St. Cloud State University]. https://repository.stcloudstate.edu/cgi/viewcontent.cgi?article=1032&context=sped_etds

Olweus, D. (1992). Bullying among school children: Intervention and prevention. In R. Peters, R. J. McMahon, & V. L. Quinsy (Eds.), *Aggression and violence throughout the life span* (pp. 100-125). Sage.

Olweus, D. (1993). Victimization by peers: Antecedents and long-term outcomes. In K. H. Rubin & J. B. Asendorpf (Eds.), *Social withdrawal, inhibition, and shyness in childhood* (pp. 315-341). Erlbaum.

Olweus, D. (2004). The Olweus Bullying Prevention Program: Design and implementation issues and a new national initiative in Norway. In P. K. Smith, D. J. Pepler, & K. Rigby (Eds), *Bullying in schools* (pp.13-36). Cambridge University Press.

Olweus, D., Limber, S. & Mihalic, S. (1999). Bullying prevention program. In D.S. Elliot (Ed.), *Blueprints for violence prevention book nine* (pp. 1-79). C&M Press.

Opydo-Szymaczek, J., Jarząbek-Bielecka, G., Kędzia, W. & Borysewicz-Lewicka, M. (2018). Child sexual abuse as an etiological factor of overweight and eating disorders - Considerations for primary health care providers. *Ginekologia Polska, 89*(1), 48–54.

Orpinas, P. & Horne, A. M. (2006). *Bullying prevention: Creating a positive school climate and developing social competence.* American Psychological Association.

Osher, D. & Kendziora, K. (2012). Building conditions for learning and healthy adolescent development: A strategic approach. In *Handbook of youth prevention science* (pp. 121-140). Routledge.

Osman, A., Gutierrez, P. M., Bagge, C. L., Fang, Q. & Emmerich, A. (2010). Reynolds Adolescent Depression Scale-Second Edition: A reliable and useful instrument. *Journal of Clinical Psychology, 66*(12), 1324–1345. https://doi.org/10.1002/jclp.20727

Öst, L.-G., Riise, E. N., Wergeland, G. J., Hansen, B. & Kvale, G. (2016). Cognitive behavioral and pharmacological treatments of OCD in children: A systematic review and meta-analysis. *Journal of Anxiety Disorders, 43,* 58–69.

Oud, M., De Winter, L., Vermeulen-Smit, E., Bodden, D., Nauta, M., Stone, L., Van Den Heuvel, M., Al Taher, R., De Graaf, I. & Kendall, T. (2019). Effectiveness of CBT for children and adolescents with depression: A systematic review and meta-regression analysis. *European Psychiatry, 57,* 33–45.

Pacer Center. (2022). *Dropout prevention.* https://www.pacer.org/parent/dropout-prevention/

Padilla, F.M. (1992). *The Gang as an American enterprise: Puerto Rican youth and the American dream.* Rutgers University.

Palincsar, A. S. & Brown, A. L. (1986). Interactive teaching to promote independent learning from text. *The Reading Teacher, 39*(8), 771-77.

Palincsar, A. S. & Klenk, L. (1992). Fostering literacy learning in supportive contexts. *Journal of Learning Disabilities, 25*(4), 211-225.

Pardini, D. A., Lochman, J. E. & Frick, P. J. (2003). Callous/unemotional traits and social cognitive processes in adjudicated youth. *Journal of the American Academy of Child and Adolescent Psychiatry, 42,* 364–371.

Parks, C. (1995). Gang behavior in the schools: Reality or myth. *Educational Psychology Review, 7,* 41-68.

Parsons, T. D., Duffield, T. & Asbee, J. (2019). A comparison of virtual reality classroom continuous performance tests to traditional continuous performance tests in delineating ADHD: a meta-analysis. *Neuropsychology Review,* 29, 338-356.

Passarotti, A. M., Trivedi, N., Dominguez-Colman, L., Patel, M. & Langenecker, S. A. (2016). Differences in real world executive function between children with pediatric bipolar disorder and children with ADHD. *Journal of the Canadian Academy of Child and Adolescent Psychiatry, 25*(3), 185-195.

Patall, E. A., Cooper, H. & Wynn, S. R. (2010). The effectiveness and relative importance of choice in the classroom. *Journal of Educational Psychology, 102*(4), 896-915.

Patel, D. R., Feucht, C., Brown, K. & Ramsay, J. (2018). Pharmacological treatment of anxiety disorders in children and adolescents: A review for practitioners. *Translational Pediatrics, 7*(1), 23-35.

Patel, R. K. & Rose, G. M. (2020). *Persistent depressive disorder (Dysthymia).* Stat Pearls. https://www.ncbi.nlm.nih.gov/books/NBK541052/

Patterson, D. S., Jolivette, K. & Crosby, S. (2006). Social skills training for students who demonstrate poor self-control. *Beyond Behavior, 15*(3), 23–27.

Pavăl, D. (2017). A dopamine hypothesis of autism spectrum disorder. *Developmental Neuroscience, 39*(5), 355–360.

Pawlo, E., Lorenzo, A., Eichert, B. & Elias, M. J. (2019). All SEL should be trauma informed. *Phi Delta Kappan, 101*(3), 37–41. https://doi.org/10.1177/0031721719885919

Pazuniak, M. & Pekrul, S. R. (2020). Obsessive–Compulsive Disorder in Autism Spectrum Disorder across the lifespan. *Child and Adolescent Psychiatric Clinics, 29*(2), 419–432.

Pearlman, A. T., Schvey, N. A., Higgins Neyland, M. K., Solomon, S., Hennigan, K., Schindler, R., Leu, W., Gilmore, D., Shank, L. M., Lavendar, J. M., Burke, N. L., Wilfley, D. E., Sbrocco, T., Stephens, M., Jorgensen, S., Klein, D., Quinlan, J. & Tanofsky-Kraff, M. (2020). Associations between family weight-based teasing, eating pathology, and psychosocial functioning among adolescent military dependents. *International Journal of Environmental Research and Public Health, 17*(1), 24.

Pearson, C. M., Miller, J., Ackard, D. M., Loth, K. A., Wall, M. M., Haynos, A. F. & Neumark-Sztainer, D. (2017). Stability and change in patterns of eating disorder symptoms from adolescence to young adulthood. *International Journal of Eating Disorders, 50*(7), 748–757.

Pennell, A., Webb, C., Agar, P., Federici, A. & Couturier, J. (2019). Implementation of dialectical behavior therapy in a day hospital setting for adolescents with eating disorders. *Journal of the Canadian Academy of Child and Adolescent Psychiatry, 28*(1), 21-29.

Perry, J. C. & Lavins-Merillat, B. D. (2018). Self-esteem and school belongingness: A cross-lagged panel study among urban youth. *Professional School Counseling, 22*(1). https://doi.org/10.1177/2156759X19826575

Perwien, A. R. & Bernstein, G. A. (2004). Separation anxiety disorder. In T. H. Ollendick & J. S. March (Eds.), *Phobic and anxiety disorders in children and adolescents: A clinician's guide to effective psychosocial and pharmacological interventions* (pp. 272–305). Oxford University.

Piacentini, J., Peris, T. S., Bergman, R. L., Chang, S. & Jaffer, M. (2007). Brief report: Functional impairment in childhood OCD: Development and psychometrics properties of the child obsessive-compulsive impact scale-revised (COIS-R). *Journal of Clinical Child and Adolescent Psychology, 36*(4), 645–653.

Picci, G., Behrmann, M. & Scherf, S. (2018). Greeble training in adolescents increases neural activation in the FFA. *Journal of Vision, 18*(10), 562–562.

Pierangelo, R. & Giuliani, G. A. (2001). *What every teacher should know about students with special needs: Promoting success in the classroom.* Research Press.

Pierangelo, R., & Giuliani, G. (2008). *Teaching students with learning disabilities: A step-by-step guide for educators.* Corwin Press.

Pierangelo, R., & Giuliani, G. (2016). *The classroom teacher's behavior management toolbox.* Information Age Publisher, Inc.

Pijper, J., de Wied, M., van Rijn, S., van Goozen, S., Swaab, H. & Meeus, W. (2016). Callous unemotional traits, autism spectrum disorder symptoms and empathy in boys with oppositional defiant disorder or conduct disorder. *Psychiatry Research, 245,* 340–345.

Ping, X., McBride, R. E. & Bruene, A. (2006). Fourth-grade students' motivational changes in an elementary physical education running program. *Research Quarterly for Exercise & Sport, 77,* 195-207.

Pisecco, S., Huzinec, C. & Curtis, D. (2001). The effect of child characteristics on teachers' acceptability of classroom-based behavioral strategies and psychostimulant medication for the treatment of ADHD. *Journal of Clinical Child Psychology, 30* (3), 413-421.

Pittig, A., Treanor, M., LeBeau, R. T. & Craske, M. G. (2018). The role of associative fear and avoidance learning in anxiety disorders: Gaps and directions for future research. *Neuroscience & Biobehavioral Reviews, 88,* 117–140.

Piven, J., Elison, J. T. & Zylka, M. J. (2017). Toward a conceptual framework for early brain and behavior development in autism. *Molecular Psychiatry, 22*(10), 1385–1394.

Planer, J., DeBar, R., Progar, P., Reeve, K. & Sarokoff, R. (2018). Evaluating tasks within a high-probability request sequence in children with autism spectrum disorder. *Behavioral Interventions, 33*(4), 380–390.

Pliszka, S. R. (2003). Psychiatric comorbidities in children with attention deficit hyperactivity disorder: implications for management. *Pediatric Drugs, 5*(11), 741–750. https://doi.org/10.2165/00148581-200305110-00003.

Pokorny, F. B., Bartl-Pokorny, K. D., Zhang, D., Marschik, P. B., Schuller, D. & Schuller, B. W. (2020). Efficient collection and representation of preverbal data in typical and atypical development. *Journal of Nonverbal Behavior, 44,* 419-436.

Pooravari, M., Pourshahriari, M. & Salehi, S. (2016). Review of literature on cognitive-behavioral therapy, behavioral parent training for aggressive behavior, and peer problem of children with conduct disorder. *International Journal of Applied Behavioral Sciences, 3*(1), 43–55.

Popham, W. J. (2001). Teaching to the Test? *Educational Leadership, 58*(6), 16-21.

Portell, M. (2019). Understanding trauma informed education. *Edutopia.* https://www.edutopia.org/article/understanding-trauma-informed-education

Powell, N. P., Lochman, J. E., Boxmeyer, C. L., Barry, T. D. & Pardini, D. A. (2017). The coping power program for aggressive behavior in children. In J.

R. Weisz & A. E. Kazdin (Eds.), *Evidence-based psychotherapies for children and adolescents* (pp. 159–176). Guilford.

Powers, C. J., Bierman, K. L. & Coffman, D. L. (2016). Restrictive educational placements increase adolescent risks for students with early-starting conduct problems. *Journal of Child Psychology and Psychiatry, 57*(8), 899–908.

Powers, M. D. & Franks, C. M. (1988). Behavior therapy and the educative process. In J. Witt, S. Elliott, & F. Gresham (Eds.), *Handbook of behavior therapy in education* (pp. 3-36). Plenum Press.

Preter, S. E., Shapiro, T. & Milrod, B. (2018). *Child and adolescent anxiety psychodynamic psychotherapy: A Treatment manual.* Oxford University.

Prince-Embury, S., & Saklofske, D. H. (2013). *Resilience in children, adolescents, and adults: Translating research into practice.* Springer.

Pua, E. P. K. (2019). *Quantifying variation in brain structure and function in autism spectrum disorders (ASD)* [Unpublished Doctoral Dissertation]. Melbourne School of Psychological Sciences.

Pullen, P. C., Lloyd, P. A. & Lloyd, J. W. (2008). Academic problems. In R. J. Morris & T. R. Kratochwill (Eds.), *The practice of child therapy*, (pp. 187-205). Routledge.

Purty, A., Nestadt, G., Samuels, J. F. & Viswanath, B. (2019). Genetics of obsessive-compulsive disorder. *Indian Journal of Psychiatry, 61*(Supplement 1), S37.

Pynoos, R. S., Weathers, F. W., Steinberg, A. M., Marx, B. P., Layne, C. M., Kaloupek, D. G. & Kriegler, J. (2015). *Clinician-administered PTSD scale for DSM-5—Child/adolescent version.* National Center for PTSD. https://www.ptsd.va.gov/professional/assessment/documents/CAPS-CA-5.pdf

Quello, S. B., Brady, K. T. & Sonne, S. C. (2005). Mood disorders and substance use disorder: A complex comorbidity. *Science & Practice Perspectives, 3*(1), 13-21.

Quintana, C., Krajcik, J., Soloway, E., Fishman, L. & O'Connor-Divelbiss, S. (2013, April). Exploring a structured definition for learner-centered design. *Fourth International Conference of The Learning Sciences* (pp. 256-263).

Rachman, S. (1976). The passing of the two-stage theory of fear and avoidance: Fresh possibilities. *Behaviour Research and Therapy, 14*(2), 125–131. https://doi.org/10.1016/0005-7967(76)90066-8

Rachman, S. (1977). The conditioning theory of fear-acquisition: A critical examination. *Behaviour Research and Therapy, 15*(5), 375–387. https://doi.org/10.1016/0005-7967(77)90041-9

Radtke, S. R., Strege, M. V. & Ollendick, T. H. (2020). Exposure therapy for children and adolescents with social anxiety disorder. In T. S. Peris & E. A. Storch (Eds.), *Exposure therapy for children with anxiety and OCD* (pp. 193–219). Elsevier.

Raines, T. C., Dever, B. V., Kamphaus, R. W. & Roach, A. T. (2012). Universal screening for behavioral and emotional risk: A promising method for reducing disproportionate placement in special education. *The Journal of Negro Education, 81*(3), 283-296.

Rajyaguru, P., Moran, P., Cordero, M. & Pearson, R. (2019). Disciplinary parenting practice and child mental health: Evidence from the UK millennium cohort study. *Journal of the American Academy of Child & Adolescent Psychiatry, 58*(1), 108–116.

Ramphal, B., Whalen, D. J., Kenley, J. K., Yu, Q., Smyser, C. D., Rogers, C. E. & Sylvester, C. M. (2020). Brain connectivity and socioeconomic status at birth and externalizing symptoms at age 2 years. *Developmental Cognitive Neuroscience, 45.* Article 100811. https://doi.org/10.1016/j.dcn.2020.100811

Rapoport, J. L. & Inoff-Germain, G. (2000). Treatment of obsessive-compulsive disorder in children and adolescents. *Journal of Child Psychology and Psychiatry, 41*(4), 419–431.

Rasing, S., Creemers, D. H., Janssens, J. M. & Scholte, R. H. (2017). Depression and anxiety prevention based on cognitive behavioral therapy for at-risk adolescents: A meta-analytic review. *Frontiers in Psychology, 28.* Article 1066. https://doi.org/10.3389/fpsyg.2017.01066

Raskauskas, J. & Modell, S. (2011). Modifying anti-bullying programs to include students with disabilities. *Teaching Exceptional Children, 44*(1), 60-67.

Ratcliff, N. & Hunt, G. (2009). Building teacher-family partnerships: The role of teacher preparation programs. *Education, 129*(3), 495-505.

Reas, D. L. & Rø, Ø. (2018). Less symptomatic, but equally impaired: Clinical impairment in restricting versus binge-eating/purging subtype of anorexia nervosa. *Eating Behaviors, 28,* 32–37.

Rees C. (2007). Childhood attachment. *The British Journal of General Practice: The Journal of the Royal College of General Practitioners, 57*(544), 920–922. https://doi.org/10.3399/096016407782317955

Rehm, L. P. (1977). A self-control model of depression. *Behavior Therapy, 8*(5), 787–804. https://doi.org/10.1016/S0005-7894(77)80150-0

Reichart, C. G., Wals, M. & Hillegers, M. H. J. (2004). Psychopathology in the adolescent offspring of bipolar parents. *Journal of Affective Disorders, 78,* 67–71.

Reis, E. M. (2002). Attention deficit hyperactivity disorder: Implications for the classroom teacher. *Journal of Instructional Psychology, 29*(3), 175179.

Research Units on Pediatric Psychopharmacology Anxiety Study Group. (2002). The Pediatric Anxiety Rating Scale (PARS): Development and psychometric properties. *Journal of the American Academy of Child & Adolescent Psychiatry, 41*(9), 1061–1069. https://doi.org/10.1097/0000458 3-200209000-00006

Reynolds, C. R. & Kamphaus, R. W. (1992). *Behavioral assessment system for children.* American Guidance Service.

Reynolds, W. M. (1989). *Reynolds Child Depression Scale.* Psychological Assessment Resources.

Reynolds, W. M. (2004). The Reynolds Adolescent Depression Scale-Second Edition (RADS-2). In M. J. Hilsenroth & D. L. Segal (Eds.), *Comprehensive handbook of psychological assessment, Vol. 2: Personality assessment* (pp. 224–236). Wiley.

Richards, D. A. & Schat, A. C. H. (2011). Attachment at (not to) work: Applying attachment theory to explain individual behavior in organizations. *Journal of Applied Psychology, 96*(1), 169–182. https://doi.org/10.1037/a0020372

Rieffe, C., Broekhof, E., Kouwenberg, M., Faber, J., Tsutsui, M. M. & Güroğlu, B. (2016). Disentangling proactive and reactive aggression in children using self-report. *European Journal of Developmental Psychology, 13*(4), 439–451.

Rienecke, R. D. (2017). Family-based treatment of eating disorders in adolescents: Current insights. *Adolescent Health, Medicine and Therapeutics, 8,* 69-79.

Ringdahl, J. E., Andelman, M. S., Kitsukawa, K., Winborn, L. C., Barretto, A. & Wacker, D. P. (2002). Evaluation and treatment of covert stereotypy. *Behavioral Interventions, 17*(1), 43-49.

Roberts, M. W. & Hope, D. A. (2001). Clinic observations of structured parent–child interaction designed to evaluate externalizing disorders. *Psychological Assessment, 13*(1), 46–58. https://doi.org/10.1037/1040-3590.13.1.46

Roberts, W. B., Jr. & Morotti, A. A. (2000). The bully as victim: Understanding bully behaviors to increase the effectiveness of interventions in the bully-victim dyad. *Professional School Counseling, 4*(2), 148-155.

Rohde, P., Lewinsohn, P. M., Clarke, G. N., Hops, H. & Seeley, J. R. (2005). The Adolescent Coping with Depression Course: A cognitive-behavioral approach to the treatment of adolescent depression. In E. D. Hibbs & P. S. Kohn (Eds.), *Psychosocial treatments for child and adolescent disorders: Empirically based strategies for clinical practice* (2nd ed., pp. 219–237). American Psychological Association.

Rojas, N. L. & Chan, E. (2005). Old and new controversies in the alternative treatment of attention-deficit hyperactivity disorder. *Mental Retardation & Developmental Disabilities Research Reviews, 11*(2), 116–130. https://doi.org/10.1002/mrdd.20064.

Rojas-Torres, L. P., Alonso-Esteban, Y. & Alcantud-Marín, F. (2020). Early intervention with parents of children with autism spectrum disorders: A review of programs. *Children, 7*(12), 294. https://doi.org/10.3390/children7120294

Roman, C. G., Decker, S. H. & Pyrooz, D. C. (2017). Leveraging the pushes and pulls of gang disengagement to improve gang intervention: Findings from three multi-site studies and a review of relevant gang programs. *Journal of Crime and Justice, 40*(3), 316-336.

Ronan, K. R., Kendall, P. C. & Rowe, M. (1994). Negative affectivity in children: Development and validation of a self-statement questionnaire. *Cognitive Therapy and Research, 18,* 509-528.

Rose, A. & Basit, H. (2020). Effects of sensorimotor problems on the performance of activities of daily living in children with autism spectrum disorder. *Journal of Health, Medicine and Nursing, 70,* 1-6.

Rosenberg, M.S., Wilson, R.J., Maheady, L. & Sindelar, P.T. (2004). *Educating students with behavior disorders* (3rd ed.) Allyn & Bacon.

Rubin, L. C. (2017). *Handbook of medical play therapy and child life: Interventions in clinical and medical settings.* Routledge.

Ruiz, N. A. L., Del Ángel, D. S., Olguín, H. J. & Silva, M. L. (2018). Neuroprogression: The hidden mechanism of depression. *Neuropsychiatric Disease and Treatment, 14,* 2837-2845.

Rutgers, A. H., Bakermans-Kranenburg, M. J., van Ijzendoorn, M. H. & van Berckelaer-Onnes, I. A. (2004). Autism and attachment: A meta-analytic review. *Journal of Child Psychology and Psychiatry, 45*(6), 1123–1134.

Rutter, M., Le Couteur, A. & Lord, C. (2003). *ADI-R. Autism diagnostic interview revised. Manual.* Western Psychological Services.

Ryan, A.L., Halsey, H.N. & Matthews, W.J. (2003). Using functional assessment to promote desirable student behavior in schools. *Teaching Exceptional Children, 35*(5), 8-15.

Rydell, A.-M. & Brocki, K. C. (2019). Cognitive and emotional profiles of CU traits and disruptive behavior in adolescence: A prospective study. *Journal of Abnormal Child Psychology, 47*(6), 1039–1051.

Sabatino, D. A., Webster, B. G., Vance, H. B. & Pumariega, A. (2001). Childhood mood disorders: History, characteristics, diagnosis and treatment. In H. B. Vance, A. Pumariega (Eds.), *Clinical assessment of child and adolescent behavior* (pp. 413-449). Wiley.

Sacco, B. & Kelley, U. (2018). Diagnosis and evaluation of eating disorders in the pediatric patient. *Pediatric Annals, 47*(6), 244–e249.

Sachs, J. (1999). The hidden conspiracy in our nation's schools. *Behavioral Disorders, 25*(1), 80-82.

Saigh, P. A., Yasik, A. E., Oberfield, R. A., Green, B. L., Halamandaris, P. V., Rubenstein, H., Nester, J., Resko, J., Hetz, B. & McHugh, M. (2000). The children's PTSD inventory: Development and reliability. *Journal of Traumatic Stress, 13*(3), 369–380.

Salend, S. J. (2005). *Creating inclusive classrooms: Effective and reflective practices for all students* (5th ed.). Merrill/Prentice Hall.

Salmivalli, C. (2014). Participant roles in bullying: How can peer bystanders be utilized in interventions? *Theory Into Practice, 53*(4), 286-292.

Samaey, C., Van der Donck, S., van Winkel, R. & Boets, B. (2020). Facial expression processing across the autism–psychosis spectra: A review of neural findings and associations with adverse childhood events. *Frontiers in Psychiatry, 11.* Article 592937. doi:10.3389/fpsyt.2020.592937

Sampson, R. (2002). *Bullying in schools* (Problem-Oriented Guides for Police Series, Guide. No. 12). U.S. Department of Justice.

Samra, C. K., & Abdijadid, S. (2020). *Specific phobia.* Stat Pearls. https://www.ncbi.nlm.nih.gov/pmc/articles/PMC7691238/

Sánchez-Jankowski, M. (1991). *Islands in the Street: Gangs and American urban society.* University of California Press.

Sánchez-Jankowski, M. (2003). Gangs and social change. *Theoretical Criminology, 7*(2), 191-216.

Sansone, R. A., Sansone, L. A., Klykylo, W. M. & Kay, J. L. (2012). The eating disorders. In W.M. Klykyko & J. Kay (Eds.) *Clinical child psychiatry* (3rd ed., pp. 289-304). Wiley.

Santarossa, A., Nabbijohn, A. N., van der Miesen, A. I., Peragine, D. E. & VanderLaan, D. P. (2019). Separation anxiety and gender variance in a community sample of children. *European Child & Adolescent Psychiatry, 28*(12), 1629–1643.

Sasson, N. J., Faso, D. J., Nugent, J., Lovell, S., Kennedy, D. P. & Grossman, R. B. (2017). Neurotypical peers are less willing to interact with those with autism based on thin slice judgments. *Scientific Reports, 7*(1), 1–10.

Scahill, L., Riddle, M. A., McSwiggin-Hardin, M., Ort, S. I., King, R. A., Goodman, W. K., Cicchetti, D. & Leckman, J. F. (1997). Children's Yale-Brown Obsessive Compulsive Scale: Reliability and validity. *Journal of the American Academy of Child & Adolescent Psychiatry, 36*(6), 844–852.

Scattone, D. (2008). Enhancing the conversation skills of a boy with Asperger's disorder through Social Stories™ and video modeling. *Journal of Autism and Developmental Disorders, 38*(2), 395-400.

Schaffer, D., Fisher, P., Lucas, C. P., Dulcan, M. K. & Schwab-Stone, M. E. (2000). The NIMH Diagnostic Interview Schedule for Children version IV (DISC-IV): Description, differences from previous versions, and reliability of some common diagnoses. *Journal of the American Academy of Child and Adolescent Psychiatry, 39*, 28–38.

Schain, R. J. & Freedman, D. X. (1961). Studies on 5-hydroxyindole metabolism in autistic and other mentally retarded children. *The Journal of Pediatrics, 58*(3), 315–320.

Schellenberg, R. C., Parks-Savage, A. & Rehfuss, M. (2007). Reducing levels of elementary school violence with peer mediation. *Professional School Counseling, 10*(5). https://doi.org/10.1177/2156759X0701000504

Schilpzand, E. J., Sciberras, E., Alisic, E., Efron, D., Hazell, P., Jongeling, B., Anderson, V. & Nicholson, J. M. (2018). Trauma exposure in children with and without ADHD: Prevalence and functional impairment in a community-based study of 6–8-year-old Australian children. *European Child & Adolescent Psychiatry, 27*(6), 811–819.

Schoorl, J., van Rijn, S., de Wied, M., Van Goozen, S. H. & Swaab, H. (2016). Variability in emotional/behavioral problems in boys with oppositional defiant disorder or conduct disorder: The role of arousal. *European Child & Adolescent Psychiatry, 25*(8), 821–830.

Schoorl, J., van Rijn, S., de Wied, M., Van Goozen, S. & Swaab, H. (2018). Boys with oppositional defiant disorder/conduct disorder show impaired adaptation during stress: An executive functioning study. *Child Psychiatry & Human Development, 49*(2), 298–307.

Schopler, E., Lansing, M. D., Reichler, R. J. & Marcus, L. M. (2005). *PEP-3, Psychoeducational profile.* Pro-ed.

Schopler, E., Van Bourgondien, M. E., Wellman, G. J., & Love, S. R. (2010). *CARS-2: Childhood Autism Rating Scale–Second Edition.* Western Psychological Services.

Schramm, E., Klein, D. N., Elsaesser, M., Furukawa, T. A. & Domschke, K. (2020). Review of dysthymia and persistent depressive disorder: History, correlates, and clinical implications. *The Lancet Psychiatry, 7*(9), 801–812.

Schreibman, L. & Ingersoll, B. (2005). Behavioral interventions to promote learning in individuals with autism. In F. R. Volkmar, R. Paul, A. Klin, & D. Cohen (Eds.), *Handbook of autism and pervasive developmental disorders: Assessment, interventions, and policy* (p. 882–896). Wiley. https://doi.org/10.1002/9780470939352.ch8

Schultz, T. R., Able, H., Sreckovic, M. A. & White, T. (2016). Parent-teacher collaboration: Teacher perceptions of what is needed to support students with ASD in the inclusive classroom. *Education and Training in Autism and Developmental Disabilities, 51*(4), 344-354.

Schutte, J. (2019). *Major depressive disorder in elementary school aged children: A training program for teachers.* University of Hartford.

Schwichtenberg, A. J., Kellerman, A. M., Young, G. S., Miller, M. & Ozonoff, S. (2019). Mothers of children with autism spectrum disorders: Play behaviors with infant siblings and social responsiveness. *Autism, 23*(4), 821–833.

Sciarra, D. T. & Ponterotto, J. G. (1998). Adolescent motherhood among low-income urban Hispanics: Familial considerations of mother–daughter dyads. *Qualitative Health Research, 8*(6), 751–763. https://doi.org/10.1177/104973239800800603

Sciberras, E., Mulraney, M., Silva, D. & Coghill, D. (2017). Prenatal risk factors and the etiology of ADHD: Review of existing evidence. *Current Psychiatry Reports, 19*(1). https://doi.org/10.1007/s11920-017-0753-2.

Scott-Goodwin, A. C., Puerto, M., & Moreno, I. (2016). Toxic effects of prenatal exposure to alcohol, tobacco and other drugs. *Reproductive Toxicology, 61,* 120–130.

Seigle, E., Walsh, N. & Weber, J. (2014). *Core principles for reducing recidivism and improving other outcomes for youth in the juvenile justice system.* New York: Council of State Governments Justice Center. https://www.njjn.org/uploads/digital-library/CSG_Core-Principles-for-Reducing-Recidivism-Improving-Outcomes-for-Youth-in-the-JJ-System_2014.pdf

Seldin, M. & Yanez, C. (2019). *Student reports of bullying: Results from the 2017 school crime supplement to the national crime victimization survey.* NCES 2019-054. National Center for Education Statistics.

Seligman, M. E. (1974). Depression and learned helplessness. In R. J. Friedman, M. M. Katz, R. J. Friedman, & M. M. Katz (Eds.), *The psychology of depression: Contemporary theory and research.* Wiley. 228-238.

Sellman, E. (2011). Peer mediation services for conflict resolution in schools: What transformations in activity characterise successful implementation? *British Educational Research Journal, 37*(1), 45-60.

Semple, R. J., Droutman, V., & Reid, B. A. (2017). Mindfulness goes to school: Things learned (so far) from research and real-world experiences. *Psychology in the schools, 54*(1), 29–52. https://doi.org/10.1002/pits.21981

Semrud-Clikeman, M., Walkowiak, J., Wilkinson, A. & Christopher, G. (2010). Direct and indirect measures of social perception, behavior, and emotional functioning in children with Asperger's disorder, nonverbal learning disability, or ADHD. *Journal of Abnormal Child Psychology, 38,* 509–519. https://doi.org/10.1007/s10802-009-9380-7.

Sexton, T. L. (2017). Functional family therapy. In M. Bennnedetto-Neitz (Ed.), *The encyclopedia of juvenile delinquency and justice.* Wiley. https://doi.org/10.1002/9781118524275.ejdj0073

Sexton, T. L. (2019). Functional family therapy: An evidence-based, family-focused, and systemic approach for working with adolescents and their families. In B. H. Fiese, M. Celano, K. Deater-Deckard, E. N. Jouriles, & M. A.

Whisman (Eds.), *APA handbook of contemporary family psychology: Family therapy and training* (pp. 171–188). American Psychological Association. https://doi.org/10.1037/0000101-011

Shader, T. M., & Beauchaine, T. P. (2020). Emotion dysregulation and externalizing spectrum disorders. In T.P. Beauchaine & S.E. Crowell (Eds.), *The Oxford handbook of emotion dysregulation* (pp. 237-248). Oxford.

Shaffer, D., Fisher, P., Lucas, C. P., Dulcan, M. K., & Schwab-Stone, M. E. (2000). NIMH Diagnostic Interview Schedule for Children Version IV (NIMH DISC-IV): Description, differences from previous versions, and reliability of some common diagnoses. *Journal of the American Academy of Child & Adolescent Psychiatry, 39*(1), 28–38. https://doi.org/10.1097/00004583-200001000-00014

Shannon, C. L., & Klausner, J. D. (2018). The growing epidemic of sexually transmitted infections in adolescents: A neglected population. *Current Opinion in Pediatrics, 30*(1), 137-143.

Shaw, W. (2019). Inhibition of dopamine conversion to norepinephrine by clostridia metabolites appears to be a (the) major cause of autism, schizophrenia, and other neuropsychiatric disorders. *Integrative Medicine for Mental Health.* https://www.immh.org/article-source

Sherburne, M. (2021). *Teen use of illicit drugs decreased in 2021, as the covid pandemic continued.* https://news.umich.edu/teen-use-of-illicit-drugs-decreased-in-2021-as-the-covid-19-pandemic-continued/

Sherrill, J. T., & Kovacs, M. (2000). Interview Schedule for Children and Adolescents (ISCA). *Journal of the American Academy of Child & Adolescent Psychiatry, 39*(1), 67–75. https://doi.org/10.1097/00004583-200001000-00018

Shore, S. & Rastelli, L. G. (2006). *Understanding autism for dummies.* Wiley.

Shute, J. (2013). Family support as a gang reduction measure. *Children & Society, 27*(1), 48-59.

Sigra, S., Hesselmark, E. & Bejerot, S. (2018). Treatment of PANDAS and PANS: A systematic review. *Neuroscience & Biobehavioral Reviews, 86,* 51–65.

Sigurvinsdóttir, A. L., Jensínudóttir, K. B., Baldvinsdóttir, K. D., Smárason, O. & Skarphedinsson, G. (2020). Effectiveness of cognitive behavioral therapy (CBT) for child and adolescent anxiety disorders across different CBT modalities and comparisons: A systematic review and meta-analysis. *Nordic Journal of Psychiatry, 74*(3), 168–180.

Sijtsema, J. J. & Garofalo, C. (2019). Social development in adolescence: Youth delinquency. In S. Hupp & J.D. Jewell (Eds.) *The encyclopedia of child and adolescent development.* Wiley online library. https://doi.org/10.1002/9781119171492.wecad423

Silove, D., Manicavasagar, V. & Pini, S. (2016). Can separation anxiety disorder escape its attachment to childhood? *World Psychiatry, 15*(2), 113-115.

Silver, R. C. (2021). *Speaking of Psychology: Twenty years after 9/11, what have we learned about collective trauma?* American Psychological Association. https://www.apa.org/news/podcasts/speaking-of-psychology/9-11-twenty-years

Silverman, W. K. & Dick-Niederhauser, A. (2004). Separation anxiety disorder. In T. L. Morris & J. S. March (Eds.) *Anxiety disorders in children and adolescents* (2nd ed., pp. 164–188). Guilford Press.

Silverman, W. K. & Moreno, J. (2005). Specific phobia. *Child and Adolescent Psychiatric Clinics of North America, 14*(4), 819–843. https://doi.org/10.1016/j.chc.2005.05.004

Simpson, J. A., Collins, W. A., Tran, S. & Haydon, K. C. (2007). Attachment and the experience and expression of emotions in romantic relationships: A developmental perspective. *Journal of Personality and Social Psychology, 92*(2), 355–367. https://doi.org/10.1037/0022-3514.92.2.355

Sitarenios, G. & Kovacs, M. (1999). Use of the children's depression inventory. In M. E. Maruish (Ed.), *The use of psychological testing for treatment planning and outcomes assessment* (2nd ed., pp. 267–298). Lawrence Erlbaum.

Skiba, R. & Peterson, R. (1999). The dark side of zero tolerance: Can punishment lead to safe schools? *Phi Delta Kappan*, 80, 372–376, 381–382.

Skiba, R. & Peterson, R. (2000). School discipline at the crossroads: From zero tolerance to early response. *Exceptional Children*, 66, 335–347.

Skinner, B. F. (1969). *The technology of teaching.* Wiley.

Slade, A. (2008). The implications of attachment theory and research for adult psychotherapy: Research and clinical perspectives. In J. Cassidy & P. R. Shaver (Eds.), *Handbook of attachment: Theory, research, and clinical applications* (2nd ed., pp. 762–782). Guilford.

Smith, C. R., Katsiyannis, A. & Ryan, J. B. (2011). Challenges of serving students with emotional and behavioral disorders: Legal and policy considerations. *Behavioral Disorders, 36*(3), 185-194.

Smith, D. D. (2007). *Introduction to special education: Making a difference.* Pearson.

Smith, K. E., Crosby, R. D., Wonderlich, S. A., Forbush, K. T., Mason, T. B. & Moessner, M. (2018). Network analysis: An innovative framework for understanding eating disorder psychopathology. *International Journal of Eating Disorders, 51*(3), 214–222.

Smith, L. D. (2015). *Male gender disparity gap: Does gender impact education.* [Unpublished Certificate of Advanced Study Thesis], Sacred Heart University, Fairfield, CT. http://digitalcommons.sacredheart.edu/edl/7

Smith, T. E. C., Polloway, E. A., Patton, J. R. & Dowdy, C. A. (2006). *Teaching students with special needs in inclusive settings* (5th ed.). Allyn & Bacon.

Smith-Battle, L., Loman, D. G. & Schneider, J. K. (2017). An umbrella review of meta-analyses of interventions to improve maternal outcomes for teen mothers. *Journal of Adolescence, 59*, 97–111.

Smothers, R. (2000). When school rules cheat kids. *Redbook, 195*(3), 88–91.

Sood, E. D. & Kendall, P. C. (2007). Assessing anxious self-talk in youth: The negative affectivity self-statement questionnaire - anxiety scale. *Cognitive Therapy and Research, 31*(5), 603–618. https://doi.org/10.1007/s10608-006-9043-8

Sosnowy, C., Silverman, C., Shattuck, P. & Garfield, T. (2019). Setbacks and successes: How young adults on the autism spectrum seek friendship. *Autism in Adulthood, 1*(1), 44–51.

Speaker, K. M. & Petersen, G. J. (2000). School violence and adolescent suicide: Strategies for effective intervention. *Educational Review*, 52(1), 65–73.

Spence, S. H. (1998). A measure of anxiety symptoms among children. *Behaviour Research and Therapy, 36*(5), 545–566.

Spence, S. H., Barrett, P. M. & Turner, C. M. (2003). Psychometric properties of the Spence Children's Anxiety Scale with young adolescents. *Journal of Anxiety Disorders, 17*(6), 605–625. https://doi.org/10.1016/S0887-6185(02)00236-0

Spence, S. H., Zubrick, S. R. & Lawrence, D. (2018). A profile of social, separation and generalized anxiety disorders in an Australian nationally representative sample of children and adolescents: Prevalence, comorbidity and correlates. *Australian & New Zealand Journal of Psychiatry, 52*(5), 446–460.

Spergel, I. A. 1995. *The youth gang problem.* Oxford University Press.

Spitzer, R., Endicott, J., Loth, J., McDonald-Scott, P. & Wasek, P. (1998). *Kiddie schedule for affective disorders and schizophrenia.* Department of Research Assessment and Training.

Spivak, H. & Prothrow-Stith, D. (2001). The need to address bullying—An important component of violence prevention. *JAMA: Journal of the American Medical Association, 285*(16), 2131–2132. https://doi.org/10.1001/jama.285.16.2131

Spruit, A., Goos, L., Weenink, N., Rodenburg, R., Niemeyer, H., Stams, G. J. & Colonnesi, C. (2020). The relation between attachment and depression in children and adolescents: A multilevel meta-analysis. *Clinical Child and Family Psychology Review, 23*(1), 54–69.

Sroufe, L. A., Egeland, B., Carlson, E. A. & Collins, W. A. (2005). Attachment and development: A prospective, longitudinal study from birth to adulthood. *Attachment and Human Development, 7(4),* 349-367. https://doi.org/10.1080/14616730500365928

Stahmer, A. C. (1995). Teaching symbolic play skills to children with autism using pivotal response training. *Journal of Autism and Developmental Disorders, 25*(2), 123-141.

Stice, E., Telch, C. F. & Rizvi, S. L. (2000). Development and validation of the Eating Disorder Diagnostic Scale: A brief self-report measure of anorexia, bulimia, and binge-eating disorder. *Psychological Assessment, 12*(2), 123-131.

Stigler, K. A., McDonald, B. C., Anand, A., Saykin, A. J. & McDougle, C. J. (2011). Structural and functional magnetic resonance imaging of autism spectrum disorders. *Brain Research, 1380,* 146–161. https://doi.org/10.1016/j.brainres.2010.11.076

Stinson, R. D. (2010). Hooking up in young adulthood: A review of factors influencing the sexual behavior of college students. *Journal of College Student Psychotherapy, 24*(2), 98-115.

Stohmann, N., Menke, K. & Silva, K. (2020). *Literature review: Teacher recruitment and retention.* https://media.gradebuddy.com/documents/1596835/9ce5e932-acc2-4ce3-8be0-fd9acf0727d1.pdf

Strandberg, A., Skoglund, C., Gripenberg, J. & Kvillemo, P. (2019). Alcohol and illicit drug consumption and the association with risky sexual behaviour among Swedish youths visiting youth health clinics. *Nordic Studies on Alcohol and Drugs, 36*(5), 442–459.

Strawn, J. R., Dobson, E. T., Ramesh, A. B., Berger, S. A. & Rynn, M. A. (2019). Pharmacologic treatment of pediatric anxiety disorders. In S. N. Compton, M. A. Villabo & H. Kristensen (Eds.) *Pediatric anxiety disorders* (pp. 359–384). Elsevier.

Strawn, J. R., Mills, J. A., Sauley, B. A. & Welge, J. A. (2018). The impact of antidepressant dose and class on treatment response in pediatric anxiety disorders: A meta-analysis. *Journal of the American Academy of Child & Adolescent Psychiatry, 57*(4), 235–244.

Streeck-Fischer, A. (2020). Complex and sequential traumatic stress disorders. In A. Hamburger, C. Hancheva & V.D. Volkan (Eds.), *Social trauma–An interdisciplinary textbook* (pp. 155–162). Springer.

Striegel-Moore, R. H. & Bulik, C. M. (2007). Risk factors for eating disorders. *American Psychologist, 62*(3), 181-198.

Stromeyer S. L., Lochman J. E., Kassing F. & Romero D.E. (2020). Cognitive behavioral therapy with angry and aggressive youth: The coping power program. In R. Friedberg & B. Nakamura (Eds), *Cognitive behavioral therapy in youth: Tradition and innovation. Neuromethods, 156.* https://doi.org/10.1007/978-1-0716-0700-8_6

Sturm, A., Kuhfeld, M., Kasari, C. & McCracken, J. T. (2017). Development and validation of an item response theory-based Social Responsiveness Scale short form. *Journal of Child Psychology and Psychiatry, 58*(9), 1053–1061.

Substance Abuse and Mental Health Services Administration. (2020). *Understanding child trauma.* https://www.samhsa.gov/child-trauma/understanding-child-trauma

Substance Abuse and Mental Health Services Administration. (2019). *2018 national survey of drug use and mental health annual national report.* https://www.samhsa.gov/data/report/2018-nsduh-annual-national-report

Sugai, G., & Horner, R. H. (Eds.). (2016). *Functional behavioral assessment: A special issue of exceptionality.* Routledge.

Sutherland-Stolting, A., Liao, B., Kraus, K., Campbell, C., & Goddard, A. W. (2020). Pathogenesis of Generalized Anxiety Disorder. In N. M. Simon, E. Hollander, B. O. Rothbaum & D. J. Stein (Eds.) *The American Psychiatric Association publishing textbook of anxiety, trauma, and OCD-related disorders* (pp. 181-196). American Psychiatric Association.

Svaldi, J., Schmitz, F., Baur, J., Hartmann, A. S., Legenbauer, T., Thaler, C., von Wietersheim, J., de Zwaan, M. & Tuschen-Caffier, B. (2019). Efficacy of psychotherapies and pharmacotherapies for bulimia nervosa. *Psychological Medicine, 49*(6), 898–910.

Swart, S., Wildschut, M., Draijer, N., Langeland, W. & Smit, J. H. (2020). Dissociative subtype of posttraumatic stress disorder or PTSD with comorbid dissociative disorders: Comparative evaluation of clinical profiles. *Psychological Trauma: Theory, Research, Practice, and Policy, 12*(1), 38–45. https://doi.org/10.1037/tra0000474

Szentiványi, D. & Balázs, J. (2018). Quality of life in children and adolescents with symptoms or diagnosis of conduct disorder or oppositional defiant disorder. *Mental Health & Prevention, 10,* 1-8.

Szucs, L. E., Lowry, R., Fasula, A. M., Pampati, S., Copen, C. E., Hussaini, K. S., Kachur, R. E., Koumans, E. H. & Steiner, R. J. (2020). Condom and contraceptive use among sexually active high schools students—Youth risk behavior survey, United States, 2019. *MMWR Supplements, 69*(1), 11-18.

Szymanski, M. L. & Zolotor, A. (2001). Attention-deficit/hyperactivity disorder: Management. *American Family Physician, 64*(8), 1355–1362.

Tak, G. S., Maheshwari, S. K., & Kaur, R. (2016). Effectiveness of psycho-education regarding eating disorders on knowledge among adolescent girls. *International Journal of Psychiatric Nursing, 2*(2), 41–45.

Tams, S. T. (2017). *Modeling longitudinal associations between parenting practices and child externalizing behavior from pre-school to adolescence* [Unpublished Doctoral Dissertation]. Ohio University.

Tasca, G. A. (2019). Attachment and eating disorders: A research update. *Current Opinion in Psychology, 25*, 59–64.

Taubner, S., Gablonski, T. C. & Fonagy, P. (2019). Conduct disorder. In A. Bateman & P. Fonagy (Eds.) *Handbook of mentalizing in mental health practice* (2nd ed., pp. 301-322). American Psychiatric Association.

Taylor, M. J., Nanney, J. T., Welch, D. Z. & Wamser-Nanney, R. A. (2016). The impact of sports participation on female gang involvement and delinquency. *Journal of Sport Behavior, 39*(3), 317-343.

Tedeschi, F. K. & Billick, S. B. (2017). Pediatric PTSD: Clinical, forensic, and diagnostic understanding. *Journal of the American Academy of Psychiatry and the Law, 45*(2), 161–169.

Teplin, L. A., Abram, K. M., McClelland, Washburn, J., & Pikus, A. K. (2005). Detecting mental disorder in juvenile detainees: Who receives services. *American Journal of Public Health, 95*, 1773–1780.

Terrasi, S & de Galarce, P. C. (2017). Trauma and learning in America's classrooms. *Phi Delta Kappan, 98*(6), 35-41. https://doi.org/10.1177/003172 1717696476

Thapar, A., Cooper, M., Eyre, O. & Langley, K. (2013). Practitioner review: What have we learnt about the causes of ADHD? *Journal of Child Psychology & Psychiatry, 54*(1), 3–16. https://doi.org/10.1111/j.1469-7610.2012.02611.x

Thapar, A. & Rutter, M. (2020). Genetic advances in autism. *Journal of Autism and Developmental Disorders*, 1–12. https://doi.org/10.1007/s10803-020-04685-z

Thapliyal, P., Mitchison, D., Miller, C., Bowden, J., Alejandro González-Chica, D., Stocks, N., Touyz, S. & Hay, P. (2018). Comparison of mental health treatment status and use of antidepressants in men and women with eating disorders. *Eating Disorders, 26*(3), 248–262.

The Council for Exceptional Children. (1992). *Children with ADD: A shared responsibility. Based on a report of the Council for Exceptional Children's Task Force on Children with attention deficit disorder.* Order No. P385.

The JED Foundation. (n.d.). *Understanding eating disorders.* https://jed foundation.org/resource/understanding-eating-disorders/

Thiemann, K. S. & Goldstein, H. (2001). Social stories, written text cues, and video feedback: Effects on social communication of children with autism. *Journal of Applied Behavior Analysis, 34*(4), 425-446.

Thijssen, J., Vink, G., Muris, P. & de Ruiter, C. (2017). The effectiveness of parent management training—Oregon model in clinically referred children with externalizing behavior problems in The Netherlands. *Child Psychiatry & Human Development, 48*(1), 136–150.

Thirumanickam, A., Raghavendra, P., McMillan, J. M. & van Steenbrugge, W. (2018). Effectiveness of video-based modelling to facilitate conversational turn taking of adolescents with autism spectrum disorder who use AAC. *Augmentative and Alternative Communication, 34*(4), 311–322.

Thomas, M. L. (2010). *Establishing street smart: A skills mastery and resistance training for adolescents: A grant proposal.* California State University, Long Beach.

Thomas, M. S., Crosby, S. & Vanderhaar, J. (2019). Trauma-informed practices in schools across two decades: An interdisciplinary review of research. *Reivw of Research in Education, 43*(1), pp. 442-452. https://doi.org/10.3102/0091732X18821123

Thompson, K. C., Stoll, K. A., Paz, C., & Wright, S. (2017). Oppositional Defiant Disorder. In S. Goldstein & M. Devries (Eds.), *Handbook of DSM-5 disorders in children and adolescents* (pp. 483–497). Springer.

Thornton, L. C. & Frick, P. J. (2018). Aggression and conduct disorders. In J. L. Matson (Ed.) *Handbook of childhood psychopathology and developmental disabilities assessment* (pp. 245–261). Springer.

Tiede, G., & Walton, K. M. (2019). Meta-analysis of naturalistic developmental behavioral interventions for young children with autism spectrum disorder. *Autism: The International Journal of Research and Practice, 23*(8), 2080–2095. https://doi.org/10.1177/1362361319836371

Tomba, E., Tecuta, L., Crocetti, E., Squarcio, F. & Tomei, G. (2019). Residual eating disorder symptoms and clinical features in remitted and recovered eating disorder patients: A systematic review with meta-analysis. *International Journal of Eating Disorders, 52*(7), 759–776.

Topor, D. R., Keane, S. P., Shelton, T. L. & Calkins, S. D. (2010). Parent involvement and student academic performance: A multiple mediational analysis. *Journal of Prevention & Intervention in The Community, 38*(3), 183-197.

Tóthová, l. (2019). Eating disorders in adolescence: social causes and consequences. *Ad Alta: Journal of Interdisciplinary Research, 9*(2), 354-357.

Treatment for Adolescents with Depression Study (TADS) Team. (2004). Fluoxetine, cognitive-behavioral therapy, and their combination for adolescents with depression: Treatment for Adolescents with Depression Study (TADS) randomized controlled trial. *Jama, 292*(7), 807-820.

Trembath, D., Sutherland, R., Caithness, T., Dissanayake, C., Eapen, V., Fordyce, K., Frost, G., Iacono, T., Mahler, N. & Masi, A. (2020). Clinician proposed predictors of spoken language outcomes for minimally verbal children with autism spectrum disorder. *Journal of Autism and Developmental Disorders, 51(2),* 564-575.

Twigg, S. (2020). Clinical event debriefing: A review of approaches and objectives. *Current Opinion in Pediatrics, 32*(3), 337–342.

University of California - Davis - Health System. (2010). ADHD, conduct disorder and smoking most strongly related to dropping out of high school. *ScienceDaily.* www.sciencedaily.com/releases/2010/07/100727142413.htm

Ünlü, E., Vuran, S. & Diken, I. H. (2018). Effectiveness of discrete trial training program for parents of children with autism spectrum disorder. *International Journal of Progressive Education, 14*(3), 12–31.

U.S. Department of Education. (2004). *Twenty-sixth annual report to Congress on implementation of the Individuals with Disabilities Education Act (IDEA).* Author.

U.S. Department of Education. (2015). *Every child succeeds act. Dec. 10, 2015.* https://www.ed.gov/essa?src=rn

U.S. Department of Education. (2017). *39th annual report to congress on the implementation of the individuals with disabilities education act.* https://www2.ed.gov/about/reports/annual/osep/2017/parts-b-c/39th-arc-for-idea.pdf.

U.S. Departments of Education and Justice (2020). *Indicators of school crime and safety,* 2020. https://nces.ed.gov/programs/crimeindicators/2020.

U.S. Department of Education Regional Education Laboratory. (n.d.). *Social emotional learning research alliance.* https://ies.ed.gov/ncee/edlabs/regions/northeast/SocialEmotional

U.S. Department of Health, Education, and Welfare, Office for Civil Rights (1978). *Section 504 of the Rehabilitation act of 1973: Fact sheet: Handicapped persons rights under federal law.* Author.

Utržan, D. S., Piehler, T. F., Dishion, T. J., Lochman, J. E. & Matthys, W. (2018). The role of deviant peers in oppositional defiant disorder and conduct disorder. In J. E. Lochman & W. Matthys (Eds.) *The Wiley handbook of disruptive and impulse-control disorders* (pp. 339-351). Wiley.

Valente, S. M. (2001). Treating attention deficit hyperactivity disorder. *Nurse Practitioner, 26*(9), 14–29.

Valiente-Gómez, A., Moreno-Alcázar, A., Treen, D., Cedrón, C., Colom, F., Perez, V. & Amann, B. L. (2017). EMDR beyond PTSD: A systematic literature review. *Frontiers in Psychology, 8,* Article 1668. https://doi.org/10.3389/fpsyg.2017.01668

Valla, J. P., Bergeron, L. & Smolla, N. (2000). The Dominic-R: A pictorial interview for 6- to 11-year-old children. *Journal of the American Academy of Child & Adolescent Psychiatry, 39*(1), 85–93. https://doi.org/10.1097/00004583-200001000-00020

van Bockstaele, B., van der Molen, M. J., van Nieuwenhuijzen, M. & Salemink, E. (2020). Modification of hostile attribution bias reduces self-reported reactive aggressive behavior in adolescents. *Journal of Experimental Child Psychology, 194.* Article 104811. https://doi.org/10.1016/j.jecp.2020.104811

van der Merwe, C., Jahanshad, N., Cheung, J. W., Mufford, M., Groenewold, N. A., Koen, N., Ramesar, R., Dalvie, S., ENIGMA Consortium PGC-PTSD, E. C. & Knowles, J. A. (2019). Concordance of genetic variation that increases risk for anxiety disorders and posttraumatic stress disorders and that influences their underlying neurocircuitry. *Journal of Affective Disorders, 245,* 885–896.

van der Velden, P. G., Contino, C., Marchand, M., Das, M. & Schut, H. (2020). Does pre-event lack of emotional support increase the risk of post-event PTSD, anxiety, depression symptoms and lack of support? A comparative population-based study among victims of threat and violence. *Journal of*

Anxiety Disorders, 75. Article 102269. https://doi.org/10.1016/j.janxdis.2020.102269

van der Zee, E. & Derksen, J. J. (2020). Reconsidering empathy deficits in children and adolescents with autism. *Journal of Developmental and Physical Disabilities, 32*(1), 23–39.

van Gelder, J. L., Averdijk, M., Ribeaud, D. & Eisner, M. (2018). Punitive parenting and delinquency: The mediating role of short-term mindsets. *The British Journal of Criminology, 58*(3), 644–666.

van Hoeken, D. & Hoek, H. W. (2020). Review of the burden of eating disorders: mortality, disability, costs, quality of life, and family burden. *Current Opinion in Psychiatry, 33*(6), 521–527. https://doi.org/10.1097/YCO.0000000000000641

van Meter, A., Moreira, A. L. R. & Youngstrom, E. (2019). Updated meta-analysis of epidemiologic studies of pediatric bipolar disorder. *The Journal of Clinical Psychiatry, 80*(3). doi:10.4088/JCP.18r12180

Van Tu, P., Ngoc, T. U., Nguyen, P. L., Thuong, N. H., Van Tuan, N., Van Hung, N., Nga, V. T., Van Quan, T. & Chu, D. T. (2020). The impact of sexual harassment on obesity in female adolescents: An update and perspective to control. *Diabetes & Metabolic Syndrome: Clinical Research & Reviews, 14(6),* 1931-1939.

Varigonda, A. L., Jakubovski, E. & Bloch, M. H. (2016). Systematic review and meta-analysis: Early treatment responses of selective serotonin reuptake inhibitors and clomipramine in pediatric obsessive-compulsive disorder. *Journal of the American Academy of Child & Adolescent Psychiatry, 55*(10), 851–859.

Vega, V. (2015). *SEL Programs: A Review of Evidenced Based Programs.* https://www.edutopia.org/sel-research-evidence-based-programs

Veliz, P. & Shakib, S. (2012). Interscholastic sports participation and school-based delinquency: Does participation in sport foster a positive high school environment? *Sociological Spectrum, 32*(6), 558-580.

Vernon, T. (2017). Pivotal response treatment: Empirically supported strategies. In J.B. Leaf (Ed.), *Handbook of Social Skills and Autism Spectrum Disorder: Assessment, Curricula, and Intervention* (pp.187-196). Springer.

Villarreal, B. (2004, February 16). Schools will continue to be safe with everyone's help. https://www.albertleatribune.com/2004/column-schools-will-continue-to-be-safe-with-everyones-help/

Vygotsky, L. S. (1978). *Mind in society: The development of higher psychological processes.* Harvard University Press.

Wade, T. D. & Bulik, C. M. (2018). Genetic influences on eating disorders. In W. S. Agras & A. Robinson (Eds.), *Oxford Library of Psychology. The Oxford Handbook of Eating Disorders* (pp. 80–105). Oxford University Press.

Walker, B., & Hoyt, L. (2015). From conflict to competence. *Reclaiming Children & Youth, 24*(1), 43–48.

Walker, H. M. (1995). *The acting-out child: Coping with classroom disruption* (2nd ed.). Sopris West.

Walker, H. M., Ramsey, E. & Gresham, F. M. (2004). *Antisocial behavior in school: Strategies and best practices* (2nd ed.). Wadsworth.

Walker, H. M., Severson, H. H. & Feil, E. G. (2014). *Systematic screening for behavior disorders (SSBD) universal screening 29, for PreK-9: Administrator's guide.* Pacific Northwest Publishing.

Walker, T. M., Robertson, E. L., Frick, P. J., Ray, J. V., Thornton, L. C., Myers, T. D. W., Steinberg, L. & Cauffman, E. (2020). Relationships among callous-unemotional traits, future orientation, optimism, and self-esteem in justice-involved adolescents. *Journal of Child and Family Studies, 29,* 2434-2442. https://doi.org/10.1007/s10826-020-01770-w

Walkup, J. T. (2017). Antidepressant efficacy for depression in children and adolescents: Industry-and NIMH-funded studies. *American Journal of Psychiatry, 174*(5), 430–437.

Wallach, L.B. (1994, June). *Violence and young children's development.* ED369578 PS022492. http://resilnet.uiuc.edu/library/wallac94.html

Waller, G. & Raykos, B. (2019). Behavioral interventions in the treatment of eating disorders. *Psychiatric Clinics, 42*(2), 181–191.

Wang, C., Geng, H., Liu, W. & Zhang, G. (2017). Prenatal, perinatal, and postnatal factors associated with autism: A meta-analysis. *Medicine, 96(18),* Article 6696. doi:10.1097/MD.0000000000006696

Warren, C. S. & Akoury, L. M. (2020). Emphasizing the "cultural" in sociocultural: A systematic review of research on thin-ideal internalization, acculturation, and eating pathology in US ethnic minorities. *Psychology Research and Behavior Management, 13,* 319-330.

Washburn, J. J., West, A. E. & Heil, J. A. (2011). Treatment of pediatric bipolar disorder: A review. *Minerva Psichiatrica, 52*(1), 21-35.

Waszczuk, M. A., Waaktaar, T., Eley, T. C. & Torgersen, S. (2019). Etiological influences on continuity and co-occurrence of eating disorders symptoms across adolescence and emerging adulthood. *International Journal of Eating Disorders, 52*(5), 554–563.

Watkins, L. E., Sprang, K. R. & Rothbaum, B. O. (2018). Treating PTSD: A review of evidence-based psychotherapy interventions. *Frontiers in Behavioral Neuroscience, 12.* Article 258. https://doi.org/10.3389/fnbeh.2018.00258

Watson, J. B. & Rayner, R. (1920). Conditioned emotional reactions. *Journal of Experimental Psychology, 3,* 1–14.

Weathers, F. W., Newman, E., Blake, D. D., Nagy, L. M., Schnurr, P. P., Kaloupek, D. G., & Keane, T. M. (2004). *Clinician-administered PTSD Scale:(CAPS).* Western Psychological Services.

Webb, L., Perry-Parrish, C., Ellen, J. & Sibinga, E. (2018). Mindfulness instruction for HIV-infected youth: A randomized controlled trial. *AIDS Care, 30*(6), 688–695.

Webster-Stratton, C. & Bywater, T. (2019). The Incredible Years® series: An internationally evidenced multimodal approach to enhancing child outcomes. In B. H. Fiese, M. Celano, K. Deater-Deckard, E. N. Jouriles, & M. A. Whisman (Eds.), APA *handbook of contemporary family psychology: Family therapy and training* (p. 343–359). American Psychological Association. https://doi.org/10.1037/0000101-021

Webster-Stratton, C. & Reid, M. J. (2018). The Incredible Years parents, teachers, and children training series: A multifaceted treatment approach for young children with conduct problems. In J. R. Weisz & A. E. Kazdin (Eds.), *Evidence-based psychotherapies for children and adolescents* (3rd ed., pp. 122–141). Guilford.

Weinfield, N. S., Sroufe, L. A., Egeland, B. & Carlson, E. (2008). Individual differences in infant-caregiver attachment: Conceptual and empirical aspects of security. In J. Cassidy & P. R. Shaver (Eds.), *Handbook of attachment: Theory, research, and clinical applications.* (2nd ed., pp. 78–101). Guilford.

Weissman, R. S. (2019). The role of sociocultural factors in the etiology of eating disorders. *Psychiatric Clinics, 42*(1), 121–144.

Weisz, J. R., Southam-Gerow, M. A., Gordis, E. B. & Connor-Smith, J. (2003). Primary and secondary control enhancement training for youth depression: Applying the deployment-focused model of treatment development and testing. In A. E. Kazdin & J. R. Weisz (Eds.), *Evidence-based psychotherapies for children and adolescents.* (pp. 165–182). Guilford.

Weitkamp, K., Daniels, J. K., Baumeister-Duru, A., Wulf, A., Romer, G. & Wiegand-Grefe, S. (2018). Effectiveness trial of psychoanalytic psychotherapy for children and adolescents with severe anxiety symptoms in a naturalistic treatment setting. *British Journal of Psychotherapy, 34*(2), 300–318.

Weller, E. B., Weller, R. A., Fristad, M. A., Rooney, M. T., & Schecter, J. (2000). Children's Interview for Psychiatric Syndromes (ChIPS). *Journal of the American Academy of Child & Adolescent Psychiatry, 39*(1), 76–84. https://doi.org/10.1097/00004583-200001000-00019

Welner, Z., Reich, W., Herjanic, B. & Jung, K. G. (1987). Reliability, validity, and parent-child agreement studies of the Diagnostic Interview for Children and Adolescents (DICA). *Journal of the American Academy of Child & Adolescent Psychiatry, 26(5),* 649–653.

Welsh, J. L., Schmidt, F., McKinnon, L., Chattha, H. K. & Meyers, J. R. (2008). A comparative study of adolescent risk assessment instruments: Predictive and incremental validity. *Assessment, 15*(1), 104-115.

Werner-Seidler, A., Perry, Y., Calear, A. L., Newby, J. M. & Christensen, H. (2017). School-based depression and anxiety prevention programs for young people: A systematic review and meta-analysis. *Clinical Psychology Review, 51,* 30–47.

Werts, M. G., Calatta, R. A. & Tompkins, J. R. (2007). *Fundamentals of special education: What every teacher needs to* know (3rd ed.). Pearson.

Wessel, L. (2017). *Vaccine myths.* American Association for the Advancement of Science.

West, K. B., Wilbanks, J. & Suveg, C. (2020). Exposure therapy for separation anxiety disorder. In T. S. Peris, E. A. Storch, & J. F. McGuire (Eds.), *Exposure therapy for children with anxiety and OCD* (pp. 143–163). Elsevier.

Weston, R., Hodges, A. & Davis, T. N. (2018). Differential reinforcement of other behaviors to treat challenging behaviors among children with autism: A systematic and quality review. *Behavior Modification, 42*(4), 584–609.

Weyandt, L. L., Oster, D. R., Marraccini, M. E., Gudmundsdottir, B. G., Munro, B. A., Rathkey, E. S. & McCallum, A. (2016). Prescription stimulant medication misuse: Where are we and where do we go from here? *Experimental and clinical psychopharmacology, 24*(5), 400–414. https://doi.org/10.1037/pha0000093

Whalen, C. & Schreibman, L. (2003). Joint attention training for children with autism using behavior modification procedures. *Journal of Child Psychology and Psychiatry, 44*(3), 456-468.

Wickelgren, I. (2012). The education of character. *Scientific American Mind, 23*(4), 48–58. http://www.jstor.org/stable/24942249

Wicks-Nelson, R. & Israel, A. C. (2006*). Behavior disorders of childhood* (6th ed.). Prentice Hall.

Wigal, S.B. (2009). Efficacy and safety limitations of attention-deficit hyperactivity disorder pharmacotherapy in children and adults. *CNS Drugs 23,* 21–31. https://doi.org/10.2165/00023210-200923000-00004.

Wigham, S., Rodgers, J., Berney, T., Le Couteur, A., Ingham, B. & Parr, J. R. (2019). Psychometric properties of questionnaires and diagnostic measures for autism spectrum disorders in adults: A systematic review. *Autism, 23*(2), 287–305.

Wilens, T. E., Adler, L. A., Adams, J., Sgambati, S., Rotrosen, J., Sawtelle, R., Utzinger, L. & Fusillo, S. (2008). Misuse and diversion of stimulants prescribed for ADHD: A systematic review of the literature. *Journal of the American Academy of Child & Adolescent Psychiatry, 47*(1), 21-31.

Williams, N. J., Scott, L. & Aarons, G. A. (2018). Prevalence of serious emotional disturbance among US children: A meta-analysis. *Psychiatric Services, 69*(1), 32-40.

Winarno, S., Muthu, K. S. & Ling, L. S. (2018). Direct problem-based learning (DPBL): A framework for integrating direct instruction and problem-based learning approach. *International Education Studies, 11*(1), 119-126.

Wing, L., Leekam, S. R., Libby, S. J., Gould, J. & Larcombe, M. (2002). The diagnostic interview for social and communication disorders: Background, inter-rater reliability and clinical use. *Journal of Child Psychology and Psychiatry, 43*(3), 307-325.

Winters, K. C., Botzet, A. M., Stinchfield, R., Gonzales-Castaneda, R., Finch, A. J., Piehler, T. F., Ausherbauer, K., Chalmers, K. & Hemze, A. (2018). Adolescent substance abuse treatment: A review of evidence-based research. In C.J. Leukefeld, T.P. Gullota, & M. Staton-Tindall (Eds.), *Adolescent aubstance abuse* (pp. 141–171). Springer.

Witt, J.C., Daly, E. & Noell, G. H. (2000). *Functional assessments: A step-by step guide to solving academic and behavioral problems.* Longmont, CO: Sopris West.

Woerner, J., Ye, F., Hipwell, A. E., Chung, T. & Sartor, C. E. (2020). Relational peer victimization interacts with depression severity to predict the timing of alcohol use initiation in adolescent girls. *Alcoholism: Clinical and Experimental Research, 44*(1), 255–263.

Wolpe, J. (1958). *Psychotherapy by reciprocal inhibition.* Stanford University Press.

Wood, S.F. & Huffman, J.B. (1999). Preventing gang activity and violence in schools. *Contemporary Education, 7*(1), pp. 19-23.

Woodward, L., Taylor, E. & Dowdney, L. (1998). The parenting and family functioning of children with hyperactivity. *Journal of Child Psychology and Psychiatry, 39,* 161–169.

World Health Organization. (2020). *Life skills education school handbook: Prevention of noncommunicable diseases.* https://www.who.int/publications/i/item/9789240005020

World Health Organization. (2022). *Suicide.* https://www.who.int/news-room/fact-sheets/detail/suicide

Xu, J., Liu, R.-J., Fahey, S., Frick, L., Leckman, J., Vaccarino, F., Duman, R. S., Williams, K., Swedo, S. & Pittenger, C. (2020). Antibodies from children with PANDAS bind specifically to striatal cholinergic interneurons and alter their activity. *American Journal of Psychiatry, 178*(1), 48-64

Xu, M., Macrynikola, N., Waseem, M. & Miranda, R. (2020). Racial and ethnic differences in bullying: Review and implications for intervention. *Aggression and Violent Behavior, 50,* 101340. https://doi.org/10.1016/j.avb.2019.101340

Yanez, C. & Seldin, M. (2019). *Student victimization in US schools: Results from the 2017 school crime supplement to the national crime victimization survey.* Statistics in Brief. NCES 2019-064. National Center for Education Statistics.

Yarımkaya, E. & Esentürk, O. K. (2020). Promoting physical activity for children with autism spectrum disorders during coronavirus outbreak: Benefits, strategies, and examples. *International Journal of Developmental Disabilities.* https://doi.org/10.1080/20473869.2020.1756115

Yoder, P., Rogers, S., Estes, A., Warren, Z., Munson, J., Hellemann, G. & McEachin, J. (2020). Interaction of treatment intensity and autism severity on frequency and maturity of spontaneous communication in toddlers with autism spectrum disorder. *Autism Research, 13*(11), 1902–1912.

Young, R. C., Biggs, J. T., Ziegler, V. E. & Meyer, D. A. (1978). A rating scale for mania: Reliability, validity and sensitivity. *The British Journal of Psychiatry, 133*(5), 429–435.

Yu, Y., Chaulagain, A., Pedersen, S. A., Lydersen, S., Leventhal, B. L., Szatmari, P., Aleksic, B., Ozaki, N. & Skokauskas, N. (2020). Pharmacotherapy of restricted/repetitive behavior in autism spectrum disorder: A systematic review and meta-analysis. *BMC Psychiatry, 20*(1), 1–11.

Zagoloff, A. & Bernstein, G. A. (2017). Separation anxiety and panic disorders in children. In S. Goldstein & M. Devries (Eds.), *Handbook of DSM-5 disorders in children and adolescents* (pp. 165–180). Springer.

Zakiei, A., Alikhani, M., Farnia, V., Khkian, Z., Shakeri, J. & Golshani, S. (2017). Attachment style and resiliency in patients with obsessive-compulsive personality disorder. *Korean Journal of Family Medicine, 38*(1), 34-39.

Zander, E., Willfors, C., Berggren, S., Coco, C., Holm, A., Jifält, I., Kosieradzki, R., Linder, J., Nordin, V. & Olafsdottir, K. (2017). The interrater reliability of the autism diagnostic interview-revised (ADI-R) in clinical settings. *Psychopathology, 50*(3), 219–227.

Zaragoza, N. (2002). *Rethinking language arts: Passion and practice.* New York: Routledge Falmer.

Zaragoza, N. (2005). Including families in the teaching and learning process. In J. Kincheloe (Ed.), *Classroom Teaching: An Introduction.* New York: Peter Lang.

Zenner, C., Herrnleben-Kurz, S. & Walach, H. (2014). Mindfulness-based interventions in schools-a systematic review and meta-analysis. *Frontiers in psychology, 5,* 603. https://doi.org/10.3389/fpsyg.2014.00603

Zhang, K., Fan, X., Yuan, J., Yin, J., Su, H., Hashimoto, K. & Wang, G. (2019). Impact of serotonin transporter gene on rTMS augmentation of SSRIs for obsessive compulsive disorder. *Neuropsychiatric Disease and Treatment, 15,* 1771-1779.

Zhang, S. & Joshi, M. (2019). Profile of hyperlexia: Reconciling conflicts through a systematic review and meta-analysis. *Journal of Neurolinguistics, 49,* 1-28. https://doi.org/10.1016/j.jneuroling.2018.08.001

Zhang, S. & Joshi, R. M. (2019). Profile of hyperlexia: Reconciling conflicts through a systematic review and meta-analysis. *Journal of Neurolinguistics, 49,* 1–28.

Zhang, S., Xia, X., Li, S., Shen, L., Liu, J., Zhao, L. & Chen, C. (2019). Using technology-based learning tool to train facial expression recognition and emotion understanding skills of Chinese pre-schoolers with autism spectrum disorder. *International Journal of Developmental Disabilities, 65*(5), 378–386.

Zhao, W. (2017). *Atypical intrinsic functional connectivity of the core face perception system in autism spectrum disorder* [Unpublished Doctoral Dissertation]. San Diego State University.

Ziser, K., Giel, K. E., Resmark, G., Nikendei, C., Friederich, H.-C., Herpertz, S., Rose, M., De Zwaan, M., Von Wietersheim, J. & Zeeck, A. (2018). Contingency contracts for weight gain of patients with anorexia nervosa in inpatient therapy: Practice styles of specialized centers. *Journal of Clinical Medicine, 7*(8). Article 215. https://doi.org/10.3390/jcm7080215

Zisser-Nathenson, A. R., Herschell, A. D. & Eyberg, S. M. (2017). Parent-child interaction therapy and the treatment of disruptive behavior disorders. In J.R. Weisz, & A.E. Kazdin (Eds.) *Evidence-based psychotherapies for children and adolescents* (3rd ed., pp.103–121). Guilford.

Index

A

A Change in the School Approach to Bullying, 438
A Human Rights Approach to Bullying Prevention, 438
A Personal Anecdote, 328
A-B-C record sheet, 66
ABC's of Rational-Emotive-Behavior Therapy, 437
Abstinence-Only Programs, 414
Accidental Pregnancy, 409
Accommodations, 72
Achenbach System of Empirically Based Assessment, 60
acquired immune deficiency syndrome (AIDS)., 405
active listening, 478
Adaptations, 72
ADD Scale for Adolescents, 143
Adderall, 135, 369
ADHD, Combined Type, 127
ADHD, Predominantly Hyperactive-Impulsive Type, 127
ADHD, Predominantly Inattentive Type, 127
ADHD-IV Rating Scale, 140
Adjusted Yearly Progress (AYP), 471
Adolescent Coping with Depression (CWD-A), 318
Adolescent Suicide, 328
Affective Development, 350
Ainsworth, 7
Alcohol, 398
Amnestic, 219
anecdotal data, 103
Anorexia Nervosa, 262
antecedent events, 469
Antecedents, 361
anterior cingulated areas, 238
Anticonvulsants, 369
antisocial, 6
Anxiety Disorders Interview Schedule for DSM-5, 173, 187
Anxiety Rating Scale for Children—Revised, 188
Applied Behavioral Analysis, 26
Approaches to Sex Education, 413
Aripiprazole, 326, 368
Assessment Measures for Eating Disorders, 277
Assessment of Bipolar Disorder, 325
Assessment of Mood Disorders, 315
At-Risk Sexual Behaviors, 403
Attachment Theory, 6
Attention Deficit Disorders Evaluation Scale - 5th ed., 133, 140
Atypical Antipsychotics, 368
Autism Diagnostic Interview, 359
Autism Diagnostic Observation Schedule, Second Edition, 360
Autistic Spectrum Disorder: An Introduction, 345
Avoidance, 219
Avoidant Attachment, 9
Avoiding the Pitfalls of Stereotyping, 478

B

baseline, 484
Beck Depression Inventory (BDI), 316
Behavior Assessment System for Children, 60
Behavior Support Plans, 29
Behavioral, 219
Behavioral Avoidance Task, 174
Behavioral Characteristics, 432
Behavioral Intervention Plan, 25
Behavioral Interventions for Aberrant Behaviors, 361
Behavioral Interventions to Promote Learning, 362
Behavioral Models, 312
behavioral rehearsal, 75
belongingness, 477
beta-hemolytic streptococcal infection, 238
Binge Eating Disorder, 264
Biological Factors, 95
Biological Models, 311
Biological Risk, 433
Bowlby, 7
Brain Function, 355
Brain Structure and Activity, 130
Bulimia Nervosa, 260
Bullying, 430
Bullying And Students Who Have Disabilities, 434

C

cardiovascular, 273
caring (empathy), honesty (reality), support (academic and emotional), and consistency, 484
Catapres, 136
Center for the Prevention of School Violence (CPSV), 416
Characteristics of Bipolar Disorder, 324
Characteristics of Gangs in Schools, 444
Characteristics of Generalized Anxiety Disorder, 228
Characteristics of Mood Disorders, 306
Characteristics of Obsessive-Compulsive Disorder, 236
Characteristics of Social Anxiety Disorder, 197
Child and Adolescent Psychiatric Assessment, 187
Child Assessment Schedule, 60
Child Behavior Checklist, 133
Child Behavior Checklist/Teacher Report Form, 140
Child PTSD Symptom Scale, 220
Child Training Intervention, 101
Childhood Autism Rating Scale, Second Edition, 358
Children that Provoke Confrontation, 476
Children's Depression Inventory, 315
Children's Interview for Psychiatric Symptoms, 187
Children's PCD Impact Scale, 239
Children's PTSD Inventory, 220
Children's Social Behavior Questionnaire, 359
Children's Yale-Brown Obsessive-Compulsive Scale, 239
chlamydia, 405
citalopram, 368
Clark Cavin, 486
Classroom as Community, 429
class-wide peer tutoring (CWPT), 475

Clinical Features of Autistic Spectrum Disorders, 349
Clinician Administered PTSD Schedule for Children and Adolescent, 220
Clozapine, 368
coaching, 75
Cognitive, 219
Cognitive Behavioral Approaches, 73, 279
Cognitive Behavioral Interventions, 176
Cognitive Behavioral Therapy (CBT), 26, 189, 317
Cognitive Behavioral Treatment, 62, 239
Cognitive Models, 313
Cognitive Strategy Training, 134
Combatting Gang Activities in Schools, 448
Community In The Classroom, 35
comorbidity, 229
compulsions, 236
Conduct disorder, 53
Conflict Resolution Through Peer Mediation, 428
Conners Parent and Teacher Rating Scales - 3rd ed., 148
Conners-Wells Adolescent Self-Report Scale, 143
Connors' Rating Scale 3rd ed., 133
Consequences, 362
Consequences of Early Childbearing, 410
Consistent features, 343
Constitutional Factors, 172
Consultation with a Dietician, 275
Contingency Management, 175
Cooperative Learning, 74
Coping Power Program, 62
Coping Questionnaire for Children—Child (or Parent) Version, 230
Cortisol, 354
cumulative method, 56
curriculum-based measurement (CBM), 142, 476

D

Dan Olweus, 430
defensive exclusion, 10
defiance disorders, 6
dehydroepiandrosterone, 57
Demographic Characteristics, 432
Dependent Use, 398
dermatological, 273
Developmental Course of Eating Disorders, 265
Dewey (1969), 429
Diagnostic Interview for Children and Adolescents, 60
Diagnostic Interview for Social and Communication Disorders (DISCO), 360
Diagnostic Interview Schedule for Children, 60, 187
Diagnostic Interviews, 359
differential reinforcement of other behaviors (DRO), 362
direct bullying, 430
direct conditioning, 198
direct instruction, 475
Direct observation, 61
discrete trial training (DT), 363, 469
Discriminating features, 343
disinhibition, 127
Disorganized Attachment, 9
disprivileging speech, 482
disproportionality, 479

Disruptive Behavior Rating Scale, 140
Disruptive Mood Dysregulation Disorder, 309
DISSECT, 73
Diversity and Its Relevance to Identification and Intervention, 479
dopamine, 122, 238, 354
drug use continuum, 398
duration, 2
Dyadic Parent-Child Interaction Coding System, 61
Dylan Klebold, 415

E

Early Warning Signs, 419
Educational Consequences, 410
Effective Approaches to School Violence, 425
Effective Use of Functional Behavioral Assessment, 425
Effexor, 136
Electrolyte imbalance, 273
Emotional, 219
Emotional regulation, 10
emotionally disturbed, 4
Enabling Factors, 450
endocrinological/metabolic, 273
environment, 469
Environmental Factors, 131, 356
Environmental Risk, 434
Eric Harris, 415
escitalopram, 368
Etiology of Autistic Spectrum Disorders, 353
Etiology of Depression in Children and Adolescents, 311
Etiology of Eating Disorders, 269
Evaluating and Responding to Threats of Violence, 421
Experimental Use, 398
externalized behaviors, 22
eye movement desensitization and reprocessing, 221
Eyeberg Child Behavior Inventory, 60

F

Face Perception, 356
Family, 230
Family Counseling, 279, 318
Family Development, 411
Family Processes, 186
Family Systems Therapy, 63
Family-Based Interventions, 62
Fear Inventory—Children, 201
FEAR plan, 230
Fear Survey Schedule for Children and Adolescents, 173
Fear Survey Schedule for Children-Revised, 173
Fluoxetine, 368
fluvoxamine, 368
forty-five-calendar-day limit, 472
forty-five-day removal policy, 473
frequency, 2
functional behavioral assessment, 23

G

Gang Impact in Schools, 444
Gang Membership and Related Activities, 441
Gang Resistance Is Paramount (G.R.I.P.), 451
gastrointestinal, 273
Gaze, 349
General Behavior Inventory, 326
General Characteristics of Eating Disorders, 264

Generalized Anxiety Disorder, 226
genetic disposition, 198
Genetic Influences, 353
genetic-biological determinism, 7
genital warts, 405
Gilliam Autism Rating Scale, Third Edition, 358
gonorrhea, 405
goodness of fit, 33
Group Cognitive-Behavioral Treatment for Adolescents, 199
Group Counseling, 280

H

head of the caudate nucleus, 238
Health-Related Consequences, 410
Helping Students Who are HIV-Positive, 406
Heritability of Fears, 172
herpes, 405
Higher-Functioning Autism, 366
History of Attempted Suicide, 335
HIV, 405
humor, 478
hyperarousal, 218, 219
Hypothalamic Pituitary Functioning, 354
Hypothyroidism, 355

I

Imitation, 350
Imminent Warning Signs, 419
Impairments in Social Interactions, 349
Implications of IDEA (2004) Regulations for Students Who Have Emotional Or Behavioral Disorders, 471
Incredible Years Training Program, 99
indirect bullying, 430
Individualized Education Plan (IEP), 472
Individuals with Disabilities Education Act (IDEA, 2004), 471
Ineffective Approaches to School Violence, 424
Information transfer, 198
Inhalants, 400
insecure attachment, 6
intensity, 2
Intentional Pregnancy, 407
interactionist perspective, 56
Internal Working Models, 9
internalized behaviors, 22
Interpersonal Counseling, 279
Interpersonal Psychotherapy (IPT), 318
Interpersonal Supports, 366
intervention intensity, 27
Interventions To Reduce Bullying in Schools, 435
Interview Schedule for Children and Adolescents, 187
Interview with the Adolescent, 273
Interview with the Parents, 274

J

Joint Attention, 349

K

Knowledge of and Access to Contraception, 414
Kohn, 485
K-SADS, 220

L

Language and Communication, 351

Language/Communication Dysfunction, 355
learner-centered software, 475
Learning and Educational Supports, 367
Learning factors, 171
Life Skills/Life Options Approach, 414
LINCS, 73
local education agency (LEA), 472

M

maintaining consequences, 67
Major Depressive Disorder (MDD), 310
maladaptive behavior, 26, 478
Marijuana, 399
Maslow, 486
Mentalization, 13
methylphenidate, 122, 135
Mindfulness, 20
modeling, 75, 175
Modifications, 72
monoamine oxidase inhibitors (MAOIs), 318
Motivation To Learn, 69
Multidimensional Anxiety Scale for Children, 188
multidisciplinary team (MDT), 481
multi-factorial, 197
multimodal, 190
Multimodal Treatment of ADHD, 138
multiple pathway method, 56
multisystemic approach, 469
Multisystemic Treatment, 64

N

National Institute on Drug Abuse (2020), 402
Naturalistic Behavioral Interventions, 363
Negative Affectivity Self-Statement Questionnaire, 230
Neobehavioristic Stimulus–Response Theory, 26
neurochemical, 238
Neurochemical Risk Factors, 353
Neurodevelopmental Disorders, 346
Neurological Risk Factors, 355
neurotransmitters, 122
Nicotine, 399
nondirective supportive therapy, 221
non-pathologizing versus problem-saturated perspective, 480
Norepinephrine, 354

O

Observation, 316
Observation Scales, 360
obsessions, 236
Obsessive-Compulsive Disorder, 234
Olanzapine, 326, 368
Operant Conditioning, 278
Operational Use, 398
oppositional defiant disorder, 89
orbital frontal cortex, 238
OxyContin, 396

P

panic attacks, 225

paradigm/pivotal response training (PRT), 364
parallel process, 12
Parent Intervention Training Program, 100
Parent Management Training, 63
Parent Teacher Association-PTA, 483
Parenting and Family Factors, 96
pediatric autoimmune neuropsychiatric disorder associated with strep, 238
Peer Group Dynamics, 433
peer mediation, 109, 428
Peer Ratings, 316
Peer Relations, 350
perseverating behaviors, 134
Persistent Depressive Disorder (Dysthymia), 314
personological variables, 469, 484
Pharmacological Interventions, 135
Pharmacological Treatment, 222, 280
Pharmacotherapy, 240
Pictorial Instrument for Children and Adolescents, 188
Play, 350
Poor Nutrition and Dietary Concerns, 130
Positive Effect of Technology and Meaningful Learning Experiences, 474
positive rapport, 470
Positive Reinforcement, 74
Post-Traumatic Stress Disorder, 214
Predisposing Factors, 450
prefrontal cortex, 122
Pregnancy, 407
Pregnancy and Birth Complications, 130
Prevalence of Adolescent Suicide, 329
Prevalence of Autistic Spectrum Disorders, 353
Prevalence of Mood Disorders, 308
Prevalence of Obsessive-Compulsive Disorder, 238
Prevention of Substance Abuse, 402
Primary and Secondary Control Enhanced Training, 318
Profile of an Adolescent Gang Member, 447
Psychodynamic Models, 312
Psychodynamic Psychotherapy, 176
Psychoeducational Profile—Third Edition, 361
Psychological Debriefing, 222
Psychological/Cognitive Risk, 434
Psychopathology, 11
Psychopharmacological Treatment of Bipolar Disorder, 326
Psychopharmacology, 318
Psychosocial Factors (Family Factors), 131
PTSD Reaction Index, 220
pulmonary, 273
Punishment, 362
Purpose Served by Gang Membership, 446

Q

Quetiapine, 326, 368

R

racoon circle, 21
Reactive aggression, 55

reciprocal peer tutoring (RPT), 475
Rehm's (1977) *self-control model*, 314
Reinforcement, 362
Reinforcing or Support Factors, 451
Relationships, 476
resilience, 470
Resistant Attachment, 8
Resolving Conflict Creatively Program (RCCP), 427
Resperidol, 136
Response Delay, 278
Response Prevention, 278
response to intervention, 27
Restitution, 107
Retrospective And Overview, 467
Reynolds Adolescent Depression Scale-Second Edition (RADS-2), 316
Reynolds Child Depression Scale, 316
Risk Factors Associated with Adolescent Pregnancy and Motherhood, 409
Risperidone, 326, 368
Ritalin, 135, 369

S

S.T.O.P. the Violence, 428
safe place, 225
Schedule for Affective Disorders and Schizophrenia for School-Aged Children, 60, 187
School Adjustment and Academic Achievement, 352
School Behavior Checklist, 61
School Structure Influences, 433
School Violence, 415
School-Based Interventions, 319, 369
Screen for Child Anxiety Related Emotional Disorders, 188
Screening for Risk Factors, 425
Screening Measures, 358
Securely attached children, 6
selective serotonin reuptake inhibitors (SSRIs), 176, 190, 318, 368
self regulation, 97
Self-Esteem Building and Social Skills Training, 427
Self-instruction, 134
self-monitoring, 134, 475
Self-monitoring Techniques, 278
self-reflection, 481
Self-Report Measures, 315
Separation Anxiety Disorder, 184
Serotonin, 354
SET-C intervention, 202
setraline, 368
setting events, 67
Sex Hormones, 355
shifting cognitive set, 97
Social Anxiety Disorder, 194
Social Cognition, 356
Social Dysfunction, 356
Social Emotional Learning, 18
Social Learning Theory, 26
Social Responsiveness Scale, Second Edition, 359
Social Skills Training, 75
Social Speech, 349
Social Use, 398
socially maladjusted, 1
Socioeconomic Consequences, 410
solution-focused approach, 480
Special Education Parent Teacher Association-SEPTA, 483
Specific Phobia, 169

Spence Children's Anxiety Scale, 188, 201
stay put provision, 471
Stereotyped, Repetitive, and Ritualistic Behaviors, 352
Stimulus Control, 278
Suicidal Volition, 334
Suicide Plan, 334
Support, 485
Sydenham chorea, 238
syphilis, 405
Systematic Desensitization, 174
systematic ignoring, 179

T

Target behaviors, 484
Teacher Report Form, 61
Teacher Training Intervention Program, 101
Teaching Acceptance of Diversity, 427
Teenage Pregnancy and Motherhood, 407
The Family Systems Model, 314
The General Semantic Approach to School-Age Bullying, 437
The Importance of Family and Community Involvement, 429
The Olweus Bullying Prevention Program, 436
The School Shooter: A Threat Assessment Perspective (National Center for the Analysis of Violent Crime [NCAVC], 2001, 421
The Suicide Interview, 333
The Victim-Turned-Aggressor, 433
Threat Management in Schools, 422
Trauma Informed Teaching, 15
Trauma-focused Cognitive-Behavioral Therapy, 221
Treatment and Education of Autistic and Related Communication-Handicapped Children (TEACCH), 365
Treatment for Adolescent with Depression Study, 319
Treatment of Comorbidities, 402
Treatment of Eating Disorders, 277
Treatment of Substance Abuse, 401
Treatment Outcomes, 281
Treatment Strategies, 361
Treatment Strategies for Mood Disorders, 317
trigger child, 476
trycyclic antidepressants (TCAs), 318

U

U.S. Departments of Education and Justice, 2020, 417
Uninformed (Misinformed) Pregnancy, 409
universal intervention, 27
Unprotected Sexual Activity: The Risk of HIV/AIDS, 405
Use of Computers, 474

V

Variable features, 343
verbal self-instruction, 179
Vicodin, 396
Video Instruction, 364
Vygotsky, 485

W

Warning Signs of Adolescent Suicide, 330
Wellbutrin, 136
Who Bullies and Why, 431
Who Gets Bullied and Why, 432
Working Collaboratively With the Families, 481
working memory, 97
Working with Teen Fathers, 413
Working with the Adolescent Mother-to-be, 411
World Health Organization, 2020, 403

Y

Young Mania Rating Scale, 326
Youth Gangs in the United States: Current Data, 443

Z

Zero Tolerance Policies and Students with Disabilities, 424

CPSIA information can be obtained
at www.ICGtesting.com
Printed in the USA
BVHW070211180123
656440BV00016B/554

9 781648 895630